Employment Law

Employment Law

James Holland LLB, PhD, Barrister

Professor of Employment Law, Associate Dean, Faculty of Business and Law,
University of the West of England, Bristol

and

Stuart Burnett MA, LLM, Barrister

Formerly Director of Operations, EEF Western, Visiting Lecturer,
University of the West of England, Bristol

OXFORD
UNIVERSITY PRESS

OXFORD
UNIVERSITY PRESS

Great Clarendon Street, Oxford OX2 6DP

Oxford University Press is a department of the University of Oxford.
It furthers the University's objective of excellence in research, scholarship, and education by publishing worldwide in

Oxford New York

Auckland Cape Town Dar es Salaam Hong Kong Karachi
Kuala Lumpur Madrid Melbourne Mexico City Nairobi
New Delhi Shanghai Taipei Toronto

With offices in

Argentina Austria Brazil Chile Czech Republic France Greece
Guatemala Hungary Italy Japan Poland Portugal Singapore
South Korea Switzerland Thailand Turkey Ukraine Vietnam

Published in the United States
by Oxford University Press Inc., New York

First published by Blackstone Press

British Library Cataloguing in Publication Data

Data available

Library of Congress Cataloging in Publication Data

Data available

Typeset by Laserwords Private Ltd, Chennai, India
Printed in Great Britain on acid-free paper by
Ashford Colour Press Ltd, Gosport, Hampshire

ISBN 978–0–19–960271–1

10 9 8 7 6 5 4 3 2 1

OUTLINE CONTENTS

DETAILED CONTENTS

PREFACE

This book is designed for use on the various Legal Practice Courses offered throughout the country. In writing the book we have tried to take into account the comments received from colleagues in other institutions concerning the particular needs of their courses as well as practitioners who also use the text, so that we hope we have at least pleased some of the people for some of the time. Each chapter deals with a specific area of employment law, but we have attempted throughout the text to show the overlap that exists between the common law and statutory rights and which pervades the subject so as to recreate the concerns that have to be foremost in a solicitor's mind when advising a client.

The book concentrates on what is usually termed 'individual employment law', touching on trade union matters only where they relate directly to this theme. Individual employment law nevertheless covers an extensive range of activities, so that we have sought to weight the chapters according to two main criteria: first, the need to address the concerns of both corporate and private clients; secondly, according to the workload of the courts and tribunals. Further, we have tried to identify the areas which cause students most concern and provide practical guidance on how these problems may be resolved.

We have listened to reviews of previous editions and thank all who have contributed, not least for the kind words. One change we were able to incorporate both from lecturers' requests and a change in the law was the division of the old Chapter 6 on discrimination into two separate chapters on equality (Chapter 6 now concentrating on 'discrimination' and the various forms of protected characteristics; Chapter 7 dealing with equal pay and atypical work). The change in law, of course, was the introduction of the Equality Act 2010 which came into effect on 1 October 2010. This Act seeks to consolidate and harmonise the law relating to discrimination and to make some amendments to the law on equal pay. As well as creating some new duties the Act addresses the problem of the piecemeal development of UK and EU anti-discrimination legislation over the last 40-plus years. The splitting of Chapter 6, however, also means that, for the second year running, we have had to re-number chapters and, for that, we apologise to all lecturers who have to adjust cross-references in their course materials.

We would like to offer our thanks to the many people who have helped us with this and previous editions. At UWE, Bristol: to the Employment law team for their thoughts and to our past students on the LPC. At the EEF: to practitioners and former colleagues for all their assistance and suggestions. We would also like to acknowledge the comments received, formally and informally, from our colleagues in other LPC-provider institutions. We hope that we have incorporated the points raised.

We would also like to express our gratitude to all the firms who have participated in the various surveys we have conducted over the years, many of which went well beyond merely supplying us with examples of their drafting practice.

Our thanks as usual to the publishers for their patience and encouragement and, specifically, to Lalle Pursglove for all her work on this edition.

The law is stated as at 1 October 2010.

James Holland
Bristol

GUIDED TOUR OF THE BOOK

Employment Law 2011 contains numerous features which have been specifically designed to facilitate your learning and understanding of employment law. To help you get the most from your text, this 'Guided Tour of the Book' highlights the features used by the author to explain the law and its application in practice.

Examples

Use these sections to gain a practical understanding of how the law is applied in realistic practical situations, and gain valuable insight into what might happen day-to-day in a solicitor's practice.

Figures

Flowcharts, diagrams, and example forms provide a visual representation to aid learning.

Summary points

The key points covered are summarised in user-friendly lists. Look at these summaries to help you consolidate your learning or to check your knowledge at revision time.

Self-test questions

These questions allow you to test yourself on particular areas of the law in preparation for exams or to assess your learning throughout the course. Use the questions to uncover areas where you might need to improve your understanding by rereading the text or by asking your lecturer. Guidance on answers can be found on the Online Resource Centre which accompanies this book.

GUIDED TOUR OF THE WEBSITE

Online Resource Centres have been developed to provide students and lecturers with ready-to-use teaching and learning resources. They are free of charge, designed to complement the text and offer additional materials which are suited to electronic delivery. The Online Resource Centre to accompany this book can be found at:

www.oxfordtextbooks.co.uk/orc/employment2011/

Student Resources

Answers to self-test questions

In this section, guidance is given on appropriate answers to the self-test questions which appear in the book.

Updates

Updates will be posted on the website when the law changes or when significant cases pass through the courts, allowing you to keep fully informed of developments. The updates are freely accessible to all and offer an easy way to keep abreast of events in this rapidly changing subject area.

Links to useful sites

This part of the site provides links and useful information which is freely accessible elsewhere on the internet. Use this resource to find relevant information quickly and easily.

Figures

Flowcharts featured in the book are available online, providing you with easily accessible visuals to help you revise.

Lecturer Resources (for registered adopters)

Test bank

A bank of questions is available to download into your assessment software. Also available in Word format, the questions allow you to provide a resource that your students can use to test themselves, or that you can use to assess their learning. Once included in your assessment software, the questions are entirely customisable, enabling you to remove questions which might be less relevant to your course, or to change the order of the questions to match the order in which topics are taught at your institution.

Each question is accompanied by feedback which shows why the selected answer is correct or incorrect, and then points the student towards the relevant page of the text if they need to reread.

ABBREVIATIONS

ACAS	Advisory, Conciliation and Arbitration Service
Age Regs 2006	Employment Equality (Age) Regulations 2006
AMRA 1988	Access to Medical Reports Act 1988
art.	Article
BERR	Department for Business, Enterprise & Regulatory Reform
BIS	Department for Business, Innovation and Skills
Convention	European Convention on Human Rights
CRE	Commission for Racial Equality
DDA 1995	Disability Discrimination Act 1995
DPA 1998	Data Protection Act 1998
DRC	Disability Rights Commission
DTI	Department of Trade and Industry
EA 2002	Employment Act 2002
EA 2008	Employment Act 2008
EAT	Employment Appeal Tribunal
EC	European Community
ECJ	European Court of Justice
EDT	effective date of termination
EHRC	Equality and Human Rights Commission
EOC	Equal Opportunities Commission
EPA 1970	Equal Pay Act 1970
EPCA 1978	Employment Protection (Consolidation) Act 1978
EqA 2010	Equality Act 2010
ERA 1996	Employment Rights Act 1996
ERA 1999	Employment Relations Act 1999
ERDRA 1998	Employment Rights (Dispute Resolution) Act 1998
ET Regs 2001	Employment Tribunals (Constitution and Rules of Procedure) Regulations 2001
ET Regs 2004	Employment Tribunals (Constitution and Rules of Procedure) Regulations 2004
ET Rules	Employment Tribunals Rules of Procedure 2001
ET Rules (Amendments) 2008	Employment Tribunals (Constitution and Rules of Procedure) (Amendment) Regulations 2008
ETA 1996	Employment Tribunals Act 1996
ETS	Employment Tribunal Service
Fixed-Term Regs 2002	Fixed-Term Employees (Prevention of Less Favourable Treatment) Regulations 2002
GMD	genuine material difference
GMF	genuine material factor
HRA 1998	Human Rights Act 1998

HSE	Health and Safety Executive
LBP Regs	Telecommunications (Lawful Business Practice) (Interception of Communications) Regulations 2000
MPL Regs 1999	Maternity and Parental Leave etc. Regulations 1999
NDC	National Disability Council
NMWA 1998	National Minimum Wage Act 1998
NMWRegs 1999	National Minimum Wage Regulations 1999
PALRegs 2002	Paternity and Adoption Leave Regulations 2002
para.	paragraph
PHA 1997	Protection from Harassment Act 1997
PHI	permanent health insurance
PHR	pre-hearing review
PIDA 1998	Public Interest Disclosure Act 1998
PTW Regs 2000	Part-time Workers (Prevention of Less Favourable Treatment) Regulations 2000
r.	rule
reg.	regulation
RIPA 2000	Regulation of Investigatory Powers Act 2000
RRA 1976	Race Relations Act 1976
s.	section
sch.	schedule
SDA 1975	Sex Discrimination Act 1975
TCE 2007	Tribunals, Courts and Enforcement Act 2007
TULRCA 1992	Trade Union and Labour Relations (Consolidation) Act 1992
TUPE 1981	Transfer of Undertakings (Protection of Employment) Regulations 1981
TUPE 2006	Transfer of Undertakings (Protection of Employment) Regulations 2006
TURERA 1993	Trade Union Reform and Employment Rights Act 1993
UCTA 1977	Unfair Contract Terms Act 1977
WTRegs 1998	Working Time Regulations 1998

TABLE OF CASES

TABLE OF UK STATUTES

TABLE OF STATUTORY INSTRUMENTS

TABLE OF EUROPEAN LEGISLATION

INTERNATIONAL TREATIES AND CONVENTIONS

1

Overview of employment law

1.1 Introduction

Employment law, on the whole, is not a conceptually difficult subject, and a good dollop of analytical common sense can often work wonders. But instinct will not provide all the answers or the best advice. Employment law can be extremely detailed at times and a solicitor needs to grasp both the detail and the overall implications in order to give proper guidance to his or her client. The interrelationship between matters such as breach of contract and unfair dismissal, for instance, can cause some confusion to those new to the subject. Nevertheless, at its best employment law is logical, dynamic, interesting, and real. At its worst it resembles the M25: it all seems to have been built at the wrong time and in the wrong place, it grinds to a halt periodically for no apparent reason, it is frequently being dug up and expanded, and sometimes seems to go round in circles.

1.2 The topics covered in the book

These can be seen from the chapter headings. They centre on the substantive law, practice, and procedure relating to the formation, operation, and termination of the contract of employment.

Collective employment law (i.e., the law concerning the rights, duties, and operations of trade unions) is not covered in this book except where it is necessary to explain the matters affecting individual rights.

1.3 The mixture of statutory and contractual rights

Modern employment law emerged out of a jumble of the Poor Laws, the history of craftsmen's guilds and trade unions, family law as applied to the behaviour of domestic servants and agricultural workers and, in the nineteenth century, the law of contract. By the 1960s one would find most employment texts set alongside contract textbooks, but, from the middle of that decade onwards, UK and European legislation has been the major driving force in the creation of employment rights and obligations.

Any questions raised in employment law may now involve: pure common law principles (mainly contractual); pure statutory principles; a combination of European Union and UK legislation and concepts; or a mixture of all the above. The lawyer who dabbles in employment law tends not to appreciate the detail (and often the conflict) involved in this mixture, so one of the recurrent themes in this book is to indicate the overlap between all these areas of law, but especially the key one of common law and statutory rules.

By way of a simple example, imagine that an employer has asked an employee to work at their Birmingham factory instead of the Coventry site (these are about 20 miles apart) but she objects. Clearly, this problem centres on what the contract of employment says or means and one would hope that the dispute might be resolved by examining the contract to see whether there is a clause detailing when the employee can be required to work at different sites—a 'mobility' clause. If the contract is silent on the point, one would have to look at whether there are any implied terms which cover the situation and, in employment law, arguments on the use and range of 'implied terms' have kept many a lawyer's family from starving.

The contractual analysis does not reveal the whole picture, however. For instance, hidden in this simple order to move site may lurk questions of discrimination based on sex, race, or disability, all involving a range of UK statutes and/or European Directives. And the position may become even more complicated if a dismissal results from the refusal of the employee to move to Birmingham.

Once dismissal has occurred (and even some resignations are deemed to amount to dismissals) the employee may have claims at common law and under statute. The most obvious common law claim is that of *wrongful dismissal,* which arises when a person is dismissed without notice or with inadequate notice and the employer had no contractually justifiable reasons for that action. The most obvious statutory claim is for *unfair dismissal* which is essentially based on two questions: (a) did the employer have a fair reason to dismiss; and (b) was that reason handled fairly (e.g., by use of proper procedures)? Many reports in newspapers or on television confuse wrongful and unfair dismissal, but they are quite different animals.

Thus the lawyer who thinks solely in terms of either common law or statutory rights may not cover all the potential claims (and there are other possibilities beyond those noted above). Equally, one needs to know where the issues will be determined. The main forum for employment disputes is that of the employment tribunals (known as industrial tribunals until August 1998), and they would have jurisdiction to determine nearly all the points raised in our example, though in contract-based matters they can only award a maximum of £25,000 and they would only have jurisdiction in the example

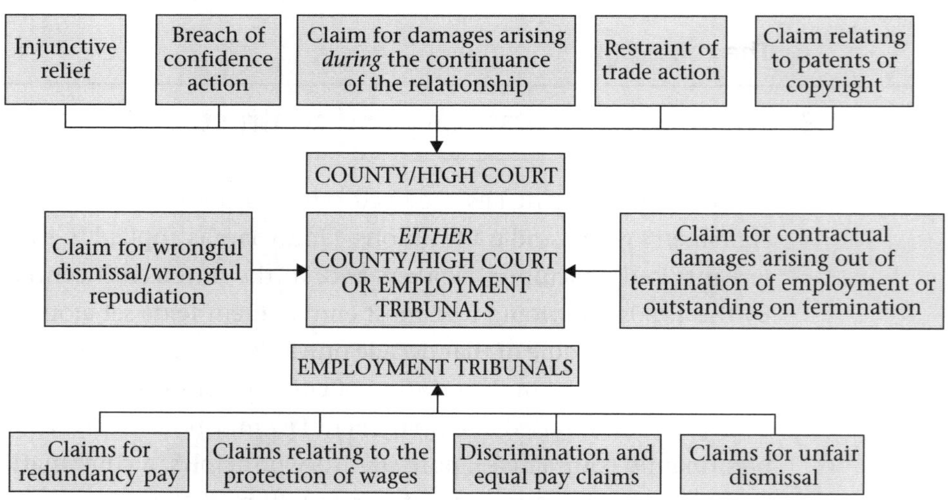

Figure 1.1 Jurisdiction of the courts and employment tribunals.

above if a dismissal had occurred as they generally cannot entertain arguments about the operation of the contract while the employment relationship is still running. The ordinary courts, however, have some overlapping jurisdiction, so all the contractual claims could be decided there, but they could not hear any discrimination claims, nor the unfair dismissal action.

Figure 1.1 sets out in diagrammatic form the various jurisdictions of the courts and tribunals. Employment tribunal practice and procedure is dealt with in **Chapter 16**.

1.4 A skeleton outline of the topics covered

1.4.1 Definition of 'employee'

Most of the rights and obligations dealt with in this book concern employers and employees; rights such as unfair dismissal, for instance, do not extend to independent contractors. The distinction is the same as you encountered at your academic stage of training in the law of torts (or obligations). Unfortunately, the term 'employee' has no workable statutory definition, so the analysis rests on a number of common law tests which explore the level of control a *company* has over an individual's work pattern, the extent to which the individual's work is *integrated* into the main work of the company, whether there are *mutual obligations* present between the parties such as the payment of sick pay and the provision of personal service, and whether the individual in all the circumstances can be said to be *in business on their own account.*

However, modern work patterns have fudged the line between employees and independent contractors, e.g., one large company we know of has more people on site who are hired through employment agencies than it has full-time employees. Further, a great deal of EU-derived legislation does not make such a clear distinction between employees and other categories so that recent legislation has tended to define rights and obligations by reference to the more expansive term 'worker'. The question of who qualifies for employment rights (dealt with in **Chapter 2**) is therefore an important one but will not concern most people as they will fall easily within the classification of 'employee'. When such problems do arise, however, they tend to centre on 'peripheral' workers such as those supplied by employment agencies and can often be extremely complicated matters.

1.4.2 The contract of employment

1.4.2.1 The form of the contract

We will deal in detail with the formation, contents, and operation of the contract in **Chapters 3** to **5**. Here we can say that a contract of employment is created like any other contract and may be made orally or in writing (or in any combination) and will be found in a mixture of express and implied terms. There is no standard format for such contracts and a solicitor should be wary of relying on general precedents that do not fit the circumstances of the case. There is a tolerated myth in employment law that each contract is negotiated on an individual basis with each employee. The reality is that most employees were simply given no option as to the contents of the contract, that many have never seen a written contract, that some think they have no contract (this applies to employers too), and that, if there are recognised trades unions in the company, they negotiated the terms of the contract (including those of non-members).

With this level of confusion over such a basic matter, it is hardly surprising, as we noted in passing above, that the employment contract is also riddled with *implied terms*. Very often these shape the contract; sometimes in a surprising way. Some, such as the duty of fidelity, cannot be excluded; others will stand unless express terms state the contrary.

1.4.2.2 Statutory intervention

There was a time when there was little statutory control over the *contents* of the contract. The first real intervention came in the 1960s with a document known as the *written statement*. The form of this statement is now prescribed by the Employment Rights Act 1996, s. 1 (ERA 1996). It is meant to provide a summary of the main contractual provisions. If an employer has not provided a contract containing all the matters which are meant to be included in the written statement he or she must provide a written statement to the employee within two months of their starting work. This is not the contract, though it can stand as very strong *prima facie* evidence of the contract and disputes regarding its alleged inaccuracies or its non-production can be referred to employment tribunals. Unfortunately, many employees have never seen one of these either.

More intervention has occurred recently covering matters such as the regulation of: the national minimum wage, maximum working hours, unauthorised deductions from wages, and the so-called 'family friendly' provisions. These are dealt with in **Chapter 4**.

1.4.2.3 The operation of the contract

Leaving aside questions of dismissal, the major concern of employees centres on how the contract is performed on a day-to-day basis. Problems will generally arise here relating to:

(a) what the terms are (a question of evidence); or

(b) what do those terms mean (a question of interpretation); or

(c) when can the employer change the terms (a question of law)?

As with our simple example above on mobility clauses, it is at this point that one first notices the real interplay between common law matters such as breach of contract and the other statutory rights and remedies. As we will explore in **Chapter 5** in particular, it is often best to approach this area by considering what the employee's response could be to any proposed interpretation or variation of the contractual terms. At one end the employee may simply put up with the employer's views, but there is a range of legal remedies which can be pursued such as seeking an injunction, suing for breach of contract, or resigning and claiming wrongful and/or unfair dismissal.

1.4.3 Discrimination and equal pay

Discrimination is dealt with in **Chapter 6** and **Equal Pay** in **Chapter 7**. Issues of age, disability, gender reassignment, marriage and civil partnerships, pregnancy and maternity, race, religion or belief, sex, sexual orientation, or trade union membership discrimination may arise during recruitment, or in the operation of the contract or at termination.

The various forms of prohibited discrimination are described in **Chapter 6** and mentioned throughout the text. Discrimination may come in different forms, e.g., *direct* and *indirect* discrimination. Direct sex discrimination comes from an obvious act of treating one person less favourably than another who does not share the first person's characteristics. Indirect discrimination arises where an employer creates a provision, criterion or practice (e.g., a change in hours of work), which at first glance looks neutral as to its effect but that is judged to be discriminatory in its operation because it puts the employee (and others who share the same 'protected characteristic') at a particular disadvantage. (e.g., as regards getting to work and still dealing with child care problems).

There are exceptions and defences to these general rules, e.g., that there is an occupational requirement (e.g., decency or authenticity points).

Enforcement is by means of application to an employment tribunal, which may make an order declaring the applicant's rights and award compensation.

1.4.4 Termination of the contract

The rights and remedies regarding termination at common law are dealt with in **Chapter 10** of this book; the statutory consequences are covered in **Chapters 11–14.** The central feature of **Chapter 10** is the concept of wrongful dismissal; **Chapters 11–13** deal with the most well-known aspect of employment law *viz* unfair dismissal; and **Chapter 14** deals with redundancy. We have hinted at how these topics interrelate in the text above.

A contract of employment can come to an end in a number of different ways:

(a) by agreement;

(b) by completion of a specific task;

(c) by expiry of a fixed-term;

(d) by automatic termination, e.g., frustration of the contract;

(e) by dismissal;

(f) by resignation.

The employment practitioner must recognise there are potentially both statutory and common law consequences.

1.4.4.1 Common law remedies

Dismissal and resignation are the most common forms of termination. In most cases either party may terminate the contract by giving adequate notice and, at common law, an employer can dismiss an employee for any reason. The only thing that matters to the common law is whether adequate notice was given. Notice periods are determined by the contract, subject to statutory minima which vary according to the length of service.

If the employer dismisses without giving adequate notice or payment in lieu of that notice, he or she may be in breach of contract. The claim is for what is termed a 'wrongful dismissal'. The employer is entitled to dismiss without notice (called a 'summary dismissal') only if the employee has committed a serious breach of the contract. Hence it is in both parties' interests to have the express terms clearly defined so that they know exactly where they stand on any given issue.

The amount of damages an employee will obtain is limited to what would have been earned during the notice period and is subject to the normal contractual rules—for example, the duty to mitigate loss.

If, on the other hand, the *employer* commits a serious breach of contract (e.g., the employer does not pay the employee) this will amount to a repudiation which the employee

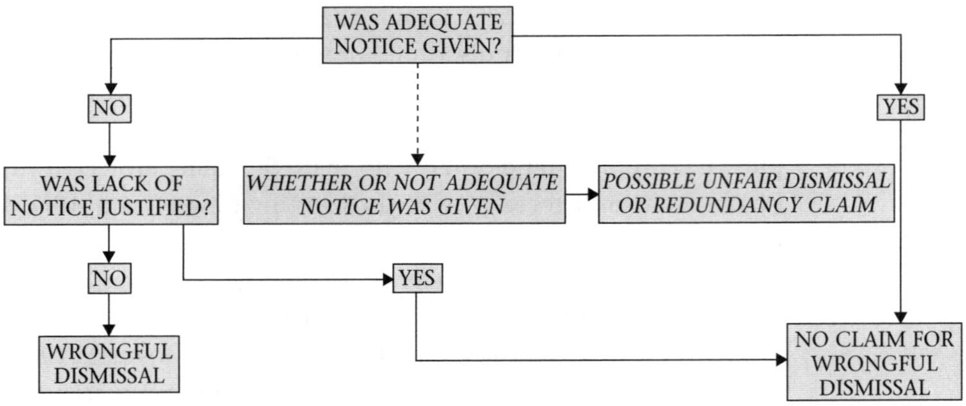

Figure 1.2 Dismissal with or without notice

may accept as terminating the contract and resign. This is termed a 'wrongful repudiation' by the employer and means that the employee will be held to have been effectively dismissed. Damages are calculated in the same way as with a wrongful dismissal. The employee who does not resign and continues in employment may of course sue the employer for damages relating to any breach.

In limited cases one of the parties may obtain an injunction to prevent a breach of contract, e.g., to prevent a dismissal taking effect until contractual procedures have been followed. An order for specific performance will not be granted, however. The real importance of injunctions lies in actions for breach of confidence and restraint of trade.

In **Figure 1.2** you can see that where dismissal is with adequate notice there are no further common law consequences. Where dismissal is without notice (and that lack of notice cannot be justified) the employee will be entitled to damages for wrongful dismissal. *Note, however, that in either case there may be statutory consequences such as a claim for unfair dismissal.*

1.4.4.2 Statutory remedies: unfair dismissal

'Unfair dismissal' is a technical term which has its own peculiar set of rules and procedures. Cases are heard exclusively in employment tribunals. Any claim must be presented within three months of what is termed the 'effective date of termination' (e.g., the end of the notice period).

Every employee is said to have the right not to be unfairly dismissed, but there are certain preliminary conditions to be met. First, the employee must qualify for the right. For instance, the right generally applies only to employees who have at least one year's continuous employment.

The employee must prove that he or she has been dismissed but, as with common law rights, a resignation may be deemed a dismissal if the employee resigned in the face of a serious breach by the employer. This is the same thing as wrongful repudiation but is called a 'constructive dismissal' in this setting.

'Fairness' is determined by a three-stage process. First, if there is any dispute on the matter an employee will have to prove they were, in law, dismissed, e.g., where there has been a resignation. Secondly, the burden is on the employer to show that the dismissal was for a 'fair reason'.

There are only six acceptable fair reasons: capability or qualifications; conduct; retirement; redundancy; statutory illegality; and 'some other substantial reason'. Dismissal for any other reason is unfair.

The third stage is to assess whether the fair reason was implemented fairly. The burden of proof here is neutral. Fairness is determined by three main factors:

- the definition contained in ERA 1996, s. 98(4) ('whether the dismissal is fair or unfair . . . (a) depends on whether in the circumstances (including the size and administrative resources of the employer's undertaking) the employer acted reasonably or unreasonably in treating . . . [the fair reason] . . . as a sufficient reason for dismissing the employee, and (b) shall be determined in accordance with equity and the substantial merits of the case');
- a vast amount of case law explaining the application of this definition in the setting of the tribunal's sense of industrial reality; and
- whether a fair procedure has been followed by the employer.

The primary remedies for unfair dismissal are reinstatement in the same job and re-engagement in a similar job. These are seldom ordered so that the main practical remedy is that of compensation.

Compensation is made up of two main elements—the basic and compensatory awards. They are assessed on different grounds *and the maximum figures are reviewed annually,* usually changing in February. The basic award is a fixed calculation, determined by reference to the age, length of service, and earnings of the employee. The maximum basic award at the time of writing is £11,400. The compensatory award is based on what is just and equitable. It is calculated on nett payments. The maximum award is currently £65,300 (both awards are subject to their usual annual change in February 2011).

Both the basic award and the compensatory award may be subject to a number of deductions, e.g., in relation to contributory fault, *ex gratia* payments made, or failure to mitigate loss.

1.4.4.3 Statutory remedies: redundancy

Redundancy is a dismissal for a particular reason. That reason is that:

(a) the business has closed down; *or*

(b) the employee's particular place of work has closed down (even though other sites may still continue); *or*

(c) the requirement for employees to do that employee's particular work has ceased or diminished.

In effect, a redundancy arises where (without necessarily any fault on the employee's part) there is a surplus of labour. Where an employee is dismissed for redundancy there may be an entitlement to a statutory redundancy payment. This is calculated in the same way as the basic award for an unfair dismissal, i.e., according to age, length of service, and pay (again, to a maximum of £11,400). The contract may also entitle the employee to a contractual redundancy payment.

Redundancy is a fair *reason* for dismissal but, as with any other dismissal, if it is handled badly by the employer it may still constitute an unfair dismissal.

We can now consider an overview of the possible consequences of dismissal. You can see in **Figure 1.3** that, whatever the reason for dismissal, and whether adequate notice was given or not, the dismissal may yet be an unfair dismissal.

The solicitor *must* be aware of this overview when giving advice to an employer. This applies at any stage: during the contract when the employer is issuing orders or varying terms of the contract, and also where a decision has been made to dismiss the employee.

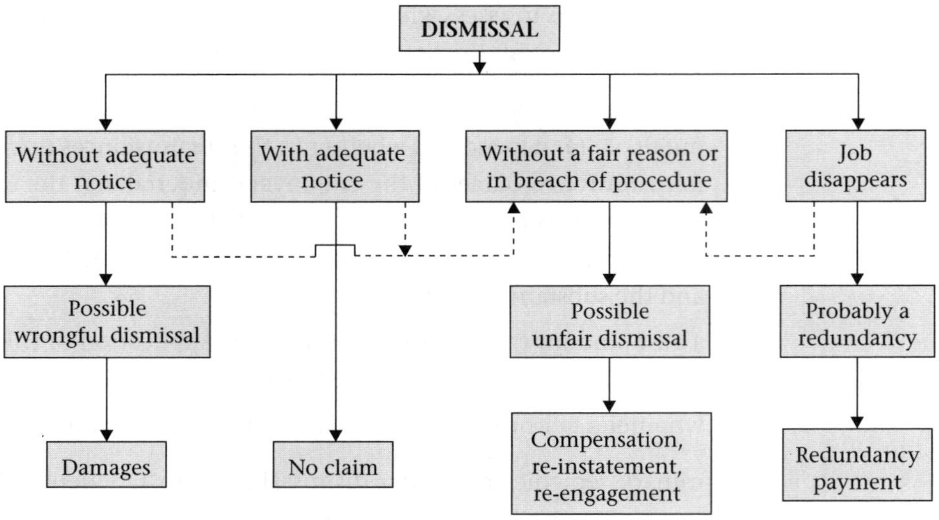

Figure 1.3 Possible consequences of dismissal.

We have not included every possible consequence in the diagram, so matters such as discrimination must also be noted (there is no maximum figure for compensation in discrimination claims).

1.4.5 Takeovers and transfer of undertakings

This topic considers what happens to the employee's rights and duties when the ownership of the business changes (it is dealt with in **Chapter 15**). In many cases the transfer of ownership will be by share acquisition and this has no effect on the employee at all. However, where a business is transferred by other means (e.g., the business or part of it is sold), the position is that all the contractual and statutory rights concerning employees (except for pensions) will be automatically transferred as well. This will apply only where the transfer is a *'relevant transfer'*, i.e., one in which:

(a) business activity passes from one legal person to another;

(b) the transfer is of an economic entity which retains its identity.

Employees will maintain their contractual and statutory rights and obligations only if they are 'employed [by the transferor] immediately before the transfer', but the term 'immediately before' is now given a loose interpretation. In essence, therefore, employees employed as part of a transferred business can regard the transferee as having been their employer all along. Thus an employee who is dismissed at any time by the transferee can bring any contractual or statutory claims against the transferee.

1.4.6 Employment tribunal procedure

Chapter 16 examines employment tribunal procedure and the special rules that apply to actions for unfair dismissal and redundancy in particular. Employment tribunals operate in much the same way as the ordinary courts but there are peculiarities that can catch the unwary. They are presided over by employment judges and are not as informal as is commonly believed. The settlement of cases before they reach the tribunal is quite common practice.

1.4.7 Protecting the employer's interests

Chapters 8 and **9** concentrate on topics which do not fall within the jurisdiction of employment tribunals, *viz*, confidentiality and restraint of trade. These are technically complicated areas which require special attention. At one time employment lawyers very often did not deal with these topics at all, leaving them to Chancery specialists; but in the modern employment law context this is no longer the case as the advice given in relation to, say, a dismissal may have major repercussions on the efficacy of restraint or confidentiality clauses.

1.4.7.1 Confidentiality

During employment an employee owes his employer a fairly strict duty to maintain the secrecy of the employer's confidential information. Once the relationship has ended, however, only certain types of highly confidential information continue to receive protection. In **Chapter 8** we will see that a difficult balance has to be struck between the employer's trade secrets (which can be protected) and the employee's know-how (which cannot). The arguments (as with restraint of trade below) are usually set in the world of interim injunctions.

1.4.7.2 Restraint of trade

Employers are often anxious to guard against direct competition once employees have left the organisation. As well as seeking to protect their confidential information, employers may also wish to ensure that an ex-employee does not have the opportunity to exert influence over the employer's hard-earned trade connexions. Restraint clauses are used by all manner of businesses, from the small high-street hairdresser who wants to prevent the ex-stylist 'stealing' his clients, to the solicitor's firm which wishes to do the same as against the partner or assistant solicitor who has moved elsewhere, through to multi-national enterprises. In all cases the restraint is presumed to be void unless it passes a test of reasonableness as between the parties in terms of the time covered by the restraint, the area affected, and the market in which the business operates.

Restraint clauses take three main forms: *non-competition* restraints which prevent the ex-employee working in that industry or at least working for named competitors; *non-dealing* restraints which prevent ex-employees accepting business from, or conducting business with, former clients; and *non-solicitation* restraints which prevent ex-employees actually initiating contact with former clients. In all cases enforcement will be granted to the minimum level needed to protect the employer's legitimate interests. The aim is to protect against *unfair* competition, not competition *per se*.

1.5 The institutions

There are three main arenas in which employment law issues are settled:

(a) *At the workplace between employers and employees, or their trade unions*

This always gets extensive publicity in the media and the image is usually one of constant warfare. The reality is that, in general, major battle-lines are not drawn here on a day-to-day basis.

(b) *In the ordinary courts*

It is a key point that we will be dealing with *contracts* of employment, and thus the normal law of contract plays a vital role in our considerations. Anything which centres on breach of contract is primarily, and often exclusively, the province of the county court or High Court and not that of employment tribunals, e.g., restraint of trade.

(c) *In employment tribunals*

These bodies were set up to deal with employment law problems and their jurisdiction is immense. Most commonly they will hear unfair dismissal, redundancy, and discrimination cases. An appeal from the decision of an employment tribunal lies with the Employment Appeal Tribunal (almost exclusively on a point of law only) and from there to the Court of Appeal (which, strictly speaking, reviews the decision of the ET, not the EAT).

In addition to all this there are other institutions which are relevant to this book and need to be noted specifically here.

1.5.1 ACAS

The Advisory, Conciliation and Arbitration Service (ACAS) seeks to promote improvements in industrial relations, e.g.:

(a) as regards collective matters in relation to the settlement of trade disputes, e.g., by arranging arbitration;

(b) to give employers, employers' associations, workers, and trade unions advice on matters of industrial relations;

(c) to provide Codes of Practice (e.g., relating to disciplinary procedures) which are not legally binding on parties but are admissible as evidence of good industrial practice so that failure to adhere to these codes may go to show that an employer acted unfairly or, if not that, can result in extra (or reduced) compensation being paid; and

(d) to promote the settlement of any complaint presented to employment tribunals, e.g., for unfair dismissal.

ACAS may now charge for its services.

ACAS now has a new function as regards unfair dismissal complaints: that of offering litigants the option of arbitration instead of going to an employment tribunal (see **11.12.2** below).

1.5.2 The Equality and Human Rights Commission

As from October 2007 the Equality and Human Rights Commission became the new single body covering equal opportunities, racial and sexual equality, disability and human rights. As well as promoting equality etc. and issuing guidance to this effect the Commission's predecessors have been held to have sufficient locus to bring judicial review actions.

1.6 European influences

Employment law has been one of the most active areas of European legislation. Thus matters such as free movement of workers, rights to receive particulars of employment, equal pay, transfers of undertakings, and redundancy consultations have all been the subject of Treaties, Regulations, or Directives of the EU.

The effect of all this is three-fold:

(a) Some legislation is directly enforceable by individuals against the state or other individuals, i.e., they can enforce rights such as equal pay under art. 141, EC Treaty, by reference to the EU legislation itself. The EU legislation may therefore be cited and relied upon in any action (having both direct applicability and direct effect).

(b) Other forms of EU legislation do not have direct applicability, though in limited cases they may have *direct effect*, which will amount to much the same thing (at least as regards vertical actions). In the case of *Faccini Dori* v *Recreb srl* [1995] ECR I-3325, the full court of the ECJ addressed the issue of the *horizontal* direct effect of Directives, i.e., the applicability of Directives, outside any enacting national legislation, to legal persons (individuals and companies) suing other legal persons. The *Faccini Dori* case made it quite clear that Directives did not have direct horizontal effect. So, all employees in the *private sector* who seek to sue their employer must rely either on the wording of the UK legislation *simpliciter* or sue the UK Government under the *Francovich* principles (*Francovich* v *Italian Republic* [1995] ICR 722). Most Directives, however, do have *vertical direct effect*, so if the employee is employed by the state he or she may be able to rely on the wording of the Directive itself. It is therefore quite possible to have different rights ascribed to different groups of employees by reason only of who they work for.

(c) Where UK legislation has been implemented to comply with EU legislation it may be interpreted in a very purposive manner. That is, the statutory interpretation techniques used by the courts and their willingness to read the UK legislation so as to comply with the spirit of the EC enactment means that a purely literal approach to such UK legislation is unsafe even when the words are unambiguous in themselves. This is known as giving the Directive *indirect effect* and may be applied to both private and public sector employees.

1.7 The Human Rights Act 1998 and employment law

In the general part of the LPC you will already have dealt with the key issues of incorporation of the European Convention on Human Rights via the 1998 Act. You will have seen that:

(a) All legislation, whenever enacted, must be interpreted in such a way as to comply with the rights granted under the Convention: HRA 1998, s. 3(1).

(b) But, in all cases, unless the UK legislation can be interpreted so as to comply with Convention rights, an Act of Parliament still takes precedence over Convention rights. This means that the *validity* of primary legislation is beyond judicial control. The same will be true of secondary legislation. However, even before the introduction of the HRA 1998, secondary legislation which was *ultra vires* its parent Act could be struck down by the normal process of judicial review. That principle can also be applied when human rights issues are involved unless the primary legislation prevents removal of the incompatibility between the legislation and human rights principles: s. 3(2)(c) and s. 6(2)(b), i.e., the incompatibility lies in the primary legislation itself. For these purposes primary legislation includes commencement orders and orders which amend primary legislation: HRA 1998, s. 21(1).

(c) All courts and tribunals must take into account the jurisprudence of the Convention, which means the decisions of the European Court of Human Rights, whenever a Convention right arises (HRA 1998, s. 2). However, UK courts are not bound to apply the decisions of the European Court. Equally, the doctrine of *stare decisis* is modified in that domestic binding precedents which are now found to conflict with Convention rights may be ignored.

(d) Certain courts (but not employment tribunals or the EAT) have the right to declare primary and secondary legislation incompatible with Convention Rights: HRA 1998, s. 4. A declaration of incompatibility only allows judges to scrutinise legislation. Such a declaration does not affect the validity of primary legislation, nor does it affect secondary legislation (subject to our comments above in (b)). Neither is the declaration directed at the litigants, so the case in hand is not affected by the declaration; it has no legal effect and is simply a 'warning shot' aimed at Parliament.

(e) There is no system of sending references (akin to art. 234, EC Treaty) to the European Court of Human Rights so that there is a possibility of conflict between the UK courts' interpretation of the Convention and that of the European Court of Human Rights (to which a 'victim' can still apply after exhausting the UK system).

(f) All public authorities must act in a way which is compatible with Convention rights: HRA 1998, s. 6. 'Public authority' includes 'any person certain of whose functions are functions of a public nature'; s. 6(3)(b). This includes courts and tribunals.

(g) Certain rights have not been incorporated e.g., art. 13 of the Convention.

(h) The areas which are likely to impact on employment law are detailed below.

1.7.1 Which employers are affected?

Action may be taken directly against a 'public authority' under the HRA 1998, s. 6 claiming a breach of Convention rights; with ordinary employers an employee would have to persuade a court that, in analysing a cause of action, existing legislation or judicial precedents should be read in the light of Convention rights. Thus there is a distinction between 'vertical' and 'horizontal' effect akin to the application of Directives in EU Law.

The term 'public authority' has not been defined in the Act but will obviously include bodies such as local authorities. This still begs the question whether all activities undertaken by a public authority are caught by s. 6 or only those which are clearly a 'public function'. It was confirmed in parliamentary debates that the definition of 'public authority' in s. 6 was intended to apply to public bodies even when acting as employers (which is not a public function *per se*). Following *Pepper* v *Hart* [1993] AC 593 on the use of Hansard this may well settle any argument on s. 6 for employment purposes so that employees of public bodies will have a direct cause of action against their employers, whereas employees of private organisations will have to take the more circuitous route.

However, the Act does recognise that there will be hybrid bodies (e.g., privatised utilities, the BBC, and professional bodies) who exercise both private and public functions.

In relation to hybrid bodies s. 6(5) states that, '. . . a person is not a public authority by virtue of sub-s. (1)(3)(b) if the nature of the act is private'.

At the time of writing, there is still a debate as to whether employment matters should be classified as public or private functions. It may well be that some such activities (e.g., health and safety matters) are classified as public whilst general employment matters are private.

1.7.1.1 Victim

A person can only rely on Convention rights against a public authority where they fall within the definition of 'victim' (HRA 1998, s. 7(7)). This generally means that the claimant must be a person who is directly affected by the alleged breach and prevents representative actions (e.g., by trade unions) except for very limited situations.

Proceedings against public authorities must be brought within one year of the act complained of.

1.7.2 Rights directly relevant to employment

1.7.2.1 Forced/compulsory labour, under art. 4 of the Convention

No forced labour claim has succeeded in Strasbourg to date, and speculations that working conditions, long hours and compulsory overtime amount to such a breach are not convincing. The employment relationship is a contractual one which both parties can terminate and, even within the relationship, existing legislation on working time, harassment etc. cover these areas adequately.

1.7.2.2 Freedom to join or not to join trade unions, under art. 11 of the Convention

Article 11 establishes the right to peaceful assembly and to freedom of association with others, including the right to form and join a trade union. Domestic law on this topic is already well-developed and this article is unlikely to have a major impact on employment law.

1.7.3 Other rights (indirectly) relevant to employment

1.7.3.1 Fair and public hearing, under art. 6 of the Convention

This is the most frequently-invoked article of the Convention. It states that '. . . everyone is entitled to a fair and public hearing within a reasonable time by an independent and impartial tribunal established by law'. Clearly this exists in the procedures adopted by the courts and employment tribunals. Some arguments have been raised that internal disciplinary proceedings are caught by this provision but these appear to be speculation for its own sake as any such decision can be 'reviewed' in a tribunal or court.

What is not so clear-cut is whether the lack of legal help/representation in tribunals might breach this article (see for instance *Airey* v *Ireland* (1979) 2 EHRR 305) or even the fact that some rights (e.g., unfair dismissal and redundancy) require qualification periods. As regards the latter point Convention jurisprudence shows (e.g., in cases dealing with limitation periods such as *Stubbings* v *United Kingdom* (1996) 23 EHRR 213) that the argument will centre on whether the qualification period is part of the substantive right to claim, say, unfair dismissal (in which case interference is unlikely) or whether it is a procedural 'add on'. ERA 1996, s. 94(1) states that an employee has the right not to be unfairly dismissed which looks like a bare declaration of the right with any qualifying period being an add on, but s. 94(2) makes sub-s. (1) subject to a range of sections including s. 108 which sets out the qualification. The point is therefore quite well-balanced.

The question of tribunals hearing cases involving their paymasters and what constitutes a public hearing have already caused some consternation and brought about changes in procedure. And on the commercial side, Part 25 of the Civil Procedure Rules was clearly drafted with art. 6 in mind, but the question of how interim injunctions and search orders operate may still occupy the attention of the courts. Whether the ACAS arbitration scheme may breach art. 6 (in that the participating parties must waive their rights to a trial) is one of those issues still under debate. We would suggest that, as the new scheme is a voluntary one, it is unlikely that art. 6 would be breached.

1.7.3.2 Respect for private and family life, home and correspondence, under art. 8 of the Convention

This does raise the thorny problem of employers monitoring staff by use of devices such as CCTV, drug testing, interceptions of e-mails, and the keeping of personnel records. There exists plenty of case law and legislation covering matters such as access to medical information and data protection, but less on monitoring employees (though see *Halford* v *United Kingdom* [1997] IRLR 471 on telephone interceptions). We can reasonably expect developments in this area (see for example, **7.8.4** on monitoring communications).

The Privy Council was recently faced with an interesting problem on the question of art. 8 in *Whitefield* v *General Medical Council* [2002] UKPC 62, [2003] IRLR 39, where a doctor with a serious history of alcohol problems was required by the General Medical Council to abstain absolutely from alcohol, to submit to random breath, blood, and urine tests, and to attend Alcoholics Anonymous. The doctor argued that together or individually these amounted to a breach of art. 8 as the conditions interfered with the right to respect for his private life. His argument was rejected on the basis that there was no authority to support the proposition that a ban on the consumption of alcohol is, *per se*, a breach of art. 8 and that he could still socialise without consuming alcohol. Further, even if these actions were a breach of art. 8(1) the conditions were lawfully imposed in the circumstances under art. 8(2) which allows for the interference in private life in limited circumstances such as the protection of health or morals. This also applied to the compulsory medical tests, which have been held to be in breach of art. 8 in other jurisdictions and circumstances.

On the facts, one has little difficulty with the analysis in *Whitefield*. Whether it gives birth to a whole range of arguments determining just how far bans by (public authority) employers on employees' 'out of work' activities will be held acceptable without breaching art. 8 (e.g., bans on smoking or taking part in dangerous sports) is more debatable.

The impact of the Human Rights Act 1998 on unfair dismissal was considered by the Court of Appeal in *x* v *y* [2004] EWCA Civ 662 concerning the activities of an employee in a public toilet, and by the EAT in *McGowan* v *Scottish Water* [2005] IRLR 167 relating to covert surveillance of an employee.

1.7.3.3 Freedom of thought, conscience and religion, under art. 9 of the Convention

The UK has specific legislation covering religious activities, e.g., Race Relations Act 1976, the Religion or Belief Regulations 2003, the Equality Act 2006 and aspects relating to working on Sundays in the ERA 1996 so that references to art. 9 for these purposes are now less relevant.

1.7.3.4 Freedom of expression, under art. 10 of the Convention

This article includes the right to receive and impart information and ideas without interference, subject to restrictions which are necessary in a democratic society. Matters such as the law of defamation, the Public Interest Disclosure Act 1998 and the duty of confidentiality already cover many aspects raised here (see **Chapters 8** and **9** below). The extent to which 'expression' extends to matters like dress codes has been the subject of speculation, though there is nothing in the Convention case law to support this.

1.7.3.5 Non-discrimination, under art. 14 of the Convention

This is not a free-standing right but relates to the provisions of the Convention itself *viz* it only prohibits discrimination in the enjoyment of one or other of the rights guaranteed by the Convention. The new Protocol 12 modifies this position.

1.8 The internet and other sources

There are numerous sites on the internet that now give access to a wide range of information on employment law. We cannot list all of those here, but a useful starting point is: www.emplaw.co.uk which is a portal to a whole host of relevant sites; www.employmentappeals.gov.uk for the EAT; www.bis.gov.uk for the Department for Business, Innovation and Skills; www.acas.org.uk for ACAS; www.opsi.gov.uk/acts.htm for recent statutes, and www.opsi.gov.uk/stat.htm for statutory instruments. Equality issues can be investigated at www.equalityhumanrights.com.

The best practitioners' text is *Harvey on Industrial Relations and Employment Law* (London: LexisNexis Butterworths) and, amongst the many journals in this field, the *IDS Brief* (Income Data Services Ltd) stands out as being informative and up to date.

2

Definition of 'employee'

2.1 Introduction

This chapter examines how the presence of an employment relationship is determined, what factors should be considered in making that determination, and what are the possible consequences of the classification.

The relevance of these questions is that they will determine:

(a) who is *responsible* for matters such as liability for tax and National Insurance contributions, injury in the workplace and damage caused to others;
(b) what contractual *rights* the company has in controlling the activities of the worker;
(c) what specific *statutory rights* the worker has acquired, such as unfair dismissal compensation, redundancy pay, maternity rights and so on.

Thus the first, and most basic, problem confronting anyone dealing with employment law is: 'How does one determine whether a worker is an employee or self-employed (i.e., an independent contractor)?' The importance to this is that few of the statutes covering the working environment relate to the self-employed. For instance, legislation relating to discrimination, together with health and safety matters, has general application but most of the statutory rights such as unfair dismissal refer only to employees. As will be seen, the mere fact that the parties reach agreement on their respective status is not the determining feature.

This chapter will adopt the following structure:

(a) The tests for an employment relationship.
(b) The benefits and pitfalls of each type of relationship.
(c) Types of employee.
(d) Vicarious liability.
(e) The statutory meaning of 'Worker'.

To most employment lawyers this area has usually been of general background relevance only. However, the basic questions raised here have surfaced more frequently in recent years.

Some employers, recognising the increased protection the law now gives to 'permanent' or 'core' employees (whether full-time or part-time), have sought to create a second tier of temporary or 'peripheral' workers with fewer rights. Sometimes this involves an attempt to categorise them as independent contractors and so not employees at all, or to devise fictions such as 'zero hours' contracts. It is also the case, however, that both EU and Government policy is moving towards doing away with the distinction between employees and independent contractors. It is increasingly common to find the term 'worker' appearing in Directives and statutes concerned with employment rights. Indeed, ERA 1999, s. 23 specifically confers upon the Secretary of State by order the power to extend statutory employment rights to workers other than employees. This means that we have a category of people who can be classed as 'employees' and to whom all the key statutory rights apply, a group of 'independent contractors' to whom none of the rights apply, and a middle-ground of 'workers' who look like independent contractors but who, in particular circumstances, may gain the same statutory employment protection rights as employees.

We will therefore first examine the practicalities of the classic distinctions of employees and independent contractors and then look at the effect of the new classification of 'worker' used in modern legislation.

2.2 The tests for an employment relationship

Various tests have been developed over the years to answer what appears to be a very simple question—how to define the term 'employee'. There is a statutory definition contained in ERA 1996, s. 230(1) but it has been deliberately left vague. It states that an 'employee' means an individual who has entered into or works under a contract of employment—which in turn is defined as a contract of service or of apprenticeship. This is less than helpful but sums up the approach of the courts *viz,* if it looks like a duck and quacks like a duck, it is a duck. Other (more legal) tests exist, as described below.

Note: to avoid confusion between the noun 'worker' and the legally-defined, statute-protected 'Worker' we have used the inelegant term 'workman' to describe the non-statutory kind. For brevity, the term also applies to women.

2.2.1 The control test

The problems associated with defining the term 'employee' or, in older terminology, 'servant' have been with us for centuries, arising long before the application of contract terminology to the employment relationship. The assessment of the presence and extent of responsibilities closely followed the analytical line as to whether the putative employer had 'control' over what the individual did and the manner in which it was done. This seemed a natural path to take. The greater the degree of control, the more likely it was that there was a contract *of* service rather than a contract *for* services; that the person was a servant rather than an independent contractor or agent. The employee sells his labour; the contractor sells a product.

The courts are concerned here to find who it is that determines the operation of the contract; who exercises the discretion? This is achieved by what may be termed a *'Who, what, where, when and how' test.* That is to say:

(a) *Who*

To what extent does the 'employer' control who does the work? The contract of employment is a contract of *personal* service, so if the workman can delegate the task or send replacements this essential element of personal service will be missing. This point was strongly emphasised in *Ready Mixed Concrete (South East) Ltd v Minister of Pensions and National Insurance* [1968] 2 QB 497, which held that a lorry driver (who had to obey a wide range of company rules) was nevertheless an independent contractor because, *inter alia,* he could, with the company's consent, arrange for a substitute driver to do his job instead. As later cases have confirmed, where a person who works for another is not required to perform his service personally *then* the relationship between the worker and the person for whom he works is unlikely to be that of employer and employee. We use the word 'unlikely' because a limited power of delegation may not be inconsistent with employee status, e.g., where the individual is allowed to delegate because of illness (see *Staffordshire Sentinel Newspapers* v *Potter* [2004] IRLR 752, EAT). However, a *general* power to delegate remains inconsistent with a contract of employment.

(b) *What*

Does the 'employer' control what work is done, e.g., the order in which jobs are undertaken?

(c) *Where*

What control does the 'employer' have over the place of work? If work is done at home or on the workman's own business premises, this will point away from an employment relationship.

(d) *When*

A similar point to 'where' which relates to the hours worked.

(e) *How*

Can the 'employer' control how the work is to be performed? With skilled workmen it becomes unrealistic to suppose that control can be exercised here. In truth, though, the courts have approached this by asking, does the 'employer' have the *right* to control activities, rather than asking whether control is *physically* exercised.

The control test is still used widely today, though usually in combination with other tests.

2.2.2 The integration test

The integration test developed to cope with the problems of controlling *how* a job is to be done. 'Integration' was never accurately defined and the test only ever really applied to fringe occupations. The formula applied was: If the workman was fully integrated into—'a part and parcel of'—the enterprise then there was likely to be a contract of service. This meant investigating whether the workman took part in administrative duties, management decisions or undertook other tasks. If some degree of **mutuality** was present, with the 'employer' providing benefits such as holiday pay, this would tend to indicate a contract *of* service. However, where a person performed only a single task, usually for only a short time, this raised the presumption of a contract *for* services.

2.2.3 Economic reality test

The control test and the integration test tend now to be subsumed into a more general balancing exercise which goes by various names—the economic reality test, the mixed test, and the multiple test. The question of who is or is not an employee is generally one of fact, not law (except in the interpretation of written contracts).

This economic reality test recognises that it is the *combination and balance* of features and the degree of emphasis that matters more than one simple checklist. So the modern approach demands that all the factors for and against the presence of an employment relationship are put into balance. Two key questions are then posed. These are:

(a) *Are these workmen in business on their own account?*

Here one looks to the financial risk and input of capital as regards equipment and varying profits. Any company, when set against an individual, will obviously have injected more capital and have taken more sizeable financial risks, so the emphasis has to be on the level provided by the workman: is it higher than one would normally expect from an employee? This entrepreneurial aspect of the test was emphasised in one of the key cases in this area, *viz Ready Mixed Concrete* v *Minister of Pensions* (see **2.2.1**) as regards lorry drivers. If a workman is in business on his own account not only will he have some chance of increasing his profits (a pieceworker could claim the same), but he will also be at some *risk* of losing money.

(b) *Is there a mutual obligation to provide work and perform tasks as directed?*
Here one looks to matters such as: is there a 'wage-work bargain', i.e., *some* obligation to provide work and *some* obligation to do that work; does the putative employer provide sick pay or holiday pay; are there set hours; and does the workman do the same tasks as ordinary employees? This last aspect of mutuality was emphasised in *Nethermere of St Neots* v *Gardiner and Taverna* [1984] ICR 612, where homeworkers, who largely regulated their own workload, were nevertheless found to be employees on the basis that in many respects they were treated the same (and did the same type of work) as their full-time equivalents.

The tests above are the guiding forms of analysis adopted by the courts, but in the end the exercise is one of balancing these features. As the Court of Appeal stated in *Hall (Inspector of Taxes)* v *Lorimer* [1992] ICR 739: although one needs to compile a detailed checklist the court must evaluate the overall effect of that detail.

2.2.4 Labels and descriptions

It may be thought that, in a contractual setting such as this, what the parties call themselves would be determinative. However, the history of this area is littered with cases where one or other party attempts to avoid liability with the use of such devices, and so the relationship is analysed under an objective test: the label is just one factor to take into account. For instance, in *Young and Woods* v *West* [1980] IRLR 201, West opted to be called self-employed although doing the same work as ordinary employees. The Inland Revenue treated him as self-employed, and all would have been well, but the company declared redundancies and, as a self-employed worker, West was not entitled to any compensation. He therefore claimed that, in reality, he was an employee all along. The Court of Appeal eventually agreed (though they also referred the matter to the Inland Revenue as regards past tax bills).

Mere labels therefore do not carry much weight. The proper approach is to consider whether the terms reflect the true intention of the parties. Thus, in *Express and Echo Publications Ltd* v *Tanton* [1999] ICR 693, the Court of Appeal noted that one should look first at the terms of the agreement and then consider whether any of those terms are inherently inconsistent with the existence of a contract of employment. If there is an inherently inconsistent term, such as clear arrangements for the provision of substitute workers on a commercial footing (i.e., a clause showing personal service is not important), the term is more likely to mean that this is not an employment relationship; if there is no inconsistency one must still look at the balance of all the terms. More recently, the Court of Appeal, in both *Protectacoat Firthglow Ltd* v *Szilagyi* [2009] EWCA Civ 98, [2009] IRLR 365 and *Autoclenz v Belcher* [2009] EWCA Civ 1046; [2010] IRLR 70, has emphasised that a tribunal must investigate whether the words of the written contract represent the true intentions of the parties, not only at the inception of the contract but at any later stage where the evidence shows that the parties have expressly or impliedly varied that agreement. Thus, the mere fact that a right to provide substitutes or not to provide guaranteed work had never been exercised, for instance, did not mean that it was not a genuine right.

It should also be stressed that the mere fact that an external body, such as HM Revenue and Customs, classes a workman as one thing or another, is only marginally important for employment law purposes.

2.2.5 Irreducible minima?

You may gather from all this (and the point is reinforced below when we look at *types* of employees) that this area can be something of a mess. The courts are constantly trying to find some overriding factors which can be used to determine all situations—often referred to as the *irreducible minima* which go to make an employment relationship—but it is the search for the Holy Grail. As the practitioners' 'bible' in this area (*Harvey on Industrial Relations and Employment Law*) concludes: 'If the obligation is merely to get the job done, then the individual is an independent contractor and not an employee; if the obligation is to do the job himself, then he could be either.' Nevertheless, the main modern contenders are as follows:

(a) The question of who exercises *control* in terms *of procedures,* e.g., the *right* to control as seen in *Ready Mixed Concrete* (above); or the presence or absence of grievance and disciplinary procedures, which was the central point in *Montgomery* v *Johnson Underwood Ltd* [2001] EWCA Civ 318; [2001] IRLR 269.

(b) The question of *who* exercises *control* in terms of the requirement of *personal service/the right to delegate.*

(c) The question of whether there is *mutuality of obligation* in terms of:

   (i) commitment, as evidenced in the presence of sick pay schemes, holiday arrangements, etc.—*Nethermere* (above, and at **2.4.5** below);

   (ii) some form of continuing consideration, as with the use of a retainer—*Clark* v *Oxfordshire Health Authority* [1998] IRLR 125 (see below at **2.4.6**); or

   (iii) some binding commitment, or express or implied guarantee of work and guarantee of service: see *Carmichael* v *National Power plc* [2000] IRLR 43, HL (below at **2.4.6**) and *McMeechan* v *Secretary of State for Employment* [1997] ICR 549 (below at **2.4.7.1**).

(d) As noted in **2.2.4** above, what the parties actually *agree*. Although not determinative, if the parties expressly negative mutuality of obligation, e.g., they agree that there is no obligation to provide work or to accept any work offered, and that the relationship is *ad hoc* and casual, then the courts will have the devil's own job to say that a casual worker (even a regular one) was employed on some form of global contract: *Stevedoring & Haulage Services Ltd* v *Fuller* [2001] EWCA Civ 651, [2001] IRLR 627. If, however, the *purpose* of the agreement is to oust the jurisdiction of the tribunal (e.g., by stating that the workman is not an employee and so cannot claim employee-related statutory rights such as unfair dismissal) then it will be struck down by the anti-avoidance provisions in s. 203 of ERA 1996.

2.2.6 Noting the basis of the question

The decisions in this area are not always consistent, but it is often useful to ask *why* the court had to make its judgment. If the matter is a simple question of money, e.g., tax liability, the court tends to take a very detached and analytical stance. If, however, the question is one of responsibility for safety as was the case in *Lane* v *Shire Roofing Co. (Oxford) Ltd* [1995] IRLR 493, one may find the Court of Appeal stretching definitions to their limit to prise the workman into the category of 'employee'. The grey area arises when the question of establishing status relates to the acquisition of rights (e.g., unfair dismissal); and, as noted above, perhaps this is the very area most likely to give rise to problems in the future.

The arguments on tax liability relate, of course, to the advantages gained by being self-employed in terms of deductions, etc. that can be made in assessing a person's yearly income. Most people are employees and so subject to the PAYE scheme, which allows for little or no leeway in the calculation of tax liability. The rules on National Insurance contributions differ according to status as well. The most recent controversy on 'employee' status and tax liability has arisen in the area of 'service providers', i.e., a person who operates a business or is engaged through an agency but works so regularly (often exclusively) for one company (e.g., providing IT services) that he or she looks to all the world like an employee. The HM Revenue and Customs' scheme, commonly referred to as IR35, creates a presumption that, under certain conditions, such people are deemed to be employees rather than self-employed.

2.3 The benefits and pitfalls of each type of relationship

Advantages to a company of hiring independent contractors	*Advantages to workmen of being independent contractors*
(a) That the company will not have to take on the administrative difficulties of tax, National Insurance, including the costs of the employer's contributions, or statutory sick pay.	(a) The workman will be able to register under Schedule D for tax purposes, gaining benefits of claiming expenses, etc.
(b) That the company is unlikely to be vicariously liable for the actions of the workmen (see **2.5** below).	(b) The workman will be free to undertake work from other sources without gaining permission from the 'employer'.
(c) That a notionally lower duty as to safety is owed to independent contractors at common law under the tort of negligence if not under the Health and Safety at Work etc. Act 1974.	(c) The workman can determine his or her own pattern of work to fit in with personal commitments or other jobs.
(d) That the company does not have to issue written statements of terms and conditions (under ERA 1996, s. 1—see **Chapter 3**).	(d) The workman may hire others to undertake the work.
(e) That the company is not responsible for the provision of training or the payment of training levies.	(e) The workman is often free to choose where the work will be done.
(f) That the company owes no duty to deal with trade unions as regards collective bargaining, redundancy consultation, or the provision of office facilities or time off.	(f) The workman may be able to negotiate better contractual terms than the equivalent employee.
(g) That the company will be dealing with commercial operators and so the contracts formed, the terms and conditions, will be viewed by courts in that setting. The company can thus hire groups of employees for specific tasks for short periods of time only.	(g) Work completed ahead of time will mean that the workman may move on to other tasks or even obtain a completion bonus.

(h) That the company cannot be liable for unfair dismissal or redundancy.	
(a) The contract of employment requires *personal* service. The employer has made the judgment as to the make-up of its workmen.	(a) Minimal financial input and risk.
(b) The employer maintains a higher level of control over employees, particularly where the company wishes the workmen to perform tasks on the periphery of the 'job description'.	(b) Fringe benefits, e.g., company cars and accommodation.
(c) This control can be emphasised by the use of disciplinary procedures and sanctions.	(c) Membership of company sick pay and pension schemes.
(d) The contract is viewed as containing a much higher degree of loyalty and good faith via the device of implied terms (see **Chapter 5**).	(d) The payment of holiday pay.
(e) Unfair dismissal actions etc. on the whole will cost less than the termination of a commercial contract. Furthermore, actions short of dismissal can be taken more easily under a contract of employment's disciplinary procedures.	(e) Greater job security in terms of increased potential for capital investment.
(f) The company does not have to pay VAT for the work undertaken.	(f) Greater job security in terms of statutory rights, e.g., unfair dismissal.
	(g) The ability to demand more money for the performance of additional tasks not defined in the contract through trade union negotiation.
	(h) The employer must indemnify the employee for expenses and liabilities occasioned in the course of employment.

2.4 Types of employee

Although the position of most workmen will never lead to litigation, specific occupations still cause problems. The questions raised above have grown in importance with the advent of different patterns of work, the move towards establishing small businesses and the massive increase in the numbers of women joining the workforce, mainly through a variety of forms of part-time jobs (e.g., temporary work, casual work, job-share schemes, and homeworking). It is fast becoming the norm to encounter employment relationships which do not fit the standard full-time pattern.

2.4.1 Crown servants

Crown servants are those individuals employed under or for a Government department or any body exercising Crown functions, e.g., civil servants. Traditionally, Crown servants have not been classed as 'employees' but have had protection against unfair dismissal. Under TULRCA 1992, s. 273, Crown servants have now gained employee status, and even those employed in the armed services have acquired certain employment rights under the ERA 1996, s. 192 and sch. 2, para. 16.

2.4.2 Directors and shareholders

Directors will not be classed as employees unless there is a contract of employment to that effect. In many cases, however, a director's duty as a fiduciary will create a greater burden of responsibility and accountability than if there were a contract of employment. The appointment of directors as employees is subject to various statutory controls. There is, however, no rule of law which prevents even a controlling shareholder from being held to be an employee too—it is a question of fact and public policy: *Secretary of State for Trade and Industry* v *Bottrill* [1999] IRLR 326—and extensive guidelines have now been laid down by the EAT in *Clark* v *Clark Construction Initiatives Ltd* [2008] IRLR 364 and modified slightly in *Secretary of State for Business, Enterprise and Regulatory Reform* v *Neufeld* [2009] EWCA Civ 280, [2009] IRLR 475.

2.4.3 Consultants

Consultants may be classed as employees if they become sufficiently integrated into the business—and note the IR35 scheme above at **2.2.6**.

2.4.4 Part-timers

Under common law no real distinction has ever been made between full-time and part-time employees. Part-time employees will, for instance, owe duties of fidelity and confidentiality and will be covered by the law on intellectual property rights (e.g., patents). And although the courts have become increasingly aware that the standard expected of part-time employees (especially where restrictions are imposed on their activities) must inevitably be less than that expected of full-timers, the residual elements of the duties will nevertheless be present.

Neither does the epithet of 'part-time' affect a person's statutory rights (see below at **11.3.2**). As the amount of work taken diminishes, however, there may be problems as to status—as with those who work at home or who are casual workers.

The Part-time Workers (Prevention of Less Favourable Treatment) Regulations 2000 (SI 2000/1551) are dealt with in **Chapter 7**.

2.4.5 Homeworkers

Once a workman is removed from the normal workplace, he gains some measure of independence as to 'control'. The more the workman can exercise discretion as to workload, timing, and organisation of work, the more he is likely to be an independent contractor. However, as was seen in *Nethermere of St Neots* v *Gardiner and Taverna* [1984] ICR 612, if these workmen are treated in much the same way as full-time employees and gain benefits as to holiday entitlements, sick pay, etc., they are more likely to be employees. There are over three million people working wholly or mainly from home—some as a result of exercising their 'flexible working' rights (see **4.7** and **4.8** below).

In *Nethermere* the company manufactured boys' trousers. They employed full-time staff in their factory and a number of homeworkers. The applicants were part-time homeworkers. Taverna had previously worked in the factory as an employee. Both had worked with the company since the late 1970s. They sewed trouser flaps and pockets using machines provided by the company. There were no fixed hours of work; but they usually worked four to five hours a day. They were paid weekly by piece-rate. They filled out time sheets and received daily deliveries. They were not obliged to accept any particular quantity of work. There arose a dispute over holiday payments, as a consequence of which the arrangement came to an end. The workmen claimed they were unfairly dismissed. The company argued they were self-employed. The Court of Appeal held that there was sufficient mutuality of obligations for the relationship to constitute a contract of employment. Although the traditional use of homeworkers has now declined, the points raised here will take on a greater significance as more and more people work from home utilising information technology as the means of performing their jobs.

2.4.6 Casuals

Presently, the two most litigated areas on the definition of 'employee' relate to casuals and 'temps'.

In certain industries, e.g., catering or agriculture, it is quite common for staff to be employed casually or seasonally. Some are employed on a regular basis, others from time to time according to demand. The more regular the 'employment', the more the workers look like employees—but what does it take before an employment relationship is triggered by this regular contact? In one of the major cases in this area (*O'Kelly* v *Trust-house Forte* [1983] ICR 728) the Court of Appeal held that some staff who worked exclusively for the hotel chain for an average of 31 hours per week, were paid weekly and received holiday pay and incentive bonuses, were still not employees because they were not compelled to take work if it was offered to them and did not receive sick pay or belong to the company pension scheme. They were deemed to be in business on their own account.

O'Kelly highlights the problem: it may well be the case that on each occasion when the workman is hired by the company there is a contract of employment for a day, a week, a month or even longer, but such intermittent periods would be unlikely to form such a cohesive whole that there could be said to be an overall employment relationship continuing during the off-periods. Without such continuity of employment the workman would not gain access to many statutory employment rights, such as redundancy payments. The rights could be present only if one could find some form of 'global' contract, spanning the gap between the periods of engagement; and to establish that one needs to find that there is sufficient mutuality of obligation between company and workman during that slack time so as to override any view that these putative employees are simply people in business on their own account.

How can such mutuality be found? One needs to find some express or implied term that work would be provided and performed when reasonably required. Thus, in *Clark* v *Oxfordshire Health Authority* [1998] IRLR 125, bank nurses were found to be employees on the basis that they were paid a retainer during the off-period; on the other hand, in *Carmichael* v *National Power plc* [2000] IRLR 43, the House of Lords held that power station tour guides who worked as much as 25 hours per week, were paid an hourly rate, given training and wore company uniforms, were not employees because their letters of appointment stated that they worked on an 'as required basis' and they were not paid between engagements.

These cases are, however, far from satisfactory in providing practical solutions which a solicitor can put in place for his or her client. First, it should be noted that on each occasion the putative employee provides his or her service, the primary tests used above (control etc.) determine whether *that particular contract* is a contract of employment or not. If it is, and that employment goes on for long enough, the employee will gain various statutory employment rights anyway (e.g., generally a year for unfair dismissal). Secondly, even if the contractual periods are for short bursts, that does not mean there *cannot* be an employment relationship. The cases have not properly explored whether these contract periods could be melded together under the rules on establishing continuity of employment so that, even with a number of short-duration contracts, statutory rights might be acquired (see below at **5.3** for the rules on continuity). Thus, we would suggest that the focus should be on whether the established rules of continuity apply and not on the nebulous problem of whether there is a 'global contract' covering the off-periods. We would submit that the existence of any global contract can be determined by the purely contractual analysis of whether there is continuing consideration during those off-periods (as in *Clark*). One should not need to go beyond that contractual analysis and explore the vague topic of 'mutuality'.

2.4.7 Temp agency workers

Employment businesses exist to supply workmen to client companies as temporary workers—or 'temps' as they are often called. The employment businesses enter into contracts with both the workman and the client company. These organisations are colloquially known as 'employment agencies', though this tag has a particular meaning in law, referring to recruitment consultants ('headhunters'). The difference is that 'headhunters' are forbidden from paying the workman; their money is made from finders' fees. As our interest lies with the status of 'temps' we shall concentrate on employment businesses (but note that older cases refer to these same organisations as 'employment agencies').

For many years, temps were not regarded as employees of either the employment business or their clients. Their position was said to be *sui generis: Ironmonger* v *Movefield Ltd* [1988] IRLR 461. But in the late 1990s the courts began to find contracts of employment, even where the contract itself specified that none existed. This did not happen on every occasion and the tide has turned again. The problem lies in the fact that there is a tripartite agreement here: the employment business 'takes on' the temp, the temp is then sent to a client company, the temp works under the general rules of the client company (perhaps receiving benefits such as sick pay), the client company pays the employment business an agreed rate, the employment business pays the temp as per *their* agreement. There are plenty of contracts floating around, but are any of them contracts of employment? Effectively, there are three possible outcomes:

- an employment contract exists between the employment business and the temp; or
- one exists between the temp and the client company (sometimes referred to as the 'end user'); or
- no employment contract exists.

2.4.7.1 Contract with the employment business?

In *McMeechan* v *Secretary of State for Employment* [1997] ICR 549 the Court of Appeal decided that there could (if the facts were right) be two contracts between a temp and an employment business: (i) an 'umbrella contract'—more often referred to as 'being on the books'; and (ii) separate contracts for each assignment given to the temp, even if the umbrella contract described the temp as 'self-employed'. In *Bunce* v *Postworth Ltd t/a Skyblue* [2005] EWCA Civ 490, [2005] IRLR 557 the Court of Appeal made it clear that it would be rare for a temp to have *any* form of employment contract with the employment business and that in those rare cases day-to-day control over the temp's activities would normally have to be present. It was thought by many that this had brought an end to such claims but the Court of Appeal did remit such a case (involving the hiring of Polish temporary workers in the hotel industry) to a different tribunal for a re-hearing in *Consistent Group Ltd* v *Kalwak* [2008] EWCA Civ 430, [2008] IRLR 505 where all the classic conditions of personal service and control were present. Despite this, one can usually say that the temp and the employment business are not parties to contracts of employment.

2.4.7.2 Contract of employment with the client company (the 'end-user')?

Again after extensive debate, the Court of Appeal, in *James* v *London Borough of Greenwich* [2008] EWCA Civ 35, [2008] IRLR 302, has now clearly established that an employment contract between the temp and the client company will only be implied where it is *necessary* to give the arrangement business efficacy. This should sound the death-knell for such arguments. However, all may change again in October 2011 when the Agency Workers Regulations 2010 are due to come into force—granting some employment rights to temps who have at least 12 weeks' 'service'.

2.4.7.3 General guidance

Until the next twist occurs it is a relatively safe presumption that a temp is employed by no one.

- It is highly unlikely (but just legally possible) that there will be an 'umbrella' agreement between the employment business and the temp which amounts to a contract of employment (see *McMeechan* and comments in *Bunce*). The more detailed the provisions in the contract as to what is to happen with each particular assignment the less likely such a contract can arise *(Bunce)*.
- Although *McMeechan* stated that there may be separate contracts of employment between the temp and the employment business for each particular assignment one still has to add all these together (with the breaks amounting only to 'temporary' cessations of employment) to get the right number of days to gain statutory rights.
- The documentation can exclude the inference of an employment relationship (e.g., an 'entire agreement' clause) but, to do this it should be very clear and not contain contradictory or conflicting statements (such conflict arose in *Royal National Lifeboat Institution* v *Bushaway* [2005] IRLR 674, EAT, so that where a temp was made permanent in the client company her continuity of employment was dated from her original start date as a temp despite wording to the contrary).
- In bringing a claim (say, for unfair dismissal) a temp is advised to proceed against both the employment business and the client company. Tribunals also have the power to join a party: Employment Tribunals (Constitution and Rules of Procedure) Regulations 2004 (SI 2004/1861), r. 10(2)(k).
- The Conduct of Employment Agencies and Employment Businesses Regulations 2003 (SI 2003/3319) affect how both employment businesses and employment agencies operate and there are separate regulations covering workmen who operate as limited companies and the specialist nursing agencies. 'Temps' are now known as 'work-seekers'—but not by most people. The Regulations lay out detailed rules on the provision of contractual documents as between all parties, including statements on whether the work-seeker is to be an employee of the employment business or is working under a contract for services. The details of these documents are outside the scope of this text but the key question as to the determination of status is not clarified in the Regulations.

2.4.8 Employees on limited-term contracts

Employers sometimes use the device of a limited-term to define the length of an acknowledged employment contract. There is nothing untoward here and the term may be short (e.g., months) or long (years) or even relate to a specific task. When the time expires or the task is completed there are no further consequences at common law, though (as will be seen in **Chapter 7** and **Chapters 11–13**) the non-renewal of a limited-term contract will constitute a dismissal for statutory purposes such as unfair dismissal. Whether the non-renewal *actually is* an unfair dismissal is a separate question.

2.4.9 Apprentices

Apprentices are a *sui generis* category of employees. The purpose of an apprenticeship is primarily that of training so that, although most of the normal rules will cover them, there are some key differences from ordinary contracts, e.g., there are restrictions on how the contract can be terminated and damages may be awarded for loss of training and status. The so-called 'modern apprenticeship agreement' is another of the tri-partite schemes (between the individual, the 'employer', and the local training organisation). The latest pronouncement by the Court of Appeal on the status of these modern apprentices is that they can be apprentices as we know them (which means they gain extra damages for loss of training): *Flett* v *Matheson* [2006] EWCA Civ 53, [2006] ICR 673.

2.4.10 Employees of unincorporated associations

The issue here is simply: 'Whom do such employees sue?' The answer has been provided by the EAT in *Affleck* v *Newcastle MIND* [1999] IRLR 405: one member of the committee should be named as respondent, in his own right and on behalf of all the other members of the committee. Any compensation should be awarded against all those on the committee at the relevant time.

2.4.11 Posted workers

The Posting of Workers Directive (96/71/EC), implemented by the ERA 1999, s. 32, covers the situations where: (a) workers temporarily work in Great Britain; and (b) workers temporarily work abroad. This requires that where a Member State has certain minimum terms and conditions of employment (see **3.4.3.1** below) these must apply to workers posted temporarily by their employer to work in that state. The contract may allow for greater benefits. It does not matter for these purposes whether the organisation posting the worker is from a Member State or not. Unfortunately, this is just the tip of the iceberg when dealing with employees working abroad and one needs to look at a whole raft of specialist legislative measures and House of Lords' decisions in the context of each type of claim before giving advice on this area.

2.4.12 Voluntary workers

Many people work on a voluntary basis (e.g., for charities); this does not make them employees. In *South East Sheffield Citizens Advice Bureau* v *Grayson* [2004] IRLR 353 the EAT held that an unpaid CAB volunteer was not an employee (for the purposes of discrimination legislation), even when paid expenses and even where the CAB would be liable to indemnify the person against negligence claims, as there was no mutuality present. The same analysis has now been applied to unfair dismissal claims in *Melhuish* v *Redbridge Citizens Advice Bureau* [2005] IRLR 419.

2.4.13 Seconded employees

There are instances where one company hires an employee's services from another company. When this arrangement becomes long term awkward questions arise as to who now employs that person. The test is essentially a factual one: where does the mutuality of obligation and element of control lie? Thus, in *Fitton* v *City of Edinburgh Council* (2008 UKEATS/0010/07/MT) the fact that the employee, seconded on an open-ended basis, opted to work under the terms and conditions of the seconding employer and held no substantive job title with her old employer (although there was a fairly loose arrangement for her to return to her old job if the secondment came to an end) led to the conclusion that she no longer worked for her original employer (when she resigned her post and claimed unfair dismissal).

2.5 Vicarious liability

An employer may be vicariously liable for the actions of employees where those actions were undertaken by the employee 'in the course of employment' and not, in the magical phrase, 'on a frolic of his own'. The traditional test has been that if the employee is performing a task which falls within the general expectations of the contract but is performing it in an unauthorised manner, the employer is still likely to be held vicariously liable. Obviously, the employer is liable for any wrongful acts which have been authorised. In *Lister* v *Hesley Hall Ltd* [2001] UKHL 22, [2001] IRLR 472, however, the House of Lords adopted a broader test: were the employee's acts and the nature of his duties closely connected? Using this test (which is similar to that used in discrimination cases), their Lordships held that an employer who was operating a children's residential school was vicariously liable for the sexual assaults on boys in the school committed by an employee-warden. The same logic was applied in *Maga* v *Trustees of the Birmingham Archdiocese of the Roman Catholic Church* [2010] EWCA Civ 256; [2010] All ER (D) 141 (Mar)—sexual abuse by a priest.

If this test is satisfied, the employer will be liable for any personal injury or other damage caused by the employee (e.g., a rugby player hitting an opponent—even where the express terms of the contract forbade this). This principle can even apply where the injured person is another employee.

The position becomes more complicated when the employee in question is a seconded employee: who bears the vicarious liability—the hiring company or the hirer? The leading House of Lords' case of *Mersey Docks and Harbour Board* v *Coggins and Griffith (Liverpool) Ltd* [1947] AC 1 established that this depended on who exercised control over how the job was done. It was thought at that time that this would usually be the permanent employer, but in *Hawley* v *Luminar Leisure plc* [2006] EWCA Civ 18, [2006] IRLR 817 the Court of Appeal held that where a doorman injured a customer the real control rested with the nightclub rather than the permanent employer for the purposes of vicarious liability so that the doorman was a 'temporary deemed employee' of the nightclub (a decision possibly influenced by the severity of the injuries caused by the doorman and the insolvency of the permanent employer). This idea of attaching legal liability to the 'user company' fits in with previous Court of Appeal authorities which had held that in some instances *both* the permanent and temporary employers could be vicariously liable for the employee's actions if the employee is 'so much a part of the work . . . of both employers that it is just to make both employers answer for his negligence'—i.e., where both 'employers' are controlling the employee's actions: *Viasystems (Tyneside) Ltd* v *Thermal Transfer (Northern) Ltd* [2005] EWCA Civ 1151, [2006] ICR 327.

2.6 The statutory meaning of 'worker'

At one time all that had to be asked was, 'Is this person an employee or an independent contractor?' If the former then all the employment rights we will cover in this book came into play; if, not, then they did not. Now, however, as we noted above, some employment rights extend to 'workers' as well as employees. The genuinely self-employed will still not fall within this definition, but 'worker' covers a wider range of people than 'employee'. For instance, the definition to be found in the Working Time Regulations 1998 (dealing with the regulation of hours of work, holidays, etc., see **Chapter 4**) and the Part-time Workers (Prevention of Less Favourable Treatment) Regulations 2000 is the same (see **Chapter 6**). The definition includes anyone who has entered into, or works under, a contract of employment and any other contract 'whereby the individual undertakes to do or perform personally any work or services for another party to the contract whose status is not by virtue of the contract that of a client or customer of any profession or business undertaking carried on by the individual', e.g., agency workers and homeworkers.

In *Edmonds* v *Lawson, Pardoe & Del Fabro* [2000] IRLR 391, the Court of Appeal held that a pupil barrister was not a 'worker' for the purpose of the National Minimum Wage Act 1998. The Northern Ireland Court of Appeal, however, extended equal pay protection (under EU law) to employment tribunal chairmen (who are statutory office-holders), classifying them as 'workers' by reference to EU legislation on equal pay and freedom of movement: *Perceval-Price* v *Department of Economic Development* [2000] IRLR 380. The EAT have also held that 'labour-only subcontractors' in the building industry who worked exclusively for one employer and undertook to provide personal service were not 'in business on their own account' and were 'workers' for the purpose of the Working Time Regulations (and so entitled to holiday pay): *Byrne Brothers (Farmwork) Ltd* v *Baird* [2002] IRLR 96. This use of the same test of 'personal service' as has been seen in defining an 'employee' was confirmed as regards 'workers' in *Community Dental Services Ltd v Sultan-Darmon* [2010] UKEAT/0532/09. This area is, not surprisingly, very fact based; so, for instance, sub-postmasters (who were not employees even under pre-WT Regs case law) are apparently neither employees nor workers—they are therefore independent contractors: *Commissioners of Inland Revenue* v *Post Office Ltd* [2003] IRLR 199.

In an attempt to bring some order to this topic the President of the EAT set out guidelines on 'spotting the worker' in *James* v *Redcats (Brands) Ltd* [2007] IRLR 296 (a case concerning the status of a courier). Here, the two key factors he identified were: (a) is there mutuality of obligations during the time the worker undertakes work for the organisation?; and (b) is the personal service involved the dominant purpose of the contract? If it is then the individual is more likely to be a 'worker'.

2.7 Summary

- Most employment rights depend upon the claimant fitting the description of 'employee', though 'workers' have been given rights under specific statutory provisions.
- Employees gain most rights; 'Workers' are generally independent contractors but may gain some statutory rights (depending on whether the wording of the legislation refers to 'employees' or 'workers'); independent contractors have no employment rights.
- The definition of 'employee' rests on utilising a series of tests which focus on control, mutuality of obligations, and the economic reality of the relationship.
- The label given to the relationship is a starting point but it is not the determining feature.
- Most problems arise with non-standard relationships such as homeworkers and 'temps'. Although each case turns very much on its facts, the courts take a pragmatic approach to such situations and tend to compare the putative employee's relationship with the employer to that of more obvious 'employees'. Recent case law has made it much more difficult for temps to argue that they have a contract of employment with anyone.

3

Formation of the contract

3.1 Introduction

The role played by the contract of employment is central to understanding all aspects of employment law. For many years contractual principles were the sole determinant of all issues within the employment relationship. Today, many features of that relationship are determined by statutory provisions, e.g., rights to claim unfair dismissal and redundancy. However, these features have not supplanted contractual theories but have been annexed to the basic contractual points, so that many issues discussed in this book require an understanding of both contractual and statutory matters.

The next two chapters describe briefly where a solicitor may discover the contractual terms. Chapter 5 will then examine what may be done with those terms. In dealing with any employment question the first port of call has to be the contract itself as made up from the express and implied terms. It is nevertheless an unfortunate feature of employment law practice that, whereas a solicitor may regard the contract as the first port of call, the employer–client tends to regard it as 'any port in a storm', often arguing *ex post facto,* and without evidence, that the contract justifies the action taken.

We can start with the fact that the ordinary rules of contract apply to contracts of employment. All the classic offer and acceptance points, the need for consideration, etc., can be seen at work here. However, there are also specially-formulated rules which apply only to employment contracts, e.g., principles of fidelity and rules of procedure. These rules have arisen for three main reasons:

(a) Employers and employees have traditionally shown complete indifference to recording accurately, or even understanding, the terms of their agreements so that *someone* has had to iron out the basic requirements (i.e., the courts and tribunals).

(b) Employment contracts generally last for an indefinite term and therefore rules have had to be created to allow the contract to change and develop with time.

(c) Employment contracts were born out of feudal and criminal law concerns. The feudal notions stretch back to legislation in the fourteenth century (1348) which set limits on the movement of labourers and on wage increases and it was not until late in the nineteenth century that actions such as disobedience to lawful orders on the part of an employee ceased to be criminal offences. When judges had to analyse the structure of the contract of employment it was hardly surprising, then, to find that they drew upon many of the old and established feudal notions of service. This is not a history lesson—it still influences the judicial view of the employment relationship, especially as regards notions of loyalty and commitment to the enterprise.

These three factors have meant that the strict rules of contract have often had to be bent a little in order to make sense in the employment setting. This 'bending' can cause problems because it leaves some uncertainty as to when distortion can occur. One of the aims of this chapter and, in particular, Chapter 5 will be to give some structure to this uncertainty.

Some commonly used concepts will inevitably be vague, and much of this can be seen in the extensive use of *implied terms* to determine the scope and intentions of the contract of employment, e.g., the requirement that the parties owe each other a duty of mutual trust and confidence. The device of implying a term is used in the same way as with ordinary commercial contracts (e.g., 'officious bystander' test), but the range of questions posed—from whether sick pay is due to the extent that an employee is expected to perform work outside the strict terms of the contract—means that a great deal of judicial inventiveness is evident, and has been necessary, over the years.

This chapter will adopt the following structure:

(a) The needs of the client.

(b) Types of contract.

(c) Sources of terms.

(d) Written statements of terms and conditions.

(e) The process of incorporation of terms.

(f) The role of trade unions in the employment relationship.

3.2 The needs of the client

The most obvious need is to obtain the best terms possible. The employee will look primarily at remuneration and benefits; the employer's concerns may be wider, stretching to matters of protecting confidentiality, rights to inventions, flexibility of operations, etc. As with any contract there is a bargain to be struck. However, this tends to give the impression of detailed haggling over terms when the reality for the vast majority of employees is quite different.

When drafting or analysing a contract of employment you will need to consider the size and resources of the administration, the requirements of the business and the market in which it operates, the types of employees involved, and the resulting industrial relations consequences of any action.

3.2.1 Needs of the employee-client

Many contracts will be the subject of long-standing agreements with trade unions so that the individual has no say in the basic format of the contract. And even when the individual does negotiate a specific contract, or negotiates certain aspects of it, e.g., pay or holiday rights, employers still effectively dictate the *form* of the contract. Thus, if involved at all, solicitors will most likely be asked to advise employees or trade unions on the structure and content of the contract, on any legal requirements, and on any pitfalls to the proposals.

If the individual employee does seek advice at the formation stage, his or her concerns will tend to centre on the *meaning and scope* of stated or unstated obligations and take the form of the following types of questions:

(a) How is pay calculated, especially regarding things such as commission rates?

(b) How are other benefits (perks) calculated?

(c) What, if any, are the requirements to be moved to other sites?

(d) What, if any, are the requirements as to overtime?

(e) What are the notice requirements?

(f) What are the pension and sickness benefit rights?

(g) What happens if I leave? Can I take a job elsewhere in the same line of business?

All these points are addressed in **Chapters 4**, **5**, and **10**.

3.2.2 Needs of the employer–client

Employers will tend to be more concerned with establishing to their satisfaction matters such as the employee's duties, flexibility of operations, and rights to vary the contract. But even here, many employers rely on their personnel (Human Resources) departments or on antiquated standard forms which have not been altered in years (but should have been). A further problem is that the contract may be made orally or in writing (or in any combination). Many employees in this country have never seen written evidence of their contract. Thus the scope for imprecision and misunderstanding is great.

Consequently, the more control that can be exercised by the solicitor at these early stages the better; from the wording of any advertisement through to the final offer letter. If such control is possible, the solicitor should be briefed clearly on points such as:

(a) Does the employer wish to hire an employee, or would an independent contractor be better suited to the needs of the business? (see **Chapter 2**)

(b) If an employee is needed, what is to be the job description and what degree of flexibility do you want from the post?

(c) Is the advertisement, appointment, or promotion in any way discriminatory? (see **Chapters 6** and **7**)

(d) What are the needs of the business in terms of working patterns, e.g., shift work, job-sharing, overtime, mobility clauses? (see **Chapter 5** in particular)

(e) Is there a special need to protect business secrets, e.g., by use of confidentiality or restraint of trade clauses? (see **Chapters 8** and **9**)

(f) What does the client want in terms of disciplinary and dismissal procedures? (see **Chapters 10**, **11** and **12** in particular)

(g) The need, if any, for any special requirements such as compulsory medical examinations or outlawing the introduction of computer disks to the workplace (this sort of term appears in an increasing number of contracts, e.g., on oil-rig platforms, where the presence of computer viruses could prove disastrous or even fatal).

3.3 Types of contract

Chapter 2 dealt with problems as to *status* (e.g., whether casual workers can be classed as employees). In this chapter we are concerned only with proven employees and the *contractual terms* themselves. Thus when we talk of 'types' of contract here we are referring to the variations in drafting styles necessary to meet specific organisational needs. The structure of employment contracts can vary tremendously, from the kind whose complexity could justify inclusion in a Tolkien novel to the rather prosaic 'I said he could start work on Monday'.

Where an employer wishes to employ workers who do not fall within the traditional definition of full-time permanent workers each *type* of worker will require special attention in the drafting of contractual terms. Issues as to formation of contract do not vary as between these different types of workers but any standard contractual terms will obviously have to be modified to take account of the employee's status in the organisation. If the employer requires distinctive provisions or working arrangements for these employees then the contract needs to reflect this explicitly.

3.3.1 Limited-term contracts

Most employment contracts are open-ended (i.e., for an indefinite term). They are usually terminated by one or other party giving notice (see **Chapter 10** for more detail). However, contracts may be made to last for a fixed term (say, six months) or for the completion of a particular task (say, until the new database is operative). Employees may be employed on a seasonal basis or to cover work for a short period (e.g., agricultural workers or shop assistants working specifically for the Christmas period). Employees may also be employed to cover for maternity or sick leave. The arrival of the agreed date, or the completion of the task, terminates the contract automatically and there are no further consequences at common law (though the position is different as regards statutory remedies such as unfair dismissal). These forms of contract are collectively known as *limited-term contracts,* the most common of which is the *fixed-term* contract. Both expressions appear in the legislation, though *limited-term* is wider and includes both fixed-term and specific-task contracts (see sch. 2, para. 3(18) of Fixed-term Employees (Prevention of Less Favourable Treatment) Regulations 2002 (SI 2002/2034), inserting new ERA 1996, s. 235 (2A) and (2B)).

The certainty that a limited-term contract possesses also brings with it a degree of inflexibility. Therefore most limited-term contracts will contain a clause permitting the contract to be terminated before expiry in the case of, for example, gross misconduct by the employee. It is also possible, strange as it sounds, to have a limited-term contract which allows for termination by either party giving notice *for any reason* to take effect before the set finish date—which makes the notion of 'fixed-term' something of a nonsense.

3.4 Sources of terms

Employment contracts are frequently a nightmare in practice. Except in the larger and better organised companies, the discovery of the precise up-to-date terms would tax even the skills of Indiana Jones on a good day.

Terms of employment are derived from a number of sources. The most obvious is that of a written contract. Unfortunately, many employees have never seen a written contract and, even if they have, it was probably issued when they started, no one can find a copy, and there is no firm evidence that it has been changed in the intervening years. Your client (employer or employee) will tell you that it *has* been altered several times, but proving this fact tends to be somewhat perplexing. Your employer–client will also justify his understanding of the terms with phrases such as: 'We've always done it that way'; 'They (the employees) all knew about it'; 'We definitely agreed that with the union sometime'; 'I would have said that in the interview'; 'I didn't think to ask—it's obvious isn't it?'; and, from the heart, 'I haven't got time for legal technicalities—I've a business to run'.

You may therefore be faced with two equally unpalatable situations—a total lack of evidence or a wealth of jumbled evidence. You must be prepared to accept, in even the best organised companies, that many 'rules' will still not appear in writing and that relevant dates of changes in practice are lost in the mists of time.

The range of source material can be extensive. You must be aware of the possible existence of:

(a) written terms;
(b) orally agreed terms;
(c) written statements (under ERA 1996, s. 1: see **3.5** below);
(d) itemised pay statements;
(e) collective agreements reached with trade unions;
(f) national and local agreements of the industry concluded between employers' associations and trade unions;
(g) works' rules and staff handbooks;
(h) custom and practice;
(i) job descriptions;
(j) job advertisements;
(k) related documents, e.g., disciplinary arrangements, grievance procedures, health and safety policies, pension booklets;
(l) a vast range of implied terms derived from the facts of the relationship, from the common law and from statute; and
(m) EU legislation, e.g., Treaties and Directives.

We shall examine these sources below. One 'source' deserves a special mention at this point: the written statement, under ERA 1996, s. 1. This is something of a sheep in wolf's clothing. As we shall see in **3.5**, written statements must be given to every employee (including agency workers) within two months of starting work; they act as summaries of the contractual terms. These documents are not, strictly, a source of contractual terms but they are nevertheless important enough to warrant particular attention.

3.4.1 The parties

In many cases there will be *three* parties involved in setting the contractual terms: the employer, the employee, and trade unions. The law works on the basis that each employee has an individual contract with the employer, but most contracts have been the subject of a collective agreement between an employer and trade union, the terms of the agreement then being translated into individuals' contracts (which may have been varied from time to time, as with an annual pay rise). Not all terms of an employer–trade union agreement are capable of being applied to individual workers; they may relate only to how the employer and trade union conduct themselves. In such cases (as with union recognition agreements) the terms do not translate into the employee's contract.

3.4.2 The express terms

As may have been gathered, employment contracts are treated with far less respect by the parties than are other contracts; many only exist as oral agreements. To quote Sam Goldwyn, the result is that, when it comes to a dispute, these oral contracts are often not worth the paper they are written on.

The most reliable source of express terms is the written contract. There you would expect to find a wide range of terms which we shall explore in **Chapter 5**, e.g., payment, hours of work, and notice requirements. There may be many other different terms, e.g., as to the maintenance of confidentiality. Equally, the contract does not have to detail every aspect of the contract so that (as with pension scheme details) reference may be made to other documents. These documents should have been given to the employee, or at least have been available for inspection at, say, the personnel/HR department.

3.4.2.1 Works' rules, employment policy statements, and staff handbooks

These documents can present particular difficulties. They usually take the form of booklets, or notices posted on boards, containing rules of practice or behaviour in the workplace. Intranet sites can also count as 'handbooks': *Harlow* v *Artemis International Corporation Ltd* [2008] EWHC 1126 (QB), [2008] IRLR 629. However, most of these various types of document tend to be nothing more than codes of conduct and are significant only because their breach might *indicate* incompetence or misconduct. They are not strictly terms of the contract. But if these rules are expressly or impliedly incorporated in the contract, or can be used to make sense of a bald statement in the contract, they may have become as much a term as any other statement, despite the fact that they probably have been imposed unilaterally.

Where an employee has signed a document which acknowledges the binding effect of the works' rules then the rules will become a term of the contract. Even without a signature, if the employer has given reasonable notice of the rules and their importance they are most likely to be classed as terms. Much will depend on the availability of the rules (e.g., handed out or displayed in a prominent place) and whether they were treated by the employer as important. The trick lies in distinguishing on the facts between a mere policy and an obligatory term: see *Grant* v *South West Trains Ltd* (C-249/96) [1998] IRLR 188 (equal opportunities policy not incorporated) and *Deadman* v *Bristol City Council* [2007] EWCA Civ 822, [2007] IRLR 888 (policy statement to treat harassment claims 'sensitively' too vague to be incorporated but the 'policy' on the make-up of the panel for hearing the grievance was clear and incorporated). It is really a question of establishing intention to create legal relations.

The arguments in this area are therefore purely contractual, but the question of incorporation is not always straightforward and even tribunal judges can approach the topic from quite different presumptions as to what is required to incorporate 'rules' which are not clearly stated as express contractual terms (see the problems relating to disciplinary procedures raised in **Chapters 10**, **11**, and **12**, for instance). Certainly, the more precise the policy's terms and the more it ties in with obvious contractual terms, the more likely incorporation has been effected.

3.4.2.2 Orally agreed terms

Oral statements have the same status as written documents. Their disadvantage is one of proof. Where there is a conflict between written and oral evidence clearly the document will have the edge. But statements made at interview, for instance, have been allowed to stand in the face of apparently contradictory written evidence. Thus, say two site engineers have been instructed to transfer from the company's Bristol plant to Coventry. Both have refused, claiming this to be outside their contractual obligations. They tell you that when they commenced work in 2003 they were given a written contract of employment which stated they would be required to work on any site in the UK 'at the discretion of Grime Ltd'. However, before agreeing to sign the contract they were assured by the HR director that their work would be limited to the Bristol area.

The written contract will be taken as binding unless evidence can be adduced to prove otherwise. The oral assurance will suffice if it can be proven, either as a collateral contract or as an overriding oral undertaking (this was so in the case on which this example is based: *Hawker Siddeley Power Engineering Ltd* v *Rump* [1979] IRLR 425). You can imagine that the question of proof could be an obstacle but, if proven, the contract would be that the employees are not required to move. With these sorts of cases in mind some employers now make use of 'entire agreement' clauses which specify that no other material or representations except those contained in the contract may amount to a contractual term: see *White* v *Bristol Rugby Club* [2002] IRLR 204 for such an example.

3.4.2.3 Custom and practice

Terms may be found by reference to established custom, though this has always been a debatable area and its use is not common today. To have effect the custom cannot be inconsistent with express terms or statutory rights. But, if a custom is reasonable, certain (i.e., can be stated precisely) and well known in the company and has been treated *consistently* as a term in the past it may be classed as a term of the contract. The employee's ignorance of the custom is not a valid point if 'everyone else' in the company or industry knew about it.

3.4.2.4 Proof of terms

You will have gathered from the above that this is not always a simple exercise, and often there is conflicting evidence. Further, in interpreting the contract the general rule, of course, is that the use of evidence as to what the parties said or did *after* the contract was made is not permitted. In reality, however, tribunals have tended to take such evidence where nothing else is available. In *Dunlop Tyres Ltd* v *Blows* [2001] EWCA Civ 1032, [2001] IRLR 629, the Court of Appeal effectively acknowledged this practice when faced with a very ambiguous agreement on the level of pay to be made for working on bank holidays. Their Lordships admitted evidence of the position before and after the date of the relevant agreement, on the basis that 'the absence of any change of practice would be a clear indication that the parties . . . intended no change in the contractual terms'. It should be stressed, however, that this case rested on a very ambiguous agreement reached some 30 years before the case itself.

3.4.3 Implied terms

A word of caution is needed regarding implied terms: in the employment setting the courts frequently operate from a set of long-established presumptions. Many of these presumptions can look rather strange because they are feudal in their origin. But the basic rules for implying terms will normally apply. Thus, in keeping with general contractual theory, terms will only be implied where they are *necessary* for the business efficacy of the contract, not simply because it would be *reasonable* so to imply them (*Liverpool* v *Irwin* [1977] AC 239). However, once a term has been found to be necessary to the contract the court will then determine the limits of that term within reasonable parameters. The idea is to make the contract workable, no more than that; and the courts will certainly avoid *writing* the contract for the parties.

A full discussion of the importance of implied terms in contracts of employment will take place in **Chapters 4** and **5**. An implied term has the same force as an express term and may even be used to resolve conflicts between express terms. However, implied terms will give way to any inconsistent express statement. The range of terms is not fixed. Implied terms will include the following:

The duties incumbent on the employer	*The duties incumbent on the employee*
The duty to pay.	A duty to act in good faith.
A limited duty to provide work.	The duty to obey lawful orders.
Duties relating to the health and safety of employees.	A duty to provide personal service.
A duty of mutual trust and confidence.	The duty to exercise reasonable skill and care.
A duty to provide proper information to employees.	The duty to take care of the employer's property.

3.4.3.1 Terms implied by law

Terms may be implied by law. For instance, the courts have created a term that employers and employees must show the other party mutual trust and confidence. Such terms are often called 'legal incidents' of the relationship and do not depend upon the intentions of the parties. Many are a matter of common sense, e.g.:

(a) a duty to act honestly;

(b) a duty on the employee's part to cooperate and obey lawful orders;

(c) a duty on the employee's part to provide faithful service, e.g., not to disclose the employer's confidential information;

(d) a duty on the employee's part not to take bribes or make secret profits from the position;

(e) a reciprocal duty of mutual trust and confidence (which is something of a minefield to define precisely—see **Chapter 5**);

(f) a duty on the employer's part not to act capriciously in operating express terms (e.g., disciplinary rules);

(g) a duty on the employee's part to be adaptable as the contract changes over time.

Others have been worked out over the years to deal with more specific situations, e.g. that:

(h) there is no *presumption* whether contractual sick pay will or will not be payable;

(i) there is no rule that the parties will act *reasonably* towards each other;

(j) the employer will ensure the reasonable safety of the employee at work;

(k) the employer is usually under no duty to provide references.

Equally, statutes have created similar irrebuttable points. Thus, for example, non-discrimination clauses relating to sex and race are automatically deemed to be part of the contract, whatever the terms may say. Clauses which seek to oust the jurisdiction of the court will be void. And the duties may take a more positive form in requiring compulsory insurance for employees or in the creation of employers' liability for the provision of defective equipment.

3.4.3.2 Terms implied in fact

Terms may also be implied from the particular conduct of the parties and by examining the parties' presumed intentions. Custom and practice is one example; documents not expressly included in the contract but used frequently by the parties may be another.

The two devices used by the courts (which will be familiar from studies of contract law) are those of the 'business efficacy test' and the 'officious bystander'. Conduct subsequent to the original agreement should be treated with caution unless it shows some form of estoppel varying the original terms. It can be useful to show what the parties *seem* to have left unstated at the outset. So, with our example above (at **3.4.2.2**) regarding the transfer of employees from Bristol to Coventry there would be scope for arguing that an implied term, arising from the *nature* of their work (they were site engineers) or custom and working practice over the last few years might exist requiring the men to move.

Of course, all this fails if there is a clear, express term to the contrary; though, even here, there is the possibility of arguing for a move under the duty to cooperate if the distance is, say, within reasonable commuting distance.

The key rule therefore has to be: would the parties have agreed to such a term if the problem had been posed to them at the outset of the contract, and is such a term necessary to make the contract work?

3.5 Statements of terms and conditions

3.5.1 The right

Most employees have the right, under ERA 1996, s. 1, to receive from their employer a statement of initial employment particulars (usually called a *written statement* of their terms and conditions). These particulars must be issued not later than *two months* after the beginning of employment. The necessary contents are detailed below. This s. 1 statement largely complies with the Proof of Employment Directive 91/533.

It needs to be stressed, however, that this written statement is *not* the contract. Rather it is very strong *prima facie* evidence of the terms. It is like an MOT certificate: it tells you what the contract/vehicle looks like at a particular moment—it is no guarantee of the real condition of the contract/vehicle or its 'roadworthiness'. Employment tribunals and courts will accept such evidence only if there is nothing in the contract proper to contradict it. Thus written or oral evidence of agreed terms, express or implied, will all prevail over a written statement. For example, in *Robertson* v *British Gas Corporation* [1983] ICR 351, the employee's letter of appointment gave details of an incentive bonus agreed with the union. The employers subsequently withdrew from the agreement with the union and ceased paying the bonus. The employee sued for the arrears of pay. The mere withdrawal from the agreement with the union did not alter the employee's contract and a written statement permitting withdrawal from the agreement as a contractual right was held to be ineffective in altering the terms of the original agreement.

Nor does this fundamental point alter simply because the employee has signed the written statement as a receipt (as in *System Floors (UK) Ltd* v *Daniel* [1982] ICR 54) or has continued in employment after it has been issued without objection. Signing a written statement *as a contract of employment,* however, will bind the employee.

Nevertheless, a written statement may be the only documentary evidence and an employee may have a hard job convincing a court or tribunal that a document, issued by the employer, does not accurately reflect the contractual agreement.

The qualifying period for this right is one month (ERA 1996, s. 198) and a qualifying employee is entitled to the statement even where the employment ends before the period of two months in case they need to make a claim against the employer and need to refer to the statement in evidence. Also, in keeping with logic, those employees who have received a document containing express terms detailing the particulars required under ERA 1996, s. 1, do not have to be given a s. 1 statement (ERA 1996, s. 7A).

Written statements are a useful way of informing employees of the general terms of the contract. They are no substitute for a properly drafted contract. Despite all this, many employees have never seen a written statement of terms (or a written contract).

3.5.2 The contents

Under ERA 1996, ss. 1–7 the written statement must contain:

(a) the names of the employer and employee;

(b) the date when the employment began;

(c) the date on which the employee's period of continuous employment began (usually the same as the start date, but work with another employer might be included);

(d) the scale, rate, and method of calculating remuneration;

(e) the pay intervals (e.g., weekly);

(f) terms and conditions of hours of work;

(g) holiday entitlements;

(h) sickness and incapacity details and entitlements;

(i) pension scheme details;

(j) notice entitlement;

(k) job title or brief description of the work;

(l) if the job is not permanent, the period for which it is meant to last, including any fixed term;

(m) the expected place of work and address of the employer;

(n) any collective agreements affecting the employment, including things such as national agreements;

(o) details of any work abroad lasting more than one month;

(p) a note specifying any grievance and disciplinary rules applicable to the employee.

If there are no details to enter under any of these heads, e.g., there is no sick pay payable, this must be so stated (s. 2).

The statement may be given in instalments but certain matters must be given in a *single document,* namely: names of the parties; start date and dating of continuous employment; method of calculating payment and pay intervals; hours of work; holiday entitlement; job title; and place of work. The statement may, exceptionally, refer to other documents to which the employee has reasonable access in respect of terms relating to sickness, incapacity, notice periods, collective agreements, disciplinary rules and procedures, and pensions.

Where a change occurs to any of the provisions mentioned above then, under s. 4, the employer must notify the employee of such changes at the earliest opportunity (and not later than a month after the change).

3.5.3 Enforcement

Should the employer fail to comply with the requirements of ERA 1996, ss. 1–7, 11 and 12 allow reference to be made to an employment tribunal. Where no particulars have been issued concerning any matter falling within s. 1, or the particulars are said to be inaccurate, the tribunal may determine what the parties have actually agreed and so what should have appeared in the statement.

However, this is almost a right without a remedy because the tribunal will not make the contract for the parties, it will not insert a term; it will simply *record* what the evidence reveals had been agreed by the parties. The tribunal will look first for evidence of express terms and then implied terms, and will also look at how the contract has actually been performed. Thus, in *Mears* v *Safecar Security Ltd* [1982] IRLR 183, the fact that employees asking for details on sick pay had not previously been paid any sick pay was damning to the question posed under s. 11.

There is uncertainty as to what is the correct approach when there is no evidence of the terms whatsoever. Should the tribunal then invent something? In *Mears* it was suggested, *obiter,* that this would be acceptable. But the Court of Appeal in *Eagland* v *British Telecommunications plc* [1992] IRLR 323 reaffirmed the rule that the tribunal should not make the contract. Thus, if the relevant term *should* have appeared in the statement then the tribunal may have to make some form of ruling; if the term in question is not one specifically covered by the s. 1 statement the tribunal should leave well alone.

Under EA 2002, s. 38 tribunals have acquired additional powers. If an employee:

- makes a claim under one of the jurisdictions set out in sch. 5 to the Act (an extensive list including an unfair dismissal claim, a redundancy payments claim, an action for breach of contract, a discrimination claim, and a minimum wages claim); **and**
- the tribunal finds in favour of the employee in respect of that claim; **and**
- the tribunal finds that the employer was also in breach of ERA 1996, s. 1 or s. 4(1) at the time the claim was made,

then the tribunal must make an award to reflect this unless there are exceptional circumstances which would make this unjust or inequitable. If the tribunal has made no award regarding the triggering claim it must award the employee two weeks' pay and may award four weeks' pay. If the tribunal has made an award regarding the triggering claim the tribunal must increase that award by two weeks' pay and may increase it by four weeks' pay. A 'week's pay' is statutorily defined in Chapter 2 of Part 14 ERA 1996. At the time of writing it is £380 gross per week (or lower if the employee is not paid this much). As with all monetary limits in employment law this amount is reviewed annually and the next review date is February 2011.

3.5.4 Written statements on Sunday working

The classic written statement has a sibling. Under ERA 1996, s. 42(1), where a person becomes a shop or betting worker he or she must receive (within two months of starting) a written statement in a prescribed form detailing rights to 'opt out' of Sunday working by giving three months' notice to do so. If the employer fails to provide this statement the employee need only give one month's notice of opting out.

This right applies to new and existing shop and betting workers, but does not apply to those employed only to work on Sunday.

3.6 The process of incorporation of terms

From the text above it will have become clear that there is rarely *one single* document constituting the contract of employment. It should also be clear that the contract of employment is not immutable; that because it deals with a continuing relationship it is subject to express and implied change.

Many terms are *incorporated in the contract by reference*. Such incorporation may occur through notification or working practice but the best insurance is that of the written contract. Equally, sometimes it might be better to leave things such as 'works' rules' on the level of non-contractual conditions.

The most common problem of incorporation, however, relates to collective agreements. An agreement between an employer and a trade union does not in itself form part of an employee's contract. If the terms are vague (e.g., that both parties will seek to promote industrial harmony), or if the terms can relate only to collective matters (i.e., how disputes are to be settled between employers and trade unions) they *cannot* form part of an individual's contract. Thus even clauses which guarantee 'no compulsory redundancies' have been held to have no contractual force: *Kaur* v *MG Rover Group* [2004] EWCA Civ 1507, [2005] ICR 625. The test is whether the term itself is appropriate for incorporation. If a guarantee of no compulsory redundancies cannot meet this test one can see that very few terms could.

Incorporation is not an automatic process. Even if there are parts of the agreement which are capable of being applied to the individual, unless they are specifically incorporated into the employee's contract neither the employer nor the individual employee is bound by them.

Membership or non-membership of the trade union is not the issue here. All employees' contracts *may* be determined by collective agreements. The most common method by which this will happen is by express incorporation, e.g., a clause that states the employee's contract is 'subject to the collective agreements for the time being in force between' the employer and trade union. The second method is by *custom*, where the practice is so well established that it has clearly become part of each employee's contract (what has been termed 'tacitly embodied' in the contract—see **3.4.2.3** above). The third method is by implication in fact. A fourth, but less common, method is by arguing that the union had ostensible or implied authority to bind the members. We would only comment that reliance on anything other than express incorporation is a dangerous game, though if the idea of *custom* is accompanied by general acquiescence on the part of the employees (as was seen in *Henry* v *London General Transport Services Ltd* [2002] IRLR 472 (CA)) then employees will have great difficulty saying at a later date (here, two years after the agreement was reached) that the collective agreement was not incorporated.

3.7 The role of trade unions in the employment relationship

Collective agreements may adopt different guises. The most obvious form of collective agreement is that conducted between an employer and the trade union in the company. But there may also be local-level agreements relating to a group of companies or an industry, and there may be national agreements along the same lines, e.g., as between employers' federations and trade union groups. In such negotiations it is common to find agreements on minimum levels of conditions (e.g., as to holiday entitlements) which would apply to the member companies or trade unions.

Agreements between trade unions and employers are not legally binding even as between these parties unless they are in writing and expressly state that they are legally binding: TULRCA 1992, s. 179.

The role and impact of trade unions, however, goes much wider than this. Although many matters concerning trade unions are outside the scope of this book it is worth noting the following:

(a) trade union rights depend largely on the trade union being 'independent' (i.e., not within an employer's control) and, more importantly, 'recognised' for bargaining purposes by the employer;

(b) those rights will include such matters as being consulted when redundancies are being made and being consulted when a business is being transferred.

Furthermore:

(c) trade unions may be sued in respect of tortious actions, usually those arising out of industrial disputes;

(d) trade unions may be joined in actions brought by employees against employers, e.g., in unfair dismissal claims where the union has brought industrial pressure to dismiss the employee (for instance, where the employee has refused to join the union);

(e) union members have specific rights concerning exclusion from trade union membership.

When considering employment law issues it would be short-sighted to think only in legal terms. The industrial relations consequences need to be accounted for too. Thus, as you will see, it may be lawful to dismiss striking employees (sometimes without any legal repercussions), but few solicitors would advocate such action apart from in extreme circumstances. An employment contract is not a one-off event like a commercial contract; the participants usually have to continue working with each other when the dispute is over and businesses normally work best when there is cooperation rather than confrontation.

3.8 Summary

- Most employment contracts are open-ended, with no fixed date for completion. These can be terminated by either party giving adequate notice.
- Other types of contract are permissible, e.g., contracts for specific periods or for the completion of specific tasks. These are known as 'limited-term' contracts. During their currency they are no different from 'permanent' contracts. The exception lies in the fact that the arrival of the fixed date or the completion of the task terminates the contract at common law and no notice is needed. There may, however, still be statutory consequences (e.g., unfair dismissal) when such contracts are not renewed.
- Terms are derived from a very wide range of sources, and employment contracts are notoriously loose in both drafting and evidence of terms. Both express and implied terms must be taken into account.

- To help overcome this employers are required to issue written statements of terms and conditions or issue contracts which cover the same prescribed headings. Many employers do neither.
- The failure to issue a written statement has limited consequences but employees may seek clarification from tribunals or use the non-issue to gain extra compensation when suing for other matters such as unfair dismissal.
- Many terms and conditions emanate from employer–trade union agreements and affect non-union members as well as unionists.
- The validity of terms may be affected by statutory obligations and rules. These are dealt with in **Chapters 4** and **5** below.

4

Statutory controls on the contents of the contract

4.1 Introduction

At the start of this book we commented on the often haphazard growth of employment law. Most of it grew out of the law of contract, itself mostly developed during the nineteenth century to reflect the preoccupation of the age with *laissez-faire* and the freedom of the parties to agree whatever terms they liked.

Much of the law that fills this book reflects a recognition by the courts of the practical reality that employer and employee are not equal partners. Most job-seekers have the stark choice of accepting the job as the employer offers it or looking elsewhere, and therefore need some protection in an unequal bargaining position. This explains the ever-growing list of common law implied terms that we noted in **Chapter 3** and shall return to in **Chapter 5**.

Statute law used to confine itself generally to termination of the contract of employment (unfair dismissal in **Chapters 11–13**; redundancy in **Chapter 14**; takeovers in **Chapter 15**), and to certain specific areas which cover employment as one among several areas of human activity (e.g., discrimination).

That position has now changed dramatically. When the National Minimum Wage Act 1998 (NMWA 1998) and the Working Time Regulations 1998 (WTRegs 1998) came into effect, we encountered for the first time (except for war-time and in specific occupations) a statutory control of the two most basic elements of the contract of employment: how much employees are paid and how long they can be required to work in return. This chapter therefore examines the limitations that statute imposes on the freedom of employer and employee to decide the terms of the contract. As well as NMWA 1998 and WTRegs 1998, we shall consider briefly some other topics, especially the 'family-friendly' measures introduced by the Employment Relations Act 1999 (ERA 1999) and the Employment Act 2002 (EA 2002). Solicitors need to know that these rights exist, but the complicated rules governing them and the detailed statutory instruments lie outside the scope of this book. The matters to be looked at are:

(a) National minimum wage.

(b) Working time.

(c) The protection of wages.

(d) Work on Sundays.

(e) Maternity rights.

(f) Paternity and adoption leave.

(g) Parental leave.

(h) Time off for dependants.

(i) Flexible working.

Perhaps we should note before we start on the detail that this is not a comprehensive list of statutory controls on the content of the contract of employment. There are quite a few other matters that space will not permit us to discuss—including tax and social security, statutory sick pay, and also the complex subject of pensions.

4.2 The national minimum wage

The national minimum wage (NMW) stands at £5.93 per hour as from 1 October 2010. There are two lower rates for workers under 22: £4.92 per hour for those aged 18 to 21 and £3.64 per hour for those aged 16 and 17. The latter rate also applies to those over 21 during the first six months of their employment if they are undergoing defined training.

The basis of the law is set out in NMWA 1998, but this is then expanded by several sets of regulations, the most important of which are the National Minimum Wage Regulations 1999 (NMWRegs 1999). While the basic principles of NMW are quite simple, the special rules to govern exceptional cases are complex. We shall therefore examine in outline:

- who is entitled to NMW;
- how the entitlement is calculated;
- administration of NMW and the remedy for infringements.

4.2.1 The scope of NMW

Under NMWA 1998, s. 54(3), the entitlement to the NMW belongs to *workers*, a broader term than merely *employees*, and the definition reproduces that used in WTRegs 1998. Workers are both those working under a contract of employment (i.e., employees) and also those working under some other contract to perform personal work or services except for those who are genuinely clients or customers of professions or businesses. The decision of the EAT in *James* v *Redcats (Brands) Ltd* [2007] ICR 1006 stresses the statutory burden of proof: it is for the employer to prove that anyone claiming to be covered by NMW is *not* a worker under this definition. The fact that the claimant was permitted to substitute someone else if she was unable to deliver packages (but by implication only if *unable* to do it, and not merely because *choosing* not to) meant that she was a worker, and not within a non-personal business relationship. The result is a broader coverage than under some of the classical tests of employee status that we discussed in **Chapter 2**.

The broad scope of the statutory definition is then restricted by NMWRegs, reg. 12. Apprentices under the age of 19 are excluded, as are apprentices under the age of 26 during the first year of their apprenticeship.

There is no exclusion of those over retirement age, and both agency workers and homeworkers are included. The only significant exclusions are those working outside the United Kingdom under NMWA 1998, s. 1(2), certain workers in family businesses (reg. 2(2) and (3)), and those undergoing work experience as trainees on certain Government schemes or as a compulsory element in undergraduate courses (reg. 12(5) and (8)).

4.2.2 Calculation of the entitlement

For most people, most of the time, the calculation of their NMW entitlement is straightforward: the number of hours worked × £5.93 or the lower figure where it applies. The time that qualifies for NMW has been interpreted broadly. Time that a night watchman spent on the employer's premises counted as working time, although he was permitted to sleep, according to the Court of Session in *Scottbridge Construction Ltd* v *Wright* [2003] IRLR 21. The same was true of a 'lifestyle support worker' at a residential care home who was occasionally required to 'sleep in'; the rate paid for this was not deemed to be an 'allowance' under the regulations (which would not be covered by the minimum rate), though an unsocial hours enhancement for payments either side of the 'sleep in' hours and a 'disturbed night' payment were, under reg. 31(1)(c): *Smith* v *Oxfordshire Learning Disability NHS Trust* [2009] ICR 1395.

Time spent training or travelling on the employer's business counts too, as does time spent at home waiting to answer the telephone on the employer's night-time service—*British Nursing Association* v *Inland Revenue* [2002] EWCA Civ 494, [2003] ICR 19. The general test is whether the worker has to be available for work (e.g., to deal with emergencies).

There is a more complex case where the worker is not paid by the hour but by reference to output and the employer does not control the length of working time. An example is traditional 'piecework', although this is now much less common in industry than was the case a generation or two ago (it usually arises these days with homeworkers). The National Minimum Wage Regulations 1999 (Amendment) Regulations 2004 require the employer to test such workers to determine the 'mean hourly output rate' and to pay workers 120 per cent of that rate.

Regulations 21–23 of the 1999 Regs contain detailed calculation methods to cover the rare cases where workers are paid an annual salary in return for annual hours. The practical problem here is that some such people may be paid a standard amount at regular weekly or monthly intervals, but if their hours of work during those periods vary they may receive less than NMW per hour actually worked in some reference periods and more in others.

The next question is how to decide whether the worker is actually being paid NMW, and which payments can be offset against the employer's liability.

Most money payments made by the employer count. Payments in kind do not (reg. 9) and neither do payments not in the nature of wages (reg. 8). There are some more detailed rules in regs 30–35. Thus, for example, reg. 31(1)(e) deals with tips and gratuities given by customers in places such as restaurants. As from October 2009, tips and gratuities do not count towards covering an employer's NMW liability.

4.2.3 Administration and enforcement

The sole administrative obligation on employers is to keep records 'sufficient to establish' that a worker is receiving NMW, and the record for each employee must consist of a single document which is retained for three years. For employees paid substantially more than NMW, this requires very little. Workers are entitled to inspect the employer's record concerning themselves.

The fundamental point about enforcement of NMW is that it is made a contractual right of every worker: NMWA 1998, s. 17. All the usual civil remedies for breach of contract then apply (see **5.8** below), and it becomes the minimum for other statutory rights. It is an offence for an employer to pay less than NMW or to fail to keep adequate records, and the officers (usually HM Revenue and Customs) are entitled to bring prosecutions.

Any employee who takes steps to secure payment of NMW is protected against suffering any detriment for doing so—NMWA 1998, s. 23. Furthermore NMWA 1998, s. 25 adds a new s. 104A to ERA 1996, so that two new sets of circumstances are added to the list where dismissal is automatically unfair. First, it is automatically unfair to dismiss an employee for seeking to be paid NMW (whether or not in the event that attempt succeeds) or as a consequence of a prosecution of the employer. Secondly, it is automatically unfair to dismiss an employee as a means of avoiding paying NMW.

4.3 The Working Time Regulations 1998

4.3.1 The origin of the regulations

The WTRegs 1998 are the implementation in Great Britain of the European Working Time Directive 93/104/EC of 23 November 1993 as a health and safety matter (opposed by the UK). The opposition from the UK led to a form of sulking in that there are several instances in the enacting regulations of 'copy-out' of Eurospeak instead of adaptation to UK legal language and this can still present us with problems from time to time.

There has been much discussion of revision of the current Directive ever since WTRegs were first introduced in this country. The provisions in the UK for opt-out from the 48-hour week that we shall discuss at **4.3.4** below have been very unpopular in much of the rest of Europe. At one time it looked as though an agreement had been reached to amend the Directive as regards opt-outs but, at the time of writing, that has faltered again.

4.3.2 The form of the regulations

Introduced as health and safety measures (when they clearly were not) working time rules are applied in the UK via the WTRegs 1998. As we shall see there are six substantive rules. The first two are limits: the 48-hour week and restrictions on nightshift. Subject to the precise rules we shall consider shortly, employers must not exceed them, and any who are found by Health and Safety Executive (HSE) inspectors to have done so risk prosecution. By contrast the remaining four (daily and weekly rest, rest breaks, and annual leave) are entitlements. Individuals denied them can bring a complaint in the employment tribunal; but where employees forgo the entitlement and choose not to complain, the employer has done nothing wrong.

4.3.3 Scope of the regulations and some definitions

As we noted at **4.2.1** above, both NMWA 1998 and WTRegs give rights to *workers*, a broader term than merely *employees*. Thus in *Redrow Homes (Yorkshire) Ltd* v *Wright* [2004] EWCA Civ 469, [2004] IRLR 720 it was held that bricklayers engaged as sub-contractors qualified as workers under this rule because they were obliged to perform work personally.

Most of the rules apply to workers of all ages, but there are a few stricter rules that apply only to those over minimum school leaving age but under 18, described sometimes as 'adolescent workers'. The rules do not apply to children: so a paper-boy was not entitled to paid annual leave—*Addison* v *Ashby* [2003] ICR 667.

Various parts of the Regulations are subject to specific exceptions, often picking up derogations available in the Directive. In addition it is possible for employers and trade unions or other employee representatives to agree to *modify or exclude* many of the Regulations, subject to certain restrictions in some cases. The original general exclusions have largely been removed by subsequent amendments, especially the Working Time (Amendment) Regulations 2003. Mobile transport workers are now generally covered by regulations specific to particular modes of transport as too are doctors in training. The only remaining general exception is the armed services, the police, and some civil protection services under reg. 18.

'Working time' is defined so as to include expressly most kinds of work experience, but more generally as time which meets the following three tests:

(a) the worker is working;

(b) the worker is at the employer's disposal; and

(c) the worker is carrying out his activity or duties.

There is some scope for speculation here. We had assumed from a classical British approach to the interpretation of a statute that *all three* elements of the definition must be satisfied for time to count as working time. Thus time while the worker is on standby would generally not count, as (a) and (c) are not satisfied, even if (b) is satisfied. The ECJ, construing the wording of the Directive in *Sindicato de Médicos de Asistencia Pública (SIMAP)* v *Conselleriá de Sanidad y Consumo de la Generalidad Valenciana* (Case C-303/98) [2001] ICR 1116, took a more purposive approach. Working time and rest periods are mutually exclusive within the scheme of the Directive, the objective of which is to grant workers minimum periods of rest. Thus doctors on call are at work if required to be present and available at the workplace, but not if they are merely required to be contactable at all times but not necessarily at the health centre.

Application of the same principle to the other main area of doubt, time when the worker is travelling on the employer's business, might suggest that the critical question will be whether the mode of travel allows the worker to rest or not.

4.3.4 The 48-hour week

By reg. 4, workers must not work on average more than 48 hours a week. The average is normally calculated over a period of 17 weeks, which can be a fixed period if so agreed between employer and worker, but by default is the last 17 weeks. In certain defined cases it can be longer—up to 26 weeks—and up to a year if some justification exists and the employer so agrees with employee representatives.

Workers who agree to work more than 48 hours may continue to do so. Employees have the choice whether to sign the opt-out. In *Barber* v *RJB Mining (UK) Ltd* [1999] ICR 679, the EAT held that reg. 4(1) had the effect of prohibiting employers from requiring employees to work more than 48 hours.

Managing executives and others *with autonomous decision-taking powers*, family workers and clergy are excluded from the 48-hour rule under reg. 20 on the basis that their working time is not measured or predetermined or can be fixed by the worker concerned. The terms we have emphasised are undefined.

4.3.5 Nightshift

There is a complicated definition in reg. 2(1) of night work and, by reference to it, of what constitutes a night worker. On the face of the definitions, it might seem that a worker is only a night worker if working at least three hours a day during night time on a *majority* of the days of work, i.e., presumably more than half. This ignores the crucial element in the regulation, 'without prejudice to the generality' of the expression, 'as a normal course'. Thus in *R* v *Attorney-General for Northern Ireland, ex parte Burns* [1999] IRLR 315, the High Court in Northern Ireland held that three hours of night work per shift had only to be a *regular feature* of the worker's pattern of working time.

Workers who fall within the statutory definition of a night worker must not work more than eight hours on average per 24-hour period (reg. 6(1)). Again there is a 17-week reference period subject to some possibilities of variation. In the case of those whose work involves *special hazards or heavy physical or mental strain* (terms that are simply copied out of the Directive), the eight-hour limit applies under reg. 6(7) to each nightshift and not to an average. The only definition supplied by the Regulations for the crucial terms is that they are to be understood by reference to an agreement between employer and worker representatives or to the risk assessment the employer carries out as part of normal health and safety management.

Those undertaking night work must be given the opportunity under reg. 7 of a free health assessment before doing so and at intervals thereafter. The form of the health assessment is not specified but it does not seem to extend necessarily to a medical examination by a doctor. Slightly more stringent requirements exist in the case of adolescent workers. The employer's obligation appears to be limited to ensuring that workers have the opportunity of a health assessment and not that they avail themselves of it.

4.3.6 Daily rest

In principle, adult workers are entitled to 11 consecutive hours rest in each 24-hour period, and adolescent workers to 12 hours (reg. 10). There are various flexibilities about the operation of the rules for adults (mostly under regs 21 and 22) but the exceptional cases are precisely defined. In *Gallagher* v *Alpha Catering Services Ltd* [2004] EWCA Civ 1559, [2005] ICR 673, airline catering workers were found to fall outside reg. 21(c). Although the *employers' activities* involved the need for continuity of service, there was no evidence that the *workers' activities* involved any such need, and that was the correct test under WTRegs 1998. The broad principle is that workers whose daily rest is not strictly in accordance with reg. 10 should have some *compensatory rest* instead (reg. 24). This term is undefined, but it seems that a commonsense approach is taken.

4.3.7 Weekly rest

Adult workers are entitled to one day off each week under reg. 11 and adolescent workers to two days off. Again there is some flexibility about the way weekly rest is arranged for adults, subject to the same principle of compensatory rest as for daily rest. In addition there is specific provision under reg. 11(2) enabling an employer to provide two days a fortnight as an alternative arrangement for adults.

The 24-hour weekly rest under reg. 11 and the 11-hour daily rest under reg. 10 are separate and additional to each other. However, despite some suggestions to the contrary, it does not seem that they must necessarily be consecutive so as to provide an obligatory 35-hour break for every shift rota.

4.3.8 Rest breaks

Adult workers are entitled under reg. 12 to a rest break of at least 20 minutes if their daily working time exceeds six hours. This means there is an entitlement to a break *after* six hours, not a break every six hours: *Corps of Commissionaires* v *Hughes* [2009] IRLR 122. There is no requirement for the break to be paid. Flexibility about the rule again depends on compensatory rest.

The rule about adolescent workers is stricter. Their break is a minimum of 30 minutes if daily working time exceeds four and a half hours. There is much less flexibility. Furthermore, if the adolescent has more than one job, daily working time must be aggregated across the jobs to determine entitlement to a break. There is no explanation of how employers are to obtain the information to operate this rule.

4.3.9 Annual leave

Workers are entitled under reg. 13 to 5.6 weeks' paid annual leave (usually 28 days). There is no service qualification. Employers may not require a worker to accept pay in lieu. The entitlement in days is obtained by multiplying the number of days in a worker's normal week by 5.6 and rounding up—never down—to the nearest half-day. The slightly odd figure of 5.6 weeks is a result of complicated methods of dealing with statutory holidays in the UK.

There are rules in reg. 16 about the calculation of payment for annual leave, which are broadly the same as for all other statutory purposes (see ERA 1996, ss. 220–229). There are also rules in reg. 15 about the notices employer and worker can serve on each other as to when leave can and cannot be taken. Some of these rules may cause practical difficulties in that they conflict with established practices in many workplaces.

If the contract provides more favourable rights than the Regulations a worker is entitled to rely on these instead.

4.3.9.1 Annual leave: workers on long-term sickness

One question that has arisen is whether a worker, away from work on long-term sickness, could elect to take annual leave and to claim payment, even if prevented by the sickness from being at work and possibly not otherwise due any payment, having exhausted any entitlement to sick pay. The Court of Appeal held in *Inland Revenue Commissioners* v *Ainsworth* [2005] EWCA Civ 441, [2005] ICR 1149 that the worker could not do so and then, on this specific point, the ECJ agreed (*Stringer* v *HMRC* (C-520/06) [2009] IRLR 219). However, the ECJ went further and ruled that where a worker is on sick leave for the whole of the holiday year and it was impossible for him to take holiday leave the worker could carry over this missed leave into another holiday year, and that there is a right to claim holiday pay in lieu for any unpaid holiday entitlement *on termination of the contract* (including from an earlier holiday year).

4.3.9.2 Annual leave: falling ill during that period

The traditional answer to the question: 'I was ill during my holiday leave, can I discount that?' was (politely), 'Bad luck'. However, the ECJ reference of *Pereda* v *Madrid Movilidad SA* (C-277/08) [2009] IRLR 959 has changed that. Here the employee fell ill just before taking annual leave and asked for a postponement of that leave. The employer refused and the ECJ held this refusal to be in breach of the Working Time Directive. It is arguable that this reasoning (based again on the health and safety aspects of annual leave) applies to employees who fall ill *during* their annual leave.

4.3.9.3 Annual leave: 'rolling up' holiday leave

Here the long-running debate has been whether it is possible for the employer to pay a 'rolled-up' rate of pay inclusive of holiday pay and then not to pay separately for holidays. This was finally resolved by the ECJ in *Robinson-Steele* v *RD Retail Services Ltd*

(C-131/04), [2006] ICR 932, where the practice was held to be contrary to the purposes of the Directive. However, where a worker's work-pattern includes days (or longer) where they are not required to be at work (e.g., some shift systems) then, provided the arrangements are not a sham and proper notice is given, leave can be scheduled during these non-working periods: *Craig* v *Transocean International Resources Ltd* [2009] IRLR 519.

A further twist to this was added in *Lyons* v *Mitie Security Ltd* [2010] ICR 628. The worker here did not give proper notice to request leave. The employer refused to pay for the lost leave or roll it over. The question raised, therefore, was whether this right to leave was inalienable or subject to conditions. The EAT held that *Stringer* (above) had decided the position where it was impossible to take leave during the leave year, but this was a different proposition. Both parties are under a duty to facilitate the taking of leave (so an employer should not act capriciously in refusing even a request made late in the holiday year) but the right is not inalienable and a worker may, in the words of the editor of IRLR, be in a position of 'use it or lose it'.

4.3.9.4 Annual leave: moving from full-time to part-time status

Finally, there is the problem that arises when a full-time employee moves to a part-time post. It is clear that from that point on their holiday entitlement must be calculated on a *pro-rata* basis with the full-time entitlement, but what happens where they have outstanding leave from the full-time days? Here, the ECJ has ruled that any loss of accrued rights is in breach of the WT Directive—though the judgment is not very clear on whether this applies where an employee chose not to use all their entitlement before the part-time switch or could not: *Zentralabbeitsreibsrat der Tirols* v *Land Tirol* (C-486/08) [2010] IRLR 631. On this basis, if an employee has, say, five unused days from their full-time position they retain these as full-time days (and not five half-days) even though moving to a part-time contract.

4.3.10 Enforcement and remedies

We noted at **4.3.2** above that the first two of the items we have just been discussing are limits enforced by inspection by HSE and possible criminal prosecution, while the remaining four are entitlements enforceable by individual claim in the employment tribunal.

HSE inspectors do not enforce the limits by any rigorous policing of employers. Indeed, it lacks the resources to enforce the Regulations effectively. In *Sayers* v *Cambridgeshire County Council* [2006] EWHC 2029, [2007] IRLR 29, the claimant claimed that her psychiatric injury resulted in part from excessively long hours. Ramsey J held that the 48-hour week limit under WTRegs did not provide her with a right of action for breach of statutory duty, but instead created only criminal liability. The apparently complete exclusion of any civil liability is perhaps surprising, given the connexion of the Directive with health and safety of workers, and we suspect that the point may be tested again.

As regards the four entitlements, reg. 30 sets out the procedure for a worker to complain to an employment tribunal. The claim must be presented within three months of the alleged denial of the right concerned. If the tribunal finds the claim well founded it must make a declaration to that effect and may make an award of compensation of an amount to reflect both the degree of the employer's fault and the amount of the worker's loss. In *Miles* v *Linkage Community Trust Ltd* [2008] IRLR 602, the EAT approved a pragmatic and practical assessment by the employment tribunal of the employer's default, which led to the making of a declaration but no award of compensation.

4.4 Protection of wages

Subject to the minimum set under NMWA 1998, it is for the parties to set the level of pay under the contract. Nevertheless, whatever level they set, Part II of the ERA 1996 provides that employers may not make deductions from workers' wages other than those required by statute and those that meet specified conditions. *Worker* is widely defined to include anyone working under a contract of service, apprenticeship or who individually undertakes to do or perform work or services personally: ERA 1996, s. 230(3).

The rules, still often referred to by practitioners as 'Wages Act' claims (referring to the 1986 statute which is now consolidated into ERA 1996), are (broadly speaking) that either:

- workers must expressly authorise the deduction or
- they must be subject to the deduction under some term of the contract which the employer has confirmed in writing.

In either case the deduction must also be one that is recognised as a permitted statutory deduction (see **4.4.2** below)

We shall see in **5.8** that there is sometimes an overlap between this rule and that giving workers a remedy in the employment tribunals for breaches of contract.

4.4.1 The meaning of 'wages'

4.4.1.1 Included in the definition

The right concerns the deductions from 'wages' and wages are defined in s. 27 of ERA 1996. Under s. 27(1), the term includes any fee, bonus, commission, holiday pay or other emolument referable to the employment, whether payable under the contract or otherwise. It also includes various payments made as a result of employment tribunal orders, statutory guarantee payments, statutory sick pay, and statutory maternity pay. Statutory holiday pay is included in the definition of wages: the outcome of the second aspect of *Stringer* v *HMRC* (above) when the case went to the House of Lords on this point ([2009] UKHL 31, [2009] IRLR 677).

The inclusion by s. 27(1) of certain non-contractual matters is enlarged in s. 27(3) by specific reference to non-contractual bonuses. The test seems to be that discretionary commission or similar payments may be *included* if it is the reasonable expectation of the parties that they will be paid: *Kent Management Service* v *Butterfield* [1992] ICR 272.

The breadth of this definition is obvious. It includes almost any payment made by the employer to the worker *qua* worker but the payment due must be work done to fall within the definition; if the failure is to pay for work promised (but not given) then that is a simple breach of contract action: *Lucy* v *British Airways* EAT/0033/08.

4.4.1.2 Excluded from the definition

By s. 27(2), the following are *excluded* from the statutory definition with the result that the protection does not extend to them and deductions made from these are a matter of pure contract law:

(a) advances of wages as a loan;

(b) expenses payments;

(c) pensions or other retirement provisions;

(d) redundancy payments;

(e) payments made to the worker in another capacity.

By s. 27(5), benefits in kind are also excluded except where they consist of vouchers or the equivalent with a fixed monetary value and *payments in lieu of notice* are excluded as they relate to termination of the employment and not to the provision of services under the employment: *Delaney* v *Staples* [1992] ICR 483.

4.4.2 Permitted deductions

Sections 13 and 14 ERA 1996 start from the premise that an employer cannot make a deduction from 'wages' except in defined circumstances. These can be quite detailed, but the broad categories where deductions will be permitted are:

(a) *Deductions authorised or required by statute.* Examples might be the collection of income tax or maintenance payments under a court order.

(b) *Deductions provided for by a term of the worker's contract of employment* where either that term is already recorded in writing to the worker, or the employer has previously notified the worker of it in writing. The deduction must also be justified on its facts, however.

(c) *Deductions expressly authorised in writing by the worker.* Examples might be payments to a pension scheme or a savings plan, or recovery in instalments of the cost of initial purchase of working clothes.

(d) *Deductions in retail employment* for the recovery of cash shortages or stock deficiencies, subject to specific controls including a limit to the deduction of 10 per cent of gross pay: see ERA 1996, ss. 17–22.

(e) *Deductions to recover an overpayment by the employer.* Although this means that an employee cannot use the Act (and therefore the employment tribunal) to challenge this deduction, the employee may still bring an action in the ordinary courts. The employer has no right to recover overpayments where no such right exists otherwise in the common law, and this is often a problem for employers when the employee has in good faith spent the money.

(f) *Deductions made because the worker is taking part in a strike or other industrial action.*

It should be noted that the agreement or consent in question must be obtained not only before the deduction has been made but also before the incident that is said to justify the deduction has occurred.

Sections 15 and 16 deal with the situation where an employee is required to make payments to the employer and the provisions mirror those of ss. 13 and 14 (thereby preventing the employer from circumventing ss. 13 and 14 by demanding reimbursement rather than making a deduction).

4.4.3 Remedies for unlawful deductions from wages

If the worker has suffered an unauthorised deduction from wages, the remedy provided by ERA 1996, s. 23 is by way of a claim in an employment tribunal. The claim must be presented within three months of the making of the deduction complained of, or (where there has been a series of similar deductions) within three months of the most recent deduction. In this instance there seems to be no limit on the retrospective period the employment tribunal may examine: *Reid* v *Camphill Engravers* [1990] ICR 435.

The employment tribunal is given little discretion as to its award if it finds the claim well-founded. It is bound to make a declaration to that effect, and also to order the employer to reimburse the money improperly deducted or received, subject only to a possible reduction of the full amount if there has been a partial authorisation or repayment: ss. 24 and 25.

4.4.4 Practical uses of the remedy in the employment tribunals

This topic may seem an obscure possibility. It is not. In practice, almost a sixth of all claims recently brought to the employment tribunals fall under this jurisdiction and we shall discuss it further at **5.7.5** below.

The point is that there is no jurisdiction for the employment tribunals to deal with alleged breaches of contract concerning current employees. The only such jurisdiction concerns people whose employment has ended. So if an employee wishes to complain about an alleged breach of contract the case must be brought in the courts, with consequently higher costs than are incurred in the tribunals. If the same claim can be presented as an alleged deduction from wages, the tribunal has jurisdiction and this possibility may be attractive to the employee.

An example may help. Suppose the issue is a dispute about the calculation of a bonus. Maybe a group of people in a sales office are paid a bonus based on sales of the company's products. When the company starts export sales the employer bases calculation of the bonus on home sales (which is all there has been until now), but the sales staff argue that it has always been based on total sales. Both sides argue that their case is a continuation of past practice and there is logic behind both contentions, depending whether the bonus was originally intended to reward the effort of the staff concerned or to reflect the success of the enterprise. The legal issue is one of construction of the rules of the bonus scheme, wherever they are to be found, whether in writing or not. An employment tribunal cannot entertain a case of construction of the contract of employment in respect of current employees, but the amount at stake for a small group of people does not seem to warrant litigation in the courts. So the employees, through their trade union perhaps, present their case to the tribunal as an alleged unlawful deduction from wages. Their bonus, they argue, should properly be based on the total sales of the company and the employer has unlawfully *deducted* the part which represents export sales. Now, when it is presented in this way, the tribunal acquires jurisdiction to adjudicate on the issue, which is legally precisely the same as it would have been in the court—construction of the contract of employment.

With a little ingenuity many contractual issues can be presented in an alternative form like this. As we shall see at **5.6** there are other ways of dealing with such issues; the relative merits of this against the others are considered at **5.7**.

4.5 Sunday working for shop and betting workers

4.5.1 The right

Under ERA 1996, Part IV, special statutory rights have been created covering employees who may be asked to work on Sundays. The legislation is somewhat convoluted but, in essence, seeks to provide shop and betting workers with the right not to work on Sundays if they so wish. The following points may be noted by way of summary:

(a) The definition of 'shop worker' in s. 232 extends beyond sales assistants to cover employees such as clerical workers, security staff, and cleaners. The definition of 'betting worker' in s. 233 covers work 'which consists of or includes dealing with betting transactions' at a track and 'work in a licensed betting office . . . open for use for the effecting of betting transactions'.

(b) Employees employed to work only on Sundays are not covered by the Act.

(c) Those who were shop workers at 25 August 1994 or betting workers at 2 January 1995 are covered provided their contracts do not, and may not, require them to work on Sundays—these are termed 'protected workers'.

(d) Any shop or betting worker who is or may be required under the contract to work on Sunday may give three months' written notice of 'opting-out' (hence 'opted-out employees'). During that notice period he or she may be required to work on Sunday.

(e) Employees may also give 'opting-in' notice, expressly agreeing to work Sundays or a particular Sunday—and, indeed, may opt in or out as the whim takes them.

(f) Questions of age, length of service, or hours worked are irrelevant for qualification for these rights.

(g) An attempt by a worker in another kind of employment, a quarry, to obtain the right not to work on Sundays by arguing under HRA 1998 that a requirement to work on Sundays infringed his right to practise his religion under art. 9 of the European Convention of Human Rights failed in *Copsey* v *WWB Devon Clays Ltd* [2005] EWCA Civ 932, [2005] ICR 1789.

4.5.2 Written statements

As we noted at **3.5.4** above, new shop and betting workers are entitled to receive a written statement in a prescribed form summarising their right to opt out of Sunday work.

4.5.3 Remedies

Both protected and opted-out workers (in the meanings defined above) have the right to complain to an employment tribunal if they suffer any detriment by reason of refusing to work on Sundays or a particular Sunday (ERA 1996, s. 45). We shall note below that they have a similar protection against dismissal or selection for redundancy for the same reason.

4.6 Maternity rights

Modern legislators have given much attention to the balance between work and family life—the 'family-friendly policies', as they are sometimes described. These are discussed in detail in **4.7–4.10** below (e.g., time-off rights relating to care). Some employers adhere to the base level of these provisions (if that) but many go beyond the statutory requirements, e.g., by providing work-based crèche facilities. Provisions relating to pregnancy and childbirth are of much longer standing, dating back originally to the Employment Protection Act 1975, although now much amended. There are four matters to consider:

(a) time off with pay for antenatal care;

(b) protection against dismissal because of pregnancy;

(c) maternity leave; and

(d) maternity pay.

The first three rights fall within the ambit of the ERA 1996, but the fourth is derived from numerous pieces of social security legislation. We shall note in **Chapter 6** that any detriment suffered by a woman because of her pregnancy constitutes unlawful sex discrimination and this point is of particular importance in relation to protection against dismissal. The employer also has special responsibilities for the health and safety of pregnant women, especially in relation to risk assessment, but such matters lie outside the scope of this book.

4.6.1 Time off with pay for antenatal care

By s. 55 of ERA 1996, every pregnant employee is entitled not to be unreasonably refused time off with pay for antenatal appointments she is medically advised to attend. There is no qualifying service and no limit to the time off.

4.6.2 Protection against dismissal because of pregnancy

By s. 99 of ERA 1996, almost any dismissal because of pregnancy or childbirth is automatically unfair and there is no service qualification. The employer is not permitted to dismiss an employee even if her pregnancy makes her incapable of doing her usual job. Indeed, if her incapability is because of some statutory restriction relating to pregnancy, childbirth, or breastfeeding or some similar recommendation of a code of practice, she is to be treated under ERA 1996, s. 66 as suspended from work and she is entitled to be paid. In an unusual exception the EAT held in *Ramdoolar* v *Bycity Ltd* [2005] ICR 368 that the dismissal of a pregnant woman for poor work performance was not unfair, because the employer did not know of her pregnancy. However, the EAT added that an employer who detects the symptoms of pregnancy and dismisses the employee before his suspicions can be proved may well find the dismissal automatically unfair.

4.6.3 Maternity leave

Part VIII of ERA 1996 (as amended by sch. 4 of ERA 1999), and in particular new ss. 71–75, sets out the structure of maternity leave. In addition we need to take account of the Maternity and Parental Leave etc. Regulations 1999 (MPL Regs 1999) as amended in 2002 and 2006 which enlarge on the statutory framework. There are three kinds of maternity leave:

(a) compulsory maternity leave;

(b) ordinary maternity leave ; and

(c) additional maternity leave.

When (b) and (c) are added together then, in most cases, an employee's statutory maternity leave entitlement will be for a period of 52 weeks (though she may elect to return earlier). We shall examine each of the rights in turn and then consider the right not to suffer detriment on account of exercising any of them.

4.6.3.1 Compulsory maternity leave

This is a health and safety requirement derived from the Pregnant Workers Directive. Under ERA 1996, s. 72 as amended, the employer is not permitted to allow the employee to work during the compulsory maternity leave period, which is the two weeks following the baby's birth.

4.6.3.2 Ordinary maternity leave

Ordinary maternity leave is covered by ERA 1996, s. 71 as amended. All pregnant employees, regardless of length of service, are entitled to a 26-week period of leave. The contract of employment subsists throughout this absence and the employee continues to benefit from her terms and conditions of employment except for remuneration. MPL Regs, reg. 9 defines remuneration for this purpose as wages or salary (and can include fringe benefits during the leave period).

The start of the ordinary maternity leave period is a matter over which the employee has some choice but it cannot commence earlier than the beginning of the 11th week before the expected week of confinement (EWC). If childbirth occurs early, ordinary maternity leave starts at once. Childbirth includes a live birth and a stillbirth or miscarriage after 24 weeks of pregnancy.

The employee returns to work after ordinary maternity leave with that whole period of absence counting for seniority and pension purposes. The right to return is to the job in which she was employed before her absence, on terms and conditions not less favourable than those that would have applied if she had not been absent. There are special provisions in MPL Regs, reg. 10 covering the position if the employee becomes redundant during ordinary or additional maternity leave.

No later than the 15th week before EWC, or as soon as reasonably practicable, she must tell the employer that she is pregnant, what her EWC is (by means of a medical certificate if the employee so requests) and when she wishes to start her leave (in writing if her employer so requests). Under the 2002 amendments the employer must respond, notifying her of the date when her maternity leave will end.

A woman returning to work after ordinary maternity leave does not need to give notice of her return unless she wishes to return early, in which case she must give her employer eight weeks' notice of her intended return date. Failure to do so will allow the employer to postpone her return.

4.6.3.3 Additional maternity leave

Under ERA 1996, s. 73, employees qualifying for ordinary maternity leave are also entitled to additional maternity leave. There is no longer a service qualification for this. The two kinds of leave remain distinct, despite the common qualification. Additional maternity leave of 26 weeks follows on after ordinary maternity leave (giving the 52 week total). The only condition imposed on the woman is that she complies with simple notification requirements.

Since 2008 the employee's contract of employment continues to subsist throughout the period of additional maternity leave as during ordinary leave. During her additional leave the woman is now entitled to all benefits under the contract excluding pay, but including fringe benefits, exactly as during ordinary leave.

The one significant remaining difference between ordinary and additional leave concerns the right to return to work. As we have noted, the right to return after ordinary leave is straightforwardly to the same job, whereas under MPL Regs, reg. 18, the employee is entitled to return after additional leave to the same job or, if it is not reasonably practicable for the employer to permit her to do that, to a job which is both *suitable* for her and *appropriate for her to do in the circumstances*. The words we have emphasised are undefined and so we await clarification from cases. In any event, her terms and conditions of employment are to be the same as would have applied to her if she had not been absent.

Under the 2008 Regulations the period of additional leave counts towards continuity of service, exactly as ordinary leave. Prior to April 2008 this was not the position for non-statutory purposes. However, if at some point in the future you find yourself pursuing some service-based, contractual right for a client where additional leave prior to that date is important, it may still be possible to base an argument on the Equal Treatment Directive 76/207 as interpreted in *Sarkatzis Herrero* v *Instituto Madrileño de la Salud* (C-294/04) [2006] IRLR 297 (when a woman deferred the start of her career for reasons of maternity leave it was in breach of the Directive, for the purposes of calculating her seniority, to postpone her start date until she actually took up the post).

The employee is required to give no notice of her intention to return if she returns at the end of the 26-week period but must give eight weeks' notice of an intention to return early (reg. 11). A statement of her intention to return at all can be required by the employer in a prescribed written form, in which event the woman must reply in writing (reg. 12).

4.6.3.4 'Keeping in touch' days

Under the 2006 amendments, employees on statutory maternity leave (ordinary or additional) may, by agreement with the employer, return to work for up to ten days without bringing the leave to an end.

4.6.4 Maternity pay

A woman is not entitled to contractual pay during her maternity leave unless her contract so provides. Instead she is entitled to statutory maternity pay (SMP). However, whereas a woman has the right to 52 weeks' *maternity leave*, SMP only lasts for nine months:

- For the first six weeks it is at the rate of 90 per cent of normal weekly earnings.
- For the remaining 33 weeks it is either 90 per cent of normal weekly earnings or a prescribed rate which is reviewed annually and is £124.88 per week. The lower rate prevails.

SMP is usually a straightforward administrative matter that causes few problems, although a woman is entitled in the calculation to the benefit of pay rises taking effect during the period prior to the leave that is used for the calculation of maternity pay, even if the rise is decided subsequently and takes effect retrospectively, as in *Alabaster* v *Barclays Bank Ltd (No 2)* [2005] EWCA Civ 508, [2005] ICR 1246. In *Gillespie* v *Northern Health Board* [1996] ICR 498, the ECJ rejected the argument that full pay was due during maternity leave.

4.7 Paternity and adoption leave

Both these rights were created under EA 2002 which amended ERA 1996 by adding new sections that we shall identify shortly. In both cases the statutory provision acts as little more than an enabling measure for delegated legislation and both are governed by the Paternity and Adoption Leave Regulations 2002 (PAL Regs 2002). There are also other more detailed sets of regulations, mostly dealing with pay. We shall give only an outline.

4.7.1 Paternity leave

The statutory basis of this right is ss. 80A and 80B of ERA 1996. For an employee to be eligible for paternity leave, three tests must be satisfied.

(a) The employee must have at least 26 weeks' service at the start of the 14th week before EWC, or in the case of an adoption at the end of the week in which the adopter is matched with the child.

(b) The employee must be the father of the child or married to or the partner (of either sex) of the child's mother or adopter. (So women may be eligible for paternity leave.)

(c) The employee must have or expect to have responsibility for the upbringing of the child.

Employees can take either one or two consecutive weeks of paternity leave. It can be taken at any time from the birth or placement up to 56 days later (or up to 56 days from EWC in the case of a premature birth). They must give the employer notice of the intention to take paternity leave by the 15th week before EWC in the case of a birth or no later than seven days after being told of being matched in the case of adoption. If it is not reasonably practical to give that amount of notice, they must give notice as soon as reasonably practical.

The rate of statutory paternity pay is the same as the later rate (after the first six weeks) of statutory maternity pay—see **4.6.4** above.

4.7.2 Adoption leave

The statutory basis of this right is ss. 75A and 75B of ERA 1996. The rules in many ways mirror those for maternity leave. Where a couple adopts, either but not both can take adoption leave. The other may be able to take paternity leave. Where there is a single adopter, it is that person who may take adoption leave and the partner may be able to take paternity leave.

In order to be eligible for adoption leave, the employee must have at least 26 weeks service at the end of the week of notification of being matched with the child. The employee must notify the employer of the intention to take adoption leave within seven days of that notification, or as soon as is reasonably practicable if that is not reasonably practicable. The employer must respond, informing the employee of the date adoption leave will end. Ordinary adoption leave lasts for 26 weeks and additional adoption leave for a further 26 weeks.

The employee must give eight weeks' notice of an intention to return early from additional adoption leave.

Statutory adoption pay is payable for nine months and its rate is the same as the later rate (after the first six weeks) of statutory maternity pay—see **4.6.4** above.

4.8 Parental leave

The next 'family friendly' right we need to consider derives from Directive 96/34/EC and is provided for in ERA 1996, s. 76, as amended by ERA 1999, sch. 4. It gives both parents a right to unpaid time off during the first five years of a child's life, or the first five years after adoption.

4.8.1 The form of the Directive

The Parental Leave Directive 96/34/EC expressly encouraged the 'social partners' at local level to agree voluntary arrangements which could become an alternative to the law in defined workplaces. Such a process is virtually unknown in this country, and there is no legal basis for it to be built upon. However, MPL Regs provide in reg. 16 for voluntary arrangements to be agreed as an alternative to the detailed default provisions in sch. 2. The difficulty of any such arrangement is the provision in reg. 21 that employees may not treat statutory and contractual rights as cumulative, but may choose whichever is better in any particular regard. Owing to the uncertainty still present, for the remainder of this section we shall concentrate on the default provisions.

4.8.2 Qualification for the right

The right to take parental leave applies to all employees with service of one year or more if they have responsibility for a child. Parental responsibility is defined by reference either to the provisions of the Children Act 1989, or to registration as a child's father.

Under ERA 1996, s. 76(5) (inserted by ERA 1999, sch. 4), the regulations implementing parental leave may specify things that are to be taken as done for the purpose of caring for a child. Such rules would limit the circumstances in which parental leave can be taken. There is no such provision in MPL Regs 1999. Consequently employees do not have to justify a request to take parental leave by reference to the circumstances.

4.8.3 The right

Each qualifying employee may take parental leave up to a total of 13 weeks for each child. Thus each parent of twins may take up to 26 weeks. Under the default provisions the leave cannot be taken in blocks shorter than a week, as confirmed in *New Southern Railway Ltd* v *Rodway* [2005] EWCA Civ 443, [2005] ICR 1162, nor for more than four weeks in any year (sch. 2, paras 7 and 8).

The right normally expires on the child's fifth birthday. Where the child is adopted it expires on the fifth anniversary of the adoption, or the child's 18th birthday, whichever is earlier. If the child is disabled (defined by reference to entitlement to a disability living allowance), the maximum leave is 18 weeks instead of 13, the right expires on the child's 18th birthday, and in this instance the default provisions do not apply the rule about minimum blocks of a week; the minimum is a day.

The employee's rights during parental leave are exactly the same as those concerning additional maternity leave—see **4.6.3.3** above. The right to return at the end of it is to the same job if the leave is four weeks or less. If leave exceeds four weeks, or it is added on to additional maternity leave, the right to return is the same as after additional maternity leave.

4.8.4 Notices and administration

Under the default provisions, the employee is normally required to give the employer 21 days' notice of an intention to take parental leave. The employer may delay the leave for up to six months if the business would unduly be disrupted and an alternative time is offered. The expiry of the right that we discussed above will be delayed to cover this postponement if necessary. The employer is entitled to ask for evidence of the employee's entitlement, but not of course for any explanation of the circumstances of the particular request.

Fathers wanting to take parental leave at the time of a birth are required to give 21 days' notice of the expected week of childbirth and of the required length of leave. They are then entitled to take the leave whenever the birth actually occurs and the employer cannot postpone it. There is a similar provision covering both parents in relation to an expected adoption.

The employee's right is to a *total* of 13 weeks' leave in relation to each child. Thus an employee who changes jobs after taking eight weeks of leave in the first two years of a child's life enjoys no entitlement during the next year, having not yet achieved the necessary service in the new job, but thereafter has a right to five more weeks in the period up to the child's fifth birthday. There is no obligation on the first employer to pass any records to the second, and monitoring of this rule may therefore cause problems.

4.8.5 Remedies

The right not to suffer any detriment and to present a claim to an employment tribunal under s. 47C of ERA 1996 (considered in relation to maternity rights at **4.6** above) also applies to parental leave. Under ERA 1996, s. 80, claims can also be presented of unreasonable postponement of parental leave.

4.9 Time off for dependants

The third of the 'family friendly' provisions that we are considering is also a result of the Parental Leave Directive 96/34/EC. Unlike parental leave, it is not subject to regulations but is set out in detail in ERA 1999, which inserts a new s. 57A into ERA 1996. The requirement in the Directive is *for time off work for urgent family reasons*; in the UK version this has become *time off for dependants*, which is probably significantly broader in its scope. The time off is unpaid.

4.9.1 Circumstances when the right arises

There are two aspects to the statutory definition of the circumstances when employees have a right to time off for dependants. First, there is the question of who is a dependant; and, secondly, there is the question of when the right arises in relation to those dependants.

A dependant is defined in s. 57A(3), (4) and (5) as:

(a) a spouse;

(b) a child;

(c) a parent;

(d) anyone else living in the same household except as employee, tenant etc.;

(e) *for certain purposes only*, anyone else who 'reasonably relies on the employee' for that help.

The circumstances are defined in precise terms in s. 57A(1). In outline, the employee must need the time off to take action related to any of the following events concerning a dependant:

(a) where any of the above dependants falls ill or is injured or assaulted, or where a dependant in categories (a)–(d) above gives birth;

(b) arranging care in relation to illness or injury—all dependants;

(c) death—(a)–(d) only;

(d) unexpected disruption or termination of arrangements for care—all dependants. An 'unexpected' event does not have to be a 'sudden' event so notice of child care problems a few days before they occurred did not invalidate the request: *Royal Bank of Scotland plc* v *Harrison* [2009] IRLR 28;

(e) unexpected incidents at school, only in relation to a child—(b).

The circumstances are thus quite tightly defined. For example, the right relates to making arrangements for the provision of care, but not to provision of care by employees themselves. In *Forster* v *Cartwright Black* [2004] ICR 1728 the EAT did not permit a claimant whose mother had recently died to use s. 57A to obtain additional bereavement leave when no need to 'take action' existed.

4.9.2 Time off

The statutory right is to unpaid time off. There is no stated limit to the amount of time, beyond the reference to *a reasonable amount* of time off in ERA 1996, s. 57A. In *Qua* v *John Ford Morrison* [2003] ICR 482, the EAT held that time off was permitted for urgent reasons such as dealing with a child who has fallen ill unexpectedly, but not regular relapses from a known underlying condition. Reasonableness related to the employee's needs and her compliance with conditions about notification to the employer; not disruption or inconvenience caused to the employer's business. In many employments, there is already a contractual right to paid time off in defined circumstances like bereavement or childbirth, but the duration is usually defined. There is no statutory reference to the interrelationship of two such rights and they therefore exist independently.

4.9.3 Notices and administration

The whole purpose of these provisions is to enable employees to deal with emergencies. There can therefore be no requirement on employees to give advance notice. They are, however, required to tell the employer the reason for the absence as soon as reasonably practicable and, unless the explanation is only being given on return to work, to state how long the absence is expected to last.

Despite the strict statutory definition of the circumstances in which the right arises, there is nothing in s. 57A to give the employer any right to demand evidence of the employee's entitlement. In *Truelove* v *Safeway Stores Ltd* [2005] ICR 589 the EAT accepted that the employee cannot be expected to communicate the need for time off in the language of the statute. A more general statement indicating the disruption of a stable arrangement was enough to indicate to the employer that an emergency had arisen so as to give rise to the right to time off. That decision, coupled with the lack of any right to evidence, seems to make it very difficult for an employer safely to refuse a request and it may be that some future case will give guidance to employers on what they may require.

4.9.4 Remedies

Under ERA 1996, s. 57B (inserted by ERA 1999), an employee can present a claim to an employment tribunal of being refused time off for a dependant and the tribunal may award compensation.

Perhaps of greater practical significance is the addition of this right to the list of those in connexion with which dismissal is automatically unfair under ERA 1999, s. 99 (see **11.8.8** below). This could cause employers a lot of difficulty in dealing with absenteeism. Employees with a poor attendance record are sometimes warned and are told that further unauthorised absence will lead to dismissal. If further absence occurs, but is in fact covered by s. 57A, it will automatically be unfair for the employer to dismiss.

4.10 Flexible working

The last of the 'family friendly' rights we need to consider is the right of the employee to ask the employer for a variation of the contract of employment in order to care for young or disabled children or (since April 2007) certain adults. It exists as s. 80F of ERA 1996, inserted by EA 2002, and is supplemented by regulations issued since 2002. Permitted requests are for changes in hours of work, place of work, or time of work.

To be eligible to make such a request employees must satisfy the following criteria:

(a) They must have 26 weeks service when making the request.

(b) The child must be 16 or under, 18 if disabled (see SI 2009/595 changing the lower age from six), two weeks after the request is made.

(c) The employee must have or expect to have responsibility for the child's upbringing.

(d) The request must be to enable the employee to care for the child.

(e) The employee must be the mother, father, guardian, adopter or foster parent of the child, or alternatively married to or the partner of such a person. From 6 April 2007 carers are included.

(f) An employee may also make a request for flexible working if caring or expecting to be caring for a person who is over the age of 18 and in need of care, and who is married to or the partner or civil partner of the employee, or a relative of the employee, or living at the same address as the employee.

(g) The employee must not have made another application to work flexibly within the preceding 12 months.

The application must be made in writing and the employer must consider it seriously. The grounds on which it may be refused are set out in detail—to summarise, they are grounds of cost, detrimental consequences, effect on other staff, or planned structural changes. In *Commotion Ltd* v *Rutty* [2006] ICR 290 the EAT confirmed that the employer is not required to produce objective justification for refusal, but the grounds must be made out. In that case the employment tribunal was entitled to find that the employer had made an outdated, 'off the cuff' response without research and that was not good enough.

An employee who is refused unreasonably or whose employer does not properly consider the request can present a claim to the employment tribunal. The tribunal can order the employer to reconsider the request and can award compensation up to a maximum of eight weeks' pay, subject to the usual statutory maximum of £380 per week. In *Shaw* v *CCL Ltd* [2008] IRLR 284 the EAT found on the facts in the case that the employer's flat rejection of the claimant's request for flexible working undermined the necessary trust and confidence between the parties and was in fundamental breach of her contract of employment, so that she succeeded in a claim of unfair constructive dismissal (see **Chapters 11** and **12**).

4.11 Summary

- All workers are entitled to the national minimum wage (£5.93 per hour for adults as from October 2010) for all hours worked.
- All workers are entitled to a limit on their weekly hours, to further limits on night shift, and to daily rest, weekly rest, rest breaks, and paid annual leave.
- Employers may not make deductions from wages without express authority and employees can often bring their contractual disputes about the amount they are paid within this rule.
- Shop workers and betting workers have the right not to be required to work on Sundays.
- Qualifying employees have 'family friendly' rights—to maternity pay and leave, to paternity and adoption leave, to time off for dependants, and to ask for flexible working.

4.12 Self-test questions

1. A 19-year-old student friend had been earning some extra money by working in a bar on Friday evenings from 7.30 to about 11.45. He has just started an additional job working in a shop on Saturday mornings from 8.00 to 1.00 pm. He gets no break and is paid £30 for five hours' work. Your friend tells you that he understands that other people get time-and-a-half for Saturdays. The shop manager told him that as a part-time worker he is not entitled to holidays.

   Your friend is fed up with feeling tired when he goes to play football on Saturday afternoon, feels he is being exploited for a poor rate of pay, and wonders if there is anything you can do to help. Do you think the shop has broken any of the rules set out in this chapter?

2. An employer has until now paid at the rate of time-and-a-half for Saturday overtime. Recently the employer announced that such additional costs made the company uncompetitive compared with others overseas and gave three months' notice that weekend overtime would henceforth be paid at time-and-a-quarter. The trade union objected on behalf of the employees but the employer was adamant that the change was necessary and the trade union responded that its members would not work overtime on that basis. In fact, the employer did not require any overtime for several weeks after the expiry of the three months, but then a request was made and several people agreed to work on a Saturday. There is some suggestion that one or two expressly asked their supervisor about payment and he replied evasively, saying that payment would be sorted out later. They were in fact paid at time-and-a-quarter. Their trade union now asks whether that payment can be challenged in the tribunals. Could you use the 'deductions from wages' jurisdiction?

5

Operation of the contract

5.1 Introduction

This chapter examines how the contract of employment operates on a day-to-day basis. The sort of questions asked by employers and employees alike tend to be:

- Which terms usually appear in a contract?
- Does the law place limitations on how those terms can be used by either party?
- How may those terms be varied over the course of time?
- What are the legal rules for resolving disputes as to the content or implementation of those terms?
- What are the rights and duties regarding the payment of wages?

In attempting to answer these points this chapter will concentrate on the common law position and will adopt the following structure:

(a) The usual terms (express and implied) and how they are used.
(b) Qualifying for employment rights.
(c) Management decisions and employees' responses.
(d) Methods of resolving disputes, short of termination of contract.
(e) Breach: summary of sanctions and enforcement.
(f) Civil remedies for breach of contract.
(g) Deductions versus breach of contract.
(h) Example of an employment contract.

5.2 The usual terms and how they are used

We saw in **Chapters 3** and **4** that the contract is made up of express, implied, and statutory terms. We have set out below the *most commonly occurring express terms* you would find in a contract, together with commentary on their purpose, scope, and operation. Some additional terms encountered in contracts will also be noted. Many of the express terms listed below correlate to the information that must be provided under the written statement detailed in **Chapter 3.**

Having looked at express terms, we will then consider the implied terms, arising from common law and from statute. There is no fixed list of implied terms and some will be more applicable to a particular contract than others.

STANDARD EXPRESS TERMS	IMPLIED TERMS
(a) The names of the parties.	*The duties incumbent on the employer*
(b) Job title.	(a) The duty to pay.
(c) Commencement date.	(b) A limited duty to provide work.
(d) The expiry date of a fixed-term contract.	(c) Duties relating to health and safety.
(e) Pay.	(d) The duty of mutual trust and confidence.
(f) Hours of work.	(e) A duty to provide proper information to employees.
(g) Place of work.	
(h) The sick pay scheme, if any.	
(i) Holiday entitlement.	*The duties incumbent on the employee*
(j) Pension scheme.	(a) A duty to act in good faith.
(k) Notice requirements.	(b) The duty to obey lawful orders.
(l) Dedication to enterprise clause.	(c) A duty to provide personal service.
(m) Disciplinary/grievance procedures.	(d) The duty to exercise reasonable skill and care.
(n) Confidentiality clause.	
(o) Intellectual property protection.	(e) The duty to take care of the employer's property.
(p) Restraint of trade clause.	
(q) Details of other benefits.	
(r) Any 'Contracting out' clause.	

Figure 5.1 Common terms of the contract.

5.2.1 Express terms

The extent of such terms, reached orally or in writing, will vary a great deal. The style of drafting is also quite variable, especially with the more complicated terms such as confidentiality and restraint of trade clauses. Therefore we have not provided 'model' clauses because these will change with the needs of the client and, more importantly, this is a matter for your course rather than this book. We have attached an example of a working contract taken from practice. We had considered using a contract which we considered to be an example of good practice, but in the end decided that a faulty contract might provide more help (and realism). This appears at the end of the chapter together with commentary so that you can see some of the clauses *in situ*.

5.2.1.1 Commonly occurring terms

(a) The *names* of the parties.

(b) *Job title* and general statement of duties.

The wider this is drafted the more built-in flexibility there is for the employer (e.g., 'clerk/typist and receptionist' allows for mobility between tasks). However, if there is ever a dispute as to performance of duties, or if the employer needs to declare the employee redundant, then an expansive list of duties may prove problematic (e.g., the job of clerk/typist might have disappeared but not that of receptionist).

(c) When the *commencement date* occurred.

This is important in establishing the employee's continuity of employment, the timing of which may affect rights to claim, *inter alia,* unfair dismissal compensation, redundancy payments, and pension rights (for details see **5.3** below).

(d) The *expiry date* of a fixed-term contract.

We noted these and other forms of limited-term contracts above in **Chapter 3.**

(e) *Pay.*

Always an essential ingredient and an apparently simple point, but if payment is determined by piece-work, commission, or is variable according to the shift pattern worked then these points need to be spelled out clearly. The application of minimum pay levels under the National Minimum Wage Act 1998 was dealt with at **4.2** above.

Included in the general description of 'pay' one might also find other benefits—'perks' and bonuses—such as company cars, accommodation, 'golden handshakes', share option agreements, private health insurance schemes, and discretionary performance-related payments. The range is extensive and, especially in relation to senior employees, quite inventive.

(f) *Hours of work,* including a statement as to the status of overtime, i.e., is overtime compulsory or merely voluntary and how is payment calculated? The number of hours worked by employees together with patterns of working (e.g., shift systems, part-time, flexitime, 'annualised hours') vary enormously but working patterns for many workers are now subject to specific constraints (see above at **4.3**).

(g) *Place of work.*

The employer's business may have more than one site. If the employer wishes to be able to move the employee from place to place it is advisable to spell this out. Equally, the employer may wish to show that the employee is only expected to work in Southampton even though there are sites in London and Plymouth (see **Chapter 14** on how this relates to redundancies in a particular place of work).

(h) *The sick pay scheme,* if any.

The employer is under no duty to provide company sick pay and many employees only receive statutory sick pay. These entitlements will be administered by the employer but they are usually much more limited than a company sick pay scheme (e.g., nothing is payable for the first three days' illness and payment is limited to 28 weeks at a fixed rate). Even where company schemes do exist there is often a sliding scale of payments, e.g., no sick pay until the employee has worked for one year, one month's entitlement for service between one and three years, and so on and it is not uncommon for employers to exclude certain types of illness from the sick pay scheme: e.g., those relating to the employee's own misconduct or generated by some activities outside work.

Some employers go beyond this and offer their employees membership of permanent health insurance (PHI) schemes (i.e., schemes drawn up by health insurance companies and offered at preferential rates to companies). Unfortunately, the wording of the sick pay scheme and that of the PHI scheme sometimes do not correlate. For instance, the PHI scheme may provide generous terms and payments (e.g., long-term incapacity payments continuing until retirement) whereas the contractual scheme will usually be framed more narrowly and allow for dismissal of incapacitated employees after (say) six months' absence. In such cases the courts may adjudge, on the wording of the various documents or by implication of terms, that the employer's contractual scheme has to give way to these more beneficial insurance provisions.

One important consequence of these cases is that, as Staughton LJ states *obiter* in *Brompton* v *AOC International Ltd and UNUM Ltd* [1997] IRLR 639, there was 'a good deal to be said for' the idea that in these circumstances a term should be implied to the effect that the employer would not terminate the contract so as to deny the employee his or her rights under the PHI scheme (at least not without having inserted some power to do so in the PHI agreement or having to pay a great deal in damages). A dismissal for good cause or a genuine redundancy, however, will not be covered by this implied term: *Hill v General Accident Fire & Life Assurance Corporation plc* [1998] IRLR 641.

(i) *Holiday entitlement.*

This area has traditionally been the domain of pure contract law. However, the Working Time Regulations (WTRegs 1998) now lay down established patterns of holiday entitlement for many workers. For those workers not covered by the Regulations, this area is still governed by the express and implied terms of the contract.

(j) *Pension scheme* arrangements, if any.

Such details will relate to any schemes operating outside the state provisions. An employer is not bound to operate a company pension scheme and an employee is not bound to join it. There are a number of different schemes available, e.g., final salary schemes and money-purchase schemes. Details are outside the scope of this book.

(k) *Notice* requirements.

This will establish what length of notice to terminate the contract is due from each party. The amount will often vary according to length of service, though there are certain *statutory minima* required under ERA 1996, s. 86 (see **5.2.4** below and **Chapter 10**). Employers may also wish to insert a term that *payment in lieu of notice* may be given by the employer. Payment in lieu simply means that the employer makes a money payment equivalent to the sum the employee would have earned during the notice period. If calculated correctly the sum equates to any damages the employee might have been awarded for the failure actually to give notice. The employer can choose to do this even if there is no clause in the contract allowing for such action. However, although no further damages will fall due, giving a payment in lieu when there is no term to that effect is technically a breach of contract and, as will be seen, this may negate any restraint of trade clause in the contract. The disadvantage to having such a clause is that it becomes an agreed contractual liability and so tax will certainly be deducted.

Notice clauses can take a variety of forms. The notice due from one party does not have to be the same as from the other, and there is no standard term which one could expect to occur in every industry. Moreover, with senior employees a whole host of ingenious devices may be found, often designed to minimise tax liabilities. One increasingly common term is the 'garden leave' clause—a mechanism whereby the employer is given notice but allowed not to work but to stay at home in the garden. This device attempts to use notice provisions to overcome some of the problems of restraint of trade clauses (see **9.10** for details).

Some employers use a clause which requires an employee to forfeit part of their final salary or holiday pay if the employee fails to give adequate notice. In *Giraud* v *Smith* [2000] IRLR 763, Kay J held that such clauses would have to constitute a genuine pre-estimate of loss in order to stand—otherwise they amounted to penalty clauses. Oddly enough, the WTRegs 1998 (see **Chapter 4**) do permit such deductions provided *some* payment is still made: *Witley & District Men's Club* v *Mackay* [2001] IRLR 595, EAT, so different analyses apply depending on how the claim is framed.

(l) *Dedication to enterprise clause,* sometimes called a 'whole time and attention clause'. This clause states the limitations under which an employee can undertake other work for a different employer, either during or after working hours. The clause, especially with senior employees, may also impose a duty to inform on colleagues' misdeeds.

(m) *Disciplinary/grievance procedures.*

Procedures have always been very important in employment law disputes. For instance, an employer's conduct in, say, an unfair dismissal action will be judged against his own published disciplinary procedure (or lack of one) in determining the fairness of any dismissal.

5.2.1.2 More specialist terms

The following terms will occur more frequently, though not exclusively, in contracts for senior employees, sales people, and research and development staff:

(a) *Confidentiality clause.*

During the currency of the contract an employer's 'secrets' will be protected by the implied terms relating to confidentiality and fidelity (see below at **5.2.3.2** and **Chapter 8**). However, an express term can serve to detail the nature of the confidential information and also serve as a warning to employees. Without such a clause there may be circumstances where junior employees who come into contact with confidential information are not bound by any duty of confidence because this was not made obvious to them.

Confidentiality clauses are also frequently drafted to protect against the use or disclosure of information once the relationship has terminated. It is a matter of some debate whether such clauses are effective and we will deal with this point extensively in **Chapter 8**. For the moment we can say that it is advisable to insert properly-drafted clauses of this nature in the contract; certainly as regards employees who are likely to handle confidential information.

(b) *Intellectual property clause.*

This clause seeks to detail ownership of copyright, designs, and inventions made by the employee during the working relationship. Such clauses cannot overturn certain statutory definitions.

(c) *Restraint of trade clause.*

Such clauses endeavour to prevent an employee working in a particular job or industry for a set time, and usually within a defined area, after the contract has ended. The effect of restraint clauses is therefore far more dramatic than any confidentiality clause. Many employers seek to rely on both types of clause in order to protect against disclosure of secrets and/or to prevent the former employee poaching the employer's trade connexions.

The presumption with restraint of trade clauses is that they are void unless:

(i) they seek to protect a *legitimate interest;* and

(ii) they are shown to be *reasonable* by reference to time, area, and the market setting. See **Chapter 9** for details.

(d) *'No-show' clauses*

These are terms which set a liquidated damages sum covering the employee's failure to join the company, having accepted the offer of the job. They have become more common in senior employees' contracts and have led to substantial damages being awarded against the no-show 'employee'.

5.2.1.3 Less common terms

The following terms, which may apply to all staff, occur occasionally but are useful:

(a) *A right to search employees.*

Companies wishing to protect against the removal of confidential documents or, more generally, against the removal of stock, are advised to insert such a clause.

There will be no general implied term to this effect and there may well now be human rights implications under art. 8 of the European Convention on Human Rights. We would suggest that the same degree of caution should be applied to searching employees' offices and desks, even though, technically, these are the employer's property.

(b) *A right to demand employees undergo medical examinations on request.*

As will be seen in **Chapter 8**, a term will not be implied which forces an employee to submit to a medical examination. An express term is necessary and often very useful. Indeed, it has become common practice in some industries (e.g., oil exploration) for the employer to have the contractual right to demand that employees undertake regular drug tests. This is defended on the grounds of health and safety; but many employers would like to see this sort of term extended to all kinds of employees. Again, art. 8 of the European Convention on Human Rights needs to be considered here (see *Whitefield* v *General Medical Council* at **1.7.3.2** above).

(c) *Suspension clause.*

This gives the employer the right to suspend an employee (i) with pay, or (ii) without pay as part of disciplinary proceedings or sanctions. It should occur in the disciplinary details (see (m) above). There will be no right for an employer to suspend without pay in the absence of such a clause, and any prolonged suspension *with* pay may be a breach of contract even with such powers in the contract as it may strike at the mutual trust of the relationship. Employees may seek to prevent long-term suspensions through applications for injunctive relief.

(d) *Lay-off and guarantee clauses.*

If an employer 'lays off' the employee (i.e., sends him or her home without pay because there is a shortage of work) this will constitute a breach of contract and may eventually be deemed a redundancy. Many industries therefore have specific rates of pay relating to short-time working, termed 'guarantee payments'. There are statutory guarantee payments as well which will operate as a minimum (at the time of writing, £21.50 per day to a maximum of five days in any three-month period).

(e) *Variation clause.*

As we will see below, although the unilateral variation of a contract by the employer is not unknown, there may be complex legal consequences (see **5.4**). Some employers therefore incorporate an express term allowing for the power to vary the contract (usually in stated circumstances). Such clauses are viewed with great suspicion by the courts and tribunals.

(f) *Maternity leave.*

Some employers offer maternity rights which are more beneficial to the employee than the bare statutory rights (see **Chapter 4** above).

5.2.2 Terms and age discrimination

Pay, benefits, and other terms and conditions that depend on age or length of service may be indirectly discriminatory under the Equality Act 2010 because older employees are more likely to benefit than younger ones. We shall see in **Chapter 6** that there are specific rules covering this situation. For instance, under sch. 9, para. 10, EqA 2010 employers do not have to justify a difference of treatment as a result of a difference in length of service between two workers if the disadvantaged worker has service of five years or less. And even where the service required to gain a benefit is longer than five years the term will not be discriminatory if the employer can demonstrate that the term 'fulfils a business need of his undertaking' (for example, by encouraging the loyalty or motivation, or rewarding the experience, of some or all of his workers). Similar exemptions apply to redundancy schemes in which those with longer service (and therefore usually older) are given higher payments than others.

5.2.3 Implied terms

Employment contracts are rarely thought out by the parties. The exact terms of contracts are often difficult to locate or are silent on many aspects. There is therefore great scope for implying terms; for instance, 'Is sick pay payable?', 'Is there a limit on overtime hours that may be worked?', 'Can the employee be asked to work at different sites?'.

The various methods of implying terms were noted in **Chapter 3** (by law, under the 'officious bystander' test, by custom, and by statute). In line with general contractual theory, terms will be implied only where they are *necessary* for the business efficacy of the contract, not simply because it would be *reasonable* so to imply them. However, once a term has been found to be necessary to the contract the court will then determine the limits of that term within reasonable parameters. Thus it may be found reasonable to imply a term that an employee will work at a variety of sites operated by the employer; it may, however, be unreasonable to include the Birmingham site when the employee normally works in Oxford.

The courts and tribunals are not afraid of implying terms, either to give a purposive interpretation to the contract or on the basis of *general* employment practice rather than by detailed analysis of the negotiations, etc. entered into by the specific parties. These general points, however, centre on how the parties would be expected to behave, e.g., to act in good faith; the courts and tribunals are more wary of accepting arguments of 'common practice' or 'general working practice' within a company without firm evidence of the fact. The generally established implied terms as to duties owed are set out below.

5.2.3.1 The duties incumbent on the employer

(a) The duty to *pay* the employee the agreed remuneration for being ready and willing to work. There is no general duty actually to supply work, though there are exceptional cases here (see (b) below).

The major statutory controls on pay are the Employment Rights Act 1996, Part II, Protection of Wages (which concerns the right for employers to make deductions from pay) and the National Minimum Wage Act 1998. The Equality Act 2010 outlaws discriminatory pay schemes.

Particular problems have nevertheless arisen over:

(i) *Sick pay.*

If there is no written or oral evidence of a contractual sick pay scheme, can such a right be implied? The Court of Appeal has stated that there is no presumption either way: *Mears* v *Safecar Security Ltd* [1982] ICR 626 (sick pay not due on the facts). One would thus have to look at all factors such as custom and practice within the company and even the seniority of the employee. If there is a term as to sick pay its duration is limited to that stated in the contract or for a reasonable period: *Howman* v *Blyth* [1983] ICR 416.

(ii) *Share purchase option schemes.*

The problem here is: what happens to the option to purchase when the contract is terminated? In *Levett* v *Biotrace International plc* [1999] IRLR 375, the contract included an option for the employee to purchase shares in the company. The right lapsed in the event of the employee being dismissed following the disciplinary procedure (it is quite common to find such terms in contracts of employment, whereby the option lapses on termination). Here, however, the employee had been summarily dismissed in breach of the disciplinary procedure. The Court of Appeal held that he was still entitled to exercise his option; the employers were not entitled to deprive the employee of his rights by relying on their own breach of contract.

Equally, wording the scheme so that employers have an 'absolute discretion' on dismissal to reduce any share option has been held not to entitle the employer to reduce it to nil: *Mallone* v *BPB Industries plc* [2002] EWCA Civ 126, [2002] ICR 1045. This is particularly interesting because, as we will see when we come to consider how each party reacts to demands made by the other (see **5.4** below), this was the first real acknowledgement by the Court of Appeal of a power to limit managerial discretion based not merely on the technicalities of 'collateral' contracts or on the presence of dishonesty, bad faith, or perversity but rather on 'irrationality'.

(b) A limited duty to *provide work*. Traditionally, only in exceptional cases will there be a duty to provide work. The most significant example occurs where the lack of work leads to an effective wage reduction, as where pay is related to commission or piece-work. A time when this is likely to be an issue is when the employee has been given notice of dismissal and not provided with work (or pay in lieu) during that time: see *Devonald* v *Rosser* [1906] KB 728. Where lack of work might have a damaging effect on reputation (e.g., in the case of actors, television personalities, or perhaps even senior business executives) there is the possibility of arguing breach of contract. And where the employer deliberately refuses to allow the employee to work for no good contractual reason, the possibility of arguing a repudiatory breach of contract becomes stronger: *Breach* v *Epsylon Industries* [1976] ICR 316. Although the above propositions have been established law for some time, the Court of Appeal decision in *William Hill Organisation Ltd* v *Tucker* [1998] IRLR 313 has confirmed that there will be cases where a right to work exists (and changing social attitudes may mean the list is wider than previously thought).

(c) A duty to *indemnify* the employee regarding expenses necessarily incurred in the course of employment. Obviously this extends to expenses such as hotel and travel costs; it may also extend to covering the employee's legal costs, but only to those relating to actions undertaken during employment.

(d) Duties relating to *safety*. In *Wilsons and Clyde Coal* v *English* [1938] AC 57, these duties were said to relate to the provision of safe fellow employees, equipment, premises, and the system of work. There are also statutory duties relating to defective equipment and compulsory insurance in addition to the responsibilities created by the Health and Safety at Work etc. Act 1974 which impose criminal liabilities in this field. There is a vast body of case law and statutory authority on duties of health and safety. More recent developments, however, have caused employers concern. The Management of Health and Safety Regulations 1992 require employers to carry out risk assessments for both physical and mental hazards at work. To this has been added case law developing the implied terms relating to *psychological* damage arising out of stress at work. In *Walker* v *Northumberland County Council* [1995] ICR 702 the employer's duty of care was extended to cover lack of attention in dealing with the workload of an (already distressed) employee.

(e) The duty of *mutual trust and confidence*. This is a rather nebulous duty and much of the case law has arisen in the context of unfair dismissal claims based on constructive dismissals (see **Chapters 11 and 12**). Just as employees have found that duties of obedience and loyalty can be vastly extended beyond the perceived agreement by implied terms, so too is an employer bound by an element of reciprocity. Thus there will be a serious breach of the duty of mutual trust (and so of the contract) if the employer victimises the employee, acts capriciously towards the employee, fails to allow *some* employees (e.g., part-timers) access to benefits, maliciously undermines an employee's authority in front of subordinates, harasses the employee, and so on. The list is open-ended and the use of this duty as a sort of 'default rule' in the governing of employment relationships has been endorsed by the House of Lords in *Malik and Mahmud* v *Bank of Credit and Commerce International SA (in compulsory liquidation)* [1997] ICR 606. In *French* v *Barclays Bank plc* [1998] IRLR 646, the Court of Appeal applied such principles to the case where an employee had been directed to move across country within the organisation and had been granted a discretionary relocation bridging loan by his employer which was then withdrawn when the employee had difficulty selling his house. The employee was forced to sell his house at a lower value than anticipated and so sued for breach of contract in respect of the shortfall. He succeeded on the grounds that the bank had breached the duty of mutual trust by seeking to change the arrangement once the employee had relied upon it.

We shall see more of this in operation in **Chapters 11–13**; we should stress, however, that this is not a duty to act reasonably, only a duty to give fair treatment under the terms of the contract. What the courts are looking for is to establish a breach of contract which makes further continuance of the relationship impossible. This will not always be the same as a finding of unreasonableness; especially if express terms allow the employer to take that particular action. Indeed, in *Johnson* v *Unysis Ltd* [2001] UKHL 13, [2001] ICR 480 the House of Lords did not see the duty of mutual trust as an overarching legal principle which might be used to control the wording of express contractual provisions (at least in relation to cases on termination of the contract). Thus it may seem unreasonable to move employees across the country every two or three years, but it is less likely to constitute a breach if a mobility clause has been incorporated in the contract. Matters such as a right to harass or discriminate cannot of course form part of an express term.

The issue of an employer's (bad faith) motives, of what constitutes a lawful order and the boundaries of mutual trust and confidence was explored in *Macari* v *Celtic Football and Athletic Club Ltd* [1999] IRLR 787. The Celtic manager, Macari, claimed the employers had acted in bad faith in dismissing him. The Court of Session, Inner House (equivalent to the Court of Appeal) held that the issue of bad faith motive was irrelevant provided the orders themselves were lawful, i.e., within the terms of the contract—even if such conduct had been proven (which, on the facts, it had not).

What is clear from all this is that the area of bad faith and the ambit of the duty of mutual trust and confidence is still open to a wide range of arguments and applications and that the 'pure contract' approach seen above is at some variance with the analysis of the same topic employed in unfair dismissal cases.

(f) A limited duty to *provide proper information* to employees regarding matters affecting rights under the contract. This implied term arises out of the decision of the House of Lords in *Scally v Southern Health and Social Services Board* [1991] ICR 771, where new employees were not informed of their rights to enhance their years of pension entitlement. This case effectively gave legal force to what is good practice anyway; but it did not create a universal rule regarding the provision of information. In *University of Nottingham* v *Eyett and the Pensions Ombudsman* [1999] IRLR 87, for instance, the High Court did not find as an implied term a duty for an employer to inform an employee taking voluntary early retirement that if he had waited a month he would have received a higher pension owing to the operation of the annual pay rise. The employer had not set out to mislead the employee but had merely implemented its general policy of offering no advice to employees on retirement provisions. In *Scally,* Lord Bridge had stated that a positive term of this nature would only be implied when the contract had not been negotiated with the individual employee, the particular term required the employee to take some action to avail him of the right and the employee could not reasonably be expected to be aware of the term without notice.

Further limitations have now been put on the term by the Court of Appeal. In *Lennon v Commissioner of Police of the Metropolis* [2004] EWCA Civ 130, [2004] IRLR 385 the Court acknowledged the existence of liability where the employer voluntarily assumed responsibility for providing information (and negligently misstated it) but distinguished this from implying a term that the employer owed any *positive* duty to provide information. Thus, *Scally* is looking more and more like a flash in the pan.

(g) One may also imply a term of *affording employees a reasonable opportunity to obtain redress of grievances:* see *W. A. Goold (Pearmak) Ltd* v *McConnell* [1995] IRLR 516.

5.2.3.2 The duties incumbent on the employee

(a) A duty to act in *good faith.* This is a wide and undefined duty which relates to the loyalty and fidelity that can be expected of an employee. This duty has had a major bearing on matters such as confidentiality, spare-time working, and employees competing with their employer. Its operation can be seen in the following examples:

(i) A duty *not to disrupt* the employer's business interests: *Secretary of State for Employment* v *ASLEF* [1972] 2 QB 455. This case concerned workers observing their contracts to the letter under a 'work-to-rule'. The disruption that followed was held to be a breach of contract. It appears therefore that the employees were held to be in breach of contract because they had observed the terms of the contract to the letter. Why this should be so is explained at **5.4.3** below.

(ii) A duty of *honesty.* This incorporates actions beyond simple theft or fraud. In *Sinclair* v *Neighbour* [1967] 2 QB 279, a betting shop manager habitually took money from the till, left IOUs, and always repaid the 'loan'. He was expressly forbidden to do this, but he continued. The summary dismissal was held to be justified. It was said that a breach occurred where further continuance of the relationship would prove impossible. That was the case here. Again, in *Denco Ltd* v *Joinson* [1991] ICR 172, the use of an unauthorised password to gain access to a computer was found to constitute gross misconduct, analogous to dishonesty.

(iii) A duty to *account for secret profits: Boston Deep Sea Fishing and Ice Co.* v *Ansell* (1888) 39 ChD 339. Most cases involve high-ranking employees taking bribes, or who have undisclosed interests which affect the employment relationship. Strictly speaking, however, this duty extends to such things as the gift from a client of a bottle of whisky at Christmas time.

Note: Points (i)–(iii) do not mean that the employment relationship is a fiduciary relationship (except in the case of certain employees such as directors). As was noted in *Nottingham University* v *Fishel* [2000] IRLR 471, an employee's duty of fidelity requires the employee to take the employer's interests into account; it does not require the employee to act in the employer's interests. In *Fishel* this meant that the head of the university's infertility unit was not under a fiduciary duty in respect of the work he did abroad (and the money earned), but he was liable to account for the money earned from work done by other university employees.

(iv) A duty to *disclose misdeeds*. There is no obligation to incriminate oneself: *Bell* v *Lever Bros* [1932] AC 161. When asked direct questions, however, there is a duty not to mislead. An intermediate area exists here under the provisions of the Rehabilitation of Offenders Act 1974. In general, this Act allows certain criminal convictions to be 'spent' after an appropriate length of time so that they do not have to be declared. What has also developed recently is the idea that there is a duty, at least incumbent on senior management whose responsibilities are affected by the actions, to notify the employer of serious breaches by fellow employees even when that involves self-incrimination: *Sybron Corp.* v *Rochem Ltd* [1983] ICR 801. This 'duty to rat' may often be made explicit or extended by the express terms. Thus in *Fishel,* although it was held that there was no *implied* term requiring the employee to inform the employer of his extra-university activities, there was a valid *express* clause to this effect. The High Court decision of *Item Software (UK) Ltd* v *Fassihi* [2003] EWHC 3116, [2003] IRLR 769 added two interesting points to this discussion:

- first, that a senior employee involved in negotiations on behalf of his employer owed a duty to the employer to disclose factors which could affect the negotiations (including his own attempts to sabotage those negotiations);
- secondly, that the activities in *Bell* v *Lever Bros* were held not to be fraudulent, and where fraud was present (as here) the *Bell* v *Lever Bros* principle could not apply, so there was a duty to self-incriminate (when the case went to the Court of Appeal the matter was decided only on the point of directors' duties and the employment angle was ignored: [2004] EWCA Civ 1244, [2004] IRLR 928). This is in keeping with other pronouncements that senior employees may well owe a duty to incriminate themselves, their positions being treated as akin to fiduciaries.

(v) A duty not to disclose *confidential information*: *Thomas Marshall (Exporters) Ltd* v *Guinle* [1978] ICR 905. This duty arises during the course of the relationship and, in some cases, will continue to operate after its termination: *Faccenda Chicken* v *Fowler* [1986] ICR 297 (see **Chapter 8**).

(vi) A duty to surrender *inventions.* Sections 39–43 of the Patents Act 1977 (as amended) deal with this point extensively. As regards most employees any invention arising out of the employee's *normal duties* will belong to the employer: *Harris's Patent* [1985] RPC 19.

(vii) A duty *not to compete* with the employer: *Hivac Ltd* v *Park Royal Scientific Instruments Ltd* [1946] Ch 169. This duty relates to actions during the currency of the contract and corresponds with 'whole time and attention' express terms. Competition cannot be prevented once the contract has been determined, subject to a valid restraint of trade clause.

(b) The duty to *obey lawful orders*. This is an essential element in the relationship. The nomenclature begs the question as to what is a lawful order. 'Lawful' in the employment context means 'contractually justified'; such orders do not necessarily have to be reasonable as well (see, for instance, *Cresswell* v *Board of Inland Revenue* [1984] ICR 508).

(c) A duty to provide *personal service* and to be ready and willing to work. Things such as taking part in a strike or other industrial action will generally amount to a breach. This will allow the employer either to withhold some or all of the wages due, or even to accept the employee's repudiation by dismissing him (see **5.4**). Illness is not a breach of this duty and, once the employee has recovered, the employer will be in breach if (subject to any express term in the contract) he insists on the employee delaying the return to work in order to undergo an examination by the company doctor and not paying the employee during that period: *Beveridge* v *KLM UK Ltd* [2000] IRLR 765.

(d) The duty to exercise *reasonable skill and care: Janata Bank* v *Ahmed* [1981] ICR 791.

(e) The duty to *take care* of the employer's property. Negligence in allowing property in the employee's care to be stolen has fallen within this heading. There are obvious limits: losing the company cat has been held to be an insufficient ground to justify dismissal. Interestingly, there is no corresponding duty placed on the employer to safeguard the employee's property.

5.2.4 Automatically imposed terms

As we saw in **Chapter 4**, terms may also be imposed by statute. For example, terms relating to sex discrimination and equal pay will automatically become part of the contract and cannot be evaded even by express agreement. The most important of these terms, for present purposes, relates to notice periods. There are requirements for the provision of minimum periods of notice laid down in ERA 1996, s. 86. *The contractual periods may be longer, but not shorter.* They operate on a sliding scale; the greater the length of service, the greater the minimum notice entitlement. The maximum statutory minimum allowed under s. 86 is 12 weeks' notice (see **Chapter 10** for a fuller explanation).

5.3 Qualifying for employment rights

Employment rights do not necessarily apply automatically to all employees. For example:

(a) unfair dismissal and redundancy rights do not usually accrue until the employee has acquired some 'continuity of employment' with that employer;

(b) the right to claim the statutory minimum period of notice on dismissal usually requires one month's continuous employment.

The detailed rules governing continuity are found in ERA 1996, ss. 210–219 and in the Employment Protection (Continuity of Employment) Regulations 1996 (SI 1996/3147). Whereas employers and employees can agree *contractual* variations to the rules, these agreements cannot affect the *statutory* rights: *Secretary of State for Employment* v *Globe Elastic Thread Co. Ltd* [1979] ICR 706 HL, and *Collison* v *British Broadcasting Corporation* [1998] IRLR 238, EAT.

It is unfortunately not uncommon for solicitors to advise on the merits of, say, an unfair dismissal case, without determining the basic qualification rights first. Thus solicitors need to establish:

(a) What rights are being claimed and whether the worker actually is an 'employee' or, in some cases such as under the WTRegs 1998, a qualifying 'worker';
(b) exactly when the employment began;
(c) exactly when it ended;
(d) any breaks in that employment; and
(e) especially if there has been a dismissal, whether the reason falls under the continuity exceptions so that no time qualification is required.

Some of the basic questions in computing continuity are:

(a) *Who must prove continuity?* Continuity of employment and the calculation of lengths of continuous employment are rebuttable presumptions. The basic presumption of continuity is set out in s. 210(5) of ERA 1996: 'A person's employment during any period shall, unless the contrary is shown, be presumed to have been continuous.' In *Nicoll* v *Nocorrode Ltd* [1981] ICR 348, the EAT held that if it is unclear whether the employee had worked the necessary number of qualifying weeks, the employee need only show some weeks count and then the burden shifts to the employer to disprove continuity.
(b) *When does continuity start and finish?* Sections 211–213 detail the start and finish dates for calculating continuity as beginning on the day on which the employee starts work, and ending with the 'effective date of termination' for unfair dismissal purposes (called the 'relevant date' in redundancies).
(c) *Which weeks count towards continuity?* Under s. 212(1), any week during the whole or part of which an employee's relations with his employer are governed by a contract of employment counts in computing the employee's period of employment, e.g., in *Colley* v *Corkindale* [1995] ICR 965 the employee only worked for five-and-a-half hours every alternate Friday; she nevertheless qualified to bring an unfair dismissal claim because the court found that there was one contract governing the intervening periods between actual work. However, this must be distinguished from the case of regular but *separate* contracts: see *Hellyer Bros* v *McLeod* [1987] ICR 526, where trawlermen employed for separate sea voyages did not gain continuity of employment.
(d) *What happens with maternity leave?* The basic rules of statutory continuity apply in such situations.
(e) *What happens when there is no contract?* The basic rule is that if there is no contract then continuity is broken. A good illustration of this is *Booth* v *United States of America* [1999] IRLR 16, where the US Government deliberately dismissed employees in the UK just short of the qualifying period for unfair dismissal (then, two years) but gave them the option to reapply for their old jobs. This dismissal and re-engagement broke the continuity of employment.
(f) *Can continuity be preserved even when there is no contract?* In limited circumstances, yes. The position is governed by s. 212(3), which states that certain weeks *will* count in computing the employee's period of employment even though the employee appears not to have a contract with the employer. These are very odd and highly technical provisions which occasionally cause problems in practice.

The weeks which count are those weeks during the whole or part of which an employee is:

(i) incapable of work in consequence of sickness or injury. Note here that if the employee has not been dismissed the contract will have continued as normal. The point of this provision is that if an employee has been absent because of illness, has been dismissed and then is re-employed at a future date, those weeks during which he was not employed may still count towards continuity provided the gap between dismissal and re-engagement was no more than 26 weeks;

(ii) absent from work on account of a temporary cessation of work. There is no definition of 'temporary'—it is a question of fact. How both parties regarded the absence would be cogent evidence, but, if necessary, one must use hindsight rather than intent to establish just how temporary it was. In *Ford* v *Warwickshire County Council* [1982] ICR 520 (a case concerning continuity of employment for part-time teachers employed only during each term and not for the school holidays), 'temporary' was said to mean 'transient'—which might exclude seasonal workers. In that case Lord Diplock also favoured a strictly mathematical approach in calculating length of service, though the Court of Appeal, in *Flack* v *Kodak Ltd* [1986] ICR 775, preferred a 'broad brush' approach, i.e., was the absence 'short' in relation to the overall employment relationship. Taking a job in the interim is not fatal to a claim of continuity (*Thompson* v *Bristol Channel Ship Repairers and Engineers Ltd* (1970) 5 ITR 85, CA) but is unlikely to cover the situation where an employee moves to a new employer, fails to settle, and quickly moves back to his old job. A 'cessation' has been defined in *Fitzgerald* v *Hall Russell & Co. Ltd* [1970] AC 984, HL: it refers to a cessation of the employee's work (not the employer's business). Thus, there was no temporary cessation in *Booth* v *USA* (above) because the work still remained;

(iii) absent from work in circumstances such that, by arrangement or custom, he is regarded as continuing in the employment of his employer for any purpose. The custom must exist when the absence begins: *Todd* v *Sun Ventilating Co. Ltd* [1976] IRLR 4; an arrangement does not have to: *London Probation Board* v *Kirkpatrick* [2005] ICR 965, EAT. Equally, the mere fact that the parties might have discussed terms and conditions on which the employee might return does not amount to an implied arrangement. The reason for the absence appears immaterial (e.g., personal reasons, employee on 'reserve list' to be called on when necessary: *Puttick* v *John Wright & Sons (Blackwell) Ltd* [1972] ICR 457).

This area has re-emerged from the shadows over the question of 'career breaks'. In *Curr* v *Marks & Spencer plc* [2002] EWCA Civ 1852, [2003] ICR 443 the Court of Appeal held that an agreed career break (here, a 'child break scheme') did not preserve continuity on the facts because there was no evidence of mutual agreement *regarding the issue of continuity*. In other words, the agreement to take the break was not enough; one needed direct evidence on the matter of continuity, e.g., an express agreement or perhaps the continuation of contractual benefits such as pension scheme arrangements.

(g) *Can some weeks which do not count still not break continuity?* The most common example arises in the case of industrial disputes. Under s. 212, if during the week, or any part of the week, the employee takes part in a strike action then the week cannot count towards calculating the total period of continuous employment but this does not break continuity.

(h) *What happens if an employee is made redundant and then re-employed at a later date?* Section 214 states that the continuity of a period of employment is broken and then re-starts afresh as regards redundancy pay entitlements only where a redundancy payment has previously been paid to the employee.

(i) *What happens when there is a change of employer?* If the employee leaves to join another company then continuity is generally broken unless that company is an associated company, or the absence and return can be classed as a temporary cessation. Where the employer changes identity the likelihood is that continuity will be maintained with the new employer (see **Chapter 15** below).

As you will see in later chapters, some rights arise immediately on employment so that no qualification period is necessary, e.g., the rights relating to discrimination, 'protective awards' in redundancies, and time off for antenatal care.

5.4 Management decisions and employees' responses

It is quite common for an employee to ask for legal advice along the lines of, 'They've told me I have to take on a different job. Can they do that?'; the context being perhaps an order to change shifts, take a pay cut, change duties, move to another site, and so on. The pragmatic advice might be unpalatable: 'No, but are you prepared to fight?'.

The corresponding question from the employer might be, 'We need to cut costs: can we change the system of working?'. There is an industrial relations' angle here too: what will the employer do in the face of individual or collective resistance? Is the employer willing to venture into brinkmanship, e.g., threatening to dismiss in the face of refusal to cooperate? It is therefore vital to know what the contract allows, whether that is legally permissible in itself, and how the terms might be open to both expansion and alteration.

In deciding on the balance between these two views you need to keep in mind all the points detailed above on express and implied terms.

5.4.1 What management can demand: lawful orders

A 'lawful order' is one which is permitted under the contract, derived from the express terms, the implied terms, or a mixture of both. Should the employee fail to obey this order he or she will be in breach of contract. If the breach is serious the employer will be entitled at common law to dismiss the employee without notice (how it is handled will determine the unfair dismissal aspect). Equally, employers can only demand that lawful orders be obeyed. An employee is free to disregard anything which falls outside the scope of contract.

As with ordinary contracts, therefore, the courts *could* have adopted the view that the parties are restricted to the originally-agreed express terms (with limited help from implied terms) and bound by nothing else. But this view does not hold true for three main reasons:

(a) Most employment contracts are for an indefinite period, terminable by notice. They may therefore last a considerable length of time and the nature of the work changes.

(b) Employment contracts are made up from a variety of sources, many of them not reduced to writing, so that certainty and proof is always a problem.

(c) The employment contract stands in the wider setting of the *employment relationship* so that the range of implied terms is more extensive than with most contracts and includes matters such as loyalty and mutual trust.

5.4.2 The employer's handling of the contract

The employer generally has the economic bargaining power to insert terms which best serve the employer's interests. Further, it is the employer who issues orders under the contract. Both these points engender a high level of managerial prerogative. What curbs are placed on managerial prerogative?

5.4.2.1 Curbs on managerial prerogative: the legitimacy of terms

There are now *statutory limitations* which make certain terms in contracts of employment illegal or ineffective. For example, those terms that:

(a) seek to license various forms of discrimination; or

(b) offend against the principle of equal pay; or

(c) attempt to diminish employee–inventors' rights; or

(d) seek generally to contract out of statutory rights (such as unfair dismissal or redundancy); or

(e) seek to exclude liability for negligence which causes death or personal injury; or

(f) offend against safety legislation; or

(g) are illegal in themselves, such as instructions to undertake criminal activities.

Away from these statutory concerns, however, there are few cases which have addressed the issue as to the *type* of terms acceptable in an employment contract. Thus, *prima facie,* employers are free to insert any terms they wish and the parties can construct any form of reasonable or unreasonable contract (restraint of trade clauses providing the rare example of common law interference: see **Chapter 9**).

Express terms generally take precedence over implied terms. We use the word 'generally' because it is not always clear whether terms 'implied by law' (sometimes referred to as legal incidents of the relationship), e.g., the duty of mutual trust and confidence, can be expunged by express terms. In *Johnstone* v *Bloomsbury Health Authority* [1991] IRLR 118, for instance, the Court of Appeal held that an express term requiring health workers to be 'available' for 48 hours over and above their normal 40-hour week could not stand in the face of the implied term to protect the employees' health and safety. However, to do this the court had to find that the express term did not create an absolute duty (only a discretionary one as to requests for overtime), and because the term was equivocal the implied term had not been overridden. If the term had created an absolute duty of absurd overtime hours the court would have faced a more difficult question. In contrast to this problem of 'basic obligations', terms implied in fact (i.e., under the officious bystander test) cannot stand against contradictory express terms.

Judicial moderation of all this has had little focus. The concept of public policy might be invoked to overcome express terms, or the uncertainty of the term or, more recently, the implying of a term that contractual rights must be implemented on reasonable grounds.

PROBLEM

An employer encounters financial difficulties. The written contract is a complicated document, laden with detailed clauses, which sets out a very generous sick pay scheme. The employer decides to reduce the benefits substantially. The union objects on behalf of its members. The employer points to page 5 of the contract, where the final clause reads: 'The employer reserves the power to alter, amend, withdraw, terminate or revoke any term in this contract for any reason by giving one calendar month's notice.' The union has come to you for advice on the legality of this action.

ANSWER

The arguments available to you are multiple. You may seek to challenge the drafting of the term. For instance, you could argue that it is uncertain because of its width or seek to rely on *contra proferentem* interpretations (which is a favoured method: see *Bainbridge* v *Circuit Foil UK Ltd* [1997] ICR 541 and *Khatri* v *Cooperatieve Centrale Raiffeisen-Boerenleenbank BA* [2010] EWCA Civ 397; [2010] IRLR 715). You could argue that such a clause permits only minor changes to be made. You might seek to argue that such a clause can only be implemented in good faith and inherently requires renegotiation rather than mere unilateral change. Arguing from basic contractual principles you could claim that the court should try to avoid a construction which effectively destroys the aim of the contract or which produces absurd consequences. Similarly you might argue that reliance on this term *in this particular way* constitutes a breach of mutual trust and confidence—that such a term can be exercised only where it is reasonable in all the circumstances so as not to damage the employment relationship irrevocably. In all these cases, however, you are on uncertain ground; the express terms clearly outflank you so that on a literal reading of the contract the odds are against your union-client on the strict wording.

Cases in this area are now becoming more common. In *Airlie* v *City of Edinburgh District Council* [1996] IRLR 516, a majority of the EAT held that a bonus scheme payable under a collective agreement (which had been incorporated into the individual contracts) *was* open to variation by the employers on the proper construction of its wording (here, 'the scheme . . . may be altered at the request of either side after consultation . . . '). The employers had consulted, failed to reach an agreement, and acted accordingly. But in *Candler* v *ICL System Services* (1996, unreported, EAT/1136/94), based on the then Wages Act 1986 (now ERA 1996, Part II), the EAT held against the employer on the wording of the clause, although not questioning the efficacy of the clause itself. The employers lost again in *Glendale Managed Services Ltd* v *Graham* [2003] EWCA Civ 773, [2003] IRLR 465 when they decided not to adhere to a nationally agreed pay rise. The employers argued that this national agreement was stated to be 'normally paid' to the employees but they had the power to withdraw it as the contract said the rate of pay would be the national rate 'as adopted by the Authority from time to time'; they had chosen not to adopt it. True, said the Court of Appeal, but only with sufficient notice so as not to breach mutual trust. The pattern has continued this way with cases holding for both sides (see *Malone* v *British Airways plc* [2010] EWHC 302 (QB); [2010] IRLR 431—insufficient evidence of mutual intention to permit a collective agreement to alter terms—and *Bateman* v *Asda Stores* [2010] IRLR 370 (EAT): staff handbook where the employer, 'reserved the right to review, revise, amend or replace the contents of this handbook), and introduce new policies from time to time...' and this was held to be incorporated into the contract itself, permitting changes to pay and conditions).

The employer will therefore argue that the clause is valid because: (i) it is an express term; and (ii) it simply reflects managerial prerogatives. The employee's arguments are more nebulous but the main ones must be: (i) to attack the wording itself on a *contra proferentem* basis; (ii) to argue that such a clause changes the nature of the contract itself and is therefore void.

We have also seen that in the cases concerning PHI schemes and share option agreements (**5.2.3.1** above) the courts have become more inventive in limiting the use of discretionary powers in the contract.

Judicial interference is therefore still somewhat unpredictable and has tended to focus more on the *use* of terms rather than their innate legitimacy. This is illustrated by the *obiter* comments of Lord Woolf MR in *Wandsworth LBC* v *D'Silva* [1998] IRLR 193 that with such terms:

(a) clear language is required to reserve to one party an unusual power of this sort;
(b) the court is unlikely to favour an interpretation which does more than enable the employer to vary contractual provisions with which the employer is required to comply (i.e., the outlawing of major changes to substantive rights);
(c) the courts should avoid constructions which produce unreasonable results.

It is certainly the case that arguments based on *implying* a power of unilateral variation are, to use the words of Fraser in *Dad's Army*, 'doomed': *Hayes* v *Securities and Facilities Division* [2001] IRLR 81, CA.

5.4.2.2 Curbs on managerial prerogative: reasonable use of terms

At the beginning of the nineteenth century practically *any* order given by an employer was lawful. Slowly, judgments began to place limitations on the employer's discretionary powers. However, it is still a well-established axiom that an employer does not have to act *fairly: Western Excavating (ECC) Ltd* v *Sharp* [1978] ICR 221. The fact that your client works for (or is) the worst employer in the city does not, in itself, matter in law.

Nevertheless, despite the avowed intentions of the EAT and the Court of Appeal that fairness is not a matter for contractual relationships, the rudiments of managerial prerogative constraints can be detected. As with so many of the recent developments of contractual theory, most of the examples have arisen in unfair dismissal cases, especially those centring round the concept of constructive dismissal. In *Cawley* v *South Wales Electricity Board* [1985] IRLR 89, for instance, the employer utilised the disciplinary procedure (technically within the contractual bounds) to demote an employee. The EAT decided nevertheless that this was an *excessive* use of the contractual power and found a breach of contract. Again, in *Woods* v *WM Service (Peterborough) Ltd* [1981] ICR 666, it was stated that 'employers will not, without reasonable and proper cause, conduct themselves in a manner calculated or likely to destroy or seriously damage the relationship of confidence and trust between employer and employee'.

There is thus a 'scale of reasonableness'. The *reasonable* use of legitimate terms (including ones that the employee does not like) carries with it no potential for breach. Neither does the *unreasonable* use of terms in itself constitute a breach. A court might concur with your employee–client's refusal to obey these orders, but you could not be certain of this (and see the discussion on 'employee adaptability' below). The employer's action needs to lie somewhere over the halfway line of the reasonableness scale, heading towards the capricious use of power and the extreme end of unreasonableness, before a breach will have occurred and your employee–client, in law at least, can legitimately choose to refuse to obey the order. The further over the halfway line, the more serious (repudiatory) the breach and, as you will see, the more the employee may have to decide whether to accept the repudiation, resign, and claim damages—or simply put up with it.

To challenge the legitimacy of the clearly-expressed terms, therefore, one must find unconscionability rather than mere unreasonableness. Thus, the Court of Appeal permitted an employer's unilateral reduction of pay (here, a car allowance) on the basis that proper notice had been given and the power was not exercised 'for an improper purpose, capriciously or arbitrarily, or in any way in which no reasonable employer, acting reasonably, would exercise it': *Wetherill* v *Birmingham City Council* [2007] EWCA Civ 599, [2007] IRLR 781. A wise employer will also note, however, that even if the contractual terms are fulfilled there is always the possibility that the exercise of such terms may amount to indirect discrimination.

A word of caution is needed here. What constitutes a lawful order falls to be decided in two quite different arenas. As a pure contractual matter (where a declaration, injunction, or damages are sought) that arena is the county court or High Court. There is a tradition for tying the rules of contracts of employment to ordinary contracts here and so things like the employee's individual needs tend to be put to one side. But matters of contract can arise in the setting of employment tribunals; both as separate issues and as adjuncts of unfair dismissal actions, redundancy claims, etc. (see **5.9**). With one eye on contractual principles, the tribunals and the EAT are not averse to implying terms which look far more like imposing a standard of reasonableness. Interestingly, in a pure contractual setting, we saw above that the Court of Appeal appears to be moving more towards an analysis based on irrationality/unreasonableness too: see *Mallone* v *BPB Industries plc* above.

Students often raise the question whether legislation relating to exclusion clauses and 'unfair terms' is relevant here. The answer is: only in extremely rare circumstances, where the employee can somehow be classed as a 'consumer' or operating under the employer's 'written standards of business': *Commerzbank AG* v *Keen* [2006] EWCA Civ 1536, [2007] ICR 623.

5.4.2.3 Curbs on managerial prerogative: discriminatory clauses

The Court of Appeal decision in *Meade-Hill and National Union of Civil and Public Servants* v *British Council* [1995] IRLR 478 brought into play the question of discrimination and the use of mobility (and similar) clauses. Here, an express mobility clause was held to be indirectly discriminatory unless the employer could justify the clause in relation to the position held by the employee, irrespective of her sex.

The appraisal of all contractual provisions against 'equality impact assessment' criteria has become increasingly important, and the sophistication of the analysis involved can easily trap the unwary. Employers need to be able to justify imposing changes in working patterns such as moving employees from part-time to full-time employment. In *London Underground Ltd* v *Edwards (No. 2)* [1998] IRLR 364, CA, for instance, the contractual issue focused on a change in shift patterns for train operators. The change was agreed with the relevant unions. Ms Edwards was the only person unable to comply with the new system. Her problem centred on childcare provisions as a single parent. The change in contractual terms was found by the EAT to constitute indirect discrimination and the employer could not justify the change in the light of its business arrangements as set against Ms Edwards' personal circumstances.

Such clauses, or variations on the general theme, appear in many contracts. Employers need to show objective reasons why such clauses are necessary rather than merely relying on the fact that the clause was lifted from a precedent book and looked useful.

5.4.2.4 Curbs on managerial prerogative: discretionary payment clauses

As we noted at **5.2.1.1(e)** above, pay is often built up from a range of different elements: basic salary, commission payments, piece-rate, and 'bonus schemes'. If the bonus can be calculated on a mathematical basis it is no different from commission or piece-rate; but sometimes there is an element of discretion built in to preserve management powers or in the hope of avoiding tax. Here, both the wording of the discretionary payment clause and the exercise of that discretion are open to argument. Employers tend to believe that the use of the word 'discretion' means absolute freedom; the case law shows otherwise.

In *Horkulak* v *Cantor Fitzgerald International* [2004] EWCA Civ 1287, [2004] IRLR 942, the Court of Appeal examined the cases on the exercise of discretion. The Court then reviewed the long-standing authority of *Laverack* v *Woods* [1967] 1 QB 278 (CA) (which established that an employer is entitled to discharge his obligations under a contract in the most beneficial way possible) and *Reda* v *Flag* [2002] IRLR 747 (where the Privy Council refused to allow an implied term of good faith to overturn an express provision, see **5.4.2.1** above). The Court concluded that it is still possible to construe an unrestricted discretion as being subject to an implied term that it will be exercised in good faith and rationally, even in the face of express provisions. The same analysis applies to cases involving discretionary share options.

Again, in *Brand* v *Compro Computer Services Ltd* [2004] EWCA Civ 204, [2005] IRLR 196—decided before *Horkulak* and not mentioned in that decision—it was held that, unless the contract makes it very clear that accrued commission on work done is not payable after termination then it is recoverable (the phrase here that payment was made if the employee remained 'in full-time employment at all times' was not specific enough to exclude the right). There is still a problem here, though. If the contract is very specific about how commission etc. is earned or accrued (thereby excluding discretion as such) then the question is one of interpretation rather than implying terms such as good faith application. Thus, in *Peninsula Business Services Ltd* v *Sweeney* [2004] IRLR 49, the EAT refused to award accrued commission in the face of a term which clearly stated that the employee only became entitled to it if in employment at the relevant date of calculation (this case was not dealt with in *Horkulak* or *Brand*).

5.4.3 Stretching the contract—employee adaptability

If the employer must adhere to an honest use of the contract, the same is certainly true for the employee. This will mean that as well as observing instructions given under the express terms of the contract, the employee is expected to be flexible in the observance of those terms. At its very basic level, this is a duty to observe the contract reasonably, or at least not to disrupt the enterprise; it has also been described as a more positive duty of cooperation. The most famous example of this arose in *Secretary of State for Employment* v *ASLEF* [1972] 2 QB 455. As part of an industrial dispute the employees decided to 'work-to-rule', i.e., to observe the absolute letter of the contract. This meant that extensive safety checks were undertaken, no leeway was allowed on manning levels, etc., and disruption to the rail network followed. The question was: could the strict observance of the contract constitute a breach of that contract? The Court of Appeal decided that it could because the purpose behind the strict observance was to cause disruption. There was an implied duty not to cause disruption. The duty was also described as the more burdensome 'duty to promote the commercial interests of the employer'. In *British Telecommunications plc* v *Ticehurst* [1992] ICR 383, the Court of Appeal further classified the withdrawal of goodwill (as part of industrial action) as a breach of contract (see also *Sim* v *Rotherham Metropolitan Borough Council* [1986] IRLR 391 on the level of duties owed by professional employees (here, schoolteachers)).

Much of the development in this area relates yet again to claims of constructive dismissal. Perhaps the clearest statement of 'employee adaptability' came in *Cresswell* v *Board of Inland Revenue* [1984] ICR 508. The employers sought to change the method of working by the introduction of computers. The employees objected, at least on the grounds that the acquisition of new skills should bring with it extra pay. The issue was whether the alteration in how the job was done could be enforced as a lawful order, or whether this was beyond the scope of the contract. It was held that employees are expected to be adaptable in performing their duties. If the change is merely as to *how* the job was done, rather than a change to the job content itself, modern employees are expected to respond favourably. Certainly, if the change is temporary an employee is expected to cooperate provided the work is suitable and the employee will suffer no disadvantage in contractual benefits or status.

Many cases have centred on employee mobility. In *White* v *Reflecting Roadstuds Ltd* [1991] ICR 733, an *express term* reserved to the employer the power to transfer employees to alternative work on grounds of business efficiency. White was not the best of employees and his performance affected the work of others in his team. He was transferred to a lower-paid job. This was held not to be in breach. One key factor was that the transfer correlated to the aims stated in the contract, i.e., it was for business efficiency. But there is no general requirement for any transfer to be made on reasonable operational grounds.

Subject to the possibility of arguing indirect discrimination, express mobility clauses therefore tend to be left alone by the courts provided they are clear and unambiguous. But if a mobility term is not clear, or is missing, there is still room for implication. Thus, if the job is of the kind where mobility might be expected (i.e., it is quite common for employees to move around in the industry, such as construction workers), or the individual employee has moved during employment, a term will be implied easily. In any other case a term might still be implied (see the constructive dismissal case of *United Bank Ltd* v *Akhtar* [1989] IRLR 507—junior employee told to move from Leeds to Birmingham at six days' notice) provided:

(a) the transfer is not actuated by malice;

(b) reasonable notice is given; and

(c) the employer does not effectively frustrate the employee's attempt to perform the contract.

But even then, the transfer is commonly limited to within commuting distance: *Courtaulds Northern Spinning Ltd* v *Sibson* [1988] ICR 451 (a heavy goods driver whose place of work was really only a starting and finishing point).

There are limits to adaptability. First, the contract may be stretched, but there comes a breaking point—usually some abuse of discretion. Secondly, *pay* has nearly always been sacrosanct: see *Burdett-Coutts* v *Hertfordshire County Council* [1984] IRLR 91 and *Rigby* v *Ferodo* [1988] ICR 29; it takes a clear term permitting a cut in wages (as in *White* v *Reflecting Roadstuds*) and no apparent abuse of that right to overcome this. There are, however, conflicting decisions of the EAT on whether the use of an express term to alter working patterns, which has an indirect adverse affect on wages or hours worked (e.g., because of changes in shift patterns), constitutes a breach of contract. In view of the comments and caveats in *White* v *Reflecting Roadstuds* and *United Bank* v *Akhtar,* it is respectfully submitted that such indirect effects should not be deemed a breach of contract. Lastly, the court or tribunal may also choose to interpret a wide clause quite narrowly, almost using the *contra proferentem* idea. For instance, in *Haden* v *Cowen* [1982] IRLR 314, the Court of Appeal took a common phrase 'the employee is required to undertake, at the discretion of the company, any and all duties which reasonably fall within the scope of his capabilities' and restricted the range of additional duties to those which would normally fall within the employee's job as a quantity surveyor. Certainly, 'adaptability' or 'flexibility' clauses do not allow an employer *carte blanche* authority to change an employee's work or conditions if these changes are unreasonable in themselves: *Land Securities Trillium Ltd* v *Thornley* [2005] IRLR 765 (EAT).

5.5 Summary of the position so far

- Terms are derived from a variety of sources. This means that the contract may be made up from a range of documents, not just one labelled the 'contract of employment' or even from oral statements.
- Many employees have never received a contract. They should at least have received a 'written statement'.

- To fill the gaps, the courts and employment tribunals have been very inventive with the use of implied terms, many of them almost trust-like in their form, such as the duty of good faith and fidelity.
- Employers have the right to demand that employees obey 'lawful orders'. These are derived from examining the express and implied terms, but they are limited in their scope by judicial and legislative intervention.
- Judicial intervention has sought to place a cap on managerial prerogative without ever going so far as to say all contracts have to be 'reasonable'. This leaves a massive interpretational gap.
- Legislative intervention (often derived from EU Directives) has imposed a number of terms which are presumed to be in the contract and which cannot be removed by negotiation or express terms to the contrary (e.g., anti-discrimination clauses).
- Because the contract is not a one-off agreement, employees are expected to show some flexibility in their working patterns (probably not so as regards pay).

5.6 Variation of contract

Under strict contract theory a contract cannot be varied unilaterally. It can be varied, either by individual agreement or through the use of collective agreements—notably where a contract is subject to 'alteration from time to time agreed with XYZ union'. The most familiar example is the annual pay increase. Consideration should also be present, although courts have paid little genuine attention to this. So, if an employer seeks to change the rate of pay or the place of work, or to insert a new restraint of trade clause, the employee is not bound in law to accept such an alteration unless the instruction is lawful, i.e., contractually justified.

Business reorganisation is the area where the real question of legitimate variation and employee adaptability arises. The employer either clearly seeks to change the terms of the contract, or argues that the proposed changes in working practice fall within the general ambit of the contract anyway. These situations may come about in a number of ways:

(a) The employer argues that the contract is clear. In this case any opposing argument must rest on the legitimacy of the terms themselves.

(b) The employer argues that, although the express terms do not sanction the change, the implied terms (derived from adaptability or custom and practice) allow for the change: see *ASLEF.*

(c) The employer argues that there is still no real change to the job, only a change in *how* the job is done: see *Cresswell* v *BIR.*

(d) The employer simply imposes the terms, offering no argument apart from economic necessity: see *Rigby* v *Ferodo,* below.

(e) The employer accepts that there is a breach but presents the argument of 'accept the change or be sacked'. This can turn into a game of 'who blinks first'.

(f) The employer formally terminates the contract and offers new contracts with different terms.

To consider the full impact of all this, it is of no value to ask 'What can (or cannot) the employer do?' The answer to that, in practical terms is: anything they can get away with.

What we need to examine instead is the possible actions that employees may take in response and their consequences.

Students are sometimes worried by this, believing there should be a list of 'cans' and 'can'ts'. There is no such list except to say that an employer has to issue 'lawful' orders as we described above. The reason why the employee's response is so important is that the power to initiate matters generally lies with the employer and it is of no use simply to ask whether an employer can, say, cut wages because the answer is always: 'Yes, if they can get away with it'. What you really need to know is how the employee intends to respond. If, for instance, the employee does not want to make waves then the employer will succeed even if the action is not strictly legitimate.

The overall position can be seen in **Figure 5.2.** Although in this chapter we are dealing only with *contractual* rights and remedies, it is worth noting here that a serious breach of contract (such as a unilateral reduction in pay) will not always amount to an unfair dismissal if the employee is dismissed for refusing to accept the change (see **Chapters 11** and **12** on the topic of business reorganisations constituting 'some other substantial reason' as a fair reason for dismissal). Equally, merely because a variation is contractually sound this does not prevent the action taken being classed as an unfair dismissal.

Figure 5.2 looks daunting at first sight but shows that out of one simple question there are numerous factors to consider. Do not therefore be put off by the complexity: in the following text we will break this diagram down and examine each particular consequence. The overall picture will then make much more sense.

Note that **Figure 5.2** takes into account both the common law claims (wrongful dismissal, wrongful repudiation, injunctions, and damages) and also notes the statutory

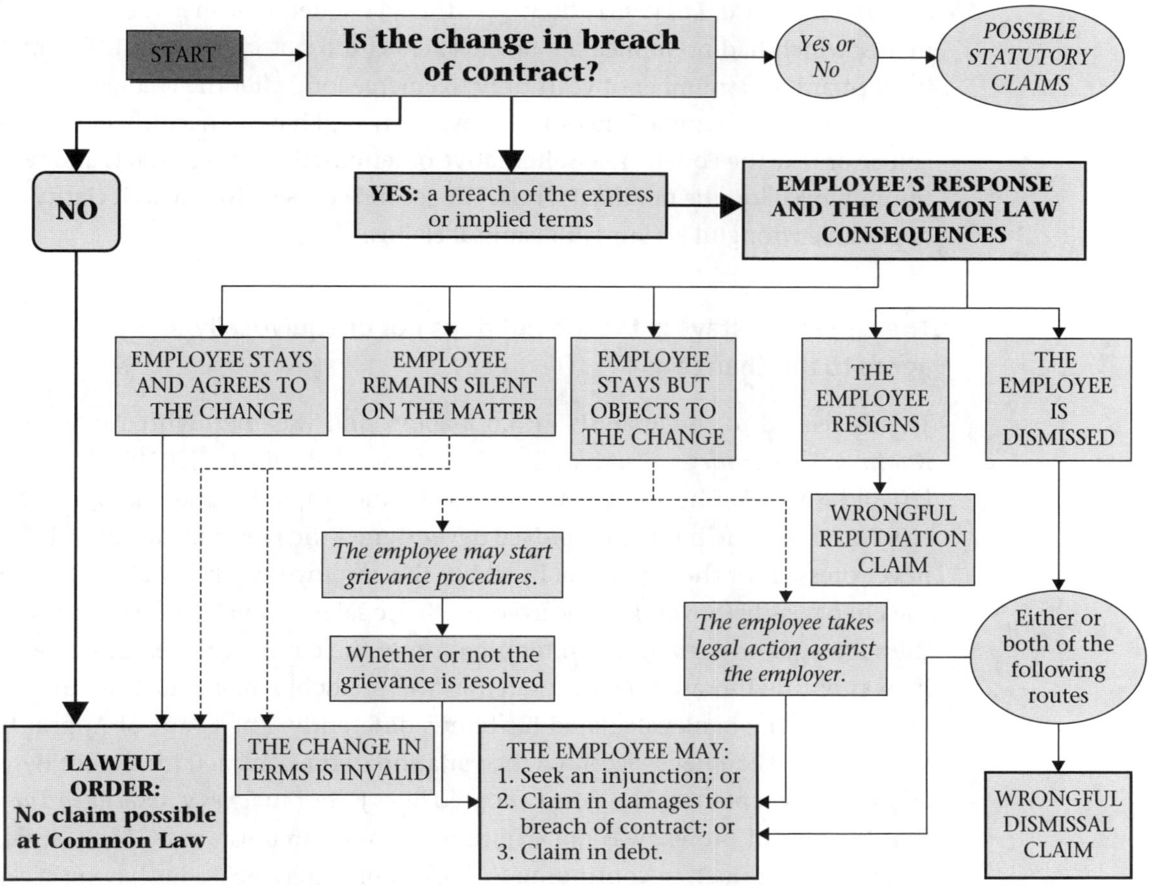

Figure 5.2 Possible consequences of variation of the contract.

claim of unfair dismissal. Changes in contractual terms may well lead to resignation or dismissal and such occurrences carry statutory consequences as well as contractual ones. As we are concerned in this chapter only with the common law position, we can simplify the discussion for the moment by ignoring the statutory consequences (their presence is simply noted as a reminder in the circular boxes at the top of each figure).

5.6.1 The employee stays in the job and agrees to the change

Most employees cannot afford to lose their job (whether on principle or by default), so it may well be that they are effectively forced to continue in their employment. They may simply have to put up with the change.

If the employee specifically agrees to or acquiesces in the alteration then sooner or later (depending on when the change is implemented) this will be deemed a legitimate change in the terms of the contract. Some 'thinking time' is permitted but doing nothing has, in most cases, been regarded as a deemed acceptance. Thus, if the employer changes the salary rates and the employees continue working under these new rates they will have accepted them.

5.6.2 The employee stays in the job but the term does not have immediate effect on the relationship

Where a change in terms *does not have immediate effect* on a particular employee, e.g., as to retirement ages or the right to move employees from one site to another, silence on the employee's part may not constitute acquiescence or agreement. In *Jones* v *Associated Tunnelling Co. Ltd* [1981] IRLR 477, the EAT stated that mere failure to object to a matter which had no immediate practical effect did not imply assent. The matter may lie dormant for a number of years only to emerge long after the change was thought to have been implemented. Thus an employer may well have to decide whether to risk this course or take the equally risky alternative of terminating the contracts and re-engaging the employees on the modified terms. The second course brings with it clarity at the cost of possible wrongful and unfair dismissal claims.

5.6.3 The employee stays in the job but does not unequivocally agree to the change

This is related to the analysis in **5.6.2** above and was highlighted most recently in *Khatri* v *Cooperatieve Centrale Raiffeisen-Boerenleenbank BA* [2010] EWCA Civ 397, [2010] IRLR 715. The employer 'redeployed' the employee and changed the employee's bonus scheme but the employee never signed the new contract and the employer never pressed for the signature. In reality the employee's job remained the same after the change as before and he received his 'basic salary' as normal (which had not been the subject of any change). On termination of the contract the employee argued that he was entitled to a bonus calculated in the pre-deployment manner (amounting to over £1m). The bank calculated his bonus differently. The Court of Appeal held that the employee had never accepted the variation in the contract: his silence here did not amount to acceptance. The Court adopted Elias J's test in *Jones* v *Associated Tunnelling*—that the lack of protest was not damning in these circumstances. The test was: is the employee's conduct, in continuing to work, 'only referable' to his having accepted the new terms?

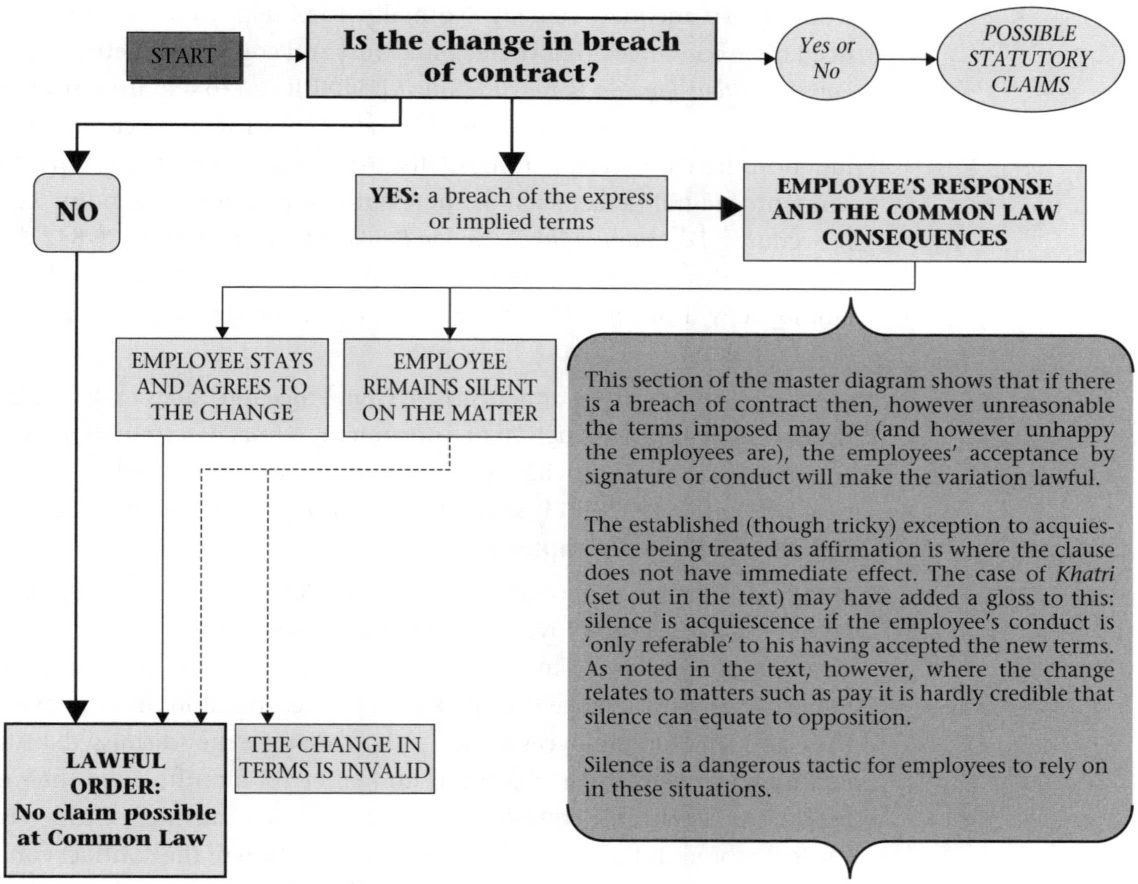

Figure 5.3 The employee stays and agrees to the change or stays silent.

5.6.4 The employee stays in the job but objects to the change

It is difficult for employees to take this course of action where they are not supported by a trade union. Nevertheless, it is possible for an employee to continue to work for an employer whilst arguing that the change is unlawful.

In the face of more immediate changes, and certainly if they relate to pay, however, the employees would have to do something to demonstrate their opposition; their objections would have to take on substance or be deemed acquiescence. There are four basic routes here:

(a) The employee may simply refuse to comply with the new terms. Obviously this has to relate to changes in things such as duties (pay, for instance, would be beyond the employee's control). This action brings matters to a head and the employer may simply respond by dismissing the employee for not obeying (what he sees) to be a lawful order. This option can therefore be a dangerous one for the employee to pursue.

(b) A second option is for the employee to continue working (under the newly-imposed terms) but voice objections to the change through devices such as the grievance procedures—a much safer option and one to be preferred to (a) above.

(c) The employee may seek a *declaration or an injunction* to prevent any unlawful variation. This does not happen frequently as more than a simple breach is required to obtain an injunction (however serious the breach) because damages would be an adequate remedy. Normally, to obtain injunctive relief the courts need to be convinced that there is still trust and confidence between the parties: *Powell* v *Brent London Borough Council* [1988] ICR 176—some cases have posed the question: is the contract still 'workable'? So, the most common use of injunctions here is to seek to restrain dismissals which have fallen down purely on some procedural defect such as their not complying with binding contractual procedures: *Dietmann* v *Brent London Borough Council* [1988] ICR 842. But, as the remedy is discretionary, there is no guarantee of effectiveness and a dismissed employee will not be able to obtain an order for *specific performance* to regain employment.

An application can be under Part 24, Civil Procedure Rules to determine a question of law or the construction of a document. A final determination of the whole action may be made provided questions of fact are not at issue: see *Jones* v *Gwent County Council* [1992] IRLR 521. *This option is not included in the diagrams* (for further explanation see **Chapter 10**).

(d) Finally, an employee may object and sue in debt or for damages: *Rigby* v *Ferodo* [1988] ICR 29. The employer sought to implement, for good economic reasons, a wage cut of 5 per cent. The employees not unnaturally objected and their union did not accept the change. No agreement was reached and the employer imposed the wage cut. The employees did not resign, nor were they dismissed. Instead, they continued to voice their objections and, after six months, sued their employer for the lost 5 per cent. The House of Lords held that they were entitled to recover the lost money as the employer's unilateral variation of the contract constituted a repudiation which the employees had neither affirmed in continuing to work nor accepted as repudiatory by resigning.

One would not argue with the principle of this case. However, four points deserve attention:

- The employers did not contend that Rigby had accepted the change, because Rigby's objections were made obvious.
- The employers did not argue that the change was lawful; their argument was the more technical one that the contract had been effectively automatically terminated by their announcement and that the employees could not therefore recover more than their contractual notice period by way of damages (12 weeks here).
- The employers were sloppy in their response to the objections. They might have dismissed the employees and offered them re-engagement on new terms.
- The level of damages was easy to assess on the facts. If the change in terms centred on working practice, as in our example about hours of work, damages would be more difficult to assess (e.g., loss of commission); there might not even be a quantifiable loss.

The full range of options open to an employee who stays on but objects to the change can be seen in **Figure 5.4** below. One key feature of taking this 'stay but sue' course was, however, highlighted by the EAT in *Robinson* v *Tescom Corporation* [2008] IRLR 408: once the employee opts for staying on and arguing his point he *must* work under the new terms whilst the issue is being resolved. If the employee refuses to accept the new terms he must either resign or take his chances on how the employer responds.

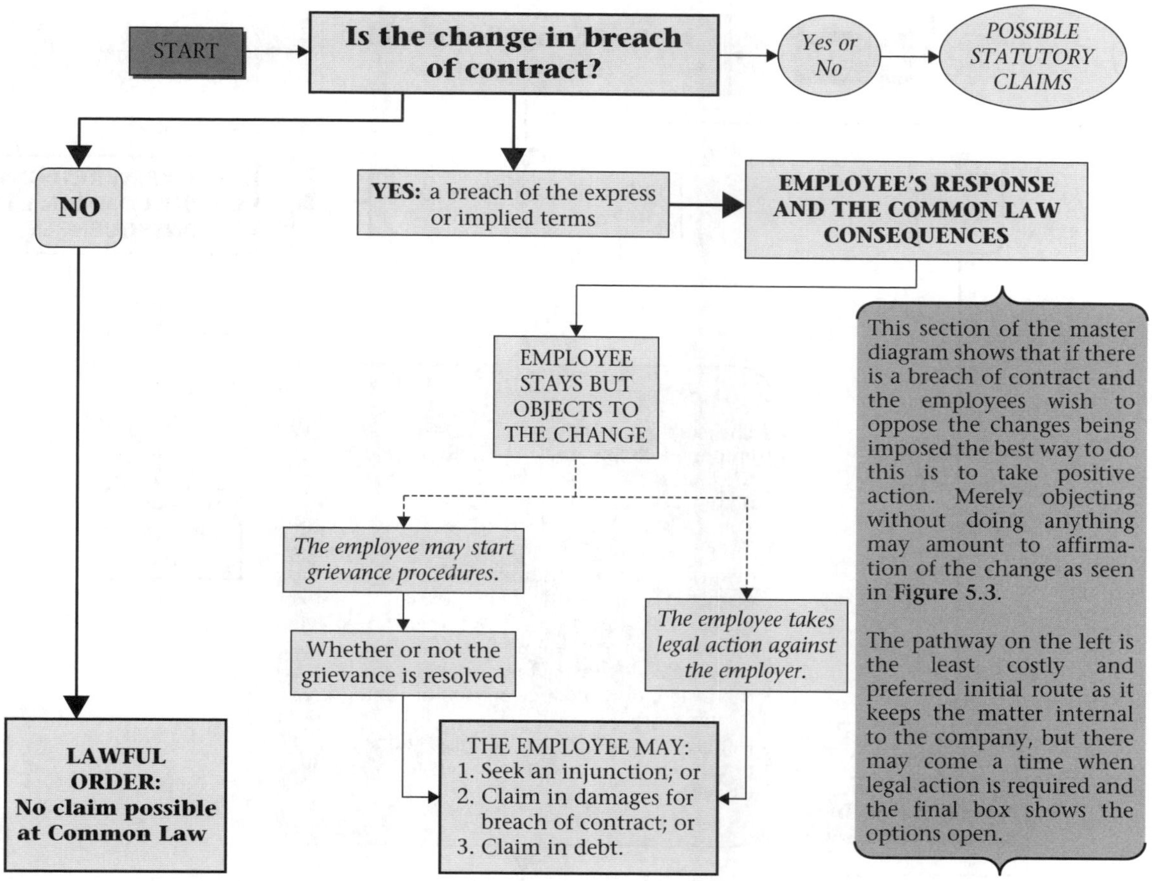

Figure 5.4 The employee stays but objects to the change.

5.6.5 The employee refuses to accept the new terms and resigns

If the employer's actions constitute a *repudiation* of the contract the employee can lawfully accept the repudiation by resigning and sue for damages. This action is strictly termed a *wrongful repudiation* claim but is sometimes referred to as 'constructive dismissal'. The term 'constructive dismissal' really belongs to claims for unfair dismissal but both terms describe the situation where an employee resigns in response to a serious breach of contract by the employer and this resignation is classed as a dismissal. The consequences flowing from an employee's resignation can be seen in **Figure 5.5**.

There is common analytical ground in determining what constitutes a wrongful repudiation and a constructive dismissal. The sorts of acts (there is an extensive range) that may be classified as repudiatory range from a failure to pay wages through to a series of minor but cumulative breaches (for a fuller list see **10.8.2** below). In all cases the employer must have committed a serious breach of the contract so the employee (or you as his solicitor) has to make a judgment call on this. If the employee gets this wrong, he or she will have simply resigned and, indeed, will be in breach himself for not giving contractual notice. Another mistake employees frequently make in this area is to wait too long before resigning (often because they are trying to find another job first). If the employee does not act promptly enough, he or she will at some stage be deemed to have affirmed the change in terms and be in the same position as if they had expressly agreed to it. Having affirmed the change the employee is no longer entitled to resign and if he does so, is again in breach. The length of time an employee may wait depends upon the

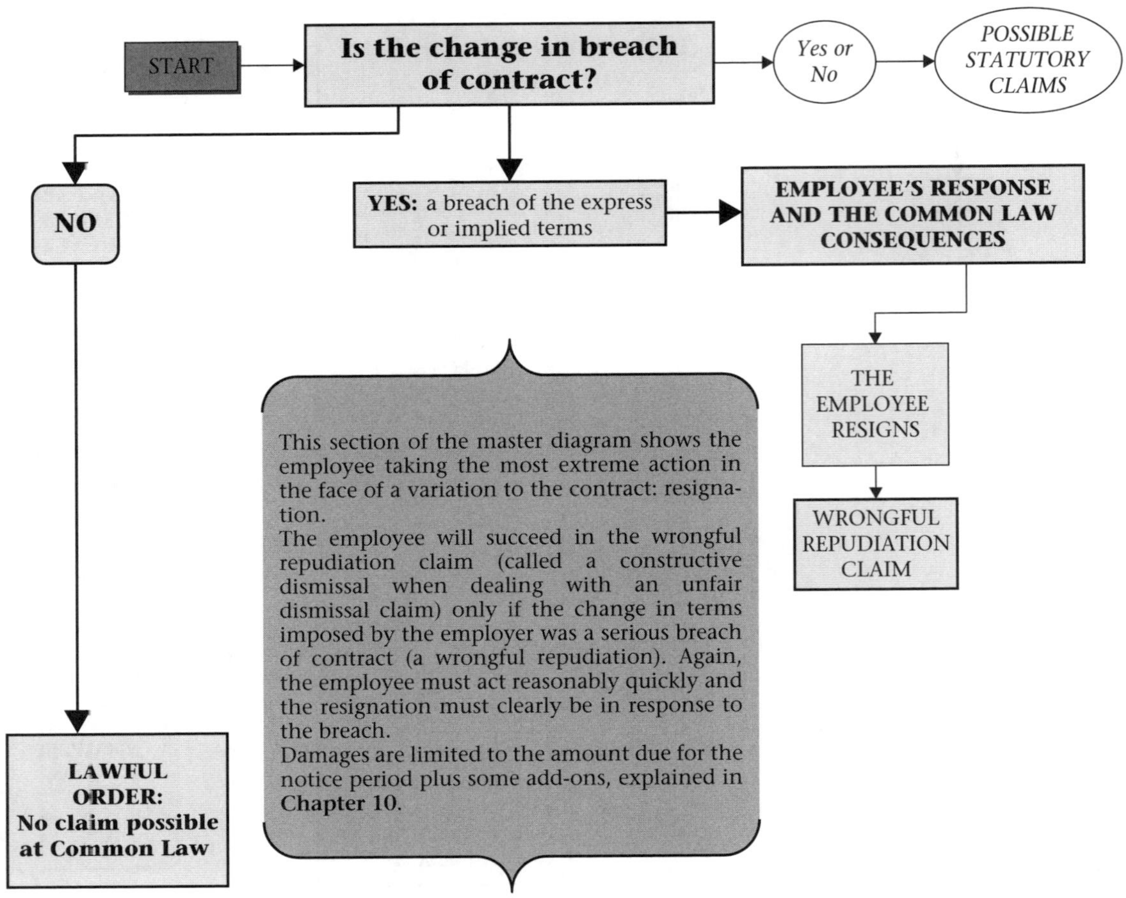

Figure 5.5 The employee resigns in the face of the change.

seriousness of the change in terms, how immediate their effect is and whether he or she maintained some form of objection. Damages for wrongful repudiation are limited to the amount the employee would have received had they been given their contractual notice.

5.6.6 The employee is dismissed

As we noted above, the employer might simply dismiss the 'non-cooperative' employee. If the dismissal is with adequate notice or payment in lieu of notice the employee has no further *contractual* claim. If the dismissal is without adequate notice there will be a potential claim for wrongful dismissal.

But remember that, at common law, the courts are only concerned with the *contractual right* to dismiss summarily, so that the employer's business reasons for the change are irrelevant here. The question is whether the employee has seriously breached the contract by not giving adequate notice. Note, in **Figure 5.6**, that we have included the possibility of a dismissed employee claiming damages/debt or seeking an injunction. The damages/debt aspect here will relate to any outstanding claims that the employee may have (e.g., for past failures to pay wages).

Whether or not the employee is given notice, he or she might also claim unfair dismissal. In such a case, the employer is likely to argue business reorganisation or misconduct (here, disobedience to a lawful order) as a defence to this action (see **Chapters 11** and **12**).

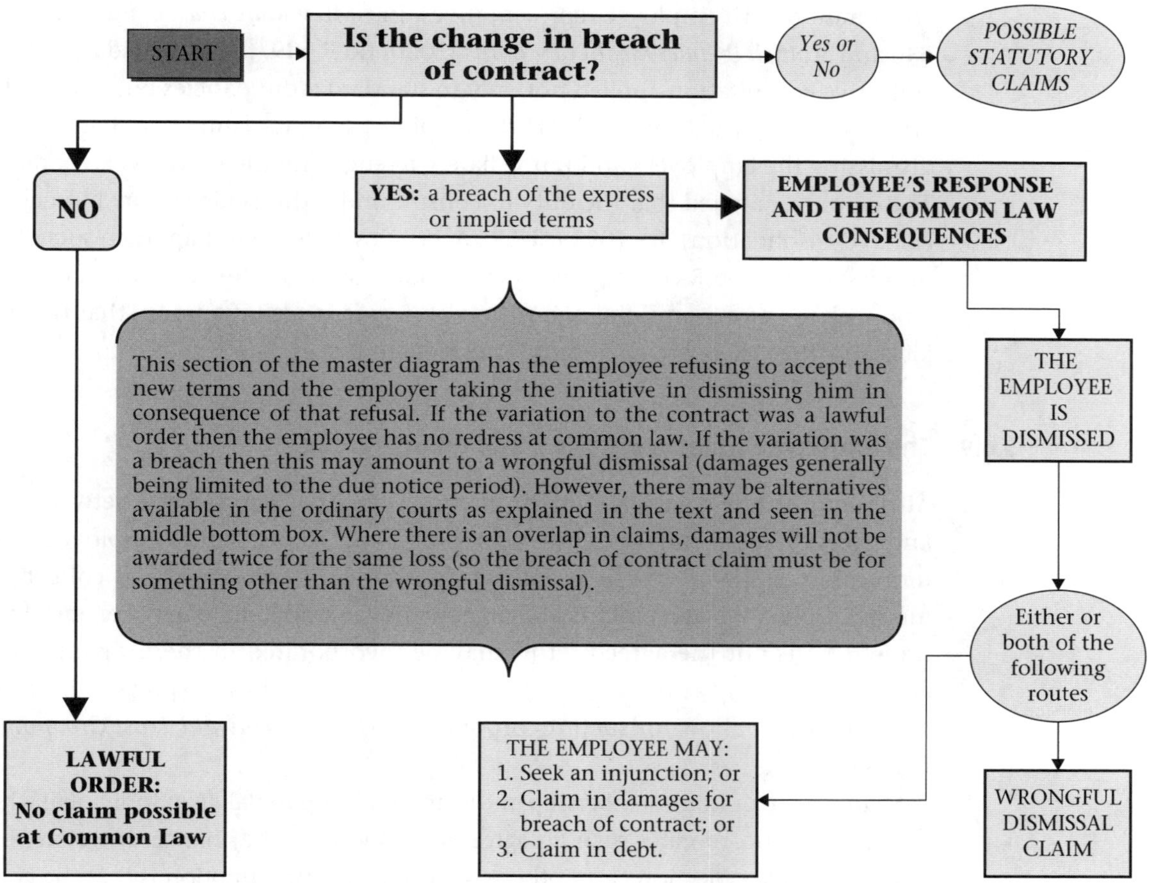

Figure 5.6 The employee is dismissed for refusing to accept the change.

5.6.7 The employee is dismissed and then re-engaged

When contemplating large-scale changes to the contract some employers believe it is easier to terminate all the contracts and re-engage immediately but on the new terms. The points noted in **5.6.4** on the giving of notice apply here. The notice must be unequivocal, so merely announcing the change (as in *Rigby* v *Ferodo),* will not be sufficient to amount to a termination and re-engagement. But if the termination is clear the employee will then be deemed to have accepted the new contract by continuing to work after the set date.

Contractually speaking, the employer gains an advantage with this option. But from an industrial relations angle this may prove disastrous; the loss of goodwill may rebound at a later stage on the employer. Equally, employees working out a notice period will most likely feel disaffected and work poorly; the alternative of paying in lieu of notice is an expensive tactic. This option is merely an extension of the 'employee dismissed' consequence and so does not appear in the diagrams.

Employees dismissed in these circumstances may also have a claim for unfair dismissal even if they are re-engaged immediately.

5.6.8 Duty to consult with trade unions

You will see below in **Chapter 14** at **14.4.2** that where dismissals arise by reason of redundancy the employer has both a duty to consult with the individual employee and, where 20 or more employees are being made redundant, a separate duty of collective consultation with employee representatives. In *GMB* v *Man Truck & Bus Ltd* [2000] IRLR 636 and *Scottish Premier Meat Ltd* v *Burns* [2000] IRLR 639, the EAT held that this duty of collective consultation applied not only to standard redundancies but also to dismissals arising out of restructuring. In *GMB* the employer sought to impose a change in terms by dismissing the employees and immediately re-engaging them on less favourable terms. The employer argued that the duty to consult under the Trade Union and Labour Relations (Consolidation) Act 1992 (TULRCA 1992), s. 188 did not apply to such 'technical' dismissals, but the EAT disagreed. This imposes quite a different burden on employers who seek to 'strong arm' the imposition of new terms (though note that the duty only kicks in where there are 20 or more affected employees).

5.6.9 The employee objects but the trade union agrees

Although the law regards contracts of employment as being made between employer and the individual employee, the reality for about 70 per cent of employees is that the terms are negotiated by the employer and trade unions (known as collective agreements). Collective agreements are virtually never enforceable between employers and trade unions but the agreed terms may be incorporated in the individual contracts and so be binding as between *employer and employee*—if the express or implied terms of the contract allow for such incorporation: *Marley* v *Forward Trust Group Ltd* [1986] ICR 891.

Membership or non-membership of the union is immaterial. If an individual whose contract already incorporates such an agreement objects to the change, therefore, he or she must make that objection clear; otherwise the general presumption is that the change has been accepted. And if the right to vary the contract according to terms incorporated by collective agreements is expressly stated in the contract, the employee will have no option (subject to such considerations as arguing indirect discrimination) but to accept the change.

It is also worth noting here that if the employer or trade union unilaterally withdraws from an existing collective agreement this has no effect upon the employee's terms unless the employee consents to the change: *Robertson* v *British Gas Corporation* [1983] IRLR 302; the change of terms is treated exactly the same as with any other variation.

5.6.10 The employees take industrial action

Industrial action takes many forms. The most obvious is the strike. Others exist: working to rule, go-slows, overtime bans, and so on. The employer and employees will therefore be in a power struggle. We have not included this in our summary diagram simply because the variety of consequences are too dependent upon the employer's response to the action.

In response to industrial action the employer may:

(a) dismiss the employees, with or without notice;

(b) refuse to accept the deficient performance and send the employees home, withholding pay;

(c) accept their partial performance but withhold wages equivalent to the time lost (see below);

(d) sue the employees for damages. Here the employee is liable only for the loss for which he or she is responsible.

The response of withholding pay is often used where the industrial action is sporadic or set for one day every week, or aimed at fulfilling only the non-contentious part of the contract: see *British Telecommunications plc* v *Ticehurst* [1992] ICR 383. Here, a longstanding dispute had developed into a 'rolling campaign of strategic strikes'. The employees refused to sign an undertaking to work normally and were told to leave the premises. Their claim for wages during this period was based on the fact that they were prepared to work, though not to comply with all the terms. The Court of Appeal held that the employer could legitimately refuse to pay for this partial performance.

It should also be noted that *an employee dismissed whilst taking part in industrial action may also lose any right to claim unfair dismissal.*

5.7 Methods of resolving disputes, short of termination of contract

If at all possible, both parties should seek to resolve differences before any termination occurs. The most obvious method is by consultation and negotiation, leading eventually to agreement.

If *employers* wish, for instance, to instigate changes they are advised to consider the practical consequences as well as the legal ones. Thus:

(a) consider the effect on the individuals in terms of future loyalty and performance;

(b) consider the effect on any relationship with trade unions;

(c) consider whether this change, if challenged, would lead to an injunction being granted or to claims for wrongful or unfair dismissal;

(d) take into account the possibility that the change may be indirectly discriminatory. Look at the effect on employees, consider whether alternatives or additional facilities are possible and be prepared to justify the change;

(e) get any agreement in writing with effect from the proposed date of change. Consider the effect of 'sleepers' in the organisation. Do not presume that simply because a change has been implemented it is legally effective;

(f) do not forget disciplinary procedures;

(g) if the change is necessary to the business it is probably worth paying for—make the change part of the annual pay negotiations thus avoiding all the problems of unilateral variation.

From the *employee's perspective* any action tends to be in response to proposed changes. Again, however, the practical and legal consequences need to be considered:

(a) consider whether the change is worth fighting in terms of job security, promotion prospects, and so on;

(b) do not resign hastily;

(c) make use of the grievance procedure;

(d) do not assume that silence equals valid opposition;

(e) consider applying for declarations or injunctions;

(f) make use of any trade union representation.

5.8 Breach: summary of sanctions and enforcement

Most of the substantive content of the following points has been made in the text at various stages. We have added this section merely to recap.

The employer is in breach	*The employee is in breach*
In response to a breach by the employer the employee may:	In response to a breach by the employee the employer may:
(a) accept the order or change as being lawful;	(a) discipline the employee (e.g., downgrading, refusal to promote, or provision of a warning);
(b) instigate grievance procedures;	(b) dismiss the employee with notice;
(c) seek a declaration as to the meaning of the contract;	(c) dismiss the employee without notice (though this is justifiable only in the face of a serious breach);
(d) seek an injunction to prevent a breach;	(d) sue the employee for any loss attributable to his or her actions (though quantifying the amount can be difficult);
(e) remain in employment but claim damages for any loss sustained;	(e) seek an injunction to prevent disclosure of confidential information or to enforce a restraint of trade clause (as regards ex-employees).
(f) resign and claim for wrongful repudiation (though this will only prove successful if the employer's breach was serious);	
(g) claim damages for wrongful dismissal, if dismissed without adequate notice;	
(h) claim in a debt action;	
(i) claim that the change constitutes indirect discrimination.	

5.9 Civil remedies for breach of contract

If the employee alleges a breach of contract there are several possible (potentially overlapping) courses of action.

5.9.1 In the civil courts

Most obviously, a breach of the contract of employment can be pursued like any other breach in the courts, either the High Court or a county court. Perhaps, for example, the employee understood at interview that a greater bonus was to be paid than has in fact been received. However, the sum involved may be unlikely to justify the expense of litigation, especially where the chance of success is poor because of the evidential difficulty of showing a clear promise. Furthermore, such litigation by an individual will not be conducive to good future working relationships. So such a remedy is really only feasible if a trade union takes the case on behalf of a number of employees in the same position, e.g., *Burdett-Coutts* v *Hertfordshire County Council* [1984] IRLR 91. The same analysis applies if the action is framed as a debt.

5.9.2 In the employment tribunal by claiming a constructive dismissal

It is open to an employee who is faced with a serious breach of the contract of employment to resign, argue constructive dismissal and to present a complaint of **unfair dismissal** to the employment tribunal. The employee must usually have one year's continuous employment with the employer in order to qualify to bring such an action. For instance, any substantial underpayment by the employer may well give good grounds for resignation, provided of course that the underpayment was in breach of contract, though a failure to give a pay increase at an annual review is unlikely to constitute a breach: *Murco Petroleum* v *Forge* [1987] ICR 282. However, reinstatement of the employee is not guaranteed even if the complaint succeeds; and the employee consequently runs a real risk of losing everything—the sum not paid and also the job. This mechanism for bringing such an issue within employment tribunal jurisdiction is dangerous territory.

5.9.3 In the employment tribunal by arguing discrimination

If the employee is able to show, for instance, that another employee of the opposite sex or of a different racial background received some benefit denied to him or her, this may be a means of bringing a claim for discrimination within the employment tribunal jurisdiction. For the purposes of the claim it may in some cases be sufficient to imagine a hypothetical employee rather than an actual example: see **Chapter 6.**

5.9.4 In the employment tribunal for action short of dismissal

Related to a discrimination action is the position where an employer subjects an employee to a detriment after the employee has sought to enforce some statutory right, e.g., where the employee has sought to enforce some of the rights noted in **Chapter 4** or has made a 'protected disclosure' against the employer in the light of the employer's unlawful behaviour. The relevance here is that if the employee's actions fall within this list and the employer responds by, e.g., demoting him, then, as well as any of the remedies noted in this chapter, there may be further remedies under Part V of the ERA 1996.

5.9.5 In the employment tribunal for breach of contract

The Employment Tribunals Extension of Jurisdiction Order 1994 restricts the tribunal jurisdiction to a claim which 'arises or is outstanding on the termination of the employee's employment'. It cannot therefore be used, for example, by current employees wishing to challenge the amount of wages paid to them, nor for claiming a breach of a compromise agreement concluded after termination: see *Miller Bros* v *Johnston* [2002] ICR 744. The maximum that can be claimed in the employment tribunal is £25,000 and matters such as personal injury claims and intellectual property rights cannot be brought before a tribunal. The phrase 'arises or is outstanding on the termination . . . ' means that an actual date has to be fixed, not a process (*Capek* v *Lincolnshire CC* [2000] ICR 878). Thus, a settlement procedure begun before termination but not concluded until afterwards was not 'outstanding' on termination, nor is it enough that an employee had a claim before termination if this was not started before that date (see *Hendricks* v *Lewden Metal Products Ltd* (1996, unreported, EAT) where an employee had not been paid sick pay for some four years but had taken no action during that time to recover it; when she raised the matter on termination it was held this did not fall within the scope of the 1994 Order).

The tribunal has no jurisdiction on misrepresentation claims: *Lakin* v *British Steel Engineering Ltd* (2000, EAT 183/99, unreported), though an argument based on a collateral contract is within the tribunal's general jurisdiction.

A novel aspect for tribunal claims is that an employer is permitted to counterclaim against the employee for breach of contract, subject to the same restrictions noted above, but only if the employee has first brought a claim *under this jurisdiction*. Employees vulnerable to counterclaims may therefore prefer to bring their claims by a different method. For example, an employee not paid outstanding holiday pay on dismissal for alleged theft will be better advised to bring a protection of wages claim than to risk an employer's counterclaim for the proceeds of the alleged theft.

The time limit for presenting the claim is three months from the effective date of termination or last date worked.

5.9.6 In the employment tribunal by arguing unlawful deduction from wages

Part II of ERA 1996 forbids employers making deductions from employees' wages except in the defined circumstances set out at **4.4** above. Wages are defined quite broadly but the sum involved must be quantifiable (i.e., a right to receive a 'bonus' is not covered though an obligation to pay a percentage of future profits would be: *Coors Brewers Ltd* v *Adcock* [2007] EWCA Civ 19, [2007] ICR 983.

5.9.7 Choosing between an unlawful deduction claim and breach of contract

It is clearly important that a solicitor realises, as a matter of tactics and law, which forum is best-suited to the breach of contract claim. The most problematic area centres on pay, for here the claimant will have to choose between a common law action in the county court, a breach of contract action in the employment tribunal, and a claim for unlawful deduction of wages, again in the employment tribunal. The problems with an ordinary civil action are noted above at **5.9.1**. The advantages and disadvantages of the tribunal actions are listed in the table below.

Protection of wages	*Breach of contract*
Unlawful deductions brought under ERA 1996, s. 23.	Under the Employment Tribunals Extension of Jurisdiction Order 1994, and ETA 1996, s. 3.
(a) Available to current employees.	(a) Only available on termination of employment.
(b) No counterclaim permitted—except that the employer may make deductions in retail employment for cash shortages and stock deficiencies.	(b) An employer's counterclaim is possible and is a self-contained cause of action which can survive the failure, withdrawal, or settlement of the employee's initial claim: *Patel* v *RCMS Ltd* [1999] IRLR 161.
(c) No limit to amount of claim.	(c) Claim limited to a maximum of £25,000.
(d) Claims for payment in lieu of notice excluded.	(d) Claims for payment in lieu of notice included.
(e) Statutory exceptions exist, e.g., loans, expenses, compensation for loss of office.	(e) A narrower set of statutory exceptions exist, e.g., those claims relating to intellectual property rights.
(f) Errors of computation are excluded (though 'errors' are narrowly construed: *Morgan* v *West Glamorgan CC* [1995] IRLR 68).	(f) The test is the factual one of whether a breach has occurred and the employer's intentions are irrelevant.
(g) The amount must be quantifiable.	

Note: None of the above affects an employee's right to bring a claim *in a county court or the High Court* for breach of contract or debt during the term of the contract or on, or after, termination.

5.10 Summary

- Terms can be found in a wide range of documents and oral statements.
- Jurisdiction for dealing with contract-based disputes lies with the ordinary courts for disputes occurring during employment.
- The exception to this arises where the claim is for an unlawful deduction from wages under s. 23 of ERA 1996: this can be heard only in the employment tribunals.
- Further, contractual disputes arising *on or after termination* can be heard in the employment tribunals as well as the courts.
- Matters such as confidentiality and intellectual property disputes can never be heard in employment tribunals.
- Other than the statutory controls dealt with in **Chapter 4**, the parties are generally free to set their own terms. However, one of the key areas of constraints which will affect a contract is that of discrimination.
- There is always the possibility that the enforcement of any term or the variation of an existing term may be discriminatory even if this was not intended by the employer (see **Chapter 6** for the consequences). No clause which is discriminatory will be allowed to stand. Direct discrimination may be easy to identify but employers need to take great care in drafting clauses which may be indirectly discriminatory, especially as regards points which do not appear obvious such as age discrimination.
- Because the employment contract is generally for an indefinite period (rather than a one-off commercial agreement) the courts and tribunals have been extremely inventive in creating implied terms, the most wide-sweeping of which is the duty of mutual trust and confidence.
- What matters most is not whether the terms in dispute are 'reasonable' but whether they are 'lawful' (contractually justified).
- The two most commonly-occurring problems with the contract of employment are: (i) trying to ascertain exactly what the contract states; (ii) dealing with situations where the employer wants to change the normal work pattern. These can overlap.
- Employees are expected to be reasonably adaptable: so 'sticking to the literal terms of the contract' is frowned upon by the courts and tribunals.
- In practical terms an employer can seek to impose or change any term: what matters in legal terms is how the employee reacts to this.
- Failure to follow disciplinary and grievance procedures (including ACAS codes and guidelines) may lead to extra compensation being payable (or the employee's claim being dismissed or reduced) in cases such as unfair dismissal claims.

5.11 Example of an employment contract

We noted at the start of this chapter that we intended to include an employment contract by way of example of industrial practice. We have chosen to include a contract that is deficient in a number of respects so that we can make some specific comments on it.

Because each LPC will develop its own methods of examining drafting and interpretation, and because there is no such thing as a 'model contract' to cover all situations, we must emphasise that this contract is not an example of good practice. Our comments in **5.11.2** are placed after the text of the contract in order for you to determine, as you read the contract, what are its strengths and weaknesses.

We have chosen to use a modified version of a real contract originally drafted in 1992 which was still in use a few years ago. Only the names, as they say, have been changed to protect the innocent.

5.11.1 The contract of employment

AN AGREEMENT made on [4th October 1992]
BETWEEN [MONTANA AND MARINO LTD] WHOSE REGISTERED OFFICE IS SITUATED AT [221B QUARTER BACK LANE, BRISTOL]
AND
[MS VICKY LOMBARDI] OF 113, ALLESLEY OLD ROAD, CLIFTON, BRISTOL IN THE COUNTY OF AVON

WHEREBY IT IS MUTUALLY AGREED AS FOLLOWS

1. SAVE Where a contrary intention appears the following terms shall hereinafter have the following meanings:

   (a) 'the Company' shall mean [Montana and Marino Ltd]

   (b) the 'Employee' shall mean Ms Vicky Lombardi

2. The Company shall employ the Employee and the Employee shall serve the Company or any of its subsidiaries in the capacity as

   Secretary, Grade A4

   or in any other such capacity as the Company may reasonably require Upon the terms and conditions hereinafter appearing. For the purpose of this employment the Employee shall reside in such place in the United Kingdom as the Company may reasonably require. The Employee shall be entitled to receive payment towards the expenses resulting from any change in residence required by the Company as set out in scales of terms and conditions laid out in the document 'Removal expenses' which may be amended from time to time. A copy of this document is available from the personnel department.

3. The Company shall pay the Employee a salary of £10,000 per annum to be paid monthly in arrears together with such expenses or allowances as may be approved. The Company shall in each calendar year review the remuneration hereunder payable to the Employee and any increase in such remuneration shall be notified to the Employee in writing and shall be substituted for the sum specified above and shall be payable as from the date specified in such notification. It is also recognised that the Employee will from time to time be required to work beyond normal working hours. Where the Employee at the date hereof or at any date hereafter is classified by the Company as being below Job Grade 6 the Employee will be paid subject to the conditions in force at that time for any overtime worked. Where the Employee at the date hereof or at any date hereafter is classified by the Company as being in a Grade 6 Job or higher his salary is deemed to include a supplement in respect of overtime and no further entitlement is due.

4. This agreement shall be deemed to have commenced on the First day of November 1992 and unless previously determined in accordance with Clause 12 of this agreement or by mutual agreement shall continue until determined by either party giving to the other one month's notice in writing expiring at any time ALWAYS PROVIDED that the period of employment shall terminate in any event on the last day of the month during which the Employee, if male, attains the age of 65 or, if female, attains the age of 60.
5. EMPLOYEES who wish to publish papers give addresses or lectures or engage in discussions on professional or technical subjects connected with their work must first seek and obtain the written consent of the Company.
6. DURING the period of his employment hereunder the Employee shall join and shall be entitled to the benefits of membership of such Pension Scheme as may be provided by the Company for the benefit of the Employee. The Employee shall contribute to such scheme in accordance with the scale of contributions from time to time in force and conform to and be bound by the rules and regulations thereof.
7. DURING his period of employment hereunder the Employee shall perform such duties and carry out such instructions and directions within the scope of his employment hereunder as from time to time may be given to him by the Company and shall obey and conform to all the general orders service regulations and notices from time to time issued by the Company and shall in all respects use his best endeavours to assist in carrying on the duties of the business of the Company in the most economical and profitable way and diligently and faithfully serve the Company and protect its interests in all things to the best of his ability and judgment.
8. DURING his period of employment hereunder the Employee shall devote the whole of his time and attention during ordinary business hours to his duties with the Company and shall not without the consent in writing of the Company previously obtained be in any way engaged in any other trade or business on his own account or with or on behalf of any other person.
9. THE Employee shall not whether during the continuance of his employment hereunder or at any time hereafter without the consent in writing of the Company previously obtained either directly or indirectly divulge or make known to any person any information relating to the business customers methods processes or secrets of the Company which may have come to his knowledge at any time during his service with the Company. Information relating to the business customers methods processes or secrets of any third party possessed by the Company and information in respect of which the Company is under an obligation of confidence towards any third party shall be deemed to be a secret of the Company for this purpose. All instructions drawings notes and memoranda relating to the said business customers methods processes or secrets made by the Employee or coming into his possession during his said service shall be the exclusive property of the Company and the Employee shall use his best endeavours to prevent the publication or disclosure of any such information or documents.
10. THE Employee shall forthwith communicate to the Company every improvement, invention, discovery, design, Trade Mark or specification which he may devise during the continuance of his employment hereunder whether

capable of legal protection or not and which might be used in connection with or relate to the business of the Company or any articles manufactured or dealt with in any of the processes or methods employed by the Company or any tools or machines or plant used by the Company. The Company will ensure that the Company and its professional advisers keep confidential all details of any invention which the Employee simultaneously claims belongs to him until either those details have entered the public domain, or it has been established that the invention belongs to the Company or the Employee releases the Company from its obligation to ensure the maintenance of confidentiality. Every such improvement, invention, discovery, design, Trade Mark or specification shall, except insofar as it may be deemed by statute to belong to the Employee, become the sole and absolute property of the Company. The Employee at any time whether during his period of employment hereunder or thereafter when required by the Company and at the Company's expense shall do and execute all acts deeds and things which may be required to enable the Company to obtain the fullest benefit and advantage from every such improvement, design, discovery, Trade Mark or specification (including the copyright in any design data in whatever form or specification) not deemed by statute to belong to the Employee.

11. THE Employee shall be entitled to such payments in respect of periods of service during which he is incapacitated due to illness or accident and to such holidays on such terms as are specified in instructions from time to time by the Company.

12. IF during his period of employment hereunder the Employee shall be guilty of any misconduct (including misconduct of a personal nature likely in any way to affect the carrying out of his duties hereunder) or of any breach or neglect of the terms of this Agreement or of the duties from time to time assigned to him the Company may without previous notice or payment in lieu of notice terminate his employment hereunder and in such circumstances he shall be paid the remuneration due to him hereunder down to the date of such termination and no more.

13. THE Employee shall not for one year after his employment hereunder ceases either on his own account or for any other person solicit or interfere with or endeavour to entice away from the Company any person who shall have been a customer of the Company during the Employee's period of service provided that this restriction shall only apply:

(i) with respect of business of the type on which the Employee was employed

(ii) to customers other than those introduced to the Company by the Employee at the beginning of his said employment.

14. ALL notices and other documents required to be served or given pursuant to this Agreement shall be deemed:

(i) to be duly served upon the Employee if left for him or sent by prepaid registered post to him at his address last known to the Company

(ii) to be duly served upon or given to the Company if served or given to the Company at its registered office and all notices and other documents sent by post shall be deemed to have Been delivered and served at the time at which they would be delivered in the ordinary course of post.

AS WITNESS the hand of an authorised official of the Company and the hand of the Employee the day and year first above written	
SIGNED	
for and on behalf of the Company:	....
in the presence of:	....
SIGNED by the above named:	....

5.11.2 Comments

5.11.2.1 General comments on style

This document will not win any 'Good English' prizes. Presumably the draftsman had rushed headlong from an intensive course in conveyancing and probate gobbledygook. The purpose of this contract seems to be that it should sound legal; certainly most employees and employers would not understand half of it—though they might be suitably impressed by this and maybe this is what your client wants. There is the risk that the more legalistic the contract appears, the more a court or tribunal will interpret it accordingly, offering little leeway for the employer to argue that the real meaning of any clause 'was common knowledge'.

Apart from the language it is also difficult to see why this contract should be used for a secretary. The intellectual property clause (clause 10) and the restraint of trade clause (clause 13) are irrelevant to this position and clearly reflect the use of one general contract designed to meet the needs of all kinds of employees. Such blanket coverage is not desirable and may have adverse effects as we shall note below.

Punctuation also appears to be a variable theme. With one eye on nineteenth-century approaches there is generally no punctuation, but then in clause 10 it appears from nowhere. Why? Lastly, the agreement was drafted in 1992. It had not been updated and suffered from this both in style and detail. The agreement was reached in advance of starting work, which is fine, but the date 'deemed' to be the starting date is in fact a Sunday. Presumably a secretary would have no reason to start work on a Sunday and so this is likely to be mere carelessness. If the employee actually contractually started work before November that earlier date will in fact be the start date. The document also fails to meet the requirements of an ERA 1996, s. 1 written statement (even in the form required in 1992).

Such a contract would sound clear warning bells. It cannot be the case that this contract is still in operation many years after the starting date. There must be other documents varying this and many forms of practice which will have done so too. So you need to be on guard: where are the real terms? If there are documents you need to find them; if there are practices you need to be told of them.

5.11.2.2 Some specific clauses

Clause 2 begins in a standard way with a job grading. In reality, the grading system for this company was changed in 1998 and there is documentary evidence to show regarding this. The phrase 'or in any other such capacity' is very wide; it was meant to mean 'in any other capacity at that grade' which would make more sense—especially if at some time the employer claims the job is redundant. But why a secretary must reside in a required place is puzzling. If this is a limitation on living within so many miles of the site then such terms usually only apply to employees who might be called upon urgently. If it is a disguised 'mobility' clause, again this is most odd for a secretary.

Clause 3 is simply convoluted. The grade A4 is below grade 6 so the secretary is entitled to overtime payments.

Clause 4 was generous in its notice period in 1992, but now falls short of ERA 1996, s. 86 requirements. The different ages of retirement for men and women are discriminatory. Even if the retirement age were the same (at 65) this would still be subject to the employer complying with the requirements now imposed as regards 'retirement dismissals' (see **Chapters 11** and **12**).

Clause 5 is irrelevant to this employee and again shows the use of a standard clause. Likewise *Clause 10* (intellectual property rights) is general waffle.

Clause 9 concerns confidentiality and may be relevant to a secretary (though we will see in **Chapter 8** that it may be ineffective anyway once employment has finished). *Clause 13* is a restraint of trade clause. It is totally inappropriate to the status of the employee and would fail.

Clause 12 concerns gross misconduct but never specifies what is meant by this.

6 Equality in employment: discrimination

6.1 Introduction and sources

The key piece of legislation in this area is the Equality Act 2010 (EqA 2010). This Act seeks to consolidate and harmonise the law relating to discrimination and to make some amendments to the law on equal pay. As well as creating some new duties the Act addresses the problem of the piecemeal development of UK and EU anti-discrimination legislation over the last 40-plus years. In doing so, the EqA 2010 repeals in full all previous Acts concerning discrimination and equal pay (such as the Sex Discrimination Acts 1975 and 1986, the Race Relations Act 1976 and the Equal Pay Act 1970), or repeals parts of Acts such as the Equality Act 2006 and revokes related statutory instruments.

The 2010 Act applies to the position where the act complained of occurs wholly after 1 October 2010 (art. 15, Equality Act 2010 (Commencement No. 4, Savings, Consequential, Transitional, Transitory and Incidental Provisions and Revocation) Order 2010 (SI, 2010/2371)). It is therefore possible that, with continuing acts, the 'old law' may still be relevant for a while yet, but the text here is based solely on the 2010 Act.

In this chapter, we shall examine:

- the prohibited acts;
- the meaning of 'discrimination' and the forms it may take;
- the defences available to an employer;
- who receives protection;
- the general and specific duties relating to the various forms of discrimination;
- procedures, burden of proof and remedies.

In **Chapter 7** we shall turn our attention to the topic of 'equal pay' together with two other heads of discrimination that are related to aspects of the *job*—rather than the person—sometimes called 'atypical work':

- part-time work; and
- fixed-term work.

We should also note here a very long-standing form of unlawful discrimination: relating to trade union membership and activities. This is not dealt with in the 2010 Act. Indeed, it takes us into the area of collective employment rights (which is outside the scope of this work) but for completeness we will touch on this towards the end of this chapter.

When all these various heads of discrimination are added together they represent more of the employment tribunals' workload than the most notorious of rights—that of unfair dismissal.

6.1.1 The European dimension

The elimination of discrimination has been one of the major strands of European social policy and the original Treaty provisions have been supplemented by several Directives. The Equality Act 2010 seeks to incorporate European Union legislation and case law into the new framework but, of course, it cannot override these Directives: they will still be relevant via the principles of direct applicability and direct and indirect effect. The most important of general application are:

- the (recast) Equal Treatment Directive 2006/54/EC which consolidated and updated the Equal Pay Directive (75/117), the Equal Treatment Directive (76/207), the Directive on Equal Treatment in Occupational Social Security Schemes (86/378), the Burden of Proof Directive (97/80), and the four major directives on gender equality, together with all their relevant amendments; and
- the Race Discrimination Directive 2000/43/EC.

Under s. 2(2) of European Communities Act 1972 regulations can be introduced through statutory instruments which are not the subject of full debate in Parliament in order to implement EU legislation, but a structured Act (as here) cannot be so easily amended. This Act therefore employs what is called a 'Henry VIII' clause (s. 203 of EqA 2010), which permits the Act to be amended by ministerial order when the minister believes it is necessary to create a 'harmonising provision' (i.e., to amend parts of the Act not covered by the EU legislation but which are affected by that legislation or simply to amend in order to comply with EU legislation).

6.1.2 The institutions

When the statutes about discrimination on grounds of race, sex, and disability were new, the implementation of each was supported by a statutory institution. Under the Equality Act 2006 the three bodies were replaced by a single Equality and Human Rights Commission (EHRC), which also has responsibility for supervision of the newer heads of discrimination such as religion or belief, sexual orientation, and age. The EHRC adopted the old codes of practice and is empowered to issue new codes and take other steps it considers will advance the cause of equality. Like its predecessors, it can provide advice and help to individuals including assistance in litigation. However, a breach of the codes does not provide a ground of complaint without evidence of such discriminatory results: *Lord Chancellor* v *Coker* [2001] EWCA Civ 1756, [2002] ICR 321.

6.2 Overview of discrimination law

- The law seeks to protect certain individuals from being discriminated against. The prohibited discriminatory actions are described in s. 39 of EqA 2010 (governing activities such as recruitment, pay, conditions or promotion opportunities).
- Section 70 of EqA 2010 effectively divides 'discrimination' as set out in s. 39 into two separate categories. When the dispute is about *non-contractual* matters (e.g., treatment of the individual, selection processes) that is the concern of the rules laid out in Part 2 of the EqA 2010, and covered in this chapter. When the dispute

concerns *contractual* matters **and the issue is about equality between men and women,** that is the concern of **Chapter 7** of this text and Chapter 3, Part 5 of the EqA 2010.

- The protection is only given to certain people (termed, in s. 4 of EqA 2010, as those having **'protected characteristics'**) and the discrimination must be **'because of'** that characteristic. The mere fact that, say, a woman is treated badly does not necessarily mean the conduct is discriminatory; the employer might treat everyone badly. The 'protected characteristics' are: age, disability, gender reassignment, marriage and civil partnerships, pregnancy and maternity, race, religion or belief, sex, and sexual orientation.
- The different forms discrimination may take are:
  - direct discrimination—where, because of a person's protected characteristic, an employer treats that person less favourably than he treats or would treat others (e.g., where the employer will not employ people over 60 or under 25).
  - indirect discrimination—where an employer creates a provision, criterion or practice (e.g., a change in hours of work) that does not in itself appear discriminatory but that may be judged to be so because it puts the employee (and others who share the protected characteristic) at a particular disadvantage. (e.g., as regards getting to work and still dealing with child care problems).
  - harassment; and
  - victimisation.
- With direct discrimination the key phrase is that the person with the protected characteristic must receive **less favourable treatment** than someone not having that protected characteristic. This means that there must be a comparator against whom the less favourable treatment is to be judged and s. 23(1) states that '... there must be no material difference between the circumstances relating to each case'. Establishing exactly who is the comparator is usually straightforward (e.g., male to female, disabled person to non-disabled) but sometimes this is an exercise that needs careful attention.
- With indirect discrimination one is comparing the effect of the provision on two groups to see if the protected characteristics' group is being put at a disadvantage. So here one needs to find a comparator group.
- Each of the protected characteristics has its own sub-set of rules and definitions deriving from the general position. The EqA 2010 has sought to standardise these rules but disability and age, for instance, are protected characteristics that have very specific rules attached to them. In the main text we shall consider the meaning of discrimination generally and then turn to see how the definitions apply to each protected group.
- Most discrimination cases are actually a battle of evidence rather than technical legal rules and such cases eat up Employment Tribunals' time.
- Associated discrimination. With regard to direct discrimination, the Act does not make any reference to the characteristics **of a particular person**. It does not talk of *that employee's* age or sex or disability, for instance, as being a protected characteristic; instead it says: 'A person (A) discriminates against another (B) if, because of a protected characteristic, A treats B less favourably than A treats or would treat others.' This is intentional. It means that an employee who, say, cares for an infirm husband, and is treated less favourably by the employer **because of this** would have a claim for discrimination (even though they themselves are not disabled). This is what is meant by 'associated discrimination'. However, 'associated discrimination'

does not apply to the protected characteristics of 'marriage and civil partnerships' and 'pregnancy and maternity'.

- Defences: there are some general defences, such as 'occupational requirement', which apply to all forms of discrimination together with additional specific ones for each protected characteristic.
- It is no defence in cases of direct discrimination for an employer to argue that they could not have discriminated because they share the characteristic of the employee. A gay man can discriminate against another gay man, a woman against a woman, a disabled person against another disabled person.
- The remedies for discrimination include an unlimited amount for compensation (compared as we shall see to the 'capped' amounts available in unfair dismissal claims).

6.2.1 Evidence in particular cases

Discrimination cases accounted for more than a third of claims in the employment tribunals in recent years. A great many involve very little law, and a lot of difficulty with the evidence.

Suppose, for example, that a client comes to you complaining of having been discriminated against. Maybe the client is a woman who has been rejected in an application for promotion in favour of a man, or an Asian applicant for a job who knows that only whites were shortlisted for interview. You ask some preliminary questions and may well find that you are drawn to one of the following two views:

(a) The unfavourable treatment received sounds as if it was very possibly discriminatory on grounds of race or sex, although you may have reservations about how the evidence will pan out. The employer has perhaps already been challenged directly by the client and claims reasons that have nothing to do with race or sex. Sometimes, however, you may establish that a junior member of management involved in making the choice has said something foolish that helps your case and undermines the employer's assertions. Unguarded emails, for instance, can often be a great benefit to claimants.

(b) Alternatively, it may seem to you that the client has all the marks of one of those people with an inflated idea of their own ability, who find it impossible to accept that an employer should find someone else a better candidate than they are, and the alleged discrimination is merely part of their denial of their own shortcomings.

Your hunch or 'gut feeling' may be important. We suggested at the start of this book that a little common sense often works wonders in understanding employment law. Nowhere is that more so than in relation to discrimination.

6.3 The prohibited acts

Section 39 EqA 2010 lays out when it will be unlawful for an employer to discriminate against or victimise prospective or existing employees. It states:

(1) An employer (A) must not discriminate against a person (B)—

(a) in the arrangements A makes for deciding to whom to offer employment;

(b) as to the terms on which A offers B employment;

(c) by not offering B employment.

So, this covers all actions from the wording of advertisements through to interviewing and recruitment.

(2) An employer (A) must not discriminate against an employee of A's (B)—

(a) as to B's terms of employment;

(b) in the way A affords B access, or by not affording B access, to opportunities for promotion, transfer or training or for receiving any other benefit, facility or service;

(c) by dismissing B;

(d) by subjecting B to any other detriment.

This is aimed at how the relationship works during the period of employment (or the reasons for its termination).

(3) An employer (A) must not victimise a person (B)—

(a) in the arrangements A makes for deciding to whom to offer employment;

(b) as to the terms on which A offers B employment;

(c) by not offering B employment.

(4) An employer (A) must not victimise an employee of A's (B)—

(a) as to B's terms of employment;

(b) in the way A affords B access, or by not affording B access, to opportunities for promotion, transfer or training or for any other benefit, facility or service;

(c) by dismissing B;

(d) by subjecting B to any other detriment.

Subsections (3) and (4) mirror the general duty but with the emphasis on victimisation.

Vicitmisation is defined in s. 27 and we shall return to this below. Section 39 goes on to deal with some specific matters relating to disability, sex, and pregnancy and maternity. We shall incorporate these into the relevant parts of the text below.

Harassment is designated a prohibited act under s. 40 of EqA 2010 and is defined in s. 26 (see below). It occurs where there is oppressive and unacceptable behaviour on the part of one party to another. An employer's responsibility for 'third party' harassment has now been extended by s. 40 beyond sex and sexual harassment matters to other forms of harassment.

6.4 What is discrimination?

6.4.1 Types of discrimination

Prior to the EqA 2010, what are now termed 'protected characteristics' often had different definitions of discrimination attached to them; the grounds for what constituted sex discrimination might be different from those for race. The Act attempts to create a standard definition, although there are still some variations on the basic theme. As noted above, discrimination in relation to any of the protected characteristics takes four basic forms. We shall deal with these in depth below. To begin, we repeat the headings given in the overview, though this time with the statutory wording:

- direct discrimination: 'A person (A) discriminates against another (B) if, because of a protected characteristic, A treats B less favourably than A treats or would treat others': s. 13(1) of EqA 2010;
- indirect discrimination: 'A person (A) discriminates against another (B) if A applies to B a provision, criterion or practice which is discriminatory in relation to a relevant protected characteristic of B's': s. 19(1);

- harassment: s.26 sets out a number of situations where this may arise but the general one is contained in s. 26(1)—' A person (A) harasses another (B) if ...A engages in unwanted conduct related to a relevant protected characteristic'; and
- victimisation: s. 27(1) defines this as, 'A person (A) victimises another person (B) if A subjects B to a detriment because (a) B does a protected act, or (b) A believes that B has done, or may do, a protected act'—a protected act includes matters such as having brought a discrimination claim against that employer.

6.4.2 Direct discrimination

Direct discrimination consists of treating one person (in this context meaning an employee, an applicant for a job or even a former employee) overtly less favourably than another, and doing so **because of** a person's protected characteristic (see s. 13 of EqA 2010). Examples might be the following:

(a) When recruiting to fill a vacant job, the employer shortlists a white candidate for interview while a black candidate with equivalent qualifications is not called for interview.

(b) The employer promotes a man to a supervisory post when a woman is apparently better suited to the job.

(c) The employer refuses to employ people aged under 30 because she believes they do not have the right work ethic.

Employers sometimes believe that if they 'didn't mean' to discriminate then they have done nothing wrong. Even accepting that many such pronouncements are frequently disingenuous, it does not matter; the employer's motives are irrelevant. It is the objective fact of less favourable treatment that matters, viewed from the standpoint of the applicant's reasonable perception. Even an employer's benign motives are irrelevant to the question whether there is direct discrimination or not.

However, because clear evidence of direct discrimination is rare (how many employers would openly admit to discrimination?), tribunals frequently have to infer discrimination from all the material facts. In reality, this means tribunals also find themselves looking for the 'why?' (the reason for the treatment) in judging whether discrimination has occurred. This helps the analysis, but these two questions are two sides of the coin, not separate issues. Trying to understand why the act in question occurred is not a search for motive or excuse, merely a step in assessing whether the 'less favourable treatment' came about **because of** a discriminatory act. For instance, a white male employee might have received a smaller bonus payment than a fellow worker on the same salary grade (who is a Muslim woman). The white male employee feels this was because the company wanted to 'look good' and that this was discriminatory—but the female Muslim employee might have recently obtained better qualifications or had a much better appraisal report.

The tribunal must be careful to consider the totality of the facts but, if it is satisfied that the protected characteristic is one of the reasons for the treatment, that is sufficient to establish discrimination. It does not have to be the only or even the main reason. Almost any less favourable treatment falls within the definition and, under s. 13(5), if the protected characteristic is race, less favourable treatment includes segregating an employee of a particular race from others.

Thus, the idea of 'less favourable treatment because of the protected characteristic' is the distinctive feature in direct discrimination claims and it involves the hunt for a comparator and a causal link.

6.4.2.1 Finding comparators

Finding comparators is not always an easy or even intuitive exercise. For example, the comparator for a male homosexual is not another male but a female homosexual: *Smith* v *Gardner Merchant Ltd* [1998] 3 All ER 852, [1998] IRLR 510. They must share the same characteristics: see *Shamoon* v *Chief Constable of the Royal Ulster Constabulary* [2003] UKHL 11, [2003] ICR 337, where the House of Lords held that a senior female police officer could not simply compare her treatment with that of two male officers doing the same job—the correct comparator had to be male police officers doing the same job *who had also received complaints about their behaviour* (as had been the case with Shamoon). A hypothetical comparator may be used. Thus, where no exact actual comparator can be found the tribunal *must* decide how a hypothetical comparator would have been treated in comparable circumstances: *Vento* v *Chief Constable of West Yorkshire Police* [2002] EWCA Civ 1871, [2003] ICR 318. Of course, arguments based on a hypothetical comparator make the claim (or at least the evidence) an even more complicated affair.

6.4.3 Discrimination by association or perception

The definition of direct discrimination given in s. 13 covers cases where the less favourable treatment is:

- because of the employee's association with someone who has that characteristic (for example, that other person is disabled and the employee in question is treated less favourably than another employee might be in, say, taking holidays because they are seen as being awkward in asking for special provisions to care for the disabled person), and
- because the employee is wrongly thought to have the characteristic (for example, a particular religious belief).

Associated direct discrimination and direct discrimination by perception apply to all protected characteristics except for: (i) marriage and civil partnership; and (ii) pregnancy and maternity. So in these instances, it must be the victim herself who is, for example, married.

6.4.4 Specific modifications to 'direct discrimination'

We shall return to the points below when dealing with the specific protected characteristics in detail but for now we should note that:

- with the protected characteristic of 'age', the different treatment of people of different ages may be justified if this is a proportionate means of meeting a legitimate aim;
- in relation to disability it is not discrimination to treat a disabled person **more favourably** than a person who is not disabled; and
- where the claimant is a man, no account is taken of special treatment afforded to a woman in connexion with pregnancy or childbirth.

6.4.5 Indirect discrimination

The idea behind indirect discrimination is that a provision that may at first glance appear neutral as to sex, race, age etc. may have hidden discriminatory consequences. So, a term that applies to everyone would appear not to be discriminatory. However, if that term disadvantages a particular protected characteristic then it may be termed 'indirectly discriminatory'. This frequently catches out employers. Section 19 of EqA 2010 states:

> (1) A person (A) discriminates against another (B) if A applies to B a provision, criterion or practice which is discriminatory in relation to a relevant protected characteristic of B's.
>
> (2) For the purposes of subsection (1), a provision, criterion or practice is discriminatory in relation to a relevant protected characteristic of B's if—
>
> (a) A applies, or would apply, it to persons with whom B does not share the characteristic,
>
> (b) it puts, or would put, persons with whom B shares the characteristic at a particular disadvantage when compared with persons with whom B does not share it,
>
> (c) it puts, or would put, B at that disadvantage, and
>
> (d) A cannot show it to be a proportionate means of achieving a legitimate aim.

Note again that there is still a need to compare like with like so the comparators have to be those who are effectively doing the same job but on whom the provision, criterion or practice has no effect (or a hypothetical equivalent). It may be best to consider a simple example.

EXAMPLE

Suppose the employers operate a system of 'flexitime', where employees have some limited choice when they may start and finish work, provided they are at work during the 'core time'. The employers decide they need to 'tighten up' the contract and insist the core time starts at 9.00 am. That rule is not directly discriminatory: it is neutral in the sense that it applies equally to everyone. However, in practice it puts women at a disadvantage compared with men because more women than men have the responsibility of getting children to school and cannot easily meet the requirement. It therefore appears to constitute indirect discrimination against any female employee who suffers a disadvantage, but it is not necessarily unlawful, as the employers may be able to defend it under s. 19(2)(d). Perhaps the main function of the department concerned is dealing with telephone and email enquiries from continental Europe, which need to be answered quickly, and there is evidence that most of them arrive during the early morning, UK time. If the woman presents a complaint the tribunal will have to consider whether the employers' rule is a proportionate means of achieving the business objective of having all available staff on hand. How much delay in starting time would the woman really need? Can the employers accommodate a small exception in her case, or is 9.00 am already perhaps a negotiated compromise when the main surge of calls is even earlier? Has the employer tried to find the woman a comparable alternative job where a later start would not matter, and what was the woman's reaction?

6.4.5.1 Provision, criterion or practice (PCP)

This phrase in s. 19 is far-reaching. It is designed to cover all manner of working arrangements but it is not specifically defined in the legislation. Instances would include: requirements to work specific hours, or to work full-time only, some redundancy selection criteria, the imposition of wide-ranging geographical mobility clauses, asking for unnecessary qualifications or experience for a job, and overtime payment schemes or work rosters that favour one type of working pattern. The real question, however, is not whether such practices may fall within the definition but, rather, whether these create a particular disadvantage for one group over another and, if so, can they be justified.

6.4.5.2 Disadvantage

The claimant must have suffered a *disadvantage* or *would have suffered one*. This is not about hypothetical situations. Instead, it covers the situation where a person is deterred from applying for a job because of the PCP in question.

One key problem here is: how do you assess 'disadvantage'? Statistics may be a convenient means of assessing this (e.g., only 10 per cent of women employees can comply with this provision but 90 per cent of men can) but are not essential and all older authorities that relied on the use of statistics alone now need to be regarded with care. Statistics are viewed by the tribunals as a starting point, but they eventually give way to additional evidence, 'common knowledge' and industrial awareness. The 'pool' of comparators will be those affected by the PCP, not just every employee.

It is certainly a difficult question of fact at times but the move over the years away from the employee having to establish that they could not comply with the condition has helped employees. Certain matters have almost shifted into presumptions, such as that women, rather than men, will be affected by changes in working patterns that have an effect on child care.

One must also bear in mind that even if the disadvantage is shown, the employer may have a legitimate reason as a defence, as occurred in the age discrimination case of *Chief Constable of West Yorkshire* v *Homer* [2009] ICR 223, dealt with at **6.7.2.2** below.

6.4.6 Harassment

Section 40(1) sets out the employer's duty: an employer (A) must not, in relation to employment by A, harass a person (B), who is an employee of A's or who has applied to A for employment. Section 40(2)–(4) go on to detail liability for 'third party' harassment, which we shall deal with below at **6.4.6.1**.

Harassment is a serious matter, both because of the devastating effect it can have on a victim's life and also because of the very large amounts of compensation the tribunals and courts have consequently been prepared to award. It covers a very wide range of conduct from at one extreme criminal assaults to at the other such verbal banter, use of nicknames, teasing and playing of practical jokes as may seem jocular and inoffensive unless one understands the victim's feelings in the circumstances in which it takes place.

Section 26 EqA 2010 defines three types of harassment:

(1) A person (A) harasses another (B) if—

(a) A engages in unwanted conduct related to a relevant protected characteristic, and

(b) the conduct has the purpose or effect of—

(i) violating B's dignity, or

(ii) creating an intimidating, hostile, degrading, humiliating or offensive environment for B.

This first type applies to all protected characteristics except for marriage and civil partnership, and pregnancy and maternity: s. 26(5).

(2) A also harasses B if—

(a) A engages in unwanted conduct of a sexual nature, and

(b) the conduct has the purpose or effect referred to in subsection (1)(b).

This second type is more specific, namely that of sexual harassment. This requires the conduct to have the same purpose or effect as the general type.

(3) A also harasses B if—

(a) A or another person engages in unwanted conduct of a sexual nature or that is related to gender reassignment or sex,

(b) the conduct has the purpose or effect referred to in subsection (1)(b), and

(c) because of B's rejection of or submission to the conduct, A treats B less favourably than A would treat B if B had not rejected or submitted to the conduct.

This third type is about a person being treated less favourably because they have submitted to or rejected sexual advances (or there is harassment related to sex or gender reassignment). The conduct must have the same purpose or effect as seen in the other types of harassment.

Section 26 concludes:

> (4) In deciding whether conduct has the effect referred to in subsection (1)(b), each of the following must be taken into account—
>
> (a) the perception of B;
>
> (b) the other circumstances of the case;
>
> (c) whether it is reasonable for the conduct to have that effect.

Section 26 centres on how an employee is treated. There is no necessity to look for a comparator. As described in *Rayment* v *Ministry of Defence* [2010] EWHC 218 (QB); [2010] IRLR 768, the standard for harassment is conduct that is 'oppressive and unacceptable'. The definition approaches the matter very much from the claimant's perspective. Thus, if a victim had made it clear that she found conduct unwelcome, the continuation of such conduct will constitute harassment. Only if it would be unreasonable to regard the conduct as harassment at all will there be a defence here.

There is no requirement for an intention to harass; conduct that has the purpose *or effect* of creating an intimidating, hostile, degrading, humiliating, or offensive environment can be harassment, even if creating such an environment was not the intention behind it. Further, the unwanted conduct no longer has to be *on the ground of* the victim's protected characteristic to fall within the definition, but only *related* to it—or indeed to that of someone else.

Many employers already have policies in place to prevent inappropriate behaviour among their workforce, and rules about harassment feature in the employment handbooks (or equivalent) of most large companies. Nevertheless the practical circumstances in which complaints of harassment arise often involve some complexity for managers and supervisors for reasons like the following:

(a) The wide range of conduct covered and the fact that the importance of seemingly trivial remarks can only be understood by the recipient concerned and in all the surrounding circumstances.

(b) Those perpetrating harassment rarely commit the outrageous or major offences. Typically they go just one small step beyond that which the victim will tolerate. So the employer will often be faced with the seemingly trivial. However, a series of incidents, even absent a single significant event, can still amount to harassment: *Reed* v *Stedman* [1999] IRLR 299.

(c) Victims are typically reluctant to complain, and will put up with unwelcome attention for a long time. However, when it eventually becomes unbearable, they expect instant remedial action from the employer.

(d) Perpetrators often claim to have believed that their attentions were welcomed. Sometimes such a claim is ludicrous; in other cases it is plausible.

In the race discrimination case of *Richmond Pharmacology* v *Dhaliwal* [2009] IRLR 336 the EAT advised tribunals to focus on three elements in harassment cases, whatever the basis of the discrimination: (i) the question of unwanted conduct; (ii) whether the *purpose or effect* (as alternatives) reasonably violated the claimant's dignity or created an adverse environment; and (iii) whether this action fell within the prohibited grounds (race, sex, etc.—merely because the parties are male and female or black and white does not *per se* make bullying discriminatory). Note also that there is a common misconception in the mind of lay people that, in sexual harassment cases, victim and perpetrator have to be of the opposite sex.

6.4.6.1 Third party harassment

An employer may be liable if a third party harasses the employer's employees. Section 40(4) defines a third party as a person other than the employer (e.g., a customer or supplier). Fellow employees are not third parties. The combined effect of s. 40(2) and (3) means that the harassment must have occurred on at least two previous occasions and the employer's liability rests on not taking reasonable steps to prevent it happening again. It does not matter for these purposes whether the third party is the same or a different person on each occasion.

6.4.6.2 General note on harassment

- Harassment applies to all protected characteristics except for: (i) pregnancy and maternity; and (ii) marriage and civil partnerships.
- It is possible to have harassment arising out of association and perception (as with direct discrimination), e.g., an employee is harassed because he has non-white friends or he is *believed* to be homosexual.

6.4.7 Victimisation

The prohibition against victimisation is laid out in s. 39 and the text for that can be found at **6.3** above. The prohibition relates to both the recruitment process and to the operation of the contract itself. Victimisation is defined in s. 27(1) as: 'A person (A) victimises another person (B) if A subjects B to a detriment because (a) B does a protected act, or (b) A believes that B has done, or may do, a protected act.' The Explanatory Notes to the Act actually classify this as a free-standing right and not a form of discrimination (as it is not tied to protected characteristics and requires no 'comparators') but it is easier to regard it so here.

A 'protected act' includes bringing proceedings under the Act as well as giving evidence of or making allegations that a person has contravened the Act. Action protected under these rules is not limited to action concerning the claimant personally. In *National Probation Service for England and Wales (Cumbria area)* v *Kirby* [2006] IRLR 508 the complainant had merely given information in connexion with another employee's complaint of racial discrimination: the EAT held that she had been victimised. Section 77 of EqA 2010 adds a new protected act, which we will come back to in **Chapter 7**. This section bans secrecy clauses regarding pay in employment contracts, so if an employee now makes or receives a 'relevant pay disclosure' and then is victimised because of this, that act falls under these protection provisions.

The classic example of a victimisation claim would be where an employee has previously brought an equal pay or race discrimination claim and is then subjected to some form of detriment by the employer (e.g. a failure to promote her). The issue would not be whether the female employee or black employee has a claim for discrimination but, rather, that they are being penalised for their previous conduct. The purpose of the legislation here is to ensure that such employees are not deterred from pursuing their claims or be punished if they do so. There must be a causal link between the victimisation and the protected act and the employer has a defence if the allegations, evidence or information were false and not made or given in good faith. There is no need to find a comparator—it is only the treatment of the victim that matters and it is possible to *infer* from the employer's conduct that there has been victimisation.

6.4.8 The employer's handling of cases of harassment and victimisation

We have noted that harassment can be a serious matter for victims whose lives are sometimes made intolerable as a result. Equally, someone wrongly accused of harassment may find there are serious consequences of trust from a partner or ostracism by other employees. Employers very often face a daunting task in dealing with cases of alleged harassment where both alleged victim and alleged perpetrator are employees, and both have the right to be treated fairly. The authors have been involved in cases where an employer, anxious to protect a victim, has taken action against a perpetrator that has led to a claim of unfair dismissal that the employer has then lost.

Solicitors may find themselves asked to advise employers what to do in such difficult circumstances. The authors offer the following suggestions:

(a) Encourage victims to complain informally and in confidence at an early stage. It was suggested in *Insitu Cleaning* v *Heads* [1995] IRLR 4 that this may best be done by means of a separate grievance procedure.

(b) Ensure that the confidence is respected, that support is given and that some action is seen to be taken, as the victim may otherwise have good grounds to resign and to claim constructive dismissal.

(c) Be careful about suspension of the alleged perpetrator, especially if the complaint of harassment appears ill-founded and/or if there are other temporary solutions like transfer to another department to avoid contact with the victim. In *Gogay* v *Hertfordshire County Council* [2000] IRLR 703, a care worker in a children's home was suspended following allegations of sexual abuse by a disturbed child and this led to clinical depression. The Court of Appeal held that the employers were in breach of the implied duty of trust and confidence.

(d) In any disciplinary proceedings, ensure that the perpetrator's rights are respected and that fair treatment results, recognising the need for some warning except when gross misconduct has occurred.

(e) Encourage complaints early enough that action can be taken before relationships have deteriorated to the point where victim and perpetrator cannot safely be left to work together.

6.4.9 Instructing, causing or inducing contraventions

Section 111 of EqA 2010 makes it unlawful for a person to instruct, cause or induce someone to discriminate against, harass or victimise another person, or to attempt to do so. The protection extends to all protected characteristics. The EHRC can enforce this section and both the recipient of the instruction and the intended victim can bring individual claims for breach of this section against the person giving the instructions, provided they have suffered a detriment as a result. However, the section only applies where the person giving the instruction is in a relationship with the recipient of the instruction in which discrimination, harassment or victimisation is prohibited.

6.4.10 Positive discrimination

A question that is often asked is whether an employer can discriminate positively, i.e., in favour of one sex or a particular racial group that may be under-represented at the workplace. Generally speaking, to discriminate *in favour* of one person is to discriminate *against* another, and the employer is given no protection against a complaint by the second. Therefore, the answer is 'No', despite some ECJ case law indicating that positive discrimination can be permissible in limited circumstances.

Duties were placed on public authorities (breach not being actionable by individuals) by the Equality Act 2006 to 'promote equality', e.g., in providing special training to help remedy under-representation but this form of positive action is well-short of positive discrimination. These have not been re-enacted yet (via Chapter 1 of Part 11 of EqA 2010) but the general positive action provisions of ss. 158 and 159 of EqA 2010 have been partially enacted. Section 158(2) states that the 2010 Act does not prohibit a person from taking any action that is a proportionate means of achieving the aim of—

> (a) enabling or encouraging persons who share the protected characteristic to overcome or minimise that disadvantage,
>
> (b) meeting those needs, or
>
> (c) enabling or encouraging persons who share the protected characteristic to participate in that activity.

Section 158(3) allows for regulations to be made that may specify action, or descriptions of action, to which sub-s. (2) does not apply. But s. 159 (which goes much further than this in terms of recruitment and promotion actions) has not been enacted except for one minor cross-reference aspect.

6.5 Defences to discrimination claims

6.5.1 General comments on defences

- Once direct discrimination is established there is one major defence of general application available to the employer—that of 'occupational requirement': see sch. 9, Part 1 of EqA 2010. An employer may also be able to plead, in rare cases, 'statutory authority'.
- Employers may have a defence against a claim of indirect discrimination if they can show that the PCP in question was a proportionate means of achieving a legitimate aim.
- Further, specific, defences or exemptions arise for some of the protected characteristics (e.g., for age discrimination an employer may calculate redundancy payments based on length of service and age—although this is clear direct age discrimination, it is permissible).

This part of the text therefore sets out the defences of general application but should be read in conjunction with any particular defences noted for the particular characteristic being examined.

6.5.2 Occupational requirement

The defence of 'occupational requirement' appears in para. 1 of sch. 9 of EqA 2010. This states that:

> A person (A) does not contravene a provision mentioned in sub-paragraph (2) by applying in relation to work a requirement to have a particular protected characteristic, if A shows that, having regard to the nature or context of the work—
>
> (a) it is an occupational requirement,

(b) the application of the requirement is a proportionate means of achieving a legitimate aim, and

(c) the person to whom A applies the requirement does not meet it (or A has reasonable grounds for not being satisfied that the person meets it).

A classic example of the application of an 'occupational requirement' would be the need to cast a woman in a role in a play—thus avoiding sex discrimination charges.
Note: This defence does not apply to cases of harassment or victimisation.

6.5.3 Statutory authority

If an act that would otherwise be unlawful discrimination is done to comply with some statutory provision then it is permissible, e.g, an employer would be able to 'discriminate' against a disabled person if health and safety regulations required this or against a pregnant woman in order to meet specific regulations protecting such women against contact with hazardous materials (see schs 22 and 23 of EqA 2010).

6.5.4 Proportionality and indirect discrimination

Employers have a defence against a claim of **indirect** discrimination under s. 19(2)(d) if they can show that the PCP or policy that causes a particular disadvantage was a proportionate means of achieving a legitimate aim. In practice the second element (legitimate aim) causes less difficulty than the first (proportionality). It will usually be possible for employers to show that the PCP meets a legitimate business aim, like the speedy handling of European enquiries in the example we used earlier. The important point is that the burden of proof in this defence lies on the employer and the presence of a legitimate aim cannot be taken for granted: employers need to establish clearly what aim they had in mind.

The wording used in the EqA 2010 is not new and the concept of proportionality is of course familiar to those who have studied European law. It allows a broad assessment of the question whether the PCP is an *appropriate and necessary* means of achieving the aim, and the likelihood is that tribunals will want to examine all the surrounding circumstances—hence the various questions we asked in the flexi-time example used above, not only about the employer's policy, but also about the circumstances in which it was introduced and the feasibility of alternatives. There is an objective balancing exercise involved in this analysis.

The employer's defence under the rules prior to 2005 was much broader—simply that the equivalent of the PCP should be *justified*—so old cases should be used with care. However, some cases had begun to reflect the new analysis. Thus in *Hardys and Hansons plc* v *Lax* [2005] EWCA Civ 846, [2005] IRLR 668, the Court of Appeal was invited on behalf of the employers to adopt a 'band of reasonableness' test in assessing the employer's argument of justification, so that (as with unfair dismissal) the employment tribunal would not merely make its own decision on what they thought a reasonable employer would do, but rather would accept that different reasonable employers might take different actions (an approach that would substantially favour employers). The Court refused and required the employment tribunal 'to make its own judgment, upon a fair and detailed analysis of the working practices and business considerations involved, as to whether the proposal is reasonably necessary'. This is certainly the position today and employers will need to show that the aim was unrelated to any discrimination practice and that they have considered all reasonable alternatives in achieving that legitimate aim.

6.5.5 Unintentional indirect discrimination

Under s. 124 of EqA 2010, in a case of indirect discrimination where the respondent proves that there was no intention to treat the claimant unfavourably, a tribunal **cannot** award damages to a claimant unless it has first considered making either a declaration or recommendation.

The mere fact that the employer claims that 'discrimination was not intended' will not be enough: in *London Underground Ltd* v *Edwards* [1998] IRLR 364 it was held that the employment tribunal was entitled to infer that a new roster was introduced with knowledge of its unfavourable consequences for the single parent applicant and an intention to produce those consequences was therefore found. Comparable logic was applied in *J. H. Walker Ltd* v *Hussain* [1996] ICR 291. Here, a rule about when holidays could be taken affected the religious observance of Muslim employees and was indirectly discriminatory: compensation was awarded.

The practitioners' bible, *Harvey*, concludes that: '*Ultimately..., "intention" seems to mean knowledge of the consequences rather than motive.*' So if the consequences are not foreseen a tribunal must consider alternative remedies before awarding compensation for indirect discrimination.

6.6 The meaning of 'protected characteristics'

This is the term used by s. 4 of EqA 2010 to describe the people entitled to bring a claim and represents no substantive change to the pre-2010 Act. The 'protected characteristics' are:

- age;
- disability;
- gender reassignment;
- marriage and civil partnerships;
- pregnancy and maternity;
- race;
- religion or belief;
- sex;
- sexual orientation.

These characteristics are then defined in ss. 5-12, aside from pregnancy and maternity, which are covered in s. 18. We shall examine the peculiarities of each of the characteristics in the statutory order set out above. The basic protection is contained in s. 39 of EqA 2010 as seen above at **6.3** ('prohibited acts').

In examining these protected characteristics the general matters on the meaning of discrimination etc. set out above will apply; we shall concentrate on variations on or additions to those themes.

6.7 Protected characteristic: age

6.7.1 Definition and relevant legislation

The EqA 2010 revoked the Employment Equality (Age) Regulations 2006 (SI 2006/1031) **except** for schs 6 (Duty to consider working beyond retirement) and 8 (Amendments to legislation).

Under s. 25(1) of EqA 2010 'age discrimination' is defined as direct discrimination because of age and indirect discrimination where the relevant protected characteristic is age. Section 5(1) of EqA 2010 states that in relation to the protected characteristic of age—

> (a) a reference to a person who has a particular protected characteristic is a reference to a person of a particular age group;
> (b) a reference to persons who share a protected characteristic is a reference to persons of the same age group.
> (2) A reference to an age group is a reference to a group of persons defined by reference to age, whether by reference to a particular age or to a range of ages.

'Age groups' can therefore be a movable feast. A 20-year-old and a 30-year-old are both in a category of 'under 40' and therefore share the same 'protected characteristics', but may be in different categories if the bar is set elsewhere. 'Age' includes **apparent** age as this will fall within the heading of discrimination by perception. So, for example, not hiring a sales executive 'because they look too young to be taken seriously' would be caught by these provisions; or, vice versa, not hiring someone who is prematurely grey because that does not fit a 'dynamic image' of the company.

6.7.2 Defences and exceptions to age discrimination

6.7.2.1 Justification

In addition to the availability of the general defence of occupational requirement, s. 13(2) of EqA 2010 provides a specific defence:

> If the protected characteristic is age, A does not discriminate against B if A can show A's treatment of B to be a proportionate means of achieving a legitimate aim.

Thus there is a defence of justification available to an employer for both direct and indirect age discrimination if the employer can show that less favourable treatment or the application of a PCP was a proportionate means of achieving a legitimate aim. The protected characteristic of age is therefore a rare example of permitting direct discrimination to be justified.

To date, employment tribunals have been reluctant to accept cost-saving as a sufficient legitimate aim on its own. Thus, for example, the employer who wants to argue that there is a better prospect of a return from the investment in training if a 22-year-old is appointed to a vacancy than a 55-year-old will probably find that the tribunal does not regard this as proportionate. Indeed, there is a strong argument that any other finding undermines the whole purpose of legislation about age discrimination. It might be different if the employer could show a particular or exceptional need to contain cost, and the disadvantaged applicant had a much shorter period left before a normal retirement age of, say, 65.

6.7.2.2 Retirement

At present an employer can require an employee to retire at 65 (sch. 9, para. 8 of EqA 2010). However, the Government has announced that it plans to scrap this rule as from October 2011. Until then, this 'default' age for retirement remains in force.

In *R (on the application of Incorporated Trustee of the National Council for Ageing)* v *Secretary of State for Trade and Industry* (C-388/07) [2009] IRLR 373, the ECJ determined that default retirement ages could in principle be valid if they were objectively and reasonably justified in the context of national law by a legitimate aim relating to employment policy, the labour market, or vocational training—and the means of achieving those aims were appropriate and necessary for the purpose. Stereotyping, as in 'capability declines once a person passes 65', is not an acceptable inference: *Seldon* v *Clarkson Wright and Jakes* [2009] IRLR 267 (EAT).

To counterbalance the present default age rule, employers must operate a procedure for anyone they wish to retire. The steps consist of a series of notices and responses (but not the need for justification) and are set out in sch. 9, part 2 of EqA 2010. If the procedure is not complied with, the employee may complain to an employment tribunal, which (if they uphold the complaint) may award compensation of up to eight weeks' pay and failure to adhere to these rules may lead to a successful claim for unfair dismissal.

Some employers operate a 'normal retirement age', which may be higher or lower than 65. Under the present rules, this is permissible provided the employer can demonstrate that the age set is not discriminatory. However, not all matters that have an age element are *ipso facto* discriminatory. Thus, in *Chief Constable of West Yorkshire* v *Homer* [2009] ICR 223 a requirement that holders of top salary positions had to possess a law degree was not discriminatory even when the employee was at an age when he could not complete the degree in time before retiring and so would not benefit from increased pay—this was a consequence of age, not age discrimination said the EAT.

Contrary to presentation in the media, tribunals have been fairly sympathetic to employers seeking to retire their workforce provided the employer acts with some common sense and can explain the retirement policy adequately.

Also contrary to popular belief, once the 'default' retirement age of 65 is scrapped this does not mean employees may continue to work for as long as they wish: employers will still be able to impose a normal retirement age but will have to justify this.

6.7.2.3 Length of service

It is at least arguable that differential treatment based on length of service (e.g., holiday entitlement) is capable of being justified on the basis we have already discussed. However, under sch. 9, para. 10, EqA 2010 employers do not have to justify a difference of treatment as a result of a difference in length of service between two workers if the disadvantaged worker has service of five years or less. The difference can relate to any benefit other than one relating to the termination of employment, and length of service can be measured in terms of total service (under the usual statutory formula) or service at a particular level.

Where the disadvantaged worker's service exceeds five years, it must reasonably appear to the employer that the use of length of service in this way fulfils a business need of the undertaking, e.g., encouraging loyalty or motivation or rewarding experience. This formula suggests that it is the belief of the employer that is paramount, rather than any objective test of the business need, but the employer's view must be reasonably based.

There has still been relatively little guidance from the courts on the tests employment tribunals should apply in assessing employers' arguments of justification. In both *MacCulloch* v *Imperial Chemical Industries plc* EAT 0119/08 and *Loxley* v *BAE Systems Land Systems (Munitions and Ordnance) Ltd* EAT 0156/08 the EAT had to examine findings by employment tribunals that age-related differences in contractual redundancy terms were justified. In the first case the tribunal had been entitled to conclude that the differences related to a legitimate aim, but the tribunal had failed properly to consider the other important question—whether the means was proportionate. In the second case, which dealt with pension arrangements in circumstances of redundancy, the tribunal had focused on pension issues and not enough on the redundancy. The requirement for detailed examination of proportionality in *MacCulloch* suggests that some employers may have difficulty in justifying differential holiday arrangements that sometimes reward employees for lengths of service very much in excess of the five-year period.

6.7.2.4 Redundancy payments

Under sch. 9, para. 13 redundancy payments made under the statutory scheme (which are age- and service-related) are exempt and employers are also permitted to operate their own age-dependent enhanced schemes provided they are based on the structure of the statutory scheme.

In some cases employers place a taper or a cap on the payments made under such redundancy schemes to employees who are nearing retirement age anyway. Although in one sense discriminatory, these mechanisms have received approval (see *Loxley* above on tapering and *Kraft Foods UK Ltd* v *Hastie* [2010] UKEAT/0024/10 on capping).

6.8 Protected characteristic: disability

Under this heading of protected characteristics the cases on the pre-2010 law show that we must have regard not only to the provisions of the statute, but also to the relevant code, the guidance and the statutory regulations. Despite the introduction of the EqA 2010 there are still some significant differences between this protected characteristic and others.

6.8.1 The meaning of disability

Section 6 of EqA 2010 (together with sch. 1) establishes who is to be considered as having the protected characteristic of disability. Section 6 states that a person has a disability if:

- that person has a physical or mental impairment; and
- the impairment has a substantial and long-term adverse effect on that person's ability to carry out normal day-to-day activities.

Each element of that definition merits closer attention.

6.8.1.1 The impairment may be *physical or mental*

The conventional view of disability probably concentrates on physical disability, but the Act also protects those with mental illnesses and those with learning difficulties. Mental illness does not have to be 'clinically well-recognised' but some kind of medical evidence is usually still required. There is no requirement for medical evidence about learning difficulties; other evidence will suffice, such as a psychologist's report. However, one of the key problems in dealing with disability based on mental illness is that of finding an appropriate comparator. Awkward behaviour may arise from the mental illness and merely comparing the disabled employee's actions to another (non-disabled but awkward) employee is unrealistic because it is the mental illness that is making the disabled employee awkward. Instead, ironically, one might have to look at a less-refined comparison, e.g., someone who did not have the illness but was, say, off work for a similar number of days, as in *Aylott* v *Stockton-On-Tees Borough Council* [2010] EWCA Civ 910.

Where the effects of the disability are plain, medical diagnosis of the cause may not be necessary: *Millar* v *Inland Revenue Commissioners* [2005] IRLR 112. The test for 'impairment', therefore, uses a 'functional' model rather than a 'medical' one: it is about what the claimant can or cannot do at a practical level. Impairment may include the *consequences* of an operation to relieve the disease: *Kirton* v *Tetrosyl Ltd* [2003] IRLR 353.

Some conditions are deemed to be a disability, e.g., where a person is certified as blind, severely sight impaired, sight impaired or partially sighted by a consultant ophthalmologist.

6.8.1.2 The effect must be *substantial*

This term is further defined in the guidance as meaning more than minor or trivial. It is undoubtedly a lower threshold than might have been expected from the use of the term 'substantial' on its own. In *Kapadia* v *London Borough of Lambeth* [2000] IRLR 699 the Court of Appeal held that uncontested medical evidence on the degree of effect is generally conclusive. The EAT has emphasised that it is a matter of fact for the employment tribunal to decide, and medical evidence must not usurp the tribunal's function.

Guidance on how to analyse this area was given in *Goodwin* v *The Patent Office* [1999] ICR 302 where the applicant was a paranoid schizophrenic but managed to care for himself, largely satisfactorily, at home. The employment tribunal had held that the effect of his impairment was not substantial and he was consequently not disabled. The EAT disagreed and in doing so gave lengthy and detailed guidance for the tribunals on how to approach the question of whether an applicant is disabled. The proper approach was to focus on things the employee could not do or could only do with difficulty and not merely on things he could do.

Paragraph 3(1) also specifically states that an impairment which consists of a severe disfigurement is to be treated as having a substantial adverse effect on the ability of the person concerned to carry out normal day-to-day activities.

6.8.1.3 The effect must be *long-term*

This means that it has lasted for 12 months or is 'likely to last for 12 months or more, or for the rest of the person's life'. Furthermore, past disability also brings the person within the definition as para. 2(2) states that: 'If an impairment ceases to have a substantial adverse effect on a person's ability to carry out normal day-to-day activities, it is to be treated as continuing to have that effect if that effect is likely to recur.' So, once a person qualifies as disabled they could remain protected for the rest of their lives. However, tribunals have struggled with the word 'likely' in this context.

The most common problem to deal with in terms of 'recurrence' arises when medication is being taken to control the illness. Paragraph 5 deals with this:

> (1) An impairment is to be treated as having a substantial adverse effect on the ability of the person concerned to carry out normal day-to-day activities if—
>
> (a) measures are being taken to treat or correct it, and
>
> (b) but for that, it would be likely to have that effect.
>
> (2) 'Measures' includes, in particular, medical treatment and the use of a prosthesis or other aid.
>
> (3) Sub-paragraph (1) does not apply—
>
> (a) in relation to the impairment of a person's sight, to the extent that the impairment is, in the person's case, correctable by spectacles or contact lenses or in such other ways as may be prescribed;
>
> (b) in relation to such other impairments as may be prescribed, in such circumstances as are prescribed.

Pre-2010 House of Lords' authority gave the word 'likely' a lower proof level, meaning of 'could well happen' rather than 'probable' or 'more likely than not' in *SCA Packaging Ltd* v *Boyle* [2009] UKHL 37, [2009] IRLR 746 where an employee had suffered hoarseness and vocal nodes problems since 1974 which could return if the medication was not taken or failed.

The same considerations apply where the person has a progressive condition. If that condition has or had an effect on that person's ability to carry out normal day-to-day activities (see below) but the effect has not yet had a substantial adverse effect, the person may be taken to have that impairment if the 'condition is likely to result in P having such an impairment' (para. 8).

6.8.1.4 The effect must be on *normal day-to-day activities*

'Normal' here means, normal for most people and will include things such as mobility, memory, speech and continence. So, usually one would look to see if the disability prevents a person from undertaking ordinary tasks. But the term has been given a broad definition. Thus, working night shifts, though not the common pattern of work, is undertaken by enough people to be 'normal day-to-day activity'. So an employee with a sleep disorder who is instructed to undertake night work might have a claim for disability discrimination. However, a person is *not* regarded as disabled if suffering an impairment that merely limits exceptionally strenuous activities or only specific kinds of job. So a person with a heart condition might not be able to lift heavy loads—that is not a 'normal day-to-day activity'. Not being able to lift ordinary loads would be covered by day-to-day activities. But each case has its complications and each individual must be treated as a special case.

6.8.1.5 Anyone with cancer, HIV infection, or multiple sclerosis

Such persons are deemed to be disabled, irrespective of the usual tests given above regarding normal day-to-day activities.

6.8.1.6 Specific exclusions

There are some *specific exclusions*. Not many pieces of legislation manage to link kleptomania, hayfever, smoking, alcoholism and body piercing but they are good neighbours here (see Part 2 of the Equality Act (Disability) Regulations 2010 (SI 2010/2128)). However, the exclusions are interpreted narrowly: thus although addiction to alcohol is excluded, depression is not—even if there is a causal link with alcoholism: *Power* v *Panasonic Ltd* [2003] IRLR 151. In *Edmund Nuttall Ltd* v *Butterfield* [2005] IRLR 751 the claimant had indecently exposed himself and was dismissed, but it was argued that his exhibitionism (one of the exclusions) was the consequence of depression. The EAT laid down the rule that the material issue was the actual reason for the offending behaviour, whether the excluded condition or the legitimate impairment. Mere exhibitionism would not be covered; but such actions driven by depression might be.

6.8.2 How can disability discrimination occur?

Following controversial debate over the interpretation and application of the old definitions of disability discrimination by the House of Lords in *London Borough of Lewisham* v *Malcolm* [2008] UKHL 43, those definitions have been amended substantially by the EqA 2010 and all previous case law needs to be viewed with extreme caution.

As well as the concepts of direct and indirect discrimination (the latter being quite difficult to apply to disability) there are two other aspects of disability discrimination that need to be noted:

- the duty to make reasonable adjustments (see **6.12.4** below); and
- the EqA 2010's newly-introduced form of disability discrimination that is contained in s. 15. This states that:

> (1) A person (A) discriminates against a disabled person (B) if—
>
> (a) A treats B unfavourably **because of something arising in consequence of B's disability**, and
>
> (b) A cannot show that the treatment is a proportionate means of achieving a legitimate aim.

This does not apply if the employer shows that he did not know, and could not reasonably have been expected to know, that the employee had the disability.

This looks peculiar at first sight but it is aimed at protecting against discrimination arising from or in consequence of the disability rather than the disability itself (which is already covered under direct discrimination). Note that the term used here is 'unfavourably' rather than the standard 'less favourably'. This means no comparator is required for this form of discrimination.

The example given in the Act's explanatory notes is: 'An employee with a visual impairment is dismissed because he cannot do as much work as a non-disabled colleague. If the employer sought to justify the dismissal, he would need to show that it was a proportionate means of achieving a legitimate aim.' Another example would be: where the disabled person is viewed as a weak or unhelpful employee because he has taken periods of disability-related absences and this has affected bonuses or promotion prospects. The person is not suffering a detriment **because** they are disabled as such, but because of the effect of that disability. This provision covers this wider situation and replaces the previous provision of 'disability-related' discrimination that had been rendered ineffective by the controversial *Malcolm* decision.

Subparagraph (1)(b) and sub-s. (2) provide the defences available. The first defence—proportionate means of achieving a legitimate aim—we have seen before as it is the now standard test for justifying indirect discrimination. The second defence relates to the employer's knowledge at the time the employer decided on taking the action that is now alleged to be discriminatory.

6.8.3 Enquiries about disability and health

New to the EqA 2010, there are now limitations on what sort of questions an employer may ask about an applicant's health. The basic position, under s. 60, is that questions may not be asked before an offer is made or the applicant has been included in a pool of successful candidates to be offered the job at a later date. The exceptions include asking questions that would be relevant to the recruitment process itself (so that some form of reasonable adjustment to the process can be made) and finding out whether a job applicant would be able to undertake a function that is intrinsic to the job, with reasonable adjustments in place as required. It is generally only for the EHRC to bring an action in relation to such activities.

6.8.4 The employer's duty to make reasonable adjustments

Under ss. 20-22 and sch. 8 of EqA 2010 the duty arises in three situations (termed 'requirements' in the Act):

- where a provision, criterion or practice puts a disabled person at a substantial disadvantage in relation to a relevant matter in comparison with persons who are not disabled. So, this covers cases on *how* the job is done;
- where a physical feature puts a disabled person at a substantial disadvantage in relation to a relevant matter in comparison with persons who are not disabled. This covers the situation of *where* the job is done;
- where a disabled person would, but for the provision of an auxiliary aid, be put at a substantial disadvantage in relation to a relevant matter in comparison with persons who are not disabled. This covers those cases where the provision of an *auxiliary aid* (e.g., special computer software for those with impaired sight) would prevent the employee being disadvantaged.

Failure to comply with any of these requirements renders that omission actionable as discrimination: s. 21. The use of the phrase 'substantial disadvantage' throughout these expressions should be noted here. Often it is thought that the duty means disabled employees are entitled to a whole range of benefits not open to others. What the duty actually refers to is making reasonable adjustments so as to ensure there is no substantial disadvantage experienced by the disabled employee in comparison to other employees.

In all cases the duty is that the employer must take such steps as it is reasonable to have to take to avoid the disadvantage or provide the auxiliary aid. An employer discriminates against a disabled person if the employer fails to comply with the duty in relation to that person. Section 20(6), (7) and (9) expand on this duty.

- Under s. 20(6), where the first or third requirement relates to the provision of information, the steps that it is reasonable for the employer to have to take include steps for ensuring that in the circumstances concerned the information is provided in an accessible format.
- Under s. 20(7), an employer is not (subject to express provision to the contrary) entitled to require a disabled person, in relation to whom A is required to comply with the duty, to pay to any extent A's costs of complying with the duty.
- Under s. 20(9), in relation to the second requirement, a reference in this section or an applicable schedule to avoiding a substantial disadvantage includes a reference to—
  - (a) removing the physical feature (which term includes the design of the building, features, fittings and furniture for instance) in question,
  - (b) altering it, or
  - (c) providing a reasonable means of avoiding it.

So, an employer is expected to take steps such as making adjustments to premises, altering working hours, providing an interpreter ('auxiliary aid' can include an auxiliary service) and much else. It may even be that the employer will have to consider moving another non-disabled employee from one post to another in order to make way for the disabled employee. These examples are subject to much further expansion in the code of practice.

Just as the meaning of 'disabled' is much wider than the conventional view of physical disability, so it is important not to think of adjustments as limited to physical steps such as providing wheelchair access. In *Archibald* v *Fife County Council* [2004] UKHL 32, [2004] ICR 954 the applicant was left almost unable to walk by complications from minor surgery and could not carry out her duties as a road sweeper. The House of Lords held that the duty to make adjustments was triggered when the employee was put at a substantial disadvantage because her disability made it impossible for her to perform the main or essential function of her job, and she was therefore at risk of dismissal, a risk that would not have arisen for a non-disabled employee. The employer had investigated transferring her to a different job (which the code of practice requires), but their Lordships felt it was insufficient for this to be on the basis of merely giving her the opportunity to participate in competitive interviews. Applying those principles in *Southampton City College* v *Randall* [2006] IRLR 18, the EAT held that the employer's duty extended to devising a new job for the complainant lecturer whose voice had been damaged by the need to shout above the noise of a machine shop.

An example where a practical limit was placed on the employer's duty is *O'Hanlon* v *Commissioners for HM Revenue & Customs* [2007] EWCA Civ 283, [2007] ICR 1359: it would be very rare for the duty to extend to providing longer periods of sick pay to a disabled employee than to one who was not disabled.

The employer is not required to make adjustments in connexion with any disability he did not know about and could not reasonably be expected to know about: sch. 8, para. 20. Further, the duty to take steps to prevent disadvantage applies only to job-related matters. In *Kenny* v *Hampshire Constabulary* [1999] ICR 27, for instance, the applicant needed personal help to use the toilet and this was held to fall outside the duty.

6.9 Protected characteristic: gender reassignment

This protected characteristic covers any person undergoing gender reassignment, or who is proposing to do so or who has already done so. Both female-to-male and male-to-female transsexuals are covered by these provisions. The employee is no longer required to be under medical supervision in order to receive protection under this heading. However, gender reassignment may well involve surgery and s. 16 of EqA 2010 prohibits an employer from treating a transsexual less favourably than injured or sick employees, where the transsexual's reason for absence is gender reassignment.

6.10 Protected characteristic: marriage and civil partnerships

This heading is straightforward and gives protection to both married couples and those in a civil partnership. People who are engaged, cohabiting or divorced, therefore, do not receive protection here though they might be protected under other heads (e.g., dismissing a woman because she has become engaged might fall within sex discrimination). Further, associated discrimination does not apply here (see s. 13(5)) so it must be the employee-victim who is married or in a civil partnership.

Marriage and civil partnership are also not included as protected characteristics in respect of harassment.

6.11 Protected characteristic: pregnancy and maternity

Section 18 of EqA 2010 covers discrimination because of:

- a woman's pregnancy or pregnancy-related illness; or
- because she takes or tries to take maternity leave.

The period during which protection is provided is the period of the pregnancy and any statutory maternity leave to which she is entitled (including any decisions taken during that time even though they may be implemented later). During this period, these types of discrimination fall within this protected characteristic and cannot be treated as sex discrimination. Because there is no comparator available (for obvious reasons) the section uses the term 'unfavourably' instead of 'less favourably'.

Section 18(6) defines the protected period for this as starting when the pregnancy begins, and ending:

(a) if she has the right to ordinary and additional maternity leave, at the end of the additional maternity leave period or (if earlier) when she returns to work after the pregnancy;
(b) if she does not have that right, at the end of the period of 2 weeks beginning with the end of the pregnancy.

6.11.1 Pregnancy-related dismissal

The dismissal of a woman because of pregnancy or childbirth will give rise to unfair dismissal rights, so that the remedies we shall consider in **Chapter 13** are available. However, the importance of the alternative right of action under EqA 2010 is that compensation for unfair dismissal is subject to a statutory maximum, while compensation for discrimination is unlimited.

Once the baby has been born and the woman has returned to work after her maternity leave, she must be treated like any other employee. Thus, for example, if her attendance record is unsatisfactory, she can fairly be dismissed for incapability provided that a man with comparable absence would be treated similarly. This rule apparently includes conditions caused by pregnancy or childbirth, provided that sickness starts **after** the return to work. In *Caledonia Bureau Investment & Property* v *Caffrey* [1998] ICR 603, the applicant's postnatal depression started during her maternity leave. Her dismissal after she was due to return to work was therefore related to maternity and unfair.

6.12 Protected characteristic: race

There are various stages in the employment relationship where race discrimination may occur, and these are listed in s. 39 of EqA 2010 and the codes of practice, e.g., advertisement, recruitment and selection, employment opportunities and dismissal. The definition of 'race' as a protected characteristic is found in s. 9 of EqA 2010. Race includes:

(a) colour;
(b) nationality;
(c) ethnic or national origins.

A racial group can be made up of two or more different racial groups so 'black Britons' could be a racial group (combining colour and nationality). The section also enables a minister to amend the Act by order so as to add 'caste' to the current definition of 'race'.

The 2010 Act has removed some of the more tricky problems of definition but there the following points are worth noting:

- 'Nationality' is acquired at birth but, as it is concerned with citizenship, it may be changed. Refusing to interview someone because they are Greek or Malaysian, for instance, would be subjecting them to a detriment based on nationality.
- 'National origins' is a larger concept than nationality and has been held to refer to race rather than citizenship: *Tejani* v *Peterborough Superintendent Registrar* [1986] IRLR 502. Thus a British person may also be 'Scottish' or 'English' and these are national origins for these purposes.
- An 'ethnic group' has been held to be broader than race alone and may include any community with a shared history and culture. Sikhs and Jews satisfy the definition; Rastafarians do not, because they are defined by religion alone (but will fall under the protected characteristic of 'religion or belief').
- Language alone (e.g., restricting employment to speakers of Welsh) does not define an ethnic group: *Gwynedd County Council* v *Jones* [1986] ICR 833.

The issue of work permits should also be noted in this context. The code of practice recommends that employers should not consider problems with job applicants obtaining work permits until decisions have been made on merit. To do otherwise runs the risk of race discrimination (even when having considered guidance from the UK Border Agency on the likelihood of success for a particular overseas applicant): *Osborne Clark Services* v *Purohit* [2009] IRLR 341.

Unsurprisingly, discrimination may be both direct and indirect. The latter might include things such as having an overly-complicated application form or using aptitude tests that require a higher standard of English than is necessary for the job.

Note also that if the protected characteristic is race, less favourable treatment includes segregating the employee from others: s. 13(5).

6.13 Protected characteristic: religion or belief

It is unlawful for an employer to discriminate on grounds of religion or of religious or philosophical belief. The protection also applies to the *absence* of such a belief, so that atheists acquire protection too. The definition extends to any *perception* of religion or belief, so that it does not have to be factually based, and it is possible to have discrimination by association (e.g., where an employee is pressured into acting against another because of that other's religion).

The explanatory notes to s. 10 of EqA 2010 give examples: 'The Baha'i faith, Buddhism, Christianity, Hinduism, Islam, Jainism, Judaism, Rastafarianism, Sikhism and Zoroastrianism are all religions for the purposes of this provision.' What is a 'philosophical belief' is a little looser. Certainly, established beliefs such as humanism and atheism would meet the standard, but anything that is less-established or looks like a cult would not be accepted so easily.

These provisions follow earlier versions, so the case law is still relevant. In *Glasgow City Council* v *McNab* [2007] IRLR 476 the EAT upheld an employment tribunal finding that the employer had discriminated against an atheist teacher when refusing him an interview for promotion in a Roman Catholic school to a post where it was considered an appointee had to be of that faith. The 'occupational requirement' (then called a 'genuine occupational requirement') exception was interpreted narrowly and the employer could not rely on it in this case.

Some cases have attracted a great deal of publicity, such as those dealing with the wearing of religious symbols and adornments. In *Azmi* v *Kirklees Metropolitan Borough Council* [2007] ICR 1154, the EAT upheld the rejection by the employment tribunal of claims of direct discrimination, indirect discrimination, and harassment brought by a school support worker who was asked not to wear the veil while teaching children. (Her claim of victimisation was allowed and this was not appealed.) The employment tribunal was entitled to find that the provision, criterion or practice was a proportionate means of achieving a legitimate aim. The wearing of crucifixes became an issue in *Eweida* v *British Airways plc* [2009] ICR 303 when the employer banned all visible adornments except those that were mandatory religious items (e.g., turbans or skull caps) and that could not be concealed. The employee insisted on wearing her crucifix outside her uniform. The EAT held that a ban on wearing such visible jewellery did not amount to indirect religious discrimination. Although it was not necessary for a belief to be shared by others in order for it to be a religious belief, nor was it necessary for it to be a mandatory requirement of an established religion, nevertheless there had to be evidence of group disadvantage, and the onus was on the claimant to prove that. The wearing of the crucifix was the employee's personal decision and there was no evidence of group disadvantage so as to satisfy the requirements of indirect discrimination.

Similar cases have concerned a registrar's refusal to conduct civil partnership ceremonies: *London Borough of Islington* v *Ladele* [2009] ICR 387 (not indirect religious discrimination as the requirement was a proportionate means of achieving a legitimate aim); and a social worker dismissed for proselytising his religious beliefs: *Chondol* v *Liverpool City Council* [2009] EAT/0298/08 (again, not discrimination but rather a question of general inappropriate conduct).

6.14 Protected characteristic: sex

This is, of course, one of the original areas in which discrimination was fought. This protected characteristic now appears in s. 11 of EqA 2010 and the provisions are straightforward: discrimination on the grounds of a person's sex is prohibited (sexual orientation being a separate protected characteristic). Discrimination may take any of the standard forms, the most problematic one for employers being that of indirect discrimination, as seen in cases such as *London Underground Ltd* v *Edwards* [1998] IRLR 364 (discussed at **6.5.5** above).

Under s. 11 a reference to a person who has a particular protected characteristic is a reference to a man or to a woman and a reference to persons who share a protected characteristic is a reference to persons of the same sex. There is a further point to note in s. 13(6)(b): that in a case where the claimant is a man, no account is to be taken of special treatment afforded to a woman in connexion with pregnancy or childbirth.

Cases on what is now termed 'occupational requirement' have established a number of 'exceptions' to sex discrimination claims. Thus, dramatic performances can draw on the occupational requirement aspect; where decency or privacy requires it this will provide an exemption, e.g., a changing room attendant; or if providing personal services like welfare or education; in domestic service involving close personal contact and in single-sex hospitals and prisons; if living accommodation is provided and cannot reasonably be equipped to provide separately for both sexes; and if the job involves work in a country (e.g., Saudi Arabia) where the law or custom requires one sex rather than the other. However, preferring men over women on the *assumption* that women will not have the physical strength or stamina to do the job or not be allowed to work in a particular country is discriminatory.

Where the discrimination concerns pay, this is a matter for chapter 4 of the 2010 Act (and the next chapter of this text): see ss. 70 and 71 of EqA 2010.

6.15 Protected characteristic: sexual orientation

This protected characteristic appears in s. 12 and is subject to the usual direct and indirect discrimination, harassment and victimisation rules so that less favourable treatment is prohibited on the ground of a person's sexual orientation—whether that orientation is towards the same sex, the opposite sex or both sexes. As under the previous regulations, the alleged discriminator's perception is included as an unlawful ground of discrimination. For instance, in *English* v *Thomas Sanderson Blinds Ltd* [2008] ICR 607 the claimant suffered homophobic banter (such as work colleagues calling him a 'faggot') even though he was not homosexual and his colleagues did not perceive him to be so (the cause of the 'banter' was that he had been to boarding school). The Court of Appeal held that this harassment fell within the (then relevant) regulations.

There is a limited operation of occupational requirements here, which has been of relevance to religious organisations with a conscientious objection to homosexuality.

6.16 Procedures, burden of proof and remedies

Section 120 of EqA 2010 sets out the jurisdiction of employment tribunals in this area, *viz,* cases involving discrimination in a work context, together with cases on the terms of collective agreements and rules of undertakings of employers, trade organisations and qualifications bodies. Enforcement in other fields is generally to the county court. There are certain respects in which the procedure in these tribunal cases is slightly different from others.

6.16.1 Employment tribunal procedure

The claim in the tribunal must be presented within three months of the act complained of (s. 123). Conduct in this area often extends over a period of time so s. 123 goes on to say that:

> (3) (a) conduct extending over a period is to be treated as done at the end of the period;
> (b) failure to do something is to be treated as occurring when the person in question decided on it.
>
> (4) In the absence of evidence to the contrary, a person (P) is to be taken to decide on failure to do something—
> (a) when P does an act inconsistent with doing it, or
> (b) if P does no inconsistent act, on the expiry of the period in which P might reasonably have been expected to do it.

Tribunals have a discretion to extend the three-month period if they think it 'just and equitable' to do so: s. 123(1)(b). This contrasts with extensions given under unfair dismissal rights, which are only provided where meeting the time limit was not reasonably practicable.

The EHRC is able to provide assistance to claimants in pursuing cases, especially if:

(a) the case raises a question of principle;

(b) it is unreasonable to expect the applicant to act alone;

(c) any other special consideration applies.

Applicants are also permitted, either before or after starting tribunal proceedings, to serve on the employer a questionnaire in a prescribed form, inviting the employer to comment on the applicant's version of events and asking specific questions. The employer is not obliged to reply, but any reply sent or the absence of a reply is admissible as evidence in the tribunal. An eight-week period is set for the employer to send the reply.

Those representing claimants often find the questionnaire procedure very useful in assembling evidence, especially where direct evidence of discrimination is lacking. It is possible, for example, to ask the employer to supply statistics about the proportions of people of one sex or racial group among the workforce, which can be compared with the local population, or among applicants for a job compared with those selected for interview or for appointment. Explanations can be required for particular treatment given to the client. Employers, on the other hand, often regard responding to these questionnaires as a time-consuming and unnecessary chore, and may if left on their own provide answers that are incomplete or less thoroughly researched or considered than they should be. Those representing respondents need to ensure that proper care is taken.

Conciliation officers from ACAS automatically receive copies of tribunal paperwork and attempt to reach settlements. In most ACAS regions certain conciliation officers are designated as having special responsibility for discrimination cases.

6.16.2 The burden of proof

Proving discrimination is often a problem. As we shall see shortly the courts have long been sympathetic to the difficult task faced by a complainant in such circumstances, but it has been made simpler by s. 136 of EqA 2010 (based on previous regulations), which implements the EU Burden of Proof Directive.

Section 136 requires that the claimant must prove facts from which the tribunal could conclude, in the absence of an adequate explanation, that the employer has committed an act of unlawful discrimination or harassment, and it is then for the employer to prove otherwise.

The rule (under the previous legislation) was examined in *Barton* v *Investec Henderson Crosthwaite Securities Ltd* [2003] ICR 1205 (EAT) and again in *Igen Ltd* v *Wong* [2005] EWCA Civ 142, [2005] ICR 931. There is a 13-point form/checklist but it is not essential for tribunals to go through these paragraph by paragraph; they must obtain their main guidance from the statutory language that required a two-stage approach. Although the tribunal would generally hear all the evidence at once, their decision-making process must involve the two stages separately. In essence:

(a) Has the claimant proved facts from which, in the absence of an adequate explanation, the tribunal could conclude that the respondent had committed unlawful discrimination?

(b) If the claimant satisfies (a), but not otherwise, has the respondent proved that unlawful discrimination was not committed or was not to be treated as committed?

The Court of Appeal in *Igen Ltd* v *Wong* emphasised the importance of *could* in (a); it may mean making an assumption contrary to reality. The employee is nevertheless required to produce evidence from which the tribunal *could* conclude that discrimination has occurred. This could include any evasive reply to a questionnaire and reference to a code of practice but the tribunal must establish there is *prima facie* evidence of a link between less favourable treatment and, say, the difference of sex and not merely two unrelated events: *University of Huddersfield* v *Wolff* [2004] IRLR 534. In *Laing* v *Manchester City Council* [2006] ICR 1519, for example, a manager treated everyone ineptly, and the EAT approved the finding of the employment tribunal that there had been no racial discrimination.

Employers should prove on the balance of probabilities that the unfavourable treatment was *in no sense* on the ground of sex or race, etc. In *EB* v *BA* [2006] EWCA Civ 132, [2006] IRLR 471 the Court of Appeal criticised the employment tribunal for not having required enough of the employer. In effect, the tribunal had looked to the claimant, a male-to-female transsexual who had been selected for redundancy because her billing level was low, to disprove merely plausible explanations by the employer, and this had denied her a fair trial.

Statistical evidence can be a very effective way of satisfying the first requirement: *West Midlands PTE* v *Singh* [1988] IRLR 186. If the case is about promotion, for example, evidence of a substantially different racial balance (or balance of the sexes) between the group from which selection is made and the group of those selected will require the employer to produce a detailed innocent justification. This is why the questions procedure can be so useful. If the employer is unable to supply statistical evidence, that itself may be evidence of having failed to meet the recommendation of the code of practice concerning ethnic monitoring.

It is usually essential to have concrete evidence of less favourable treatment. Sometimes it is possible to produce a comparison with an actual person of the opposite sex or a different racial group, but in *Balamoody* v *United Kingdom Central Council for Nursing, Midwifery and Health Visiting* [2001] EWCA Civ 2097, [2002] ICR 646, the Court of Appeal accepted that it would often be impossible to do so and that a hypothetical comparator would suffice. It is essential that the employment tribunal draws its inferences from findings of primary fact and not just from evidence that is not taken to a conclusion, as the Court of Appeal emphasised in *Anya* v *University of Oxford* [2001] EWCA Civ 405, [2001] ICR 847. An employer may behave unreasonably or dismiss unfairly in circumstances that involve no unlawful discrimination.

6.16.3 Compensation to be awarded

- Compensation to be awarded in the event of a successful claim of discrimination is to be calculated by the tribunal as an amount that is just and equitable to reflect the loss suffered by the applicant and there is no statutory limit. Tribunals may make a declaration regarding the rights of the complainant (and the respondent);
- may make an order for compensation;
- may make a recommendation stating that the respondent should take specific action within a particular period. This may be aimed at the wider workforce, not just the complainant;

- in cases of indirect discrimination where there is a finding that there was no intention to discriminate, must first consider declarations and recommendations before awarding compensation.

The rules are the same as for awards of damages in the county court, and damages for injury to feelings are often awarded. There have been some large awards for injury to feelings, but the Court of Appeal has now held in *Vento* v *Chief Constable of West Yorkshire Police* [2002] EWCA Civ 1871, [2003] ICR 318 that there should be three broad bands which, after recent case law applying inflation rates are: between £18,000 and £30,000 for the most serious cases involving a lengthy campaign of discriminatory harassment; between £6,000 and £18,000 for serious cases not meriting an award in the highest band; and between £500 and £6,000 for less serious cases, such as an isolated or one-off act of discrimination. In *Laing Ltd* v *Essa* [2004] EWCA Civ 2, [2004] ICR 746 it was confirmed that the test was one of causation rather than foreseeability. Where more than one form of discrimination is established, the tribunal must examine injury to feelings under each of them, although it may not be necessary to fix separate sums where there is overlap: *Al Jumard* v *Clwyd Leisure Ltd* [2008] IRLR 345. If s. 14 of EqA 2010 is brought into effect at some date 'dual discrimination' claims will be permitted.

6.17 Trade union membership and activities

The last of the heads of unlawful discrimination we identified at the start of the chapter is that which arises from trade union membership or activities. This is on the fringe of the topics covered in this book, since it consists of individual rights related to collective employment law. The following is therefore only a very brief outline of the relevant statutory provisions, all of them taken from TULRCA 1992.

By s. 137 of the Act, it is unlawful to discriminate in making offers of employment on the basis of:

- trade union membership or non-membership; or
- willingness to become a trade union member.

By s. 144, it is unlawful to take any action short of dismissal against an individual employee for the purpose of:

- stopping the employee from being a trade union member;
- stopping the employee from taking part in trade union activities;
- forcing the employee to join some trade union; or
- forcing the employee to join a particular trade union.

The scope of this section is much narrower than the definition of discrimination at **6.2** above. It clearly includes the employer's intention. The action must be direct and must be for the *purpose* of deterring or forcing. Action for some other purpose that happens to affect unionists and non-unionists in a discriminatory way is not included, and neither is action taken against the union rather than against the individual.

By s. 152, any dismissal where the main reason is the employee's trade union membership, non-membership, or participation in activities is automatically unfair.

(See **Chapters 11** and **12** for a fuller explanation.) Particularly heavy penalties follow for the employer. Furthermore, it is possible for the employee apparently dismissed for such reasons to seek an order continuing the employment until a tribunal hearing can be held about the fairness of dismissal: see s. 161, 'interim relief'.

By s. 153, it is unfair to select an employee for dismissal for redundancy on the basis of trade union membership, non-membership, or activities. See **Chapter 14**.

Claims about all these matters must be presented to the employment tribunal within three months of the allegedly discriminatory act or of the dismissal. The tribunal may only prolong that period if satisfied that it was 'not reasonably practicable' for the claim to be presented in time. See **Chapter 16**.

6.18 Summary

- The concern of this chapter has been where the dispute is about *non-contractual* matters (e.g., treatment of the individual, selection processes). **Chapter 7** of this text will deal with contractual matters (e.g., pay).
- Those receiving protection under this legislation must fall within one of the 'protected characteristics': age, disability, gender reassignment, marriage and civil partnerships, pregnancy and maternity, race, religion or belief, sex, or sexual orientation.
- The different forms discrimination may take are:
  - direct discrimination, which may include 'associated discrimination' except as regards the protected characteristics of 'marriage and civil partnerships' and 'pregnancy and maternity';
  - indirect discrimination;
  - harassment; and
  - victimisation.
- With direct discrimination the key phrase is that the person with the protected characteristic must receive **less favourable treatment** than someone not having that protected characteristic. This requires a comparator to be found. The comparator may be hypothetical.
- Indirect discrimination requires a comparator group. A provision, criterion or practice that is found to be indirectly discriminatory may still be justified if it is based on a legitimate aim and the application of the provision etc. is proportionate to the aim.
- Each of the protected characteristics has its own sub-set of rules and definitions deriving from the general position.
- There are defences of general application, such as 'occupational requirement', which apply to all forms of discrimination together with additional specific ones for each protected characteristic.
- The remedies for discrimination include an unlimited amount for compensation (compared as we shall see to the 'capped' amounts available in unfair dismissal claims).

6.19 Self-test questions

1. The Department for Work and Pensions has a dress code under which all staff are required to dress 'in a professional and businesslike way'. Men are required to wear a collar and tie but women merely 'to dress appropriately and to a similar standard'. The code goes on to ban denim clothing, lycra leggings, shorts, cropped tops, trainers, and baseball caps. Matthew Thompson, an administrative assistant whose work does not bring him face-to-face with the public, objects to the rule about collar and tie and brings to the employment tribunal a claim of direct sex discrimination. What factors should decide whether he succeeds?
2. What are the key elements that define whether someone is disabled under EqA 2010?

7

Equality in employment: equal pay and atypical work

7.1 Introduction and sources

The topic of 'equal pay' first saw legislative daylight in the Equal Pay Act 1970. Those provisions have now been replaced by Part 5, **Chapter 3** ('Equality of Terms') of the Equality Act 2010 (EqA 2010).

This chapter covers two areas which are related to the issues discussed in **Chapter 6** but which have a different slant from the normal 'discrimination' angle. As we noted at the start of **Chapter 6**, s.70, EqA 2010 effectively divides the concept of 'discrimination' (as explained in s. 39) into two separate categories. When the dispute is about *non-contractual* matters (e.g., treatment of the individual, selection processes), that is the concern of the rules laid out in **Chapter 6** of this text and Part 2 of the EqA 2010. When the dispute is about *contractual* matters relating to equality, that is the concern of this chapter, together with **Chapter 3**, and Part 5 of the EqA 2010.

Part 5 EqA 2010 deals with equality between the sexes as regards contractual rights and it establishes the principle that women and men should receive the same pay and other contractual terms for doing the same job. Part 5 EqA 2010 is not concerned with general anti-discrimination provisions or 'protected characteristics' (e.g., based on race, age or disability): it is about inequality between the sexes. It is possible to bring a claim for both sex discrimination and breach of the equality duties in the right circumstances.

At the end of this chapter we shall examine 'atypical' work. Attempts to provide part-time and fixed-term workers with equal rights to full-time employees did not occupy legislative attention until relatively recently and grew out of EU Directives and ECJ case law. Part-time workers now receive protection under the Part-Time Workers (Prevention of Less Favourable Treatment) Regs 2000 (SI 2000/1551); fixed-term workers are covered by the Fixed-Term Employees (Prevention of Less Favourable Treatment) Regs 2002 (SI 2002/2034).

7.2 The principle of equal pay

The principle of equal pay for men and women is contained in art. 141 of the Treaty of Rome, the treaty which established the (then) European Economic Community. It is directly enforceable in the courts of the UK. Section 64, EqA 2010 gives effect in the UK to the principle that women should receive the same terms as men (and vice versa) for work which is equal to the work of the comparator of the opposite sex. For simplicity we will generally refer here to a woman's right to comparison with a man (since this is the basis of most inequality and litigation) but the principle applies both ways.

Under s. 66 of EqA 2010, every employee's contract of employment is deemed to include an equality clause, unless one already exists, and s. 66(2) explains that a sex equality clause has the effect that if a woman's employment terms are less favourable to a comparative male the woman's terms are modified so as not to be less favourable; and if the woman does not have a term which corresponds to a term of the man that benefits that man, the woman's terms are modified so as to include such a term.

A similar provision (referred to as a sex equality rule) is implied into the terms of pensions schemes.

7.2.1 General remarks about equality clauses

As art. 141 EC Treaty has direct effect an individual can bring a claim under it, or under EqA 2010 or both. The mechanism by which equal pay is achieved in the UK is *contractual*. So, once the existence of an equality clause is established it can be enforced like any other contractual term. The parties may not contract out of these rules.

The scope of s.66 includes *all* contractual terms and not only pay or remuneration. The only significant exception is that preventing men from claiming any statutory restriction on the employment of women or any benefit related to pregnancy or childbirth.

Lack of pay equality may well be generated by overt or inherited discrimination, and comparisons can only be drawn between men and women (as we have said, no other protected characteristics come under this heading) but the topic of equal pay is quite distinct from sex discrimination. It is about matching jobs and the pay and conditions that goes with them and, unlike sex discrimination, there must be a real (not hypothetical) comparator.

Indeed, s.70, EqA 2010 makes it explicit that sex discrimination provisions have no effect in relation to a term of the woman's contract that is modified by, or included by virtue of, a sex equality clause or rule, or would be so modified or included but for the presence of a 'material factor' defence—see below. Further, neither the inclusion of a less favourable term nor the failure to have an equality term will be counted as sex discrimination.

The exception to this is where an equality clause cannot be deemed to operate because, say, there is no comparator. Here, s. 71 allows claims to be brought where a person can show evidence of direct sex discrimination. As we commented in **Chapter 6**, evidence of direct discrimination is not easy to find and the example given in the explanatory notes has probably not been heard in industry for 30 years, *viz*, an employer tells a female employee, 'I would pay you more if you were a man'.

7.2.2 Which terms?

The equality clause operates in relation to *each individual term* of the woman's contract. It is therefore no defence for the employer to argue that, taken overall, the woman is treated as favourably as the man, and that a benefit in one term must be offset against a detriment in another: *Hayward* v *Cammell Laird* [1988] ICR 464. By contrast, in *Degnan* v *Redcar and Cleveland Borough Council* [2005] EWCA Civ 726, [2005] IRLR 615, the Court of Appeal refused to interpret the *Hayward* principle as allowing a woman to make a string of comparisons, selecting different male comparators for different elements of the remuneration package, and thereby claiming a total hourly monetary rate higher than any single male comparator. Further, the right does not incorporate a proportioning device: if a job evaluation revealed that the woman's work was 75 per cent of the value of the man's this does not mean she is entitled to be paid 75 per cent of the man's pay.

7.3 What types of work are covered?

Section 64, EqA 2010 establishes the types of work to which the Act applies. It states that the key 'equal pay' sections of the Act (ss. 66–70) apply where:

- a person (A) is employed on work that is equal to the work that a comparator of the opposite sex (B) does; and that
- references to the work that B does are not restricted to work done contemporaneously with the work done by A.

This leaves hanging the question of what is 'equal work' and we shall examine that shortly. However, the second bullet point should be noted here as this permits comparisons to be made with a woman's predecessor in the post. The employer, for instance, might have decided to save money by offering the post at a lower rate than was paid to the previous (male) holder. This may have nothing to do with sex discrimination. However, if a woman is new to the post she can use that old rate of pay as the basis for a claim.

7.3.1 Equal work

This is dealt with in s. 65. There are three forms of determining 'equal work'. A's work is said to be equal to B's if it is—

(a) like B's work;
(b) rated as equivalent to B's work; or
(c) of equal value to B's work.

We shall follow the statutory pattern in explaining what these terms mean.

7.3.2 Equal pay for like work

'Like work' is defined in s. 65(2) and (3):

(a) A's work and B's work are the same or broadly similar, and
(b) such differences as there are between their work are not of practical importance in relation to the terms of their work.

(3) So on a comparison of one person's work with another's for the purposes of subsection (2), it is necessary to have regard to—
(a) the frequency with which differences between their work occur in practice, and
(b) the nature and extent of the differences.

Thus the consideration whether the man and the woman are doing like work is a practical one, with the emphasis on what is actually done rather than what the contract might in theory require.

7.3.3 Equal pay for work rated as equivalent

This is covered in s. 65(3)–(5). Subsection (3) states:

> A's work is rated as equivalent to B's work if a job evaluation study:
>
> (a) gives an equal value to A's job and B's job in terms of the demands made on a worker, or
> (b) would give an equal value to A's job and B's job in those terms were the evaluation not made on a sex-specific system.

The term 'sex-specific' is explained in sub-s. (5) as being a system that 'if, for the purposes of one or more of the demands made on a worker, it sets values for men different from those it sets for women'.

So, the job evaluation should involve an *analytical process* and not merely be a comparison of the whole job. Some job evaluation schemes used in business (e.g., approaches such as 'paired comparisons'—which consists of evaluating the job as a whole with each other job in turn and awarding comparative points according to overall importance) have previously been held not to satisfy the statutory definition: *Bromley* v *Quick* [1988] IRLR 249. Taking a purposive approach under the EU Directive (now 2006/54/EC) in *Redcar and Cleveland Borough Council* v *Bainbridge* [2007] EWCA Civ 929, [2008] ICR 238, the Court of Appeal held that 'rated as equivalent' must include male jobs rated *lower* than the woman's if the woman was paid less than those comparators. Ideally, jobs should be broken down into components (known as factors) and clear scores for each component should then be awarded to produce a final overall mark. It should be as objective and measurable an approach as is possible.

The scheme itself must be *non-discriminatory*. For example, there must not be excessive emphasis on the physical strength required.

7.3.4 Equal pay for work of equal value

The third possible comparison a woman can introduce is with a man who is not doing the same work and whose work has not been rated as equivalent, but who is claimed to be doing work of equal value. The fact that she is in a job where there are men doing the same job or work rated as equivalent does not prevent her from finding another man elsewhere in the company with whom to make this different comparison: *Pickstone* v *Freemans* [1988] ICR 697. However, if, say, there are four women doing a job alongside 30 men doing the same job and they are all paid less than the alleged comparator the argument for equality is somewhat diminished.

Section 65(6) states that A's work is of equal value to B's work if it is—

> (a) neither like B's work nor rated as equivalent to B's work, but
> (b) nevertheless equal to B's work in terms of the demands made on A by reference to factors such as effort, skill and decision-making.

EXAMPLE

In an engineering factory, the factory nurse claims she is doing work of equal value to that of the foreman (a male) in a production department. Who can say whether she is right or not? Their two jobs have almost nothing in common. The outstanding features of his (much physical effort, uncongenial working conditions, long experience on the shop floor, extensive supervisory responsibility) are factors that have to be set against hers (good manual dexterity, care for others). Depending on the weight given to any of those factors it seems very difficult to produce any desired result from an evaluation. Nevertheless, when the issue of equal value is referred to a tribunal, the tribunal (adopting a procedure we shall consider shortly) is obliged to answer the question whether the jobs were indeed of equal value. The answer has to be 'yes' or 'no': there is no 'not proven' option on the grounds that the question was too difficult or that the jobs were too different to compare properly. On these facts, once an investigation has started to look at issues such as effort, skill and decision-making, and the training and qualifications required to do the two jobs, it is very likely the nurse's job would be found of at least equal value to the foreman's.

Section 131, EqA 2010 sets out the method by which an employment tribunal may assess 'work of equal value'. This may involve appointing an independent expert (as designated by ACAS) to prepare a report. However, if a job evaluation study has already been conducted a tribunal must follow this unless it has good reason to suspect that the evaluation is discriminatory or unreliable. A tribunal does not have to appoint an expert: it may choose to determine the question of equal value itself.

7.3.5 Pay secrecy clauses

New to the topic of equal pay are the provisions of s. 77 of EqA 2010, which outlaw **some** 'gagging clauses' on pay. Until now it was quite common to find terms in a contract that sought to prevent employees discussing or revealing their level of pay, both within and without the organisation. Such clauses may have helped preserve confidentiality in its widest sense, but they also prevented women from assessing how their pay equated or did not equate with fellow employees.

Gagging clauses as between colleagues, which seek to prevent discussions on pay in order to establish the presence of inequality or discrimination, are now unenforceable. A disclosure by a colleague (or former colleague) may now be made or received if done so for the purpose of finding out whether there is a connexion between pay and a person having (or not having) a particular protected characteristic. This provision does not, however, allow discussion of salary to people outside the company, such as competitors, and general 'gagging clauses' are still enforceable (so, a discussion, say, between two men as to their levels of pay that might reveal different treatment could still be the subject of a gag).

The provision or receipt of the information is also deemed a protected act for the purposes of victimisation within s. 27, EqA 2010 (see **Chapter 6**).

7.4 How are comparators found?

This is dealt with in s. 79. Comparators may come from a range of sources:

- The obvious one is another person doing the same job who is paid more. We have seen in **7.3** above that *predecessors* may be used for comparison purposes: what of successors? *Walton Centre for Neurology and Neurosurgery NHS Trust* v *Bewley* [2008] ICR 1047 held that a woman cannot compare herself with her *successor* in the job because, often, the employer has to pay more to recruit a new employee than was paid to a predecessor, irrespective of the sex of the two people, and because a hypothetical comparator was not available to claimants under the law at the time. However, now that it is possible in some circumstances to make use of the hypothetical comparator (see below) that point is at least moot.
- The comparator may be someone who is employed by the complainant's employer or by an associate of that employer, provided the complainant and the

comparator *work at the same establishment*: s. 79(3). It is not a purely geographical test. So, a local authority or large corporation may well have a number of different sites but may still constitute one 'establishment' for these purposes. Employers are associated if (a) one is a company of which the other (directly or indirectly) has control, or (b) both are companies of which a third person (directly or indirectly) has control.

- Further, if the comparator does not work at the same establishment he may still be used provided common terms apply at the establishments (either generally or as between the complainant and the comparator employees): s. 79(4). 'Common terms' does not only mean identical or the same, but also sufficiently similar for a fair comparison to be made—*British Coal Corporation* v *Smith* [1996] ICR 515, HL (canteen workers and cleaners held to be in the 'same employment' as their male comparators in different establishments employed as surface mineworkers). The rule has been held to be broad enough to permit a comparison between two Scottish local authorities, although they acted independently of each other, in *South Ayrshire Council* v *Morton* [2002] ICR 956, Court of Session. However, it did not extend to two government departments when pay was determined departmentally, and central pay bargaining had been abandoned in *Robertson* v *Department for Environment, Food and Rural Affairs* [2005] EWCA Civ 138, [2005] ICR 750.

Although there is no such 'same employer' requirement under art. 141 the case law has established that there must still be some form of 'single source' generating the terms and conditions. A claimant who meets the requirements of s. 79 does not also have to meet those of art. 141.

7.4.1 Hypothetical comparators

We have already noted, but it is worth repeating, that it has long been the position that equal pay claims could not make use of a 'hypothetical comparator'. The EqA 2010, however, has brought about **limited** change here. Section 71 states that:

> (1) This section applies in relation to a term of a person's work—
> (a) that relates to pay, but
> (b) in relation to which a sex equality clause or rule has no effect.
>
> (2) The relevant sex discrimination provision (as defined by section 70) has no effect in relation to the term except in so far as treatment of the person amounts to a contravention of the provision by virtue of section 13 or 14.

This is slightly convoluted. Section 71 states that in some cases a claim about contractual terms may be treated as a pure discrimination claim and thus allow for the use of a hypothetical comparator. Say a woman has no comparator to base a case on but has evidence that the employer is discriminating against her, e.g., she discovers documents that demonstrate that he 'got her cheaply'—that if he had had to employ a man he would have had to pay more, The real or deemed equality clause is of no effect because of the lack of a comparator but if the treatment of the employee amounts to direct discrimination the employee may bring a claim under those headings (i.e., sidestepping s. 70 even though the complaint relates to a contractual term) and this means the employee can now make use of a hypothetical comparator.

7.5 Maternity equality clauses

Section 74, EqA 2010 deals with the position of equal pay while a woman is on maternity leave. The first issue concerns the calculation of the maternity pay itself and this provision makes it clear that the 'maternity equality clause' must reflect the pay and bonuses she would have received had she not been on maternity leave (i.e., any increases). The clause also ensures that a woman's pay on her return to work following maternity leave must take account of any pay increase that she would have received if she had not been on statutory maternity leave.

In keeping with the pattern of the Act, under s. 76 the pregnancy and maternity discrimination provisions of the Act do not apply where a maternity clause or rule operates. However (again), where there is discrimination concerning non-contractual matters relating to maternity then the rules concerning sex discrimination are triggered (e.g., the non-promotion of a pregnant woman).

7.6 Defences to equal pay claims

Once it has been established that a woman doing like work, work rated as equivalent or work of equal value to a man is being paid or treated less favourably, then it is presumed that this is because of the difference of sex. The employer may be able to rebut this by showing that the disparity cited is really down to 'material factors' (what used to be called 'genuine material factors' under the old legislation—the word 'genuine' now being seen as redundant) which are relevant and significant and which do not themselves directly or indirectly discriminate against the worker because of her sex (s. 69). If the disparity reveals indirect discrimination the employer must show that it is a proportionate means of meeting a legitimate aim. Based on pre-2010 case law, this means that if the material factor is 'tainted by sex' (as the House of Lords termed it) the employer will have to go further and establish that these actions were objectively justified. One recent pre-2010 example is *Blackburn* v *Chief Constable of West Midlands Police* [2009] EWCA Civ 1208, [2009] IRLR 135 where a night-shift scheme (which excused officers, including the claimants, who had childcare responsibilities or medical problems) was found to be indirectly discriminatory but objectively justified: the objective of the scheme was to reward those who worked nights and to pay those who did not work nights the same as those who did rather defeated the whole purpose. The fact that other forces adopted different schemes was not taken as relevant.

The long-term objective of reducing pay inequality will always count as a legitimate aim: s. 69(3). For instance, following a re-organisation some (male) employees have their pay protected for a short time as their original pay was above the level now ascribed to that job. Provided the employer can show that this is a legitimate means of removing pay inequalities, this will be a defence.

7.6.1 What is a material factor?

The factor in question must be 'material' and this means 'significant and relevant', incorporating a range of personal and extrinsic circumstances that justify why one person should be paid more than another even though they are 'doing the same job'. The distinctions drawn may cause a great sense of injustice but may be a material factor for equal pay purposes. The best way to think of this is: if two *men* were paid differently for doing what is apparently the same job there would be no equal pay problem but there would still be an industrial relations need to demonstrate why this is so. A material factor does not necessarily have to make good sense: it only has to be the cause of the difference and not be tainted by sex. Some headings illustrate the range of possibilities for a material factor, the success of which depends very much on the facts:

- *Market factors such as skills shortages or those which may reflect a market situation.* Organisations will sometimes offer better pay to people joining them than is offered to existing same-grade employees in order to 'recruit at market level'. Although the ECJ expressed doubt in *Enderby* v *Frenchay Health Authority* [1994] ICR 112 as to whether market forces constituted a sufficient material factor under art. 141 of the Treaty of Rome to justify a difference in pay between speech therapists and pharmacists, in *Rainey* v *Greater Glasgow Health Board* [1987] ICR 129 the House of Lords held that market forces could indeed be a material factor. However, market forces will not be a sufficient material factor if in truth they represent discrimination on historical grounds of sex. And given that an employee may now use a predecessor as a comparator the employer's use of this defence would be very limited unless it could be demonstrated that the new job differed significantly in some way from the old. 'Market forces' arguments may well have had their day, though whether 'recession-driven' arguments may successfully take their place is arguable.
- *Geographical variations.* Rates of pay vary across the country according to variations in the cost of living so an employee in Sunderland may be paid less than his or her equivalent in the same company but based in London.
- *Performance-related pay, productivity bonuses, and shift-work compensation rates.* The key issue which can undo these potentially valid material factors tends to be historical discriminatory practices that are often found embedded in these schemes.
- *Experience and length of service.* Many employers operate pay structures that add pay increments depending on service. It is seen as a good reward for loyalty, but as more women than men tend to take career breaks it is capable of discriminatory results. In *Cadman* v *Health & Safety Executive* (Case C-17/05) [2006] ICR 1623, the ECJ held that employers do not have to provide special justification for basing pay on length of service unless the worker produces evidence raising 'serious doubts' about its inappropriateness in the particular circumstances. Service, they decided, goes hand-in-hand with experience and rewarding experience is generally a legitimate aim of pay policy. In *Wilson* v *Health and Safety Executive* [2009] IRLR 282 the EAT, whilst stating their support for the ECJ's analysis, nevertheless required the employer to demonstrate justification in relation to a service-related provision and issued guidelines for tribunals for assessing the issue of 'serious doubts' (a high hurdle to clear for the claimant), including hearing this as a preliminary point.
- *Pay protection schemes* such as 'red circling' where an employee is demoted as a result of a re-organisation but they are kept on their previous level of pay for some (usually defined) time. If this is just a method of perpetuating past discrimination then no material factor exists. Even where this is not the case, pay protection schemes will work only in the short term; they cannot be used to perpetuate historical pay differentials.

7.7 Remedies in relation to equal pay

7.7.1 Jurisdiction and time limits

An employee or former employee may present a claim to the employment tribunal that the equality clause in the contract of employment is being contravened. The claim may be for breach of an equality clause or rule or to apply for a declaration as to meaning. In what is termed a 'standard' case the claim must be brought within six months of appointment or the end of the employment contract (s. 129). 'Standard' refers to the ordinary indefinite type of contract. Where the case is not a 'standard' one, the following time limits apply:

- With a 'stable work case' (but not if it is also a concealment or incapacity case (or both)): the period of six months beginning with the day on which the stable working relationship ended. A 'stable work case' is where there is a series of fixed-term or short-term contracts with breaks. Under the previous legislation on the same wording, it was held in *Slack* v *Cumbria County Council* [2009] EWCA Civ 293, [2009] IRLR 463 that where the employer had in the past terminated the old contract and issued a new one (with a clear expression that the later one superseded the older) time began to run from that termination and so fixed the point of backdating.
- A 'concealment case' (but not if it is also an incapacity case): the period of six months beginning with the day on which the worker discovered (or could with reasonable diligence have discovered) the qualifying fact. This arises where the employer deliberately conceals information from the employee.
- An incapacity case (but not if it is also a concealment case): the period of six months beginning with the day on which the worker ceased to have the incapacity. 'Incapacity' here means a person aged below 18 or one whose mental capacity is impaired.
- A case which is a concealment case and an incapacity case: the period of six months beginning with the later of the days on which the period would begin if the case were merely a concealment or incapacity case.

One danger employees face in all these cases is in knowing the date from which time runs. For instance, where there is a major change in terms and conditions, sufficient to amount to the issuing of a new contract then, strictly, time has begun to run from that change date. However, the Court of Appeal has shown some imagination and sympathy here (in *North Cumbria University Hospitals NHS Trust* v *Fox* [2010] EWCA Civ 729, [2010] IRLR 756) by holding that where there is a stable employment relationship (i.e., no actual break in the employment relationship or change in the nature of the work) the technical contractual change does not affect time to bring a claim.

7.7.2 Arrears due

Arrears of pay are limited to six years. However, retrospective claims for longer periods are permitted if the employer has concealed necessary information for the claim to be brought (s. 132(4)). Retrospective claims about pension schemes' membership can go back to 8 April 1976 (the date of a key ECJ judgment in this field: *Defrenne* v *Sabena* (Case 43/75) [1976] ICR 547); and complaints regarding the accrual of rights within the scheme can go back to 17 May 1990 (the date of another ECJ judgment, *Barber v Guardian Royal Exchange Assurance Group* (C 262/88) [1991] 1 QB 344, [1990] ECR I-1889).

7.7.3 Burden of proof

As with discrimination cases seen in **Chapter 6**, a reverse burden of proof operates here. So, once the claimant has established the case at a basic level the tribunal must hold that there is a contravention unless the employer can establish otherwise (s. 136).

7.7.4 Obtaining information

One major barrier any potential complainant faces is that of obtaining the information on which to base their case. We noted above the removal of 'gagging clauses' in certain instances. Section 138 adds to this in procedural terms, permitting the aggrieved party to ask questions, either posed directly to the employer or on a form. The questions and the answers are admissible as evidence in a case brought under the Act (whether or not they are contained in the prescribed form). The court or tribunal may also draw inferences from a failure by the respondent to answer the questions posed within eight weeks or from evasive or equivocal answers.

However, in certain specified circumstances the court or tribunal cannot draw such inferences e.g., where it is reasonable for the respondent to say that to answer differently would have prejudiced criminal proceedings or revealed the reason for criminal proceedings being withdrawn or not being brought (s. 138(5)).

7.7.5 Transfers between tribunals and courts

Section 140 enables courts and tribunals to transfer cases (in either direction) where appropriate to the actions involved.

7.7.6 Applications by employers

There is a little used provision, carried forward from the old law, and now set out in s. 127(3) of EqA 2010, that enables an employer to seek clarification from the tribunal of the meaning of an equality clause where a dispute arises in relation to the effect of that clause: this is a rare example of the opportunity for an employer to initiate tribunal proceedings.

7.8 Part-time workers

The Part-time Workers Regulations (PTW Regs 2000) provide a statutory basis of protection. The regulations bought into force the Part-time Workers Directive (97/81/EC). Part-time workers have the right under PTW Regs 2000 not to be treated less favourably than their employer treats a comparable full-time worker. There thus needs to be a comparison with a full-time worker, defined generally as one who is employed by the same employer under the same type of contract, engaged in the same or broadly similar work and working or based at the same establishment as the part-time worker. This cannot involve a hypothetical comparator.

In this case, conditions of employment have to be applied *pro rata*. There are circumstances, however, where the *pro rata* principle laid down by reg. 5(3) is not straightforward. In *McMenemy* v *Capita Business Services Ltd* [2007] CSIH 25, [2007] IRLR 400, a part-time employee who worked on Wednesdays, Thursdays, and Fridays claimed that he was disadvantaged because more bank holidays fall on Mondays than on any other day. The Court of Session held that he had indeed suffered a disadvantage, but that it flowed from the fact that he did not work on Mondays, not from his part-time status, as a full-time employee who worked from Tuesday to Saturday would have been treated similarly. This basis of finding that there had been no unlawful discrimination is of course specific to the facts, as in many employments it would be impossible to find such full-time comparators. Many employers in fact approach such issues on the 'gain-on-the-swings, lose-on-the-roundabouts' principle of overall fairness and the decision does not consider whether that is acceptable. In *Sharma* v *Manchester City Council* [2008] ICR 623 (and again in *Carl* v *University of Sheffield* [2009] UKEAT/261/08 (also considering the Scottish equivalent case which disagreed with *Sharma*)), the EAT accepted that the employment tribunal had only to be satisfied that part-time status was the 'real reason' for less favourable treatment for a claimant to succeed; there was no requirement for the claimant to prove that it was the *sole* reason, despite the wording of the Directive.

Workers can complain to an employment tribunal if the employer treats them less favourably, or dismisses them or subjects them to a detriment for a reason related to the exercise of rights under the regulations. There is a defence available to the employer if the unfavourable treatment can be justified on objective grounds. Compensation can be awarded but does not include injury to feelings. Workers are entitled to a written statement of reasons for less favourable treatment.

The initial surge of complaints to the employment tribunals in 2001 after the Regulations came into force (most of them about the pensions rights of part-timers) has not been maintained since and while ERA 1999, s. 20 made provision for the issue of codes of practice about part-time work, none has yet been produced.

7.9 Fixed-term workers

The Fixed-Term Regs 2002 are also the result of a European Directive, in this case the Fixed Term Work Directive 99/70/EC, and follow a very similar pattern to PTW Regs 2000. It is unlawful to treat a fixed-term employee less favourably than a comparable permanent employee. The *pro rata* principle applies again. Less favourable treatment may be justified objectively and there is express provision that it may be justified for one condition of employment to be less favourable, if, taken overall, conditions of the fixed-term worker are as good as those of the permanent person—reg. 4. Fixed-term workers are entitled to a written statement of the reasons why they are less favourably treated, and they also have the right to be informed by the employer of available permanent vacancies.

When the employer failed to renew a fixed-term contract in *Department of Work and Pensions* v *Webley* [2004] EWCA Civ 1745, [2005] ICR 577, that omission was held not to be less favourable treatment within the meaning of these regulations.

The fact that a fixed-term contract contains a provision allowing it to be terminated earlier by notice does not deny the worker the protection of the regulations: *Allen* v *National Australia Group Europe Ltd* [2004] IRLR 847.

People who have been employed for four years or more under successive fixed-term contracts have the right under reg. 8 to be treated as permanent employees unless the employer can justify objectively the continued use of fixed-term contracts.

7.10 Summary

- The major part of this chapter concerns disputes about *contractual* matters relating to equality. Non-contractual matters relating to equality, such as sex discrimination, are treated differently and were the concern of **Chapter 6**.
- Part 5, EqA 2010 deals with equality between the sexes and it establishes the principle that women and men should receive the same pay and other contractual terms for doing the same job.
- Under s. 66 of EqA 2010, every employee's contract of employment is deemed to include an equality clause, unless one already exists, and contracts may be deemed modified accordingly to deal with this.
- Terms must be treated as discrete items. There is no argument available to employers that the man and woman's contract demonstrates 'overall equality'.
- There are three forms of determining 'equal work'. A's work is said to be equal to B's if it is: (a) like B's work, (b) rated as equivalent to B's work, or (c) of equal value to B's work.
- This means that A must find a comparator of the opposite sex. In nearly all cases this must be a real, not hypothetical, comparator.
- The employer may defend an 'equal pay' action by showing that there are 'material factors' that are relevant and significant **and** that do not themselves directly or indirectly discriminate against the worker because of her sex.
- Claims must generally be brought within six months of appointment or termination
- As with discrimination cases seen in **Chapter 6**, a reverse burden of proof operates.
- Arrears of pay are limited to six years. Pensions-based claims may extend further back.
- The Part-time Workers Regulations provide a statutory basis of protection for such workers. Part-time workers have the right not to be treated less favourably than their employer treats a comparable full-time worker.
- The Fixed-Term Regs 2002 follow a very similar pattern to PTW Regs 2000. It is unlawful to treat a fixed-term employee less favourably than a comparable permanent employee. Less favourable treatment may be justified objectively, e.g., for one condition of employment to be less favourable, if, taken overall, conditions of the fixed-term worker are as good as those of the permanent person.

8 Protecting business secrets

8.1 Introduction

8.1.1 Scope of Chapters 8 and 9

The next two chapters deal with the complex topics of confidentiality and restraint of trade. Questions of protecting *confidential information* can arise both during the employment relationship and afterwards; the *restraint of trade doctrine* applies only to ex-employees. The remedy for an alleged breach (of either type of duty) is by way of a claim for damages in the ordinary courts, usually accompanied by an application for injunctive relief. Employment tribunals have no jurisdiction over confidentiality or restraint matters.

For reasons of space, neither **Chapter 8** nor **9** will deal with intellectual property rights such as patents, copyright, trademarks, or design rights, though all these areas may be relevant to higher-ranking employees and researchers.

8.1.2 Introductory comments on confidentiality

This chapter deals with the protection of information. Every business, from the small backstreet engineering company to the large multinational, will generate business secrets of some nature. These may take the simple form of customer lists, discount concessions, or manufacturing know-how. Equally, the information may take the form of formulae, inventions, secret recipes, or technical data and drawings. All these items are at least *capable* of attracting the protection of the law. The size and importance of the company is not the determining feature; nor will the perceived value of the information be conclusive of any classification of secrecy. The problems of protecting confidential information are quite real. Recent research has shown that over 65 per cent of professionals have admitted to having stolen commercially sensitive information, and departing employees often take with them e-mail lists, customer lists, and technical specifications. Computer misuse is a particular problem.

Anyone claiming that another has breached their confidence must show three things:

(a) the law would class the information as possessing the necessary quality of confidence about it; and

(b) the information was imparted in circumstances which conveyed an obligation of confidence; and

(c) there was unauthorised use of that information.

The information does not have to be contained in a document but it must have an identifiable source.

8.2 How will a duty of confidentiality arise?

Mere receipt of information is not enough to generate a duty of confidentiality. The recipient of the information must accept or realise that the information is to be treated as confidential before any duty will be imputed to him or her. This is tested objectively. Employees will acquire a duty of confidentiality by way of express or implied terms. Third parties (e.g., the companies that employees move to) may also be caught by the duty of confidentiality.

8.2.1 Express terms of the contract

Employers use two key express terms to protect confidential information: *confidentiality clauses* and *restraint of trade clauses. A* confidentiality clause only seeks to prevent the use or disclosure of information. Here is a fairly standard draft:

> 'The employee shall not either during his appointment or at any time for two years after its termination: disclose to any person(s) (except those authorised by the Company to know or as otherwise authorised by law); use for his own purposes or for any purposes other than those of the Company any information of a confidential or secret nature which may be made known to the employee by the Company or any customer or supplier of the Company or which may be learned by the employee during his employment, including, in particular, information which relates to: (a) research and development; (b) technical programmes, technical data, and operations; (c) manufacturing formulae, processes, and techniques; (d) customers' details and specific requirements. Saving that, in all cases, this list of confidential items is not to be treated as closed or exhaustive of the employee's duties.'

We will deal with restraint clauses in **Chapter 9**. These clauses seek to close off the opportunities available to an employee to disclose information by prohibiting the employee working (in some capacity) for another employer. For the moment, here is an example:

> '*Non-Dealing with Clients:* For a period of 12 months after termination of the Employment, the Employee shall not directly or indirectly (and whether on his own account or for any other person, firm, company, or organisation) deal with any person, firm company, or organisation who or which at any time during the preceding 12 months shall have been a client customer of, or a person or company in the habit of dealing with, or any person or company who has been in negotiations with, the Company, and with whom or which the Employee has had direct dealings or personal contact as part of the Employment so as to harm the goodwill of the Company or any other Group company or so as to compete with the Company or any other Group Company.'

Employers should set out in clear terms what the responsibilities of the employee are as regards information gained in the course of employment, otherwise, as in *United Indigo Chemical Co. Ltd* v *Robinson* (1932) 49 RPC 178, an injunction to restrain a former employee from using 'secret processes' learned during employment may be refused on the grounds that access to the information was freely available within the company and the employee had never been told that what he had learned was to be regarded as confidential.

Although the law will usually imply obligations necessary for the protection of confidential information the inclusion of an express clause is recommended as an additional precaution. Certainly one would expect such clauses to appear in contracts with scientific, research, technical, and other skilled or professional employees. The advantages of the inclusion of an express term are:

(a) it makes obvious to a court the employer's 'subjective' assessment regarding the importance of confidentiality;

(b) in borderline situations it may be that a clear policy will convince a court that certain information deserves to be labelled 'confidential';

(c) such clauses serve as a warning to employees;

(d) a negative formulation of the duty (i.e., that disclosure will constitute a breach) may serve as the basis for an injunction.

8.2.2 Implied terms of the contract

The existence of a duty of confidentiality is treated as axiomatic in the employment relationship because a violation of confidence is a breach of the duty of fidelity or good faith which is an intrinsic part of every employee's contract. Indeed, the courts treat this so seriously that even the *possibility* of a breach of confidence may prevent employees being permitted to work for others in their spare time: *Hivac Ltd* v *Park Royal Scientific Instruments Ltd* [1946] Ch 169.

The implied duty is usually expressed as a *negative* responsibility, i.e., a duty not to use or disclose confidential information acquired during the course of employment (*Thomas Marshall (Exporters) Ltd* v *Guinle* [1978] ICR 905), not to make unauthorised copies of documents (*Robb* v *Green* [1895] 2 QB 315), nor deliberately to memorise documents for further use after the relationship has ended (*Johnson & Bloy* v *Wolstenholme Rink plc and Fallon* [1987] IRLR 499). The duty covers all levels of employees who come into contact with confidential information.

The duty of confidentiality owed by an employee whilst the contract subsists is now different in nature from that owed by former employees. In *Faccenda Chicken* v *Fowler* [1986] ICR 297, it was said that the only implied term which continues after the contract has ended is that the employee must still respect the employer's *trade secrets* to the same extent as when the contract subsisted; the employee is free to make use of all other information. We will return to this below in **8.6**.

8.3 What makes information confidential?

Anyone seeking an injunction to restrain the use or disclosure of confidential information will be called upon to specify the secrecy element; to give clear particulars of the information. It will not suffice for an employer merely to say that there is *some* confidential information in need of protection. In *Thomas Marshall* v *Guinle* (**8.2.2** above), Megarry V-C laid out the basic requirements:

(a) the information must not be in the public domain already;

(b) the employer must believe that the information is of a kind whereby disclosure would harm the business;

(c) those beliefs must be reasonable. For instance, what has the employer done to protect the secrecy of the information? How widely is the information disseminated within the organisation?

(d) the information must be judged in the light of the usage and practices of the particular industry or trade;

(e) the maintenance of secrecy must not offend the public interest.

8.3.1 What kind of information is capable of attracting protection?

The range is extensive. The list would include chemical formulae; customer lists; sales figures; drawings; industrial designs; fashion designs; details of an invention currently under development; information contained in computer programs; computer access codes; an e-mail contact list; discount concessions given to customers; delivery route plans; research papers; financial and other reports; and, of course, state official secrets. All of these items and more are *capable* of being classed as confidential. The information may be of a technical, commercial, or even personal nature, but it should have what has been termed a 'basic quality of inaccessibility' about it. The mere fact that other companies are willing to pay for the information in question does not, however, mean the information is confidential: *Potters-Ballotini* v *Weston-Baker* [1977] RPC 202. Equally, confidential information does not have to be *novel* to draw protection. It is the *security* of secrets that matters, not inventiveness.

Whilst the employment relationship continues, the employer can rely heavily on the duty of fidelity to ensure that secrets are protected. The grade of that information (trade secret or merely confidential) does not really matter.

8.3.2 What is expected of the employer?

Employers are well-advised not to rely on the implied terms alone but also to ensure that employees are informed as to their duty in respect of confidential information and told of any changes in company policy, or to the status or responsibility of the employee, or to changes in access to information. Employers should restrict access to confidential information and detail in writing any information which might not normally be classified as confidential in that industry but which the employer has special reason to regard as such. As regards the ability of employers to monitor employees' communications as part of a security policy, see **8.8.4** below.

8.3.3 Information in the public domain

Although information in the public domain is no longer confidential, how that product was developed may still be protectable. For instance, just because an item has been constructed from *materials* which themselves are in the public domain does not mean the *preparatory information* fails the confidentiality test, for the ingenuity in constructing the finished item may be the confidential information, not the final product *per se*. The fact that competitors or others might eventually ascertain how and why the information was used to produce an item, e.g., the basis for combining certain features, does not destroy confidentiality—at least in the meantime: see *Weir Pumps Ltd* v *CML Pumps Ltd* [1984] FSR 33.

8.3.4 The springboard doctrine

Inextricably tied in with the 'public domain' point is the 'springboard doctrine'. The doctrine was the brainchild of Roxburgh J in *Terrapin Ltd* v *Builders' Supply Co (Hayes) Ltd* [1960] RPC 128. The springboard doctrine is used by the courts in two ways:

(a) 'Theft': here an individual is making use of information which he or she has taken (effectively stolen) from the former employer, such as customer lists: *Roger Bullivant* v *Ellis* [1987] ICR 464. The basis for the claim is the breach of confidence (not merely any breach of contract) by the employee during the currency of the contract. This breach is deemed to continue to have an effect even after termination and can therefore form the basis of a claim for damages and injunctive relief. The 'springboard advantage' is that the employee has gained an unfair competitive edge by stealing the information rather than compiling it himself. The springboard doctrine has also been applied to restraint of trade cases where the employees do not 'steal' information as such but act in a way during the term of their contracts which breaches their duty of fidelity. The doctrine was applied in this way to prevent ex-employees from poaching their former employer's clients and taking staff with them to a rival business in *UBS Wealth Management (UK) Ltd* v *Vestra Wealth LLP* [2008] EWHC 1974 (QBD), [2008] IRLR 965.

(b) 'Competitive edge from insider knowledge': this arises when the information has entered the public domain but the *background knowledge* of the product or process gives the employee an advantage or headstart over those who also have access to that publicised information. Here the employee will not be allowed to take advantage of such an edge to take the appropriate short cuts in development of the product. He will have to wait until the market has been deemed to 'catch up'. This is a difficult one to apply in practice.

A key point to the 'springboard injunction' is that it can operate even if there is no express contractual clause preventing use or disclosure, particularly as regards (a) above. Thus, in *Crowson Fabrics Ltd* v *Rider* [2008] IRLR 288 the copying of the employer's 'Supplier Bible' amounted to a springboard advantage even though the contract was silent on this point. This sort of injunction can be very useful in practice because the information does not have to be of a highly confidential nature for it is the unfair advantage gained by the ex-employee that is the key feature. Consequently, information which might otherwise not be protected can be protected if the springboard doctrine applies.

8.3.5 The maintenance of secrecy must not offend the public interest

8.3.5.1 What is the public interest?

In *Gartside* v *Outram* (1857) 26 LJ Ch 113 at p. 114, Sir Wiliam Page Wood V-C declared that: 'There is no confidence as to the disclosure of iniquity'. Under the common law, therefore, an employee was not acting in breach of confidence by disclosing the employer's wrongdoings: *Lion Laboratories Ltd* v *Evans* [1984] 2 All ER 417. The case law shows that disclosure had to be made to the appropriate bodies, usually the police, regulatory and professional bodies, or even Royal Commissions (newspapers have been occasionally accepted but with criticism: *Initial Services Ltd* v *Putterill* [1968] 1 QB 396). Criminal behaviour is not a prerequisite. The defence has, however, not extended to the 'public good', e.g., disclosing the employer's suppression of the apocryphal everlasting lightbulb.

8.3.5.2 Public Interest Disclosure Act 1998

This Act affords special protection for 'whistle-blowers' in defined circumstances. The Act is convoluted at best, but its aim is to give protection to workers (not just employees, but also independent contractors and third-party contractors) who disclose specified forms of information using the procedures laid out in the Act. That protection focuses on providing rights to workers in cases of action short of dismissal being taken against them as well as dismissal itself following their disclosure of information. We will return to the dismissal aspect more fully in **Chapter 11**.

Our concern here is to note the types of information that fall within the Act and the procedures to be utilised in order to gain protection.

The information disclosed

The Public Interest Disclosure Act 1998 (PIDA 1998) created a new s. 43B to the ERA 1996. Section 43B provides that for a worker to gain protection:

(a) the disclosure in question must be a 'qualifying disclosure';

(b) the worker must have followed the correct procedure on disclosure; and

(c) the worker must have suffered a detriment or have been dismissed as a result of all this. The detriment can be at the hands of the employer, the ex-employer or even a different employer (e.g., someone who fails to appoint the person when they hear of a previous protected disclosure).

A 'qualifying disclosure' means one that, in the reasonable belief of the worker, tends to show one or more of the following (occurring anywhere in the world):

(a) a criminal offence has been committed or is likely to be so;

(b) a person (not necessarily the employer) has failed, is failing or is likely to fail to comply with any *legal obligation* to which he or she is subject. *Parkins* v *Sodexho Ltd* [2002] IRLR 109 EAT held (with some doubt) that the idea of a 'legal obligation' was not limited to statutory obligations and could encompass complaints made by the employee that the contract had been breached;

(c) a miscarriage of justice has occurred or is likely to occur;

(d) the health or safety of any individual has been, is being or is likely to be endangered;

(e) the environment has been, is being or is likely to be damaged;

(f) information tending to show any matter falling within any of the above has been, is being or is likely to be deliberately concealed.

Note that the standard is the *reasonable belief* of the worker, but the protection does not apply where the worker commits a criminal offence in making the disclosure. Equally, 'illegal' activities prior to disclosure, such as hacking into the employer's computers to show that the employer was not complying with data protection rules, are not protected: *Bolton School* v *Evans* [2006] EWCA Civ 1653, [2007] IRLR 140. This appears to limit an employee's opportunity to demonstrate the employer's questionable activity where all the information lies with the employer. However, other decisions have shown that the standard of 'reasonable belief' is not that high an obstacle. This is because reasonable belief is judged against the standards of good faith, so an employee can be mistaken but still act in good faith (what the Americans call the 'pure heart but empty head test'): see *Babula* v *Waltham Forest College* [2007] EWCA Civ 174, [2007] IRLR 347. However, where there is a predominant ulterior motive for making the disclosure this may destroy the element of good faith: *Street* v *Derbyshire Unemployed Workers Centre* [2004] EWCA Civ 964, [2005] ICR 97 (e.g., personal antagonism).

There must actually be a 'disclosure' of 'information', not just a mere general allegation or expression of opinion. Slade J gave an example in *Cavendish Munro Professional Risks Management Ltd* v *Geduld* [2010] ICR 325: if an employee stated that 'The wards have not been cleaned for the past two weeks...' that would convey information as part of an allegation; but if all that was said was 'You are not complying with health and safety requirements', that would be a mere allegation and not covered by the Act.

The procedures

The Act sets out the ways in which a disclosure may be made in order to gain protection. These are:

(a) disclosures to the worker's employer or other responsible person: s. 43C of ERA 1996;

(b) disclosures made in the course of obtaining legal advice: s. 43D;

(c) disclosures to a Minister of the Crown, under s. 43E, where the worker's employer is an individual appointed under any enactment by a Minister of the Crown;

(d) disclosures to a 'prescribed person': s. 43F. The list of prescribed persons is set out in the Public Interest Disclosure (Prescribed Persons) Order 1999 (SI 1999/1549) and includes people such as the Information Commissioner, the Civil Aviation Authority, the Environment Agency, and the Health and Safety Executive.

Additionally, where the worker cannot follow the above procedural lines of communication, disclosures which are made in good faith and without personal gain (except as provided for under an enactment) will be permitted to other people:

(a) in 'other cases' which fall within the guidelines laid out in s. 43G. Essentially these are instances where the worker reasonably believes that the employer will subject them to a detriment if they follow the procedure noted in s. 43C; or where there is no 'prescribed person' and the worker reasonably believes that evidence may be concealed or destroyed; or where disclosures have been made to the relevant people before. The reasonableness of the worker's actions are decided by reference to matters such as the seriousness of the relevant failure, whether the disclosure is made in breach of the duty of confidentiality, etc.

(b) in cases of 'exceptionally serious' breaches: s. 43H. The bypassing of the noted procedures is again allowed where the worker acts in good faith and without personal gain. In determining the reasonableness of the worker's actions, it is specifically provided that regard must be had to the identity of the person to whom the disclosure was made, i.e., as with the common law before, merely running to the press without thought is frowned upon.

Once a whistle-blowing worker has complied with the above requirements, he or she will gain protection from a dismissal related to the disclosure etc., as set out in **10.8.8.3** below. Any term in the worker's contract which purports to prevent any worker from making a protected disclosure (i.e., a gagging clause) will be void.

8.4 The duty owed by employees

As we have seen, the identification of the employee's duties is a fairly straightforward exercise: an employee will be forbidden from competing with the employer during the currency of the contract if harm is likely to be occasioned. So, how is the employee's duty formulated? We shall explore the following:

(a) What level of information is protected?

(b) The role of honesty.

(c) The positive duty to disclose details about oneself and others.

8.4.1 What level of information is protected?

Can trivia be the subject of a duty of confidentiality? One would think not; though defining trivia might prove difficult. So the fact that the company chairman has a cat called Henry is hardly deserving of protection. However, information need not be complex in order to attract protection. As was noted in *Coco* v *Clark (A. N.) (Engineers) Ltd* [1969] RPC 41, the simpler the idea the more likely it is to require protection. In the same case, however, Megarry J also noted that 'equity ought not to be invoked to protect trivial tittle-tattle, however confidential'.

However, in different contexts information may be trivial or important. What biscuits the chairman has with his tea strikes a chord of irrelevancy, unless the information reveals that the company produces biscuits and these are either 'test' biscuits or biscuits from another manufacturer. And when pieces of information are put together the sum might be greatly more significant than the parts—the individual pieces of the jigsaw might now reveal a discernible picture. The safest presumption to make, therefore, is that during the currency of the contract any doubt is likely to be decided in favour of the employer, certainly if that information is passed to a competitor.

8.4.2 The role of honesty

An employee is expected to act with honesty. With regard to confidentiality the most obvious example of this is that the employee will not be permitted to copy or memorise confidential documents for use after the contract ends (see 'springboard doctrine' at **8.3.4** above). Companies often include such a term demanding 'delivery up' of such items as books, records, computer software, memoranda, lists, and other documents relating to the business of the company on termination of the contract.

Thus, copying and deliberately memorising lists (see *Roger Bullivant* v *Ellis* at **8.3.4**) have been held to be actions which restrict the employee's use of that information. The same with copying an e-mail list of contacts: *Pennwell Publishing (UK) Ltd* v *Ornstein* [2007] IRLR 700. And in the area of unfair dismissal the EAT has held accessing computer files using another employee's identity code and password can amount to gross misconduct: *Denco Ltd* v *Joinson* [1991] ICR 172.

8.4.3 The extent to which the duty requires positive action by the employee

As well as the duty *not to disclose* confidential information, an employee (at least a senior employee) also owes a positive duty to surrender information relevant to the relationship, e.g., where an employee detects patterns in the market which might have an adverse or beneficial effect on the employer's business: see *Sanders* v *Parry* [1967] 1 WLR 753, *Industrial Development Consultants* v *Cooley* [1972] 1 WLR 443, and *General Nutritions Ltd* v *Yates, The Times,* 5 June 1981. In *MacMillan Inc.* v *Bishopsgate Investment Trust plc* [1993] 1 WLR 1372, however, the Court of Appeal limited this general duty to information obtained *in the course of employment.*

There is no common pattern of practice in this area. Some precedents do indeed include an express duty to surrender information gained in the course of employment, including disclosure of any soliciting from competitors. Managers are often subject to a term to disclose to their seniors adverse developments in the market, e.g., that a supplier is known to be in trouble, and failure to do so can amount to gross misconduct (see *Dunn* v *AAH Ltd* [2010] EWCA Civ 183, [2010] IRLR 709). However, most contracts (if dealing with positive duties at all) focus on a term requiring the employee to do all that is reasonable to *prevent* disclosures. This clause is, again, aimed mainly at those in managerial positions.

The idea of positive duties becomes more problematic when it involves self-incrimination. In the absence of fraud there is no duty to volunteer information regarding the employee's own misconduct: *Bell* v *Lever Brothers* [1932] AC 161. However, in *Swain* v *West (Butchers) Ltd* [1936] 3 All ER 261, it was held that employees were under a duty to notify their employer of the misconduct of their fellow employees. When these two principles were combined in the case of *Sybron Corp.* v *Rochem* [1983] ICR 801, the finding was that there is a duty, at least incumbent on senior management whose responsibilities are affected by the actions, to notify the employer of serious breaches by fellow employees even when that involves self-incrimination (as was the case here).

In this context one should also note the limited effects of the Rehabilitation of Offenders Act 1974 regarding statements of 'spent' convictions and the fact that for some occupations employers have to conduct checks with the Criminal Records Bureau.

8.5 The duty owed by former employees

Most disclosures or use of information are likely to occur once the employee has left the company. It is here that the real battle lines are drawn and the courts are wary of imposing the same level of duty on former employees as they place on existing employees. Partly, this is because once the employee has left then any fetters placed on the exercise of that person's skill, expertise, technical competence, or general ability to earn a living could be disastrous to the employee (see also **Chapter 9**).

This is an area which demands that the practitioner makes a number of judgment calls, often based on commercial or scientific practices. Many LPC students find that 'flow charts' can at least help to reduce some of the problems and so we have tried in **Figure 8.1** to map out the basic analytical structures employed by practitioners. This diagram shows you the overall pattern of analysis, but we shall repeat parts of the diagram with commentary to accompany the relevant text.

The key questions we need to address are:

- Does it matter how the contract came to an end?
- What sort of information is protectable? In particular, can an employer prevent an employee making use of the employee's own skill and knowledge acquired during his employment?
- If the information is protectable, does this mean that all confidential information gains protection or are there further limitations?
- What is the protection offered by the law (i.e., what are the remedies for breach of confidence)?

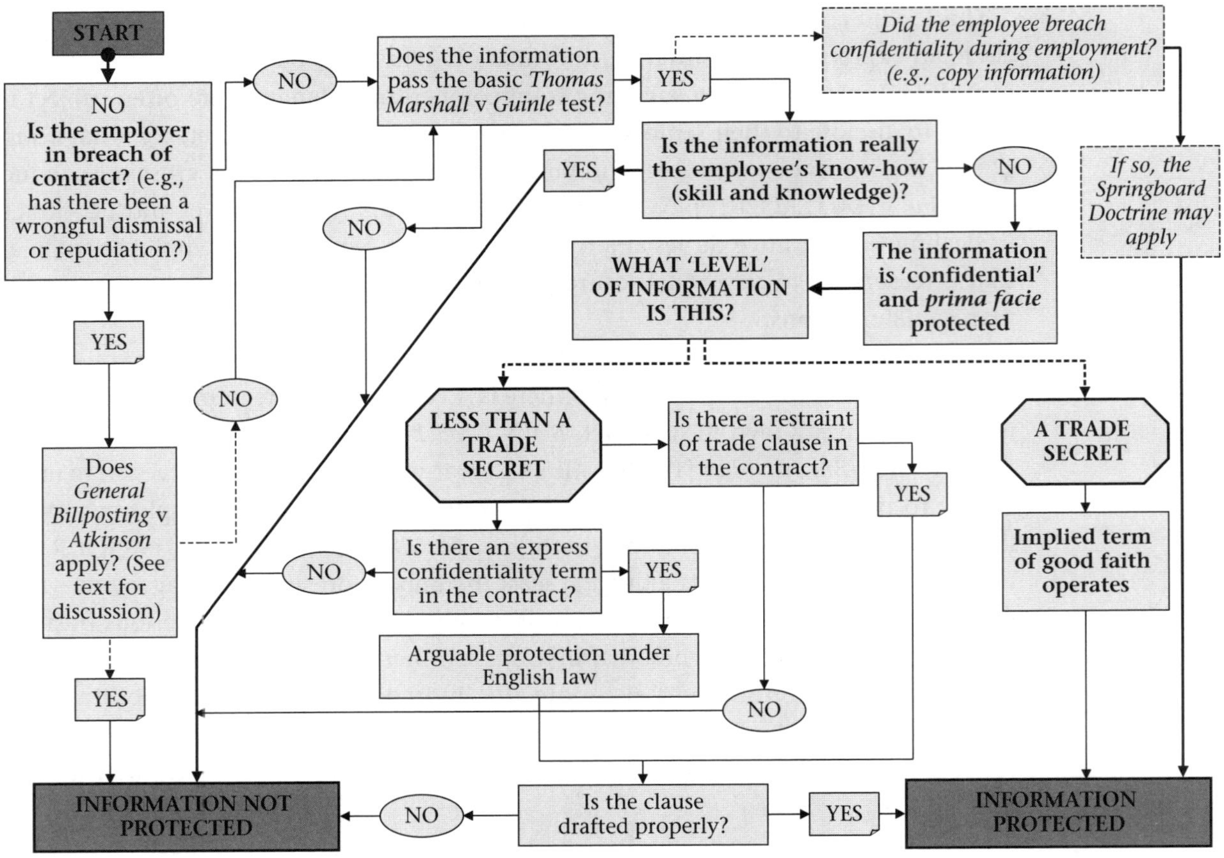

Figure 8.1 Diagrammatic summary.

8.5.1 The importance of how the contract came to an end

Figure 8.2 highlights the fact that, in some instances, ex-employees may be relieved of any post-termination duties owed to their former employer. So the first question addressed in the flow chart is: has the employer committed a breach of contract by *wrongfully dismissing* the employee or *wrongfully repudiating* the contract of employment? Wrongful dismissal will be covered in depth in **Chapter 10**. For the moment, we can say that a wrongful dismissal occurs where the employer terminates the contract without giving the employee due notice; a wrongful repudiation occurs where the employer breaches the contract and the employee resigns as a consequence. In 1909 the House of Lords held that a wrongful dismissal or repudiation destroyed the efficacy of a restraint of trade clause.

However, there has been no direct authority on whether a wrongful dismissal or wrongful repudiation affects the validity of either the implied term or any express term of *confidentiality,* and practitioners have been divided on this one. The only case to comment on the topic of confidentiality has been *Campbell* v *Frisbee* [2002] EWCA Civ 1374, [2003] ICR 141, where, on an appeal based on an application for summary judgment, Lightman J had to decide whether an express confidentiality term survived a repudiatory breach (here, an alleged assault by the model, Naomi Campbell on her ex-personal assistant). Their relationship, however, was one of a contract *for* services so any comments on the position of employees had to be *obiter.* Lightman J held: (a) that Ms Campbell's confidentiality regarding her private life was a form of property and this could not be destroyed by a repudiatory breach; (b) (*obiter*) the same would apply to employment relationships had this been one (an observation itself based on more *obiter* statements in a Court of Appeal case on restraint of trade, *Rock Refrigeration Ltd* v *Jones* [1997] ICR 938). Ms Frisbee's appeal from this decision to the Court of Appeal was successful, but only on the ground that the issue of law involved was not suitable for summary determination under Part 24 CPR. Lord Phillips MR did, however, comment (again *obiter*) at [22] that,

> We do not believe that the effect on duties of confidence assumed under contract when the contract in question is wrongfully repudiated is clearly established. While we do not consider that it is likely that Miss Frisbee will establish that Lightman J erred in his conclusions in a manner detrimental to her case, it cannot be said that she has no reasonable prospect of success on the issue.

This comment indicates that a wrongful dismissal or repudiation may not now destroy the duty of confidentiality—but nothing has been decided on this since. **Figure 8.2** illustrates this argument in the overall structure. If there has been no breach or the case law makes the breach irrelevant, the next step in the analysis is to apply the *Thomas Marshall* v *Guinle* test first noted above at **8.2.2**.

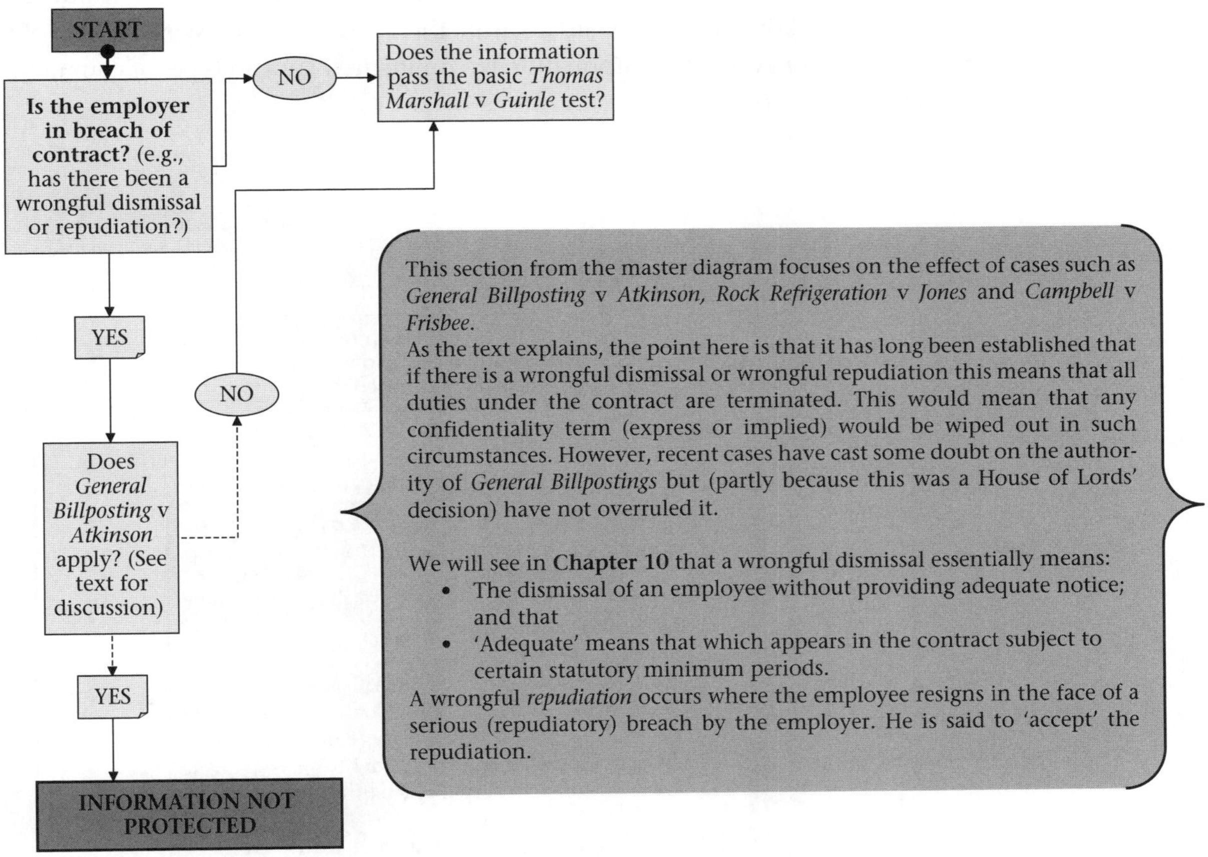

Figure 8.2 Effect of termination on the duty of confidentiality.

8.5.2 Information: the basic protection

The *Thomas Marshall* v *Guinle* test is essentially a simple one, requiring us to determine whether or not the employer has done something which shows the information is confidential and that it is not already in the public domain. Its place in the analysis is set out in **Figure 8.3**.

8.5.3 Copied and memorised information

Figure 8.3 shows us that something does not become part of the employee's know-how merely because he or she has copied or memorised the information. In *PSM International plc* v *Whitehouse* [1992] IRLR 279 the Court of Appeal noted that there was a difference between the typical confidential information cases that involved using or disclosing information, and those of the 'copying and taking' variety (such as *Robb* v *Green* and *Roger Bullivant* v *Ellis*) where the information in question takes a more tangible form and could be protected under the springboard doctrine. It was suggested that the 'springboard doctrine' we saw above could be used as *an alternative method* of protecting information that did not qualify as a trade secret. In line with this the Court of Appeal has confirmed that information that is carried away in the employee's head does not automatically belong to the employee (*Johnson & Bloy* v *Wolstenholme Rink plc and Fallon* [1987] IRLR 499). Nor does ownership of the information depend on whether the information was or was not learned with the deliberate intent to misuse. Even where the employee has memorised information without any thought of misuse, it is an objective test whether that information belongs to the employer or not: *SBJ Stephenson* v *Mandy* [2000] IRLR 233.

If the information can be classed as something other than the employee's know-how and is not covered by the springboard doctrine the next stage is to ask: what *level* of information is it? For even if the information is 'confidential', not all types of confidential information will be protected.

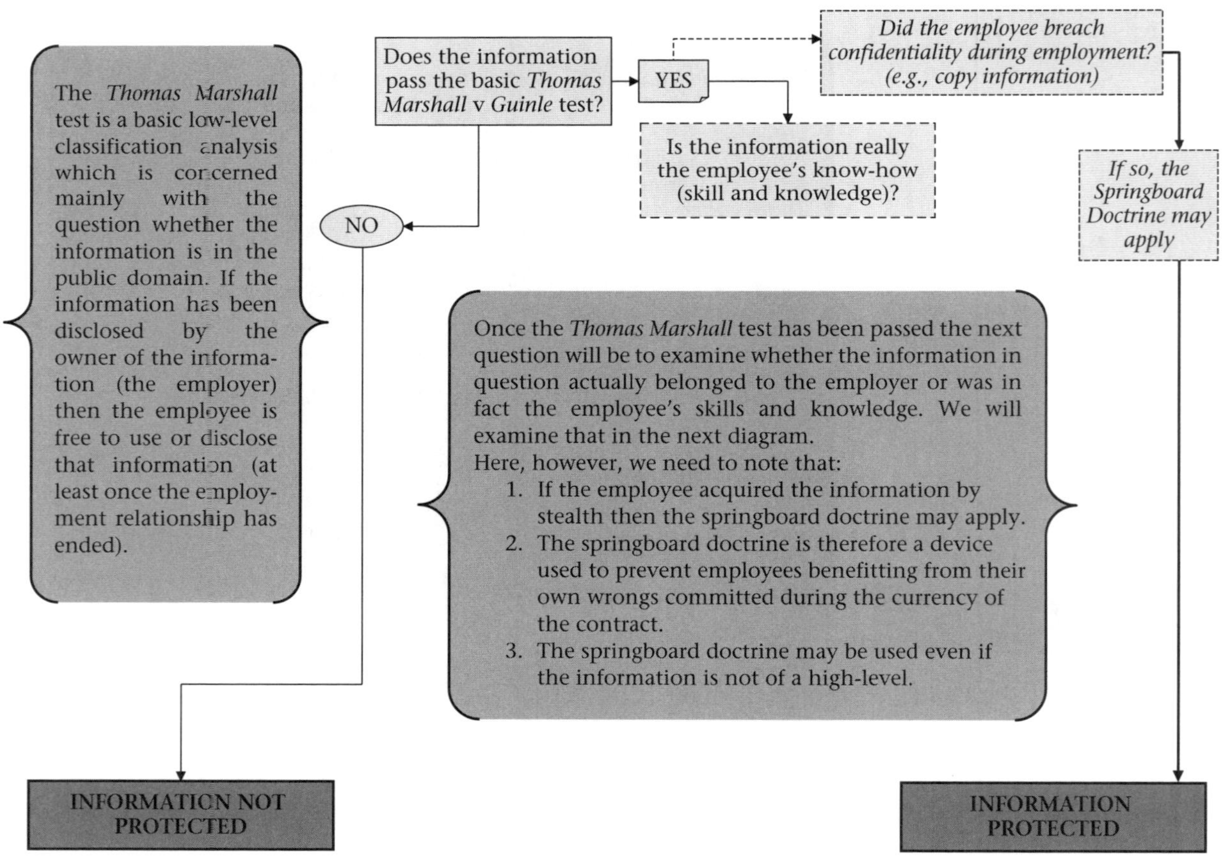

Figure 8.3 The *Thomas Marshall* and Springboard Tests.

8.5.4 Information: distinguishing employees' know-how

The information may have survived any possible argument of wrongful repudiation; it may have survived the *Thomas Marshall* test, but it may still not belong to the employer if it amounts to the employee's 'know-how'. Exactly what information will constitute an employee's know-how (otherwise referred to as the employee's 'skill and knowledge'), as opposed to the employer's confidential information, is a difficult judgment call even for experienced practitioners. We would suggest that, in essence, *technical information* is likely to belong to the employer whereas *the technique* of performing the job belongs to the employee.

In *FSS Travel and Leisure Systems Ltd* v *Johnson* [1998] IRLR 382 (a restraint of trade case based on the protection of confidential information), for instance, the Court of Appeal again confirmed that the exercise of an employee's skill, experience, know-how, and general knowledge cannot be controlled by a former employer. This will apply whether that employer is claiming the information is a trade secret or under an express confidentiality clause. Indeed, the *FSS Travel* case shows how difficult the line between know-how and confidential information can be to draw sometimes. Here the company was seeking to show that, as the ex-employee programmer knew that a program could be run to produce a certain effect (e.g., to obtain credit card bookings), the knowledge of this *design solution* could be applied in competitors' systems so that mere disclosure of the solution could be damaging to the company. Thus, it was not the detailed knowledge of the 2,852 programs that was at issue but the knowledge of what the programs could achieve by way of problem-solving. The company's claim failed; this was skill and knowledge.

Although the cases cannot be said to describe clear tests, certain features can be discovered in order to identify employees' know-how. Anything which relates to general methods

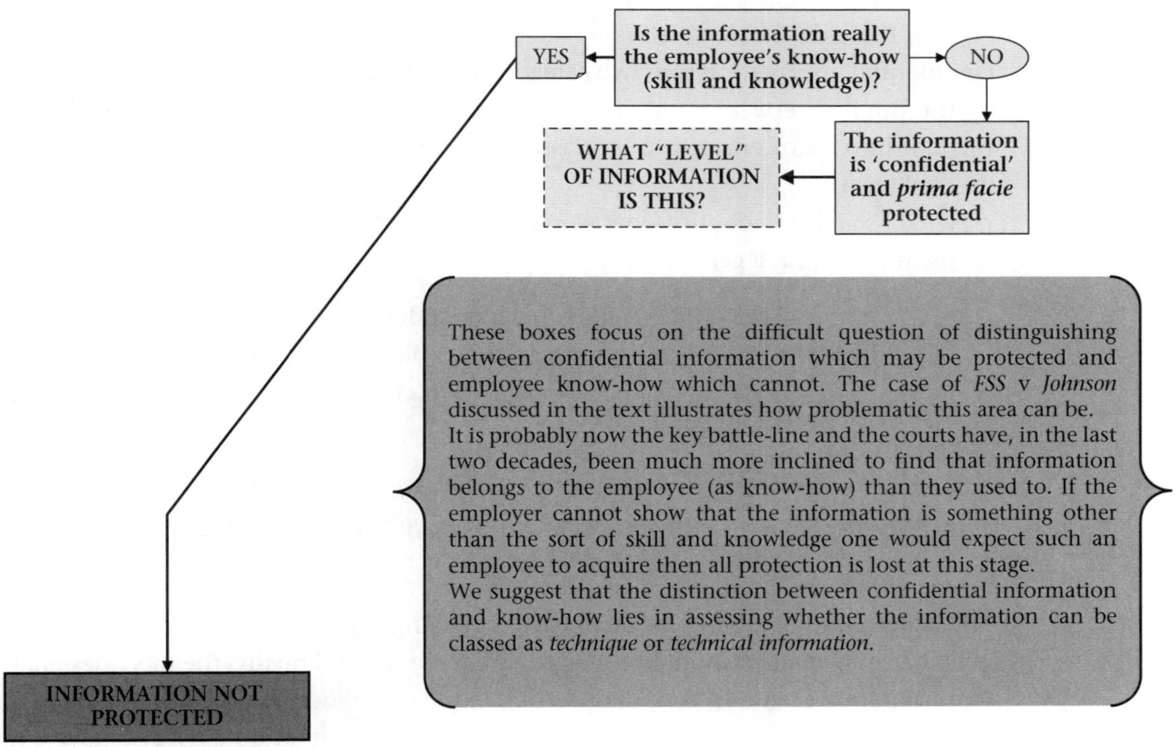

Figure 8.4 The employee's skill and knowledge.

of performing the company's business rather than information related to particular negotiations or transactions is likely to be classed as know-how. Equally, knowledge which is not 'readily separable' from the employee's general knowledge and which is 'inevitably', 'necessarily', or 'naturally' acquired in the course of employment will also be know-how. Thus, methods of working and industrial practices will be more difficult than facts and figures to label as one or the other. In *Ocular Science Ltd* v *Aspect Vision Care Ltd* [1997] RPC 289 at 370 Laddie J put it this way:

> [F]or public policy reasons, an employee is entitled to use and put at the disposal of new employers all his acquired skill and knowledge. That is so, no matter where he acquired that skill and knowledge and whether it is secret or was so at the time he acquired it. Where the employer's right to restrain misuse of his confidential information collides with the public policy, it is the latter which prevails.

8.5.5 Levels of information: defining trade secrets

One would be forgiven for believing that the employer had jumped all the necessary hurdles by now but **Figure 8.5** tells us otherwise. An employer does not gain protection for every piece of information in his possession: the information must be either a *trade secret eo nomine* (by that name) or *information akin to a trade secret.* That protection arises from the continuing nature of the implied duty of good faith/fidelity which is present in all employment relationships and which is deemed to run on even after the contract has been terminated.

Until the case of *Faccenda Chicken* v *Fowler* [1986] ICR 297 the term 'trade secret' simply meant anything that was not the employee's know-how. Use of this 'know-how' could not—and still cannot—restrict the activities of former employees; but anything which was not part of an employee's know-how was referred to as the employer's 'trade secret' and *prima facie* could be protected. That was the traditional distinction. However, in *Faccenda Chicken* Neill LJ created a further distinction, dividing an employer's confidential information into two categories: (a) trade secrets, which could be protected by the implied term of good faith; and (b) information which, though confidential, was not important enough to be classed as a trade secret and so not protected by the implied term.

Neill LJ sought to identify what would make information a 'trade secret'. He listed the following points as a general guide:

(a) *The nature of the employment*—where 'confidential' material is habitually handled by the employee this may impose a high obligation of confidentiality.

(b) *The nature of the information itself*—a limited circulation list for the information may indicate a higher level of secrecy.

(c) *Whether the employer impressed on the employee the confidentiality of the information.*

(d) *Whether the relevant information can be easily isolated from other information which the employee is free to use or disclose.*

The courts have obviously become wary of making the criteria too restrictive in deciding what information should be classed as a trade secret. Equally, the mere designation of information as either 'confidential' or a 'trade secret' does not determine the matter, though in borderline cases it may be persuasive. The information must also have passed the *Thomas Marshall* v *Guinle* [1978] ICR 905 basic test (see **8.3**).

As Neill LJ noted, it is impossible to provide a definitive list of trade secrets or their equivalent. Secret processes of manufacture provide obvious examples, but innumerable other pieces of information are *capable* of being trade secrets. With a heavy defensive *caveat* our suggestions for classification are:

(a) The information must provide a competitive edge so that disclosure would cause significant harm to the employer.

(b) The information must be inaccessible to the rest of the industry.

(c) There must be proof that serious attempts have been made to limit and safeguard the dissemination of the material within the company.

(d) The 'pure and applied research' cases tend to cause fewer problems so that it is reasonably safe to give the tag of trade secret to:

  (i) inventions (patentable and not patentable);
  (ii) technical or design data and specifications;
  (iii) specific technical processes of construction and manufacture;
  (iv) test performance figures for a new product;
  (v) chemical and other formulae;
  (vi) craft secrets;
  (vii) secret recipes.

Which business secrets are the equivalent of trade secrets is a more difficult question. The names and commercial preferences of customers, for instance, can obviously amount to sensitive information and, in some cases, might be so highly confidential and useful to a business as to amount to a trade secret. That commercial information might be as deserving of the same level of protection offered to more traditional 'scientific' trade secrets was

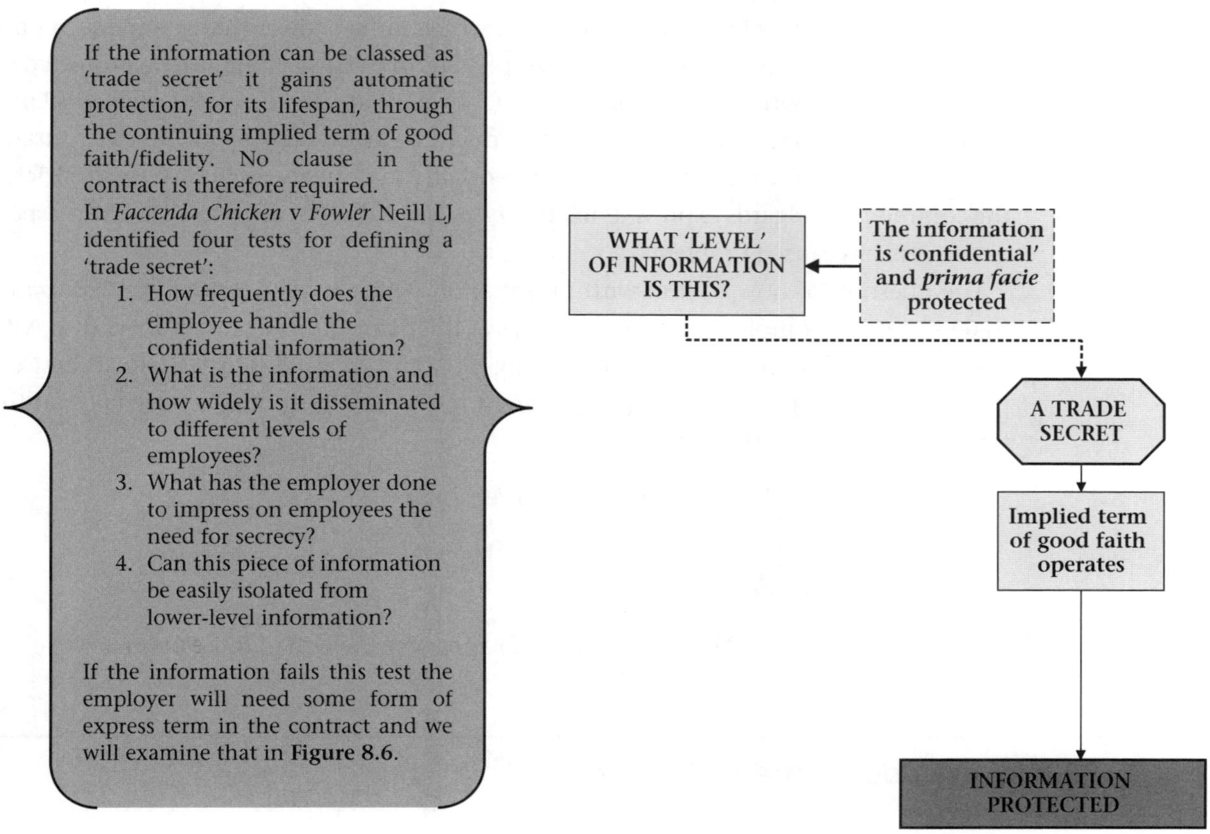

Figure 8.5 Trade secrets and the implied term of good faith.

a principle recognised in *Lansing Linde Ltd* v *Kerr* [1991] 1 All ER 418. There, for instance, Butler-Sloss LJ commented that the term 'trade secret' has to be 'interpreted in the wider context of highly confidential information of a non-technical or non-scientific nature'. With that in mind, we offer the following points as to what business secrets may amount to trade secrets:

(a) manufacturer's 'know-how' (as distinct from the employee's know-how). By this we mean the *particular applications* of technology unique to that company and which are not part of public knowledge. This might extend to things such as specific and detailed 'quality control' procedures developed by the company;
(b) customer lists when connected to things such as discount or purchasing policies and which are not otherwise available. Although customer pricing lists were not protected in *Faccenda,* this should not be taken as a rule of universal application because (as was noted by Staughton LJ in *Lansing Linde* v *Kerr* and again in *Frayling Furniture Ltd* v *Premier Upholstery Ltd* (1998, unreported, ChD) and in *SBJ Stephenson v Mandy*) the importance of these lists and their relative secrecy may matter a great deal to particular companies' business;
(c) operative tenders and quotations which have not been published;
(d) detailed plans for expansion and market projections;
(e) computer software containing novel features;
(f) access codes for computers and secure areas.

8.5.6 Levels of information: other confidential information

Neill LJ's guidelines for determining whether information meets the test of being a trade secret are used widely; but there was a more controversial aspect to his Lordship's judgment. Neill LJ also decided that information which ranked lower than a trade secret not only failed to gain the protection of the implied term but also could not be protected by the use of an express confidentiality clause. This was a surprise to practitioners. His Lordship then speculated that such information might be protectable by means of a restraint of trade clause. There was no express confidentiality term in *Faccenda Chicken* so, strictly, the comments as regards express terms are *obiter.* Nevertheless, as you will see, this aspect of the case has caused problems.

The question of how to deal with information which is confidential but less than a trade secret is a complicated one, but it lies at the heart of how practitioners deal with matters of confidentiality, both from a litigation and drafting perspective. To best explain this, therefore, instead of going straight to the next diagram we have laid out the text in section **8.6** in the following order:

- Description of *Faccenda Chicken* v *Fowler.*
- The case law since *Faccenda Chicken.*
- The practical effects.

The relevant diagrams (**Figures 8.6** and **8.7**) appear at the end of **8.6.3** below.

8.6 *Faccenda Chicken* v *Fowler*

Fowler was employed as a sales manager for the company. He established a system of selling fresh chickens from refrigerated vans and subsequently resigned from Faccenda

Chicken to set up a similar competing business. He took a number of Faccenda's employees with him. It was alleged that Fowler and the others had used and disclosed information, derived from Faccenda's operations, in their new business. The information related to delivery routes, customers' addresses, delivery times, and pricing policy. Faccenda sought an injunction to prevent the use and disclosure of this information. The contract did not contain a restraint of trade clause or a confidentiality clause so protection could only be gained through the continuing implied term of good faith/fidelity.

8.6.1 The decision

In the Court of Appeal, Neill LJ gave the only judgment. His Lordship generally confirmed the decision of Goulding J in the High Court and reiterated that the duty of confidentiality owed in employment relationships is based purely on contractual, not equitable, principles—thus focusing on express and implied terms in the contract. His Lordship identified two categories of information:

(a) *trade secrets*, which are protected by the implied term of good faith; and

(b) *everything else*, ranging from trivia through skill and knowledge and onto the borders of trade secrets.

On the facts, the information was not classed as a trade secret. Further, as there was no express clause in the contract the information was not protected by any other means so Fowler *et al.* could do with it what they wanted.

8.6.2 The unresolved practical issue

So far so good, but then came the *obiter* observations from both Goulding J and Neill LJ as to what would have been the position *had there been* an express confidentiality clause or a restraint of trade clause in the contract. Goulding J indicated that 'express terms' or 'restraint of trade clauses' could be used to protect information which was not a trade secret. Neill LJ said the same but used the phrase 'restrictive covenants'. These asides have caused some practical difficulties:

- We do not know whether the phrases 'express terms', 'restrictive covenants', and the like are meant to mean that *both* express confidentiality clauses and restraint of trade clauses can provide protection, or whether only restraint clauses can so operate.
- If the phrases mean that both restraint and express confidentiality clauses can be used to protect information which is lower than a trade secret then this helps employers greatly, as information not protected by the implied term can be covered by a well-drafted express term. This is the way practitioners viewed the law before *Faccenda* but it is probably not what Neill LJ, in particular, meant.
- More likely, Neill LJ meant that lower-level information could only be protected by using a restraint clause. Unfortunately, Neill LJ indicated that 'it was clear' from the case law that a restraint of trade clause seeking to protect against the disclosure of confidential information would only be enforceable if the information was a trade secret or its equivalent. But, as we have noted, if the information is already of such a high level, the implied term of good faith will protect it anyway.
- All this means that Neill LJ was saying (*obiter*) that an express confidentiality clause could not add any further protection to the implied term already there but that a restraint clause *could* if the information was akin to a trade secret (which, he

seemed to forget, was already protected by the implied term of good faith anyway, so this point just goes around in a circle).

- Perhaps the key point here is the very practical one that it is very difficult to police a confidentiality clause (when do you know what was said to whom?) but a restraint clause, which stops someone working for a competitor, is more obvious in its observance and breach.

Had both the High Court and the Court of Appeal avoided making such *obiter* comments, the decision in *Faccenda* would have been a useful illustration of the categorisation of types of information according to the industry in which they arise. The *obiter* points have caused problems since their utterance (and it should also be noted in passing that the two principal cases cited by Neill LJ do not support his conclusions anyway: see *Printers & Finishers Ltd* v *Holloway* [1965] 1 WLR 1 and *Worsley (E.) & Co. Ltd* v *Cooper* [1939] 1 All ER 290).

8.6.3 The case law since *Faccenda Chicken*

Faccenda has been accepted as the leading authority on this area by all levels of court (though the *obiter dicta* on express confidentiality clauses have not been reviewed directly by the House of Lords).

Most LPC courses do not deal in depth with this area anymore so we shall simply list the key cases here for your reference: *Balston Ltd* v *Headline Filters Ltd* [1987] FSR 330; *Roger Bullivant* v *Ellis* [1987] ICR 464 (CA); *Poly Lina Ltd* v *Finch* [1995] FSR 751; *Lancashire Fires Ltd* v *S. A. Lyons & Co. Ltd* [1996] FSR 629 (CA); *Poeton Industries Ltd* v *Horton* [2000] ICR 1208 (CA). These cases have not had to tackle the issue directly. They do, however,

If the information is not a 'trade secret' it is not protected by the implied term of good faith. Therefore, the only other mechanism available to gain protection is a well-drafted 'express term'. Unfortunately, the cases are not settled as to whether an express confidentiality clause can protect information which is classified as lower than a trade secret.
The section from the master diagram below traces the consequences of an express confidentiality clause providing or not providing protection under the present law.

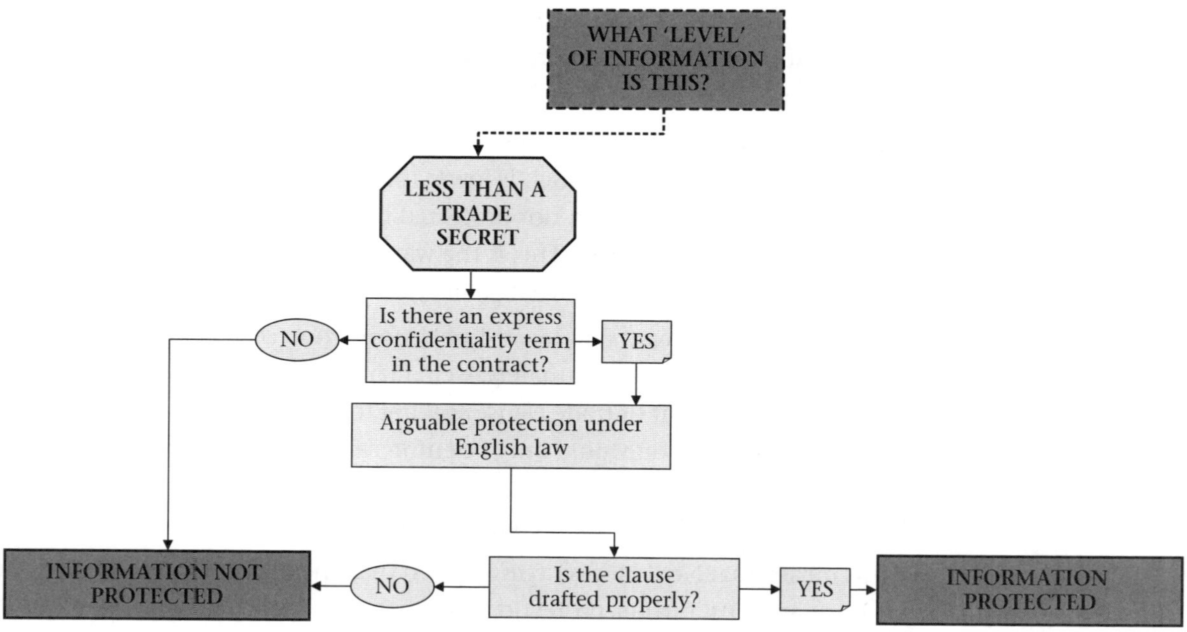

Figure 8.6 Protecting lower-level information by use of an express term.

In *Faccenda Chicken* v *Fowler* Neill LJ appeared to indicate that information falling below the 'trade secret' level could still receive protection through the employer's use of a restraint of trade clause. As noted in the text, we have some difficulty with this because restraint clauses are something of a blunderbuss device and, when used in connexion with the protection of information, have traditionally been reserved for high-level information or 'trade secrets'. On this basis, Neill LJ's *obiter* comments would lead us in a circle, but the position has never been definitively tested. If such a clause does offer protection it must still be drafted to fit the circumstances and pass the 'reasonableness' test.

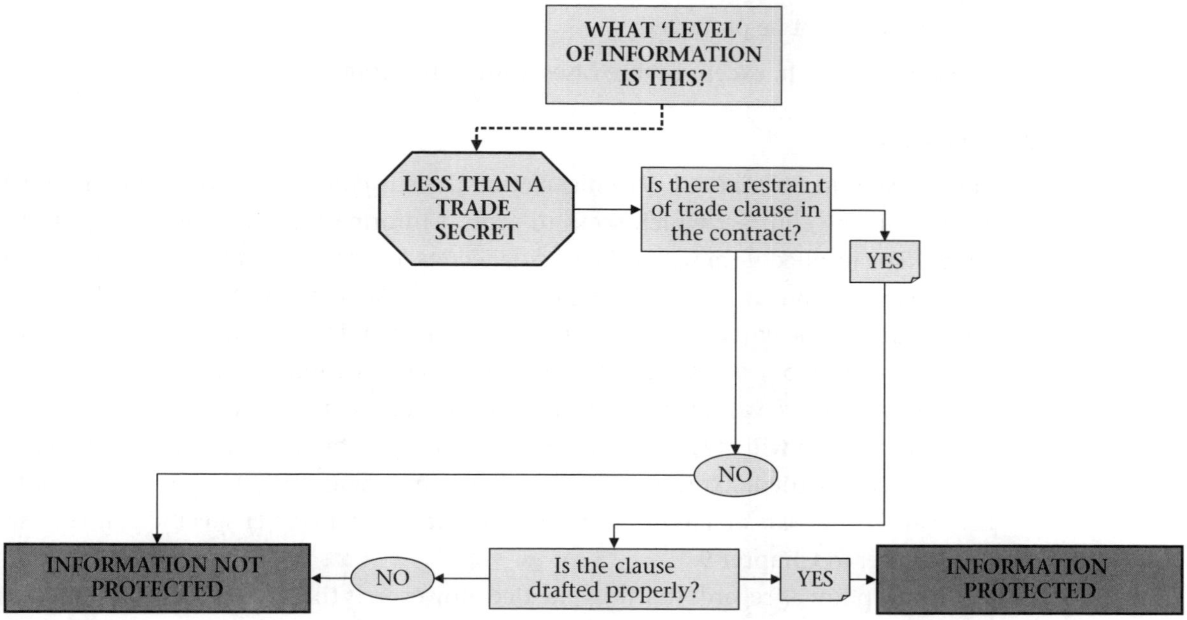

Figure 8.7 Protecting lower-level information by use of a restraint clause.

recognise that some form of protection can be gained by express terms, and Scott J (as he then was) recognised in *Balston* that it is pointless allowing for an express term to protect trade secrets as they are already protected.

We really should not be in this position where we do not know whether an express confidentiality clause or a restraint of trade clause can or cannot protect information once the employment contract has ended. In effect, the courts have sidestepped the problem and concentrated instead on extending the boundaries of what is meant by 'trade secret' to bring more commercial information within the protection of the implied term of good faith. Perhaps this is more pragmatic.

If we look at all this in diagrammatic form, **Figures 8.6** and **8.7** demonstrate the analytical pathways. You will see that, whether you are dealing with an express confidentiality clause or a restraint of trade clause based on the preservation of confidence (or both), and even if it is accepted that these clauses can protect information lower than a trade secret, you must still look to the actual drafting of the clauses (especially in the case of restraint terms) to see whether they do in fact provide the protection sought.

8.6.4 The practical effects of *Faccenda Chicken* and drafting strategies

8.6.4.1 Practical effects

There are probably no fewer than *six* ways of classifying information:

(a) *trade secrets,* which will gain automatic protection by the continuing effect of the implied term;

(b) *high-level confidential information;* so high-level that it is equivalent to a trade secret and protected by the implied term;

(c) *confidential information,* falling short of such protection but which may be the subject of a reasonable restrictive covenant (either a confidentiality clause or restraint of trade clause);

(d) *copied or memorised information,* which will be protected by the springboard doctrine because it involves a breach of fidelity occurring *during* the relationship;

(e) *skill and knowledge,* which inevitably becomes part of the employee's experience and cannot be protected;

(f) *trivia,* which, except in rare cases, cannot be protected.

8.6.4.2 Drafting practice

The decision in *Faccenda Chicken* means that there is *prima facie* little value in inserting a clause in the contract which seeks to protect information once the relationship has ended. The implied term will protect trade secrets (or their equivalent) and nothing else can be covered. But an express clause might nevertheless achieve two things: first, it may help to determine whether particular information could be regarded by the courts as attaining the level of trade secrets; secondly, it may deter employees.

Alternatively, we would say that the inclusion of an express term is vital in order to give information which is not automatically protected by the implied term any chance of being safeguarded. Express terms may appear in two forms: (a) as part of the contract itself; and (b) as part of a termination agreement. We shall cover specific points relating to the latter in **Chapter 9**.

The key point as regards drafting practice, however, is that *even if* Faccenda Chicken *is correct* there is a great deal to gain and very little to lose by inserting such a clause. For, if *Faccenda Chicken* is right, the clause will be ignored; but if *Faccenda Chicken* is wrong and the draftsman has not inserted such a clause, then protection will be lost for all but 'trade secrets'. The full 'belt and braces' approach, of course, demands the use of a restraint of trade clause as well.

Thus, if your client asks whether a former employee can be stopped from disclosing some lower-level confidential information, your answer might have to be: 'Possibly not'. But turn the point around: if you wish to give your client any chance of protection in the future you will need to insert an express confidentiality clause and/or a restraint of trade clause. In a slightly different context the Court of Appeal has affirmed this approach. In *Brooks* v *Olyslager OMS (UK) Ltd* [1998] IRLR 590 the employer and employee reached a compromise agreement concerning the employee's resignation. The employee later told an investment banker a few 'home truths' about the management style and financial stability of his former employer. The company heard about this and refused to pay the balance of the agreement, claiming there should be an implied term in the agreement that the employee would not disclose information of a sufficiently high degree of confidentiality as to amount to a trade secret. The Court of Appeal disagreed: the information did not fall into the category of trade secret, merely being information concerning the reason for the employee's resignation and matters which might be seen as detrimental to the company. An express term may still, on the facts, not have saved the day; but it would have provided a fighting chance.

The most secure line to take is that anything which is not clearly part of an employee's know-how should be included in an express confidentiality term. Materials such as general research data, details of drawings, costings, accounting information, customers' credit ratings, the contents of forthcoming catalogues, company-produced quality maintenance manuals (if not already a trade secret), restricted circulation memos and minutes of meetings, problems encountered in the development of a product or reasons why certain matters were rejected, and personnel records such as salary packages would therefore seem appropriate to this category. One might also include in this clause any item which may only be debatable as a trade secret (e.g., customer lists or sales strategies).

8.6.5 Precedents

Our surveys of practice have revealed a fair degree of commonality in the definitions of confidential information being protected. Most precedents include a general ban on the use or disclosure of trade secrets or other confidential information and then provide a (non-exhaustive) list of examples. In addition to the items mentioned above, common items were: customer requirements; trade arrangements; marketing strategies; mark-ups; the affairs of clients; expansion plans; the movements of senior employees; litigation in progress; potential customer lists; and various terms on computer information.

Most draft precedents also include a specific clause on the 'delivery up' of documents, papers, computer disks, etc. on the termination of employment. Some prohibit writing papers, giving lectures, etc. *during* employment without the express permission of management.

8.7 Remedies for breach of confidence

Any unauthorised disclosure of information during the currency of the contract is likely to amount to a breach of contract; a serious one if the effect is to cause harm to the enterprise (potential or actual). Disciplinary action may result. Realistically, however, these responses strike at the symptom and not the cause. What the employer wants is to prevent the use or disclosure of the information and to recover any lost profit.

Many judges have commented that the duty of confidentiality is of minimal value to an employer because of the difficulty of enforcement. The alternative sometimes suggested by the courts is for employers to rely more on the insertion of a restraint of trade clause which will prevent the employee from working in the industry. But while it is true that restraint clauses are generally a more effective means of impeding ex-employees, they are not a panacea because (i) it is likely that such clauses can only protect trade secrets anyway and (ii) they are far more likely to fail for lack of reasonableness than any confidentiality clause.

Thus the first 'remedy' is prevention: insert both confidentiality and restraint of trade clauses in order to protect confidential information. Failing prevention, the remedies available for breach of the duty will include:

Permanent remedies	*Interim remedies*
Injunction.	Interim injunction.
Delivery up or destruction of documents.	Order for delivery up of documents.
Damages.	Search order (formerly called an *Anton Piller order*).
An account of profits.	
Declaration as to confidentiality.	

To this list the Civil Procedure Rules have added: interim declarations (r. 25(1)(b)); pre-action disclosures (r. 31.16); and summary judgments (under Part 24), now obtainable by both claimant and defendant.

Note: To avoid repetition, injunctions are discussed in **Chapter 9** regarding confidentiality and restraint of trade (at **9.11**) and more generally in **Chapter 9** (at **9.10**).

However, it is useful to note here the comments of Laddie J in the *Ocular Science* case on drafting statements of case ([1997] RPC 289 at 359). These show that the claimant must be able to provide full and proper particulars of all the confidential information in question. The defendant must know what breach is being alleged; it is not enough to rely on a loose contention that a 'package' of information is confidential.

With this burden placed on the claimant it also follows that the claimant should not be obstructed in establishing the evidence. Thus, it is also possible for the claimant to obtain a disclosure order requiring the employee to give up the names and addresses of business contacts, irrespective of whether those contacts had been made before or after termination of employment. When it comes to lists of post-termination contacts, however, the defendant's own confidentiality is in need of *prima facie* protection. The best way to achieve this is by way of undertakings from the defendant's solicitor as to use of that information: *Intelec Systems Ltd* v *Grech-Cini* [1999] 4 All ER 11.

8.7.1 The parties

The employer may well join the new employer as a third party, but there are difficulties attached to this. First, this will inevitably slow things down. Secondly, one of the factors the court takes into account in awarding an injunction (see **9.11** below) is the ability of the defendant to pay any damages that might be awarded at trial; the joining of a company with all its resources is therefore disadvantageous to the applicant. Thirdly, there is the question of proving that the new employer received the information knowing of the breach or at least turning a blind eye to its potential. In *Thomas* v *Pearce* [2000] FSR 718 the Court of Appeal made it clear that the test is one of honesty not reasonableness.

8.7.2 Springboard injunctions

In some cases an employer may be able to obtain an injunction even where the information is not a trade secret: see above at **8.3.4**.

8.7.3 Database rights

Databases can take a lot of time and money to create. They are valuable pieces of information and they are open to abuse from copying. The EC Database Directive 96/9/EC addressed this issue. As well as extending copyright protection in this area this Directive also created a creature known as a 'database right'. In the UK this was implemented as a property right through the Copyrights and Rights in Databases Regulations 1997 (SI 1997/3032). The right is infringed where all or substantial parts of the database are extracted or re-utilised (reg. 16) and employees who fall foul of this may be liable under the regulations through the application of breach of copyright remedies (reg. 23).

8.7.4 Defences to breach of confidentiality

Aside from arguing that the information is simply not confidential at all, the two main defences are: (a) publication; and (b) just cause. We touched on publication at **8.3.3** above regarding 'the public domain'. 'Just cause' was covered at **8.3.5** above in the discussions on public interest.

Some further points need to be made on publication. Although publication destroys confidentiality, two points need to be noted:

(a) The case law shows (notably *Attorney-General* v *Guardian Newspapers Ltd (No. 2)* [1988] 3 All ER 545 (CA)—the *Spycatcher* case) that *partial* publication may not destroy confidentiality as long as the information retains the 'basic attributes of inaccessibility' i.e., it is not *generally* available to the public.

(b) Publication by the *defendant* may (strange as it sounds) destroy confidentiality. Although one would think the defendant should not profit from his or her own wrong (see *Speed Seal Products Ltd* v *Paddington* [1986] 1 All ER 91), Lord Goff in *Spycatcher* expressed the view that once disclosed, by whatever means, the information was no longer confidential. This would affect the calculation of damages aspect (i.e., dating the termination of the duty), though the defendant would still probably be bound by the springboard doctrine.

8.8 The employee's right to confidentiality

In addition to the human rights implications noted at 1.7 above, there are four main areas to note here:

(a) The Data Protection Act 1998.

(b) The Access to Medical Reports Act 1988.

(c) The provision of references.

(d) The interception of communications.

8.8.1 The Data Protection Act 1998

The aim of this Act is to allow employees access to data held on them by 'data controllers' (i.e., their employer). Employees have the right to challenge inaccuracies and claim compensation for any ensuing loss. The Office of the Information Commissioner has issued guidance notes and a draft Code of Practice: see the website at *www.ico.gov.uk* and, under the Criminal Justice and Immigration Act 2008, has powers to impose fines for unlawful processing of personal data.

8.8.1.1 Outline of the provisions

At the heart of the Data Protection Act 1998 (DPA 1998) lie eight principles around which the Act is structured, enforced, and interpreted (see sch. 1). There is an obligation on all data users to observe these principles, e.g., that the information shall be processed fairly and lawfully; that 'personal data' (a term which includes expressions of opinions) shall be accurate and, where necessary, kept up to date; that personal data shall not be kept for longer than is necessary; that unauthorised processing shall be guarded against; and that personal data should not be transferred outside the EC unless that recipient country has adequate levels of data protection. The Act confers on the Information Commissioner extensive powers of enforcement.

8.8.1.2 The meaning of 'data'

In addition to computer-based information the 1998 Act extended the meaning of 'data' to information which is 'recorded as part of a relevant filing system or with the intention that it should form part of a relevant filing system', e.g., personal files (s. 1(1)(c)). A 'relevant filing system' is defined at s. 1(1) as:

> any set of information relating to individuals to the extent that, although the information is not processed by means of equipment operating automatically in response to instructions given for that purpose, the set is structured, whether by reference to individuals or by reference to criteria relating to individuals, in such a way that specific information relating to a particular individual is readily accessible.

In the case of *Durant* v *Financial Services Authority* [2003] EWCA Civ 1746, the Court of Appeal considered the meanings of 'data' and 'relevant filing system'.

(a) *Data*

'Data' will relate to an individual if they are: 'information that affects [a person's] privacy, whether in his personal or family life, business or professional capacity'. The Court held that this will include information which is biographical in a significant sense. The Information Commissioner's comment is that this means that, 'Simply because an individual's name appears on a document, the information contained in that document will not necessarily be personal data about the named individual.' The Information Commissioner gives examples of personal data: information about the medical history of an individual, an individual's salary details, information concerning an individual's tax liabilities, information comprising an individual's bank statements, and information about individuals' spending preferences: see also *Common Services Agency* v *Scottish Information Commissioner* [2008] UKHL 47, [2008] 1 WLR 1550 on the meaning of personal and sensitive data in relation to requests made to public authorities under the freedom of information legislation.

(b) *Relevant filing system*

The Court of Appeal gave a narrower meaning to 'relevant filing system' than many had thought to be the case. It is limited to a system:

(i) in which the files forming part of it are structured or referenced in such a way as to clearly indicate at the outset of the search whether specific information capable of amounting to personal data of an individual requesting it under section 7 is held within the system and, if so, in which file or files it is held; and

(ii) which has, as part of its own structure or referencing mechanism, a sufficiently sophisticated and detailed means of readily indicating whether and where in an individual file or files specific criteria or information about the applicant can be readily located.

This means that not all manual filing systems are covered by the Act: only manual filing systems broadly equivalent to computerised systems in ready accessibility are within the system of data protection. The Information Commissioner's website provides a number of working examples.

8.8.1.3 Accessible records

The question of 'relevant filing systems' does not arise in relation to *accessible records,* so that in such cases, rights of access are much wider. Section 68 defines this term as covering health records, certain educational records (set out in sch. 11), and certain public records (set out in sch. 12). A 'health record' is one which consists of information relating to the physical or mental health of an individual which has been made by or on behalf of a 'health professional' (see s. 69) in connexion with the care of that individual.

8.8.1.4 Sensitive personal data

This term covers racial or ethnic origin, political opinions, religious beliefs, trade union membership, physical and mental health, the employee's sexual life, and the commission of an offence or proceedings relating to an offence (s. 2). There are specific *additional* restrictions placed on the processing of such information (see sch. 3). Problems are beginning to surface here with regard to the standing of 'sickness absence' records by employers.

8.8.1.5 Employees' rights

An employee, as a 'data subject', has certain rights under the Act (see generally s. 715). These can be broadly categorised as:

(a) the right to be informed, in response to a written request, that personal data about him or her is being processed;

(b) the right of access (on payment of a fee) to personal data held by the employer. This must be communicated in an 'intelligible form';

(c) the right to apply to a county court or to the High Court to have inaccurate data corrected or deleted;

(d) the right, in certain cases, to be informed of the logic involved in computerised decision-making;

(e) the right to compensation for damage caused by any breach of the Act as well as in certain cases of distress;

(f) the right to complain to the Commissioner that the principles of the Act have been broken.

Section 7 allows certain information or parts of it not to be disclosed if information relating to another individual would be revealed, and sch. 7 lays out the exemptions relating to the general rights, e.g., in relation to references supplied by the employer, data processed in connexion with proposed redundancies, company takeovers, or negotiations on pay increases.

8.8.1.6 Contractual and other obligations

Under s. 56 employers (or prospective employers in the case of recruitment) commit a criminal offence if they seek to require an employee or third party to supply them with certain records (i.e., emanating from certain data controllers (e.g., a chief officer of police) and relating mainly to criminal convictions) unless required by an enactment or by showing that, in the circumstances, this was justified as being in the public interest.

Under s. 57 any term or condition of a contract is void in so far as it requires an employee to supply any record which has been obtained by the employee under s. 7 and which consists of the information contained in any health record as defined by s. 68(2): see **8.8.1.3** above.

8.8.2 Access to Medical Reports Act 1988

Under the provisions of the Access to Medical Reports Act 1988 (AMRA 1988) a person may apply to gain access to medical reports relating to that person which are to be, or have been, supplied by a medical practitioner for employment or insurance purposes.

8.8.2.1 The basic right

An employer may request a medical report on physical or mental health matters (made after 1 January 1989) concerning an employee at any time. The medical report must be for 'employment purposes', but no distinction is drawn in the Act between existing and prospective employees, or for that matter with those undertaking a contract *for* services. AMRA 1988 allows an employee or prospective employee to withhold consent to a medical report being sought. This will apply whatever the contract states. Further, under s. 3 the employer seeking a medical report *cannot* do so unless the employee has been notified of this right *and* the employee notifies the employer that consent is given.

The right to withhold consent is a fine theoretical right but, in the end, of less practical significance than it first appears because the employer will still have to make a decision (e.g., to employ or even to dismiss) on the evidence available. And what the Act does not permit is the suppression of *particular* items of information by the employee.

8.8.2.2 Outline of the Act's provision

- AMRA 1988 concerns reports made by a 'medical practitioner' (as defined in the Medical Act 1983) who is or has been responsible for the clinical care of the individual. Thus, the Act seems to be aimed at the employee's general practitioner, consultant, or psychiatrist who has treated the employee on a continuing basis. Company doctors appear to be exempt from the Act unless there is this element of continuity present in providing 'care'.
- The employee must also be notified of his or her right to withhold consent, a right of inspection, and a right to request that amendments be made before submission of the report. Equally, information may be withheld by the medical practitioner from the employee where disclosure would be likely to cause serious harm to that individual or others, or would be likely to reveal information about another person, or the identity of the supplier of the information. This last point does not apply where the affected individual has given consent or is a health professional involved in the care of the employee.

8.8.2.3 The effect on employers

Aside from the detailed administrative requirements, AMRA 1988 did not effect changes to the law of confidentiality. Neither did the Act create extra rights of protection from dismissal, etc. Thus, although an individual may obtain an order securing compliance with the terms of the Act (s. 8), there is no separate right of damages.

8.8.2.4 Requesting medical examinations

Where the request relates to prospective employees there are few restraints placed on employers, save the practical one of deterring employees who might object to the examination. The reporting medical practitioner will owe a duty of care to the prospective employee to produce an accurate assessment. But as regards existing employees, express terms allowing an employer to demand a medical examination and report are necessary. Such a clause will still be subject to the provisions of AMRA 1988. It would seem extremely unlikely that a refusal by an employee to consent to the release of the report could be construed as misconduct which might justify a dismissal; although an employee's refusal to submit to *any* medical examination where there is justifiable concern, or a valid dispute, as to suitability to perform the job may be held to constitute misconduct.

There is, however, no implied duty to participate in medical examinations: *Bliss* v *South East Thames Regional Health Authority* [1987] ICR 700. Exceptions might occur, though, where there is a justifiable need for a report, e.g., following an accident. Mandatory medical examinations may also, in some cases, be a breach of human rights (see **1.7** above).

8.8.2.5 Testing employees

It is estimated that about 8 per cent of the workforce in Britain are subject to some form of drug testing. On blood and urine, the ECHR has determined that individuals have the right not to be subjected to such testing but these cases did not arise in the employment context.

Two cases have considered the relevance of art. 8 ECHR to this analysis. In *O'Flynn* v *Airlinks The Airport Coach Co. Ltd* [2002] Emp LR 1217, the applicant was dismissed after testing positive for cannabis in a random drugs test. The dismissal took place before the Human Rights Act 1998 came into force, so art. 8 could not be relied on in any event. However, the EAT considered whether the Convention would have made any difference and concluded that it would not. They said that they had difficulty seeing how the zero-tolerance policy operated by the employer interfered with the employee's right to a private life, save to the extent that she could not report for duty with drugs in her system. In any event, they would have held any interference to have been justified under art. 8(2) for public safety reasons, given that she could be called upon to serve hot drinks on moving coaches.

The Privy Council has strengthened this approach with *Whitefield* v *General Medical Council* [2003] IRLR 39 where a general practitioner appealed against conditions imposed on his registration by the Health Committee of the General Medical Council. These conditions included complete abstention from alcohol at all times and submitting to random blood and breath tests. He argued that these restrictions were disproportionate to the object to be achieved and deprived him of the enjoyment of social drinking on family occasions contrary to his rights under art. 8(1). The Privy Council rejected his appeal and took the view that there was no authority supporting a view that an absolute ban on alcohol infringed a right to private family life and rather chastely reminded him that he was free to enjoy a social life with non-alcoholic drinks. They also held that any interference would have been permissible under art. 8(2) in any event, for public safety reasons.

8.8.2.6 Employee's declarations

Prospective employees do not owe a duty to volunteer information about themselves but do owe a duty not to misrepresent their position. This will include, in some cases, information concerning spent criminal convictions under the Rehabilitation of Offenders Act 1974. Where employees have been asked direct questions at an interview, on an application form, or during the course of their employment, they will come under a duty not to mislead or be fraudulent. Following this line, it is becoming quite common for companies to make use of questionnaires on health matters. Apart from questions which may be discriminatory (direct or indirect) there is no legal bar as such on this type of investigation, though again we may have to take account of human rights issues.

If an employee is taken on under false pretences this may well justify a later dismissal when the concealment is discovered. This principle applies to concealment of physical or mental illness, at least where such illness affects the job: *O'Brien* v *Prudential Assurance Co. Ltd* [1979] IRLR 140. Most health questions posed on application forms are very general in nature and it is not uncommon for an employee to be able to 'interpret' these questions in their favour without wandering into the area of misrepresentation.

8.8.3 References

8.8.3.1 The common law position

At common law an employer is not obliged to provide references, though the specific rules of bodies created under statute (e.g., financial institutions) may mean that an employer is bound to do so and these rules may require the inclusion of specific information so that any failure may amount to a breach of contract between the employer and employee: *TSB Bank plc* v *Harris* [2000] IRLR 157. The general common law rule is also subject to the law on discrimination. Thus, the provision of defective references (or even the refusal to give references) because an employee has previously brought a sex discrimination claim against the employer may amount to discrimination under Equal Treatment Directive 76/207: *Coote* v *Granada Hospitality Ltd* (Case C-185/97) [1998] IRLR 656 (ECJ). And here, the EAT was prepared to stretch the words in the Sex Discrimination Act 1975 (SDA 1975), s. 6(2) ('a woman employed by him') to include *ex-employees*.

Employers will owe the *recipient* of references a duty of care under the principles of negligent misstatement. It is quite common, and good practice, for a new employer to make any offer of employment subject to the receipt of satisfactory references; the meaning of 'satisfactory' is essentially a subjective one: *Wishart* v *National Association of Citizens Advice Bureaux* [1990] IRLR 393.

The *employee* will have an action against the employer who provides faulty references for defamation and malicious falsehood, though not for breach of confidentiality, if permission for full disclosure has been given. References are therefore subject to qualified privilege and the key point, in defamation or malicious falsehood, will be the presence or absence of malice.

An employee also has a cause of action in negligence against the employer for any failure to use reasonable skill and care in the provision of references: *Spring* v *Guardian Assurance plc* [1994] ICR 596. This House of Lords' decision has caused employers some consternation. The Court of Appeal has now added a gloss, and further problems, to this area. In *Bartholomew* v *London Borough of Hackney* [1999] IRLR 246 the Court dealt with the position where references were provided which detailed (beyond the information actually requested) that the employee had left Hackney after disciplinary action had been taken against him, this action only ceasing when the employee had agreed to voluntary severance. The reference did not give a full explanation of the position (e.g., that the employee had been counter-claiming race discrimination). Although finding against the employee on the facts, the Court indicated that the mere accuracy of a reference is not enough to provide protection to an employer; what is required is a broader test of 'fairness'—although the reference need not be comprehensive, it must not give an unfair overall impression of the employee.

One aspect of 'fairness' is that if employers provide negative information on employees they will be at risk if the employees have not had the opportunity to comment on these complaints. Thus, in *Cox* v *Sun Alliance Life Ltd* [2001] EWCA Civ 649, [2001] IRLR 448, an ex-employee succeeded in his claim against his former employer on facts very similar to *Bartholomew,* because whereas in *Bartholomew* it was held that the statements did not ultimately give a false impression, here the references were seriously inaccurate and the allegations cited had never been put to the ex-employee.

8.8.3.2 Effect of Data Protection Act 1998

Schedule 7 of the DPA 1998 (dealing with exemptions from the provisions of s. 7) lays out certain rules as regards access to references. References given in confidence by the data controller (the employer) relating to the employee are exempt from the provisions of s. 7 if given for the purposes of education and training, the appointment to any office, or the provision of services.

Employees may therefore gain access to references given by previous employers if held on their present employer's files, but as the author's identity would be revealed by such an investigation this access seems to fall within the exceptions to s. 7 so that the ex-employer's permission would most likely have to be gained first.

8.8.4 The interception of communications

Many employees now have access to computers as part of their work. The development of e-mails and the growth of the internet have begun to cause problems for employers in terms of monitoring their employees' communications. The issues involve abuse of company time and facilities, employees accessing pornographic internet sites, confidential information being disclosed through e-mails, etc., and (in this great age of constant quality-control) the need for employers to standardise or regulate telephone and written communications. The more employers intercept such communications, the more they open themselves to problems of infringement of privacy (see *Halford* v *United Kingdom* [1997] IRLR 471, regarding the tapping of telephone calls without prior warning).

8.8.4.1 Surveillance

It is estimated that about 80 per cent of all employees are subject to monitoring or surveillance of some form in the workplace. Surveillance may take many forms, given the wide availability and low cost of employee-monitoring technology. There is also some indication that disciplinary proceedings/dismissals for breaches of e-mail and internet policies now outnumber proceedings for breaches of health and safety regulations, dishonesty, and theft. No distinction is made in the various pieces of legislation between systematic monitoring and occasional monitoring.

The starting point for any analysis of the legality of this now has to be art. 8(1) ECHR which states that: 'Everyone has the right to respect for his private and family life, his home and his correspondence.' Article 8 rights were extended to the workplace in *Niemietz* v *Germany* (1992) 16 EHRR 97 (search of a lawyer's office), where the ECHR stated that the term 'private life' does not exclude professional and business activities.

Although (debatably) the Human Rights Act 1998 only applies to cases involving 'public authorities', courts and tribunals are also public authorities within the Act so that, in reaching any decision, they must operate within the Convention (see **Chapter 1** above). Article 8 may therefore be used indirectly in relation to the acts of a private employer (or, debatably against a public authority undertaking a private act as per HRA 1998, s. 6(5)).

Halford v *United Kingdom* also established the idea of the 'reasonable expectation of privacy' at the workplace. American authorities would indicate that 'reasonable expectation' includes both a *subjective* expectation which is *objectively* reasonable. This leaves open the question whether an employer can remove the 'reasonable expectation of privacy'. In *Halford* this was not an issue as there was no waiver/warning, but the cases dealing with contracting-out regarding the related articles, 9 and 10 ECHR, strongly suggest that workers may 'opt out' or be deemed to have opted out of the protection of Convention rights in the employment context.

8.8.4.2 The statutory framework on accessing information

Interception of communications occurs when the contents of the communication can be read by a third party. The Regulation of Investigatory Powers Act 2000 (RIPA) governs the interception of communications over both public and private networks (if attached to a public system). It creates criminal liability and a civil tort of unlawful interception.

Under these regulations it is unlawful for a person, without authority, intentionally to intercept a communication in the course of its transmission by means of the postal service or public telecommunications system. The employer may *monitor* communications and *not be in breach where:*

- the employee and other sender/recipient have consented; or
- the employer has reasonable grounds to so believe; or
- the employer does other acts which comply with RIPA.

Monitoring of *traffic data* is not covered by RIPA. Instead, this is covered by the Telecommunications (Lawful Business Practice) (Interception of Communications) Regulations 2000 (LBP Regs). These regulations authorise monitoring and recording of all communications (telephone or e-mail) *without consent*:

- to ensure compliance with regulatory practices, e.g., Financial Services Authority requirements;
- to ensure standards of service are maintained, e.g., in call centres, to prevent or detect crime;
- to protect the communications system—this includes guarding against unauthorised use and potential viruses;
- to determine the relevance of the communication to the employer's business, i.e., picking up relevant messages when someone is away from work.

The monitoring should be limited to cases where it is necessary and relevant to the employer's business needs (thus *obviously* private communications do not fall within the permission to monitor, etc.). The LBP Regs require businesses to make all reasonable efforts to inform users of possible interception (there is no requirement to get consent). However, the LBP Regs also allow employers to monitor (but not record) for the purpose of determining whether the communications are relevant to the system controller's business (and thus open up employees' e-mail accounts).

The Information Commissioner's code of practice, *Monitoring at work: an employer's guide,* states that any monitoring of e-mails should only be undertaken where: the advantage to the business outweighs the intrusion into the workers' affairs; employers carry out an impact assessment of the risk they are trying to avert; workers are told they are being monitored; information discovered through monitoring is only used for the purpose for which the monitoring was carried out; the information discovered is kept secure; employers are careful when monitoring personal communications such as e-mails which are clearly personal; employers only undertake covert monitoring in the rarest circumstances where it is used for the prevention or detection of crime.

Further, the Information Commissioner's guidance indicates that the employer should only undertake acts such as monitoring where there is a clear problem which needs to be examined. The theme throughout the codes is transparency. If monitoring takes place, then save in exceptional circumstances the employer should ensure that employees know what is being done, how it is being done, and the reasons for it.

The Information Commissioner has also issued a wide range of codes covering matters such as the use of CCTV cameras in the workplace.

8.8.4.3 Storage of information

This is covered by the Data Protection Act 1998 as detailed above.

8.9 Summary

- The duty of confidentiality is concerned with protecting information which is central to the employer's business, the use or disclosure of which would cause harm to the employer.
- Once employment has been terminated the employer's confidential information may still be protected by the implied duty of fidelity which will continue even though the relationship has ended.
- But, confidential information will generally be protected only if it can be classified as a trade secret. There is no one common definition of 'trade secret' that can be applied to all organisations.
- What cannot be protected is the employee's 'know-how' acquired during employment and which he wishes to use in another employment.
- There is some debate as to whether an express term of confidentiality can extend protection to information which falls outside the definition of trade secret.
- An ex-employee may be prevented from using or disclosing his ex-employer's confidential information for a defined limited period, or forever, depending upon the nature of the information.
- The normal method of enforcement of a confidentiality term is by means of an injunction. Any application will be dealt with under the *American Cyanamid* principles.
- Employees also have rights of confidentiality. These centre mainly on the Data Protection Act 1998 and anti-surveillance legislation.

A combined 'self-test' question covering the topics raised in this chapter and the next will appear at the end of **Chapter 9**.

9

Restraint of trade

9.1 Introduction

Employers are often anxious to guard against direct competition from former employees. The only sure way to guarantee this is to remove them from the marketplace for a limited period of time, and the only way to do this legitimately is by means of a restraint of trade clause. Restraint of trade clauses seek to curtail the employee's opportunity to gain employment and are so subject to stringent analysis, justification resting solely on the prevention of *unfair* competition.

In this chapter we will examine the doctrine of restraint of trade under the following general headings:

(a) What constitutes a restraint of trade?

(b) Importance of how the contract was terminated.

(c) How reasonableness is determined: legitimate interests.

(d) How reasonableness is determined: reasonableness of drafting.

(e) Drafting and interpretation.

(f) Implied restraints.

(g) Restraints during employment.

(h) Preparatory actions.

(i) Garden leave.

(j) Injunctions.

9.2 What constitutes a restraint of trade?

9.2.1 Definition

A restraint clause is designed to stifle competition from ex-employees. When faced with such a clause the courts will presume the restraint to be *void* unless the employer can show it is reasonable. Reasonableness is assessed in two stages:

(i) is there a 'legitimate interest' to protect? and

(ii) is the wording of the clause acceptable?

We shall return to 'legitimate interest' at **9.5** below. As to the wording used, there are four headings to be considered in determining reasonableness:

(a) reasonableness in terms of the *'market'* in which the parties are operating and the appropriateness of the clause in relation to that employee;

(b) reasonableness in terms of *time*;

(c) reasonableness in terms of *area* covered;

(d) *public policy*.

A major caveat is necessary: each case turns very much on its facts. One cannot say that a one-year restraint, for instance, will always be reasonable or that a worldwide restraint is automatically unreasonable. Indeed, in *Dairy Crest Ltd* v *Pigott* [1989] ICR 92, the Court of Appeal made it clear that even authorities concerning the same trade (here a milkman) were not to be regarded as binding precedents. The basic rule is that an employer cannot be protected from competition *per se*, only from *unfair competition*.

Any practitioner in this area will tell you that merely relying on standard terms, without seeking to modify them according to the client's needs, is a particularly disastrous tactic. Thus it has been said that the client who demands to be given a standard clause is misguided and the solicitor who provides one is a fool.

9.2.2 Types of restraint

The most common types of restraint are:

(a) *Non-competition restraints* (i.e., preventing the employee working in that industry as a whole, or at least with named competitors). These are the most draconian clauses and are viewed with great suspicion by the courts.

(b) *Non-dealing restraints* (i.e., preventing employees accepting business from or conducting business with former clients or specifically named former clients). These are still treated carefully, especially as they may affect third party rights. For instance, even if a former customer prefers to take his business to the employee in the new job rather than continue dealing with the employer, any action by the employee may still constitute a breach of contract (see *John Michael Design plc* v *Cooke* [1987] ICR 445).

(c) *Non-solicitation restraints* (i.e., preventing employees actually initiating contact with former clients, though not barring the employee from dealing with such clients who transfer their business without solicitation). Non-solicitation clauses are usually less dramatic in their effect and, in many cases, procure a more sympathetic reception from the courts; though this does not necessarily ensure their success. We will deal with non-solicitation clauses later as a separate topic (see **9.8.5** below).

(d) *Non-poaching restraints* (i.e., preventing the employee from soliciting former colleagues to join him in the new venture).

9.2.2.1 Termination agreements

Although most restraint clauses arise under the ordinary terms of the contract, some will be found in termination agreements negotiated with departing employees (usually senior employees). Confidentiality agreements may appear here too. Obviously, the employer will have to pay for these, but the clauses themselves will be treated in the same way as those arising in the employment contract. If a covenant is introduced for the first time at this stage, or an existing one is varied, any monies paid may be subject to tax.

9.2.3 Which type of restraint to choose

Many employers will wish you to draft a clause that would make a pact with the devil look like an attractive alternative. For the most part, this should be resisted if only because a clause which seeks to restrain an employee more than is necessary will fail on this ground alone. Therefore, one should ask what level of protection is necessary to protect those interests, starting with non-solicitation clauses and moving on to non-dealing and then non-competition clauses. Tactics may also play a part here. Your client may insist upon a non-competition clause in order simply to scare off ex-employees. If so, you need (in writing) to advise that the clause is likely to fail. Equally, from the employee's perspective, one might accept the imposition of a draconian clause on the basis that it will never stand up in court so why worry about it! Whatever the ethical points here, both tactics carry dangers. These dangers may be summarised as follows:

9.2.3.1 From the employer's perspective

(a) Such a wide clause may well alienate an otherwise loyal employee.

(b) The opportunity to draft a potentially workable clause may be lost.

9.2.3.2 From the employee's perspective

(a) The court may find a way to 'blue-pencil' (i.e., edit) the clause so that a clause, assumed to be unlawful, becomes binding.

(b) The court may narrow the ambit of wide-ranging phrases (e.g., restrict the term 'business' to a particular aspect of the company's business) even though the strict meaning of the words might not allow for this and, in doing so, catch the unwary employee who has agreed to the clause believing it meant something else.

(c) Precedent, or at least *stare decisis,* is treated with caution in this area. Even the same clause (appearing in slightly different circumstances) may not be treated with consistency.

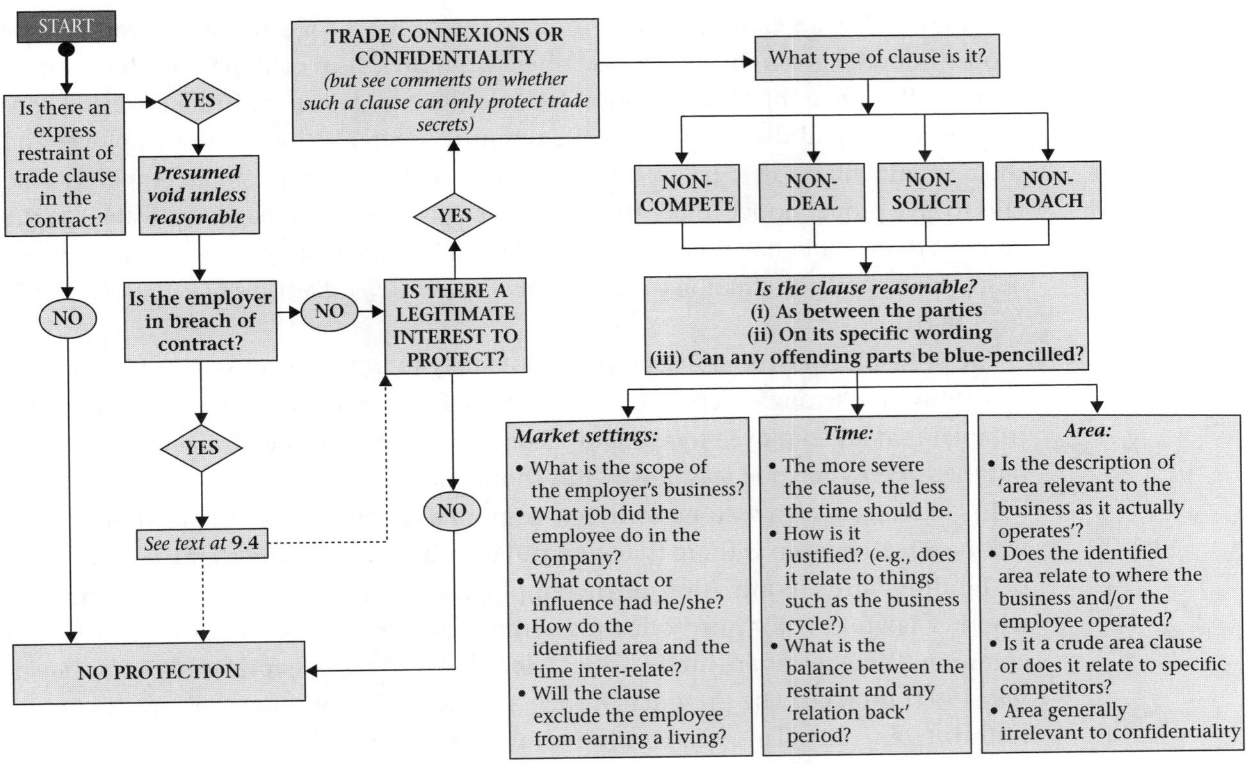

Figure 9.1 Diagrammatic summary.

9.2.3.3 The basic approach

As with confidentiality in **Chapter** 8 we have tried, in **Figure 9.1**, to map out the basic analytical structures employed by practitioners as regards restraint of trade. This diagram shows you the overall pattern of analysis and the text below follows the pattern of the diagram.

9.3 Is there an express term?

The courts will not imply a restraint of trade to the employer's benefit. They will, however, interpret a term in the contract which seeks to restrain an employee's activities but which masquerades as an ordinary term of the contract as being in restraint of trade and strike it out. *Marshall* v *NM Financial Management Ltd* [1997] IRLR 449 is a good example of this. Here, the contract stipulated that commission should be payable to an employee after termination of the contract *only if* the employee did not enter into competition with the former employer. By another name this was a restraint clause.

The next point to note in the diagram is the presumption described above: even if there is an express restraint of trade clause, it will be presumed void unless reasonable. We will leave aside analysing 'reasonableness' for the moment and presume the clause in question passes this test.

9.4 The importance of how the contract was terminated

9.4.1 Wrongful dismissal

At common law an employer can terminate the contract for any reason provided the proper notice is given. In such a case, there is no breach of contract and the restraint clause will survive the termination of the relationship. However, if the dismissal constitutes a wrongful dismissal this will amount to a repudiation by the employer and the restraint will cease to be even potentially effective. So, although an employer who fails to give proper notice under the contract is only open to damages equivalent to the amount that should have been paid or worked in the first place, the wrongful dismissal destroys any post-termination covenants: see *General Billposting Co. Ltd* v *Atkinson* [1909] AC 118 (HL).

The principles of *General Billposting* do not apply to unfair dismissals, only to wrongful dismissal or wrongful repudiation cases. Whether they might apply to a finding by a tribunal that an employee was unfairly (constructively) dismissed is open to question, but there seems no good reason why this should not be so.

To guard against this, some contracts contain a statement that the restraint clause will be effective even if there is a wrongful dismissal. They state that the clause will be binding 'after termination of the employment however that comes about and whether lawful or not', or 'following termination for whatever reason'. Although common, these terms are ineffective: *Living Design (Home Improvements) Ltd* v *Davidson* [1994] IRLR 69. The presence of such a clause does not, however, invalidate the restraint generally. This was confirmed in *Rock Refrigeration Ltd* v *Jones* [1997] ICR 938 (CA). It is also worth noting that in *Rock Refrigeration* the Court also took time to take a little side-swipe at *General Billposting* which may yet have practical effects.

Both Simon Brown and Philips LJJ (*obiter*) questioned whether *General Billposting* accorded with current legal principle in the light of the House of Lords' decision in *Photo Productions Ltd* v *Securicor Transport Ltd* [1980] AC 827. That case had held that an exclusion clause in a contract could survive a fundamental breach. Their Lordships' point was that if this is so then perhaps a restraint clause can survive a wrongful dismissal.

9.4.2 Justifiable dismissal

A dismissal without notice or with inadequate notice may still be a lawful dismissal if there is a contractually justifiable reason. In dismissing the employee the employer has accepted the repudiation of the contract by the employee. The employer is therefore still able to rely on the restraint covenants.

9.4.3 Resignation by the employee

If the employee resigns without giving notice, in the face of repudiatory conduct by the employer, he or she will have accepted the repudiation so that the restraint clause will cease to have any effect, as with a wrongful dismissal. If the employee gives notice, however, it seems that this will preserve the restraint clause: *Normalec* v *Britton* [1983] FSR 318.

9.4.4 Dismissal with payment in lieu of notice

Payment in lieu of notice is not a breach of contract if the contract so allows for it. If the contract does not allow for this then payment in lieu is a technical breach even though no damages would be due: *Rex Stewart Jeffries Parker Ginsberg Ltd* v *Parker* [1988] IRLR 483 (CA). The technical breach will invalidate the restraint clause.

9.4.5 Transfer of the business

As will be seen in **Chapter 15**, when a business is transferred existing employment rights are generally transferred as well. In *Morris Angel & Son Ltd* v *Hollande* [1993] IRLR 169, the question raised was whether a restraint of trade clause was subject to this rule. The Court of Appeal decided that a restraint clause entered into by the transferor company and the employee could be enforced by the transferee (purchaser) of the business. But in this case, the employee's contract was terminated very soon after the transfer so that the 'inherited restraint' related directly to contacts, etc. gained by the employee in the *transferor's* business. The position is unclear where there is a larger gap.

As will also be seen in **Chapter 15**, there is a general rule that any alteration to an employee's contractual rights following a relevant transfer is invalid if the reason for the alteration relates to the transfer of the business. In *Crédit Suisse First Boston (Europe) Ltd* v *Lister* [1998] IRLR 700, a business was taken over and new terms (some better than before, some worse) were introduced by the transferee. One disadvantageous change to the employee was the replacement of a 12-month non-solicitation clause with a three-month non-solicitation clause coupled with a three-month non-competition clause. The Court of Appeal held that, as these changes were detrimental to the employee and were as a result of the transfer, they were invalid (despite the fact that, on balance, the employee's position after all the changes, including monetary payments, was at least neutral).

9.5 Legitimate interests

As you can see from **Figure 9.1**, at the heart of all that follows is the first aspect of 'reasonableness', namely that the employer must be seeking to protect a legitimate proprietary (business) interest. The restraint must afford adequate, but no more than adequate, protection to the employer's interest. It is legitimate to:

(a) seek to prevent the potential disclosure of confidential information;

(b) seek to prevent the employee making use of the employer's trade connexions.

These are the standard touchstones, though a court can always recognise other legitimate interests.

9.5.1 Legitimate interest: preventing the potential disclosure of confidential information

We noted in **Chapter 8** that it is uncertain (following the *obiter* comments in *Faccenda Chicken* v *Fowler* [1986] ICR 297, CA) whether an express confidentiality clause can have any effect. Thus employers are often advised to insert a restraint of trade clause if they wish to protect confidential information which is important but not a trade secret. The advantage to a restraint clause is that a breach is more easily detectable and policed than the mere act of disclosing information. We have voiced the opinion that the use of a restraint clause is not justifiable simply to protect confidential information lower than a trade secret, but the 'belt and braces' practical thing to do is to insert both restraint and confidentiality clauses side by side.

9.5.2 Legitimate interest: preventing the employee making use of the employer's trade connexions

The debate flowing from *Faccenda Chicken* is not relevant to trade connexions: these are protectable legitimate interests.

9.5.2.1 Trade connexions: what are they?

There are a number of aspects hidden in the term 'trade connexions'. There are categories to which the term clearly applies, namely:

(a) the employer's customers and clients;

(b) the employer's suppliers.

There are categories where the application is likely to be made, namely:

(c) existing employees.

And there are categories where the application is more debatable, namely:

(d) the employee's previous client base;

(e) customers who no longer deal with the employer;

(f) future potential customers.

We shall examine these interests in turn.

9.5.2.2 Trade connexions: customers, clients, and suppliers

These categories—(a) and (b) in the list above—are sometimes referred to as the employer's 'goodwill' because they sum up the range of the employer's contacts and therefore the operational value of the business. Most cases will be concerned with these types of trade connexions. A solicitor's clients are treated no differently here from, say, a milkman's customers: the professional connexion with those clients does not carry with it some form of implied restraint of trade: *Wallace Bogan & Co.* v *Cove* [1997] IRLR 453.

9.5.2.3 Trade connexions: existing employees

The starting point for (c) is that recruiting another employer's employees is not unlawful provided those employees are not induced to breach their existing contracts. But can an employer set up a restraint of trade clause which prevents one of its own former employees from 'stealing away' (poaching) fellow employees when she leaves? Can the employer's own employees be regarded as 'legitimate interests'? In *Dawnay, Day & Co. Ltd* v *De Braconier D'Alphen* [1997] IRLR 442, the Court of Appeal reviewed what was becoming a long line of cases and decided that an employer did have a legitimate interest in maintaining a **stable workforce** within the limits of reasonableness, unhelpfully adding that 'it does not always follow that this will always be the case'. On this basis, it is suggested that any *non-poaching* clause can relate only to employees who were former colleagues, and probably only to those of senior status, though, like many 'rules' in this field, this is not a certainty (see, for instance, *SBJ Stephenson* v *Mandy* [2000] IRLR 233 where Bell J allowed a clause which protected against the poaching of all staff on the basis that the prime assets of the company—an insurance brokerage—were its staff).

Where solicitors' precedents contain such a clause, the majority of these do indeed refer to 'senior employees' or similar descriptions (e.g., 'skilled employees' as defined in the contract). Some extend this category to employees above a certain (defined) level of seniority or pay, or those who have to report to the board, or those with whom the employee has had direct contact (or combinations of these), or to those who are also similarly covered by a restraint clause. A small percentage give more limited definitions of 'forbidden employees'; mainly those whose work involved the handling of confidential information or who had influence over customers.

9.5.2.4 Trade connexions: the employee's previous client base

The employee may have legitimately brought to the business useful connexions which he or she now wishes to carry forward to the next employment. To what extent have these connexions become the 'property' of the employer? In *M&S Drapers* v *Reynolds* [1956] 3 All ER 814 (concerning a salesman), the Court of Appeal viewed such contacts as still belonging to the employee. In contrast to this, in *Hanover Insurance Brokers Ltd* v *Schapiro* the former employee—a *senior* employee—was offered no such sympathy. It is likely that the longer an employee works for a particular employer, the more their 'property' in their previous contacts is eroded. The legitimacy of inserting an express clause in the contract to counter such possibilities, akin to partnership agreements, does not appear to have been reviewed by the courts.

9.5.2.5 Trade connexions: past and future customers

In *Hinton & Higgs (UK) Ltd* v *Murphy and Valentine* [1989] IRLR 519, a clause attempting to restrain contact with the employer's 'previous or present' connexions was declared unreasonable because of the width of the term 'previous clients'. The category needed to be defined and limited. Equally employers have not been able to guard against the ex-employee dealing with the employer's potential **future** customers (*Konski v Peet* [1915] 1 Ch 530) unless the departing employee has made some initial contact with the customer before leaving: *Rex Stewart Jeffries Parker Ginsberg Ltd* v *Parker* [1988] IRLR 483.

Sometimes an employee leaves just when the employer and a customer are at the stage of negotiating potential contracts. It is unlikely that any restraint could legitimately cover such potential contacts. An exception was seen in *International Consulting Services (UK) Ltd v Hart* [2000] IRLR 227 where the High Court held that, in principle, such trade connexions could be protected even where the employee's contact with the customer was unconnected with those negotiations and fell outside the 'relation back' period in the contract of 12 months, but here the employee had been in a central and influential position within the company during the negotiations.

9.6 What type of clause is it?

We outlined the four main types of restraint clauses in **9.2.2** above. The severest restraint is a non-competition clause. Courts take a lot of persuasion to enforce one of these unless the employer shows a very good reason, e.g., the time factor is very short and/or the area covered is small. The courts are more relaxed with, say, a non-solicitation clause as this only seeks to prevent the former employee approaching the employer's contacts for a set period or within a specified area.

You can see in **Figure 9.2** that the clause has to be reasonable as between the parties and reasonable on its specific wording. We shall now examine these ideas in **9.8** below, but first we should note the idea of 'blue-pencilling'.

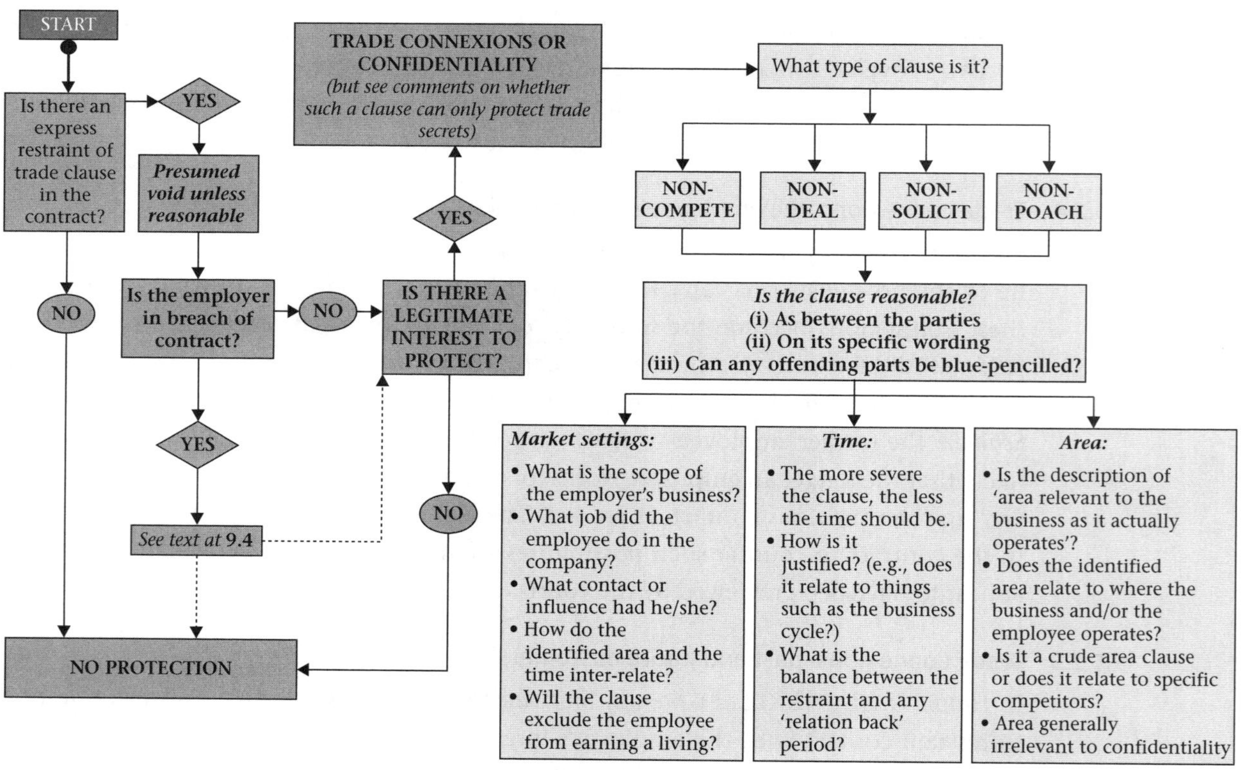

Figure 9.2 Determining reasonableness.

9.7 Severance and 'blue-pencilling'

'Blue-pencilling' means that the courts may, within limitations, remove words or sentences which are felt to make the clause unreasonable. The courts have no general power to rewrite a restraint to make it reasonable. They may give some interpretation to the wording, but it is not the courts' function to make contracts. What they have long accepted, however, is the idea of editing the clause—or applying the infamous blue pencil.

The remaining part of the clause is then allowed to stand and be effective. In *Sadler* v *Imperial Life Assurance of Canada* [1988] IRLR 388, three conditions were stated as necessary for severance (or 'blue-pencilling') to occur:

(a) the unenforceable provisions could be capable of being removed without the need to add to or modify the remaining part;

(b) the remaining terms continue to be supported by adequate consideration; and

(c) the removal of the words does not change the character of the clause, i.e., make the contract substantially different from that which was originally agreed.

In truth this will occur most often when there are separate clauses: one clause may be struck out leaving the other (narrower) clause operative. A final clause stating that 'each undertaking is a separate and distinct undertaking and the invalidity or unenforceability of any part of any of them shall not affect the validity or enforceability of the remainder' can prove useful and appears frequently in practice.

Asking a court to 'blue-pencil' is the equivalent of clutching at straws and what is never tolerated is a clause which states that the restraint will be effective 'so far as the law allows': *Davies* v *Davies* (1887) 36 ChD 359.

9.8 How is reasonableness determined?

The traditional dimensions to be measured in restraint cases have been those of *time and area*. Although the unreasonableness of either factor by itself may invalidate the restraint, the factors do overlap a great deal. Thus a restraint that is too wide in geographical terms will generally fail, but it may be saved if the time limitation is short. Likewise, a lengthy restraint may be valid especially where the geographical limitation is not extensive.

In the text below we have analysed the concept of 'reasonableness' in relation to the headings of:

(a) the market setting;

(b) time; and

(c) area.

We have created these headings merely as a device to help explain the courts' reasoning. They overlap and interact; one affects the other.

9.8.1 When is reasonableness determined?

Reasonableness is determined by looking at the point the agreement was entered into (i.e., the date of the contract, any amendment or separate agreement). Promotions and changes in job titles, which effectively involve new contracts, can therefore have an effect on the reasonableness of any clause: what was reasonable for a salesperson with numerous contacts may not be suitable for an office-bound sales manager. It is common practice, therefore, to draft clauses which refer to events at the point of termination such as the prevention of the solicitation of customers 'who have been clients of the employer during the last 12 months prior to the termination of the contract'.

9.8.2 Width of the clause: reasonableness in terms of the 'market setting'

In every case the court has to relate the restraint to the market setting of the company and the individual in question: what is the scope of the employer's activities and what did the employee do? It is not reasonableness as an abstract concept that matters but rather reasonableness in relation to the *particular* contract of employment.

9.8.2.1 The scope of the employer's business

The first question to ask is: what sort of business are we dealing with? The effects (and therefore the reasonableness) of a standard clause will be different, for instance, when dealing with a butcher's business, a finance company, an estate agency, or a national frozen foods company. It may well be reasonable to have a 12-month restraint for an accountant because clients will probably visit the practice annually to submit their tax returns but the same period would be difficult to justify where a butcher leaves a shop and customers return weekly or monthly.

The next question is: where is the employer's business located? The type of restraint that is acceptable (reasonable) can often be affected by the company's location. Say, for instance, that you have a restraint of not competing within a two-mile radius of the business. Would it make a difference if the business was located in the centre of London as opposed to a provincial town such as Taunton? In both instances a two-mile restraint might, in the abstract, appear reasonable, but those two miles may well cover many more customers in the heart of London than in Taunton. Paradoxically, the whole market for the service might be wiped out in a small town whilst not being significantly affected in London. So, the key point is: what business are we trying to apply this to? A two-mile radius restraint for a hairdresser in Taunton probably cuts out most of Taunton. It cuts out a large slice of London too, but there are other areas where the employee might set up shop. So, one cannot say that, say, a two-mile radius restraint is automatically reasonable in every case: one has to look at the market in which the employer operates.

It is, of course, also true that location may be completely irrelevant. A person can be situated in London and still *deal* with customers in Bristol, for instance, by means of telephone, advertisement, fax, internet, or letter as well as by personal proximity. Such was the position in *Office Angels Ltd* v *Rainer-Thomas and O'Connor,* regarding an employment agency. Here, a clause which sought to prevent the employee engaging in or undertaking the trade or business of an employment agency within an area of 1.2 square miles from the relevant branch looked reasonable but was held void. The clause was not over-demanding but, again, client contact was generally made by telephone. The actual siting of any rival office was largely irrelevant and the clause was meaningless.

Thus, a small radius restraint might be unreasonable and restraint extending to the whole of the UK, European Union, or even worldwide could be reasonable, *depending on the market in which the business operates*. Most draft contracts we have seen, therefore, would only employ a ban on competition within a certain 'radius' from the employer's business in relation to small businesses such as hairdressers, butchers, etc. where the catchment area is defined by the siting of the business. The use of 'radius' is not applicable to many other types of business today though it was applied to solicitors in *Hollis* v *Stocks* [2000] IRLR 712, where the Court of Appeal upheld a one-year, ten-mile radius non-competition clause against an assistant solicitor which also forbade the solicitor representing any clients at specified police stations and a named magistrates' court. The Court of Appeal interpreted the phrase 'work within ten miles from the firm's office' to mean 'to work as a solicitor' and, looking at the geography of the East Midlands, the proximity of large towns not covered by the restraint, and the general work of the solicitor's practice, held that the clause was reasonable.

In summary, the employer must be able to show a functional correspondence between the activities prohibited under the restraint and the activities of the business. It may very well be the case, for instance, that a non-solicitation clause would be the highest level of protection acceptable and all others would fail.

9.8.2.2 The job done and the status of the employee

At its simplest level the employer needs to be able to justify the fact that the job done and the position held by the employee warrants the imposition of a restraint. For instance, area restraints may be appropriate for salesmen and confidentiality restraints may be justifiable for researchers, but having one standard restraint that applies to both plus, say, manual workers, is hard to justify. The case of *Marley Tile Co. Ltd* v *Johnson* [1982] IRLR 75 provides a good example of the sort of thing to be considered. Here, the clause in question sought to restrain the employee (a salesman) from soliciting, canvassing, or dealing with customers of the employer in products made, sold, or fixed by the company or in other similar products in any area in which he had been employed by the company for a period of one year after termination. The restraint covered *any area* in which the employee had worked during the year prior to leaving. In that year the employee had worked mainly in Devon, but several months before leaving he had also worked in Cornwall. This meant that the possible number of customers covered by the clause was in the region of 2,500 and the range of products was enormous. The restraint was held to be void—it could not legitimately apply to products the employee never dealt with (see also *Commercial Plastics Ltd* v *Vincent* [1965] 1 QB 623).

Junior employees may get more gentle treatment from the courts than their seniors. However, care should be taken when dealing with employees who have gained expertise in a particular field to the exclusion of all else. If the restraint effectively prevents them working within that field it is likely to fall foul of the test for reasonableness.

EXAMPLE

Your client is a salesman in the drapery trade. His contract contains a non-solicitation clause set to last for five years and is applicable to the employer's connexions who had been customers during the three years prior to termination. He wants to know whether he is likely to be restrained from working for a rival company.

This is based on the case of *M&S Drapers* v *Reynolds* [1956] 3 All ER 814. The Court of Appeal refused the restraint, partly on the grounds that the employee did not hold a position which warranted such a restriction. That was in 1956: today such a lengthy clause, even for a more senior employee, would be difficult to justify. Ask yourself: 'why does the employer need a five-year restraint covering customers from the last three years of the employee's employment?' What is the justification? One aspect of the justification might be that the employee has had extensive contact with these customers. The time still looks excessive but, as we shall see, this idea of 'contact' is much more important than status in assessing reasonableness.

9.8.2.3 The level of contact between the employee and the trade connexion

Here we ask:

(a) does the employee have to have had *contact* with the trade connexion before a restraint is valid; and, if so,

(b) what level of contact is necessary?

To answer question (a): the long-standing approach has been that contact is necessary. Usually this has meant *physical contact,* but repeated indirect contact can change this and those who procure business *without direct contact* have been held to fall within the ambit of restraint clauses. This is because frequency of contact coupled with some degree of attachment can generate reliance and influence. The closer the contact and the more reliant on the employee the customer/supplier becomes the more justifiable the restraint: *Scorer* v *Seymour Johns* [1966] 1 WLR 1419 and *Office Angels Ltd* v *Rainer-Thomas and O'Connor* [1991] IRLR 214. What is more debatable is whether an employee's *reputation* can be considered as a trade connexion (and therefore a legitimate interest) because it has long been established that mere personal attributes cannot be the subject of a restraint. In *Austin Knight (UK) Ltd* v *Hinds* [1994] FSR 52 Vinelott J noted that it was possible that influence might exist via *reputation* (at least in a business operating in a tightly knit market) although on the facts would not infer such influence. It is suggested that, if any form of restraint is permissible, it is most likely to be that of preventing solicitation of existing clients, rather than a general ban on acting within the general field of, say, financial services.

To answer question (b): on the whole it would be unwise for an employer to rely on merely proving *some form* of contact. The courts are really looking for the degree of *influence* that could be exerted by the employee over the customer or client: *Hinton & Higgs (UK) Ltd* v *Murphy and Valentine* [1989] IRLR 519. In analysing the degree of influence the court must set the 'employer's hold' over the customer against the type of contact the customer has with the employee (the level of reliance), the seniority of the employee, the nature of the goods or services, and the frequency of contact.

EXAMPLE

The owner of a hairdresser's business is tired of losing staff to rivals. She particularly values the work of the new stylist, and the receptionist who gets on very well with customers. She wants to know, in principle, whether she can impose a restraint of trade clause on either or both employees.

Receptionists will come into contact with all customers, but the degree of influence is infinitely less than is likely with the particular stylist and, though a restraint might prove to be effective, the argument favours the employee. But if we move to the stylist there is greater justification for the imposition of a restraint clause. So now, if that stylist sets up in business a short distance away it is arguable that some customers may well follow (see *Marion White Ltd* v *Francis* [1972] 3 All ER 857). However, this argument will only succeed where *influence* is shown—unless there are other factors present such as deceit: *East* v *Maurer* [1991] 1 WLR 461.

For some reason, hairdressers have long occupied the minds of judges in this area. In *Steiner (UK) Ltd* v *Spray* (1993, unreported, LEXIS transcript) the Court of Appeal was again concerned with this trade. Affirming the test of *influence* the court approved a *non-competition* clause on the basis that a ban on solicitation was irrelevant in this business and that non-dealing was impossible to police. Their Lordships were, however, influenced by the fact that the clause covered an area of only three-eighths of a mile for six months.

9.8.2.4 Contact: relationship with employee's past dealings

In practice, both non-dealing and non-solicitation restraints tend to relate the restraint to contacts which the employee made during some period prior to termination. For instance, a clause which seeks to restrain an employee from dealing with customers or suppliers of the company for 12 months from termination will frequently contain a 're-lation back' phrase such as:

> who are at the date of termination of the employment and who shall have been at any time in the preceding 12 months a customer of . . . the Company and with whom the employee has had direct dealings or personal contact as part of that employment.

The 'relation back period' of prior dealings/contact tends to be either of six or 12 months. In assessing reasonableness the courts often balance the length of the restraint against the length of the 'relation back' period: see *Dentmaster (UK) Ltd* v *Kent* [1997] IRLR 636, CA.

9.8.3 Width of the clause: reasonableness in terms of time

The middle of the three 'reasonableness' boxes in **Figure 9.2** is 'time'.

9.8.3.1 Time in relation to confidential information

'Time' is the key element in relation to the protection of confidential information. The restraint can last no longer than the projected useful life of that information. An obvious difference lies in the considerations applied to ex-employees of organisations famed for their 'secret recipes' and those, say, in the fashion industry, where the secrecy of next season's designs has a limited lifespan. It may be reasonable in the former case to impose a lifetime ban; in the latter case, probably no more than a few months. Highly technical information will probably have a short lifespan, both because of the speed at which technology changes and also because an employee could not retain enough detail of the information for too long. So the vital question for a draftsman to ask the employer is: what is the lifespan of the information? The cynical practitioner then reduces this period by at least 25 per cent.

It must also be the case that different employees, or at least groups of employees, will have access to varying levels and types of confidential information. Thus, a restraint clause applied without variation to all employees is likely to fall foul of the reasonableness test because a one-year restraint, whilst reasonable in relation to the head of computer design, may be too great when applied even to a computer programmer or a technician.

9.8.3.2 Time in relation to trade connexions

A more relaxed attitude to lengthy or unlimited restraints has been taken by the courts in relation to trade connexions: *Fitch* v *Dewes* [1921] 2 AC 158—a solicitor's managing clerk who interviewed about half of the firm's clients was prevented from practising within seven miles of Tamworth Town Hall for an unlimited time. But this case does not set a general pattern. Before a restraint runs its course any advantage gained by the former employee will begin to fade. Knowledge of the market will become out of date and, more importantly, connexions will be lost. With this in mind, Jessel MR suggested a very workable test in *Middleton* v *Brown* (1878) 47 LJ Ch 411, at p. 413: that the duration of the restraint should be limited to the time it takes for a replacement employee to demonstrate his effectiveness to customers.

We would propose that any time limit must be justifiable both in relation to the 'replacement employee' idea coupled with an investigation into the *cycle* of the employer's business, i.e., how often contracts are renewed or repeat customer contact expected. We used the example of a firm of accountants being in contact with clients only every 12 months in **9.8.2.1** above as part of identifying the appropriateness of a restraint to the nature of the employer's business: here we see how that assessment of 'market setting' can overlap with the assessment of acceptable time periods.

9.8.4 Width of the clause: reasonableness in terms of area covered

This is the final box in **Figure 9.2**. The key point here is that the size of the area is related more to density of population than mere acreage. It is thus an oversimplification to state that the wider the area the more likely it will be unreasonable; although it is a convenient rule of thumb.

Both UK and worldwide bans have succeeded. In *Littlewoods Organisation Ltd* v *Harris* [1976] ICR 516, a director concerned with mail order catalogues was restrained from employment within the UK for one year. *Under Water Welders and Repairers Ltd* v *Street and Longhorne* [1968] RPC 498, concerned a diver under a three-year worldwide restraint. With the increasing presence of national and multi-national companies in the marketplace, the problems as to which area is to be covered by the restraint will be ever-increasing.

9.8.4.1 Area in relation to confidential information

Where the justification for a restraint rests on the protection of information, its geographical ambit may have to be very wide. After all, information knows no real boundaries. Thus, the general 'market' in which the employer operates is a justifiable 'area'; and that area might these days be the UK, Europe, or even worldwide.

The restraint based on protecting confidential information is most likely to be aimed at preventing competitors from benefiting from the employee's expertise. It is a better tactic for an employer to limit a restraint to named competitors or competitors within a defined area: *Littlewoods Organisation Ltd* v *Harris* [1977] 1 WLR 1472. Here the restraint was for one year. The clause was drafted to prevent Harris working for Littlewoods' major rival, Great Universal Stores (GUS). Harris left Littlewoods and went to work for GUS. The clause (which was effectively worldwide in its scope) was construed as applying only to the UK (because that was the only place where Littlewoods and GUS were rivals) and only to the type of business in which GUS competed with Littlewoods. With these limitations (and debatable interpretations) the clause was held to be enforceable.

The *Littlewoods* case also illustrates the point that the courts are quite capable of adopting a generous interpretation where the overall package appears reasonable. For instance, in *Turner* v *Commonwealth & British Minerals Ltd* [2000] IRLR 114, the restraint was worded so as to apply to geographical areas which fell within the company's influence but in which the employees had not worked. The clause might have failed on the same analysis as *Marley Tile Co. Ltd* v *Johnson* (see **9.8.2.2** above), but the Court of Appeal construed the clause as only applying to those areas in which the employees *had* worked, thereby saving the restraint.

9.8.4.2 Area in relation to trade connexions

The reasonableness of geographical restraints in relation to trade connexions is more problematic. Because non-dealing or non-competition clauses are crude devices the courts must do two things: first, they must survey the actual width of the employer's operations; secondly, they must determine whether the restriction effectively negates the former employee's potential *influence* over the company's connexions. On the first point, for instance, if a company operates only in Coventry, a restraint extending to Newcastle would go beyond what is necessary. This form of analysis works very well with localised businesses but note the comments on 'radius' restraints above.

When the employer's business is less localised the definition of a reasonable area has to rest on the factual point of understanding the employer's business and the appropriateness to the employee. It can no longer be the case that merely because the employer operates across the whole UK, the restraint should also cover such an area. The clause should relate to the siting of the employer's competitors and/or the employee's activities. Indeed, many clauses now try to relate the restraint to 'customers' (either in general form or even specific names—see **9.8.5.2** below) so that 'area' has become much less of a determining factor than it used to be.

9.8.5 Non-solicitation covenants and trade connexions

The general rules described above apply equally to non-solicitation covenants as to non-dealing and non-competition clauses. We have separated out this area only because it brings with it some extra matters for consideration. Non-solicitation clauses relate to the protection of trade connexions only. The time qualification in the restraint will therefore be germane, though the question of the area covered is usually irrelevant. Oddly enough, there appears to be no case where a non-solicitation clause has been held void purely on the grounds of its duration; but this does not negate the need for the employer to show it is reasonable on the facts.

9.8.5.1 What constitutes solicitation?

Solicitation involves action by the employee: the enticing or active attraction of connexions away from the former employer. The terms 'soliciting' and 'enticing' have not, however, been defined authoritatively. We would suggest that anything which seems to carry an invitation to defect, rather than merely provide information, will amount to soliciting. Certainly, being approached by a former customer of the employer is not solicitation; and to prevent this activity the employer will need to have inserted a non-dealing clause.

Apart from the more obvious act of contacting connexions directly and overtly, it is also probable that *indirect* approaches such as advertising in newspapers and trade journals will constitute solicitation if they contain some form of inducement. Merely informing clients that one has left the old employer is not solicitation—the solicitation part would come with any 'I can now be contacted at. . .' statement.

If the solicitation clause has a geographical limit the issue of advertising material which spills over into the forbidden zone could present a problem. There appears to be no direct case law on this point, though in *Cullard* v *Taylor* (1887) 3 TLR 698, a solicitor restrained from operating within a particular area who sent letters to clients residing in the area was held to be in breach of the restraint; and New Zealand authority (*Sweeney* v *Astle* (1923) 42 NZLR 1198) indicates that advertising which spills over into the protected area so that customers become aware of the employee's position will be outlawed. If such is the position then the question of time constraint becomes particularly important if the clause is to be seen as reasonable rather than punitive.

9.8.5.2 Which connexions are covered?

These need to be capable of identification. The conclusive factor will then be whether the clause is protecting against influence being exerted by the former employee. Thus, in *Gledhow Autoparts* v *Delaney* [1965] 1 WLR 1366, the clause sought to restrict the activities of a salesman. The clause prohibited solicitation 'within the districts in which the traveller operated'. Many of the customers had no contact with the employee. The clause was therefore wider than necessary and void (see also *Marley Tile Co. Ltd v Johnson* [1982] IRLR 75).

The comments on prior contact noted above at **9.8.2.3** apply equally here and are not repeated.

We should also note again that if a clause is otherwise reasonable it will not be deemed unreasonable simply because the employer's connexions state they are unlikely to continue doing business with the employer anyway: see *John Michael Design plc* v *Cooke* [1987] ICR 445.

9.8.6 Public policy considerations

Strictly speaking, the whole doctrine of restraint of trade is based on the concept of public interest; the balancing of an individual's liberty with principles of freedom of contract. Courts can therefore 'fall back' on pronouncements of public interest or public policy in order to strike out clauses which, though reasonable perhaps as between the parties, offend some vague judgment as to what is acceptable.

One thing which is certain about public policy is that it is not immutable. As a starting point, however:

(a) If the restraint has passed the tests of legitimate interest as well as temporal and spatial reasonableness it will fall on the employee to prove that it is nevertheless contrary to public policy: *Herbert Morris* v *Saxelby.*

(b) It will not be contrary to public policy simply on the grounds that the employee's interests are more adversely affected than the employer's interests are protected. Except in the extreme cases where the employee is prevented from working at all the effect on the employee is not really a consideration addressed by the courts. The test is not based on the *balancing* of interests: *Allied Dunbar (Frank Weisenger) Ltd* v *Weisenger* [1988] IRLR 60.

(c) It was suggested in *Faccenda Chicken* v *Fowler* that the use to which an employee puts confidential information may have an effect on the court's approach to the protection sought, e.g., seeking to earn a living is viewed as potentially warranting protection but merely *selling* the information will lose the court's favour.

Other examples of courts invoking 'public policy' to strike out clauses include: *Bull* v *Pitney-Bowes* [1967] 1 WLR 273, where a pension scheme contained a clause stating that if a retired employee entered into any form of competition with the employer that employee's pension rights would be affected; and *Kores Manufacturing Co. Ltd* v *Kolok Manufacturing Co. Ltd* [1959] Ch 108 (a reciprocal agreement, made between two companies, restraining the employment of each other's former employees held to be contrary to public policy).

But public policy does not always damn restraint clauses. Thus in *Bridge* v *Deacons* [1984] AC 705 the Privy Council perceived the value of restraint clauses as providing a means whereby the young can replace the old. And in *Kerr* v *Morris* [1987] Ch 90 the Court of Appeal did not agree that doctors in general practice formed a special class which was exempt from the applications of restraint of trade clauses.

It would also appear that a defective restraint cannot be saved by the fact that during the time it should have applied the employee also received some post-termination payments: *TSC Europe (UK) Ltd* v *Massey* [1999] IRLR 22, ChD.

9.9 Drafting and interpretation

9.9.1 The problems in giving meaning to the clause

The basic premise is that an employer stands or falls by what is written in the restraint clause. Here is a typical restraint clause:

Non-competition

For a period of 6 months after termination of the Employment, the Employee shall not (whether directly or indirectly) be engaged or interested whether as principal, servant, agent, consultant or otherwise in any trade or business which by virtue of its location competes with any trade or business being carried on in the United Kingdom at the date of termination of the Employment by the Company and in which trade or business the Employee has been involved as part of his Employment.

It does not make for light reading, partly because the tradition of not using punctuation (which died out elsewhere in legal documents years ago) still rears its ugly head in this area. Further, the clause often makes no sense at all when actually applied to the employer and employee, because it has simply been lifted from a book of precedents. It is therefore advisable to make the meaning of any clause as clear as possible. Phrases such as 'engage', or 'undertake', or 'carry on a business' are somewhat flexible expressions which may bear a different meaning in a given context. A solicitor must make sure the context fits. If the contract is silent or ambiguous on a particular point it will most likely be construed against the employer.

As a matter of drafting practice, therefore, it is imperative that any restraint clause actually reflects both a legitimate interest *and* the relevance of that clause to the employee's work. The easiest clauses to draft are those which prohibit actions on a sweeping basis. They are equally the most dangerous clauses because they cannot hope to cover all eventualities. Even an immaculately worded contract which contains only one general clause intended to cover the entire workforce will probably be drafted too widely to cover specific situations or will not be appropriate to grades of employees.

9.9.1.1 Narrowly-drafted clauses

Clauses which are very specific will generally not be read as protecting wider interests. The courts will not write words into a clause to make it effective. If an interest needs protecting the restraint clause must be drafted to achieve this. At its simplest, this will mean that a non-solicitation clause will fail to prevent employees dealing with customers *who contact them*.

9.9.1.2 Construing wide wording

Courts may choose to read wide wording in a restricted way so as to make it workable. Thus, sometimes the courts have limited the application of any restraint, however widely worded, to the employer's actual business interests. In *Business Seating (Renovations) Ltd* v *Broad* [1989] ICR 713 a non-solicitation clause failed to say what the '*business* of any customers or clients' actually was. The court interpreted the clause by reference to other clauses in the contract to define the business as that of the repair and renovation of office furniture; but the court could simply have struck out the clause for ambiguity. Indeed, this is exactly what happened in *Mont (J. A.) (UK)* v *Mills* [1993] IRLR 173. The clause was again too general and did not attempt to focus on the need to protect confidential information; its defects were not a 'mere want of accuracy of expression'. It is advisable to define the 'business' involved, especially in multi-product companies.

Recently, some level of unspoken disagreement has emerged in the Court of Appeal as to the most appropriate style of interpretation to be used. A literal (or *contra proferentem*) approach was seen in *Mont* v *Mills* (Glidewell, Beldam, and Simon Brown LJJ), *Ingham* v *ABC Contract Services* (unreported, 1993: per Russell and Leggatt LJJ) and the approach was specifically approved by Sedley and Simon Brown LJJ (perhaps not surprisingly) in *Wincanton* v *Cranny & SDM European Transport Ltd* [2000] IRLR 716. In *Hanover* v *Schapiro,* however, the Court had adopted a far more purposive approach (Dillon and Nolan LJJ) and in *Beckett Investment Management Group Ltd* v *Hall* [2007] EWCA Civ 613, [2007] IRLR 793 the Court permitted a clause, drafted in favour of a holding company which effectively dealt with no one, to be applied to the subsidiary companies on the basis of 'practical reality'. It is not surprising that their Lordships, in all cases, have expressed the need for a full hearing of a case to resolve what is a fundamental divergence of principle.

The draftsman's dilemma is this: where the restraint clause does not specifically state the interest which the covenant is intended to protect the court can look at the wording and the general circumstances to ascertain the parties' intentions, but it can also hold that the wording is simply too wide to protect anything. But where the covenant *does* state the interest of the employer, the court is likely to follow that wording and limit the scope of the protection. Thus spelling out the legitimate interest gains the advantage of definition and certainty, but runs the risk of limitation. What the courts will not tolerate from the ex-employee are 'colourable evasions'—minor and meaningless alterations of status on the behalf of the employee (e.g., a change in job title) made simply to avoid the exact wording of the restraint. An employee who argues that acting as an assistant to, say, an architect, is not in breach of a restraint which forbids him 'carrying on that profession', will see little sympathy from the courts. Setting up a limited company under which to continue in the same trade will also count as a colourable evasion: *Gilford Motors* v *Horne* [1933] Ch 935.

9.10 Restraints during employment

The doctrine of restraint applies to post-termination events. Cases that use the term to refer to restrictions during employment (see *Schroeder (A) Music Publishing Co. Ltd* v *Macaulay* [1974] 1 WLR 1308 and *Davis (Clifford) Management Ltd* v *WEA Records Ltd* [1975] 1 WLR 61) have not been concerned with employment law at all, but rather with commercial contracts (and most recently relating to exclusive contracts for 'exploited' songwriter-performers).

There are important analytical distinctions between the two types of term. First, courts are reluctant even today to upset express terms relating to the operation of the contract, e.g., terms relating to hours, pay, etc. At the same time, courts have always subjected restraint clauses to a detailed and rigorous analysis. Secondly, an express term relating to the currency of the contract is presumed **valid** unless shown otherwise; restraint clauses are presumed to be void. Thus both restraint of trade and servile incidents may be based upon the same *common rule* of preventing undue restrictions on personal liberty, but one should be clear as to which is being used.

Having said that, however, there are borderline instances in employment law. In *Tullett Prebon plc* v *BGC Brokers LP* [2010] EWHC 484 (QB); [2010] IRLR 648, for instance, Jack J held that a term that required repayment of a signing fee if the employee did not serve out the full term of the contract was not a 'restraint of trade'.

9.10.1 Express terms

These usually appear in the form of 'whole time and attention'. Frequently they state as their justification the prevention of competition. An express term can indeed limit the activities of employees undertaken in their spare time. Any restriction the employer imposes on the employee will not deprive the employee of earning any livelihood and therefore will most likely be tolerated by the courts. At least this should hold true with full-time workers; contracts with part-time workers or consultants will be viewed more in the employee's favour.

9.10.2 Implied terms

In the absence of an express term the employee (at least senior employees) will still be bound under the duty of fidelity to use the employer's time for the employer's purposes, i.e., not to pursue other activities during working hours—at least if those activities are in competition with the employer, cause harm to the employer's interests, e.g., by divulging (or having the potential to divulge) confidential information (see *Hivac Ltd* v *Park Royal Scientific Instruments Ltd* [1946] Ch 169), or cause harm to the relationship (e.g., by undertaking work which adversely affects the proper fulfilment of the employment contract).

It follows that some low-ranking staff will have greater freedom as to the use of their spare time and cannot be so easily limited: *Nova Plastics Ltd* v *Froggatt* [1982] IRLR 146 (odd-job man not in breach when working for a competitor in his spare time). Proof of real or potential harm to the employer would be necessary for any restriction to have effect.

9.11 Employees' preparatory actions before termination

9.11.1 Preparatory acts

If an employee is planning to resign and set up in business, he or she will have made some preparations. Any business venture will need some planning. If the employee uses the employer's time and facilities to do this then this action will constitute a breach of contract: *Wessex Dairies Ltd* v *Smith* [1935] 2 KB 80, where the employee milkman (on his last day of employment) set about informing customers of his plans to set up in business on his own account.

Some latitude is given to enterprising employees. In *Laughton* v *Bapp Industrial Supplies* [1986] IRLR 245, the two employees wrote to their employer's clients informing them of their intention to set up in business on their own account and asking for product lists, price lists, and general terms. They were summarily dismissed when this was discovered by the employers. The EAT held that their actions did not amount to a breach of fidelity; their actions were *merely preparatory*. The position would have been different if they had used the employers' time and equipment (such an example would be seen in the later case of *Crowson Fabrics Ltd* v *Rider* [2008] IRLR 288 where employees 'overstepped the line' setting up e-mail accounts and actively soliciting customers); or even if there had been express terms forbidding such action. In *Balston Ltd* v *Headline Filters Ltd* [1987] FSR 330, a director's *intentions* to set up in a competing business were held not to be a breach of fiduciary duty or breach of fidelity; neither were his actions which were undertaken during his notice period but at a time when he had been released from his duties. But in *Marshall* v *Industrial Systems & Control Ltd* [1992] IRLR 294, the employee was in breach when he formed concrete plans with a fellow employee to steal away the business of the employer's best client. And again, in *Adamson* v *B&L Cleaning Services Ltd* [1995] IRLR 193 the EAT found the dismissal of a foreman to be fair when he had sought to tender for a contract in competition with his employer. This was a breach of fidelity and distinguishable from *Laughton* v *Bapp*. The Court of Appeal has also noted that where an employee can be classed as a fiduciary (usually because he is a director as well as employee) preparatory acts are treated much less leniently: *Helmet Integrated Systems* v *Tunnard* [2007] IRLR 126. However, in this particular case the Court was keen to point out that it will not imply a term that an employee cannot prepare to compete and any express terms would be read *contra proferentem*. We also noted in **Chapter 8** that the 'springboard doctrine' may be used to prevent ex-employees benefitting from their breaches of fidelity to their former employer whilst setting up their new business: *UBS Wealth Management (UK) Ltd v Vestra Wealth LLP* [2008] EWHC 1974 (QBD), [2008] IRLR 965.

These cases tended to focus on acts of preparation as distinct from substantive actions. What is not entirely clear, however, is whether potentially harmful acts such as soliciting customers, suppliers, or even fellow employees, *pursued in the employee's own time*, will constitute a breach of fidelity. There are indications (see *Thomas Marshall* v *Guinle* [1978] ICR 905 at 925 and *Hivac Ltd* v *Park Royal Scientific Instruments Ltd* [1946] Ch 169 at 178) that the answer would be that a breach has occurred. Certainly this should be the case where the contract contains a 'whole time and attention' clause.

9.11.2 Going beyond preparatory acts

If the employee is simply planning to leave the company to join another (e.g., attending interviews), it follows from the above discussion that this will **not** constitute any breach of fidelity. Care must be taken here to distinguish preparatory acts, such as attending interviews, from acts such as copying confidential information or memorising data or diverting business opportunities. In *Sanders* v *Parry* [1967] 1 WLR 753, for instance, an assistant solicitor agreed with one of his principal's clients to resign and set up in business, in premises provided by the client, taking with him the client's business. Havers J commented that the employee was 'knowingly, deliberately and secretly acting, setting out to do something which would inevitably inflict great harm on his principal'. Thus, such actions will constitute a breach of contract and open up the possibility of injunctive relief.

The 'poaching' of employees, even whole teams, by a rival company has become more common recently. One senior employee may be taken on by a rival organisation and then that person will use their knowledge and contacts to enlist groups of former colleagues to join them. This may involve breaches of confidentiality and inducement to breach contracts. Such was the case in *Tullett Prebon plc* v *BGC Brokers LP* [2010] EWHC 484 (QB), [2010] IRLR 648 where the senior ex-employee sought to use other managers as 'recruiting sergeants' for their respective teams.

9.12 Garden leave

The rather horticultural term 'garden leave' refers to attempts to hold the employee (who usually wishes to terminate the contract) to his or her notice period. The idea is that the employee will not be forced to work during that notice period but may stay at home (in the garden!) and still be paid. If successful, the effect of such a clause is that it operates as some form of indirect restraint as the employee cannot work for any competitor during this time because of the employee's continuing duty of fidelity. Contacts and confidential information thus become less and less useful. Injunctions have been granted to this effect. Such relief is discretionary.

The case law really began with *Evening Standard Co. Ltd* v *Henderson* [1987] ICR 588. Henderson sought to leave to work for a rival newspaper, giving only two months' notice instead of the 12 required. The company sought to put him on garden leave. An injunction was granted because the company was not seeking to compel Henderson to continue working as such, nor was the company refusing him the right to work, nor would it be seeking damages from him for not working. But an injunction was refused on similar facts in *Provident Financial Group plc* v *Hayward* [1989] ICR 160 because the Court of Appeal found that the employer's position would not be seriously affected by the employee's actions. In *GFI Group Inc* v *Eaglestone* [1994] IRLR 119 a 20-week notice period/garden leave was held to be arbitrary and the garden leave was reduced to 13 weeks.

It is advisable to have an express 'garden leave' provision in the contract, rather than merely rely on the notice provision covering this by implication: see *Eurobrokers Ltd* v *Rabey* [1995] IRLR 206 but there is no bar on seeking to rely on the implied right to keep an employee to his notice. In *Eurobrokers* the employee resigned and the employers sought to bind him to an express six-month garden leave clause. He declined to observe this and an injunction was granted enforcing the period. The court noted that the employer had expended a great deal of money in developing contacts for the employee and that this period represented a reasonable time for the employer to cement new relations with those customers.

William Hill Organisation Ltd v *Tucker* [1998] IRLR 313 saw the Court of Appeal again refuse to grant a 'garden leave' injunction where there was no express term allowing for this, holding that the employer was under an obligation to let this senior employee perform his job, not just receive his wages (which is a little odd given that the employee actually wanted to leave his job to work elsewhere). Therefore, on a 'belt and braces' approach it is advisable for an employer to include both a garden leave clause and a payment in lieu clause in the contract. The case did not end there. Morritt LJ went on to comment that in the case of a garden leave injunction being sought, 'it had to be justified on similar grounds to those necessary to the validity of the employee's restraint covenant in restraint of trade . . . '. The same point was made again by Morritt LJ in *Symbian Ltd* v *Christenson* [2001] IRLR 77. This case also contains the controversial view of Sir Richard Scott V-C that, during garden leave periods, an employee no longer owed a duty of good faith or fidelity to his employer.

Where an employer seeks to enforce both a garden leave clause and a restraint clause there is a persuasive argument that the overall effect might be unreasonable. Some contracts therefore specify that if the garden leave is enforced the restraint will be reduced accordingly. Following the Court of Appeal decision in *Crédit Suisse Asset Management Ltd* v *Armstrong* [1996] IRLR 450, however, we now know that (except in extreme cases) there is no juridical basis for such a set-off. The Court also confirmed its powers in deciding on the permissible length of garden leave clauses in any particular case.

It is also sometimes argued that a garden leave clause should be unenforceable where employees need to be allowed to work to preserve their particular skills. There is the basis for an argument here but the employees involved must come, so to speak, with clean hands. Where they have committed an act of serious misconduct that led to their being given notice, they will not get the sympathy of the court: *SG & R Valuation Services Co* v *Boudrais* [2008] IRLR 770. They will lose any 'right to work' and have to serve out the notice (even when they are being suspended during that time). This case also demonstrated that whereas a court will usually look for an express garden leave term, in some instances an employer (as here) can rely on notice clauses alone through the device of implied terms.

The reasonableness of garden leave clauses is determined at the time of enforcement rather than the time of contracting.

9.13 Injunctions

Though a claimant may have a remedy of damages as of right there exists the additional or alternative discretionary remedy of an injunction. However, if damages will compensate the claimant fully an injunction will not be granted. Neither will the court grant an injunction which amounts to an order for specific performance.

9.13.1 Basic rules for injunctions

Injunctions come in two forms: interim (pending a full hearing of the issues) and final (granted at the conclusion of the full action). In either case they may be limited in duration or perpetual in their effect. The granting of injunctions is a discretionary remedy. The key section of the Civil Procedure Rules is Part 25.

As far as employment matters are concerned, interim injunctions have the greater prominence. Despite the fact that the interim injunction really does not decide the merits of the case at all, the granting of such injunctions can effectively determine the issue. For instance, if the lifespan of a restraint of trade clause is one year it is unlikely that the full action will be heard before its expiry. Thus where an employer is faced with an employee or former employee who is about to divulge confidential information, breach copyright, destroy the novelty of a patentable invention and so forth, the effectiveness of an injunction can come into play. Even in advance of any breach it is possible to obtain a *quia timet* (because he fears) injunction.

Almost inevitably, where an interim injunction is granted the claimant will have to undertake to pay any damages due should the final action determine that the injunction was not justified. In some cases, the court will require proof that this undertaking can be honoured. It is also possible for a defendant to seek to avoid the full implications of an interim injunction by offering to the applicant or the court an undertaking in relation to some or all of the relief sought.

9.13.2 *American Cyanamid* v *Ethicon*

The decision of the House of Lords in the patent case of *American Cyanamid Co.* v *Ethicon Ltd* [1975] AC 396 established the position as regards *with notice* applications for prohibitory injunctions. In these cases evidence is normally given by witness statement, to the exclusion of cross-examination. The employer does not have to show a *prima facie* case to obtain an injunction preventing, for example, the breach of a restraint of trade or confidentiality clause. Rather, the test is whether:

(a) there is a serious issue to be tried at the full hearing. This is a low-level test. In *Arbuthnot Fund Managers Ltd* v *Rawlings* [2003] EWCA Civ 518, Chadwick LJ stated (at [30]) that the question at this interim stage is, '[W]hether it is plain and obvious that the restraint will fail after examination at a trial. If it is not plain and obvious—because the determination as to what is in the interests of the parties and in the interests of the public must await a trial—then the clauses must at this stage be regarded as having a reasonable prospect of being upheld'; and

(b) if there is, whether the 'balance of convenience' favours the granting of the injunction. This aspect has been described as a shorthand phrase for 'the balance of the risk of doing an injustice' or 'the balance of hardship'. The primary factor in deciding this question is whether damages at trial would be a sufficient remedy. If they would be, this negates the need for an injunction. However, damages are often not an adequate remedy in this area as (especially in confidentiality cases) once the 'cat is out of the bag' the injury caused may well be uncompensatable in monetary terms. Equally, if the defendant is unlikely to be able to pay any damages awarded this points towards an injunction being granted—and if the applicant cannot give a cross-undertaking on damages this makes the granting of an injunction less likely. The focus of 'balance of convenience' often amounts to gauging the cost to the employer of allowing the employee to use/disclose or continue to use/disclose the secret as against the possibility that the employee will be unable to work in the industry. The cases show that the employer's needs are usually seen to be paramount, though some notice was taken of the employee's (unopposed) claim of potential job loss in *Corporate Express Ltd* v *Lisa Day* [2004] EWHC 2943 where the remaining part of the restriction was quite short. A very good and straightforward application of this balancing act can be seen in *Steffen Hair Designs* v *Wright* [2004] EWHC 2995, where a 'half-mile radius' non-competition injunction was granted against a hair stylist working for a competitor some two hundred yards away, but this was limited in scope to cover only ex-clients of the stylist's previous employer (effectively turning it into a non-dealing clause—which is very practical but highly questionable as it involves rewriting the contract to turn a non-competition clause into one of non-dealing).

In *Lawrence David* v *Ashton* [1989] ICR 123, the Court of Appeal stated that the *American Cyanamid* principles will *normally* apply to restraint of trade and confidentiality cases. The court will then seek to make an order for a speedy trial of the full action, usually on the application of the defendant. If, however, a speedy trial is not possible the judge is placed in something of a dilemma: to tie down the employee for a lengthy period so that long-term employment prospects might be adversely and seriously affected; or to allow the employee to continue working for the competitor so that, even if the restraint is finally found to be valid, the employer's remedy is purely a pyrrhic one. In such instances (as was noted specifically in *Lansing Linde Ltd* v *Kerr* [1991] ICR 428 by the Court of Appeal), the judge at the interim hearing may have to investigate the substantive merits of the case in order to decide whether or not to grant the injunction. Thus, if the full action cannot be tried before the period of the restraint has expired (or almost expired), the court's decision could for most practical purposes effectively determine the issue at the interim stage. Equally, there is little point in granting an interim injunction concerning confidential information where there can be no further material damage to the employer.

As a basic approach, therefore, if a speedy trial is not possible a judge will have to consider, in a limited way because of the availability of evidence, the actual merits of the case. Indeed, in *Series 5 Software Ltd* v *Philip Clarke* [1996] FSR 273 Laddie J made the point that assessing the merits of the case was not in itself contrary to the spirit or intentions of *American Cyanamid*. Laddie J reviewed the authorities in depth and concluded that Lord Diplock in *American Cyanamid* had not intended to exclude consideration of the strength of the parties' cases; what was intended was that the court should not at this stage attempt to resolve difficult issues of fact or law. Thus it is necessary that a clear view of the evidence adduced can be gained by the judge without great debate before the relative strengths can be considered. The application of the *American Cyanamid* principles, as modified by *Series* 5, remains the position as regards interim injunctions applications based on restraint of trade clauses relating to the protection of trade connexions. With applications relating to the protection of confidential information (based on the implied term, any operative express terms, or any restraint justified by the protection of information) matters have taken a different route because of the impact of the Human Rights Act 1998.

9.13.3 Impact of the Human Rights Act 1998

Article 10 ECHR states:

> 1. Everyone has the right to freedom of expression. This right shall include freedom to hold opinions and to receive and impart information and ideas without interference by public authority . . .
>
> 2. The exercise of these freedoms, since it carries with it duties and responsibilities, may be subject to such formalities, conditions, restrictions or penalties as are prescribed by law and are necessary in a democratic society . . . for the protection of the reputation or the rights of others, *for preventing the disclosure of information received in confidence* . . . [emphasis added]

In cases involving the publication of material concerning others, therefore, this article (via the Human Rights Act) has to be considered. In terms of the granting of interim injunctions, the procedural method of dealing with this is set out in s. 12(3) of HRA 1998 which states: 'No [relief affecting the exercise of a Convention right to freedom of expression] is to be granted so as to restrain publication before trial unless the court is satisfied that the applicant is likely to establish that publication should not be allowed.'

High-profile case law has sprung up in this area (sometimes involving the potential conflict between art. 10 and art. 8—respect for private and family life): see, for instance, *Douglas* v *Hello! Ltd* [2001] QB 967, on the infamous wedding photos of Michael Douglas and Catherine Zeta-Jones; *A* v *B (a company)* [2002] EWCA Civ 337, [2002] 3 WLR 542 on the sexual exploits of a footballer; *Venables* v *News Group Newspapers Ltd* [2001] Fam 430, on the identities of the killers of James Bulger and the more technically biased case of *Imutran Ltd* v *Uncaged Campaigns Ltd* [2001] 2 All ER 385, where a group campaigning for the cessation of animal experiments sought to publish confidential information belonging to a pharmaceutical company. These cases have generally been concerned with the freedom of the press or the protection of reputation. None of the cases had to consider, as part of the *ratio*, what was meant by the phrase in s. 12(3): 'the applicant is likely to establish that publication should not be allowed'. That problem fell to the Court of Appeal in *Cream Holdings Ltd* v *Banerjee* [2003] EWCA Civ 103, [2003] 2 All ER 318. As Sedley LJ puts it: how likely is 'likely'? The Court of Appeal held that the word 'likely' means *'a real prospect of success, convincingly established'*—a standard higher than that expected under *American Cyanamid* but lower than the notion of 'more probable than not'. 'Real prospect' here means 'not fanciful' rather than 'on the cards'.

As was noted in *Cream Holdings,* however, this test is just the first step; it is still open to the court to decide on the merits available to it whether to grant or refuse the injunction (indeed, in *Cream Holdings* itself the Court of Appeal was divided on the application issue). Simon Brown LJ put it this way: 'That is not, of course, to say that, whenever the [likely to succeed] test is satisfied, the court will grant interlocutory relief [sic] . . . . Often the court will not think it right to exercise that discretion in favour of prior restraint unless it is indeed satisfied that the claim will more probably than not succeed at trial' (at [61]). This is because, as Simon Brown LJ further commented (at [56]) on the move away from the original *American Cyanamid* principles, 'there will indeed be a number of claims for injunctive relief which will now fail when earlier they would have succeeded; they will fail because the court is required by s. 12(3) actually to consider the merits . . . '.

It is possible that human rights issues may arise in an employment context and trigger a s. 12(3) analysis but most employment-based cases will not centre on issues such as freedom of expression and privacy in the way these terms have so far been used in human rights jurisprudence. Nevertheless, the potential is always there. *Cream Holdings* itself involved an ex-employee in-house accountant passing information about alleged company malpractices to a local newspaper. The employee was under a duty of confidentiality and was in breach of this by relating her stories to the newspaper. Much of the detail of this case is contained in a closed judgment owing to the nature of the information, but, since the court affirmed the granting of the injunction, we must conclude that the presence of the duty was enough to persuade the court to continue with the temporary stop to publication (together with the fact that the delay in publication would not destroy the newsworthiness of the article itself). Nor did the well-established principle that there can be no confidentiality in iniquity (i.e., the company's alleged misconduct) prove to be a major decisive factor (but contrast, for instance, Sedley LJ's comments at [87] with those of Arden LJ at [96]). The injunction did not, however, relate to disclosures made by the accountant to relevant professional and supervisory bodies under the Public Interest Disclosure Act 1998.

9.13.4 Summary of rules regarding interim applications

There are different standards to apply in justifying the granting of interim injunctions depending upon the basis for the claim.

(a) Where the issue is one of the protection of trade connexions *only* the normal *American Cyanamid* principles should apply.

(b) The merits of the case may nevertheless have to be examined where a speedy trial is not possible. This is a matter of discretion and the courts should rarely attempt to resolve complex issues of disputed fact or law: *Series 5*.

(c) Any case involving the disclosure of confidential information may bring with it human rights implications in the form of art. 10 ECHR and even, possibly, art. 8 rights. If so, the procedures described in s. 12(3) of HRA 1998 must be adhered to. If not, one presumes that the *American Cyanamid/Series 5* principles continue unabated (though this is not clear and it seems safer to work on the basis that s. 12(3) is the guiding light).

(d) Although *American Cyanamid* was distinguished in *Cream Holdings,* and a different test used, in many practical ways the test under s. 12(3) is not that dissimilar to the one created by Laddie J in *Series 5* (though generated by different considerations).

9.13.5 Search orders

The idea of search orders (formerly ***Anton Piller*** orders) is derived from the case of *Anton Piller KG* v *Manufacturing Processes Ltd* [1976] RPC 719. They represent the final link in a chain of orders which seek to deal with physical evidence. Along with freezing orders (formerly *Mareva* injunctions) they have been described as the law's nuclear weapons. Search orders have now been placed on a statutory footing: Civil Procedure Act 1997, s. 7. They are dealt with in CPR, r. 25.1(1)(h) and by Practice Direction 25.

The effect of search orders (to varying degrees) is to allow the claimant immediate access to the defendant's premises to search for and seize documents and other evidence such as information stored on computer. The purpose behind such orders is to prevent dishonest defendants dealing with the evidence in a manner prejudicial to the case. Circumstances have to be exceptional for a search order to be made. There must be an extremely strong *prima facie* case, the extent of possible damage must be serious, there must be clear evidence that the other party is likely to disobey any court order, and the items to form the subject of the order must be clearly identifiable. An order might be made, for instance, where an employee is secretly making 'pirate' copies of the employer's copyright work and selling them abroad. An order will not be made where the claimant is simply on a 'fishing expedition'.

Care must also be taken where the right of inspection (and consequent search) might actually reveal the other side's trade secrets, etc. An undertaking for damages will be required and the court demands that the applicant comes with 'clean hands' so that all matters even remotely relevant to the case must be disclosed. The order must be served by an independent solicitor who must explain the effect of the order to the defendant and inform the defendant of the legal right to seek legal advice before complying with the order.

An application for a search order may be refused where there is the possibility of self-incrimination regarding criminal offences on the provision of the evidence by the defendant. This privilege does not, however, extend to the possibility of physical violence being meted out to the defendant by his associates should he comply with the order (*Coca-Cola Co. & Schweppes Ltd* v *Gilbey* [1996] FSR 23).

9.14 Summary

- A restraint of trade clause seeks to prevent unfair competition from ex-employees by restricting their activities after termination of the contract.
- Restraints of trade come in four main forms. Ranging from the severest to the mildest these are:

  a. *non-competition restraints* (i.e., preventing the employee working in that industry as a whole, or at least with named competitors);

b. *non-dealing restraints* (i.e., preventing employees accepting business from or conducting business with former clients or specifically named former clients);

c. *non-solicitation restraints* (i.e., preventing employees actually initiating contact with former clients, though not barring the employee from dealing with such clients who transfer their business without solicitation);

d. *non-poaching restraints* (i.e., preventing the employee from soliciting former colleagues to join him in the new venture).

- Restraint clauses are presumed to be void unless they are reasonable. Reasonableness depends upon the employer showing that there was a 'legitimate interest' to protect (e.g., customer contacts) and that the wording of the clause is reasonable as between the parties in terms of the length of the restraint, area covered, the status of the employee, and the general market conditions.
- Restraint clauses are usually concerned with preventing the ex-employee making use of his customer contacts made when he was employed by the former employer, but such clauses can be used to prevent the dissemination of the employer's information by precluding the ex-employee from operating within the same field of business. It is therefore possible for a contract to contain an implied duty of fidelity relating to confidential information, an express term on the same subject, and have a restraint clause which seeks to do the same thing.
- Restraint clauses come in varying degrees of severity e.g., *non-competition clauses* seek to prevent the ex-employee working in a particular industry for a defined period, whereas *non-solicitation clauses* only seek to prevent the ex-employee approaching clients of the former employer. The more draconian the clause, the stricter the test of reasonableness applied by the courts.
- Enforcement is by way of injunction. Interim injunctions are governed by the rules emanating from *American Cyanamid* v *Ethicon*.

9.15 Self-test question on Chapters 8 and 9

Your client is Phoenix Guitars of Bristol. The company manufactures guitars and guitar parts and employs 26 employees. Your Principal wishes you to provide some preliminary guidance notes on a key question: if *Phoenix Guitars Ltd* go ahead and dismiss one of their employees (Mr Setters), will they still be able to enforce the confidentiality and restraint of trade clauses against him? The Personnel Director, Mr Burek, briefs you as follows:

1. **The business:** *Phoenix Guitars Ltd* is a long-established company which makes and sells a range of standard hand-made guitars and guitar parts to retail outlets, plus custom-made guitars for individual customers (ranging from ordinary guitar players to internationally renowned rock stars). It is located in Bristol. It has a network of sales across the UK to specialist guitar shops and general musical outlets but receives the custom-made orders directly from the public through telephone, internet, or personal contact. The company derives its raw materials (various kinds of hardwood, electrical fixtures, etc.) from across the world.

2. **The work undertaken by Setters:** Mr Setters is the senior (of two) product designers. Mr Setters has been with the company for five years. His contractual notice period is two months. His work involves creating new designs for sale to the retail outlets together with designing the custom-made guitars we produce for individual customers. His work is mainly factory-centred, but involves some contact with those customers who get in touch with us directly as well as with the retail outlets that stock our goods. He reports directly to the managing director. Mr Setters has access to a wide range of information which the company regards as confidential, *viz:*
   (i) Customers' (retail and personal) specific requirements, especially in the case of long-established relationships;
   (ii) Future expansion plans;
   (iii) Details of contracts with suppliers around the world, including discounts obtained.

   This information is held in electronic and paper form and Mr Setters is aware of the importance to the company of all this information. The establishment of customer contacts is very dependent on the reputation of employees.
3. **Recent events:** A couple of weeks ago we held an investigation into Setters' conduct during a presentation team's visit to a potential client. At dinner one evening he informed the potential client that '*Phoenix* may be a market leader now but they are not investing enough in general research or advertising for the future'. The potential client immediately asked us to respond to this. We recalled Setters immediately and instigated disciplinary procedures. Setters has insisted that this was 'only general talk and taken out of context'. Nevertheless, we are considering dismissing him. However, we have received reliable information that Setters has already been in negotiations with a rival company (*Andrea Amati*) and that they are on the verge of offering him a contract of employment. It would also seem that Setters has been talking to his fellow designer about transferring with him to *Andrea Amati.*
4. **Competitors:** We have two main competitors within the UK: *Le Strad Ltd* (whose headquarters are in Birmingham) and *Andrea Amati (Musical Instruments) Ltd* (in London). There are, of course, numerous American, Japanese, Korean, and Mexican companies operating worldwide, including within the UK, but these produce mass-market guitars and parts. Ours is a specialist operation and we do not compete directly with these large-scale production companies. Until now, *Andrea Amati* has concentrated on the European market (in which we have no interest). However, we have firm evidence that *Andrea Amati* is seeking to expand its share of the UK market in the near future and plans to offer new designs centred on a very competitive pricing policy. Such a development could affect our market share adversely. We do not therefore want to lose any of our key employees to any of our competitors, especially *Andrea Amati.* We believe that Mr Setters is likely to use or disclose our trade secrets in these areas if he leaves or is dismissed.
5. **Likelihood of damage to the company:** Should Setters leave and disclose our trade secrets he will cause us substantial harm in that the financial deals and design/production methods we use, together constitute business processes which provide us with a competitive edge over our rivals. *Andrea Amati Ltd* is a major rival who is seeking to mirror our activities and undercut our

prices. Our new business strategy has emerged after intensive analysis and is near completion. The life-span for the information in Mr Setters' possession can be conservatively calculated as three years in terms of business strategy/redesigns.

Setters has good contacts with both customers and suppliers and would undoubtedly make use of these in any new business venture. It is a fickle market; some would transfer their allegiance from us and follow him, especially if his new employer were to undercut us.

Extracts from Setter's contract of employment relating to restraint and confidentiality terms

8. CONFIDENTIALITY

8.1 The Employee acknowledges that during the course of his employment with the Company he will receive and have access to confidential information of the Company and he will also receive and have access to detailed client/customer lists and information relating to the operations and business requirements of those clients/customers.

8.2 The Employee shall not (other than in the proper performance of his duties or with the prior written consent of the Board or unless ordered by a court of competent jurisdiction) at any time either during the continuance of his employment or after its termination disclose or communicate to any person or use for his own benefit or the benefit of any person other than the Company or any Associated Company any confidential information which may come to his knowledge in the course of his employment and the Employee shall use his best endeavours to prevent the unauthorised publication or misuse of any confidential information provided that such restrictions shall cease to apply to any confidential information which may enter the public domain other than through the actions of the Employee.

8.3 For the avoidance of doubt and without prejudice to the generality of Clause 8.1 the following is a non-exhaustive list of matters which in relation to the Company are considered confidential and must be treated as such by the Employee:-

8.3.1 any secrets of the Company or any Associated Company:

8.3.2 marketing strategies and plans;

8.3.3 customer lists and details of contracts with or requirements of customers;

8.3.4 pricing strategies;

8.3.5 discount rates obtained from suppliers or given to customers and sales figures;

8.3.6 lists of suppliers;

8.3.7 any invention technical data know-how or other manufacturing or trade secrets of the Company or any Associated Company and their clients/customers.

9. RESTRICTIONS ON ACTIVITIES FOLLOWING TERMINATION

9.1 For a period of TWELVE MONTHS after termination of the Employment, the Employee shall not directly or indirectly (and whether on his own account or for any other person, firm, company, or organisation) deal with any person, firm, company or organisation who or which at any time during the preceding TWENTY FOUR MONTHS shall have been a customer of or in the habit of dealing with the Company, and with whom or which the Employee has had direct dealings or personal contact as part of the Employment so as to harm the goodwill of the Company or any Associated Company or so as to compete with the Company or any Associated Company.

9.2 For a period of SIX MONTHS after termination of the Employment, the Employee shall not canvass solicit or approach or cause to be canvassed, solicited or approached in relation to a business which may in any way be in competition with the Company, the custom of any person who at the date hereof or at any time during the period of TWENTY FOUR MONTHS prior to the Termination Date shall have been a client or customer of the Company or any Associated Company.

9.3 The covenants given by the Employee in sub-clauses 9.1 and to 9.2 inclusive above will not cease to apply in the event that the Employment is terminated by the Company in breach of contract.

10

Termination of the contract at common law

10.1 Introduction

A contract of employment can come to an end in a number of different ways:

(a) by agreement;

(b) by completion of a specific task;

(c) by expiry of a fixed term;

(d) by automatic termination, e.g., frustration of the contract;

(e) by dismissal;

(f) by resignation.

These forms of termination describe the basic layout of the chapter. However, we are also interested in the consequences of any termination, so that we will adopt the following additional headings:

(g) Justifiable and wrongful dismissals;

(h) Post-termination duties;

(i) Damages and other remedies;

(j) Outline of tax considerations.

Under each of the headings (a)–(f) there may be statutory as well as common law consequences. We shall concentrate on the common law consequences in this chapter, but will make cross-references to certain statutory points where there is a substantial overlap.

The points raised in **Chapters 3**, **4**, and **5** should also be noted regarding the structure and operation of the contract. We saw there, for instance, that where the employer makes unilateral changes to the contract there may be a number of consequences such as wrongful dismissal claims, wrongful repudiation claims, and the granting of injunctions. But clearly there does not have to be an attempt at altering the contract before resignations and dismissals may occur. A termination of the contract may occur for a variety of reasons, e.g., because of the employee's misconduct or incapability, or because there is a redundancy. Before examining these consequences we need to note the other, less common forms in which a termination may occur.

10.2 Termination by agreement

The parties are free to agree at any time that the contract may terminate on the happening of certain circumstances. They might also agree at any time that if the contract comes to an end in specific or general circumstances then an agreed sum (a 'golden handshake') will be payable. This will stand as liquidated damages (enforceable if a genuine pre-estimate of loss).

Agreements simply to end the contract are not common. Usually there will be a dismissal or resignation. As a consensual termination cannot by its very nature amount to a dismissal the courts are naturally suspicious of these arrangements because, without some form of a dismissal, statutory rights such as unfair dismissal will be nullified. Indeed, ERA 1996, s. 203 forbids any *exclusions* of statutory rights. Therefore the burden of proving the presence of a genuine agreement and absence of an exclusion of rights is an onerous one. Anything that smacks of duress, fraud, or general bad faith will find disfavour and so be classed as a dismissal. The areas that have caused most problems are:

(a) *Apparent resignation.*

The employer and employee may agree to termination without notice so that the employee can take another job more easily. This is genuine and unlikely to cause problems. But where a resignation has arisen from an employer's statement along the lines of 'resign or be sacked', the courts are reluctant to accept this as a valid agreement. We shall deal with this more fully at **10.8.1**.

(b) *Employees' concessions.*

In granting extended leave of absence employers have developed a practice of asking for a written undertaking that, should the employee fail to return by a set date, the parties agree that this will automatically terminate the contract. In *Igbo* v *Johnson Matthey Chemicals Ltd* [1986] ICR 505, the Court of Appeal outlawed such terms; to find otherwise, it was noted, could lead to every contract containing a clause whereby the employee 'agreed' that if late to work on Monday mornings this would automatically terminate the contract.

The most common *valid* consensual terminations therefore relate to contracts for the completion of specific tasks and non-renewal of fixed-term contracts.

10.3 Termination by completion of a specific task

A termination in these circumstances used not to count as a dismissal for common law or statutory purposes, but such contracts are now classed as 'limited-term' and subject to the rules noted below: see EA 2002, sch. 2, paras 3(7) and 13.

10.4 Expiry of limited-term contracts

Both contracts for the completion of a specific task and fixed-term contracts technically fall under the general description of 'limited-term'. 'Task' contracts will include things such as employees doing so-called 'seasonal' or 'casual' work who have contracts for a short period or task that ends when the period expires or the task is completed (e.g., agricultural workers or shop assistants working specifically for Christmas or another busy period). The most commonly occurring limited-term contract, however, is the fixed-term one. We will generally use the phrase 'limited-term' below. Where we refer to 'fixed-term' this is simply because that is the best example, but the regulations still apply to both forms of contract.

A fixed-term contract usually has clear start and finish dates. The contract may last weeks, months, or years. At common law the arrival of the agreed date terminates the contract automatically and no further consequences flow from this. The contract has terminated by effluxion of time and no advance notice by either party is necessary.

It should be noted, however, that the expiry *and non-renewal* of any limited-term contract *will constitute a dismissal for statutory purposes* and employees on 'limited-term' contracts have also gained protection from receiving less favourable treatment than other employees under the Fixed-Term Employees (Prevention of Less Favourable Treatment) Regulations 2002 (SI 2002/2034) noted above in **Chapter 7**.

10.4.1 Limited-term contracts and notice provisions

Odd though it sounds, it is possible to have limited-term contracts which expressly allow for termination (by either party giving notice) which will take effect at an earlier date than the set finish date: *Dixon* v *BBC* [1979] ICR 281. The reasons for this are again tied in with preserving statutory rights. Do not worry about the apparent illogicality of it all.

Some fixed-term contracts will delineate the stated period but permit indefinite continuance after the final date. A notice period applicable to this second stage will then be specified. In these circumstances the parties may give notice during the fixed term to terminate the contract at the end of the fixed term (and so before the extension has begun) or to take effect at some time during the extension: *Costigan* v *Gray Bovier Engines Ltd* (1925) 41 TLR 372.

If a limited-term contract is terminated prematurely the amount of damages will be either for the given notice period (if there is one) or else for the remainder of the term (see **10.10** below). There may also be an action for unfair dismissal or redundancy.

Where a limited-term contract is about to end employers often notify employees of this fact. There is no requirement to do so, but it does make for sound practice. However, employers should be wary of issuing any such letter in the form of 'giving notice'; such words may invite a tribunal to conclude that the dismissal occurred for reasons other than expiry of the term and this may revive arguments about unfair dismissal.

10.4.2 Waiver/contracting-out clauses

Such clauses state that an employee will not be able to claim *statutory* rights such as unfair dismissal and redundancy payments on the expiry and non-renewal of the contract. Although these clauses can still be found in a number of contracts, they are of decreasing validity (see **10.3.6** below).

10.4.3 Successive terms

It has been quite common for employers to use a succession of fixed-term contracts rather than create a contract of indefinite duration. The reason for this was to add on waiver clauses and thereby seek to avoid any liability for unfair dismissal or redundancy. Under reg. 8 of the Fixed-Term Employees (Prevention of Less Favourable Treatment)

Regulations 2002 (SI 2002/2034), such employees are now regarded as ordinary employees (i.e., the contract will be regarded as having no temporal restrictions) if:

(a) the employee was employed on a fixed-term contract before the start of the present contract, or the current fixed-term contract has been renewed; *and*

(b) the employee's period of continuous employment is four years or more; *and*

(c) the employment of the employee under a fixed-term contract was not justified on objective grounds. That justification must be present either at the time of the last renewal or, where the contract has not been renewed, at the time it was entered into. This means that a burden is placed on the employer to justify the continuing use of fixed-term contracts. The term 'renewal' includes any extension.

Under reg. 9, an employee on a limited-term who believes they should be classed as a permanent employee may request a statement from the employer confirming or denying this, with reasons. If the employer does not respond, or denies permanency, an employee may also make an application to the tribunal for such a declaration (reg. 9(5)). These points may be modified by way of a collective agreement with a trade union or through a workforce agreement (see sch. 1).

10.4.5 Probationary periods

These are devices commonly used by employers when hiring or promoting employees. They purport to offer some form of 'trial period'. In fact they are generally meaningless. Unless the wording specifies such they are *not* fixed-term contracts of any nature and dismissal can occur during the course of the probationary period: *Dalgleish* v *Kew House Farm Ltd* [1982] IRLR 251. They are a traditional warning to employees, nothing more. New employees will generally only have a claim if the employer acts in breach of the contract, e.g., by not giving adequate notice of dismissal. This is because unfair dismissal rights *generally* do not accrue until there has been one years' service. Existing employees who are promoted and put on a 'probationary' period maintain any existing rights they have to claim unfair dismissal.

10.5 Automatic termination

10.5.1 Frustration

Frustration of a contract occurs when unforeseen circumstances, which are beyond the control of either party, make it impossible to perform the objectives of the contract. The most common examples of the doctrine of frustration applying to employment contracts are illness, death, and imprisonment. A frustrating event terminates the contract automatically, except where the event relates to the employer and the claim is for redundancy; in this case the employee's rights are preserved.

If the 'frustrating event' has been *caused* by the fault of one party, that party cannot rely on it. The burden of proof lies with the party claiming frustration of the contract.

10.5.1.1 Frustration and sickness

The application of the doctrine of frustration to employment contracts, especially where illness is the issue, should be treated with great caution. Cases like *Condor* v *Barron Knights Ltd* [1966] 1 WLR 87, where a pop group drummer was unable to 'drum' for the seven nights per week required, are rare examples of frustrating events. Guidelines on when illness will frustrate a contract have been laid down: see, for instance, *Egg Stores (Stamford Hill) Ltd* v *Leibovici* [1977] ICR 260. Thus the following factors need to be considered:

(a) What is the nature of the illness?

(b) How long has the incapacity lasted?

(c) How long is it likely to continue?

(d) What are the terms of the contract, e.g., as to sick pay?

(e) How long was the employment set to last?

(f) What was the nature of the employment, e.g., was he or she a key employee?

(g) For how long has the employee been employed?

Questions of frustration tend to arise either when there is an accident or illness which will obviously have long-term effects, or where the position with a long-term illness employee has been allowed to drift. This may seem unlikely, but it happens, e.g., an employee is off work, the sick pay scheme becomes exhausted, the employers lose contact with the employee and then maybe a year or more later someone decides to 'tidy up the books'. They then discover the employee—or 25 such workers in one case dealt with by the authors.

On the other hand, the acceptance of medical certificates and retention of the P45 does not necessarily mean the frustration *has not occurred.* This is because the matter is beyond the control or the intentions of the parties—it has either happened or not happened: *Hart* v *Marshall & Sons (Bulwell) Ltd* [1977] ICR 539. The right to receive notice does not survive a frustrating event.

The key point is whether performance of the contract has now become impossible, or at least radically different from the original undertaking. The doctrine can also apply to contracts where a short period of notice is due (see *Notcutt* v *Universal Equipment Co. (London) Ltd* [1986] ICR 414); but whatever the type of contract, reliance on the doctrine is generally inadvisable—the employer would be wiser to decide whether or not to dismiss for incapacity. First, as will be seen in **Chapter 12**, the test for fairness in ill-health dismissals bears a remarkable similarity to the issues raised in frustration. Secondly, if there is the prospect of recovery then, unless there is an issue of 'key worker', this will usually mean there is no frustration.

10.5.1.2 Frustration and imprisonment

The second possibility of a frustrating event occurs when the employee is sent to prison. This makes turning up for work slightly difficult. In *Shepherd* v *Jerrom* [1986] ICR 802, the Court of Appeal decided that imprisonment is capable of frustrating the contract (here, an apprentice received a sentence of between six months' and two years' borstal training). The longer the sentence the more likely the frustration; though again one must relate this to the actual contract—status of the employee as a key worker, length of notice period, whether there is a fixed-term contract, etc. The same considerations will apply to restrictive bail conditions and being placed on custodial remand: see *Four Seasons Healthcare Ltd* v *Maughan* [2005] IRLR 324 (contract was not frustrated during the period where an employee was suspended from work whilst on bail awaiting trial).

10.5.2 Winding up of the company

The compulsory winding up of a company will operate as a notice of dismissal. A resolution for voluntary winding up will, in most cases, also constitute such notice; at least where the business is being discontinued. An employee may then have a claim for wrongful dismissal.

10.5.3 Appointment of a receiver

The appointment of a receiver by the court or as an agent for the creditors will again constitute an automatic termination of the contracts of employment. Not so, it appears, with an appointment by the debenture holders, at least for junior employees whose positions effectively remain intact.

10.5.4 Changes in a partnership

The retirement of a partner operates as a dismissal at law. Most employees will simply be re-engaged, however, and the employees' continuity of employment is preserved under ERA 1996, s. 218(5): *Stevens* v *Bower* [2004] EWCA Civ 496. The practical effects are therefore minimal. The dissolution of the partnership does, technically, bring about a termination. So, where re-engagement does not occur the employee may claim wrongful dismissal plus any statutory rights.

10.5.5 Transfer of the business

At common law, where the business is sold, this will operate as a termination; but the position now has to be read in the light of the Transfer of Undertakings (Protection of Employment) Regulations 2006 (SI 2006/246), as discussed in **Chapter 15**, so that if there is a 'relevant transfer' under these Regulations it is most likely that the contracts of employment will simply be transferred along with the sale. Consequently there will be no dismissal and continuity of employment gained with the old employer will be deemed to have been with the new employer. The basic idea behind the Regulations is that nothing should really have changed simply because the business has been transferred.

10.6 The meaning of dismissal

The meaning of 'dismissal' is central to employment law. It ranges from 'being given the sack' through to resignations which are deemed dismissals. The area contains technicalities which can trap the unwary solicitor, and it is for the employee to prove dismissal if the employer challenges the claim (e.g., following a resignation). Employees may therefore find themselves 'dismissed' (as legally defined) for the purposes of common law and statutory claims in the following circumstances:

(a) where the employee is given the sack (see **10.6.1** below);

(b) where the employer uses language which amounts to dismissal (see **10.6.1**);

(c) where the employer intimates a future dismissal (see **10.8** below);

(d) where the employer says 'resign or be sacked' (see **10.8**);

(e) where the employer repudiates the contract and the employee resigns (see **10.6.3** and **10.8**);

(f) where a fixed-term contract is not renewed. This applies only to statutory claims such as unfair dismissal (see **10.4** above).

At common law the consequences of being dismissed are that if the employer has acted in breach of contract the employee will be able to sue for damages. This is known as a *wrongful dismissal action*. As we will see, the assessment of damages is governed by ordinary contractual principles. In employment contracts this generally means that an employee will be able to sue for the amount that he or she should have received as a notice of termination payment.

In **Chapters 11–14** we will see how a dismissal may lead to other *statutory* forms of compensation, i.e., unfair dismissal compensation and redundancy payments.

10.6.1 Being sacked

A dismissal will normally occur when the employer terminates the contract *with or without notice*. The decision to dismiss must be *communicated,* orally or in writing, to be effective. Where notice is given by post (which is not too clever when seen from an unfair dismissal angle) there is no debate as to 'postal rules' applying: the notice is communicated when the employee reads or could reasonably have been expected to read the letter (*Brown* v *Southall and Knight* [1980] ICR 617).

In most cases the act of dismissal will be obvious: 'you are dismissed'; 'you're sacked'; 'collect your P45 and get out'; 'I'm giving you four weeks' notice', and so on. The 'sack', by the way, comes from the days when a dismissed worker would be handed his bag of tools; the message was obvious.

Problems will arise when the words used are not clear, were meant merely as a censure or are said in anger (and perhaps regretted). The basic rule has to be: how would a reasonable person understand the words? If the reasonable man would perceive the words as amounting to a dismissal, they will constitute a dismissal; if the employee is wrong then he or she has resigned and is in breach of the contract. There is always the possibility, however, that the words (though not an overt dismissal) were such as to destroy the mutual trust and confidence in the relationship and so amount to a wrongful repudiation/constructive dismissal. Claims in the alternative are therefore advisable, i.e., the employee was dismissed on *x* date; alternatively, if the words did not amount to an overt dismissal they destroyed the mutual trust and confidence and so amounted to a repudiation.

Harsh words can therefore produce a 'dismissal' by a number of routes. A fascinating line of cases has developed on the meaning of language in industrial and commercial settings. Consider the following:

(a) 'Go, get out, get out'—not a Victorian melodrama but the case of *Stern (J &J)* v *Simpson* [1983] IRLR 52;

(b) 'You're finished with me'—*Tanner* v *Kean* [1978] IRLR 110;

(c) 'If you do not like the job, fuck off'—*Futty* v *Brekkes (D & D) Ltd* [1974] IRLR 130.

None of these utterances amounted to a dismissal *in the circumstances*. This is a key point. In *Futty* v *Brekkes,* the employee was a fish filleter on Hull docks; and, strange though it seems, such language is not abnormal on Hull docks. The case stands out in the memory not because of the language used (there are many variations on this theme), but because of the attempt to define the term as: 'If you are complaining about the fish you are working on, or the quality of it, or if you do not like what, in fact, you are doing, then you can leave your work, clock off, and you will be paid up to the time when you do so. Then you can come back when you are disposed . . . '. And the same would not necessarily hold true if the characters were a bank manager and junior clerk—more so if said in front of customers.

Words spoken in anger can cause more problems. The act of dismissal can be clear but then regretted. In *Martin* v *Yeoman Aggregates Ltd* [1983] IRLR 49, a retraction within five minutes of an angry outburst was held sufficient to counter the dismissal even though the employee insisted he had been dismissed. This owes more to the promotion of good industrial relations practice than pure logic. It is a question of degree whether the words are withdrawn too late.

10.6.2 Intention

The courts have not been consistent on the status to be given to intention. If an employer intimates dismissal but does not intend this to be the case, should this make any difference?

We have seen that if the words are *ambiguous* the general test to be applied is what would reasonably be understood from the context. The same should hold true for *unambiguous* language, and this appears to be so following the Court of Appeal's decision in *Sovereign House Security Services Ltd* v *Savage* [1989] IRLR 115. However, as with words spoken in anger, an employee will be best advised to get confirmation of dismissal before taking any further action.

The latest authority on this concerns a *misunderstanding* by the employer. In *Willoughby* v *CF Capital Ltd* [2010] UKEAT/503/09 the employer was faced with budget cuts and discussed with the employee the possibility of the employee becoming self-employed. The employer believed the employee had agreed to this and sent her a letter terminating employment. Not surprisingly the employee treated this as a dismissal. The employer then sought to withdraw the letter on the basis of having made a mistake. The case was remitted to another tribunal, but the EAT was firmly of the view that the dismissal could not be retracted: it was intentional albeit mistaken.

10.6.3 Resigning

A dismissal may also occur when the employer repudiates the contract (e.g., by some radical alteration of the terms) and the employee accepts this repudiation by resigning. Strictly this is known as *wrongful repudiation* by the employer; though when used nowadays in relation to unfair dismissal it is usually referred to as 'constructive dismissal'. Some people incorrectly refer to both common law and statutory claims under the heading of constructive dismissal; it is not the worst sin in the world.

This topic is discussed more fully in **10.8** below.

10.7 Justifiable and wrongful dismissals

The word 'justifiable' can cause some initial problems here. Remember that we are concerned only with common law rights in this chapter, so a dismissal is 'justifiable' when it is not in breach of contract. It is irrelevant for these purposes whether it was 'fair' in all the circumstances. So, if an employee is dismissed with proper notice the common law will not be bothered that the employee had been loyal to the company for 20 years and has been treated abysmally, or that the dismissal was really motivated by sex or race discrimination. These factors are irrelevancies as far as the common law is concerned.

EXAMPLE 1

Anna is an employee who falls ill. She has worked for the company for five years and this is the first time she has been absent from work. Unfortunately the employer has suffered a bad spate of malingerers taking time off. This has caused immense organisational problems. The employer decides to make an example of someone and dismisses Anna. The employer gives proper notice under the contract.

It would be very unlikely that this constituted a wrongful dismissal, although one would need to see the exact terms of the contract to be sure, e.g., the contract may have a mandatory disciplinary procedure. The action does, however, seem very unfair to Anna. This is not the concern of the common law. The common law does not care whether the employer might have been a central character in a Dickens novel. If there is an 'unfair dismissal' here Anna will have to take that to an employment tribunal.

10.7.1 Justifiable dismissals: notice given

Since any contract of employment can be lawfully terminated by the giving of proper notice it is irrelevant *why* the employer decides to dismiss. The only exceptions to this general power to dismiss arise (rarely) when the contract specifies that dismissal can be only for certain defined reasons or that (even more rarely) the contract lasts for life: see respectively *McLelland* v *Northern Ireland General Health Service Board* [1957] 1 WLR 534 and *Ivory* v *Palmer* [1975] ICR 340. As we noted in **Chapter 5**, however, if the contract makes certain procedures mandatory before a dismissal can occur then an injunction may be obtained to prevent dismissal until the procedures have been completed.

10.7.1.1 Proper notice

Proper notice is determined according to the terms of the contract. A payment in lieu of notice is an acceptable way of meeting the requirements. Both forms of giving notice are subject to the minima stated in ERA 1996, s. 86, which are as follows:

Length of service	*Minimum notice entitlement*
less than one month	no notice due
after one month	1 week
after 2 years' completed service	2 weeks
after 3 years' completed service	3 weeks
after 4 years' completed service	4 weeks
for each year of completed service	one additional week's notice
after 12 years' service	12 weeks
BUT:	
after 13 years' service	still only 12 weeks
after 20 years' service	still only 12 weeks

The statutory minimum period of notice therefore has a ceiling of 12 weeks. To determine an employee's notice entitlement, therefore, one should ask:

(a) What does the contract state? Usually this is solved by examining the express terms, though occasionally one may have to resort to devices such as custom and practice to determine the period.

(b) Is this equivalent to or greater than the s. 86 notice required?

(c) If not then apply s. 86 minimum notice.

Section 86 uses the term 'not less than [*x weeks*]': the courts and tribunals do not have to award only the minimum period. It is still open to the tribunal or court to award 'reasonable notice'. However, the idea that 'reasonable notice' may be awarded often gives the impression that courts and tribunals are quite creative in assessing notice entitlement.

That idea should be discarded. Where courts have turned to reasonable notice either the contract has been unclear or the facts have been extreme, e.g., an employee of senior status with 25 years' service being awarded six months' notice.

EXAMPLE 2

An employee has been employed for eight and a half years. When new machines are introduced on to the production line he is dismissed as surplus to requirements. His contract stipulates that he is entitled to one month's notice. The employer duly pays wages in lieu of the employee working the notice.

The payment in lieu of notice is irrelevant here. However, on these facts the notice does not meet the s. 86 minimum, which should be eight weeks. Note that portions of years are not generally counted and that any questions of 'reasonable notice' will not be admitted on these facts.

Limited-term contracts are treated no differently, *provided there is a notice clause.*

Where notice is given the date of termination must be ascertainable. There is no dismissal if all that is given is a general warning of dismissal unless the warning is so specific that it amounts to an ultimatum and therefore an anticipatory breach: *Greenaway Harrison Ltd* v *Wiles* [1994] IRLR 381.

Sections 87–91, ERA 1996 deal with rights once notice has been given. For instance, subject to the technicalities of s. 87(4) (see *Scotts Co. (UK) Ltd* v *Budd* [2003] IRLR 145), if the employee falls sick during the notice period he is entitled to be paid, even if not otherwise entitled to sick pay. But, under ss. 88(2) and 89(4), any payments made to the employee by the employer (e.g., statutory sick pay) go towards meeting the employer's liability under these sections.

10.7.1.2 Waiving rights to notice

The parties are free to agree to give shorter notice than would normally be required or even to waive notice. Provided such variations are genuine there will be no breach of contract and therefore no damages payable: *Baldwin* v *British Coal Corporation* [1995] IRLR 139.

10.7.1.3 Notice and age discrimination

As mentioned in earlier chapters, the idea of preventing age discrimination extends to terms and conditions of the contract. Thus, varying notice periods which depend on length of service (and therefore indirectly to age) may be seen as discriminatory—this time as against younger employees.

The s. 86 statutory notice periods probably fall within s. 191 and sch. 22 EqA 2010 which provides that the provisions in the Act will not 'render unlawful any act done in order to comply with a requirement of any statutory provision'. But this is not certain because s. 86 lays down *minimum* periods, not mandatory ones. Nevertheless, it is likely that an employer adhering to s. 86 notice periods will be safe.

Contractual notice periods based on length of service do not receive the protection of s. 191 but may be saved by sch. 9, para 10 EqA 2010 (service-related benefits exceptions). Under this regulation contractual rights dependent on up to five years' service are exempted and anything over this can be justified if the employer shows the term fulfils a business need for the undertaking, e.g., by rewarding loyalty.

Payments in lieu of notice provide a further problem as they do not fit within sch. 9 and therefore will be discriminatory unless they are objectively justified as constituting a proportionate means of achieving a legitimate aim.

10.7.2 Justifiable dismissal: no notice given

When an employee is in serious breach of contract (e.g., commits an act of serious misconduct) the employer has a number of options available. These include:

(a) doing nothing;

(b) disciplining the employee;

(c) suing the employee for damages;

(d) dismissing the employee with notice;

(e) dismissing the employee without notice.

This is in line with ordinary contract principles that the innocent party may, in the face of a repudiation by the other party, affirm the contract as it stands or accept the repudiation. Thus a dismissal without notice (known as a *summary dismissal*) will be justified where the employee's actions show that further continuance of the relationship is impossible: *Sinclair* v *Neighbour* [1967] 2 QB 279 (here, dishonesty).

It follows, therefore, that the contract of employment itself is of vital importance in assessing whether the employee's conduct justifies dismissal without notice. The contract may define terms such as 'gross misconduct', or it may lay down specific procedures for dealing with any dismissal point, e.g., that no dismissal may occur until the employee has been given an opportunity to state a case. The more technical the contractual terms become the more likely it is that the employer will be in breach by not following them. So it might be that, even in the face of obvious misconduct, an employer will have to adhere to the procedures laid out in the contract *if the terms specifically set out what must happen before a dismissal can occur*: *Dietmann* v *Brent London Borough Council* [1988] ICR 842.

This does not establish a rule that a breach of disciplinary procedures will render a dismissal wrongful, though, because:

(a) if the dismissal is with proper notice (or payment in lieu) no further damages will be payable—though there is the possibility that the employee might obtain an injunction to prevent dismissal *until* the procedures have been complied with;

(b) most procedures are drafted more loosely than the *Dietmann* example. The issue is therefore one of construction of the particular contract.

If notice is *not given* the employer will have to justify this. If it is not justified the employee will recover damages for wrongful dismissal. Justification for dismissal without notice depends solely on the employer having a sound *contractual* reason for so dismissing. This will mean that the employee must have committed a serious breach of contract (see *Laws* v *London Chronicle (Indicator Newspapers) Ltd* [1959] 1 WLR 698). *The breach may be of express or implied terms*. Examples of serious breach by an employee will include:

(a) refusal to obey a lawful order;

(b) failure to cooperate;

(c) a deliberate and persistent failure to follow contractual instructions;

(d) dishonesty (in its widest sense);

(e) assault;

(f) prolonged absenteeism;

(g) disclosing confidential information;

(h) failing to disclose the misdeeds of subordinates;

(i) gross negligence;

(j) drunkenness at work;

(k) most forms of industrial action.

However, it is usually stressed by judges that each case turns on its facts. Certainly this will be true when dealing with one-off incidents. Whereas the normal approach would be that a one-off incident is not a repudiation of the contract, that clearly cannot be a universal rule. A pilot bouncing the company jet, for instance, does not deserve a second chance. But should the pilot be dismissed with or without notice? Would you say that the same result would be reached with a salesman who crashed a company car? And an accumulation of petty incidents may also amount to a serious breach: *Pepper* v *Webb* [1969] 2 All ER 216.

The more serious the breach the more likely a summary dismissal will be justified.

10.7.2.1 Contractual term

Employers sometimes attempt to set out a right to dismiss without notice on the occurrence of certain events, other than gross misconduct. This is a questionable practice in itself; but, certainly, the wording of such clauses will be construed *contra proferentem*: *T&K Improvements Ltd* v *Skilton* [2000] IRLR 595, CA, where a clause allowing dismissal 'with immediate effect' on failing to reach sales targets was held not to permit dismissal without notice. A similar approach to contractual terms was seen in **10.7.1** above.

10.7.3 Wrongful dismissals

10.7.3.1 Definition

A dismissal *without notice or with inadequate notice* will constitute a wrongful dismissal unless the employer was acting in response to a serious breach of the contract by the employee.

Payment in lieu of notice, unless specifically allowed for in the contract, will also constitute a technical breach of contract. For the most part this is an irrelevancy, given that damages for wrongful dismissal would amount to the same sum, but classifying this as a technical breach may have an effect on matters such as the efficacy of restraint of trade clauses: see *Rex Stewart Jeffries Parker Ginsberg Ltd* v *Parker* [1988] IRLR 483, above at **9.4.4** and below at **10.9**.

Employers often refer to 'instant dismissal'. This is in fact a vague term and should not be taken at face value. Certainly, an employee might be 'instantly dismissed' when he or she is dismissed without notice; but the employee or the employer may also use the term 'instant dismissal' to describe a dismissal with payment in lieu or a dismissal with notice where the employee is not required to work out the notice. There can therefore be important differences between 'instant dismissals' and 'summary dismissals' and you need to be sure which you are talking about (a point missed by the employers in *Skilton* above).

Figure 10.1 illustrates the possible consequences of dismissing with or without adequate notice. The right-hand side of the diagram illustrates the fact that damages are unavailable at common law if the contract is terminated lawfully. The far left-hand side

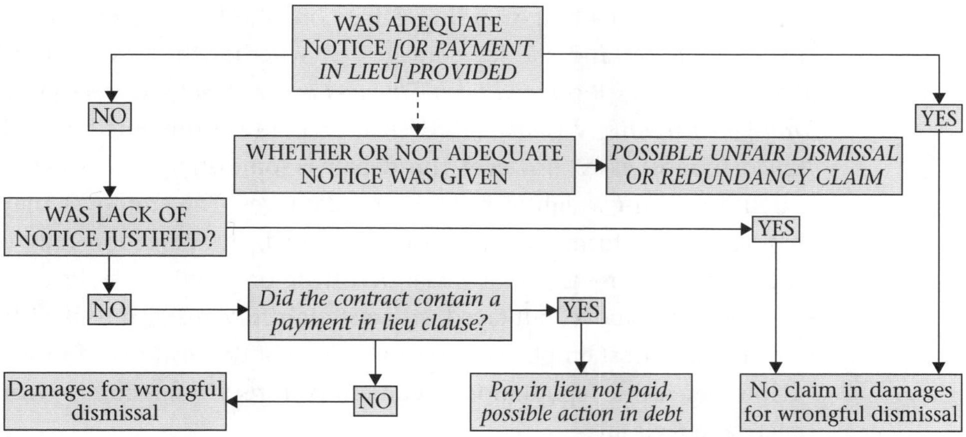

Figure 10.1 Dismissal with or without notice.

shows that the mere fact that notice has not been given does not conclude the analysis: the lack of notice may be justified. The section concerning payments in lieu of notice takes account of the decision in *Abrahams* v *Performing Rights Society* [1995] IRLR 486 and we will return to discuss the significance of this decision at **10.10.3** below.

The diagram also notes the possibilities of an unfair dismissal claim flowing from either type of dismissal. This point will be taken further in **Chapter 11** but highlights the fact that there may be a dismissal which is both unfair and wrongful, a fair but wrongful dismissal and even an unfair but lawful dismissal.

10.7.3.2 Relationship with repudiation

A wrongful dismissal is sometimes viewed as another form of repudiation of the contract. If this is so then, as in the ordinary law of contract, the repudiation does not automatically bring the contract to an end—it must be accepted by the innocent party. An unaccepted repudiation, it is said, is a thing writ in water. The innocent party has a choice whether or not to accept the repudiation. The argument is that when the employee is told to go (in breach of contract) he or she should be able to say, 'No. This is in breach and I do not accept the repudiation.' In practice, this simply shows us that law and reality do not always coincide. But there can be cases where this point matters.

We have already seen some spin-off practical points that have developed from the debate. Since a repudiation does not have to be accepted by the innocent party then a breach by the employer during the currency of the contract can be met with various tactics, e.g.:

(a) It is now well-established that employees faced with a repudiation may object to the breach but remain in employment and sue for damages: *Rigby* v *Ferodo* [1988] ICR 29 (discussed in **Chapter 5**);

(b) We have also seen that, even when a dismissal is about to occur or has just occurred, an employee may be able to invoke the courts' help. Injunctions can be granted to restrain dismissals or declare dismissals invalid which do not comply with mandatory contractual procedures: *Dietmann* v *Brent London Borough Council* [1988] ICR 842, although this does not mean that the rules of natural justice will be imputed to contracts of employment generally.

Trying to relate this to wrongful dismissal is more difficult. Assume that an employer has just told the employee that he is dismissed without notice. Does the employee have to accept this?

There has been a long-standing debate on whether an employee must simply accept this repudiation and sue for damages, or whether there is some other remedy available: see *Gunton* v *Richmond-upon-Thames London Borough Council* [1980] ICR 755; *London Transport Executive* v *Clarke* [1981] ICR 355; and comments by Lord Oliver in *Rigby* v *Ferodo*. In most cases, however, this debate is somewhat sterile since there is no practical benefit in having a right other than for damages. The employee may object but, given that specific performance will not be ordered, the objection may be futile. Thus, an employee may prevent a dismissal occurring or may have a dismissal nullified on the grounds noted above, but faced with a straightforward dismissal without notice there is nothing that most employees can do but accept the dismissal and sue for damages.

However, if the 'repudiation' argument is correct in relation to wrongful dismissal the practical effects are:

(a) the employee, by accepting the *de facto* position, will have in law accepted the wrongful repudiation by the employer. The employee will therefore, technically speaking, have resigned (see below) rather than have been overtly dismissed;

(b) there may be a difference in calculating the exact date of termination.

10.7.3.3 Proof of conduct

The employer will have to justify any dismissal *without notice*. Normally proof will relate to the facts known at the time of the dismissal. However, the employer is also entitled to rely on evidence *not known to him at the time of dismissal: Boston Deep Sea Fishing and Ice Co.* v *Ansell* (1888) 39 ChD 339. This is because the arguments are based on whether or not there has been a breach of contract. The employer's knowledge or lack of it does not affect the materiality of the breach.

EXAMPLE 3

The employer summarily dismisses an employee for theft. The employer has no proof, only strong suspicions. Some weeks after the dismissal the employer discovers the proof. The employer may use this subsequently discovered information in order to prove the employee's breach of contract, thereby justifying the dismissal without notice. The same logic applies even if the employer had *no reason* to dismiss but later discovered one.

By way of advance warning, however, the rules regarding proof in an unfair dismissal action are different. There the employer can rely only on facts known *at the time of dismissal*. Thus out of one incident of dismissal there may be different rules of proof depending on whether one is claiming for wrongful or unfair dismissal.

10.8 Resignation

An employee may resign at any time by giving proper notice under the contract. The minimum s. 86 period is one week; and this does not alter with length of service. The contract may set any notice requirement.

If an employee leaves without serving proper notice then he or she is in breach of contract. The employee will be liable for damages, though specific performance will not be ordered. The employee may, however, still be subject to a restraint of trade clause.

The fact that the employer has accepted the employee's repudiation of the contract is ignored because the employee will not be allowed to profit from his or her own breach.

Once a lawful resignation has been given it cannot be withdrawn except:

(a) with the employer's permission; or

(b) where the resignation came in the heat of the moment and is retracted quickly; or

(c) where the resignation was in breach of contract and the employer has not yet obviously accepted the repudiation.

However, an employee is entitled to resign, with or without serving notice, and claim damages where the employer has repudiated the contract (see 'wrongful repudiation' below).

The discussion on 'resignation' and its effect should be read in conjunction with the topic of 'constructive dismissal' in **Chapters 11** and **12**. When this is taken into account you will see that a resignation may amount to an unfair dismissal as well as to a wrongful repudiation at common law.

10.8.1 Meaning of 'resignation'

In most cases an employee will resign to take up another job elsewhere. If the employee gives proper notice (and there is no question of restraint of trade) no further problems will occur. There can be no claim for wrongful or unfair dismissal or for redundancy payments and the employer cannot force the employee to remain in employment. The employer may indeed waive all or some of the notice because an employee who is set to leave can prove disruptive (intentionally or otherwise).

We are concerned here with *apparent* resignations which might turn out to be *dismissals*:

(a) resignations in the heat of the moment;

(b) pressure from the employer;

(c) the employer's bad faith;

(d) voluntary redundancies and early retirement.

10.8.1.1 Resignations in the heat of the moment

Employees, like employers (see **10.6.1**), are allowed some leeway with heated outbursts. If the words spoken are ambiguous there is the preliminary point as to whether they constituted a resignation at all. If the words are unambiguous the employer is entitled to take these at their face value and the employee must live with the consequences. However, an employee is allowed to retract within a reasonable time if the words were spoken in anger: *Kwik-Fit (GB) Ltd* v *Lineham* [1992] ICR 183. An employer who refuses to allow a reasonable retraction will have dismissed the employee from that point.

10.8.1.2 Resignations under pressure

Employees who resign following an invitation to 'resign or be dismissed' may still have a claim for wrongful or unfair dismissal—were they pushed or did they jump? But advance warning of dismissal *at some future time* does not constitute pressure and so is not a dismissal (nor is this enough to amount to a repudiatory breach by the employer). If the employer were to indicate that the future termination will be in breach of contract, however, then this will amount to an anticipatory breach which the employee may act upon immediately.

There may be a fine line between these two points. The key aspect is whether there is to be found in the employer's words an *ascertainable future date of dismissal;* if there is then any resignation may be treated as a dismissal.

EXAMPLE 4

A month ago the employer told the employee that the factory would be closed down in 11 months' time. The employee has just resigned and wishes to claim a redundancy payment on the basis that he has been dismissed.

Although there is a final date when the employee's contract will seemingly come to an end this is not enough. The employee might be dismissed before then, or the redundancy may never come about. The resignation is just that: there is no further claim based on a 'dismissal' (see *International Computers Ltd* v *Kennedy* [1981] IRLR 28).

The real cases of 'resign or be sacked' therefore arise when the employee is clearly going to face some form of disciplinary procedure and is 'given the honourable choice'—a sort of industrial hara-kiri option. This may indeed be honourable, but it is also possible that it is a dismissal. It is not a dismissal simply to instigate disciplinary procedures, nor even to offer the employee a way out of the proceedings. Such conversations become dismissal when the employer threatens dismissal by other words: when the conversation is effectively, 'We are going to dismiss you come what may, go now'.

10.8.1.3 Resignation generated by the employer's bad faith

This bears a close resemblance to pressurised resignations. In *Caledonian Mining* v *Bassett and Steel* [1987] ICR 425, the employers had announced the proposed closure of the workplace. No date was actually given. The employers informed the employees that they could arrange transfers to another site some distance away. Alternatively, they said that they had reached agreement with the National Coal Board so that the employees could change employers, stay in the area, but take a wage cut. The employees chose this option. They then claimed redundancy pay from Caledonian Mining, who replied that the employees had resigned and so were not entitled. It was held that the employers had acted in bad faith and had inveigled the employees into resigning in order to deprive them of their statutory rights. Therefore this constituted a dismissal.

10.8.1.4 Voluntary redundancies and early retirement

In many cases where redundancies are announced the employer will first ask for volunteers. Any subsequent termination could be classed as a resignation, a dismissal, or even a consensual termination. In order to claim a redundancy payment the employee must have been dismissed.

Early retirement schemes usually take a considerable amount of time to work out problems with dates, pension arrangements and so on. Such cases are therefore more likely to constitute a mutual agreement termination (provided the agreement was genuine) rather than dismissal or resignation.

10.8.2 Wrongful repudiation

What constitutes a *serious breach* of contract on the employer's part? Examples would include:

(a) a failure to pay wages;

(b) harassment (including harassment by other employees);

(c) victimisation by the employer or senior staff;

(d) unilaterally changing the employee's job content or status;

(e) humiliating employees in front of others including the use by a manager of foul and abusive language, whether or not the employer argues that that is part of the 'normal working environment': *Horkulak* v *Cantor Fitzgerald International* [2003] IRLR 756;

(f) unwarranted demotion or disciplinary sanctions;

(g) falsely accusing an employee of misconduct or incapability;

(h) unilateral variation in contract terms, e.g., a change in hours or pay;

(i) requiring a substantial transfer of location (certainly if without reasonable notice);

(j) suspension without pay where the contract does not allow for this—and even *with pay* if prolonged.

A series of breaches may also fall within the definition of repudiation, though this is always more difficult to substantiate unless the employee has kept careful records.

Many of these points tend to be classified as a breach of the implied term of *mutual trust and confidence* owed by the employer to the employee. Clearly the list is not closed.

It should also be remembered from **Chapter 5** that an employee does not have to resign in the face of a repudiatory breach. If the contract is still capable of being performed the employee may remain and seek other remedies, e.g., suing for breach, or may simply put up with the breach.

10.9 Post-termination duties

In **Chapters 8** and **9** we noted that a breach or even a technical breach may have the effect of invalidating post-termination terms such as restraint of trade clauses: see *Rex Stewart Jeffries Parker Ginsberg Ltd* v *Parker* [1988] IRLR 483. A wrongful dismissal will invalidate a restraint of trade clause: *General Billposting Co. Ltd* v *Atkinson* [1909] AC 118. Even a payment in lieu will invalidate a restraint clause *unless* the contract expressly allows for this form of termination.

10.10 Damages and other remedies

10.10.1 Damages

Employment contracts are no different from other contracts, in that the basis for awarding damages is to fulfil the reasonable expectations of the parties—to put the injured party in the same position as if the contract had been performed properly: *Hadley* v *Baxendale* (1854) 9 Exch 341. Damages for wrongful dismissal are therefore based on the contemplation of the parties—which means payments that would have fallen due in the notice period. The limitation period is six years (three months if claiming in an employment tribunal).

Employment tribunals have jurisdiction to hear wrongful dismissal claims (and other contractual claims arising from or outstanding on termination). However, their jurisdiction is limited to awarding £25,000 maximum. This should be borne in mind when deciding on the appropriate forum in which to make the claim and *Fraser* v *HLMAD Ltd* [2006] EWCA Civ 738 should be taken as a salutary lesson. Here the employment tribunal awarded the employee damages for wrongful dismissal but capped the award at £25,000. The Court of Appeal held that the employee was not entitled to bring proceedings in the High Court to recover the excess even though he had 'reserved his right' to do so. The practical advice is: (a) choose the forum carefully; and (b) if an error has been made as to forum, seek to withdraw that part of the claim from the tribunal and pursue the matter in the ordinary courts. Bear in mind, however, that under tribunal rules, withdrawn claims cannot be reactivated in the tribunal.

It is worth noting in this context that an employee may have a claim under the law of contract *and* under ERA 1996, Part II for any outstanding wages on termination. These are claims which are distinct from wrongful dismissal claims (see **4.4** and **5.9** above). Further, as noted above in **Chapter 5** and at **10.7.1.3**, there are arguments that service-related notice periods are discriminatory in that they favour older employees. We have no authority yet on this so we will work on the basis that discrimination is not a key factor.

10.10.1.1 Employees' damages

In the abstract one could argue that when the employee is wrongfully dismissed (especially if jobs are scarce) the loss could be enormous. But at any given time and for any reason an employment contract may be lawfully terminated by one or other party giving the notice required under the contract. Thus, in assessing what has been lost one needs to know the maximum that could have been gained had the parties behaved properly in bringing the contract to an end. The maximum that could have been gained in the overwhelming majority of employment contracts is payment for the notice period. Thus damages are limited to the amount that would have been paid if notice had been properly given, or any shortfall between the payment due and that which was made.

Where an employee has resigned and successfully claims *wrongful repudiation* of the contract, the amount of damages will be equivalent to a wrongful dismissal claim and the same rules as to calculation will apply.

To the basic figure of wages one needs to add (at least in some cases) other sums which could have been gained *during that notice period.* Thus, to the basic wages figure one might add:

(a) fringe benefits, e.g., a company car, medical insurance;

(b) tips, to which the employee was contractually entitled (usually given as estimated value);

(c) commission and bonus to which the employee was contractually entitled;

(d) share options and payments under profit-sharing schemes;

(e) pension loss—at its lowest level an amount representing the employee's contributions;

(f) backpay (including holiday entitlements);

(g) interest from date of dismissal to date of hearing.

As with so many of these lists, therefore, one needs to know the terms of the contract in order to determine quantum. These additional elements, however, are given *for the length of the notice period* and not as general, life-long sums. The loss of the company car will therefore be calculated according to its value to the employee for the eight-week (or other) period of notice. Reference is made here to tables such as those compiled by the AA to determine value.

10.10.1.2 Damages not related to the notice period

In some circumstances the damages for wrongful dismissal may actually be *greater* than the notice period. If, for instance, an employee has been dismissed without notice and in breach of contractually binding disciplinary rules (e.g., the procedure clearly laid down in the contract was not followed) the damages may be calculated in this way:

(a) take the date of dismissal and calculate how long it *would have taken* to comply with the contractual disciplinary scheme;

(b) add the notice due from the imaginary date of the disciplinary hearing properly conducted.

We will return to this at **10.10.6.2** below in examining the role of injunctions.

Occasionally you will find an employee who has been dismissed just before a key date in their employment relationship. For instance, they might have been dismissed just short of a year's service (which is the point where most employees gain the right to claim unfair dismissal), or maybe the dismissal occurs just short of an anniversary of their employment which, if they had passed this point, would have meant they gained a better pension or redundancy payment. To what extent can an employee claim damages to take account of such 'lost opportunities'?

We start with a long-standing presumption derived from *Laverack* v *Woods* [1967] 1 QB 278, CA: that an employer must be assumed to discharge his contractual responsibilities in the manner most favourable to him. So, if an employer dismisses an employee at a time which best suits the employer then there is nothing wrong with this and no damages will be awarded for lost opportunity. This may be a dangerous game in terms of brinkmanship and rules have been developed in the area of unfair dismissal which sometimes come as a shock to such employers but the basic principle remains the same, as confirmed in *Harper* v *Virgin Net Ltd* [2004] EWCA Civ 271, [2004] IRLR 390.

Employers can get things wrong (sometimes innocently). In *Silvey* v *Pendragon plc* [2001] EWCA Civ 784, [2001] IRLR 6, for instance, an employee was dismissed with payment in lieu of notice. As we shall note below, the date of dismissal when payment in lieu of notice is given is deemed to be the date of the dismissal itself and not the date when notice would have expired had it been worked. This meant here that the employee lost out on an accrual to his pension which, if he had worked his notice, he would have acquired. The Court of Appeal found that the payment in lieu was not authorised in the contract and was therefore a technical breach (even though no damages could be paid as Silvey had received the proper sum). But this finding meant that Silvey could claim a sum to which he would have been entitled had it not been for this repudiatory breach.

Every few years the basic principle of damages being limited to notice (plus add-ons) is challenged. The aim is to overcome the fact that, as we shall see, compensation for *unfair dismissal* is 'capped' and claimants (especially highly-paid ones) need to find a device whereby the common law can be used to obtain damages at large.

One such challenge that ran for a while is the argument that there is an implied term in the contract not to be unfairly dismissed. This died a death in *Fosca* v *Birkett* [1996] IRLR 325. The House of Lords' cases of *Johnson* v *Unisys Ltd* [2001] UKHL 13, [2001] ICR 480 and *Eastwood* v *Magnox Electric plc* [2004] UKHL 35, [2004] 3 WLR 322 then cut short the argument that the implied term of mutual trust and confidence could be used to allow a claim for unfair treatment connected to a dismissal (we shall deal with these in more detail at **10.10.1.6** below). The latest in the line of cunning arguments is *Edwards* v *Chesterfield Royal Hospital NHS Foundation Trust* [2010] EWCA Civ 571. Here the argument was that a dismissal following a failure to follow an express contractual disciplinary procedure (which, had it occurred, said the employee, would have found in the employee's favour) meant that the employee could claim for *all* loss that resulted, not just the loss for notice plus how long the procedure would have taken. The Court of Appeal agreed with this, to the surprise of many, though this case has not been heard on its merits (it was an appeal from an order made under CPR Pt 24) and, even in its present form, is set for further appeal.

10.10.1.3 Injured feelings

Damages are not generally awarded for loss of future prospects or injured feelings: *Addis* v *Gramophone Co. Ltd* [1909] AC 488 and *Bliss* v *South East Thames Regional Health Authority* [1987] ICR 700. However, loss of reputation (stigma damages) has now been recognised as a head of damage by the House of Lords in *Malik and Mahmud* v *Bank of Credit and Commerce International SA (in compulsory liquidation)* [1997] ICR 606, emanating from breach of the implied term of mutual trust and confidence (specifically, not to run a corrupt and dishonest business so as to damage the employees' future employment prospects). This head of damages has so far been given a narrow application, so the fact that an unjustifiable, even capricious, dismissal diminishes future job prospects does not trigger *Malik* damages.

Although injury to feelings may be excluded, we noted above at **5.2.3(d)** that an employer owes a duty of care not to injure an employee. This has been a growth area for litigation, with two main angles: (i) the tortious one of causing psychological injury in the form of stress; and (ii) the contractual one of acting in such a way as to breach the duty of mutual trust and confidence.

10.10.1.4 Psychological injuries: the safety angle

In *Page* v *Smith* [1995] 2 WLR 644 the House of Lords held that, as a matter of general principle, physical and psychological injury are subject to the same test of foreseeability. The first major case to deal with stress in the workplace was *Walker* v *Northumberland County Council* [1995] ICR 702. Here, the employers knew the employee was under stress as he had already taken time off work for this, but they failed to take this into account in piling on even more work when he returned. The employers were held liable for the psychological injury that followed. In various cases this notion was then tested in cases which did not involve a 'second incident'.

In the joined cases of *Sutherland* v *Hatton* [2002] EWCA Civ 76, [2002] ICR 613 the Court of Appeal held that the ordinary principles of employer's liability applied to stress-at-work cases. The case went on appeal to the House of Lords under the name *Barber* v *Somerset County Council* [2004] UKHL 13, [2004] ICR 457 where their Lordships held that an employer's duty is to take positive thought for the safety of the workers *in the light of what the employer knows or ought to have known.* The key point that emerges from *Barber* is that this is a general *positive* duty to take some steps to be aware of pressures on employees, not one which only applies where the employer is aware of a vulnerable employee. This is not an absolute duty, however, and where the evidence does not support the view that the employer should have known about the stress etc., then no liability can follow.

The topic was examined again by the Court of Appeal in six more joined cases under the lead name of *Hartman* v *South Essex Mental Health and Community Care NHS Trust* [2005] EWCA Civ 6, [2005] IRLR 293. Scott Baker LJ cites with approval the guidelines drawn in *Hatton.* These guidelines survived the House of Lords' decision and include examining things such as: the nature and extent of the work done by the employee, signs from the employee of impending harm to health, the size and scope of the employer's operation, its resources, and the interests of other employees in any redistribution of duties. It is not enough to merely set up a counselling service and hope the problem goes away; the employer's duty is to act on the knowledge available: *Intel Corporation (UK) Ltd* v *Daw* [2007] EWCA Civ 70, [2007] IRLR 355. This is even more so when the employee is returning to work after physical or psychological injury: an employer should ideally have in place an adequate return-to-work programme.

10.10.1.5 Psychological injuries: harassment

The Protection from Harassment Act 1997 (PHA 1997) was devised to deal with the problem of stalkers but in *Majrowski* v *Guy's and St Thomas's NHS Trust* [2006] UKHL 34 the Court of Appeal and then the House of Lords (on different reasoning) held that:

(a) an employer could be vicariously liable for an employee's breach of statutory duty provided the legislation does not expressly or impliedly exclude such liability; and
(b) the PHA 1997 had no such exclusion and therefore applied to employment situations, e.g., in the case of bullying by work colleagues.

This decision takes us beyond the bounds of negligence as described above because, once harassment has been found, the next test is whether the employer is vicariously liable on the facts (now subject to a wider and less employer-friendly test of 'work connexion') and, if this is found, the Act creates strict liability (so that foreseeability is irrelevant). Harassment is undefined in the PHA 1997, but it has to be a course of conduct not just a single incident and will include causing the victim alarm or distress through speech as well as conduct (s. 8(3)). However, as the Court of Appeal commented in *Conn* v *Council of City of Sunderland* [2007] EWCA Civ 1492, [2008] IRLR 324 the conduct must cross the boundary from that which is unattractive or even unreasonable into something oppressive and unacceptable.

Section 3(2) states that 'On such a claim, damages may be awarded for (among other things) any anxiety caused by the harassment and any financial loss resulting from the harassment'. Note that the use of the word 'anxiety' sets a much lower standard than proving 'personal injury' and that the limitation period under the PHA 1997 is six years instead of the personal injury three-year period.

10.10.1.6 Psychological injuries: mutual trust

Running alongside the *safety* argument has been a debate about whether an employer's actions (which might produce psychological injury) might constitute a breach of the implied term of mutual trust and confidence. Once the case of *Malik* had extended the duty to matters such as how an employer's conduct affects an employee's reputation (see above at **10.10.1.1**), the opportunity to argue an extension of the duty of mutual trust to conduct which causes psychological harm became ever-present. The limits of *Malik* are being well and truly tested.

The first major test arose in *Johnson* v *Unisys Ltd* [2001] UKHL 13, [2001] ICR 480 where the Court of Appeal [1999] ICR 809 and then the House of Lords revisited the area in the context of a dismissed employee who claimed that his summary dismissal (based on allegations made against him) represented a breach of the term of trust and confidence leading to severe psychiatric illness and financial damages. Their Lordships held that, though *Addis* v *Gramophone Co. Ltd* might be reviewed in modern circumstances, here the position was clear: there was no need to develop the common law to overlap this remedy. Further, whereas *Malik* may be applicable to breaches of contract arising *during* the employment relationship, it was not relevant to the manner of the *termination*.

This apparently simple distinction has complications: what happens where an employer commits a breach of mutual trust (say, in terms of false allegations or bad faith disciplinary measures) and the employee is eventually dismissed or resigns? Is the breach one occurring 'during' the contract and so actionable as a common law claim under *Malik*, or one related to termination and so *not* actionable under *Johnson?* After a fair amount of debate, inevitably cases arose where a dismissal did result and the *Johnson* v *Unisys* distinction had to be tested. In the joined cases of *Eastwood* v *Magnox Electric plc* and *McCabe* v *Cornwall County Council* [2004] UKHL 35, [2004] 3 WLR 322 the House of Lords pronounced on this position. Their Lordships decided that a common law claim for psychological injury arising from a breach of the duty of mutual trust will only arise where the cause of action has accrued *before* dismissal.

Unfortunately (as their Lordships recognised) the distinction between discipline and dismissal can become very fudged and, if dismissal does result, we shall see that injury to feelings, etc. is not something which an employment tribunal can award as part of unfair dismissal compensation either. This is not helpful and we have seen further complications above with the case of *Edwards* v *Chesterfield Royal Hospital NHS Foundation Trust* in which the Court of Appeal held that career-long loss of earnings based on the breach of a contractual disciplinary procedure was not excluded by the *Johnson* reasoning.

10.10.1.7 Employers' damages

It should be noted that employers are also entitled to sue for damages where the employee has not served proper notice according to the contract (the contract is the only real issue here as the ERA 1996, s. 86 minimum for employees is fixed at one week). Employers may also counterclaim in any contractual claim brought by an employee (but not under an ERA 1996, Part II claim).

The amount of the employer's damages in these circumstances will be limited to the sum needed to find a replacement. A general clause which allows employers to deduct a sum of money from any final payment owed to an employee (e.g., outstanding pay) when the employee leaves without giving notice is not a genuine pre-estimate of loss and so likely to be classed as a penalty clause: *Giraud* v *Smith* [2000] IRLR 763. Such 'recovery' clauses can be drafted so as to amount to genuine estimations, though: see *Neil* v *Strathclyde Regional Council* [1984] IRLR 14, on recovering the costs of a training scheme. If another employer has induced the employee to break his or her contract that employer will also be liable. But these are not usually real, practical issues. If employers need to do something in these circumstances they will either seek an injunction to hold employees to their notice period ('garden leave' injunctions), or seek to enforce a restraint of trade clause (see **Chapter 9**).

Tullett Prebon Group Ltd v *El-Hajjali* [2008] EWHC 1924 (QB), [2008] IRLR 760 gave us the unusual position of an employer suing successfully for a 'no-show' on the part of the new employee. The employment contract contained an express term dealing with what would happen if the prospective employee did not start work and this was deemed to be a liquidated damages clause (amounting to nearly £300,000).

None of this of course affects an employer's right to sue the employee for breach of contract *simpliciter*. Usually it will not be worth the employer's time or money but, should the employee be covered by insurance for their actions then the employer may well take up this option: see *Lister* v *Romford Ice and Cold Storage Co Ltd* [1957] AC 555. Indeed, in *Safeway Stores Ltd* v *Twigger* [2010] EWHC 11 (Comm); [2010] 3 All ER 577 a group of employees entered into a price-fixing agreement that laid the company open to fines for breach of competition law in excess of £10m. The employer sought to recover this amount from them (or, realistically, via the insurance cover) for breach of their contracts and the employees applied to have the claim struck out, attempting to rely on the maxim *ex turpi causa non oritur actio* (one cannot benefit from one's own wrongdoing, i.e., that the company bore the blame as the offending party for its employee's actions). However, Flaux J in the Commercial Court rejected the employee's arguments for strike-out and allowed the case to proceed to trial.

10.10.2 Deductions from employees' damages

Nothing in life, so they say, is free. The employee may well have a good claim for wrongful dismissal, but deductions can be made from any award. First, the employee cannot avoid tax liabilities so the award will generally be made net of tax and National Insurance. This applies to all cases where the damages are under £30,000.

If the award exceeds £30,000 complications set in. The basic rule is that the courts must decide on the loss and then add to this figure ('gross up') an amount representing the tax which will eventually have to be paid by the employee. This grossed-up figure represents the damages awarded against the employer, and the employee can then sort out the tax position with HM Revenue and Customs. Thus, if a court calculates that the damages come to £60,000 it may have to award £80,000 so that the employee will actually get £60,000 after the taxman has made a request the employee cannot refuse (see *Shove* v *Downs Surgical Supplies Ltd* [1984] IRLR 17).

There are different methods used for grossing up. The two main methods depend in part on the level of detailed information available to the court/employment tribunal. The *Shove* approach is the more accurate. It involves the following steps:

1. Take the value of gross salary and benefits.
2. Calculate taxable value of 1 above.
3. Calculate tax and NI payable after deduction of allowances.
4. Deduct tax and NI from gross salary and benefits.
5. Multiply this net figure of annual loss by period of damages/compensation.
6. Make any deductions for mitigation.
7. Make deductions for accelerated receipt.
8. Deduct £30,000.
9. Gross up taxable slice and add back the £30,000.

In all cases, damages may be reduced because of the 'duty' to mitigate any loss. This means that the victim of any breach must minimise the loss, not act unreasonably to increase the loss, and account for any benefits received. The burden of proving failure to mitigate lies with the employer.

Deductions from damages

Usually deducted	*Not usually deducted*	*Debatable*
Payment in other work (including fringe benefits, commission, shares, etc.).		Failure to make use of appeals procedure. The most recent EAT authority (*Lock* v *Connell Estate Agents* [1994] IRLR 444) disapproves of such a deduction being made.

(Continued)

Any payment in lieu received.	Payment in lieu, where the basis of the claim is a debt action: *Abrahams* v *Performing Rights Society* [1995] IRLR 486—below.	Money from temporary or short-term employment. The chain of causation may not be broken where employee finds new work and then that employment fails.
Sum representing failure to take reasonable steps to find new employment (i.e. failure to mitigate).	No deduction for failure to mitigate where ex-employee has failed to make profits in new (self-employed) enterprise.	Offer of re-employment by employer. Always debatable, but must certainly be made or repeated after dismissal: *Shindler* v *Northern Raincoat* [1960] 1 WLR 1038.
Jobseekers' allowance, to the extent that this constitutes a net gain: *Westwood* v *Secretary of State for Employment* [1985] ICR 209.	Private pension payments: *Hopkins* v *Norcross* [1994] ICR 11, CA—possible with caveat that contract may disallow this.	Compensatory award for unfair dismissal: *O'Laoire* v *Jackel International Ltd* [1990] ICR 197.
Income support to the extent that this constitutes a net gain.	Statutory redundancy payment and the Basic Award element of Compensation for unfair dismissal.	Failure to make a claim for social security benefits: *Secretary of State for Employment* v *Stewart* [1996] IRLR 334.
Tax, NI, and pension contributions.	Insurance moneys or charitable payments other than by employer.	Sick pay.
Accelerated receipt (usually only in cases of very long-term notice periods or remainders of fixed-term contracts), of 5–10 per cent deduction.		*Ex gratia* payments by the employer. These are certainly deductible if clearly intended to compensate employee for dismissal.

Note: Deductions in unfair dismissal cases are treated differently (see **12.4** below).

10.10.3 Action for debt

In *Abrahams* v *Performing Rights Society* [1995] IRLR 486 the Court of Appeal added a new gloss to this area. Here, the parties had failed to reach agreement concerning the extension of the employee's fixed-term contract. Instead, the employee agreed to continue working *'under the terms of his existing contract'* for two years. That fixed-term contract had contained a clause allowing for two years' notice or payment in lieu to be given.

After only six months of the new contract the employer dismissed the employee summarily. Following considerable debate as to the exact meaning of the phrase 'under the terms of his existing contract', it was held that the employee was still entitled to two years' notice or payment in lieu (a trifling sum of £232,292). In a case full of twists and turns, the central question then became whether, on what appeared to be a straight-forward wrongful dismissal, the employee had to mitigate his loss on the principles described above.

In an uncommon reversal of arguments, the *employer* contended that this was indeed a wrongful dismissal and so subject to mitigation. The employee argued that where, as in this case, the contract of employment expressly provides that the employment may be terminated by the employer on payment of a sum in lieu of notice, any summary dismissal is a *lawful* termination, not a breach of contract, and the amount unpaid constitutes a debt (which is not subject to mitigation). The court agreed with the employee:

(a) the provision in the contract for payment in lieu gave rise to a contractual entitlement and therefore created a debt; and, *obiter,*

(b) even if the notice provision were to be regarded as liquidated damages, no duty to mitigate would apply.

Amongst the many practical implications to this case we would note the following:

(a) most senior employee contracts (and many others) incorporate a payment in lieu provision, so the ramifications of this case are extensive;

(b) many of these contracts use this clause so as to take advantage of the reasoning in *Rex Stewart Jeffries Parker Ginsberg Ltd* v *Parker* and avoid any technical breach of contract (see above at **10.9**);

(c) employers and their solicitors must therefore balance the potential sums due *as a debt* against the need for restraint of trade protection when drafting the contract.

The decision in *Abrahams* has had a mixed reception. In *Gregory* v *Wallace* [1998] IRLR 387, *Hutchings* v *Coinsee Ltd* [1998] IRLR 190, and *Cerberus Software* v *Rowley* [2001] IRLR 160 the Court of Appeal has confirmed the basic principle in *Abrahams* that a payment in lieu clause can create a debt rather than a contractual claim but placed emphasis on the wording of the clause itself. If the clause reserves to the employer the *right* to decide whether to make the payment or not it is more likely that any non-payment can only be recovered in a claim for damages rather than debt (and so be subject to mitigation).

10.10.4 Where there is no dismissal

We have so far fixed on wrongful dismissal. It may be that the employee is not dismissed and yet suffers loss. Such was the case in *Rigby* v *Ferodo* [1988] ICR 29 (discussed in **Chapter 5**), where the employees, faced with a pay cut in breach of contract, remained in employment and sued for damages representing their lost wages.

The employee may likewise always sue for any other form of breach of contract. A difficulty arises here, however. *Rigby* v *Ferodo* was an easy case because the quantum was the lost wages. If the employee is suing for a breach relating to an unlawful order, e.g., to move to another site or undertake different responsibilities, damages will be more difficult to quantify. This problem has not really been addressed by the courts.

Again, a claim under ERA 1996, Part II, Protection of Wages, should be noted here as a possibility.

10.10.5 Limited-term contracts

We repeat in this context that damages for breach of a limited-term contract will be for the remainder of the term *unless* the contract contains a notice provision, in which case damages will be for that notice period.

Clearly, if the remainder of the term is the relevant period the employee will be claiming a large sum in many cases. Here tax implications will come into their own. However, some heed must be taken of the fact that instead of earning a £25,000 salary each year for the next, say, three years the employee will be getting this money in one fell swoop. The courts therefore take account of this *accelerated receipt* and reduce the award to reflect this. A rule of thumb deduction has been 5 per cent but recent judicial comments have indicated a willingness to equate this with the personal injury figure of 2 per cent.

10.10.6 Equitable remedies

These discretionary remedies do not have a strong foothold in employment contracts, especially if they amount to a request for an injunction for specific performance.

10.10.6.1 Declarations

An employee (or employer) may seek a declaration by the court as to the contractual position and rights of the parties. There must be a genuine grievance to pursue—the courts are not prone to giving lecture courses. A declaration is not a decision, it is an opinion. It cannot require the parties to undertake a particular act—though it would seem generally inadvisable to ignore it.

10.10.6.2 Injunctions

The courts are not keen to turn service into servitude and will therefore be loath to come to any decision which smacks of specific performance of the contract. Damages will usually suffice here as a remedy so, *unless damages are inadequate,* injunctions will not be granted. The concern of *employers* seeking injunctive relief regarding the maintenance of confidentiality, 'garden leave' clauses and restraint of trade was dealt with in **Chapter 9** (at **9.12**). Those points will not be repeated here.

An *employee* may seek an injunction in three main circumstances:

(a) to prevent a dismissal occurring which will be in breach of contractually enforceable rules of procedure;

(b) to prevent a dismissal taking place at all;

(c) to get the employee's job back.

It is unlikely that an injunction will be granted for the last point: *Marsh* v *National Autistic Society* [1993] ICR 453. Injunctions preventing dismissals in any circumstances are again a rare event. However, injunctions to hold the dismissal until procedures have been adhered to have become more common. Thus, although a dismissed employee will not be able to obtain an order for specific performance to *regain* employment, it is feasible that a court would grant an interim injunction requiring the dismissal not to take effect *unless and until* the employer had complied with the contractual terms (e.g., disciplinary procedures).

The decisions are not consistent in this area but it seems that injunctions may be granted (remember it is a discretionary remedy) where:

(a) the dismissal is in breach of a mandatory contractual procedure (usually relating to disciplinary action; but this may also extend to things such as redundancy selection procedures: *Anderson* v *Pringle of Scotland Ltd* [1998] IRLR 64). Injunctions can be granted to restrain dismissals which do not comply with set contractual procedures: *Dietmann* v *Brent London Borough Council* [1988] ICR 842;

(b) trust and confidence has been maintained between the parties, i.e., the parties are still content to continue working together (judged on rational, not purely subjective, grounds: *Powell* v *Brent London Borough Council* [1988] ICR 176), or at least the contract is still 'workable'.

Injunctions come in two forms: interim (pending a full hearing of the issues) and final (granted at the conclusion of the full action). In most cases a prohibitory interim injunction will be granted or refused on the *American Cyanamid* principles (from *American Cyanamid Co.* v *Ethicon Ltd* [1975] AC 396—see **Chapter 9**).

10.10.6.3 Part 24, Civil procedure rules

One of the problems in this area is that if an employee fails to obtain an interim injunction preventing dismissal this will effectively decide the issue, because by the time the full action comes to trial the issue will be dead and buried except for damages.

Thus we noted in **Chapter 5** the case of *Jones* v *Gwent County Council* [1992] IRLR 521, where a novel and interesting approach to these problems was taken when RSC Ords 14A, r. 1 was used to prevent a letter of dismissal being effective. RSC Ords 14 and 14A have now been amalgamated into CPR, Part 24. This part covers applications by claimants or defendants for summary judgment and allows a court to determine any question of law or construction of any document at any stage in the proceedings (there must be no dispute of fact) where the question is suitable for determination *without a full trial* and that determination will decide the claim.

In *Jones* a catalogue of ineptly handled disciplinary hearings took place until Jones eventually received a letter of dismissal. Jones sought an injunction to restrain the council from dismissing her pursuant to the letter until full trial. Chadwick J held that, for the purposes of Ord. 14A, the status of the purported dismissal letter could be determined as easily in the current hearing as at full trial. That being so, the letter of dismissal was not a valid and effective dismissal because it did not comply with the disciplinary procedures set out in the contract. Further, it was held that under Ord. 14A the presence or absence of mutual trust *was irrelevant.* A permanent injunction was therefore issued restraining the council from dismissing Jones *pursuant to its dismissal letter* and an interlocutory injunction was granted restraining the council from dismissing unless proper grounds existed after carrying out the correct procedure.

Part 24, CPR could thus prove to be a very effective weapon for employees where the dispute is only about the meaning of documents, e.g., in cases of threatened demotion or dismissal which hinge on the wording of the contract. The number of cases making use of this device is steadily increasing; although use of RSC Ord. 14A in *Abrahams* v *Performing Rights Society* was the subject of some critical comment from Hutchinson LJ. Whether Part 24, CPR could be applied to confidentiality or restraint of trade cases is debatable. If there is no dispute as to fact so that 'reasonableness' is purely a point of law, there seems no reason why this should not be the case.

10.10.6.4 Judicial review

Judicial review is not relevant to employment law except in very limited circumstances. These were defined in *McLaren* v *Home Office* [1990] ICR 824 as being (i) that the decision was made by a public body; or (ii) where an employee or employer is entitled to refer disputes on the employment relationship to a disciplinary or other body established by statute.

10.11 Outline of tax considerations

This section makes no attempt to describe in detail the various schemes employed by companies to deal with taxation matters, merely to note some key points to be considered when termination is effected.

Where employment is terminated an employee may sometimes be entitled to or offered different financial packages, ranging from redundancy payments and notice payments through to retirement sums and 'golden handshakes'. In each case there may be tax liability and each element of any package has to be examined closely for sometimes part of a package may be caught by tax whilst others parts are exempted in some form. It is not the case (as is often presumed) that the first £30,000 paid to an employee on termination is exempt from tax. It depends what elements make up that £30,000 (or any sum for that matter). The key Act is the Income Tax (Earnings and Pensions) Act 2003.

10.11.1 Normal rule

Earnings derived from employment are subject to tax and monies paid on the termination of a contract will be subject to tax in the same way that wages are where there is a contractual obligation to make that payment and this still applies even when:

(a) the payment is expressed as being discretionary; and

(b) the contract is silent on the point but such payments constitute normal practice.

This will apply equally to express terms allowing for payment in lieu of notice (*EMI Group Electronics Ltd* v *Caldicott (Inspector of Taxes)* [1999] IRLR 630) and will apply to other benefits such as the retention of company cars. Where the contract (or practice) does not allow payment in lieu of notice employers may still, theoretically, deduct tax; but most will pay gross as the first £30,000 here is not taxable in the employee's hands under ss. 401–405, Income Tax (Earnings and Pensions) Act 2003. The Revenue has issued guidance notes on tax and pay *in lieu* of notice: see www.hmrc.gov.uk/bulletins/tb63.pdf.

10.11.2 Compensation for loss of office

Ex gratia payments (e.g., 'golden handshakes' and compromise agreements) will not be subject to the general rule provided they do not relate to services rendered and are not a contractual right. In such cases the first £30,000 is not taxable. The £30,000 figure applies to termination of employment not to the tax year so staggering the payment over two tax years is of no effect.

As *any prior agreement* may be subject to tax, various schemes have been devised to help reduce the chance of tax being charged where there is no contractual obligation but termination terms are being negotiated. Such tactics involve complicated assessments of liabilities for relevant tax years.

10.11.3 Damages for wrongful dismissal

The basic principles in this area were set out in *British Transport Commission* v *Gourley* [1955] 3 All ER 796. The employee should be placed in the same position as if the contract had been performed properly. The *Gourley* principle means that deductions must be made from any award for tax, as described in **10.10.2** above.

Where there is a contractual right to a payment in lieu (necessary if the employer wants to use this device and still protect the restrictive covenants in the contract) that payment will fall to be taxed as earnings. HMRC regard non-contractual payments in lieu as subject to the same rule but agree that where there is no contractual entitlement to a payment in lieu and the employer fails to make one or makes an inadequate payment then any money regained by the employee is treated as damages and not taxable for the first £30,000. Genuine agreements to terminate will be treated the same way.

10.11.4 Statutory payments

Such payments are taxable, but in general are treated as exempt from tax up to £30,000.

(a) The basic award in unfair dismissal (see **Chapter 13**) is payable as a gross figure.

(b) The compensatory award in unfair dismissal is already calculated on a net pay figure so no further adjustment is necessary.

(c) The 'Additional award' in unfair dismissal is payable as a gross figure.

(d) Statutory redundancy pay (see **Chapter 14**) is payable gross. The current limit is £11,400 and so does not trouble the £30,000 exemption rule, but of course this may form part of a package which does take an employee over that figure.

(e) Contractual redundancy pay, strictly, should be treated as a contractual right and subject to tax. However, HM Revenue and Customs have issued a Statement of Practice on this (SP1/94) to the effect that if the scheme is a genuine redundancy payment no tax will be taken. The amount will still go towards the calculation of the £30,000.

10.12 Summary

- A contract of employment may be terminated in a number of ways, most commonly dismissal and resignation.
- The common law is only concerned with the contractual aspects of termination so its focus is on whether or not adequate notice was given to terminate the contract.
- A dismissal made without adequate notice is a wrongful dismissal and the employee will be able to recover damages to the amount of notice that should have been given.
- Just because a dismissal has been without notice does not mean it is wrongful. The employer may be able to justify this by referring to a serious breach of contract by the employee which brought about the dismissal.
- The employer is permitted to rely on evidence of the employee's breach even if this was not known at the time of dismissal.
- A resignation brought about by the employee's acceptance of the employer's repudiatory breach allows the employee to claim wrongful repudiation of the contract. Damages are treated in the same way as wrongful dismissal claims.
- Although the parties are free to determine what notice is due on termination from either side, there are statutory minimum periods of notice which alter according to length of service.
- These periods of notice (and other terms for that matter) must not be discriminatory. As regards any term which is service-related there may be problems with age discrimination.
- The assessment of damages is subject to the normal contractual rules so that issues of actual loss, mitigation, and taxation all come into play. Damages are generally not awarded for injured feelings, but stress claims may be tagged on to other contractual damages.

11

Unfair dismissal: dismissal and fair reasons

11.1 Introduction and overview

11.1.1 Jurisdiction

This chapter is concerned with the most important (or at least the most notorious) of the statutory rights: the right to claim unfair dismissal. The sole arena for deciding these claims is the employment tribunal; unfair dismissal actions *cannot* be heard in the ordinary courts. The bulk of employment tribunals' workload is made up of unfair dismissal cases. Many are settled before going to a tribunal; most of the cases heard are decided in favour of the employer. Appeal lies to the Employment Appeal Tribunal (EAT) on 'a question of law' (a term which has been given an increasingly narrow ambit by the EAT and the Court of Appeal).

11.1.2 Relationships with wrongful dismissal

Right at the start the differences between *wrongful dismissal* actions and *unfair dismissal* actions should be noted. We have seen that wrongful dismissal is concerned with awarding damages for breach of contract. Unfair dismissal rights centre on the *reason for* the dismissal and *the manner* in which the dismissal was handled. It is quite possible to have the following combinations:

(a) a dismissal which is unfair but which is not wrongful;

(b) a dismissal which is wrongful but which is not unfair;

(c) a dismissal which is both unfair and wrongful;

(d) a dismissal which is neither unfair nor wrongful.

11.1.3 Overview of unfair dismissal actions

This overview relates to the issues we will be covering in **Chapters 11**, **12** and **13**.

- Only employees, not independent contractors, have the right to claim unfair dismissal: s. 94 of ERA 1996. The right extends to those employed in casual or part-time work and to those who have limited-term contracts, but some employees are excluded from the right (e.g., those working outside Great Britain).
- In most cases an employee must have been employed for one year to qualify for the right, though there is an ever-growing list of exceptions.

- There is no upper or lower age for claiming unfair dismissal, though compulsory retirements are still possible provided certain procedures are followed (this is set to change in October 2011).
- To claim the right an employee must have been dismissed. The term 'dismissal' can include a termination of the contract arising from a resignation—known in this context as a 'constructive dismissal'. A constructive dismissal only arises where the employer has seriously breached or repudiated the contract and this has been accepted by the employee in resigning. If challenged, it is for the employee to show a 'dismissal' occurred.
- There are six potentially fair *reasons* for dismissal set out in s. 98(2) of ERA 1996. They are: capability, conduct, retirement, redundancy, statutory illegality, and 'some other substantial reason'. If the employer cannot show one of these reasons the dismissal is unfair.
- Even if the dismissal is for a fair *reason,* this will not make it a fair dismissal: there is a second limb. Where the fair reason is conduct, capability, redundancy, statutory illegality, or 'some other substantial reason', s. 98(4) of ERA 1996 *fairness* is judged by examining whether the employer acted reasonably or unreasonably in treating the reason as sufficient to justify dismissing the employee. This breaks down into two key tests: (i) whether a fair procedure was used; and (ii) whether the decision to dismiss fell within the 'range of reasonable responses open to a reasonable employer'. As we shall see, however, 'retirement' dismissals are treated as a special case and are subject to slightly different rules for determining 'fairness' under s. 98ZG of ERA 1996.
- The extent to which a company adheres to its procedures (and how these follow the ACAS Code and Guidelines) is extremely important in judging questions of fairness.
- A dismissal will be automatically unfair in certain circumstances (set out at **11.8.8** below). Examples include dismissal for reason of pregnancy and dismissals because the employee made a legitimate public interest disclosure.
- If a finding of unfair dismissal is made the tribunal should consider whether to direct that the employee should be reinstated in their job, but this is hardly ever ordered so the main remedy is compensation. Tribunals award compensation under two main headings (see **Chapter 13** for details):
  - The basic award (a sum of money calculated on a fixed formula relating to age and years of service). The maximum sum that can be awarded (for 2010–11) is £11,400. This figure is updated every February.
  - The compensatory award. This is assessed on the basis of what the tribunal considers just and equitable and it is sub-divided into: (i) loss from date of dismissal to the tribunal hearing; and (ii) future loss. The maximum compensatory award that can be awarded is £65,300. This figure is also updated every February. Some dismissals, e.g., relating to public interest disclosures, are not subject to the statutory maximum.
- Deductions may be made from these awards e.g., for contributory fault, even resulting in a finding of unfair dismissal leading to no compensation.

11.2 Preventive measures

Most employers these days are aware of the importance of being able to justify dismissal decisions and of the need to follow correct procedures. But many dismissals (especially in small companies) can result from hasty management decisions and it is not uncommon for employers to sit on problems (e.g., an employee's incompetence) and then expect to be able to dismiss without any warning having been given to the employee, without any consultation, and immediately. Another common practice is to dismiss for the event *following* the big one, i.e., the employer misses or dodges the opportunity to dismiss for the misconduct which would have been easy to defend but, almost as a knee-jerk reaction, dismisses for an event that is not justifiable.

You may not have control over any of this because usually the parties will come to you with a *fait accompli* rather than in advance for advice. However, if you can advise your client prior to dismissal there are some general industrial relations and personnel points to note. The reasons why these pieces of advice are given here will become clear later when we look at how employment tribunals judge the fairness of dismissals.

There are two main practical categories in which the employer will wish to dismiss:

(a) *Maintaining standards.*

Employers regard it as important to maintain standards of acceptable behaviour on the part of employees, relating for example to quality of workmanship, rate of output, punctuality, attendance, and working relationships with other staff. Employees who fail to meet these standards will (or at least should) generally be warned about their shortcomings but dismissal is the final sanction that can be used.

(b) *Relationship impossible to maintain.*

The employee's actions here will include dishonesty (especially in a position of trust), sexual misconduct and harassment of other staff, and assault.

Quite often both strands are present in a single case so that the position can become muddied and the employer may need advice on analysing the reason for any dismissal. For instance, senior management may centre on the maintenance of standards whilst supervisors focus on the effect of misconduct on fellow workers. When evidence is given as to why dismissal occurred it is clearly better if everyone is in general agreement, and this is better sorted out *before the dismissal.*

Before any dismissal employers should also be advised to examine other available courses of action and to:

(a) make proper use of their disciplinary procedures (which should comply with the ACAS Code);

(b) consider the effect on remaining employees in terms of future loyalty and performance (arising from leniency or excessive severity);

(c) consider the effect of any decision on supervisors, e.g., undermining their authority;

(d) consider the effect on any relationship with trade unions;

(e) consider all the alternatives if business reorganisation or redundancy is the reason for dismissal.

If dismissal is inevitable, try to control the manner of the dismissal. Your checklist should include:

(a) consider the terms of the contract;

(b) make sure that all the evidence is available and clear;

(c) make sure that the employer genuinely believes that dismissal is a reasonable course of action;

(d) make sure that all the relevant procedures have been complied with;

(e) make sure that any hearing is properly conducted;

(f) make sure that dismissal is consistent with previous practice within the company.

11.3 Qualifying for the right

Although ERA 1996, s. 94 states that every employee has the right not to be unfairly dismissed, there are certain conditions to be met. We noted these qualification aspects in **Chapter 5**. So, if we assume that your employee–client has asked you for advice following a dismissal, you need to ascertain, to begin with, that:

(a) your client was in fact an employee; and

(b) your client had one year's continuous employment (although there are many exceptions to this rule: see **11.8.8** below); and

(c) your client has fulfilled his or her part in any company dispute resolution procedures; and

(d) your client is not prevented from claiming because of the application of international law; and

(e) your client does not fall within a miscellaneous excluded category; and

(f) your client is still within the three-month limitation period which begins at the effective date of termination (the EDT).

These points are expanded below.

11.3.1 Service

The length of time an employee has spent with his or her employer (the continuity of employment) has always been a vital factor in determining whether or not he or she qualifies for unfair dismissal rights. The general requirement is for one year's service. Thus, in most cases, an employee dismissed before the expiry of one year will have no claim. Further, employing a person on a fixed-term contract for just less than one year so as to avoid liability for unfair dismissal is not 'less favourable treatment' for the purposes of the Fixed-term Employees (Prevention of Less Favourable Treatment) Regulations 2002 (SI 2002/2034)—even when it is the government trying to avoid liability under its own regulations: *Department for Work and Pensions* v *Webley* [2004] EWCA Civ 1745, [2005] ICR 577.

11.3.1.1 The effective date of termination

The period of continuity ends at the effective date of termination (EDT) and the limitation period for bringing claims starts at this point. The EDT is not necessarily the date when an employee is told that he or she is dismissed: *it varies according to whether notice is given or not.* Any notice given begins to run on the day after notification. So the EDT is defined in ERA 1996, s. 97(1), as follows:

Action taken	*Date of EDT*
The employee is given notice (whether or not all the notice is worked and whether or not the correct notice was given).	The date the notice expires
The employee is dismissed with payment in lieu of notice.	The date of dismissal
The employee is summarily dismissed (i.e., without any form of notice).	The date of dismissal
A limited-term contract comes to an end.	The end date in a fixed-term contract or completion of task in a task contract

The distinction between the first and second actions may seem to be one of semantics; sometimes this is true. But the basic difference is that in the first instance the employee is either given the choice of working out the notice, or the employer insists on some work, e.g., to tidy-up existing jobs or to pass on operational information to other employees; payment in lieu, on the other hand, is of immediate and unchallengeable effect. The position can, however, be complicated further. The way the employer expresses (orally or in writing) the dismissal and making of the payment in lieu may also affect the EDT. If the employer makes it clear that he is dismissing the employee immediately but paying him his notice entitlement, the EDT is that date of notification (this is the usual pattern). However, if the employer gets carried away (or has no concept of the problems) and talks about dismissing with notice but giving a payment in lieu instead of asking for notice to be worked, the EDT is the date the notice would have expired (see *Adams* v *GKN Sankey Ltd* [1980] IRLR 416).

Employers frequently use the third option described above (pay in lieu) because, provided there is no contractual term guaranteeing payment in lieu, it may avoid the tax liability due for the notice period. These distinctions prove to be a common point of confusion and need to be treated very carefully. For instance, although the third option may have tax advantages if there is no contractual right to dismiss with payment in lieu this is still a technical breach of contract which will render any restraint of trade clause ineffective (as we saw at **8.9**).

A novel way of calculating EDT was seen in *Kirklees Metropolitan Council* v *Radecki* [2009] EWCA Civ 298, [2009] IRLR 555. The employee had been suspended and was negotiating a compromise agreement. The employer removed him from the payroll on the date given in the draft ('subject to contract') agreement. Radecki did not sign this and discussions dragged on. When Radecki lodged a complaint of unfair dismissal the defence was that he was out of time, basing the EDT on the payroll removal date. The Court of Appeal agreed with this: the council had, by repudiation or otherwise, brought the contract to an end for these purposes.

If there is a letter of dismissal the EDT takes effect from the time the employee reads that letter.

11.3.1.2 Appeals

If an employee is dismissed he or she may well appeal against that decision using the company's disciplinary/grievance procedure. The question then arises: if the dismissal is confirmed on appeal, is the employee's date of dismissal the original date of the decision or the confirmation of that decision at the culmination of the appeals procedure? In most cases, unless there is express contractual provision to the contrary, the *original date* will count: *West Midlands Co-operative Society Ltd* v *Tipton* [1986] ICR 192. Thus any summary dismissal runs from that date and any notice given runs from that date too. If, however, the employee is suspended *pending a decision to dismiss,* the time can only run from the actual decision to dismiss. The employee's case becomes even easier to argue where that suspension is on full pay: *Drage* v *Governors of Greenford High School* [2000] IRLR 314.

11.3.1.3 Varying the EDT

It is not open to the parties to agree an EDT which is different from the normal method of calculation: *Fitzgerald* v *University of Kent at Canterbury* [2004] EWCA Civ 143, [2004] ICR 737. The effective date of termination is a statutory construct which depends on what has actually taken place and not on what the parties agreed. Note, however, that the parties may agree to vary the notice *period,* e.g., where the employee has been given notice but wishes to leave earlier. A genuine variation such as this will mean that the EDT moves as well.

11.3.1.4 Extending the EDT by the statutory minimum notice period

Under ERA 1996, s. 97(2), the EDT may be deemed extended in certain circumstances by adding on to it the s. 86 statutory minimum period of notice (see **9.7.1.1** above for how that period is calculated).

EXAMPLE

An employee is dismissed summarily after 51 weeks' service. Strictly, she does not have the requisite one year's (52 weeks') service to claim unfair dismissal. However, s. 97(2) allows the employee the fiction of adding on the s. 86 notice that should have been given (here, one week) in calculating the EDT. Thus the employee gains the one year's qualification and can claim unfair dismissal. This device lessens the opportunities for unscrupulous employers to engage in brinkmanship tactics.

Note, however, that only the s. 86 notice can be used this way. The contractual notice (which may be longer) is irrelevant. The statutory extension also applies where the employee has waived his right to notice or has received payment in lieu of notice because such matters relate only to the employee's contract and do not affect his statutory rights: *Secretary of State for Employment* v *Staffordshire County Council* [1989] ICR 664. This method of extending the EDT also applies to constructive dismissal claims. However, if the summary dismissal was contractually justified (e.g., because the dismissal was for gross misconduct or other serious breach by the employee) then this device cannot be applied.

As well as ensuring statutory rights in borderline situations the same technique can be used to calculate years of service for compensation purposes; so a dismissal close to four years' service would normally count as three years (because only whole years are considered), but the use of the s. 86 notice might take the qualification over the line into four years' service. This might affect the quantum of an employee's entitlement to, say, redundancy pay.

11.3.1.5 Exceptions to the service qualification

Some unfair dismissals do not require a one-year qualification period. These are set out in ERA 1996, s. 108 and TULRCA 1992, s. 154. Most of these types of dismissal are also deemed 'automatically unfair', so we have detailed these reasons in a table under that heading at **11.8.8** below.

11.3.2 Hours worked and minimum age

Under ERA 1996, s. 210(4) an employee does not have to work for any set number of hours per week in order to qualify for statutory rights such as unfair dismissal, redundancy, or maternity leave. There is also no minimum age for claiming unfair dismissal.

11.3.3 Retirement age

The rule whereby an employee lost all rights to claim unfair dismissal at age 65 was removed in 2006. However, some companies have a 'normal retirement age' for employees. In many cases this is set below 65, though not always. If companies have no such requirement the default retirement age is presently 65. Subject to what we say below at **11.8.4**, where employees reach 65 or have a 'normal retirement age' then any dismissal *for retirement* at that age is potentially fair. This begs the question: how do you determine whether there is a 'normal retirement age'?

11.3.3.1 Determining 'normal retirement age'

This is a technical term and does not just mean the date employees generally or commonly retire. It has been the subject of much case law. In *Waite* v *GCHQ* [1983] ICR 653, the House of Lords held that the normal retirement age was *prima facie* to be determined by what the contract said even if some employees happened to be kept on past the stated age of, say, 60. However, if the employees' reasonable expectations are that they will work past this age (e.g., because the evidence is that nearly everyone does so) there is probably no normal retirement age and the default of 65 comes into play. One of the key factors here is that one is not looking for a normal retirement age for the company as a whole but the age which applies to the *group of employees* to which the employee in question belongs. For instance, there may be different ages for clerical staff and manual workers. Even employees sharing the same job title have been found to be in different 'positions' under closer examination—and one person can constitute a group here: *Wall* v *British Compressed Air Society* [2003] EWCA Civ 1762.

The test was developed further in *Brooks* v *Telecommunications plc* [1991] IRLR 4, where the EAT held that one should determine a normal retirement age by:

(a) identifying the undertaking in which the employee is employed (in case this is a multi-site company);

(b) identifying which employees hold the *particular position* also held by the employee in question; and

(c) establishing the normal retirement age *for that group* of employees.

To this, the Court of Appeal has set out 10 common sense guidelines for determining normal retirement age. These start with the rebuttable presumption that the contract provides the answer, before subjecting this to a reasonable expectations test by looking at company practice: *Barclays Bank plc* v *O'Brien* [1994] IRLR 580.

Under s. 98ZE of ERA 1996, where an employee has a normal retirement age below 65 and is dismissed at or after that age, retirement is not to be taken to be the reason (or a reason) for dismissal if having that normal retirement age amounts to unlawful age discrimination. To avoid being age discrimination the NRA must be justified as being 'a proportionate means of achieving a legitimate aim'.

11.3.4 Working outside Great Britain

Some employees spend some or all of their time working abroad. Because the ERA 1996 says nothing about territorial range, jurisdiction over such contracts is now determined by the rules of international law such as the Brussels Convention on Jurisdiction and Enforcement of Judgments in Civil and Commercial Matters and the Rome Convention on the Law Applicable to Contractual Obligations (transposed respectively into our law via the Civil Jurisdiction and Judgments Act 1982 and the Contracts (Applicable Law) Act 1990). These focus on where the employee's work has some connexion with the UK. The test is essentially: during the whole of the contract's duration, where does the employee habitually carry out his work? If his habitual place of work cannot be determined, the applicable law is that in which the place of business through which he was engaged is situated unless the circumstances show that the contract is more closely connected with the law of another country.

In addition, the Posting of Workers Directive (96/71/EC) deals with the position where a person is posted temporarily abroad for a limited period (either from the UK or to the UK) and was implemented in the UK via the ERA 1999. Article 6 of the Directive provides: 'In order to enforce the right to the terms and conditions of employment guaranteed in Article 3, judicial proceedings may be instituted in the Member State in whose territory the worker is or was posted, without prejudice, where applicable, to the right, under existing international conventions on jurisdiction, to institute proceedings in another state.'

The leading case is the joined cases of *Serco Ltd* v *Lawson; Botham* v *Ministry of Defence;* and *Croft* v *Veta Ltd* [2006] UKHL 3, [2006] IRLR 289. Here, the House of Lords attempted to give guidance as to when an employee fell within the jurisdiction of the tribunals for unfair dismissal purposes. Their Lordships held that the idea of 'employment in Great Britain', developed by the Court of Appeal, was the general yardstick. The terms of the contract and prior conduct would be factors to consider, but the common sense approach was to look at the employee's base and particularly where the employee was working when dismissed.

It would therefore be unusual for an employee based abroad to fall within the scope of unfair dismissal legislation but, if the employee was posted abroad (e.g., a foreign correspondent) or the territory in question was effectively a 'British enclave' (an armed forces base: *Botham's case;* or remote outpost such as Ascension Island: *Lawson's case*), such expatriate employees could gain protection. This is because the connexion between the employment relationship and the UK was a strong one.

11.3.5 Contracting out

The general position is that it is not possible to contract out of statutory rights except where there is an ACAS conciliation or a compromise agreement under ERA 1996, s. 203 (see **11.12** below).

11.3.6 Limited-term contracts

We noted in **9.4.2** that, in the past, clauses commonly appeared in limited-term contracts which permitted the contracting-out (or waiver) of the employee's statutory rights to claim unfair dismissal or redundancy payments on expiry and non-renewal of the term. However, under: (i) ss. 18(1) and 44 and ERA 1999, sch. 9 a limited-term contract entered into on or after 25 October 1999 can no longer exclude rights relating to unfair dismissal; and (ii) under EA 2002, s. 45 and sch. 2, para. 3(13)–(17) and the Fixed-Term Employees (Prevention of Less Favourable Treatment) Regulations 2002 (SI 2002/2034), para. 5, the same applies to redundancy payments rights where the dismissal occurs on or after 1 October 2002. However, any waiver/contracting-out clauses entered into before these respective dates will remain valid until the term expires so you may still (just) encounter valid waiver clauses in the case of lengthy fixed-term contracts. One limitation on this is that such waivers cannot be included in any renewal or extension of the limited term.

You may also encounter the position where there has been a succession of limited terms. The non-waiver provisions above apply to these but there is a further point: where the *renewal* of a fixed-term takes the total of successive terms over four years employment is deemed to be permanent as from the renewal date or the date on which four years was attained.

11.3.7 Excluded categories

There are a number of miscellaneous categories. The most common ones are:

(a) the police force. This includes all those who have the powers or privileges of a constable;

(b) share fishermen, i.e., masters and crews of fishing vessels who take a share in the profits of the catch;

(c) employees working under illegal contracts.

11.3.7.1 Employees working under illegal contracts

This category deserves special comment. As with the ordinary law of contract, a contract of employment which is illegal will be unenforceable. No rights, under common law or statute, will therefore flow from a dismissal. The most obvious example is a contract designed to evade tax liabilities: *Napier* v *National Business Agency Ltd* [1951] 2 All ER 264 (agreement to classify wages as expenses). In some cases the illegal part of the contract may be severed, leaving the rest to stand. For example, an unlawful restraint of trade clause will not affect the validity of the remainder of the contract and discriminatory clauses can be ignored or modified.

If the employee is innocent of the fact of illegality it seems that he or she may still claim unfair dismissal rights. The test is subjective and relates to ignorance of the relevant facts, not ignorance of the law. Likewise, if the employee gains no advantage from the illegality (e.g., participates in a VAT evasion) it is likely that the right to claim unfair dismissal is not damaged: *Hewcastle Catering Ltd* v *Ahmed and Elkamah* [1991] IRLR 473. And a short-term illegality may have the effect only of breaking the employee's continuity of employment, which can start again after the duration of the illegality.

11.3.8 Limitation period

In general, the employee must present any claim within the three-month limitation period which begins at the EDT: ERA 1996, s. 111(2). The period begins on the EDT itself and 'month' means calendar month, so one must find the EDT, take the date of the day before the EDT and project this forward three months. Thus a dismissal on 3 October must be presented *on or before 2* January of the following year (3 January is too late). This topic is dealt with more extensively in **Chapter 16**.

11.4 Burden of proof

Before turning to the detail of what is meant by fairness and unfairness, it is important to note that there are three stages in an unfair dismissal action and the burden of proof at each stage is different. Thus:

(a) the *employee* (if challenged) must prove there was a dismissal. This may be an issue where the employee has resigned but claims constructive dismissal;

(b) the *employer* must show that the dismissal was for one of the six accepted *fair reasons;*

(c) the burden of proving the *fairness* of the dismissal is neutral.

We will now examine what is meant by 'dismissal', 'fair reason', and 'fairness'.

11.5 The meaning of 'dismissal'

We noted in **Chapter 10** that the term 'dismissal' is a technical term which can occasionally confuse, and one which can certainly trap the unwary. Employees may therefore find themselves 'dismissed' (as legally defined) in the following circumstances:

(a) where the employee is 'given the sack';

(b) where the employer uses language which amounts to dismissal;

(c) where the employer intimates a future dismissal;

(d) where the employer says 'resign or be sacked';

(e) where the employer repudiates the contract and the employee resigns;

(f) where a limited-term contract is not renewed;

(g) on retirement.

Points (a)–(f) were discussed in detail in **Chapter 10** at **10.6** and **10.8** and we will consider retirement in more depth below.

11.6 Constructive dismissal

11.6.1 A resignation which is deemed a dismissal

We saw in **Chapter 10** that when an employee resigns this may still constitute a dismissal for common law purposes (termed a 'wrongful repudiation'). The position is the same as regards *statutory rights* and is governed by ERA 1996, s. 95(1)(c). This states that a resignation will amount to a dismissal if 'the employee terminates the contract under which he is employed (with or without notice) in circumstances in which he is entitled to terminate it without notice by reason of the employer's conduct'.

In this statutory context this is known as 'constructive dismissal'. But the definition leaves a problem: what sort of conduct by the employer *entitles* the employee to resign and claim unfair dismissal?

11.6.2 The *Western Excavating* test

The issue of 'entitlement' was determined by the Court of Appeal in the key case of *Western (ECC) Ltd* v *Sharp* [1978] QB 761. Lord Denning MR held that one must use a **contractual** analysis so an employee is entitled to resign and claim unfair dismissal only if:

(a) the employer's actions are a significant breach of contract (an employer who is merely acting unreasonably is not necessarily in breach of contract, but we shall see that the two can overlap substantially);

(b) the resignation is obviously related to the employer's conduct; and

(c) the employee responds quickly.

11.6.3 Are all breaches repudiatory?

The short answer to this question is 'no': *Western Excavating* v *Sharp* established that a *serious* breach is required. Moreover, in *Hilton* v *Shiner* [2001] IRLR 727, the EAT confirmed and applied previous *dicta* to the effect that the employer's conduct must have been without reasonable and proper cause. For instance, instigating disciplinary action against an employee would not *per se* be a breach of mutual trust and confidence if there appeared good grounds for doing so. A gloss was added to this by the EAT in *Morrow* v *Safeway Stores* [2002] IRLR 9 that, once a breach of mutual trust has been found, this implied term is so fundamental to the workings of the contract that its breach automatically constitutes a repudiation—a tribunal cannot conclude that there was such a breach but, on the facts, hold that it was not serious. Like many EAT decisions, if one starts trying to apply this to real situations these two judgments do not sit together comfortably. It is suggested that the solution seems to be that a tribunal must make a clear finding of serious breach/no breach, incorporating the *Hilton* v *Shiner* aspect and, if there is a breach, must make a finding of constructive dismissal accordingly.

So, in general terms, the *Western (ECC) Ltd* v *Sharp* analysis still holds good. The test was held to be a contractual one because, to repeat the key statutory phrase, the conduct must be so serious as to 'entitle [the employee] to terminate [the contract] without notice by reason of the employer's conduct'. But over the years the boundary between 'serious breach' and 'unreasonableness' has been tested often.

11.6.4 Type of conduct required to bring a claim

In *Malik and Mahmud* v *Bank of Credit and Commerce International SA (in compulsory liquidation)* [1997] ICR 606 Lord Steyn provided us with the then key test: a constructive dismissal entails showing that the employer has, without reasonable and proper cause, conducted himself in a manner calculated or likely to destroy or seriously damage the relationship of mutual trust and confidence.

11.6.4.1 Classic examples

A good example of the general application of a contractual analysis of 'dismissal' occurred in *Cawley* v *South Wales Electricity Board* [1985] IRLR 89. The employer utilised the disciplinary procedure (technically within the contractual bounds) to demote an employee by many grades. The EAT decided nevertheless that this was an excessive use of the contractual power and found a breach of contract. In reality, many cases have to turn on a judgment call. The line between merely unreasonable conduct (which is not a constructive dismissal) and seriously unreasonable conduct (which will be) has to be a question of fact: *Brown* v *Merchant* [1998] IRLR 682. Another variation of this can occur when salespeople have their areas or range of products changed under company reorganisations. If the contract defines area, commission, etc. any change by the employer will at least technically constitute a breach. But even if the contract is unclear on these matters (yes, it does occur) one would expect the courts to find an implied term to the effect that the company should at least come to some agreement concerning the impact on commission: *Star Newspapers Ltd* v *Jordan* (1993, unreported, EAT 709/91). Wider still, in *Woods* v *WM Service (Peterborough) Ltd* [1981] ICR 666, it was stated that employers will not, without reasonable and proper cause, conduct themselves in a manner calculated or likely to destroy or seriously damage the relationship of confidence and trust between employer and employee. Examples of constructive dismissal actions other than failure to conduct grievance procedures properly are:

(a) harassment (including harassment by other employees) and any discrimination that is statutorily barred (e.g., sex or race);

(b) victimisation: *Gardner* v *Beresford* [1978] IRLR 63;

(c) unilaterally changing the employee's job content or status: *Coleman* v *Baldwin* [1977] IRLR 342;

(d) humiliating employees in front of others: *Isle of Wight Tourist Board* v *Coombes* [1976] IRLR 413;

(e) unwarranted demotion or disciplinary sanctions: *Cawley* v *SWEB* (above); or improper use of disciplinary sanctions such as issuing a final warning for a minor offence, as happened in *Stanley Cole (Wainfleet) Ltd* v *Sheridan* [2003] ICR 297;

(f) falsely accusing an employee of misconduct or incapability: *Robinson* v *Crompton Parkinson Ltd* [1978] IRLR 61;

(g) unilateral variation in contract terms, e.g., a change in hours or pay: *Woods* v *WM Service (Peterborough) Ltd* (above);

(h) deliberately withholding pay: *Cantor Fitzgerald International* v *Callaghan* [1999] IRLR 234;

(i) demanding that the employee undertakes a substantial transfer of location (certainly if without reasonable notice);

(j) suspension without pay where the contract does not allow for this—and even with pay if prolonged;

(k) failure to support a manager in the light of well-known operational difficulties;

(l) failure to provide a working environment that is reasonably suitable for the performance of contractual duties;

(m) failure to investigate properly the possibility of finding alternative work for an employee who is suffering from work-related stress or failure to make reasonable adjustments to working conditions in the case of an employee suffering from a disability: *Nottinghamshire County Council* v *Meikle* [2004] EWCA Civ 859, [2005] ICR 1.

These are just examples and one would need to investigate the alleged breach very carefully. For instance, as we noted extensively in **Chapter 5**, an employee is expected to be adaptable in the operation of the contract. Therefore, what appears to be a unilateral variation of the contract may prove to be no such thing in law. Equally, the breach must be *serious* and much will depend upon the particular facts and the particular contract—though points such as harassment and victimisation will be easier to argue.

11.6.4.2 The 'last straw'

It is usually one breach that is in issue, but the idea of a 'last straw' can also apply so that a history of incidents can be drawn together: see *Lewis* v *Motorworld Garages Ltd* [1986] ICR 157. There does not necessarily have to be temporal proximity between the events, but the larger the gap the weaker the case becomes. The 'last straw' does not have to be a breach itself; it is the overall picture that counts. Nevertheless, the 'last straw' must contribute to the alleged continuing breach of mutual trust: *Omilaju* v *Waltham Forest* LBC [2004] EWCA Civ 1493, [2005] ICR 481.

11.6.4.3 Additional reasons for leaving

The mere fact that an employee has other, additional, reasons for leaving (e.g., to go to a different job) does not mean that the effective cause of the resignation has ceased to be the employer's breach. Neither does a delay of a few weeks in order to find such work damn the employee's case automatically.

11.6.4.4 Anticipatory breach

A constructive dismissal can arise by way of anticipatory breach but where an employer tells the employee that he will impose changes to the contract and will do this by giving proper notice to terminate and then re-engage on the new terms, this is not an anticipatory breach or a constructive dismissal: *Kerry Foods* v *Lynch* [2005] IRLR 681 (EAT). It will be a dismissal for statutory purposes when it occurs, however, and the mere fact that the employer has said he will re-engage does not prevent a claim for unfair dismissal being successful.

11.6.4.5 Construction of the contract

Particular care should be taken where the only issue is the *construction of the contract* itself. Authorities (occasionally used in employment cases) have indicated that the employer's conduct has to show that he clearly intends not to be bound by the contract before a breach will occur. This is an uncertain and little-used area: see *Brigden* v *Lancashire County Council* [1987] IRLR 58.

11.6.4.6 Who breached first?

We saw in **Chapter 10** that an employer may use any evidence, whenever discovered, to show an employee was in breach of contract. As you will see below the rules on unfair dismissal require the employer to show what was in his mind at the moment of dismissal, so subsequently discovered information is not strictly admissible. However, because constructive dismissal actions are a cross between common law and statute an employer can bring evidence to show that the employee had breached the contract before the potential dismissal event even if the employer did not know this at the time he himself was repudiating the contract: *RDF Media Group plc* v *Clements* [2007] EWHC 2892 (QB), [2008] IRLR 207. Here, an employer's adverse published comments on an employee (who was about to join a competitor) might have been repudiatory had not the employer subsequently discovered that the employee had already leaked confidential information in breach of contract.

RDF was a common law claim concerning restraint of trade clauses. The question posed in *Aberdeen County Council* v *McNeill* [2010] IRLR 374 was whether the same logic should apply to constructive dismissal claims. The EAT in Scotland thought it should, so that where an employee resigned during a misconduct investigation (claiming breach of mutual trust in its handling) the employer defended the claim by referring to the bullying and harassment charges that had brought about the investigation: the argument being that the employee had breached the implied term of mutual trust and confidence first.

The editors of the Harvey Bulletin rightly point out that this 'You started it' argument could have serious ramifications, especially where the employee's breach was not actually connected to the alleged repudiatory breach by the employer (and how far back would such a 'trigger' operate?). The *RDF* case has already been subject to criticism and *Aberdeen* v *McNeill* likewise but, for the moment, this 'skeletons in the cupboard' point needs to be treated cautiously as a potential trap for claimants (i.e., before resigning, make sure there is nothing lurking in the past which may be used by the employer).

To this we can add a further problem (present in repudiation cases even without the *RDF* analysis): when does an employer's conduct amount to affirmation of a breach by the employee? In *Cook* v *MSHK Ltd* [2009] EWCA Civ 624, [2009] IRLR 838 the Court of Appeal applied the same acceptance/affirmation test to an employer's conduct in the face of an alleged repudiatory breach by the employee as already applied to employee's faced with repudiatory breaches, i.e., make clear the non-acceptance or be deemed to have affirmed the breach.

11.6.5 Resignations following faulty grievance procedures

In a constructive dismissal claim it is for the employee to prove the fact of 'dismissal' and, where a constructive dismissal follows on from a resignation based on the allegation of a failure in the operation of a grievance procedure, a tribunal has to somehow decide whether that failure is a serious breach of contract.

Buckland v *Bournemouth University Higher Education Corporation* [2010] EWCA Civ 121, [2010] ICR 908 laid to rest a heated debate in this area. The case arose from a marking dispute between lecturers in which Professor Buckland's original marks were altered (and so approved) without reference to him. Professor Buckland lodged a grievance but resigned even when an inquiry's report supported him as he felt the report did not go far enough.

The Court of Appeal re-established the *Western Excavating* contractual approach (which had been under attack in recent EAT cases) and then went on to consider whether an employer may 'cure' a repudiatory breach (here by holding an inquiry). The Court followed normal contractual principles and held that only an anticipatory repudiatory breach can be so cured. These two tests together meant that the employee had been constructively dismissed.

11.6.6 Apparent resignations

Problems can arise with apparent resignations which turn out to be nothing of the sort, e.g., resignations in the heat of the moment. As we saw in **Chapter 10**, employees are allowed some leeway with heated outbursts. If the words spoken are ambiguous there is the preliminary point as to whether they constitute a resignation at all. If the words are unambiguous the employer is entitled to take these at their face value and the employee must live with the consequences. This approach has been confirmed in *Hogan* v *ACP Heavy Fabrications Ltd* (1994, unreported, EAT 340/92) where the EAT held that there is no obligation on the employer formally to accept the employee's resignation where the employee has responded to a clear breach by the employer. The EAT indicated that an employer *would have to accept the resignation* if the employee simply resigned without giving proper notice; which only adds to the confusion because it means an employer effectively has to judge its own actions. However, an employee is allowed to retract within a reasonable time if the words were spoken in anger or the intellectual capability of the employee is in question: *Kwik-Fit (GB) Ltd* v *Lineham* [1992] ICR 183. An employer who refuses to allow a reasonable retraction will have *dismissed* the employee from the point.

Inviting employees to resign is often seen by employers as an honourable way of avoiding dismissing them so that, in future job applications, the employees will not have the stigma of 'dismissal' on their record. However, such invitations may in themselves constitute a breach of mutual trust and confidence if, say, in the context of a non-disciplinary hearing an employee is advised to consider this course of action (see *Billington* v *Michael Hunter and Sons* (unreported, UKEAT/578/03/DM)); nor does the tag 'without prejudice' aid the case, as this may not always prevent such discussions or letters being used in litigation: *BNP Paribas* v *Mezzotero* [2004] IRLR 508, where the EAT held communications were only privileged under the 'without prejudice' rule where they were made in a situation where there was a genuine attempt to settle an extant dispute.

11.6.7 Consequences of showing a constructive dismissal

Proving a constructive dismissal means nothing in itself. There is no statutory remedy for being constructively dismissed (though there may be a wrongful repudiation claim at common law). All that a constructive dismissal proves is that the employee was dismissed. This can be seen in **Figure 11.1** below. As you will see later in this chapter, once an employee has established a constructive dismissal the question of the fairness of that dismissal has to be decided in the normal way.

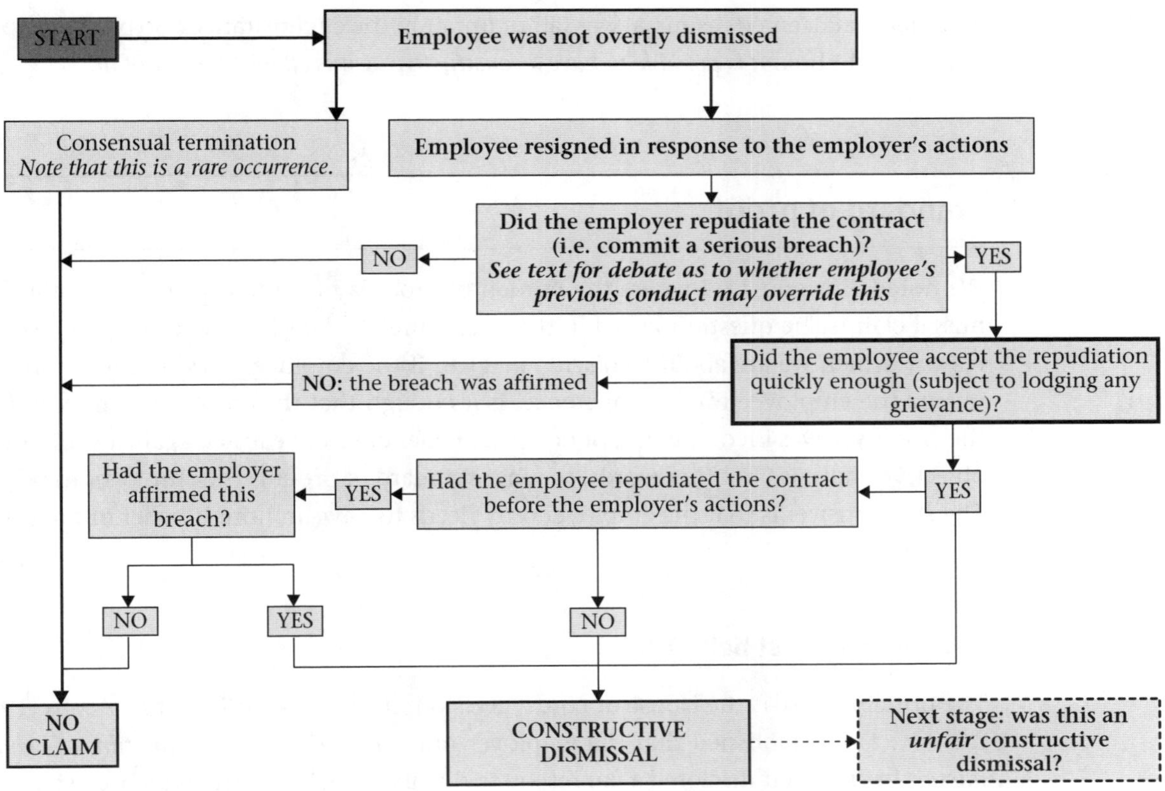

Figure 11.1 Showing a constructive dismissal.

EXAMPLE

Suppose Aquitaine Ltd employs Eleanor on terms that include a mobility clause. Aquitaine asks Eleanor to move to a newly acquired site close by. Eleanor is unhappy and raises various objections. Aquitaine does its best to meet these objections but Eleanor is quite uncooperative and refuses to move. In desperation, Aquitaine issues an instruction to Eleanor to move on a stated date, having met all the practical difficulties. Eleanor still refuses, resigns, and claims unfair dismissal.

If the mobility clause is not as watertight as the company had hoped Eleanor may succeed in persuading the employment tribunal that there was a constructive dismissal, but, as you will see when we look at 'fairness', it is unlikely that the tribunal will find that it was an unfair (constructive) dismissal. Whether this action amounts to indirect discrimination is another matter.

11.6.8 What should the employee do when faced with a serious breach?

We have not yet dealt with the question of how swiftly the employee must act in the face of the breach. All the case law since *Western Excavating* has stressed that, if the breach is supposedly repudiatory, the employee must act quickly and resign within a reasonable time in response to that breach. If the employee did not act quickly enough he or she was said to have *affirmed* the breach and lost the right to claim constructive dismissal.

The case law shows us that a delay of a few days, even a month, will not usually be fatal provided the employee has objected to the conduct. If the employee then resigns in the face of the breach he or she is said to have *accepted the repudiation*.

We have summarised the requirements for a constructive dismissal action in the diagram opposite (**Figure 11.1**). We should stress that **Figure 11.1** does not tell the full story because once a constructive dismissal has been proven the tribunal must then consider whether that deemed dismissal was fair or unfair in the circumstances. So please note the bottom-right box: *it is possible to have a constructive dismissal which is still fair.*

11.7 Standard of proof

We noted above in **11.4** where the burden of proof lay for each stage of an unfair dismissal claim. The question raised in this section relates specifically to the issues of 'fair reason' which we are about to discuss in **11.8.** If the employer says that he or she dismissed the employee for incompetence, is it enough that the employer simply *believed* the employee was incompetent, or does that belief have to be tested against some wider, objective analysis? In other words: to what standard of proof is the employer to be put? The short answer is that the employer only needs to have an honest belief in the reason he puts forward.

11.7.1 What is an honest belief?

The principal case is the House of Lords' decision in *Devis (W) & Sons Ltd* v *Atkins* [1977] AC 931. This established that the employer must *honestly believe at the time of the dismissal* that the facts disclosed a fair reason to dismiss. Provided there is an honest belief it does not matter that the employer was mistaken. Thus, if an employer honestly believes that the employee has committed theft and dismisses for that reason (misconduct), it is irrelevant at this stage whether the employee did or did not commit the theft.

Most employees will not believe your advice when they are told this. They will argue that the employer has no right to dismiss them unless the offence can be proven. They will be wrong. In an unfair dismissal claim, positive proof of the offence is not required.

Practically speaking, of course, in order for the employer to show this honest belief he or she will have to show that the evidence was at least *capable* of generating the conclusion. Waking up one morning and 'honestly believing' an employee is incompetent is clearly not enough. Thus, although the employer does not have to *prove* the incompetence, the decision to dismiss must flow from an *honest belief based on reasonable grounds.* Indeed, in some cases the employer does have to show that the reason for dismissal exists and mistake is no defence, e.g., redundancy dismissals and dismissals on grounds of statutory requirements.

11.7.2 Timing of the belief

As the test is one of honest belief it follows that the employer can only rely on evidence known to him at the date of dismissal. Any evidence which comes to light after the dismissal relating to the employee's conduct *during* the relationship cannot be relied upon as it could not have been known to the employer at the point of dismissal. So, if an employer dismisses for theft (honestly believing the employee was guilty) this will constitute a fair reason. The tribunal will then have to decide whether it was fairly handled. If, subsequent to the dismissal, the employer discovers new facts which show that the employee had committed other acts of misconduct these facts are irrelevant in judging the fairness or unfairness of the dismissal—they were not in the employer's mind at the moment of dismissal. Note the contrast here with the common law position where the employer *is entitled* to rely on evidence not known to him at the time of dismissal: *Boston Deep Sea Fishing and Ice Co.* v *Ansell* (1888) 39 ChD 339 (see **Chapter 10** at **10.7.3.3**).

'Honest belief' is not always a restricting influence: in *St Anne's Board Mill* v *Brien* [1973] ICR 444 the employees were dismissed because, after proper investigations, the employer believed they were unreasonably refusing to obey a lawful order. The employees had refused to work with a colleague because they said he was dangerous and had caused the injury of another employee. The employer believed otherwise. Some time after the dismissal it was shown that the employees were correct. But this did not matter. The employer had acted fairly on the evidence reasonably available at the time of dismissal.

The case of *West Midlands Co-operative Society Ltd* v *Tipton* [1986] ICR 192, added an interesting angle to this. The employees here were dismissed and then were refused the right to an internal appeal under the disciplinary procedure, as granted in the contract. Part of their case was that the employer had acted unfairly in not allowing them to appeal. But any appeal must logically come after a dismissal and so, strictly, is irrelevant under *Devis* v *Atkins.* The House of Lords resolved this by treating the matter of appeals as part of the *continuing process of the dismissal.* Not necessarily logical, but good common sense.

Lastly, it should be noted that although subsequently discovered events are generally irrelevant to the fairness of the dismissal, they *can* be taken into account in the following situations:

(a) where the evidence relates *directly* to the reason for the dismissal and helps to substantiate that reason;

(b) in assessing the level of compensation (see **11.13.3** below);

(c) where the event occurs during the employee's notice period, e.g., the employee dismissed on grounds of ill-health recovers before the expiry of the notice or the redundancy situation is rectified. The employer is expected to react to this change: *Williamson v Alcan (UK) Ltd* [1978] ICR 104.

This reasoning means that the 'reason' has to be assessed both in relation to the point at which notice is given and the termination itself. A fair redundancy selection, for instance, might become unfair if the circumstances of the business change in this period: see *Stacey* v *Babcock Power Ltd* [1986] ICR 221, *Alboni* v *Ind Coope Retail Ltd* [1998] IRLR 131 and *West Kent College* v *Richardson* [1999] ICR 511.

In *Devis* v *Atkins* the main concern of the House of Lords was to outlaw the use of *fresh reasons* by an employer to justify a dismissal. That point is still sacrosanct. Thus the order of analysis is:

(a) What was the reason for the dismissal?

(b) Was that reason a fair reason under ERA 1996, s. 98?

(c) Did the employer handle the dismissal fairly in treating that reason as a sufficient reason for dismissal?

11.8 Potentially fair reasons

As can be seen in (b) and (c) above, assessing fairness involves a two-stage process.

It cannot be over-emphasised that these stages are *separate* and will be considered in sequence by the employment tribunal. Employers frequently misunderstand the process and suppose that an outstandingly good reason (e.g., strong evidence of theft) somehow makes up for a poor handling of the situation (e.g., not giving the employee a chance to explain). Nothing can be further from the truth. If the handling is unfair the dismissal will most likely be unfair, no matter how good the reason.

Thus, proving that the dismissal was for one of the fair reasons set out below does not mean that the employer has won. This is just the first stage. If the employer *cannot* show a fair reason, however, the employee will win at this stage and, as will be seen in **11.8.8**, some reasons may be classed as *automatically unfair* irrespective of how they were handled.

11.8.1 The reason or principal reason

Under ERA 1996, s. 98 the burden of proof lies with the employer to show a defence under one of the headings detailed below as the *reason or principal reason* for dismissal.

In the text below we will first note some basic rules on assessing 'reasons', then we will give the basic requirements of each potentially fair reason and then turn to the fairness of their operation in **Chapter 12**. The six fair reasons for dismissal are:

(a) capability (s. 98(2)(a));

(b) conduct (s. 98(2)(b));

(c) retirement (s. 98(ba));

(d) redundancy (s. 98(2)(c));

(e) statutory illegality (s. 98(2)(d));

(f) some other substantial reason (s. 98(1)(b)).

11.8.1.1 Multiple reasons

The employer may have more than one reason for the dismissal; the notion of a 'principal reason' does not mean 'a single reason'. But the section does prevent an employer relying on a 'shotgun approach' of detailing every unsatisfactory aspect of the employee's work in the hope that one will hit the target: *Smith* v *Glasgow City District Council* [1987] ICR 796. The weakness with multiple reasons (certainly those which are interdependent) is that as the structure of reasons becomes more complicated the questions of proof become more difficult to establish clearly. The most common overlaps arise:

(a) when the employer cites different incidents to justify the dismissal, e.g., various forms of misconduct; and

(b) between misconduct and incapability, e.g., a history of intermittent absences could be a case of incapability (e.g., health) or misconduct.

An exception to this overlap occurs where the reason is 'retirement'. That either stands or falls as a reason on its own.

11.8.1.2 The label given by the employer

Tribunals do not have to accept an employer's stated reason. The reason can be rejected as a fraud or as a mistake. A discovered fraud—for example, dismissing an employee because of trade union activities but citing incapability—will lead to a finding of unfair dismissal at this stage. But where there is simply a genuine mistake of labelling on the employer's part at the time of dismissal the tribunal may have more sympathy if the facts relied upon by the employer as constituting the reason for the dismissal were clear to the employee at the time of termination: *Abernethy* v *Mott, Hay and Anderson* [1974] ICR 323. The key element, therefore, is that if the employer consistently relies on the same *facts* to justify the dismissal a change of *legal reasons* may not be fatal. It will nevertheless be a dangerous course of action to dismiss for one stated reason and then plead another in the tribunal.

Where employers have sought to soften the blow of dismissal by labelling it as a 'redundancy' when no redundancy actually exists they run the risk of being trapped by that stated reason. The same applies where the reason given is retirement.

11.8.1.3 ERA 1996, s. 92

Section 92 allows an employee to demand from the employer written reasons for the dismissal. There must be a specific request and the employer must reply within 14 days of that request. Any unreasonable refusal or lies by the employer may lead to the employer having to pay the employee two weeks' pay (whether dismissed unfairly or not). The employer's statement is admissible in any proceedings. Except for women dismissed while pregnant or on maternity leave, qualification for this right requires one year's service. There is, however, no upper age limit.

11.8.1.4 Disagreement as to reasons

As well as the obvious case where an employer gives a reason (say, misconduct) and the employee denies this, there may be cases where the employee puts forward another reason—what he or she says is the *real* reason—for the dismissal. For instance, the employer may cite misconduct and the employee may claim the real reason was that he disclosed evidence about the employer's nefarious activities to the police. If the employee is right then the employer has not shown a fair reason and, in this example, the employee will gain much more compensation (see **11.8.8.3** on public interest disclosures). In such instances, if a tribunal finds that the employer was wrong it does not automatically mean the employee was right. That claim must still be investigated, with the employee producing 'some evidence' not just mere assertion: *Kuzel* v *Roche Products Ltd* [2008] EWCA Civ 380, [2008] ICR 799.

11.8.1.5 Pressure of industrial action

The ERA 1996, s. 107, states that, in assessing the reason for dismissal, the employment tribunal must ignore pressure placed on the employer to dismiss arising from threats etc. of industrial action made by third parties, e.g., other employees or trade unions. Expressions of disgruntlement about the employee from third parties do not fall within this section. But if fellow employees say that they will go on strike unless an employee becomes a member of a union, that is the area covered by s. 107.

11.8.2 Capability as a fair reason

Section 98(3) of ERA 1996 defines capability as 'capability assessed by reference to skill, aptitude, health or any other physical or mental quality'. This breaks down into three sub-headings:

(a) *Qualifications.*

Cases in this area are rare. Section 98(3)(b) states that qualifications means 'any degree, diploma or other academic, technical or professional qualification relevant to the position which [the employee] held'. What amounts to qualification (as opposed to a licence or permit, for instance) has been given a narrow interpretation in *Blue Star Ship Management Ltd* v *Williams* [1978] ICR 770. The qualification must be connected substantially to the employee's job.

(b) *Incompetence.*

Employees are incompetent when they cannot perform their duties as required under the terms of the contract. It is rare for one-off incidents of incompetence to justify a dismissal, though not impossible; where, for example, bad workmanship causes the employer a massive loss. Examples of incompetence include: slow completion rates; making misjudgements or mistakes; lack of adaptability; inability to work with colleagues; and inability to deal with clients.

(c) *Ill-health.*

If an employee's absence from work (either on prolonged absence or on an intermittent but frequent basis) means that he or she is unable to do the job, an employer is entitled to rely on this as the reason for dismissal. Unjustified absence (e.g., being caught painting the house while drawing company sick pay on the pretext of back pain) will probably count as *conduct* (see **11.8.3** below). Employers who categorise ill-health absence as *capability,* on the other hand, are not necessarily doubting that the reason is perfectly genuine: the employee may simply be incapable of attending often enough to comply with the contract.

It is often thought that if the employer's actions caused the illness or injury the employer cannot then dismiss for reasons of incapability. This view is incorrect, but the more troublesome question is whether employers owe some extra duty to sick employees if they are responsible for the illness. Various EAT judgments have given some or no sympathy to this view. The Court of Appeal's view in *McAdie* v *Royal Bank of Scotland* [2007] EWCA Civ 806, [2007] IRLR 895 was to endorse the findings of the latest EAT decision and hold that an employer can dismiss in such cases but should be seen to 'go the extra mile' in handling any dismissal.

11.8.3 Conduct as a fair reason

The difference between conduct and capability is often that the employee can improve conduct but capability can imply something about the employee's innate ability that cannot be changed (in the same way that the authors might improve their attendance record at an athletics club but will never run a mile in under four minutes). Some issues, such as excessive absence or incompetence, may fall under both heads and the choice of one over the other may rest on how far the employee is believed to be at fault—doing one's best, albeit one's incompetent best, is better argued as capability for instance.

The heading therefore covers a diverse range of activities, such as:

(a) disobedience to lawful orders;
(b) gross insubordination;
(c) abusive language;
(d) theft;
(e) fraud;
(f) taking bribes;
(g) drunkenness at work;
(h) possessing a personality which amounted to a disabling and negative approach to the job and destroyed the trust and confidence between employer and employee;
(i) disclosing confidential information;
(j) gaining unauthorised access to computer files;
(k) assault;
(l) intermittent absenteeism;
(m) persistent lateness;
(n) taking unauthorised and prolonged leave; and even
(o) conduct occurring outside the employment relationship which has a direct bearing on the contract of employment.

There is no requirement that the misconduct must have been gross: the culmination of a series of incidents over which warnings have been issued will also fit the bill.

11.8.4 Retirement as a fair reason

The *compulsory* retirement of an employee is a potentially fair reason for dismissal (s. 98(ba) ERA 1996). Unlike the other fair reasons, however, for this reason to be acceptable certain procedures have to be followed—otherwise the retirement will *not* be taken as the reason (or a reason) for dismissal. Schedule 9 EqA 2010, paras 8 and 9, creates exceptions to age discrimination regarding retirement and states that whether or not the reason for a dismissal is a retirement shall be determined in accordance with the conditions set out in ss. 98ZA–98ZF ERA 1996. In the sections below we consider the effects of different retirement ages.

11.8.4.1 Retiring at 65 or above

The 'default' age for retirement has been set at 65 so any dismissal for retirement will be for a fair reason, if:

- as set out in s. 98ZB(1) and (2), there is no 'normal retirement age' in the company for that group of employees and the employee retires at or after 65; or
- as set out in s. 98ZD(1) and (2), the 'normal retirement age' is 65 or higher and the employee retires at or after that age,

provided in both instances that the procedures laid out in sch. 6, para. 2 of the Employment Equality (Age) Regulations 2006 are followed (see below for details). Employees may also have claims for unlawful discrimination running alongside or instead of unfair dismissal claims where the reason for dismissal relates to age. This means that any normal retirement age less than 65 has to pass the non-discrimination test.

11.8.4.2 Retiring earlier than 65

Where the employee's 'normal retirement age' is below 65 and the employee retires at or after that retirement age, this will also be a fair reason for dismissal (see s. 98ZE(1)). Again, the sch. 6 procedures must have been followed and the 'normal retirement age' must not be discriminatory (s. 98ZE(2)).

11.8.4.3 Schedule 6, para. 2 procedures

These are straightforward and require the employer:

- to inform the employee in writing of the date on which he intends the employee to retire and of the employee's right to make a request to continue working past the retirement age. This must be done not more than one year and not less than six months before the proposed retirement date; and
- to consider that request at a meeting where the employee may be accompanied by a fellow worker (if it is not reasonably practicable to hold a meeting an employer must still consider representations made by the employee); and
- to consider any appeal made by the employee.

The word 'consider' should be noted. It does not mean 'negotiate' and does not even require the employer to provide reasons for refusal.

11.8.4.4 Terms and other sources of information

Under para. 2(2), the duty to notify applies regardless of any term in the employee's contract of employment indicating when his retirement is expected to take place, any other notification of, or information about, the employee's date of retirement given to him by the employer at any time, and any other information about the employee's right to make a request given to him by the employer at any time.

11.8.4.5 Schedule 6, para. 4

If the employer fails to notify the employee six months in advance of the proposed retirement as per sch. 6, para. 2, he will still have an ongoing duty to do so, 'until the fourteenth day before the operative termination'. This looks like a peculiar provision but its importance can be seen in the next section.

11.8.4.6 Section 98ZF ERA 1996

Imagine that a tribunal is faced with a retirement dismissal where the para. 2 procedures have not been followed. At first sight this cannot therefore be a fair reason for dismissal. However, if:

- the dismissal is at or after 65 and there is no retirement age; or
- the dismissal is at or after the normal retirement age when that age is higher than 65; or
- the dismissal is at or after the (non-discriminatory) normal retirement age but that is set below 65,

Then:

- the tribunal must take into account the matters listed in s. 98ZF to determine whether what has happened may still amount to a fair reason for dismissal.

The s. 98ZF matters are:

- whether or not the employer has notified the employee in accordance with sch. 6, para. 4;
- if the employer has so notified the employee, how long before the notified retirement date the notification was given;
- whether or not the employer has followed, or sought to hold a meeting with the employee in accordance with sch. 6, para. 7.

11.8.4.7 Failure to follow procedures

If the employer fails to comply with either sch. 6 or s. 98ZF procedures he is prevented from using 'retirement' as a fair reason and the dismissal is automatically unfair. Further, a finding that a dismissal was not actually for 'retirement' may also give rise to a claim for age discrimination.

11.8.4.8 What may prevent a retirement being a fair reason?

Retirement will *not* be a fair reason for dismissal where:

(a) The sch. 6 procedures have not been followed.

(b) The sch. 6 procedures *have* been followed but the contract terminated before the intended date of retirement.

(c) There is a normal retirement age lower than 65 and it is found to be unlawful discrimination.

(d) There is no 'normal retirement age' and the dismissal occurs before 65 (s. 98ZA).

(e) There is a 'normal retirement age' (whether above or below 65) but the employee was dismissed before that age (s. 98ZC).

Of course, with (b), (d) and (e) dismissals there may be other fair reasons why an employee is dismissed e.g., conduct.

11.8.4.9 Breach of procedures: a separate cause of action

Under sch. 6 para. 11 an employee may complain to a tribunal that the employer has failed to comply with para. 2 procedures. If the tribunal decides there was a breach of para. 2 it shall award up to eight weeks' pay (the meaning of 'a week's pay' is discussed in **Chapter 12** below).

11.8.5 Redundancy as a fair reason

To make someone redundant is to *dismiss them* for reasons of redundancy. Redundancy has its own particular rules which are dealt with in **Chapter 12**, but one may have a fair or unfair dismissal for reasons of redundancy. The meaning of 'redundancy' is given in ERA 1996, s. 139(1) and (6). This provides a highly technical definition. In general terms s. 139 states that a redundancy occurs in three situations:

(a) where there is a cessation of the business;

(b) where there is a closure of the employee's particular workplace;

(c) where there is a cessation or diminution in the requirements for employees to do work of a particular kind (i.e., there is a surplus of labour for that particular type of job).

Tribunals will rarely second-guess an employer's decision to declare a redundancy.

11.8.6 Statutory illegality as a fair reason

In rare cases it may become legally impossible to continue to employ the employee, e.g., on the expiry of a work permit, or where a teacher has been declared unsuitable by the Department for Children, Schools and Families. The ERA 1996, s. 98(2)(d), states that such occurrences provide a fair reason for dismissal where the employee 'could not continue to work in the position which he held without contravention (either on his part or on that of his employer) of a duty or restriction imposed by or under an enactment' (thus statutory instruments are included in the definition). It is for the employer to show that any continued employment would have contravened the statute etc.

It is also now a criminal offence under s. 8 of the Asylum and Immigration Act 1996 to employ a person who does not have permission to work in the UK.

11.8.7 Some other substantial reason as a fair reason

Under ERA 1996, s. 98(1)(b), the employer can show 'some other substantial reason of a kind such as to justify the dismissal of an employee holding the position which the employee held'. This sounds like some sort of major catch-all category. It is. The words are not read *eiusdem generis* with the other fair reasons. The most common forum in which this reason is argued, however, is that of a business reorganisation falling short of redundancy, e.g., where the workload remains the same but certain employees are deemed unsuitable for the new requirements of the business or will simply not put up with the changes to their terms or status and resign.

The line between dismissal for reasons of business reorganisations and dismissal by reason of redundancy can be a fine one. However, the key point is whether the statutory definition of redundancy is fulfilled or not: put simply, did the requirement for employees to do their particular work cease or diminish? If all that has happened is that there is a reorganisation of the way existing work is performed then the fact that an employee is replaced by someone with different skills or doing a slightly different job does not mean there is a redundancy. For instance, in *Shawkat* v *Nottingham City Hospital NHS Trust (No. 2)* [2001] EWCA Civ 954, [2001] IRLR 555, the Court of Appeal held that when the hospital merged two departments so that a thoracic surgeon was required to also take on cardiac work (and refused to do so and was dismissed) there was no redundancy as there was no diminution in the employer's need for employees to carry out thoracic surgery.

Other examples of 'some other substantial reason' have been:

(a) a refusal to accept the imposition of a restraint of trade clause. This is a good example of 'some other substantial reason' in action as the Court of Appeal stressed in *Willow Oak Developments Ltd* v *Silverwood* [2006] EWCA Civ 660, [2006] IRLR 607 that even if the clause is unreasonable in itself this does not matter in establishing that there is a *reason* for dismissing. The reasonableness of the clause might go to determine whether the employer acted fairly but does not affect the existence of the reason unless the employer has acted whimsically or capriciously or the reason is inadmissible because of discrimination;

(b) a refusal to accept a change in terms relating to hours, or pay or job content;

(c) discovering that the employee had originally concealed medical problems from the employer;

(d) where heavy pressure to dismiss was brought to bear on the employer by a valued customer (though it is advisable to have a term in the contract allowing for such dismissals) and the employer still needs to look at the extent of any injustice to the employee;

(e) a mistaken belief that continuing to employ the employee would be in breach of a statute: *Klusova* v *London Borough of Hounslow* [2007] EWCA Civ 1127, [2008] ICR 396;

(f) reasonably believing (mistakenly as it turned out) that an employee had resigned;

(g) termination of employment as chief executive as an automatic consequence, under the express terms of the contract, of the termination of a directorship: *Cobley* v *Forward Technology Industries plc* [2003] EWCA Civ 646, [2003] ICR 1050.

This area is full of unpredictability. The temptation is to over-use it because it provides what has been described as an 'employer's charter'. This label is probably accurate in relation to business reorganisations, but the examples cited above should not be treated as precedents. Sometimes it is useful to plead it on behalf of the employer 'in the alternative': see **Chapter 14**.

11.8.8 Automatically unfair reasons

Certain reasons for dismissal are deemed automatically unfair. This means that, once the tribunal finds that the reason for the dismissal was one of these reasons they *must* make a determination that the dismissal was unfair. As with ordinary unfair dismissal claims the burden of proof is on the employer to establish the reason for the dismissal but, if the employee does not have one year's service, the Court of Appeal has held that it is for the employee to prove the dismissal was for an automatically unfair reason: *Smith* v *Hayle Town Council* [1978] ICR 996. Once a finding of automatically unfair dismissal has been made, some reasons carry with them what is termed a **minimum basic award** (see **Chapter 12**). The relevant points in the table below are: 1, in limited cases, and 5, 7, 8, and 9).

11.8.8.1 Summary of unfair dismissal qualification rights

We noted above that, for most dismissals, an employee must have one year's service to qualify for unfair dismissal rights. There are exceptions, and most of these exceptions are also deemed automatically unfair dismissals. The table below illustrates this.

	Reason for dismissal	*Service qualification*	*Automatically unfair?*
1	Dismissals relating to a transfer of an undertaking.	*One year*	*Yes, but the employee may lose this protection in defined circumstances: see* ***Chapter 13***
2	'Retirement dismissals' where the appropriate procedures have not been followed.	*One year*	Yes
3	Dismissal where the worker exercised or sought to exercise, the right to be accompanied (or accompanied another worker) at a disciplinary hearing or a retirement meeting.	None	Yes

4	Dismissals falling within ERA 1996, s. 99 (leave for family reasons), e.g. those relating to pregnancy, childbirth, maternity, maternity leave, parental leave, or to an employee taking time off to care for certain dependants (described in s. 57A).	None	Yes
5	Dismissals relating to health and safety matters which fall within ERA 1996, s.100.	None	Yes
6	Dismissals of certain shop and betting workers who refuse to work on Sundays, as set out in ERA 1996, s. 101.	None	Yes
7	Dismissals relating to the enforcement of the Working Time Regulations, as set out in ERA 1996, s. 101A.	None	Yes
8	Dismissals of occupational pension scheme trustees within the ambit of ERA 1996, s. 102.	None	Yes
9	Dismissals of certain employee representatives falling within ERA 1996, s. 103.	None	Yes
10	Dismissals under the Public Interest Disclosure Act 1998, as set out in ERA 1996, s. 103A: the so-called 'whistle-blower provisions' (see below at **11.8.8.3**).	None	Yes
11	Dismissals relating to the assertion of statutory rights as set out in ERA 1996, s. 104 (including employees dismissed for reasons connected with flexible working arrangements under SIs 2002/3207 and 2002/3236): see below at **11.8.8.2**.	None	Yes
12	Dismissals in relation to national minimum wage claims falling within ERA 1996, s. 104A.	None	Yes
13	Dismissals relating to the claiming of tax credits under the Tax Credits Act 1999, as set out in ERA 1996, s. 104B	None	Yes
14	Dismissal of part-time workers under ERA 1996, s. 108(i) who have, or have sought to, exercise rights set out in reg. 7, paras 1 and 3 of the Part-time Workers (Prevention of Less Favourable Treatment) Regulations 2000 (SI 2000/1551).	None	Yes
15	Dismissals where the principal reason is that the employee has exercised, or sought to exercise, certain rights relating to limited-term contracts. For details, see reg. 6(3) of the Fixed-Term Employees (Prevention of Less Favourable Treatment) Regulations 2002 (SI 2002/2034).	None	Yes
16	Dismissal relating to the performance of jury service, under ERA 1996, s. 98B(1), as amended by ERA 2004, s. 40(3).	None	*Yes, but the employee may lose this protection in defined circumstances set out in s. 98B(2)*
17	Dismissals for a conviction which is 'spent' under the Rehabilitation of Offenders Act 1974: s. 4(3)(b) unless the employee falls within a category excluded from the provisions of the Act.	*One year*	Yes

18	Dismissal for trade union activities and membership as defined in TULRCA 1992 s. 152 (as amended by sch. 2, ERA 1999). *Note that taking industrial action is not counted as a 'trade union activity'.*	None	Yes
19	Dismissal (in defined circumstances) for taking part in official industrial action—known as 'protected industrial action' under TULRCA 1992, s. 238A.	None	Yes
20	Dismissal of employees for a defined reason connected with the recognition or de-recognition of a trade union: TULRCA 1992, sch. A1, paras 161 and 164.	None	Yes
21	Dismissals relating to the Transnational Information and Consultation of Employees Regulations 1999.	None	Yes
22	Dismissal in connexion with reg. 30 of the Information and Consultation of Employees Regulations 2004 (SI 2004/3426).	None	*Yes, though with exceptions regarding disclosure of confidential information*
23	Dismissal in connexion with the establishment of a European Public Limited-Liability company under reg. 42 of the European Public Limited Liability Company Regulations 2004 (SI 2004/2326).	None	*Yes, though with exceptions regarding disclosure of confidential information*
24	Dismissals arising out of suspension on medical grounds as defined in ERA 1996, s. 64(2) (*note, this is a narrow category related to employees who work with dangerous substances and is not the same as a dismissal because of illness*).	*One month*	*No*

Where an employee is *selected for redundancy* and the reason for that selection is one of the automatically unfair reasons noted above then that selection is automatically unfair and normal qualifying periods do not apply (see TULRCA 1992, s. 153 and ERA 1996, s. 105). **However, the automatic unfairness provisions do not apply to selection for redundancy where points 1 or 3 in the table above apply.**

A selection for redundancy for reasons of trade union membership, activities or recognition issues will fall within the automatically unfair provisions: TULRCA 1992, s. 153 and sch. A1 para. 162.

If the reason for dismissal is discriminatory an action may be brought for that discrimination (see **Chapter 6**) rather than being tied to an unfair dismissal action. In either case there are no qualification periods and a dismissal for, say, reasons of sex discrimination, will be automatically unfair (though not so with disability discrimination). However, where a tribunal finds a dismissal to be both unfair and discriminatory it will set-off the awards to avoid double recovery. Given that compensation for discrimination is not subject to any upper limit (whereas unfair dismissal claims are—see **Chapter 13** below), a distinct discrimination claim should always be considered if there is evidence to support this.

Two points covered in the table above require further explanation.

11.8.8.2 Asserting statutory rights

Under ERA 1996, s. 104, if the employee complains to the employer that certain statutory rights have been infringed then any dismissal by the employer in response to this is automatically unfair. Thus retaliatory action by the employer now carries with it specific penalties. It does not matter that the employee's claim was wrong, nor that it was not correctly labelled, as long as it was made in good faith. The first case in this area (*Mennell* v *Newell & Wright (Transport Contractors) Ltd* [1996] ICR 607) reinforced the interpretation of the 'good faith' test as being of the 'pure heart but empty head' variety. The Court of Appeal stated that:

(a) the employee must have made an allegation to his employer that a statutory right was being infringed;

(b) the allegation need not be specific, provided it has been made reasonably clear to the employer what right was claimed to have been infringed;

(c) it does not matter whether the statutory right has actually been infringed, nor need the allegation be correct as to the employee's entitlement to the right, provided the claim is made in good faith;

(d) the onus will lie on the employee to establish that he was dismissed for his assertion of a statutory right.

The term 'reasonably clear' has been given a liberal interpretation by the EAT: the employee is not required to spell out the infringement.

The 'relevant statutory rights' are set out in s. 104(4) of ERA 1996. They include:

(a) any right conferred by the Act for which the remedy for its infringement is by way of a complaint or reference to an employment tribunal' (e.g., minimum notice, right to receive a written statement, health and safety dismissals)—the list is extensive;

(b) rights concerning the protection of wages under ERA 1996, Part II;

(c) rights conferred under TULRCA 1992 concerning union activities.

A twist has now been added to the concept of 'asserting' a right. Item 8 in the table above relates to dismissals for refusal to comply with a requirement (e.g., overtime) which would itself contravene the Working Time Regulations. It is clear from *McLean* v *Rainbow Homeloans Ltd* [2007] IRLR 14 (EAT) that such a refusal is not 'asserting' a statutory right but is a separate head of 'automatic unfairness' and so not subject to the rules just described in (a)–(d) above. All that is required, say the EAT, is that the employer has refused to accede to a requirement which would have breached the Regulations and the dismissal is because of that refusal.

11.8.8.3 Public Interest Disclosure Act 1998

We noted the main provisions of this Act in **Chapter 8** (at 8.3.5). The purpose of the Act is to permit employees to make certain disclosures about the activities of their employers without suffering any penalty for having done so. This is achieved through the insertion into ERA 1996 of two new sections: s. 47B and s. 103A.

Section 47B(1) of ERA 1996 (as inserted by PIDA 1998, s. 2) states that: 'A worker has the right not to be subjected to any **detriment** by any act, or any deliberate failure to act, by his employer done on the ground that the worker has made a protected disclosure.'

Section 103A (as inserted by PIDA 1998, s. 5) states: 'An employee who is **dismissed** shall be regarded for the purposes of this Part as unfairly dismissed *if the reason (or, if more than one, the principal reason) for the dismissal is that the employee made a protected disclosure.*' The employee only has to act in 'good faith' when making the allegations in order to come under the umbrella of 'protected disclosure' and the burden of showing bad faith is on the employer. However, this is not a licence for employees' flights of fantasy: there must be a clear causative link between the detriment/dismissal and the disclosure before protection is given (see *London Borough of Harrow* v *Knight* [2003] IRLR 140). A detriment may occur even after the employee has left the organisation, e.g., with the refusal to provide references: *Woodward* v *Abbey National plc* [2006] EWCA Civ 822, [2006] IRLR 677.

There are different compensation rules depending on whether the employee suffered a detriment or a dismissal. Where the claim is for detriment s. 49(1)(b) calls for an assessment of loss akin to discrimination claims so that there is no statutory limit on the amount and damages for injury to feelings may be included. In the case of a dismissal there is also no statutory limit on compensation but injury to feelings is not included. This leaves the problem of assessing compensation when a 'detriment' turns into 'dismissal' (e.g., the employee cannot take the detriment any longer and resigns). Here, detriment losses are taken up to the point of termination, dismissal losses from that point: *Melia* v *Magna Kansei Ltd* [2005] EWCA Civ 1547, [2006] ICR 410.

11.8.9 Automatically fair reasons

The basic premise of ERA 1996, s. 98 is that although the reason may be *fair* this does not mean that the dismissal is fair; this has yet to be decided. However, in the case of dismissal involving national security the tribunal may never get to debate the issue of fairness: see ERA 1996, s.10.

Some confusion has been added to this area by the EAT in *B* v *BAA plc* [2005] All ER (D) 321 (May) which held that the tribunal must still investigate the reasonableness of such dismissals to see whether alternative courses of action could have been taken (e.g., redeployment). This is a very surprising decision and we will have to see if it stands future tests.

11.9 Summary

The three chapters covering unfair dismissal are central to any study of employment law and the law can be quite technical and complex at times. We provided an overview of unfair dismissal actions at the beginning of this chapter and the reader is referred to that section. **This summary provides some additional, more detailed, points better understood once you have read this chapter.**

- In most cases an employee must qualify for the right to claim unfair dismissal by being employed for at least one year. We have seen that there are numerous exceptions to this rule, most of which tie in with 'automatically unfair' dismissals.
- The non-renewal of limited-term contracts does not naturally trigger thoughts of unfair dismissal but it still counts as a dismissal for statutory purposes and we have seen that this area can cause particular problems for employers.
- Although the list is quite short, some employees are expressly excluded from bringing a claim, e.g., those who work outside Great Britain.
- Employees cannot opt out (or be persuaded to opt out) of their unfair dismissal rights.
- Unfair dismissal actions depend first on establishing a 'dismissal'. A constructive dismissal is not a cause of action in itself. If a constructive dismissal is proven the

tribunal must still decide whether the dismissal was fair in all the circumstances (see the next chapter).

- Compulsory retirement dismissals are treated differently from the other fair reasons in as much as they have their own prescribed procedures both for determining the existence of a fair reason and the question of fairness.
- Some reasons for dismissal are classed as automatically unfair; the list is extensive.

12

Unfair dismissal: determining fairness

12.1 Introduction

In **Chapter 11** we considered how employees qualify for the right to claim unfair dismissal, the meaning of 'dismissal' and the six fair reasons an employer may use to justify such a dismissal to defend a claim for unfair dismissal. If the employer cannot show a 'fair reason' then the dismissal will be automatically unfair. If the employer is successful at that stage (which is not a difficult hurdle) the next issue is to examine whether that 'fair reason' was handled fairly. Therefore, in this chapter we turn our attention to the way in which employment tribunals determine whether the dismissal was fair or not.

The question of 'fairness' is a judgment call and depends very much on the facts. Nevertheless, we can detail some general points that tribunals will look at for each 'fair reason'. In **Figure 12.1** below we can see the pathway that tribunals trace in analysing an unfair dismissal case. **Figure 12.1** is concerned only with the way 'fairness' is determined. It does not deal with the financial consequences of any particular finding; that is left until the next chapter.

What is meant by 'fairness' tends to be something of a mixture of fact and law. The 'fact' part relates to investigating the way in which the employer relied on the cited fair reason; the 'law' relates to general guiding principles that have been established over the years. The best way to describe fairness, therefore, is by recounting some general principles used by tribunals and then relating them to the particular fair reasons.

12.2 General principles of fairness

The Employment Rights Act 1996 (ERA 1996), s. 98(4) states:

> the determination of the question whether the dismissal is fair or unfair (having regard to the reason shown by the employer)—
>
> (a) depends on whether in the circumstances (including the size and administrative resources of the employer's undertaking) the employer acted reasonably or unreasonably in treating it as a sufficient reason for dismissing the employee, and
> (b) shall be determined in accordance with equity and the substantial merits of the case.

Leaving aside 'retirement' dismissals for the moment, the s. 98(4) test may be broken down into *two* pervasive questions:

(a) Did the employer utilise a *fair procedure*?

(b) Did the employer's decision to dismiss fall within the *range of reasonable responses* open to a reasonable employer?

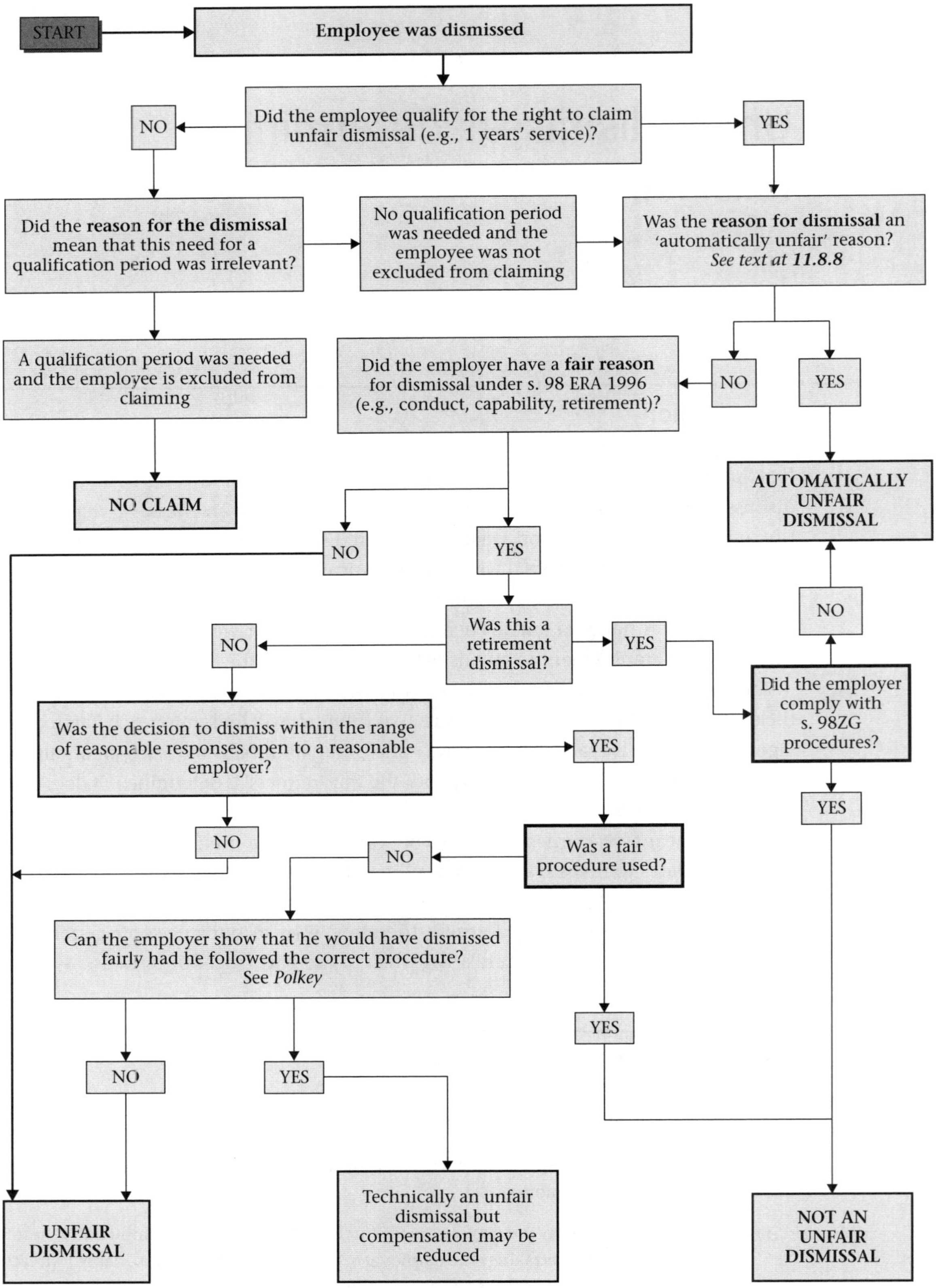

Figure 12.1 Determining fairness.

The burden of proof regarding *fairness,* it will be remembered, is *neutral.* But all this really means is that the employer does not bear the burden when the facts are doubtful or in dispute. The reality is that, since the employer made the decision and generally has the greater access to information, the tribunal effectively expects the employer to show *why* the decision was made and *how* it was reasonable.

The impact of the Human Rights Act 1998 on unfair dismissal was considered by the Court of Appeal in *X* v *Y* [2004] EWCA Civ 662. Although no breach of human rights was found in this case (which centred on art. 8 ECHR—'privacy') Mummery LJ set out some suggestions on dealing with human rights points, especially as regards actions taken against private employers. The statement must be *obiter* but it is nevertheless extremely useful. His Lordship suggested the following framework of questions at [64]:

(1) Do the circumstances of the dismissal fall within the ambit of one or more of the articles of the Convention? If they do not, the Convention right is not engaged and need not be considered.

(2) If they do, does the state have a positive obligation to secure enjoyment of the relevant Convention right between private persons? If it does not, the Convention right is unlikely to affect the outcome of an unfair dismissal claim against a private employer.

(3) If it does, is the interference with the employee's Convention right by dismissal justified? If it is, proceed to (5) below.

(4) If it is not, was there a permissible reason for the dismissal under the ERA, which does not involve unjustified interference with a Convention right? If there was not, the dismissal will be unfair for the absence of a permissible reason to justify it.

(5) If there was, is the dismissal fair, tested by the provisions of s. 98 of the ERA, reading and giving effect to them under s. 3 of the Human Rights Act 1998 (HRA 1996) so as to be compatible with the Convention right?

In *McGowan* v *Scottish Water* [2005] IRLR 167 the EAT in Scotland dealt with art. 8 again, this time regarding covert surveillance of an employee's home: the employee was thought to be falsifying timesheets on call-out times. Although recognising that such surveillance 'raised at least a strong presumption that the right to have one's private life respected is being invaded' no breach was found as the action was held to be proportionate to the case.

12.3 The first general aspect of fairness: fair procedure

It has always been a key feature of employment law that an employer must operate a fair procedure when dismissing an employee. An employer contemplating a dismissal must therefore be aware of the significance of:

- the ACAS Code and Guidelines; and
- the employer's own contractual procedures

and we will deal with each of these in turn.

12.3.1 The ACAS Code and Guidelines

Under TULRCA 1992, s. 199 ACAS may issue codes of behaviour. A new statutory Code has been issued to accompany the Employment Act 2008. The Code is not legally binding. Notwithstanding the fact that a failure to follow any part of this Code does not, in itself, make a person or organisation liable to proceedings, employment tribunals will take the Code into account when considering relevant cases. Perhaps even more importantly, a tribunal will be able to increase or decrease any award of compensation by up to 25 per cent where an employer or employee unreasonably fails to follow the Code. Similarly, arbitrators appointed by ACAS to determine relevant cases under the ACAS Arbitration Scheme will take the Code into account.

The Code represents a common sense approach to industrial relations matters and generally recommends the use of informal action to resolve matters followed by formal action (such as a first warning, second, and final warning). It sets out procedures designed to help the employee correct the behaviour. The full Code can be accessed through www.acas.org.uk. Here are some highlights:

On disciplinary procedures:

- deal with issues promptly and consistently;
- establish the facts before taking action;
- make sure the employee is informed clearly of the allegations;
- allow the employee to be accompanied and to state their case;
- make sure that the disciplinary action is appropriate to the misconduct or incapability;
- provide employees with an opportunity to appeal.

On grievances:

- the employee should clearly inform the line manager of the nature of the grievance;
- the employee should be allowed to bring a companion to any hearing;
- the action taken should be appropriate to the grievance;
- an appeal system should be in place.

12.3.2 Contractual procedures

Tribunals are also interested in the employer's own contractual procedures and whether these have been adhered to. The more elaborate these are the more complications set in when the employer finds he cannot comply with them. The risks are obvious. Thus, in one case the authors once dealt with, a Cornish company had, as its final appeal, the involvement of the parent-company chairman. He was in Switzerland and did not speak English. When this procedure was tested it was found wanting and came under severe criticism.

Company disciplinary codes often spell out what is meant by 'gross misconduct' or 'gross breach of duty'. If these clauses pretend to give *exhaustive* definitions they lose the possibility of flexibility in the face of the unexpected and employers may be caught by their own wording. Some provisions should also be made in the contract for determining when a warning becomes 'stale', e.g., three or six months for an oral warning, six months for a written warning, and 12 months for a final warning. No tribunal will allow reference to be made to a warning given five years previously as proof of compliance with the disciplinary code (though these earlier incidents might be referred to in the hearing as evidence of the employment history).

If the employer wishes to impose suspension without pay as a penalty this must be spelt out in the contract; otherwise it will be a breach which may, in itself, lead to claims for contractual damages, or even constructive dismissal.

12.3.3 Failure to operate the contractual procedures properly

The question is simple: what happens if an employer fails to operate a dismissal procedure properly but, had he done what he was meant to do, it is very likely that the dismissal would have been fair? Should a tribunal find that the failure in procedure 'made no difference' to the outcome and so decide the dismissal was not unfair, or should it call it an unfair dismissal but reduce any compensation (possibly to zero). Throughout the 1980s the 'it makes no difference' test ruled so tribunals would engage in a 'what if?' exercise, perhaps conclude that the employee was doomed anyway and so decide there was no unfair dismissal. Then the House of Lords laid this to rest in *Polkey* v *A.E. Dayton Service Ltd* [1987] AC 344, deciding that this all-or-nothing test was too simplistic. Instead, the test should be: make a finding of unfair dismissal but assess the chances of whether the employee *might* have been dismissed had the procedure been followed—or by looking at future employment prospects within the company generally (e.g., the likelihood of a redundancy occurring soon)—and reduce the compensation if necessary. Under the Employment Act 2002, a statutory form of the 'it makes no difference' test was created and became the governing test—but the Employment Act 2008 re-instated the *Polkey* test as from April 2009.

This in turn means that the case law which flowed from *Polkey* is relevant again. In *Duffy* v *Yeomans & Partners Ltd* [1995] ICR 1 and again in *Lord Mayor and Citizens of the City of Westminster* v *Cabaj* [1996] ICR 960 the Court of Appeal held that there is no proposition of law that *any* failure in procedure leads inevitably to a finding of unfair dismissal. The *Polkey* test is not that blunt a weapon. Instead, one should:

(i) ask whether the consequences of the breach in procedure effectively denied the employee 'due process' by impeding his ability to defend his position; and

(ii) why did the employer not follow his own procedures? Thus minor breaches may well be passed over but a failure which affected the general fairness of the procedures would be damning.

12.3.4 Relevance of appeals procedures

In *West Midlands Co-operative Society* v *Tipton* [1986] ICR 192 the House of Lords held that the appeals' procedure was an integral part of deciding the question of fair procedure. Indeed, a properly conducted appeal can remedy some procedural deficiencies in the original hearing.

12.3.5 A fair hearing

In misconduct dismissals especially, but also with incapability and 'some other substantial reason', the employee should have a chance to state a case. In *Clark* v *Civil Aviation Authority* [1991] IRLR 412, the EAT stated that a hearing should adopt the following pattern:

(a) Explain the purpose of the meeting.

(b) Identify those present.

(c) If appropriate, arrange representation.

(d) Inform the employee of the allegations.

(e) Indicate the evidence—in writing or by calling witnesses.

(f) Allow the employee to ask questions (though there is no legal obligation to allow the employee to cross-examine witnesses: *Santamera* v *Express Cargo Forwarding*

[2003] IRLR 273). In some cases fellow employees might be reluctant to be seen acting as informants. In *Linfood Cash & Carry Ltd* v *Thomson* [1989] ICR 518 the EAT established guidelines for dealing with instances where the employees might be in fear of being named.

(g) Allow the employee to call witnesses.

(h) Listen to the arguments raised.

To this we would add that the hearing needs to be seen to be fair, so that staff who were involved in earlier stages which generated this hearing should not also act as judge and jury. In particular, an appeal should not (wherever possible) be heard by the same panel which decided to dismiss.

12.3.6 Right to be accompanied

Under ERA 1999, s. 10 a *worker* (defined in s. 13) is entitled to be accompanied at a disciplinary or grievance hearing by a single companion where the hearing 'could result in . . . the administration of a formal warning . . .'. The right is not absolute: the request must be a 'reasonable' one so, within that setting, an employer can refuse to allow certain individuals who might prejudice the hearing to accompany the worker (see ACAS Code at paras 15 and 36). The person accompanying the worker must be either a trade union official or another of the employer's workers.

The label attached to any disciplinary hearing ('informal' or 'formal') is irrelevant; the right is triggered where the warning will become part of the employee's disciplinary record: *London Underground Ltd* v *Ferenc-Batchelor* [2003] IRLR 252. It is not that common these days for an employer to issue oral informal warnings and keep no record at all, so this decision widens the right substantially.

However, a meeting called to investigate an issue is not a disciplinary hearing (*Skiggs* v *South West Trains Ltd* [2005] IRLR 462) and only if it becomes apparent during the meeting that disciplinary action may occur does the s. 10 right kick in—at which point the meeting should be terminated and a fresh one started later. If the employer fails to comply with this the worker may present a complaint to an employment tribunal under s. 11, the maximum compensation being two weeks' pay. Under s. 12, a worker dismissed as a consequence of seeking to exercise these rights or for making a complaint to an employment tribunal will be regarded as automatically unfairly dismissed.

Legal representation at internal hearings is always a thorny issue (especially as s. 10 does not mention such characters). Most companies prohibit this. However, following *Kulkarni* v *Milton Keynes Hospital NHS Foundation Trust* [2009] EWCA Civ 789, [2009] IRLR 829 employers (or at least employers who are public authorities for the purposes of the Human Rights Act 1998) may have to change their rules. The decision here was that legal representation must be allowed so as to comply with art. 6 ECHR (*obiter* as there was also a contractual right present) where the effect of the proceedings might 'deprive an employee of the right to practice his or her profession' (e.g., a doctor—as here—or lawyer, accountant etc.). Apparently, though, where all that is at risk is the loss of a specific job (e.g., with a cleaner) this right does not arise. This approach was extended in *Governors of X School* v *R(G)* [2010] EWCA Civ 1, [2010] IRLR 222. The proceedings in question here would not normally qualify under the ACAS Code so as to attract legal representation, but they concerned allegations of inappropriate behaviour with a young person made against a teaching assistant. The Court felt that in such cases any determination by an internal panel would have a substantial influence or effect on future statutory proceedings. On that basis the Court held that legal representation was necessary.

It is suggested that the engagement of art. 6 is not of universal application to ordinary dismissal cases even concerning public authorities; the facts need to be quite specific and the impact of the proceedings quite severe before the article becomes relevant.

12.4 Second general aspect of fairness: range of reasonable responses

In this part the tribunal sets what has happened against the actions of the 'reasonable employer' (a hypothetical figure drawn from the extensive experience of employment tribunal panels). This part of the assessment is derived from *British Leyland (UK) Ltd* v *Swift* [1981] IRLR 91 (and *Iceland Frozen Foods* v *Jones* [1983] ICR 17). The question posed will be: is it possible that a reasonable employer, faced with these facts, would have dismissed? For instance, let us imagine that an employee has committed theft; the employer has investigated the matter thoroughly and has to decide whether to dismiss. The range of options open to the employer could include:

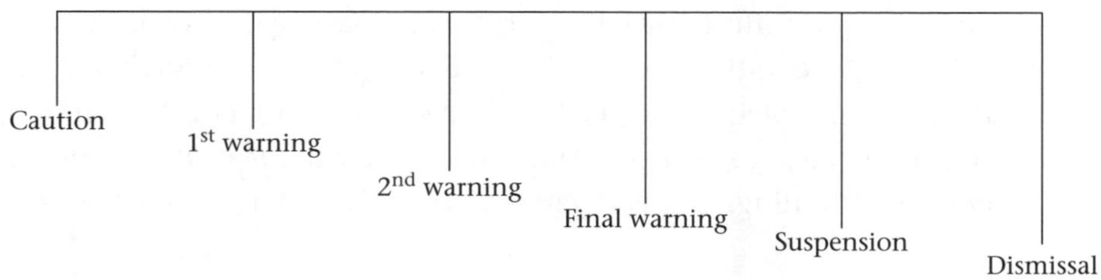

Figure 12.2 Range of reasonable responses.

Some employers may not have dismissed in these circumstances; they may have gone to a final warning instead: but if the decision to dismiss falls within *the band of reasonableness* then this will show fairness. The theft example would satisfy this test, even though with a long-serving employee *some* employers might stop short of dismissal (for example, because of the employee's disciplinary record: see *Strouthos* v *London Underground* [2004] EWCA 402, [2004] IRLR 636). With questions of frequent lateness, absenteeism, incapability, or refusal to obey an order the debate opens out a little. However, what the tribunal should not do is to substitute its own standard of reasonableness—the test is whether the employer acted as a reasonable employer, having regard to the size and administrative resources available. Thus, the employer's beliefs that the grounds for dismissal justified the action have to be weighed against the tribunal's *perception* of reasonable practice based on its experience of industrial practice. The decision to dismiss may be one the employer would always follow, but the key question is whether the rest of industry would be so like-minded.

Where an employee has already been subject to various stages of the disciplinary process it is not too difficult to justify the final decision to dismiss. Most problems will arise when stages are bypassed or, in the case of gross misconduct, omitted. There the tribunal has to be clear that a reasonable employer could have dismissed in the circumstances. After some debate at the end of the last century the Court of Appeal confirmed the range test in *Foley* v *Post Office; HSBC (Formerly Midland Bank)* v *Madden* [2000] IRLR 827: the role of employment tribunals is not to impose their own standards of reasonableness, but to test the employer's actions against those of a reasonable employer.

In *Sainsburys Supermarkets Ltd* v *Hill* [2002] EWCA Civ 1588, [2003] ICR 111, the 'range of reasonable responses' test was held to apply equally to the procedures used as to the penalty being imposed (the dismissal). And, as we have seen at **11.5** above, this test is also relevant to the notion of 'dismissal' in a constructive dismissal claim based on the inadequate operation of a grievance procedure.

12.4.1 Relationship with grievance procedures

It is often thought that once an employee launches a formal grievance then any disciplinary proceedings must be held in abeyance until the grievance is heard. There is no such rule, though; if the contract stipulates for this the employer would be ill-advised to do otherwise.

We should note that this problem may of course arise under any heading of 'fair reason' but its most usual home is in misconduct cases, e.g., an employee is to be called to a disciplinary hearing concerning his conduct towards a customer; before that really gets started he lodges a grievance against his line manager citing failure to support him or bullying behaviour.

12.5 Fairness in capability and qualifications dismissals

Where an underlying reason could have been classed as conduct *or* capability, we noted in **11.8.3** that *conduct* may be more appropriate where the employee is easily able to improve with a little effort; *capability* is more appropriate if it is accepted by the employer that the employee either is or has become incapable of meeting the requirements (perhaps because the job has changed). With *conduct* the emphasis on handling the dismissal fairly is one of giving a chance for improvement; with *capability,* on compassionate treatment over such things as investigating alternative and more suitable work.

12.5.1 Qualifications

We noted above that the qualification must be connected substantially to the employee's job. So, if an employee loses his or her driving licence this will merit dismissal only if the licence was vital to the job and the employer has considered other alternative jobs within the company. A requirement for an employee to pass a key examination or aptitude test would fall within this category: *Blackman* v *Post Office* [1974] ICR 151 (a salutary point perhaps!).

12.5.2 Competence

If an employer claims that an employee was fairly dismissed for incapability the employment tribunal will expect clear evidence, not just some vague subjective assessment that the employee 'couldn't cut it'. As a basic checklist, therefore, the following matters should be considered:

(a) How good is the evidence of incompetence? Is it objectively proven, e.g., after a proper investigation?

(b) Was there a proper appraisal system in operation, or at least some formal way in which the employee could know of the defective performance?

(c) Were warnings given? In particular, was it made clear what would be the consequences for failure to improve?

(d) Were the warnings/objectives impossible to meet? For instance, an instruction that unless the company obtains a market share of 80 per cent by the end of the year the employee–manager will be dismissed may or may not be pure fantasy.

(e) Were any opportunities for training or retraining given?

(f) What form of supervision was operative?

(g) Were alternatives considered?

(h) What consideration was taken of the employee's status, length of service, and past performance?

(i) Have incompetent employees been dismissed in similar circumstances in the past?

The relevance of some of these factors will depend upon the size of the company. For instance, a small, backstreet engineering company will not have the facility to look at many (if any) alternative jobs.

With incompetence dismissals emphasis has to be placed here on giving an opportunity to the employee to improve and listening to the employee's opinion, e.g., are the demands impossible to fulfil? Equally, if the employee challenges the employer's assessment it would be advisable to allow the employee (if feasible) the chance to demonstrate his or her case: *Morgan* v *Electrolux* [1991] IRLR 89. In that case the employee was found to have overbooked piece-work. In explaining her activities she asked to demonstrate her work speed. This request was refused. The Court of Appeal held that the employers had not acted reasonably in denying her this opportunity.

As with gross misconduct, there may also be gross incompetence which will justify dismissal without previous warnings, but greater care needs to be taken with incompetence. Indeed, if a single incident is that important it often involves an overlap between incompetence and misconduct, e.g., *Alidair Ltd* v *Taylor* [1978] ICR 445, where a pilot 'bounced' the company jet.

12.5.3 Ill-health

Dismissals on the grounds of ill-health have always been treated more cautiously by employment tribunals than any other potentially fair reason. Two forms of absence for ill-health may arise: intermittent absences and those lasting for prolonged periods. In the latter case it may be that the contract is frustrated (though for reasons noted in **Chapter 10** at **10.5.1** reliance on this should be avoided). General guidelines on dealing with sickness dismissals have been proffered in a number of cases, e.g., *Spencer* v *Paragon Wallpapers Ltd* [1977] ICR 301 and *East Lindsey District Council* v *Daubney* [1977] ICR 566. From these cases we can draw up a list of actions expected of the employer.

When dealing with long-term absence there is a duty on the employer to ascertain the true position, to discuss the future with the employee (and possibly his or her doctor), and to look for alternative work. When dealing with intermittent absences the employer needs to make the employee aware of the standard required, giving the employee time to meet this and perhaps attempting to resolve the issue via medical investigations and analysing the possibility of alternative work. Thus, the employer should:

(a) investigate the nature of the illness;

(b) investigate the likely length of absence;

(c) assess the impact on the business (i.e., does that employee hold a key position?). The more important the employee is to the business the more the absence cannot be tolerated for any great length of time. It is therefore perhaps ironic that the more valued employee might have to be dismissed sooner than the lesser employee in order to find a replacement. Temporary replacements provide an answer, but not realistically in key positions, for few recruits would be found on this basis;

(d) assess the impact the absence will have on other employees, i.e., the increase in *their* workload or the effect on their pay if part of a team working on commission or bonuses;

(e) take account of available medical evidence. This will often mean that the employer will have to obtain appropriate medical reports;

(f) take notice of the employee's length of service and any contractual sick pay scheme;

(g) consider alternative work;

(h) consult the employee over the issues noted above (warning an employee to get better is somewhat futile, but an employer may have to indicate at some time that the position cannot go on forever).

There are three points that need some elaboration:

12.5.3.1 Obtaining proper evidence

The aspect of discussion and consultation is useful not only to keep the employee informed of developments, but also to ascertain exactly what the position is at any time. Dismissing shortly before the employee is set to return does not, for instance, exemplify good management. Equally, if the employer needs medical evidence in order to make a decision the employee's assistance is needed; more so under the provisions of the Access to Medical Reports Act 1988 and the Data Protection Act 1998 (see **Chapter 8**). In all cases tribunals must decide (i) as a matter of fact, what level of consultation was necessary or desirable; and (ii) whether the process employed was adequate in the circumstances. A failure to seek medical advice damages the employer's argument of fairness. The employee's own GP, or possibly a specialist, is the obvious source to provide independent medical assessments (especially if there is a conflict of medical opinion). However, unless there is an express contractual power to request the employee to undergo a medical examination the employer cannot force the employee to do so. Any such *demand* would constitute a repudiatory breach: *Bliss* v *South East Thames Regional Health Authority* [1987] ICR 700 (request for a psychological examination). But if the employee does refuse to cooperate the employer is entitled to make a decision on the facts available.

12.5.3.2 Intermittent absences

These pose a different kind of problem. The employer's tolerance of such situations does not have to be *infinite*. Warnings following consultation may be more appropriate here because of both the disruptive effect of short-term but frequent absence and also the possibility that there is a question of misconduct as well as or instead of incapability. Medical evidence may prove useful here too, though if an employee has been diagnosed as suffering from, say, back trouble which flares up periodically this evidence does not actually resolve the problem.

12.5.3.3 Relationship with contractual sick pay scheme

Most companies operate a sick pay scheme (as noted at **5.2.3.1** above) and a frequently asked question is: can an employer dismiss someone who is still on sick leave? The usual advice is, yes, but with great caution. If the employee commits an act of gross misconduct during the sick leave or fails to cooperate with the reasonable requests of the employer whilst on sick leave that will justify dismissal for misconduct: *Briscoe* v *Lubrizol Ltd* [2002] EWCA Civ 508, [2002] IRLR 607; likewise if the employer has to make people redundant, being ill is no safeguard against selection: *Hill* v *General Accident Fire & Life Assurance Corporation plc* [1998] IRLR 641.

But the real problem comes where the employer wishes to dismiss *because* of the employee's absence owing to illness. Tribunals have long accepted that an employer may have to dismiss someone, despite the presence of a clause which seems to 'guarantee' an employee a period of sick leave, if genuine business needs drive them that way e.g., in the case of a key employee. The question is then whether the dismissal is handled fairly.

At **5.2.3.1** we noted that a conflict has developed (as it often does in employment) between the form of analysis used by the ordinary courts and that used by employment tribunals in dealing with dismissals of employees who are on contractual sick leave. We saw that a recent run of cases has, by reliance on express or implied terms, concluded that an employee can only be dismissed *for cause* (e.g., redundancy) whilst on sick leave, especially if the dismissal would adversely affect any health insurance entitlements. The ordinary courts are concerned only with the contractual analysis. Thus, in *Hill* v *General Accident,* Lord Hamilton (in the court of Session, Outer House—the equivalent to the High Court) stated that: 'Where provision is, as here, made in the contract for payment of salary or other benefit during sickness, the employer cannot, solely with a view to relieving himself of the obligation to make such payment, by dismissal bring that sick employee's contract to an end.' An implied term is created to this effect that can only be ousted by clear express wording.

What of the position as regards unfair dismissal? There is no case directly covering whether the presence of private health insurance, for instance, prevents the employer from dismissing fairly on ill-health grounds, but in a related area such a limitation has been placed: *First West Yorkshire Ltd* v *Haigh* [2008] IRLR 182. Here, the EAT held that an employer had not acted within the range of reasonable responses when dismissing a long-term sick employee without considering how he might qualify for 'early medical retirement' under their pension scheme (coupled here with a finding that the employer had chosen the dismissal route for purely financial reasons and also because the employer had failed to obtain proper medical evidence as to how long the illness would last).

12.5.4 Overlap with disability discrimination

In **Chapter 6** we noted the main provisions of disability discrimination in relation to recruitment, terms, promotion opportunities, etc. The legislation also has relevance as regards any dismissal based on a person's disability. The term 'dismissal' when applied to the protected characteristic of disability is likely to include the non-renewal of limited-term contracts and constructive dismissal, although there is no definition given in the Act.

Thus a disabled person who has been dismissed has two main statutory claims:

(a) a discrimination action under the Equality Act 2010; and

(b) an unfair dismissal action under ERA 1996.

There can be considerable overlap in the substantive analysis of these claims. There is nothing in the EqA 2010 to prevent an employee from also claiming unfair dismissal under ERA 1996 either exclusively or in the alternative and a finding of unfair dismissal will not mean that the statutory cap in unfair dismissal action (currently £65,300) will, by a side wind, limit the open-ended compensation possible under a discrimination claim: see *Beart* v *HM Prison Service* [2005] EWCA Civ 467, [2005] ICR 1206.

However, the dismissal of a 'disabled person' is not automatically unfair. Neither does EqA 2010 specifically alter the general provisions of s. 98 of ERA 1996. Certainly, if an employee falls within the provisions of EqA 2010 it is highly unlikely that it will be sufficient for an employer merely to show that the disabled employee was incapable under s. 98(2)(a) in order to defend an unfair dismissal claim. Effectively, where a 'disabled person' is dismissed or subjected to any other detriment then, in any unfair dismissal action defended on the grounds of capability, the tribunal will have to take into account the requirements of good practice and, as seen in the House of Lords' disability discrimination case of *Archibald* v *Fife Council* [2004] UKHL 32, [2004] IRLR 651 this may mean making extensive arrangements for transferring jobs, etc. as part of the duty to make 'reasonable adjustments'. This does not mean that an employer cannot take into account absences which are disability-related; it simply means that where the sickness is tied in with a disability the employer has to be able to justify any actions as regards the disability as part of defending the unfair dismissal claim: *Royal Liverpool Children's NHS Trust* v *Dunsby* [2006] IRLR 351.

The safest advice for all employers must therefore be that an employer must have in mind, when dealing with an employee who is ill or who has absences from work (or who might be made redundant), the requirements of EqA 2010.

There are advantages to pursuing a claim directly under EqA 2010, e.g., no age limit; no qualifying period of employment; the specific inclusion of 'injury to feelings' as a head of compensation; and no limit on the amount of compensation that may be awarded. However, to succeed in a claim under the EqA 2010 the employee must have been the subject of 'discrimination' as set out in the Act. This might be difficult to establish in any given case. An unfair dismissal claim, although initially less attractive, might still prove to be the better course of action.

It is possible for there to be an unfair dismissal under s. 98 of ERA 1996 but for a disability discrimination claim to fail where the employee may not be able to establish all elements for the latter claim (e.g., the employer's actions were justified) but in assessing the overall reasonableness of the employer's actions in an unfair dismissal claim they are found wanting. The converse is less likely.

12.6 Fairness in misconduct dismissals

In the text below we consider the special requirements affecting conduct dismissals. The forms of misconduct can be legion. However, standard methods of dealing with misconduct dismissals emerge from the cases. The employer needs to show:

(a) an honest belief that the employee was guilty of the offence;

(b) that there were reasonable grounds for holding that belief; and

(c) that these came from a reasonable investigation of the incident(s).

This is not an immutable checklist and, given that the burden of proof as to fairness is neutral, minor failures under these principles will not inevitably damn an employer's case: *Boys' and Girls' Welfare Society* v *McDonald* [1996] IRLR 129.

These principles were first clearly stated in relation to dishonesty dismissals in *British Home Stores* v *Burchell* [1980] ICR 303, and have been approved on wider grounds since then. They are therefore often referred to as the '*Burchell* principles'. They demonstrate that *conclusive proof is not necessary*. So the employer is required to formulate an opinion and then to decide whether, on that evidence, a dismissal is justified. The tribunal will then examine the basis for the belief and then go on to determine whether a reasonable employer would have dismissed in those circumstances.

There is no requirement to find some form of *mens rea* in the employee's actions. The test is simpler than this: did the employee commit the act complained of? For example, say an employee has assaulted another employee. The employee claims that the other employee provoked him by teasing him about his inability to carry out a temporary task. The employee also says that he cannot remember hitting the other person; that he 'blacked out'. Provided the dismissal is dealt with fairly (see below) the employer is not expected to launch into criminal law in order to establish the state of the employee's mind. Equally, an employer does not have to cogitate on whether there is a line to be drawn between intent and commission where the employee has been discovered, about to commit an act, e.g., a theft: *British Railways Board* v *Jackson* [1994] IRLR 235.

A general checklist for misconduct dismissals would therefore be:

(a) The employer must adhere to the spirit of the *Burchell* principles, or the evidence must be so obvious (or there is a confession) that it fulfils the same function.

(b) The employer must adhere to the company's procedures (which should fit with the ACAS Code). Employers often have elaborate procedures and many (for good reason) will have 'informal' stages or what are sometimes called 'fair blame policies' that seek to settle matters before disciplinary proceedings are engaged. The danger is that once these formal proceedings are engaged the employer may be deemed to have determined that the conduct in question is of a minor nature by its use of the informal stage; if recourse is made to formal disciplinary proceedings at a later date this may therefore be seen as inconsistent action and outside the range of reasonable responses: *Sarkar* v *West London Mental Health NHS Trust* [2010] EWCA Civ 289, [2010] IRLR 508.

(c) The employer must have conducted a proper hearing. This merely gives force to natural justice points but it may be that where the consequences of any decision are particularly serious (e.g., leading to withdrawal of professional licences or deportation for loss of work permit) the standard expected of the employer's investigations will be particularly high: *Salford Royal NHS Foundation Trust* v *Roldan* [2010] EWCA Civ 522, [2010] IRLR 721.

(d) The employer should review the status of previous warnings.

(e) The employer should note the employee's disciplinary record.

(f) The employer should take note of the employee's length of service.

(g) The employer's policy of dealing with misconduct should show consistency.

(h) Alternatives to dismissal should be considered.

(i) The relevance of criminal proceedings, or acquittals or convictions should be considered.

Some of these matters, such as the conduct of a fair hearing, have been noted above. One or two deserve further elaboration. A misconduct dismissal does not have to be for gross misconduct. A series of lesser incidents might bring about a fair dismissal if proper procedures have been followed. Gross misconduct will more easily justify moving straight to dismissal, without going through warnings, but otherwise all forms of misconduct fall under the same general guidelines.

12.6.1 What is 'gross' misconduct?

Many contracts define what is regarded as gross misconduct. If they are so tightly drawn that they provide an exhaustive list it will be difficult to add to this. But most contracts merely give the primary examples. These would include: dishonesty (usually whatever the amount and whatever the form), fighting at work and assault, disclosure of confidential information, setting up in a competing business (at least as regards senior employees), and gross insubordination. The list will vary from industry to industry though. Thus, 'fighting' might take various forms. A snowball fight in a foundry, where pieces of metal, etc. may be on the floor, could prove dangerous and an employee could fairly be dismissed for participating. Equally, an offence may be serious without being gross misconduct, e.g., where an employee incompetently fails to deal with invoices and so loses the company money. He or she may have committed a serious offence but, if the amount is small, this will hardly be gross negligence. In the end, the definition of 'gross misconduct' is relevant only:

(a) to show why the employer bypassed the warnings stage and went straight to dismissal;

(b) in relation to *wrongful dismissal,* to show why summary dismissal was chosen.

12.6.2 The employee's disciplinary and service history

The point of emphasis here is that in each case the employer is dealing with an individual, therefore that individual's history in the company is a major component of any decision to dismiss. This is especially true where the dismissal relates to conduct which is not gross misconduct.

As a rule of thumb, employers will treat long-serving employees with a little more leniency because of the loyalty factor. Thus, although this does not afford complete protection, a reasonable employer will at least take service into account in deciding whether to dismiss or impose some lesser penalty. But if the employment record shows a history of disciplinary problems, this can equally damn the employee and if warnings for other matters are still operative this will have a major influence on the decision to dismiss. Normally one would expect an employer to issue the next-level warning. If some stages are to be omitted the employer will need to justify this.

In some cases an employee may have a history of warnings but these may have expired (most warnings are given a limitation period of three months, six months etc. depending on their level). Employers frequently ask whether they can take such expired warnings into account. The traditional answer has always been 'No' but the Court of Appeal has decided that though taking into account expired warnings may not generally be good industrial practice there is nothing in the language of ERA 1996, s. 98(4) to prohibit this if the employer can show it was reasonable to do so: *Airbus UK Ltd* v *Webb* [2008] EWCA Civ 49, [2008] ICR 561.

12.6.3 Consistency of treatment

There are two matters here. There should be consistency in dealing with employees involved in the same incident, e.g., a fight. But, wider than this, there should be some consistency across the years in dealing with types of offence. This may apply even when the management personnel has changed over the years: *Proctor* v *British Gypsum Ltd* [1991] IRLR 7. Here the EAT stated three points on consistency of treatment:

(a) An otherwise fair dismissal might be classified as unfair in the light of inconsistency of treatment.

(b) Though ERA 1996, s. 98 demands consideration of the *individual's* case, comparisons may be valid if they reveal a pattern that it is understood in the company that such conduct will be overlooked, that the comparisons reveal that the reason given for dismissal is not genuine, or that the cases are analogous.

(c) Changes in circumstances, e.g., an increase in theft, might well justify changes in policy (though some form of prior notification would be necessary). In such cases, acting severely as a deterrent to others may be acceptable.

The Court of Appeal issued further guidance on 'consistency' in *Paul* v *East Surrey District Health Authority* [1995] IRLR 305. Whilst not overturning any of the above, there is a recognition that similar incidents are not that common across the years when examined carefully and employers do have some flexibility. Thus, an employer may take account of mitigating personal circumstances (or aggravating circumstances), how contrite the employee is, and the levels of seriousness of the offences involved. Points (a) and (b) above also received specific approval. Nevertheless, the quite common cry of the employer that 'We will make an example of this one' is therefore prone to attack.

Linked with this is the problematic area of suspected theft when the employer can pinpoint a group of employees but cannot identify the guilty individual or individuals specifically. Should the employer dismiss one, some, all or none? The cases reveal that, provided the employer's investigations are reasonable and all other factors have been taken into account, dismissing *all* of the group will be a fair method of dealing with the problem: *Monie* v *Coral Racing Ltd* [1981] ICR 109. The employer must be convinced on 'solid and sensible grounds' that one or more *of that group* has committed the act. The employer does not, however, *have* to dismiss all the members of the group (this is where the other factors may be relevant, e.g., past disciplinary record). This principle has been extended to other situations where it is impossible directly to apportion blame to a group, e.g., for faulty workmanship.

12.6.4 The relevance of criminal proceedings

Employers are not required to await the outcome of criminal proceedings before deciding on dismissal (unless, as with some NHS trusts' contracts, the contract so specifies). Equally, employers cannot dismiss simply because an employee has been charged with an offence. First, the mere fact of being charged is irrelevant and, secondly, the offence will ultimately have to have some bearing on the employment relationship to justify the dismissal: *Singh* v *London Country Bus Services Ltd* [1976] IRLR 176.

This means that employers will have to conduct their own investigations before any decision to dismiss is likely to be fair: *Lovie Ltd* v *Anderson* [1999] IRLR 164. Evidence supplied to employers by the police or other bodies may be treated as reliable by the employer but must still be tested as much as possible before being acted upon. All this is quite awkward in practice because the employee (unless confessing) is hardly liable to prove cooperative! Indeed, the Court of Session in Scotland and the English EAT have disagreed over the appropriateness of employer investigations. Perhaps the key point is that the employer, on the evidence available (which may include statements made to the police), has to be sure that dismissal is the right course; any doubts may mean having to wait. Usually, if an employer drags out a disciplinary procedure they will pay the penalty as being judged to have acted unreasonably. Where ongoing police investigations are present delay is less likely to be viewed as unconscionable.

A conviction does not absolve the employer from some investigation of the matter, but this relates more to matters such as mitigation; an employer is certainly entitled to treat a conviction as proof of guilt: *P* v *Nottinghamshire County Council* [1992] ICR 706. But neither will an eventual acquittal turn an existing properly conducted dismissal into an unfair dismissal. Further, if the employer does await the outcome of the trial a dismissal following acquittal may still be fair because the standards of proof are different and other matters may have come out at the trial. Employers who state that *they will be bound* by the outcome of the trial are in a difficult position: any subsequent dismissal will most likely be unfair.

12.6.5 Concluding points on misconduct

Because the forms of misconduct are so various, all that can be given here are the general guidelines. These will hold true in each case, but the considerations for absentee dismissals, dismissals for fraud, fighting, disobedience, and so on will each have their variations in terms of appropriate forms of procedure and investigation. Most importantly, the employer must be able to demonstrate, as regards whichever type of misconduct is pertinent, that the decision to dismiss that particular employee for that particular offence was warranted.

This is particularly true where activities external to the employment relationship are at issue. Here, questions of privacy and human rights may be engaged. The latest pronouncement in this field (*Pay* v *United Kingdom* [2009] IRLR 139) confirms the usual balancing approach seen in art. 8 ECHR (privacy) cases. Here, a probation officer's external activities involving a company concerned with bondage and sado-masochistic role-playing were assumed by ECHR to be 'private' but the dismissal/breach of privacy was still found to be justified under art. 8(2) ECHR because of the nature of his work.

One further point worth emphasising arises where the employee is dismissed for misconduct in refusing to obey an order from the employer. Most employees believe that if the order was unlawful (i.e., in breach of the contract) they cannot be dismissed fairly for refusing to obey it. In many cases the lawfulness of the order will indeed affect the fairness of any dismissal, but it is only a factor in the equation. If the employer has, for instance, given ample warning of any change being implemented, consulted sufficiently and acted reasonably any resulting dismissal in the face of the employee 'sticking to the contract' may not be unfair.

12.7 Fairness in retirement dismissals

The fairness of retirement dismissals is not subject to the general principles described above.

For a retirement to be a fair *reason* for dismissal under s. 98(2)(ba), the employer must comply with the points set out in ss. 98ZA–ZF of ERA 1996. But that still leaves the question whether that fair reason was handled fairly. To answer that question we need to look at an additional set of procedures. These are contained in s. 98ZG of ERA 1996.

Section 98ZG states that the dismissal will be *automatically fair* provided the employer has:

- given proper notification to the employee of her right to request to continue to work beyond the retirement date or, failing that, given proper notification prior to the fourteenth day before dismissal;
- considered that request;
- considered any appeal against a decision not to allow the employee to continue working.

If the employer fails to comply with any of these points, the dismissal is *automatically unfair*. However, it is also possible (somewhat bizarrely) that, where the NRA or age requirements have been respected but there is a fault in the application of the duty to inform, the tribunal still has a discretion under s. 98ZG of ERA 1996 to consider whether the dismissal is fair where the employer has complied with the continuing duty to inform the employee up to two weeks before the intended retirement date.

12.8 Fairness in redundancy dismissals

With a redundancy dismissal the tribunal will be concerned to discover whether the redundancy was implemented fairly. It is rare for a tribunal to question the need for redundancy; that is a business decision for the employer to make (unless there is bad faith): *James W. Cook & Co. (Wivenhoe) Ltd* v *Tipper* [1990] ICR 716. Instead, the area most rife for debate is that of *selection* for redundancy. Thus if selections for redundancy are badly handled and the selection criteria are not objectively justifiable, there may be an unfair dismissal for reason of redundancy (a full discussion of these points occurs in **Chapter 14** generally, and specifically at **14.5**). Indeed, certain dismissals for redundancy will be automatically unfair.

The burden of proving that any of the above reasons apply lies with the employee. Thus the fact that trade unionists are selected does not in itself breach any provisions: the selections have to be *because* the employees were trade unionists, or had asserted a statutory right, etc.

In ordinary cases the employer may still have acted unfairly. Thus an employer must also:

(a) ensure that the selection criteria were objectively justifiable and applied fairly;

(b) undertake proper individual and/or collective consultation; and

(c) ascertain whether suitable alternative employment is available.

Hence the selection process and the procedure for decision-making and implementation will be called into question in deciding fairness.

Selection for redundancy because of a person's disability is not automatically unfair but will have to be justified, and that justification must be both material to the circumstances of the particular case and substantial.

12.9 Fairness in statutory illegality dismissals

We have already noted that it is for the employer to show as a fact that any continued employment would have contravened the statutory rule in question in order to claim this as a fair reason for dismissal. As with other 'fair reasons', the citing of an enactment does not absolve the employer from showing that the dismissal was handled fairly. The problem of the illegality, for instance, might only have a short life-span and so might easily be corrected, or the illegality might affect only part of the employee's duties so that alternative work or a change in duties could be looked at. In other words, if the situation can be remedied the employer would be unwise to dismiss before checking this.

12.10 Fairness in dismissals for 'some other substantial reason'

12.10.1 A catch-all category?

In the text below we consider the special requirements affecting 'some other substantial reason' dismissals. The tag of 'catch-all' does indeed apply to this area, dragging along with it all the lack of definition inherent in the phrase. Thus if the dismissal does not fall within any of the other five fair reasons it *might* come within this heading. For example, in *A* v *B* [2010] IRLR 844 the employer faced a difficult problem concerning alleged child sexual abuse. Information was supplied to the employer by the Serious Organised Crime Agency that one of its employees, a senior civil servant, had been charged with sex crimes in Cambodia. The employee was 'totally exonerated' but further allegations by official bodies were made that he was a continuing threat to children. The employee was summarily dismissed despite there being no proven misconduct on his part. In what Underhill J described as a difficult judgment, the employer was held to have 'some other substantial reason' for dismissal (official notification of a possible threat to children and the potential impact on public opinion of continuing to employ the individual) and to have acted fairly in the circumstances.

Many employers will plead this catch-all in the alternative, e.g., if the dismissal was not for redundancy it was for 'some other substantial reason etc.' such as a business reorganisation; or if the employer was mistaken about the effect of a statutory rule and dismissed for statutory illegality, the honest belief might be pleaded as 'some other substantial reason'.

However, by far the most common form of 'some other substantial reason' is that of business reorganisations. We noted in **Chapter 5** that where an employer effects a change to the employee's terms and conditions a range of alternative consequences is possible at common law, e.g.:

(a) the change may be lawful via the express or implied terms of the contract;
(b) the employee might simply accept the change (reluctantly or otherwise);
(c) the employee might object and seek an injunction or damages;
(d) the employee might refuse to accept the change and be dismissed, in which case there may be a claim for wrongful dismissal;
(e) the employee might resign and claim wrongful repudiation.

To this we have added, in the earlier stages of this chapter, that:

(f) the employee might refuse to accept the change and be dismissed, in which case there may be a claim for unfair dismissal; or
(g) the employee might resign and claim constructive unfair dismissal.

Whichever way the unfair dismissal claim comes about, the employer can argue that the fair reason was 'some other substantial reason' under ERA 1996, s. 98. How will this be analysed by the employment tribunal?

12.10.2 Business reorganisations

Employers frequently wish to reorganise parts of a business in order to increase efficiency. Often this will simply involve a change in working patterns or methods, and, as seen in *Cresswell* v *Board of Inland Revenue* [1984] ICR 508 in **Chapter 5**, this may not involve any variation of the employment contract at all. An employee who refuses to cooperate and who resigns in the face of such changes will have no claim for wrongful repudiation at common law or for unfair dismissal because there will have been no dismissal. If the employee refuses to cooperate and is dismissed there may be a claim for wrongful or unfair dismissal; but from the unfair dismissal perspective the fair reason could be incapability or misconduct (and fairness would be decided accordingly).

If the change does constitute a breach of contract the employer may still argue that the dismissal was not unfair because of the business reorganisation. The tribunal is not allowed to second-guess the employer's business decision, so the employer can establish the 'fair reason' quite easily, e.g., insisting on the insertion of restraint of trade clauses because of recent problems with ex-employees joining competitors: *RS Components* v *Irwin* [1973] ICR 353. The test was once quite stringent: was there a 'pressing business need' for the change? However, greater leniency is now evident so that all that is needed is a 'sound business reason' (see *Hollister* v *National Farmers' Union* [1979] ICR 542), or even merely that the change was beneficial to the operation of the company. A mere assertion that there is a business reason is not enough, but employers are only expected to show the factual *evidence* as the basis for making their business decision.

The question of fairness still has to be decided, however. As with any unfair dismissal claim, the manner in which the employer handled the dismissal is still important. The tribunal is therefore seeking to find out whether the reorganisation was effected in a reasonable way. One of the difficulties that crops up here is that just because the employer is acting reasonably in seeking to implement the change it does not automatically follow that the employee is acting unreasonably in refusing to accept it. All manner of reasons may be relevant, e.g., family commitments or travel arrangements and, again, one must also consider the question of indirect discrimination arising from any reorganisation (see, for instance, *London Underground Ltd* v *Edwards (No. 2)* [1999] ICR 494).

The tribunal will therefore need to look at:

(a) whether the employer consulted with the employee and any employee representatives;

(b) whether the employer considered alternative courses of action;

(c) whether the terms were those which a reasonable employer would offer;

(d) what is the balance of advantages and disadvantages to both parties;

(e) whether the majority of employees have accepted the change.

No one factor is given greater weight than another and the whole context of the reorganisation needs to be examined: *St John of God (Care Services) Ltd* v *Brooks* [1992] IRLR 546. Again, however, one needs to be aware of the possible impact of DDA 1995. For instance, employers must now look at making reasonable adjustments to working arrangements and physical features of premises in relation to disabled employees. These adjustments include such matters as altering working hours, modifying equipment, and assigning a different place of work. Thus, these matters must be taken into account in effecting a business reorganisation otherwise there is a likelihood that the change in terms etc. will be seen as unreasonable.

12.11 Constructive dismissal and fairness

It is a common assumption that a constructive dismissal is automatically unfair. This view is wrong. All that a finding of constructive dismissal does is to show that the employee (despite having resigned) was in fact *dismissed*.

The question of fairness is a separate matter. Constructive dismissal asks whether the employer's conduct was repudiatory. It is a contractual test and, as with any other dismissal, the employer's breach of the contract is not what the idea of 'fairness' centres on. *Thus there may be fair or unfair constructive dismissals.* If you look back at **Figure 11.1** you will see that it only dealt with the analysis of whether or not there had been a constructive dismissal; it said nothing about fairness. It only told half the story because, once a constructive dismissal has been found the tribunal's attention then shifts to the analysis in **Figure 12.1**—as with any other unfair dismissal action.

Having said this, in many cases it will be quite unusual for an employment tribunal to be convinced that a constructive dismissal was nevertheless fair in all the circumstances. For instance, in *Cawley* v *South Wales Electricity Board* [1985] IRLR 89, an employee had been seen (by a member of the public) urinating out of the back of a SWEB van as it travelled down a main street. Apparently the employee had bladder trouble and the whole incident arose out of a practical joke being played by his workmates. The employee was at first dismissed but on appeal this was turned into a heavy demotion. He complained that, although the demotion was allowed for in the contract, its implementation was an abuse of power. He resigned and claimed that he was (unfairly) constructively dismissed. The tribunal found constructive dismissal and never really directed its mind to the question of fairness. However, on appeal the two points were found to be so closely intertwined that the general points had been covered. So it will be with most misconduct constructive dismissals.

The major exception to all this arises with constructive dismissals based on business reorganisations. Here the two questions of serious breach and fairness are quite distinct. Let us say, for example, that an employer decides unilaterally to change the terms of the contract for good economic reasons. The employees object. The employer insists, and eventually your employee–client resigns and claims unfair (constructive) dismissal. There is probably very little difficulty in showing a serious breach of contract by the employer here (though one cannot be sure of this without considering such factors as implied terms and employee adaptability: see **Chapter 5**). But, assuming that a serious breach can be shown, there is a constructive dismissal. We are also assuming that the employee qualifies to bring a claim for unfair dismissal in the first place otherwise all we are left with is a common law claim for wrongful repudiation.

Now, the next question is: was this dismissal unfair? The employer may claim business reorganisation as 'some other substantial reason' and this is not the most difficult hurdle to overcome. Thus it is quite likely that, although the change was a repudiation of the contract, and although the employee was contractually entitled to refuse to accept the alteration, any resulting dismissal may well not be unfair.

Your employee–client may well have difficulty accepting this point (along with some of the others noted above). Your employer–client may be equally surprised.

You can analyse a constructive (unfair) dismissal claim from either of two angles:

- you can use **Figure 11.1** to determine whether the resignation will count as a dismissal at all and then go on to examine whether, if it is a constructive dismissal, that dismissal was fair or unfair; or
- you can start with **Figure 12.1** and determine whether the employee qualifies for claiming unfair dismissal (because, if he does not all the rest is irrelevant), then go back to the analysis in **Figure 11.1** to consider whether the resignation is a constructive dismissal and return to **Figure 12.1** to look at fairness.

There is no one answer to which method to use but it is probably better to follow the first route because even if your client will not qualify to claim unfair dismissal he or she may still be able to bring a wrongful repudiation action (the test for wrongful repudiation and constructive dismissal being practically identical).

12.12 Industrial action

Under ERA 1996, s. 16 and sch. 5, the relevant provisions in TULRCA 1992, i.e., ss. 238–239, were amended and a new section (s. 238A) inserted. The dismissal of an employee *because* he or she is taking part in *official* (otherwise called 'protected') industrial action will be *automatically unfair* if:

(a) the dismissal takes place within the period of 12 weeks beginning with the day the employee started to take industrial action; or

(b) it takes place after the end of that period and the employee had stopped taking industrial action before the end of that period; or

(c) it takes place after the period, and though the employee had not stopped industrial action, the employer had not taken defined procedural steps (defined in s. 238A(6)) to resolve the dispute.

12.12.1 What is industrial action?

Industrial action may take many forms, including a strike, a work-to-rule, a go-slow, or an overtime ban. The question of what is and what is not industrial action in any particular set of circumstances is *a question of fact* for the employment tribunal. The action does not need to be in breach of contract: *Power Packing Casemakers Ltd* v *Faust* [1983] ICR 292. In this case the employees refused to work non-contractual overtime (so there could hardly be a breach) as part of wage bargaining tactics. What was present in *Faust,* however (and is generally required), is some pressure, some disruption of the employer's business for industrial relations reasons, e.g., pay demands. Rendering only partial performance of a contract as part of an industrial action campaign (i.e., 'we will do x but not y', when x and y are part of the contract) is still industrial action and the employee may lose some or even all of his pay, despite the partial performance.

Although there is no statutory definition of 'industrial action', 'strike' is defined in ERA 1996, s. 235(5) as '(a) the cessation of work by a body of employed persons acting in combination, or (b) a concerted refusal, or a refusal under a common understanding, of any number of employed persons to continue to work for an employer in consequence of a dispute . . .'. This must be done to compel the employer to accept the employees' view on bargaining positions or for showing sympathy with other workers. This definition has, however, been limited to determining continuity of employment; so essentially the definition of strike is also a question of fact.

12.12.2 What is 'taking part'?

This has proved to be a problem area as regards employees who are on holiday or sick when the action occurs, or who feel unable to go into work because they are afraid to cross picket lines.

It is vital to know who is 'taking part' because the employer must be careful (at least with official action once the protected period seen in **12.10** has passed) to treat all those taking part, at the moment that one participant is dismissed, in the same way. Thus an employer does not want later to discover that an employee was not dismissed along with others taking part in an official action, because this would mean that the employees who were dismissed would once again be able to claim unfair dismissal. The employer's ignorance is no defence and the employee's motives are also irrelevant: *Coates & Venables* v *Modern Methods & Materials Ltd* [1982] ICR 763. Again, participation is a question of fact.

The employer therefore has to be sure, before dismissing anyone, *which* employees are taking part. For to dismiss the relevant employees *but miss one* will be a fatal error; and to dismiss someone who *is not taking part* will mean that that individual will have a good claim for unfair dismissal. The burden lies on the employer. As regards those employees who are absent from the company (e.g., those on sick leave), the employer needs to ascertain by reasonable investigation whether they are *associated* with the action: *Hindle Gears Ltd* v *McGinty* [1985] ICR 111. However, it is permissible, where the action is causing massive disruption, for the employer to dismiss everyone with unauthorised absence first and then investigate afterwards. One point to note, however, is that if an employee originally took part in the industrial action and returned to work before any dismissals occurred, he or she is not participating at the relevant time. Any dismissal will have to be judged on ordinary principles of fairness.

12.12.3 Rules vary according to the type of action

Industrial action can be classed in a number of ways depending on whether a trade union has sanctioned the action. Thus, if a trade union supports the action it is referred to as '*official action*' and the employee gains certain protection from this tag. If a trade union does not support the action this is called '*unofficial action*' and the industrial action is not protected. Industrial action will be unofficial *unless:*

(a) the employee is a union member and the action has been authorised or endorsed by the union; or

(b) although the employee is not a union member, some of those taking part are and the action has been authorised or endorsed by the union (see TULRCA 1992, s. 237).

An employee who is dismissed whilst taking part in *unofficial action* has no right to complain of unfair dismissal even if others are not dismissed: TULRCA 1992, s. 237 (but note s. 238A: there is a day's grace allowed if the action was official and then was repudiated by the union).

Where none of the participants is a union member the action is sometimes called '*not unofficial action*'. This means that it is not protected action within s. 238A, but is covered by s. 238 which, broadly, allows the employee to claim unfair dismissal if all those taking part were not treated the same by the employer.

12.13 Action short of dismissal

Before we turn to the remedies for unfair dismissal we should note that, in certain cases where an employee has action taken against him short of dismissal he will gain rights to obtain a declaration against the employer or compensation. The aim here is that where an employee has sought to enforce rights under the contract and is then subjected to a detriment by the employer as a result of this but is not dismissed, he should have some right of recourse against the employer. We will not cover all the detailed provisions here, but, in outline, the grounds contained in Part V, ERA 1996 (ss. 44–49) are:

(a) cases where the employer has carried out activities in connexion with health and safety matters (s. 44);

(b) cases where the employee has refused to work on Sundays (s. 45);

(c) cases involving the working time regulations (s. 45A);

(d) cases concerning the actions of trustee of occupational pension schemes (s. 46);

(e) cases concerning employees acting as employee representatives under TULRCA 1992 (s. 47);

(f) cases where employees have sought to enforce rights relating to trade union activities or membership (TULRCA 1992, s. 146 as amended);

(g) cases involving employees who have sought time off in certain defined circumstances (s. 47A);

(h) cases where employees have made protected disclosures (s. 47B);

(i) cases where employees have sought leave for family and domestic reasons (s. 47C);

(j) cases involving employees seeking to enforce tax credits rights (s. 47D); and

(k) cases involving applications for flexible working (s. 47E).

The remedies for such actions are set out in ERA 1996, s. 49. Awards may be made that include a sum for injury to feelings (akin to discrimination claims and using the *Vento* guidelines applied in such cases—see **Chapter 6**): *Virgo Fidelis Senior School* v *Boyle* [2004] IRLR 268 (a case of disciplinary action being taken by the school against a teacher following a protected disclosure).

12.14 Other methods of dispute resolution

12.14.1 Settlements and conciliation

Many cases are settled before the hearing. Any settlement concluded through an ACAS officer, reached orally or in writing, is binding on the parties. An ACAS officer is always given the employee's ET 1 (the equivalent to a statement of claim) and the employer's ET 3 (the defence). The officer will then seek to conclude a settlement between the parties.

A settlement can be reached at any stage in the proceedings. Settlements through ACAS are usually put down in writing on a form known as a COT 3.

For years this was the only way to ensure that a settlement was binding on the parties. However, under ERA 1996, s. 203(2)(f) and (3) the parties may now reach their own binding compromise agreement. In outline:

(a) the agreement must be in writing;

(b) it must relate to the particular complaint;

(c) the employee must have received advice from a relevant independent adviser; and

(d) the employee's adviser must be insured or have indemnity provided for members of a profession or professional body.

The issue of settlements and the considerations involved are dealt with more fully in **Chapter 16**.

12.14.2 ACAS arbitration scheme

In May 2001, a voluntary arbitration scheme was introduced under the auspices of ACAS as an alternative to going to an employment tribunal for dealing with simple unfair dismissal disputes. It was designed to relieve some of the workload of tribunals. The scheme is limited in its form and only applies to cases of alleged unfair dismissal or claims under flexible working legislation. Even then, ACAS also strongly recommends that questions of EU law are left to employment tribunals. Both parties must agree, in writing, to go to arbitration and this agreement contains certain waivers, e.g., a very limited right of appeal against the arbitrator's decision. The ACAS arbitrator may conduct proceedings anywhere (e.g., at the workplace), those proceedings are held in private, no oath is administered, the arbitrator will take a strong inquisitorial role, and the matter will be decided on general grounds of fairness, not the rules developed under unfair dismissal case law (e.g., the range of reasonable responses test). Once both parties have signed an agreement to go to arbitration under the Scheme, an employment tribunal can no longer hear the claim.

A full description of the scheme can be found at www.acas.org.uk. The Arbitration Act 1996 does not apply to this scheme.

12.15 Summary

We provided an overview of unfair dismissal actions at the beginning of **Chapter 11** and summary points relating to the definition of dismissal and what constitutes a fair reason for dismissal at the end of that chapter. This summary provides additional points which focus on 'fairness'.

- Unfair dismissal actions depend first on establishing a 'dismissal'. Constructive dismissal is not a cause of action in itself. If a constructive dismissal is proven the tribunal must still decide whether the dismissal was fair in all the circumstances.
- If the employer has shown a fair reason the burden of proof is neutral as to whether this reason was handled fairly. However, most of the evidence tends to be in the employer's possession and, in a tribunal action, it is the employer who usually goes first. The legal burden may not be on the employer, but the reality is that the employer has to demonstrate: (i) that the employer utilised a fair procedure; and (ii) that the decision to dismiss fell within the range of reasonable responses open to a reasonable employer.
- Many, if not most, successful unfair dismissal claims centre on the employer's failure in conducting a fair procedure.
- Compulsory retirement dismissals are treated differently from the other fair reasons in as much as they have their own prescribed procedures both for determining the existence of a fair reason and the question of fairness.
- Some reasons for dismissal are classed as automatically unfair; the list is extensive.
- If a tribunal finds that an employee has been unfairly dismissed it may order reinstatement or re-engagement, but this rarely occurs so the most commonly used remedy is that of compensation. Whereas the basic award depends entirely upon a fixed formula relating to length of service (subject to deductions), the compensatory award focuses on what has been lost up to the date of the hearing and what is the likely projected loss. The touchstone is a 'just and equitable amount'. This, too, is subject to deductions.

13

Remedies for unfair dismissal

In this chapter we consider the remedies available in unfair dismissal cases. At the end of the chapter we will go through a worked example of assessing compensation.

13.1 The range of remedies available

13.1.1 Reinstatement

Reinstatement means to be put back in the same job with compensation for loss between dismissal and reinstatement. If reinstatement is requested by the employee the employer can refuse to reinstate only where it is reasonable to do so, e.g., where the mutual trust and confidence has been shattered. The employee is not obliged to request reinstatement, nor is the tribunal bound by any request. Indeed, the employee can have a change of mind at any time. However, tactically some employees request reinstatement (although they do not really want it) because a refusal *may* increase the amount of compensation. This tactic can also backfire.

An unreasonable refusal by the employer to reinstate where it would have been practicable to do so may lead to an *additional award* being given in addition to the *basic award* and the *compensatory award* (see below). Though reinstatement is the primary remedy (as emphasised in *Polkey* v *A. E. Dayton Services Ltd* [1987] AC 344), it has traditionally occurred in fewer than 2 per cent of cases.

13.1.2 Re-engagement

This consists of returning the employee to a similar job or to a job with an associated employer. Re-engagement is subject to the same tests as reinstatement.

13.1.3 Compensation

The two main elements are the basic award and compensatory award. They are assessed on quite different grounds which are discussed in detail below. The figures which form the basis for calculating these awards are now changed annually according to the Retail Price Index changes for September of each year (see ERA 1999, s. 34) and are usually brought into effect in the following February (at the time of writing we do not know whether this index will share the fate of other government-based calculations, such as state pensions, and be changed to the lower consumer prices index instead of the RPI—a difference of over 1.5 per cent at the time of writing). The principles for assessing compensation are set out in ERA 1996, ss. 118–126 (as amended).

The figure of a 'week's pay' described below is presently £380. It is next due for adjustment in February 2011.

13.1.4 The additional award

Where a tribunal has ordered reinstatement or re-engagement (generally referred to here as re-employment) and the employer has not complied with this the tribunal must make an additional award, unless the tribunal is satisfied that it was not practicable to comply with the order. Where the employer has unreasonably refused to re-employ the employee an additional award of 26–52 weeks' pay on top of the basic and compensatory awards can be ordered by the employment tribunal (ERA 1996, s. 117(3)(b) as amended by ERA 1999, s. 33(2)).

13.1.5 Interim relief

Under ERA 1996, s. 128, employees who have been dismissed may apply for 'interim relief' in a limited number of cases. The claim must be presented before the end of the period of seven days immediately following the EDT. Where the tribunal finds that it is likely that on final determination the tribunal will find that the reason for dismissal falls within:

- s. 100(1)(a) or (b) ERA 1996—health and safety-related dismissal;
- s. 101A(d)—working time-related dismissal;
- s. 102(1)—occupational pension scheme trustee-related dismissal;
- s. 103—employee representative-related dismissal;
- s. 103A—protected disclosure-related dismissal; or
- para. 161(2) sch. A1, TULRCA 1992—trade union membership and activities-related dismissal,

it may order continuance of the contract or, ultimately, award compensation. Interim relief actions are not common.

13.2 Assessing the basic award

This is calculated on length of service. It is a fixed formula. When a client asks how much he or she will get or have to pay in an unfair dismissal case, this is the one figure that provides some level of certainty. The formulation is set out in ERA 1996, s. 119(2). It is almost identical to the redundancy entitlement.

CALCULATION:	[AGE factor] × [SERVICE] × [WEEK'S PAY]
AGE:	For any service where the employee was 41 or over the factor is 1.5
	For any service between the ages of 22 and 41 the factor is 1
	For any service below the age of 22 the factor is 0.5
SERVICE:	Subject to a maximum of 20 years
WEEK'S PAY:	Subject to a maximum of £380 per week

The maximum basic award is therefore £11,400 i.e., 1.5 × 20 × 380.

The method of calculating this can be seen in the following examples.

EXAMPLE 1

An employee is aged 56 at the time of dismissal and has 10 years' service with the company (only complete years can count). He earns £450 per week. To calculate the basic award you must take the length of service as at the EDT and count back from the employee's present age to see how many years of service fall into each age bracket. This tells you that here all the years of service fall within the age bracket of 'over 41'. Therefore the factor for each of these years will be 1.5. As the employee earns more than the maximum 'week's pay' he is limited to the £380. Thus 1.5 × 10 years × £380 gives a figure of £5,700 (i.e., 15 × £380).

EXAMPLE 2

Where the employee's years of service straddle two of the age brackets the computation becomes more difficult. If we take the same employee but change his age to 46 the method of calculation becomes: (1.5 × 5 years) plus (1 × 5 years) × £380 giving a figure of £4,750 (i.e., 12.5 × £380). This is because five years of his service fall within the age bracket of '41 or over' and are given a multiple of 1.5, but the remainder fall within the age bracket '22–41' and are only given a multiple of 1.

The Department for Business, Innovation and Skills (formerly the Department for Business, Enterprise & Regulatory Reform (BERR)) issues a 'ready reckoner' for calculating these figures (called a PL808). **Figure 13.1**, derived from the PL808, shows the calculations for unfair dismissal. We have taken 16 as the start date as this is the 'school-leaving age'.

13.2.1 Minimum basic award

Under ERA 1996, s. 120(1) a minimum basic award of £4,700 will be made where the reason for dismissal is one specified in ERA 1996, ss. 100(1)(a) and (b), 101A(d), 102(1), or 103 (see **13.1.5** above for what these relate to).

13.2.2 Minimum basic award and certain redundancy cases

In some cases (detailed in ERA 1996, ss. 138 and 141) an employee may be made redundant but be offered re-engagement immediately or soon after dismissal. There are detailed rules as to whether a refusal by the employee to be re-engaged destroys his right to claim redundancy pay. Section 121 ERA 1996 sets out an employee's rights to a minimum basic award in such instances.

13.2.3 Reductions in the basic award

The situations where a tribunal may reduce the basic award are listed in **13.4** below and are dealt with in ERA 1996, s. 122.

Service (years)	1	2	3	4	5	6	7	8	9	10	11	12	13	14	15	16	17	18	19	20
Age (years)																				
17	½																			
18	½	1																		
19	½	1	1½																	
20	½	1	1½	2																
21	½	1	2	2½	3															
22	½	1	1½	2½	2½	3														
23	1	1½	2	2½	3	3½	4													
24	1	2	2½	3	3½	4	4½	5												
25	1	2	3	3½	4	4½	5	5½	6											
26	1	2	3	4	4½	5	5½	6	6½	7										
27	1	2	3	4	5	5½	6	6½	7	7½	8									
28	1	2	3	4	5	6	6½	7	7½	8	8½	9								
29	1	2	3	4	5	6	7	7½	8	8½	9	9½	10							
30	1	2	3	4	5	6	7	8	8½	9	9½	10	10½	11						
31	1	2	3	4	5	6	7	8	9	9½	10	10½	11	11½	12					
32	1	2	3	4	5	6	7	8	9	10	10½	11	11½	12	12½	13				
33	1	2	3	4	5	6	7	8	9	10	11	11½	12	12½	13	13½	14			
34	1	2	3	4	5	6	7	8	9	10	11	12	12½	13	13½	14	14½	15		
35	1	2	3	4	5	6	7	8	9	10	11	12	13	13½	14	14½	15	15½	16	
36	1	2	3	4	5	6	7	8	9	10	11	12	13	14	14½	15	15½	16	16½	17
37	1	2	3	4	5	6	7	8	9	10	11	12	13	14	15	15½	16	16½	17	17½
38	1	2	3	4	5	6	7	8	9	10	11	12	13	14	15	16	16½	17	17½	18
39	1	2	3	4	5	6	7	8	9	10	11	12	13	14	15	16	17	17½	18	18½
40	1	2	3	4	5	6	7	8	9	10	11	12	13	14	15	16	17	18	18½	19
41	1	2	3	4	5	6	7	8	9	10	11	12	13	14	15	16	17	18	19	19½
42	1½	2½	3½	4½	5½	6½	7½	8½	9½	10½	11½	12½	13½	14½	15½	16½	17½	18½	19½	20½
43	1½	3	4	5	6	7	8	9	10	11	12	13	14	15	16	17	18	19	20	21
44	1½	3	4½	5½	6½	7½	8½	9½	10½	11½	12½	13½	14½	15½	16½	17½	18½	19½	20½	21½
45	1½	3	4½	6	7	8	9	10	11	12	13	14	15	16	17	18	19	20	21	22
46	1½	3	4½	6	7½	8½	9½	10½	11½	12½	13½	14½	15½	16½	17½	18½	19½	20½	21½	22½
47	1½	3	4½	6	7½	9	10	11	12	13	14	15	16	17	18	19	20	21	22	23
48	1½	3	4½	6	7½	9	10½	11½	12½	13½	14½	15½	16½	17½	18½	19½	20½	21½	22½	23½
49	1½	3	4½	6	7½	9	10½	12	13	14	15	16	17	18	19	20	21	22	23	24
50	1½	3	4½	6	7½	9	10½	12	13½	14½	15½	16½	17½	18½	19½	20½	21½	22½	23½	24½
51	1½	3	4½	6	7½	9	10½	12	13½	15	16	17	18	19	20	21	22	23	24	25
52	1½	3	4½	6	7½	9	10½	12	13½	15	16½	17½	18½	19½	20½	21½	22½	23½	24½	25½
53	1½	3	4½	6	7½	9	10½	12	13½	15	16½	18	19	20	21	22	23	24	25	26
54	1½	3	4½	6	7½	9	10½	12	13½	15	16½	18	19½	20½	21½	22½	23½	24½	25½	26½
55	1½	3	4½	6	7½	9	10½	12	13½	15	16½	18	19½	21	22	23	24	25	26	27
56	1½	3	4½	6	7½	9	10½	12	13½	15	16½	18	19½	21	22½	23½	24½	25½	26½	27½
57	1½	3	4½	6	7½	9	10½	12	13½	15	16½	18	19½	21	22½	24	25	26	27	28
58	1½	3	4½	6	7½	9	10½	12	13½	15	16½	18	19½	21	22½	24	25½	26½	27½	28½
59	1½	3	4½	6	7½	9	10½	12	13½	15	16½	18	19½	21	22½	24	25½	27	28	29
60	1½	3	4½	6	7½	9	10½	12	13½	15	16½	18	19½	21	22½	24	25½	27	28½	29½
61 and above	1½	3	4½	6	7½	9	10½	12	13½	15	16½	18	19½	21	22½	24	25½	27	28½	30

Figure 13.1 Calculating the basic award (adapted from PL808 (rev 6)).
Note: If the employee earns less than £380 per week it is that lower figure that will be used in the calculation, subject to the national minimum wage rate as described in **4.2** above: *Pagetti* v *Cobb* [2002] Emp LR 651.

13.3 Assessing the compensatory award

The method of calculation is set out in ERA 1996, s. 123. Compensation is based on what is 'just and equitable in all the circumstances having regard to the loss sustained by the complainant in consequence of the dismissal' and the tribunal must be satisfied that there was a causal link between the dismissal and the loss suffered: *Simrad Ltd* v *Scott* [1997] IRLR 147. It is calculated on *net* payments.

The maximum compensatory award is £65,300 (see ERA 1996, s. 124).

Tribunals have long used one leading case as the basis for calculating the compensatory award: *Norton Tool Co. Ltd* v *Tewson* [1973] 1 All ER 183.

We have noted above that discrimination claims (e.g., sex or race) are not subject to any 'capping' of compensation. Section 37, ERA 1999, lists the following reasons for an unfair dismissal as also not being subject to any cap:

- a dismissal falling under the 'whistleblower' provisions of the Public Interest Disclosure Act 1998 and ERA 1996, s. 103A;
- a dismissal falling under ERA 1996, ss. 100 and 105(3) (automatically unfair dismissal where the reason relates to health and safety).

A selection for redundancy based on these reasons will also be automatically unfair and not subject to capping.

13.3.1 The *Norton Tool* principles

Under the principles enunciated in *Norton Tool,* certain general principles for calculating loss have been laid down. These include the following headings:

- immediate loss of wages;
- future loss of wages;
- loss of fringe benefits;
- the manner of dismissal;
- loss of statutory employment protection rights;
- loss of pension rights.

13.3.1.1 Immediate loss of wages

This heading deals with loss dating from the EDT to the date of hearing. This normally is an easy calculation. If notice or payment in lieu of notice has been given, the employee's loss will date from the expiry of that period worked or the period covered by the payment. The corollary to this is that, if notice has not been given, loss flows from the date of dismissal (in effect compensating the employee for not receiving a notice payment).

The following special cases should be noted:

- Section 123(4) ERA 1996 states that, in assessing loss, 'the tribunal shall apply the same rule concerning the duty of a person to mitigate his loss as applies to damages recoverable at common law . . .'. Thus, if the employee obtains a new job at a lower rate of pay before the tribunal hearing the amount received will be deducted from this heading of loss. Equally, if the employee does not do all that is expected to mitigate loss, a sum will be deducted.
- There must be proof of loss. If an employee is unfit to work in the period following dismissal there is an argument that there was no loss of earnings during that time. In *Dignity Funerals Ltd* v *Bruce* [2005] IRLR 189, the Court of Session (Inner House) accepted this idea but held that if the dismissal was a cause of the inability to work (in this case psychiatric illness) then an award, in full or in part, was still due (and see *Burlo* v *Langley* below).

- Where the employee obtains a new job which pays better than the old one the EAT settled (after long debate) in *Whelan* v *Richardson* [1998] IRLR 114 for a method of taking account the payment but not penalising the employee further, if the payment exceeded the loss for this period, by continuing to deduct the excess from the award of compensation.
- Certain social security payments have to be accounted for. If the employee receives benefits between the EDT and the hearing, including incapacity benefit in most cases (*Morgans* v *Alpha Plus Security Ltd* [2005] IRLR 234, EAT) but excluding income support and housing benefits, then these sums are treated in a special way. The tribunal must formally identify the loss for the period between dismissal and hearing (after deductions have been made) in its judgment. That sum (known as the 'prescribed element') is then withheld until the Department for Work and Pensions has determined how much it wishes to reclaim under the Employment Protection (Recoupment of Jobseeker's Allowance and Income Support) Regulations 1996 (SI 1996/2349). Once the recoupment figure is known the excess (if any) is paid to the employee.

  The slightly vague phrase above, 'in most cases', regarding incapacity benefit is there because in some cases a person may receive incapacity benefit but still be able to work (e.g., wheelchair users). In such cases it would be inappropriate not to award compensation because of this payment: *Sheffield Forgemasters International Ltd* v *Fox* [2009] IRLR 192.

13.3.1.2 Immediate loss and the notice period

Here we ask: what happens where the employee has not been given some or all of his due notice and has found a new job during that time? Is the notice period (or at least the statutory minimum) to be regarded as sacrosanct (e.g., as a debt) and so not subject to mitigation, or should this period be treated like any other claim in damages and any sum received set off against the notice due? *Norton Tool* suggested that it was good industrial practice not to apply the rules of mitigation to the notice period, or at least to what is now the s. 86 minimum notice entitlement. So, you would be forgiven for thinking that this problem should have been sorted out, but it has not: there has been over 30 years of debate. In *Babcock FATA Ltd v Addison* [1987] ICR 805 the Court of Appeal endorsed the *Norton* Tool approach but held that an employee who had received a *payment in lieu of notice* could not claim that sum again as part of any unfair dismissal compensation—there was no loss for that period to compensate. In *Burlo* v *Langley* [2006] EWCA Civ 1778, [2007] ICR 390 the Court of Appeal again held that the *Norton Tool* principle survives but decided that if an employee is dismissed without notice or payment in lieu of notice but was sick during the period when notice would have run then her loss was the sick pay she should have received and not her full wages for that period. Thus the amount attributed to that notice period in any unfair dismissal compensation should be limited to that payment she would have received had she worked through her notice.

Section 123(4) ERA 1996 clearly requires tribunals to take into account the rules of mitigation of loss in awarding compensation, but at the moment we have the *Norton Tool* principle which effectively disapplies this as both regards overt and constructive dismissals for reasons of 'good industrial relations practice'—accompanied only by some particular exceptions to that principle.

13.3.1.3 Future loss of wages

This involves a degree of informed guess-work. The tribunal will need to establish how long the applicant is likely to be unemployed, what are the employee's attributes and skills, what the market is for such skills, and whether he or she might have been dismissed for redundancy anyway in the near future. The tribunal will therefore seek to make an award relating to the employee *as an individual,* so that similarly-aged employees dismissed at the same time might still receive different compensations. The award is discretionary.

If the employee has already found another permanent job which is better paid there will probably be no loss under this heading; if less well paid, the tribunal will have to judge when (if at all) the equivalent payment will be reached. These general statements are subject to the points made above in *Whelan* v *Richardson,* and also to those made by the Court of Appeal in *Dench* v *Flynn & Partners* [1998] IRLR 653. Here, an employee had been dismissed, had lodged a claim for unfair dismissal and then taken up new permanent employment, but within two months of starting had then terminated that employment. The question was whether, once the employee took up the (eventually aborted) permanent position, that event marked the end of the period for which she could claim compensation from her original employer.

The Court of Appeal said that the question for the tribunal is whether the unfair dismissal can be regarded as a continuing course of loss when the employee is subsequently dismissed by her new employer with no right to compensation after a month or two in her new employment. Logic, if not sympathy, indicates that the chain of causation has been broken but the Court held that it might not be: tribunals must assess as a question of fact what is a just and equitable compensation and in doing so they must determine *why* the new employment did not last. If there was good reason why it did not last (e.g., where the new job might only last for the probation period—and did), its presence does not in itself break the chain of causation between dismissal and loss.

Cases such as *Leonard* v *Strathclyde Buses Ltd* [1998] IRLR 693 have made it clear that the test for causation should be one of applying common sense—what are the natural and direct consequences of the dismissal?—rather than intricate legal arguments on remoteness. Nevertheless, the reasonableness of the dismissed employee's actions subsequent to dismissal will come under scrutiny. Thus, for instance, what should be the position where an employee's response to dismissal is to set up in business (which will have a major lead-in period before profits can be made) or decides to go to university to increase his or her marketability? Should the immediate financial loss which results from these decisions still be attributable to the employer's actions? The latter example was seen in *Khanum* v *IBC Vehicles Ltd* (2000, unreported) where an obviously progressive employer dismissed Khanum for attending an open day at a university. She had great difficulty in finding another job—there was evidence she had been blacklisted—and, after 10 months, enrolled on a university degree course. It was accepted in evidence that, given the job market, this was a reasonable course of action and the chain of causation remained unbroken (unlike the earlier case of *Simrad Ltd* v *Scott* [1997] IRLR 147 where a decision to retrain was a matter of choice rather than need).

13.3.1.4 Loss of fringe benefits

These can be included: for example, company cars or accommodation or even the difference in value between shares sold back to the company by the employee on termination (at the then market value) and the new market value of those shares at the date of the hearing.

13.3.1.5 The manner of dismissal

In *Johnson* v *Unisys Ltd* [2001] UKHL 13, [2001] ICR 480 the House of Lords rejected a claim in contract for damages for injury to feeling arising *from the manner of dismissal.* In doing so, Lord Hoffmann contemplated (unfortunately, out loud) whether, instead, an employment tribunal might be able to compensate for injury to feelings in an unfair dismissal action. This was news to employment lawyers but sparked a raft of cases where this was pleaded. In turn this led to the House of Lords (including Lord Hoffmann) holding that Lord Hoffmann's words were *obiter*: *Dunnachie* v *Kingston upon Hull City Council* [2004] UKHL 36, [2004] 3 WLR 310. Further, the natural meaning of the word 'loss' in s. 123 of ERA 1996 did not admit damages for injury to feelings or psychiatric injury as part of unfair dismissal compensation.

We should note three things here:

- compensation in discrimination actions *can* include an award for injury to feelings;
- an award for injury to feelings can be made in relation to an action short of dismissal (see *Virgo Fidelis Senior School* v *Boyle* above);
- damages can be awarded for injury to feelings where the cause of action accrues before dismissal (see the joined cases of *Eastwood* v *Magnox Electric plc* and *McCabe* v *Cornwall County Council* [2004] UKHL 35, [2004] 3 WLR 322 above—which consisted of the same House of Lords' panel as in *Dunnachie*).

13.3.1.6 Loss of statutory employment protection rights

When an employee starts a new job he or she will generally have to work for one year before any unfair dismissal rights accrue. This heading provides some compensation for that loss, although the figure is nominal (usually about £300). Tribunals may also award compensation for loss of ERA 1996, s. 86 statutory notice rights (usually assessed at half the employee's statutory entitlement, e.g., four weeks for eight years' service).

13.3.1.7 Loss of pension rights

The losses under this heading can be very high. Odd then, you may think, that the exact principles for determining loss have never really been worked out. One document which seeks to provide help here is *Compensation for loss of pension rights—Employment Tribunals (2003)*, produced by a committee of Employment Tribunal chairmen and the Government Actuary. This sets out two alternative methods of calculating loss: (i) the simplified approach (essentially the sum of the contributions an employer would have made but for the dismissal); and (ii) substantial loss approach (which involves the use of actuarial tables). This is what is said on the two approaches:

> Section 4.11. *The simplified approach* ... involves three stages (a) in the case of a final salary scheme, the loss of the enhancement to the pension already accrued because of the increase of salary which would have occurred had the applicant not been dismissed, (b) in all cases, the loss of rights accruing up to the hearing and (c) the loss of future pension rights. These last two elements are calculated on the assumption that the contribution made by the employer to the fund during the period will equate to the value of the pension (attributable to the employer) that would have accrued. In the case of a final salary scheme, it may be necessary to make an adjustment to the employer's contribution as discussed in section 6.5. No such adjustment is necessary in the case of a money purchase scheme because the scheme is personal to the employee.
>
> 4.13. *The substantial loss approach,* by contrast, uses actuarial tables comparable to the Ogden Tables to assess the current capitalized value of the pension rights which would have accrued up to retirement. There may be cases where the Tribunal decides that a person will return to a job at a comparable salary, but will never get a comparable pension . . . . In such cases the substantial loss approach may be needed even where the future loss of earnings is for such a short period. But it must be remembered that loss of pension rights

is the loss of a fringe benefit and may be compensated by an increase in salary in new employment.

The EAT bravely waded into this quagmire in *Greenhoff* v *Barnsley Metropolitan Borough Council* [2006] ICR 1514. The steps recommended (in this sequence) involve a tribunal:

(a) identifying all possible benefits that the employee could obtain under the pension scheme;

(b) setting out the terms of the pension relevant to each possible benefit;

(c) considering in respect of each such possible benefit first the advantages and disadvantages of applying what we have described as 'the simplified approach' or 'the substantial loss approach' and also any other approach that might be considered appropriate by the Tribunal or by the parties;

(d) explaining why they have adopted a particular approach and rejected any other possible approach; and

(e) setting out their conclusions and explaining the compensation they have arrived at in respect of each head of claim so that the parties and this Appeal Tribunal can then ascertain if they had made an error.

An employee who draws a pension early following a dismissal does not have to offset this money against any unfair dismissal compensation: *Knapton* v *ECC Card Clothing Ltd* [2006] ICR 1084 (EAT). Equally, where an employee is unfairly dismissed but finds a new job quickly there may still be a large sum due in respect of pensions' loss (e.g., where the employee was in a 'final salary' scheme and now has to join a less advantageous one).

13.3.2 Increased compensation

A tribunal may increase an award by no more than 25 per cent where the employer fails to comply with a statutory code and that failure was unreasonable. As we have noted above, ACAS has issued a statutory code to cover discipline, dismissal and grievance practices.

Section 3(2) Employment Act 2008 (EA 2008) inserts a new s. 207A to TULRA 1992 to achieve this. This section 'applies to proceedings before an employment tribunal relating to a claim by an employee under any of the jurisdictions listed in Schedule A2'. This schedule lists claims such as unfair dismissal and redundancy but also includes claims relating to equal pay, discrimination, the national minimum wage and other more technical areas of employment law. So, an employee bringing a claim for discrimination who demonstrates that the employer has failed to follow, say, a proper grievance procedure, may be entitled to an uplift in any compensation.

More particularly here, this is where an employer who has ignored proper procedures in dismissing an employee will find that the tribunal has a discretion to increase the compensation payable.

We should also repeat at this stage the point made back at **3.5.3** that another, different, adjustment may be made: ERA 1996, s. 124A (inserted by EA 2002, s. 39) states that, where an award of compensation for unfair dismissal falls to be increased under s. 38 EA 2002 (failure to give statement of employment particulars), the adjustment shall be in the amount awarded under ERA 1996, s. 118(1)(b) (the compensatory award) and shall be applied immediately before any reduction under s. 123(6) or (7) (contributory fault on the part of the employee).

13.4 Deductions from the overall award

Deductions may be made from both the basic award and compensatory award figures. These deductions are generally at the discretion of the tribunal. In the summary chart below you will see that there are a number of reasons why deductions can be made.

The new s. 207A of TURCA 1992 described immediately above also allows for a tribunal to reduce any award of compensation by no more than 25 per cent where an ACAS Code applies and the employee has failed unreasonably to comply with that code (e.g., did not take full advantage of the grievance procedures). Section 124A ERA 1996 states that, where an award of compensation for unfair dismissal falls to be reduced the adjustment shall be in the amount awarded under ERA 1996, s. 118(1)(b) (the compensatory award) and shall be applied immediately before any reduction under s. 123(6) or (7) (contributory fault on the part of the employee).

13.4.1 The *Polkey* reduction

Where a tribunal finds that a dismissal was unfair it may still reduce the award payable by any amount if it is convinced that, had the employer followed the correct procedures it was likely that the dismissal would have been fair. So, if the tribunal thinks it was only a matter of time before the employee would have been dismissed (usually for a different and fair reason) or there was only a minor defect in the procedures used and had this been corrected the employee would have been dismissed fairly it will make a finding of unfair dismissal but only award compensation to reflect this 'lost time' or minor defect.

Because this is an exercise in speculation the tribunal will require evidence to work on (e.g., of future risk to that person's job or to the industry as a whole) but the fact that there are uncertainties does not mean a tribunal should avoid the question: *Scope* v *Thornett* [2006] EWCA Civ 1600, [2007] ICR 236.

You will note from the table at **13.4.2** below that any *Polkey* reductions are taken only from the compensatory award. We should also note some key questions as regards *Polkey*:

- Does the *Polkey* reduction apply only to 'procedural' defects? The answer is 'no', though practically this will have to be the source for most such arguments: see, for example, *Lambe* v *186K Ltd* [2004] EWCA Civ 1045, [2005] ICR 307.
- Compensation should still be awarded if the evidence shows the employer *would not* have dismissed, even if he *could* in fact fairly have dismissed (see the Court of Appeal decision in *Trico-Folberth Ltd* v *Devonshire* [1989] ICR 747).
- Some processes adopted by the employer can be *so* unfair or so fundamentally flawed that it is impossible to formulate the hypothetical question of what percentage chance the employee had of still being dismissed even if the correct procedure had been followed: *Davidson* v *Industrial & Marine Engineering Services Ltd* (EAT) (unreported, EATS/0071/03) 24 March 2004 (on redundancy procedures).

13.4.2 The types of deductions made

Deductions from the basic award	*Deductions from the compensatory award*
(i) Any amount for an unreasonable refusal on the employee's part to be reinstated.	(i) Recoupment of benefits including some part of sickness and invalidity benefits.
(ii) Any amount for conduct before dismissal whenever discovered. There need be no causal link with the dismissal.	(ii) Mitigation, as with ordinary contractual principles.

(iii) Any amount for contributory fault.	(iii) Any contractual redundancy payments which are in excess of the statutory scheme.
(iv) Any statutory redundancy payments already made, but only if the dismissal is for redundancy.	(iv) Any *ex gratia* payments.
	(v) Any contributory fault.
	(vi) No more than 25 per cent of the award (under s. 207A of TULRCA 1992).
	(vii) An amount representing the likelihood that the employee would have been dismissed sometime in the future anyway (e.g., for redundancy)—the *Polkey* reduction.

The basic award is not reduced for a failure to mitigate loss, even where the employee has not actually suffered any financial loss (e.g., on getting a new and better paid job immediately). Also, it should be noted that, even where the tribunal has made a finding of contributory fault on the part of the employee and reduced the compensatory award by a discretionary percentage, it still has a discretion whether to reduce the basic award as well, and may (because the two awards rest on different principles) legitimately decline to do so: *Optikinetics Ltd* v *Whooley* [1999] ICR 984.

Where an employer has reached a settlement on compensation with the employee, or has made an *ex gratia* payment, it is advisable that the ambit of either payment is made clear. If the payment or settlement is not expressed to cover the basic award as well as the compensatory award, there is a danger that the employee will still be entitled to the full basic award (see *Chelsea Football Club and Athletic Co. Ltd* v *Heath* [1981] ICR 323).

The next question is: at what point are the deductions made?

13.4.3 Order of making deductions

The basic award calculation is relatively straightforward, even when deductions are involved. With compensatory award calculations, however, tribunals have to estimate the employee's actual loss and attempt to award a 'just and equitable sum' on the facts. The exercise of discretion thus brings with it obvious problems. What is not so obvious at first glance is the importance of deciding in which order to make any deductions.

The order in which one applies percentage reductions (e.g., for contributory fault or failure to mitigate) may mean that vastly different figures are reached depending upon that order. For instance, say an employee is earning £20,000 net per annum and is dismissed. The tribunal finds an element of contributory fault to the extent that the employee was 50 per cent to blame for the dismissal. The employee has mitigated his loss by immediately finding a new job but it only pays £10,000 net. Ignoring basic award etc., what is the loss? If you apply the percentage reduction first, you get: (i) 50 per cent of £20,000 = £10,000; then (ii) deduct the £10,000 earned, as mitigation—leaving you with no loss. But if you deduct the mitigation amount first (£20,000 less £10,000), this leaves £10,000; apply the 50 per cent reduction and you have £5,000 per annum loss.

The cases in this area have been all over the place because the tribunals and courts have been in disagreement as to what elements go to calculating *the actual loss suffered as a result of the dismissal* and what factors go to *reducing loss,* e.g., if an employer makes an *ex gratia* payment to the dismissed employee, does that reduce the actual loss suffered or should you calculate loss and then take away the *ex gratia* payment made? As with the simple example above, the answer can make a big difference.

The conflict in the case law has thankfully been simplified by a line of cases starting with the decision of the Court of Session in *Heggie* v *Uniroyal Englebert Tyres Ltd* [1999] IRLR 802. These cases, together with all the comments on deductions in the text above give us the list below for determining the order for making deductions. We start with the general rule that any percentage reductions should be made after straightforward cash deductions have been implemented and that the last thing to apply is the statutory cap on compensation (presently £65,300). The only exception to this rule is where the dismissal was for redundancy and the employer has already paid a contractual redundancy payment that is greater than the statutory maximum (presently £11,400)—this is a 'cash' payment but ranks as the second last item. So, the order is:

- deduct any payment already made (e.g., *ex gratia* or *payment in lieu)* other than a contractual redundancy payment;
- make deductions relating to mitigation or for failure to mitigate;
- make any *Polkey* reduction;
- adjust in favour of either party up to 25 per cent for failure to follow the ACAS Code;
- make any reduction for contributory fault;
- deduct any contractual redundancy payment to the extent that it exceeds the basic award;
- apply the statutory cap.

A word of warning based on experience: tribunals in different regions often apply their own methods of calculating the order of deductions.

13.5 The overlap between unfair dismissal and wrongful dismissal

We noted at the start of **Chapter 11** that it is quite possible to have the following combinations:

(a) a dismissal which is unfair but which is not wrongful;

(b) a dismissal which is wrongful but which is not unfair;

(c) a dismissal which is both unfair and wrongful;

(d) a dismissal which is neither unfair nor wrongful.

This overlap often causes confusion to those new to the area. The following points are therefore repeated by way of guidance.

13.5.1 Jurisdiction overlap

Employment tribunals have sole jurisdiction to deal with statutory rights such as unfair dismissal and redundancy pay claims. However, in cases such as wrongful dismissal and wrongful repudiation an applicant may choose whether to pursue these claims in the ordinary courts or in an employment tribunal under ETA 1996, s. 3. Employees may pursue actions for wrongful dismissal etc. in a tribunal even though they are not claiming unfair dismissal or redundancy payments.

In the ordinary courts there is no limit to a claim for breach of contract. By contrast, any claim for contractual damages in a tribunal is limited to a maximum of £25,000 (this amount has not changed in years)—even where there are a number of claims involved. The limitation period for such claims is the same as for unfair dismissal (three months from the EDT). Further, tribunals are still restrained from deciding upon contractual points *during* the currency of the employment relationship (e.g., whether an employee's contract has a mobility clause) as well as all matters such as personal injury claims and restraint of trade disputes.

13.5.2 The substantive overlap

Common law wrongful dismissal and wrongful repudiation claims (described in **Chapter 10**) are concerned only with whether the employee received adequate notice according to the contract and ERA 1996, s. 86 statutory minima (plus the fringe benefits relating to that notice and minus any deductions). Unfair dismissal claims are concerned with the *reason why* and the *manner in which* an employee was dismissed. Whether or not an employee was dismissed with adequate notice is irrelevant to an unfair dismissal claim. Thus:

EXAMPLE 1

An employee has worked for a company for 10 years. He is dismissed without notice for absenteeism.

(a) He might have a claim for wrongful dismissal in the ordinary courts or in an employment tribunal if his employer cannot justify the summary dismissal. Justification depends upon whether or not the employee's actions constituted a repudiation of contract which the employer was accepting by dismissing him.

(b) He might (at the same time) have a claim for unfair dismissal in an employment tribunal, *whether or not he was wrongfully dismissed*.

(c) He has no claim for redundancy pay as there is no redundancy situation here.

EXAMPLE 2

An employee (of ten years' service) is dismissed owing to a surplus of labour because the company's sales have been hit by a recession.

(a) He might have a claim for wrongful dismissal if he does not receive adequate notice (here, at least ten weeks).

(b) He appears to have a claim for redundancy pay. Likely as not the employer will simply pay the statutory (and perhaps contractual) amount due. There would be no need to go to a tribunal on this aspect.

(c) He may still have a claim for unfair dismissal on the grounds that:

  (i) the redundancy was conducted unfairly (e.g., selection procedure); or

  (ii) there was no redundancy situation—it was a sham; or

  (iii) the employer correctly claims there was a business reorganisation and not a redundancy situation.

EXAMPLE 3

An employee is told that major changes will be made to her terms and conditions of employment (e.g., pay levels). She refuses to accept these and resigns.

(a) She may have a claim for wrongful repudiation in the ordinary courts or in an employment tribunal. She will claim that she has accepted the employer's repudiation of the contract by resigning. Her claim will be for her notice period.

(b) She may have a claim for unfair dismissal, but first she will have to prove she was constructively dismissed.

(c) She may have a claim for redundancy pay, in that she might prove she was constructively dismissed but the employer shows that this was for reasons of redundancy and was fair in all the circumstances.

(d) In addition she may also have a claim based on discrimination (direct or indirect).

13.5.3 The financial overlap

It has long been established that an employee should not benefit from 'double recovery'. Thus any payments, or awards, made for the notice period should be accounted for when assessing loss from date of dismissal to date of hearing. With the introduction of limited contractual jurisdiction for employment tribunals it has been much easier to assess the relevant loss (including therefore both wrongful and unfair dismissal awards) in one fell swoop. In assessing unfair dismissal claims tribunals:

(a) first assess the loss relating to the basic award;

(b) then assess the compensatory award, which in turn is split into the two elements of:

  (i) loss between the EDT and the date of hearing—the prescribed element; and

  (ii) future loss.

As seen above, the tribunal's assessment of the 'prescribed element' takes into account the notice period (and whether it was given or not). Under the principle preventing 'double recovery' the employee will not obtain compensation covering the period from dismissal to hearing *and* be awarded notice entitlement if the notice has already been paid or served out: only the actual loss is compensated. A problem can arise, however, where the tribunal awards compensation (say, £90,000), which includes a figure representing unpaid notice entitlement (say, £10,000), and then, the £90,000 has to be reduced to the statutory maximum of £65,300. Effectively, the employee has been deprived of his or her notice as this has been swallowed up in the capping exercise. One way round this is for the tribunal to first award damages for the wrongful dismissal under its contractual jurisdiction and then turn to considering the compensatory award. True, in this example it will still be capped, but the difference in the actual amount awarded is marked. There seems nothing in principle to prevent this.

In the unlikely event that an employee has succeeded in a separate county court action for wrongful dismissal claim *before* having the tribunal hearing, the tribunal can still make the normal award but will not give compensation for loss covered by the notice period.

Note: The basic award remains unaffected by all this. That is due to the employee irrespective of any wrongful dismissal claim or proper notice payment because it is equivalent to a redundancy pay claim.

13.6 Calculating the compensation

13.6.1 Tax implications

The possibility of being awarded £65,300 compensation brings with it a need to examine whether tax might be payable on the award. There are two elements to be borne in mind.

- The first is that tribunals have traditionally assessed the compensatory award on the basis of net pay (though this is not strictly a requirement) because that figure represents the actual loss an employee suffers. This equates with how wrongful dismissal damages are assessed (see *British Transport Commission* v *Gourley* [1956] AC 185, HL). In most cases, therefore, there will be no further tax implications on any award made because problems only arise where £30,000 or more is awarded.

- The second element arises where the £30,000 threshold is exceeded. Here, the compensatory award may count as employment income under s. 62 and Chapter 3 of Part 6, Income Tax (Earnings and Pensions) Act 2003 and so be subject to tax. Section 401(1) states that: 'This Chapter applies to payments and other benefits which are received directly or indirectly in consideration or in consequence of, or otherwise in connexion with: (a) the termination of a person's employment . . . '. Section 403(1) states that: 'The amount of a payment or benefit to which this Chapter applies counts as employment income of the employee or former employee for the relevant tax year if and to the extent that it exceeds the £30,000 threshold.'

The effect of all this is that, on any tribunal award or compromise agreement of £30,000 or greater, the employee will receive a tax demand on the amount over £30,000. Therefore, for the employee to gain the actual amount assessed by the tribunal, some 'grossing up' is necessary so that the employee will have the correct amount net after payment of tax (i.e., in order for the employee to actually receive, after all tax is paid, say £35,000, the tribunal may have to award £40,000).

This begs the further question: can tribunals award more than the £65,300 cap as a grossed-up figure so that, when tax is later paid under s. 401, an employee will have actually received the £65,300? On the wording of ERA 1996, s. 124 (inserted by ss. 33 and 37, ERA 1999) this appears unlikely as it says 'The amount . . . of the compensatory award . . . shall not exceed [£65,300]'.

It should also be noted that payments made for wrongful dismissal, payments in lieu of notice, the basic award, the compensatory award, *ex gratia* payments, and statutory or contractual redundancy payments will all have their own rules as to tax, but they all go to the calculation of the £30,000 trigger point. Liability for National Insurance contributions follows tax liability.

The assessment point for tax will be the tax year in which *payment is received*. This may matter where the dismissal and hearing do not fall within the same tax year and the employee is unemployed at the time of hearing.

EXAMPLE

An employee who is awarded £70,000 (by a combination of the awards/damages noted above) will have this reduced to £65,300 by the capping restriction. Any tax due would then be calculated on the £65,300 figure. No grossing up would be available because the tribunal has reached its limit. Thus, instead of the £70,000 (or even the £65,300) which the employee has been awarded, there will be a subsequent tax bill on the excess of the award over £30,000. For instance, the employee would at some future date receive a bill from the Revenue assessed on, say, 40 per cent of the excess (here 40% × £35,300 = £14,120). This obviously means that out of the original tribunal assessment of £70,000 the employee only ends up with £51,180 (£65,300–14,120) in his pocket.

13.6.2 The calculation

Below is an example of how an unfair dismissal claim can be assessed in terms of the technically complex area of compensation. So, on the basis of all that we have discussed above we may now consider a fairly simple worked example. In this case, John Collins, aged 40, was employed at Hall & Lee Ltd for the past 10 years. He was dismissed on the grounds of frequent absenteeism. His appeal within the disciplinary procedure failed. He earned £500 per week gross. He was given 10 weeks' pay in lieu of notice and has remained unemployed since his dismissal some 20 weeks ago (the present date being the date of the hearing). You represent the company and, on the facts, you had previously advised reaching a settlement. The company had offered £3,500; you could not persuade them to go higher and their offer was rejected. You will argue that the dismissal was not unfair but, on the facts, you are not optimistic. Thus, you also intend to argue that the applicant contributed to his dismissal owing, amongst other things, to his aggressive attitude at the disciplinary hearing. You have already advised that the employer is likely to lose because Hall & Lee did not adhere strictly to their own procedures and really dismissed Collins in order to set an example for the workforce. Further, you have grave doubts over some of the company's witnesses. You have calculated that the compensation figure is likely to top £7,000.

The employment tribunal has now made a finding of unfair dismissal. All your fears were realised, except that you think you may have convinced the tribunal that Collins contributed to his dismissal. You are hoping for a 50 per cent reduction.

The tribunal must now assess the level of compensation due. Fortunately for you and the tribunal there is no loss of pension calculation to be made here. The 'recoupment of benefits' figure is calculated at £2,000 for our purposes.

We must consider three basic steps and then make a final calculation. These steps are laid out in **Figures 13.2–13.5**.

Note: In all these tables the figures apply to dismissals occurring before 1 February 2011.

To obtain the final figure payable to the employee we need to make the following calculations given in **Figure 13.5**. Note that in these calculations we have not made any *Polkey* reductions because the evidence given in our example was that the employee was dismissed as an example to others so dismissal was not inevitable and no procedures could have corrected this.

Steps to be taken	*Amount*	*Notes on making the calculation*
Step 1: Calculate the employee's *gross* weekly pay (including the value of fringe benefits).	£500	This is equivalent to £26,000 and just about at the national average wage.
Step 2: Impose a ceiling of the maximum weekly wage allowed in calculating the Basic Award.	£380	This is equivalent to approximately £20,000 per annum. As the employee's weekly wage is £500, it will be capped at £380 for the purposes of calculating the Basic Award. If the claimant is earning less than £20,000 then the actual (lower) figure will be used, e.g., £10,000 per annum equals approximately £192 per week.
Step 3: Make an initial calculation of the Basic Award. On the facts given we know that the claimant has 10 complete years' service.	£380 × 10 £3,800	The maximum figure is £11,400. Here the claimant only has a multiple of 10 to be applied as all his service falls below the age of 40 *(see **Figure 13.1** for the relevant multiples).*
Step 4: Make any necessary deductions.	£3,800 *less* £950 £2,850	Deductions may be made by the tribunal for the reasons set out at **13.4** above. Here, the sum of £950 represents a 25% contributory fault decision.
Step 5: The Basic Award	£2,850	This figure will now be carried forward to the final calculation in **Figure 13.5** below.

Figure 13.2 Method of calculating the basic award.

Steps to be taken	*Amount*	*Notes on making the calculation*
Step 1: Calculate the employee's *net* weekly pay (including the value of fringe benefits).	£382	Note that this is the net figure after deductions for tax and National Insurance. The £380 'weekly pay' figure does not apply here even if the net wages exceeds it *(this figure has assumed no pensions contribution).*
Step 2: Calculate the loss from the date of dismissal to the date of hearing.	£382 × 20 = £7,640	This assumes a 20-week gap between dismissal and hearing as stated in the instructions. The actual gap may of course be greater or smaller, depending on the complexities of the case and tribunal date pressures.
Step 3: Calculate the sum received (if any) in relation to earnings for this period.	£382 × 10 = £3,820	We are told that the claimant received 10 weeks' pay in lieu as per the minimum statutory entitlement. This has to be accounted for.
Step 4: Deduct the sum calculated in step 3 from the loss in step 2.	£7,640 *less* £3,820 = £3,820	The sum here is the net payment, but note that some employers pay the gross salary re notice—in which case it would be the gross sum that needs to be accounted for.
Step 5: Make any necessary further deductions.	£3,820 *less* £955 = £2,865	Deductions may be made by the tribunal for a number of reasons. Here the tribunal has deducted 25% for contributory fault.
Step 6: The Prescribed element *(being the loss between date of dismissal and hearing after appropriate deductions).*	£2,865	This sum will not be paid over to the employee immediately. The employer must wait for notification of deductible social security benefits and then pay over the remainder to the employee. **This figure will be carried forward to the final calculation in Figure 13.5 below.**

Figure 13.3 Method of calculating the prescribed element in the compensatory award.

Steps to be taken	*Amount*	*Notes on making the calculation*
Step 1: Assess loss from date of hearing to some point in the future.	£382 × 15 = £5,730 *plus* £450 = £6,180	The tribunal will refer to the *Norton Tool* principles as described in the text. A key part of this calculation is the fact that the tribunal must assess how long they think the claimant will remain unemployed or suffer other loss (e.g., if in employment but at a lower wage). Here we have taken an estimate of 15 weeks at the net weekly sum. We have then added a figure for the remaining heads under *Norton Tool.*
Step 2: Make any necessary further deductions.	£6,180 *less* £1,545 = £4,635	Deductions may be made by the tribunal for a number of reasons. Here the tribunal has deducted 25% for contributory fault. Note: as with the 'Prescribed element' calculation, we have taken the position that the tribunal is satisfied that the claimant has not received any payments which mitigate loss – nor has there been a failure to find suitable work.
Step 3: The calculation of future and other loss.	£4,635	**This figure will be carried forward to the final calculation in Figure 13.5 below.**

Figure 13.4 Method of calculating other/future loss in the compensatory award.

Steps to be taken		
Step 1: Gather together the various amounts as previously calculated.	Source of figures	Amount
Basic Award figure	From **Figure 13.2**	£2,850
Additional Award figure	*not relevant here*	£0
Prescribed element in the compensatory award	From **Figure 13.3**	£2,865
Net compensatory award figure for future loss	From **Figure 13.4**	£4,635
Step 2: Add together all parts of the compensatory award to obtain what is called the 'Monetary Award'.	From **Figure 13.3** and **Figure 13.4**	£7,500
Step 3: Add the Basic Award to the Monetary Award to obtain the total award. Note that the prescribed element will not be paid over to the employee until the 'recoupment' figure has been calculated.	From **Figure 13.2**	£10,350 (but £2,865 held back until recoupment ascertained)
Step 4: Ascertain the recoupment figure.	From the text in **13.6.2**	£2,000
Step 5: Deduct the recoupment figure from the running total to obtain the sum the employee will actually receive.	£10,350 minus £2,000	£8,350

Figure 13.5 Making the final calculation.

13.7 Summary

- If a tribunal finds that an employee has been unfairly dismissed it may order re-instatement or re-engagement, but this rarely occurs so the most commonly used remedy is that of compensation.
- An additional award may be payable where re-instatement or re-engagement is ordered but unreasonably refused.
- The basic award depends entirely upon a fixed formula relating to length of service. It is subject to deductions. The maximum basic award is £11,400. This is based on gross pay.
- The compensatory award focuses on what the employee has lost up to the date of the hearing and what is the likely projected loss. The touchstone is a 'just and equitable amount'.
- The compensatory award is subject to deductions and these deductions occur in a particular order. The maximum compensatory award (for dismissals after 1 February 2010) is £65,300. This is based on net pay.

Note, from **Chapters 11** and **12**, that some 'automatically unfair' dismissals are not subject to the statutory compensation cap.

Where an employee is awarded more than £30,000 there may be tax implications.

14

Redundancy

14.1 Introduction

This chapter examines the meaning of redundancy, the obligations of the employer, and the circumstances in which the law may give a redundant employee some redress. Rights to a redundancy payment first arose in 1965 and are now found in the Employment Rights Act 1996 (the ERA 1996).

First and foremost, it needs to be stressed that *redundancy is merely a particular reason for dismissal*. It is one of the 'fair reasons' for dismissal seen in **Chapters 11–13**. Clients—both employers and employees—often miss that obvious point and use 'make redundant', 'downsizing', or even 'allowing jobs to fall away' instead of 'dismiss' in the belief it sounds less harsh. We shall refer to 'dismissal for redundancy'.

Why, then, is dismissal for redundancy any different from dismissal for anything else? The answer is that the dismissed employee may have any of four claims against the former employer, three of which are peculiar to this reason for dismissal:

(a) a complaint of wrongful dismissal. This is the one possible claim that is the same as for any other dismissal;

(b) a claim for a statutory redundancy payment;

(c) a complaint of unfair dismissal by reason of redundancy;

(d) a claim for a higher level of severance payment based on some alleged contractual entitlement.

We shall return to those four possible claims in **14.5**. Meanwhile, though, we need to ask two important preliminary questions in *every* individual case:

(a) *Has there been a dismissal?*

This is dealt with in **14.2** below. The definition of dismissal for the purpose of entitlement to a redundancy payment is slightly broader than for the other purposes.

(b) *Was that dismissal for redundancy?*

This is dealt with in **14.3** below. The essence of redundancy is that the employee's job must have disappeared, possibly along with the jobs of other employees.

After looking at those preliminary questions we shall consider in **14.4** a list of steps an employer needs to work through in handling a redundancy fairly, a list drawn mostly from decided cases on unfair dismissal. That will bring us back to the employee's point of view in **14.5**.

The chapter will therefore be set out in the following four sections:

(a) The definition of dismissal.

(b) The definition of redundancy.

(c) Duties of the employer in carrying out a redundancy.

(d) Remedies for the redundant employee.

There is one final introductory comment to make. In general this book deals only with individual employment law: the law involving the employer and the employee. It does not attempt to cover collective employment law involving employers and trade unions, or other employee representatives. In the present chapter some blurring of that rule is necessary. For instance, if an employer failed to comply with a duty to consult employee representatives about which employees were selected for dismissal, that may appear to have little to do with the individual employees. However, the solicitor representing one of them will want to argue that proper consultation might have led to a different method of selection and to the dismissal of someone else instead of the client. Possibilities like that mean that we must mention in outline some of these collective matters at various points in the text. Those advising clients who need to know more may find useful the ACAS advisory booklet, obtainable from its website at www.acas.org.uk.

14.2 The definition of dismissal

As we have seen, redundancy is a particular *reason* for dismissal. It is not something alternative to dismissal. So whether a particular set of circumstances constitutes a dismissal has to be measured against the tests that we considered in **Chapters 10** and **11**. In **Chapter 10** we noted that at common law a contract can end in various ways: resignation by the employee, dismissal by the employer, operation of law, and termination by mutual consent. As with unfair dismissal, dismissal is defined for purposes of redundancy payments more broadly than that. Indeed, the two definitions in ERA 1996, s. 95 and s. 136 are almost the same, and we shall concentrate here on specific points relating only to redundancy payments. In both matters, doubt can arise whether particular events do actually constitute a dismissal.

14.2.1 Uncertain dismissals

In practice the most common circumstance in which doubt arises as to whether there has been a dismissal is the giving by an employer of advance warning of redundancy. As we shall see shortly, employers are required to consult employees before issuing formal notices and such advance warnings are common. Sometimes the distinction between a warning and notice is a fine one.

The basic rule is that for a dismissal to be effective it must enable a precise date of termination to be ascertained: *Morton Sundour Fabrics Ltd* v *Shaw* (1967) 2 ITR 84.

In *ICL* v *Kennedy* [1981] IRLR 28, the employer announced on 12 October 1979 that a factory was to be closed by the end of September 1980. K resigned so that her employment ended on 2 November 1979 and, *inter alia*, claimed that she was under notice of dismissal. The EAT held there was no dismissal. A general statement about closure did not permit precise ascertainment in October 1979 of *when* the particular employee would be dismissed.

14.2.2 Constructive dismissals

As we noted in **Chapter 11**, an employee is entitled to resign without notice if the employer has committed a serious or 'fundamental' breach of the contract of employment. Such a resignation is called a constructive dismissal, and under s. 95(1)(c) of ERA 1996 it qualifies as a dismissal for purposes of unfair dismissal law. By s. 136(1)(c) of ERA 1996 it similarly qualifies for purposes of entitlement to a redundancy payment. The statutory language is almost identical and the cases set out in **Chapters 11** and **12** therefore also apply here.

A constructive dismissal for redundancy might arise in circumstances like this. The production director in a company retires and is not to be replaced, at least for the time being. His secretary is told to go to work for the production manager. She refuses on the grounds it is a more junior post and resigns. If the secretary's contract was specifically as secretary to the production director, this is probably a constructive dismissal for redundancy. There will be no constructive dismissal for redundancy or anything else if her contract required her to perform whatever secretarial duties the employer requires. In that case she has been given an instruction within the terms of the contract.

14.2.3 Dismissals for redundancy payment purposes

There are three sets of circumstances set out in ERA 1996 which might not obviously seem to constitute a dismissal by the employer but which nevertheless qualify as such for purposes of entitlement to a redundancy payment:

(a) rejection of an alternative job during or after a trial period;

(b) anticipation of the employer's notice;

(c) resignation because of lay-off or short-time.

Case (c) rarely occurs. An employee who has been kept on short-time for a defined period may resign and serve notice on the employer that the resignation is a dismissal under s. 148 of ERA 1996 but in the modern job market this is uncommon. Cases (a) and (b) occur more often, however, and require further attention.

14.2.3.1 Trial periods for alternative jobs

An employer can escape the obligation to make a redundancy payment by offering a different job as an alternative to dismissal. The employee must be given a trial period in the new job—see **14.4.7** below. Rejection of the alternative job during the trial period is treated as a dismissal, but entitlement to a redundancy payment will depend on the reasons for rejection—see **14.4.7.1**.

14.2.3.2 Anticipation of the employer's notice

It often happens that the employer gives the employee notice of dismissal for redundancy and, during the notice period, the employee manages to find another job which it is necessary to start as soon as possible. Can the employee leave early and still claim a redundancy payment?

Such a resignation is regarded as a dismissal for redundancy and a redundancy payment is due provided the requirements of s. 136(3) of ERA 1996 have been met:

(a) The employee must be under actual notice of dismissal and not merely have received some vague or preliminary warning.

(b) The employee must give written notice of resignation. It must be submitted to the employer close enough to the original termination date that the outstanding period is less than the employee's contractual notice.

(c) The employer must not have served on the employee a counter-notice requiring the employee to remain in employment until the original termination date. If that is done, entitlement to a redundancy payment depends on an assessment by the employment tribunal of whether it would be just and equitable to award all or part of it in the light of the employer's reasons. See ERA 1996, s. 142.

There is a way of avoiding these requirements, established in *CPS Recruitment* v *Bowen* [1982] IRLR 54. B resigned in advance of the obligatory period, but it was held that the circumstances constituted a *consensual variation* of the date of termination set by the employer. That was sufficient to qualify as a dismissal by the employer, and a redundancy payment was due.

14.2.4 Volunteers for redundancy

An employer wishing to reduce the size of the workforce will often invite employees to volunteer to leave, perhaps offering some enhanced severance payment as an inducement, and/or giving the opportunity to those approaching retirement age to retire early with some augmentation of pension.

The question arises whether such circumstances constitute a dismissal for any purpose. There is no general answer: everything depends on the facts. Sometimes the termination of employment will be by mutual consent and there will be no dismissal by the employer: *Birch* v *University of Liverpool* [1985] ICR 470. Most *early retirements* are likely to be of this kind. In other cases, however, the employee may merely have intended to enquire what the severance payment might be, and if the contract is terminated in the absence of any clear mutual consent that termination is likely to be a dismissal.

14.3 The definition of redundancy

The essence of a dismissal for redundancy is that the employer requires fewer people. Redundancy can be contrasted with capability, conduct, or the other reasons contemplated in s. 98(1) and (2) of ERA 1996, in that those other reasons imply some criticism of the employee, whose job then needs to be filled by someone else. Redundancy involves no criticism and no need to replace. Employees dismissed for redundancy may have been brilliant performers at their job; they lose their jobs solely because the employer is affected by circumstances often (if inelegantly) described as a redundancy situation.

14.3.1 The statutory definition

The statutory definition of redundancy is contained in s. 139(1) of ERA 1996:

> 139.—(1) For the purposes of this Act an employee who is dismissed shall be taken to be dismissed by reason of redundancy if the dismissal is wholly or mainly attributable to—
>
> (a) the fact that his employer has ceased or intends to cease—
> (i) to carry on the business for the purposes of which the employee was employed by him, or
> (ii) to carry on that business in the place where the employee was so employed, or
>
> (b) the fact that the requirements of that business—
> (i) for employees to carry out work of a particular kind, or
> (ii) for employees to carry out work of a particular kind in the place where the employee was employed by the employer,
>
> have ceased or diminished or are expected to cease or diminish.

That definition is a good example of a statutory provision that is at first sight unintelligible and yet which uses precise words that practitioners will need to borrow when drafting documents. It will be found to envisage four possible sets of circumstances, each of which we shall consider further below:

- The employer is shutting down the business entirely. (The business disappears.)
- The employer is shutting down the business in the place where the employee works. (The place of work disappears.)
- The employer eliminates the work the employee does, either generally or in the particular place of work. (The job disappears in its entirety.)
- The number of people doing that job is to be reduced but not eliminated. (Fewer people are required in the job.)

Before we proceed any further, it is worth spotting two key omissions from the definition in s. 139(1):

(a) Nothing is said about the reasons *why* the employer's requirement ceases or diminishes. Indeed, s. 139(6) reinforces that point and states that the reduction may be permanent or temporary and for whatever reason. So a reduction in the workforce because of a loss of orders and a reduction because of a wish to increase profits are both covered: *Cook* v *Tipper* [1990] ICR 716.

(b) There is no suggestion of any objective test of the needs of the business. An employment tribunal will not normally go behind the employer's assessment of what the requirement was, at least in relation to examining whether the definition of redundancy is satisfied. (The question of whether the employer acted reasonably is another matter: see **14.4.1** below.)

14.3.2 The business disappears

If the employer ceases business, there is rarely in practice any dispute that the ending of employees' employment was by reason of redundancy. The only complication arises when the employer ceases business but someone else takes over. In many such cases there is no dismissal and no redundancy because employment is automatically taken over by the new owner—see **Chapter 15 (Takeovers and transfer of undertakings)**.

14.3.3 The business survives but the job disappears

The other three cases—paragraphs (a)(i) and (b)(i) and (ii) in the statutory definition—are not quite so straightforward. At one time, there was much argument about the correct construction of the statutory language. The uncertainty has been removed by the decision of the House of Lords in a Northern Irish case, *Murray* v *Foyle Meats Ltd* [1999] ICR 827. Before returning to that case it may help to explain the problem.

As a solicitor in practice you will find that private clients often misunderstand completely the legal notion of redundancy. They complain that the employer has described their dismissal as for redundancy but it cannot be so: their work remains to be done and it is in fact being shared out among other former colleagues. Someone has told them that it is always jobs and not people who are redundant; on that reasoning their job clearly remains in existence. You will need to take the client back to the statutory language and explain that it is the *requirement of the business* for employees that matters. So the 'someone' is making a meaningless distinction. Yet you may still find that the statutory language causes problems.

Sometimes the uncertainty relates to the *work of a particular kind* that the employee was employed to do. In *Cowen* v *Haden* [1983] ICR 1, for example, Mr Cowen had been employed as a divisional contracts surveyor, having previously been a regional surveyor, until a heart attack made it difficult for him to travel and he was promoted to a more static job. He argued that the work he actually did was as a surveyor and that, when the employers decided to eliminate the particular job of divisional contracts surveyor, they should not simply have dismissed him as the holder of that post but rather should have made a selection from all surveyors. In the jargon that has since become widely used, the employee interpreted his work in that case by reference to a *function test*; the employer had used a *contract test*. The Court of Appeal held that it was the terms of the contract that mattered and the case became authority for the contract test.

In other cases an analogous question arises in a different form and relates to the place where the employee was employed. Lots of employees nowadays have some sort of mobility clause in their contracts, entitling the employer to move them, perhaps in defined circumstances or with defined notice, to other sites. If there is a surplus of employees at one site but not at another, it becomes important whether the place of work is to be defined by the terms of the contract including the mobility clause (a *contract test* again) or by reference to what actually happens and where the employee in fact works (the *factual* or *geographical* test).

In *Safeway Stores plc* v *Burrell* [1997] ICR 523, the EAT adopted a radical new approach which supposedly reverted to the language of the statute and resolved the conflict between the two tests. Mr Burrell was employed as petrol station manager at a supermarket. There was to be a major reorganisation of the management structure and B was invited to apply for a more junior job as petrol filling station controller. His duties as controller would be less than those set out in his contract as manager, but substantially the same as the work he actually performed. The two lay members of the employment tribunal applied the function test and concluded B was not redundant; the chairman felt bound by the *Cowen* v *Haden* authority to find that he was indeed redundant. The EAT held that both the contract test and the function test were predicated on a misreading of the statute and suggested that the correct approach was similar to the sequence of questions we set out at the start of the chapter:

(a) Was the employee dismissed?

(b) If so, had the requirements of the employer's business for employees to carry out work of a particular kind ceased or diminished, or were they expected to cease or diminish?

(c) If so, was the dismissal of the employee caused wholly or mainly by the state of affairs identified at (b)?

Glosses were laid on this in subsequent decisions until the House of Lords pronounced on the issue in *Murray* v *Foyle Meats Ltd* [1999] ICR 827. Murray was employed in a slaughterhouse and was described like everyone else as a 'meat plant operative'. In fact he worked exclusively in the slaughter hall. The employer decided to reduce the number of 'killing lines' from two to one and to reduce the number of staff accordingly. The industrial tribunal (Northern Ireland has not changed the name) had to address the question we have been discussing, applied in this case to the equivalent Northern Irish statutory wording: should they regard the work as that specified in the contract (the contract test) or should they consider what Murray actually did (the function test)?

The House of Lords described the statutory language as 'simplicity itself' and regarded both the contract test and the function test as 'missing the point'. They expressly approved the reasoning of the EAT in *Safeway Stores* that we summarised earlier. First a tribunal must ask whether there exists in a particular case one of the sets of economic circumstances described in s. 139 of ERA 1996, and secondly they must ask whether the dismissal was *attributable* to those circumstances. This pragmatic approach based on the statutory language must now be regarded as authoritative but it must be said that this approach seems to make the statutory words *work of a particular kind* in s. 139(1)(b) superfluous and there just may be some scope for further consideration in due course.

In *Shawkat* v *Nottingham City Hospital Trust (No. 2)* [2001] EWCA Civ 954, [2001] IRLR 555, the Court of Appeal used the *Murray* principle to rule that the question whether a business reorganisation did or did not amount to a redundancy was a question of fact for the employment tribunal to decide (this is often a difficult line to draw).

14.4 Duties of the employer in carrying out a redundancy

A succession of statutes, beginning with the Redundancy Payments Act 1965, and a vast body of case law has now created an extensive list of duties for the employer to fulfil when reducing the size of the workforce. Failure to follow the steps the law expects may make resulting dismissals unfair. We shall therefore now proceed to examine the topic from the employer's standpoint. A solicitor advising a company how to handle a redundancy will need to cover the nine interlinking steps in **Figure 14.1**:

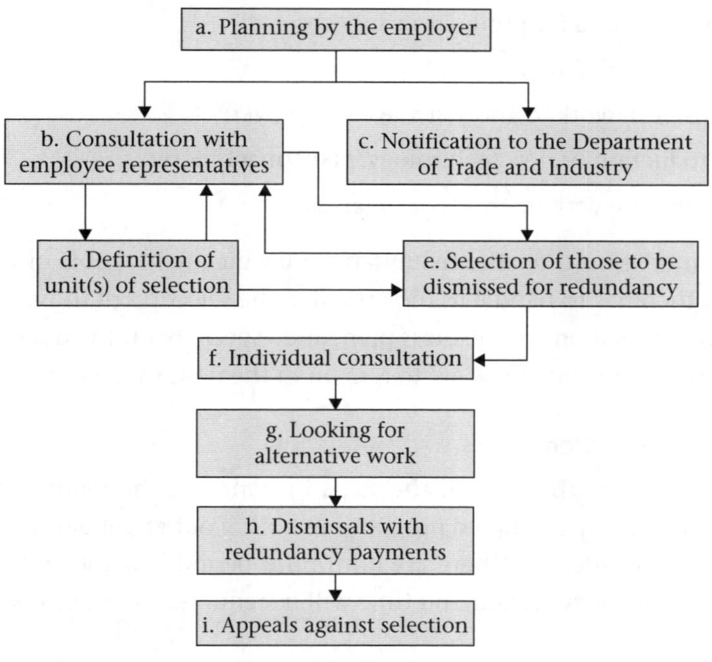

Figure 14.1 Scheme for handling a redundancy.

As the steps are drawn mostly from decided cases about unfair dismissal, this is also a useful checklist for a solicitor advising *either* party about such a complaint. Although the steps are set out in sequence, they interrelate closely and the list must also be viewed as a whole.

Although some of the steps may sound like common sense, some such organised approach by the employer is essential to avoid missing something important. The employment tribunals will often expose dismissals for redundancy to particularly close scrutiny. Perhaps it is out of concern that, because employers tend to select for retention the best workers and to dismiss the poorest performers, an unscrupulous employer can use a redundancy to lose those who contribute least but are not so bad as ever to have been warned under a disciplinary procedure. A systematic approach is good evidence that the employer is behaving compassionately and fairly. In practice employers are most often found at fault in tribunal hearings about unfair dismissal in connexion with steps (e), (f), and (g).

14.4.1 Planning the redundancy

The employer's wish to reduce numbers employed normally reflects some kind of business planning and employers often reach fairly clear decisions about what they wish to do. We shall see shortly that an essential part of the proper handling of a redundancy is consultation of employees and possibly also their representatives—see **14.4.2** and **14.4.6** below. It is therefore important that the solicitor contributes to the planning process while redundancies remain a *proposal* and before a firm *decision* to dismiss has been made.

14.4.1.1 The needs of the business

The employer needs to identify clearly why the redundancy is necessary at all. In due course the reason may have to be disclosed to employee representatives and the Department for Business, Innovation and Skills. The form HR 1 which can be used for notification to the Department suggests the following reasons: the employer may find that more than one is appropriate, or that other reasons beyond those on the list are involved:

(a) lower demand for products or services;

(b) completion of all or part of contract;

(c) transfer of work to another site or employer;

(d) introduction of new technology/plant/machinery;

(e) changes in work methods or organisation.

The reason or reasons for the redundancy may dictate in whole or in part the way the employer then has to handle it. In particular, the selection of those to be dismissed will depend very much on the business plan, and especially on the question of what activities (and therefore what jobs) are to remain in the new, smaller organisation.

14.4.1.2 A programme of action

After being guided through all the steps in handling the redundancy, the employer will need to draw up a detailed programme setting out target dates for the various steps we are now considering. There are minimum periods for the collective consultation described in the next section and time will be required for other steps in the sequence.

14.4.1.3 Examining alternatives to redundancy

Except where the employer manages to achieve the required reduction in a workforce by volunteers, redundancy always involves the dismissal of people through no fault of their own and with likely consequent hardship in many cases. The tribunals expect employers to recognise the human cost of redundancy and to regard dismissal as a last resort in reducing costs. Other options should be explored, such as the reduction of overtime, or ceasing sub-contract work.

The point is reflected in a leading case on the handling of redundancies by an employer: *Williams* v *Compair Maxam* [1982] ICR 156. In the course of its decision the EAT set out five principles to be followed by the employer—see later at **14.4.5.2** for the full list. The first reads as follows.

1. The employer will seek to give as much warning as possible of impending redundancies so as to enable the union and employees who may be affected to take early steps to inform themselves of the relevant facts, consider possible alternative solutions and, if necessary, find alternative employment in the undertaking or elsewhere.

As with so many of these duties on the employer, the important point for the tribunal is not whether the employer has actually adopted any of these alternatives to dismissal, but rather that there is evidence that they were considered seriously. The employer must seek to reach agreement with the employee representatives about ways of avoiding or minimising dismissals for redundancy—see **14.4.2** below.

14.4.1.4 Fixing the number of dismissals

As we have seen, the statutory definition of redundancy speaks of the employer's *requirement* for people to do work. The implication is important. It is not some objectively determined requirement of the business but the *employer's* requirement, and in practice the tribunals almost always accept that it is the employer's responsibility to decide how many people the business needs.

Sometimes it is tempting to challenge the 'need for' redundancy on behalf of the dismissed employee on the basis that the employer could perfectly well have kept the employee in employment. This may be worth trying if the employer has failed to consider alternatives, or if it appears that the so-called redundancy is in truth a cover for dismissal for some other reason. Experience suggests it will rarely do much for the dismissed employee to argue in effect that the employer should have run the business in some other way. The employment tribunals will not 'second-guess' the employer and speculate what they might have done in the employer's shoes.

14.4.2 Consultation

14.4.2.1 The duty to consult employee representatives

Whenever 20 or more people are to be dismissed for redundancy, the employer is required to consult employee representatives. This is part of collective employment law and beyond the scope of the book, but any failure by the employer to consult collectively as the law requires may tend to make individual dismissals unfair and this topic cannot be ignored. The duty to consult arises when the employer makes 'strategic or commercial decisions' or 'changes in activity' which compel the employer to plan for redundancies: *Akavan Erityisalojen Keskusliitto AEK ry* v *Fujitsu Siemens Computers Oy* ECJ (C-44/08), [2009] IRLR 944.

The duty appears in TULRCA 1992, s. 188. That section talks of the duty being triggered when redundancies are 'proposed' whereas the parent Directive uses the term 'contemplated'. The *Akavan* decision above concerned this sort of distinction (in Finland) and, as the editors of *Harvey* suggest, the case rightly concentrates on whether the consultation is real and genuine rather than fine linguistic distinctions.

A solicitor advising a private client may find the following points of help in deciding whether it is worth exploring further. Anyone wanting to know more about this topic should refer to one of the standard works on collective issues or on redundancy.

(a) The statutory duty to consult arises if 20 or more dismissals are proposed. Minimum periods (of 30 or 90 days) are specified depending on the number involved.

(b) Where the employer normally negotiates terms and conditions of employment with a trade union, consultation must be with union representatives. In those circumstances the tribunals will probably expect the employer to discuss all redundancies with the union, even where fewer than 20 are involved. In cases of 20 or more where there is no union recognition, representatives must be elected.

(c) Amongst the matters about which the employer will need to consult are means of avoiding dismissals altogether, reducing the numbers to be dismissed, and mitigating the consequences and also the proposed method of selection—see **14.4.4** and **14.4.5** below.

(d) 'Consultation' is defined by the statute as an attempt to reach agreement with the representatives. It does not necessarily mean 'negotiation'.

(e) A claim that the employer has failed to consult as required may be presented to the employment tribunal by the trade union or other employee representatives, or (subject to some restrictions) by any of the employees who have been dismissed as redundant.

(f) This collective consultation about proposed redundancy is quite separate from the individual consultation about selection for dismissal—see **14.4.6** below. Neither replaces the other.

(g) It is now dangerous to rely on some of the older cases that suggest that individual notices of dismissal may be issued during the period of consultation, so that notice and consultation periods run concurrently, provided consultation is not made a sham. The current view, as in *Middlesbrough Borough Council* v *TGWU* [2002] IRLR 332, is that it undermines consultation if the employer names those to be dismissed or issues notices for dismissal while the topics at (c) above are supposedly still under active discussion. The ECJ has gone further still, ruling that the Directive requires consultation to take place *before* the issue of individual notices.

(h) Agreements resulting from collective consultation must be regarded with care, like any other collective agreement, as they may not be legally enforceable. In *Kaur* v *MG Rover Group Ltd* [2004] EWCA Civ 1507, [2005] ICR 625, the Court of Appeal held that an agreement providing that there was to be no compulsory redundancy was not apt to be incorporated into individual contracts of employment.

14.4.2.2 Remedy for failure to consult

If a claim has been presented to the employment tribunal that the employer has not consulted as required and the claim is established, the tribunal has a mandatory duty under TULRCA 1992, s. 189(2) to make a declaration to that effect. It has a discretion to make a 'protective award'. This is effectively an order to the employer to keep the redundant employees in employment, or at least to pay their wages, for a defined protected period.

The maximum possible protective award is 90 days, which can be a significant extra cost for the employer. There may, however, be an even greater consequence. A serious procedural failing like inadequate collective consultation (especially if of sufficient culpability as to have caused the employment tribunal to have exercised its discretion to make a protective award) may well lead to a finding of unfair dismissal since the decision of the House of Lords in *Polkey* v *A. E. Dayton Services* [1988] ICR 142—see **14.4.6** below. An award of compensation is not automatic but could well follow if it can be shown that better consultation might have changed the final result.

Where a solicitor acting for a private client suspects that collective consultation was required but has been inadequate or absent, it is always worth investigating whether anyone has made a claim about that failing. If so, a copy of the decision should be obtained, or, if the other case remains to be decided, an application should be made to the employment tribunal to delay listing of the individual claim until after the collective claim has been decided.

If no claim has been presented, an attempt should be made to find out why not: for example, a trade union may have consented to a curtailment of the consultation process in order to obtain some other benefit (like notice to be paid in lieu in order to escape tax) for its members and any criticism of the employer in such circumstances could be counterproductive.

14.4.3 Notification to BIS, the Government Department

An employer proposing to dismiss as redundant between 20 and 99 employees must notify the Department for Business, Innovation and Skills (BIS) 30 days before the first dismissal takes effect. If 100 or more employees are to be dismissed the period is 90 days. The precise details are set out in TULRCA 1992, s. 193.

Although the statute speaks of notifying the Secretary of State, in practice the duty is easily met by completing the standard form HR 1, obtainable from the Department. A copy of the form must also be given to employee representatives.

The form HR1 is reproduced at the end of this chapter.

14.4.4 Definition of the unit of selection

We noticed in **14.3** above that the definition in s. 139(1) of ERA 1996 allowed four kinds of redundancy:

(a) the business disappears;

(b) the place of work disappears;

(c) the job disappears in its entirety;

(d) fewer people are required in the job.

Case (d) is different from the other three: not everyone doing the particular job is to be dismissed, but only one or more out of several. Which employees will the employer choose to dismiss and which to retain? This is the very important question of selection, to which we shall return shortly in **14.4.5**.

First, though, there is an important preliminary point: what exactly is 'the job' in which fewer people are required? If that sounds like a non-issue, it is certainly not in practice. For example, many modern methods of production demand considerable versatility from a workforce. So a particular person may operate this machine today, that machine tomorrow, and have been doing something else entirely yesterday. To say that the redundancy affects work on one machine in particular reduces selection to a game of musical chairs in which the music stops whenever the employer happens to make the selection. The group from which a selection is made is known as the 'unit of selection'.

This issue is not at all easy for the employer. If the unit of selection is defined too narrowly, employees who are selected will complain that a wider group should have been considered, in which case they themselves might well have kept their jobs. If the unit of selection is drawn too broadly, there will be some employees who argue that the work they were doing remains wholly unaffected by the redundancy, so that their dismissal was not really for redundancy at all. In some circumstances different people could pursue the two arguments about the same selection.

This idea of selecting employees who are not directly affected by the redundancy is often referred to as a *bumped redundancy*. In *Church* v *West Lancashire NHS Trust* [1998] ICR 423 the EAT decided that earlier case law statements permitting such 'bumping' were in fact *obiter* and held that bumped redundancies were not redundancies at all—they were simple dismissals. However, the House of Lords, in *Murray* v *Foyle Meats Ltd* [1999] ICR 827 (see **14.3.3** above) specifically approved the reasoning of the EAT in those earlier cases and held that a tribunal must first ask whether there exists in a particular case one of the sets of economic circumstances described in s. 139 of ERA 1996, and secondly whether the dismissal was attributable to those circumstances. Under that pragmatic approach, which takes an overall view of the employer's requirements, 'bumping' may now fall within the definition of redundancy.

Those cases guide the employment tribunal in the view it should take if the employer *chooses* to adopt an approach of bumping. There is no clear rule of law that tells the employer how to define a unit of selection. Provided regard is had to the principles in *Safeway Stores plc* v *Burrell* (see above at **14.3.3**), the employer is usually free to define the job in whichever way best suits the business. Sometimes, though, the choice is limited. In the example we considered of the versatile machine operators, it is almost inevitable that the unit of selection must include all machine operators.

Cases where the employer will need to take particular care in defining the unit of selection include the following:

- where there is some versatility or flexibility amongst employees affected by the redundancy (as above);
- where people with similar skills or doing a similar job are employed in several departments or functions: should the employer take each such group separately or together?
- where people doing similar but not identical work are employed on different grades or their equivalent, reflecting different degrees of skill: is it appropriate to divide the function into several units or to take it all together, and (if the latter) how does the employer ensure a result giving the right balance of 'chiefs and Indians'?

In all these instances, the important point is that the employer should have considered the choice of the unit of selection with some care and be able to justify the result logically to an employment tribunal. There are no general rules of law as to which answer should be given. So the solicitor acting for a dismissed employee will usually achieve more by showing that the employer failed to address the point than by arguing that a particular choice lay outside the band of reasonableness.

So far this question of the unit of selection has been examined only in relation to the fourth kind of redundancy, where the job is not to be eliminated but numbers are just to be reduced. Perhaps it is already obvious that the point is in fact of somewhat wider application. When in case (c) we speak of the job as *disappearing*, exactly the same consideration needs to be given to what may be the job. It is not good enough for the employer to treat a particular employee as redundant on the basis that that individual's job has disappeared if one of the examples described above raises doubt about the definition of that job. Similarly in case (b), an employee who is required to be mobile between several places of work may be unfairly selected for redundancy if that is done solely on the basis of his or her happening to be working at a particular site that is being closed on the day the selection is carried out—see **14.3.3** above.

This issue of the choice of the unit of selection is one that ought to be included in collective consultation about the redundancy. Sometimes, even where employee representatives are unwilling to agree with the employer a method of selection for dismissal from within the unit, it is still possible for the two sides to reach agreement about the definition of the unit. The employer will need to consider properly any suggestions put forward by employee representatives: hence the arrows in both directions in **Figure 14.1**.

14.4.5 Selection

We now need to turn to the aspect of the employer's handling of the redundancy which is perhaps more likely than any other to lead to a claim in the employment tribunal of unfair dismissal—the selection of which employee or employees in the unit are to be dismissed and which retained.

Employees and trade unions often prefer the employer to select for dismissal on the basis of length of service alone, arguing that this is impartial, well understood by those affected and consequently generally accepted as fair. The practice of 'last-in-first-out' is widely referred to by its initials: LIFO.

The employer probably has quite a different view. If the workforce is being drastically reduced, it is extremely important to the employer that the business retains those key skills that are essential to its survival. Some process of evaluating employees' skills and suitability is therefore required.

At one stage there was widespread public belief that LIFO was the normal way to select for redundancy, and it is possible to detect something close to a legal presumption to that effect in some early cases. However, in reality, other forms of evaluation of employees had become common, following on from guidelines laid down by the EAT in 1982: *Williams* v *Compair Maxam* [1982] ICR 156. By 1987 LIFO had been described as outdated: *Suflex* v *Thomas* [1987] IRLR 435 (but most people still think this is how redundancies are dealt with). The guidelines make *Compair Maxam* the leading case on selection, but various others have followed since.

We need to consider two main kinds of case—those where some method of selection has been established on a previous occasion, and those where, because no such precedent exists, a method has to be designed from scratch.

14.4.5.1 Use of established criteria, customary or agreed

Until 1994 there was an important rule that the selection of an individual employee for dismissal on the ground of redundancy would be *automatically unfair* if it was in breach of a customary arrangement or agreed procedure. The Deregulation and Contracting Out Act 1994 repealed the rule of *automatically* unfair dismissal. It does not give employers a free hand to ignore all past practice or to break existing agreements. Any such action by the employer is now assessed alongside any other consideration of reasonable behaviour under ERA 1996, s. 98(4).

14.4.5.2 Design of a method of selection

What if there is no satisfactory past practice to rely on? How should the employer select who is to go and who to stay?

There is no single right answer to the question but the most common solution by far is to choose a set of criteria and to mark each employee under each of them, to add up the resulting scores, and to select for dismissal those whose total is lowest. We shall look further at this method shortly. It is not the only possibility, however.

Occasionally employers are still content to select on the basis of LIFO despite all its shortcomings and the potential for this to be classed as age discrimination against younger employees who are likely to have shorter service than older employees. The employer must justify the selection as a proportionate means of achieving a legitimate aim.

Sometimes the decision rests on a single criterion. For example, if a company has a European sales force of two, one of whom speaks French and the other French and German, it is possible that the second will need to stay and the first to be dismissed, irrespective of their relative sales abilities. The only alternative choice would limit the sales territory available to the company.

Occasionally, the needs of the business can be set out in a sequence of decreasing priorities, so that they can be applied as a series of criteria. So, for example, if the redundancy arises from a decision to reduce the scope of operations in the business, discontinuing one or more activities in order to concentrate on others, the employer may decide first to choose for dismissal those with no experience at all of the continuing activities. Other criteria may then follow to choose a second and third group.

More often, the various factors all have some part to play and it is better to apply them simultaneously. This brings us back to the score-sheet approach we have already mentioned as the most common, certainly amongst large employers. An example of a score-sheet, or 'matrix' as it is often described, is shown at **Figure 14.2**. It is quite common to attach different weighting factors to the different criteria and to have some predetermined tie-break arrangement to distinguish those with equal totals. The tie-break may well be length of service.

Because the matrix approach is so common, much of the guidance to be drawn from the cases is actually expressed in those terms. Indeed the leading case on methods of selection—*Williams* v *Compair Maxam* [1982] ICR 156—is based on that approach. We have already encountered the first of five principles set out by the EAT in that decision. It is now necessary to set out the remainder.

1. The employer will take steps in collaboration with any trade union to avoid dismissals altogether.
2. The employer will consult the union as to the best means by which the desired management result can be achieved fairly and with as little hardship to the employees as possible. In particular, the employer will seek to agree with the union the criteria to be applied in selecting the employees to be made redundant. When a selection has been made, the employer will consider with the union whether the selection has been made in accordance with those criteria.
3. Whether or not an agreement as to the criteria to be adopted has been agreed with the union, the employer will seek to establish criteria for selection which so far as possible do not depend solely upon the opinion of the person making the selection but can be objectively checked against such things as attendance record, efficiency at the job, experience, or length of service.
4. The employer will seek to ensure that the selection is made fairly in accordance with these criteria and will consider any representations the union may make as to such selection.
5. The employer will seek to see whether instead of dismissing an employee he could offer him alternative employment.

EXEMPLARY MANAGEMENT LIMITED

ASSESSMENT FOR REDUNDANCY SELECTION – JANUARY 2009

Employee's Name .... Department .... Clock No ....

Job .... Date of start .... Date of birth ....

	D 1 points	C 2 points	B 3 points	A 4 points	Factor	Score
1 Length of service as at 31 December 2006	Less than 2 years	2 years but less than 5	5 years but less than 10	10 years or more	X2	
2 Attendance record **a) Days absent during 2005–06**	More than 20	20 or less but more than 10	10 or less but more than 5	5 or less	X1	
b) Number of absences	11 or more	6–10	3–5	0–2	X1	
3 Quantity of work	Requires supervision to achieve acceptable level.	Average worker for the grade, normally achieves expectations without frequent supervision.	Always achieves targets and often exceeds them.	An exceptionally good worker, consistently exceeding targets by a substantial amount.	X3	
4 Quality of work	Correction of errors is often necessary; work needs to be checked.	Occasionally makes errors requiring correction, but quality usually acceptable.	Seldom makes errors. Usually reliable.	Almost never makes mistakes. Consistently reliable.	X3	
5 Versatility	Limited to skills of own job.	Can carry out tasks closely related to usual job.	Can undertake a broad range of work within department or discipline.	Capable of a wide range of work within the discipline and outside it.	X4	
6 Adaptability	Tends to resist change.	Adapts to change slowly.	Generally accepts change and adapts well to new ideas.	Shows a positive attitude to change and adapts on own initiative.	X3	

Total

Assessment performed by .... Date ....

Approved by .... Date ....

Checked by HR Department .... Date ....

Figure 14.2 An example of a redundancy selection matrix.

Since those five principles were first set out in 1982 there has been some criticism of the EAT for adopting the approach in that and several other cases of setting out guidelines for future reference as if they were a statute or a code of practice. Nevertheless, the principles have never been overturned and remain valid. Indeed subsequent cases have tended to enlarge them. We can therefore set out some advice for employers in designing a matrix:

(a) Discuss it with trade unions or employee representatives and 'seek to agree ... criteria': *Williams* v *Compair Maxam*.

(b) Include some factors on the list that are capable of objective measurement and are not solely subjective opinion: *Williams* v *Compair Maxam*. Subjective judgments can be given a greater objectivity if two or more people are involved.

(c) Ensure that enough guidance is given to those doing the marking that they clearly understand what they are to do. In practice, however, a competent manager or supervisor is unlikely to experience much difficulty if the categories are clearly defined.

(d) Be careful of vague factors like attitude which appear to give excessive scope for personal prejudice, but do not necessarily exclude them if relevant: *Graham* v *ABF* [1986] IRLR 90.

(e) It is best to include length of service as a factor, although there is no definite authority that its omission is wrong. Using it merely as a tie-break is probably not enough: *Westland Helicopters* v *Nott* (1989, unreported, EAT/342/88). See the remarks at **14.4.5.2** above, however, about the risk of age discrimination. The matrix at **Figure 14.2** gives the maximum mark for length of service to those who have been employed for 10 years or more, a common practice before the rules on age discrimination. Some may now prefer to remove any preference based on service longer than five years, so as clearly not to offend the regulations, but many consider that in this context longer service represents a proportionate means of achieving the legitimate aim of rewarding loyalty.

(f) Avoid any selection criterion which is directly or indirectly discriminatory on grounds of sex, race, or the other prohibited heads, or trade union membership or activities. See **Chapter 6** about sex and race etc; **14.4.5.3** below about trade union membership.

(g) Exercise particular care when a factor such as rate of work, quality of output, or attendance record may be influenced by the employee's disability: see **6.8** above about disability discrimination.

(h) Ensure that the assessments are made accurately and fairly according to the criteria: *Williams* v *Compair Maxam*. Although this sounds like common sense, simple errors often occur in practice, e.g., misreading a sickness record or making a mistake of arithmetic.

(i) Give some thought to whether employees selected for dismissal will be permitted to see the marks scored by other employees in the unit of selection—during individual consultation, on appeal, only during employment tribunal proceedings (see **16.8.3** below), or never. This is a difficult issue: most employers do not wish to risk demotivating those who, unbeknown to themselves, were 'near misses' for selection.

The example of a matrix in **Figure 14.2** attempts to reflect that advice. In an example at the end of the chapter we shall look at one that does not. While tribunals are unwilling to fault an employer's method of selection simply on the basis that they might have done differently—see, for example, *British Aerospace plc* v *Green* [1995] ICR 1006—many established methods are very susceptible to challenge, especially on the grounds of disability discrimination.

14.4.5.3 Selection related to trade union membership or activities

Under s. 153 of TULRCA 1992, a selection for redundancy is automatically unfair if the reason for it is the employee's trade union membership or activities.

Selection based on trade union membership or activities does not have to be deliberate. An evaluation influenced by trade union activity, perhaps because a shop steward was unable to achieve as high an output as some others because of the amount of time spent on trade union business, may well be caught by this rule.

14.4.6 Individual consultation

After the process of selection, the employer will have decided who is to stay and who to go but the employees concerned do not yet know. The next step is to inform them.

The law makes it very clear that this step involves much more than merely conveying information. Redundant employees have the right to be consulted individually about their redundancy before notice of dismissal is given. The leading case on this individual consultation is the House of Lords' decision in *Polkey* v *A. E. Dayton Services* [1988] ICR 142. As this requirement forms part of the concept of reasonableness in unfair dismissal it has been possible to argue that consultation is inappropriate or superfluous in particular cases, although the circumstances in which the tribunals have been prepared to accept such an argument have become fewer as a consultative approach to employment relations generally has become more established. In *Mugford* v *Midland Bank* [1997] ICR 399, for example, it was suggested that the employer would have to show that consultation would have been an utterly futile exercise.

What is the employer actually obliged to do? *Rowell* v *Hubbard Group Services* [1995] IRLR 195 gives useful guidance on the need for consultation to be proper and genuine. The following is an indication of the approach tribunals expect:

(a) Do not rush the process. Encourage the employee to be accompanied by a colleague. Recognise that the employee may be in a state of some shock from the announcement, and allow time for a response.

(b) Explain to the individual why the particular job is affected by redundancy at all.

(c) Explain why this particular employee is at risk of selection for redundancy, but do nothing at this stage that could be interpreted as giving notice of dismissal. If an assessment matrix has been used, show it to the employee and explain the marks given. In *Alexander* v *Bridgen Enterprises Ltd* [2006] IRLR 422 the EAT held that the employer's failure to provide such particular information made dismissal unfair. While such disclosure is not mandatory in every case, the employee must have sufficient information to understand selection and to challenge it—*Davies* v *Farnborough College of Technology* [2008] IRLR 14.

(d) Give the employee and/or the representative a few days to express any views about (b) or (c) and consider them properly and genuinely. In particular, examine any representation which suggests that the assessment may have been performed incorrectly.

(e) Discuss whether there is any possibility of alternative work—see **14.4.7** below—or any other alternative solution.

(f) Do not finalise the redundancy list or issue any notices of dismissal until the process of individual consultation has been completed. Alterations may be required.

(g) Hold a second interview to confirm the selection if no alternative solution has been found. Issue notice of dismissal only at this stage.

The processes of collective consultation with employee representatives and individual consultation are not alternative processes. However extensive the first, the second is necessary too: see *Rolls Royce Motors* v *Price* [1993] IRLR 203. In practice, however, the required scope of individual consultation may well be reduced in practice by collective consultation, especially if the trade union or other employee representatives have agreed some aspects of the redundancy: see *Mugford* v *Midland Bank plc* [1997] ICR 399. In cases where there has been no collective consultation, individual consultation needs to be especially thorough and to include at least some elements of the topics considered at **14.4.2.1** above.

Solicitors advising smaller employers may well find that these requirements are not well understood. There are still employers without previous experience of handling a redundancy who believe that the whole process can be completed effortlessly in a couple of hours. Thus, whilst selection of individuals may be the most common issue in tribunal applications concerning large companies, lack of consultation is very common amongst smaller ones.

14.4.7 Alternative work

The employer will next want to consider the possibility of alternative work for a redundant employee. Curiously this step arises for two quite different reasons. First, the employer, by making an offer of suitable alternative work, may escape the liability of making a redundancy payment if the employee unreasonably refuses it: ERA 1996, s. 141. Secondly, and quite unconnected with that express statutory provision, there is the general requirement on the employer as part of acting reasonably to seek alternative solutions to whatever problem caused the redundancy, including looking for alternative work for the employee who might otherwise be dismissed. Without that step dismissal may be unfair. We shall look at both aspects in turn.

14.4.7.1 Alternative work as an alternative to a redundancy payment

The rule in s. 141 of ERA 1996 permits two possible kinds of offer by the employer as a means of avoiding a redundancy payment: an offer of employment which is identical to the old job in all respects, and an offer of some different job which is suitable for the employee. The first is unusual in practice and generally arises only if the employer, having dismissed the employee, then finds that the dismissal was a mistake and that the business now has a continuing requirement for that employee after all. In either case, though, the entitlement to a redundancy payment is lost only if the employee unreasonably refuses the offer. In the more common case of a different job, the two elements of a *suitable* job and an *unreasonable* refusal must be considered separately.

The question whether the offer is of suitable employment is primarily a matter of objective fact for the tribunal to assess: *Cambridge and District Co-op* v *Ruse* [1993] IRLR 156. All aspects of the job can be taken into account, including, for example, the level of skill involved and not only the pay and conditions: *Standard Telephones and Cables* v *Yates* [1981] IRLR 21.

The question whether the employee has refused the offer unreasonably often requires consideration of broadly the same matters, but viewed this time from the subjective standpoint of the individual employee: *Carron* v *Robertson* (1967) 2 ITR 484. It is not necessary to imagine the viewpoint of a notional reasonable employee nor to take account of the views of other people who may have been made the same offer: *Everest's Executors* v *Cox* [1980] ICR 415 and *Fowler (John) (Don Foundry)* v *Parkin* [1975] IRLR 89. Thus, for example, if the employer closes one factory and offers alternative jobs at another a few miles away, some employees who have farther to travel to work in consequence may be found to have refused reasonably, whilst others living close to the new jobs may have refused unreasonably.

It is not entirely clear from the cases how far reasons for a reasonable refusal have to be related to the job. The better view seems to be that there must be some connexion. Refusal for a wholly extraneous reason like the wish to take another job would almost certainly be unreasonable.

14.4.7.2 The timing of such an offer

For an offer of alternative work to be effective in denying an employee a redundancy payment the new job must start no later than four weeks after the ending of the old job: ERA 1996, s. 141(1). The offer must be made before the old job ends.

In every case where the employee accepts different, alternative work the first four weeks of performing the new job are to form a trial period, unless the parties expressly agree a longer period for purposes of retraining. At any time during that period or at the end of it, the employee can reject the new job and elect to be treated as dismissed for the purposes of receiving a redundancy payment: ERA 1996, s. 138.

14.4.7.3 Alternative work as part of reasonableness

The cases such as *Williams* v *Compair Maxam* [1982] ICR 156—and in particular the first of the five principles we set out at **14.4.1.3**—as well as the codes of practice make it clear that the employer should always try to avoid dismissals for redundancy if possible. In almost every case that requirement will oblige the employer to take the trouble to look on behalf of every redundant employee for possibilities of continuing employment in the same company or in 'associated' companies, i.e., other companies within the same group of companies: *Vokes* v *Bear* [1974] ICR 1.

In some groups of companies where there are many plants scattered over a wide area, the requirement in *Vokes* v *Bear* is demanding. Other cases such as *Quinton Hazell* v *Earl* [1976] ICR 296, make it clear that the duty of the employer is to take reasonable steps to look, but not to conduct an exhaustive search. The employer is not permitted to eliminate some possibilities because of an assumption that the employee will not be interested, perhaps because the alternative job is of a lower status: *Avonmouth Construction Co.* v *Shipway* [1979] IRLR 14. The employee should be given the chance to decide, and this is one of the purposes of the individual consultation we considered at **14.4.6** above (see also *Huddersfield Parcels* v *Sykes* [1981] IRLR 115).

14.4.7.4 'Bumping'

We noted the idea of 'bumping' above at **14.4.4**—where a redundant employee A is capable of doing other jobs in an organisation and would like to take B's job thereby displacing B who is dismissed instead. Maybe B, for instance, has much shorter service. The general rule is that the employer is not required to accede to A's wish. Indeed, most employers refuse to do so, reflecting the view of the EAT in *Elliott Turbomachinery* v

Bates [1981] ICR 218 that bumping, a term they described as 'singularly inelegant and esoteric', was a recipe for industrial unrest amounting to chaotic proportions if applied wholesale and indiscriminately. (Note that, since the House of Lords decision in *Murray* v *Foyle Meats Ltd* [1999] ICR 827 mentioned at **14.4.4**, employers can no longer safely resist bumping by arguing that B's dismissal falls outside the definition of redundancy.) However, A may sometimes be able to present the same case in a different way: by arguing that A and B are doing such similar jobs that they should have been considered together and the unit of selection was in fact too narrowly defined (again see **14.4.4**). If A proposes bumping during individual consultation the employer is at least under some duty to consider the proposal seriously—*Lionel Leventhal Ltd* v *North* EAT/0265/04.

14.4.8 Redundancy payments

The original reason for a separate legal category of dismissal for redundancy was that it qualified the employee for a redundancy payment, subject to certain rules (when there was no such thing as unfair dismissal). So the next duty for the employer is to see what redundancy payment is due to each of the dismissed employees. There are two matters to consider: statutory redundancy payments and contractual severance terms. In addition, of course, there is an entitlement to notice or pay in lieu. The position sometimes appears complicated by the way contractual payments are expressed, so as to include both a statutory payment and pay in lieu of notice. It is, however, convenient for us to look at each in turn.

14.4.8.1 Statutory redundancy payments

In essence the statutory scheme of payments is very simple. As the calculation of the amount (unlike possible entitlement) is scarcely ever in issue, we shall do no more than to sketch the rules in outline. Under ERA 1996, s. 162, the redundant employee is entitled to a number of weeks' pay, depending on both age and service. There is no entitlement whatever below two years' service.

The definition of 'service' is the same as for other statutory purposes: see ERA 1996, ss. 210–219 and also **5.4**—s. 211(2). If a redundancy payment was made at some earlier point in the employee's service but the employee was then re-employed, continuity of service runs only from that date—see s. 214.

A week's pay is similarly the same as for other statutory purposes: the normal pay for the normal hours if pay does not fluctuate; the average of the previous 12 weeks if it does; and subject in all cases to the statutory maximum of £380, apparently now also subject to the national minimum wage: see ERA 1996, ss. 220–229 for the detailed rules.

The calculation is almost the same as for a basic award of compensation for unfair dismissal as set out in **Figure 13.1** above:

CALCULATION:	[AGE factor] × [SERVICE] × [WEEK'S PAY]
AGE:	For any service where the employee was 41 or over the factor is 1.5
	For any service between the ages of 22 and 41 the factor is 1
	For any service below the age of 22 the factor is 0.5
SERVICE:	Subject to a maximum of 20 years
WEEK'S PAY:	Subject to a maximum of £380 per week

The maximum statutory redundancy payment is therefore £11,400, i.e., 1.5 × 20 × 380. As we noted with regard to the basic award in **Chapter 13** these figures are usually updated in February of each year.

Disqualifications of those under 18 or over 65 were removed in 2006. As with calculating the EDT for unfair dismissal, if the employee was dismissed with less than the minimum statutory notice appropriate to length of service and thereby failed to meet the minimum of two years' service, or just missed the anniversary of starting so as to obtain one more year's service, it is possible to read forward the date of termination of employment accordingly.

14.4.8.2 Contractual severance payments

There are many employers which have set up their own schemes of redundancy or severance payments (sometimes known by some other name) in excess of the statutory scale. We have used the term 'severance payment' in this book to distinguish such contractual payments from statutory redundancy payments, but that terminology is not standard and it should not be assumed to apply elsewhere. There is a risk that such schemes (which often provide benefits related to age, length of service, or both) may offend the rules on age discrimination. Employers will in general need to justify such schemes as a proportionate means of achieving a legitimate aim under the Equality Act 2010 but there is an express exemption for schemes based on the statutory scheme.

A scheme is based on the statutory scheme if it uses as its base the idea of 'week's pay' and uses a multiplier as with the statutory scheme. However, the 'week's pay' can be real pay rather than limited to the £380 and the multiplier for years of service can be more generous than the statutory scheme. Thus a contractual scheme that uses actual week's pay (say £600, which is about £31,500 per annum), the usual age multiplier e.g., 1.5 for service over 41) and then a further multiplier of 2 would give an employee with ten years' service (all at 41 or above) £18,000 as opposed to a £5,700 statutory payment. Such schemes, especially if couched as voluntary severance schemes, can help ease the pain of redundancies.

Employers may adopt completely different schemes. Then the test (in relation to any age discrimination claims) is whether the scheme can be justified. In *MacCulloch* v *Imperial Chemical Industries plc* [2008] IRLR 846 and *Loxley* v *BAE Systems Land Systems (Munitions and Ordnance) Ltd* [2008] IRLR 853 the EAT determined that schemes that were not within the exemption could nevertheless be justified. The EAT, especially in *MacCulloch*, stressed that tribunals must consider properly both parts of the statutory rule—that the differences relate to a legitimate aim, and that they are a proportionate means of achieving it. The EAT accepted that the reward of loyalty through service-related payments was a legitimate aim, as also was greater protection for older workers who would probably find it more difficult to obtain another job after redundancy.

An important question, when employees are then dismissed for redundancy, is whether the better scheme has become a contractual entitlement or not. The tests are no different in this matter from any other examination of contractual status discussed in **Chapter 3**. A scheme that was mentioned in the staff handbook in a section dealing with benefits and rights in *Keeley* v *Fosroc International Ltd* [2006] EWCA Civ 1277, [2006] IRLR 961 was held to be apt for incorporation in the contract of employment, even if its detail was only set out elsewhere. Particular attention will be paid to the circumstances in which the scheme was first introduced and the apparent beliefs of the parties at the time: see, for example, *Lee* v *GEC Plessey Telecommunications* [1993] IRLR 383.

Many employers, aware of the danger of establishing a contractual entitlement that might be a financial embarrassment on a future occasion, take care to explain that better terms are specific to a particular redundancy.

It should not be assumed that any superior set of terms automatically becomes a contractual entitlement because used once or more in the past: it will be necessary to produce some evidence to turn mere practice into a contractual term. The question of whether mere past practice has been turned into a contractual entitlement depends on a detailed examination of all the surrounding circumstances as listed in *Albion Automotive Ltd* v *Walker* [2002] EWCA Civ 946.

14.4.8.3 Cancellation of contractual arrangements

Most of the cases that have reached the courts have concerned employers who have established (intentionally or not) some contractual scheme of enhanced severance payments and who have then wanted to abandon it. A company of some 500 employees and a severance payment scheme that yields an average of £20,000 per employee has a potential liability of £10 million. This is likely to exceed the total value of the business if it is put up for sale, and the consequence of such schemes is often serious for the future of the business concerned.

In such circumstances some employers have sought to bring such schemes to an end and to replace them with something poorer, or even with nothing at all except the statutory scheme. Where these schemes have become part of the contract, the mechanism for doing so is the same as for introducing any other change in the terms of employment as discussed in **Chapter 5**. Employees or their representatives may agree to the abandonment of the severance scheme, but this is obviously rather unlikely when the employer has no significant inducement to offer. More likely the employer will have to terminate the employment of all the employees on the existing terms of employment and then offer re-engagement on terms that are identical in all respects except for the loss of the severance scheme.

Such a mass ending of employees' contracts of employment is, of course, a dismissal and the people concerned will be able to bring complaints of unfair dismissal. The employment tribunal will still have jurisdiction to hear those complaints even though the employees may have accepted the new jobs under protest: see *Hogg* v *Dover College* [1990] ICR 39. The employer will classify the dismissals as for a substantial reason, and the question whether the employer acted reasonably in so dismissing the employees will enable the employment tribunal to examine the importance of ending the severance payment scheme.

The employer will need to consult employee representatives about this mass dismissal under the provisions discussed at **14.4.2** above. This is not because the employees are truly redundant under the definition we have been considering throughout the chapter; clearly they are not. It is because there is a special definition of redundancy for the purposes of collective consultation, introduced to comply with the European Directive on multiple dismissals. Collective consultation is required about all dismissals not related to the individual employee. The employer may therefore find that the very act of seeking to end generous severance payments is argued by employees to constitute a redundancy, and to give rise to an entitlement to the payments. However it is unlikely that any scheme of contractual severance payments will in fact depend on such a definition.

14.4.9 Appeals

Most employers who operate some formal mechanism for selecting employees for dismissal for redundancy then provide an opportunity for those selected to appeal against that decision. This is usually separate from and subsequent to the individual consultation we considered at **14.4.6**. There has been no clear authority requiring such a stage: indeed, in *Robinson* v *Ulster Carpet Mills* [1991] IRLR 348, the Northern Ireland Court of Appeal expressly found that it was not necessary.

Where some appeal opportunity is provided, it must comply with the rules of natural justice. In particular the person hearing it must not be in a position of bias by having been involved in the decision to dismiss. So employers need to ensure that selection is made low enough in a management hierarchy to leave someone more senior to hear the appeal.

14.5 Remedies for the redundant employee

So far, this chapter has looked at redundancy from the point of view of giving advice to the employer before dismissals have taken place. Now it is necessary to look at the other side of that coin and to consider the redress available to an employee who has been dismissed. The principles apply equally, of course, whether the solicitor acts for the dismissed employee or for the ex-employer. As we noted at the start of the chapter, any redress at all depends on establishing that there has been a dismissal, but there are then four possibilities that we shall need to consider in turn:

(a) a complaint of wrongful dismissal, i.e., a claim for notice or pay in lieu of notice;

(b) a claim for a statutory redundancy payment;

(c) a complaint of unfair dismissal, seeking reinstatement, re-engagement or compensation;

(d) a claim for a contractual severance payment.

14.5.1 Wrongful dismissal

The same rules about the employee's right to notice apply to a dismissal for redundancy as to any other dismissal. If the employee appears not to have been given due notice or pay in lieu, you should refer to **Chapter 10**.

There is just one special point that is probably peculiar to dismissal for redundancy. Some severance payment schemes provide a total sum including pay in lieu, a statutory redundancy payment and an additional payment, without any specific identification of the amount of the component parts. At one stage there was a tax benefit to be gained from this device but the loop-hole has now been blocked. Nevertheless the approach remains in some severance payment schemes and it is worth checking that an individual client who seems not to have received pay in lieu of notice is not in fact covered by a scheme of this kind.

14.5.2 Statutory redundancy payments

We have already considered the method of calculating a statutory redundancy payment at **14.4.8.1** above.

An employee with more than two years' service is entitled to a statutory redundancy payment and can present a claim of non-payment or insufficient payment to the employment tribunal. In practice most employers are aware of the need to pay redundancy payments and such cases are nowadays rare, except where there is a dispute as to whether the dismissal was for redundancy.

A typical case where redundancy may be in dispute as the reason for dismissal is provided by the example of constructive dismissal for redundancy we considered at **14.2.2** above. The employer gives the employee (the production director's secretary) an instruction to change job (to be secretary to someone else), regarding it as a lawful instruction within the existing contract. The employee regards the proposed job as of lesser status and outside the terms of the contract, refuses to move, and resigns in protest. The employee's entitlement to a redundancy payment will depend upon the true construction of the contract, and that may be a matter for the employment tribunal.

14.5.3 Unfair dismissal

Of the four possible remedies, the one most often adopted is a claim to the employment tribunal of unfair dismissal. We have seen in **Chapter 11** that there are six potentially fair reasons for dismissal and that redundancy is one of them. Under ERA 1996, s. 98(4), the employer must act reasonably in dismissing for the stated reason. The advice to employers we have been considering in **14.4** above is distilled from cases of alleged unfair dismissal, and therefore reflects the tribunals' view of what constitutes reasonableness when the reason is redundancy. So a solicitor acting for either party will need to establish the facts and then to match them against the nine stages in **Figure 14.1**.

Before we return to that sequence there are two preliminary questions worth asking:

- Was the dismissal truly for redundancy?
- Is the dismissal automatically unfair?

14.5.3.1 Was the dismissal truly for redundancy?

The dismissed employee may have received a dismissal letter which refers to a redundancy, but the solicitor acting for the dismissed employee doubts whether that is really an accurate description. It is worth examining the facts against the definition of redundancy we considered at **14.3** above.

Sometimes an employer will describe the dismissal of an employee (perhaps quite a senior person) as a 'redundancy', where that person is considered not to have been performing very well but who the employer does not wish to retain while going through the disciplinary procedure. The redundancy in such circumstances may be rather obviously false: perhaps steps are already being taken to recruit a replacement, thereby demonstrating that the employer's requirement for people to do work of that kind has neither ceased nor diminished. Since the burden of proof as regards the *reason* for dismissal rests with the employer (unlike the burden of proof as regards *reasonableness* which is neutral), the employer who has wrongly described a dismissal in this way will find it difficult to satisfy that burden and the dismissal will be unfair.

The employee may well be unclear whether dismissal in the context of a business reorganisation is for redundancy or not. We have already discussed the topic in relation to dismissal for some other substantial reason in **Chapters 11** and **12**. As we noted at **14.3.3**, the question whether there is a redundancy depends on application of the statutory definition as required by *Murray* v *Foyle Meats Ltd* [1999] ICR 827, and that is a matter of fact for the employment tribunal to decide. A finding that the dismissal was for 'some other substantial reason' (here, a business reorganisation) will mean no redundancy payment is due.

14.5.3.2 Is the dismissal automatically unfair?

An employment tribunal is *bound* to find a selection for redundancy unfair under TULRCA 1992, s. 153 if it was based intentionally or otherwise on trade union membership or activities. This finding is mandatory and does not depend on any question of reasonableness under ERA 1996, s. 98(4). The solicitor representing the employee has only to show that the reason for dismissal was redundancy, that other similar employees were not dismissed and that the reason for selection of this employee reflected trade union membership or activities, whether the employer discriminated deliberately or not. This right covers trade union representatives, safety representatives, and those functioning as employee representatives for the purposes of consultation about the redundancy.

This kind of challenge to a selection for redundancy has become more common. Employees selected for dismissal often have a difficult task in challenging the method of selection adopted by the employer and *dicta* in *British Aerospace plc* v *Green* [1995] ICR 1006 imply that the task will become no easier. It is suggested in that case that it is sufficient for the employer to show a good system of selection and that it was fairly administered, and that ordinarily there is no need for the employer to justify all the assessments on which the selection for redundancy was based. Against that background, challenge under s. 153 becomes an attractively safe mechanism for attacking the employer's selection. There is no parallel provision of automatic unfairness if the selection can be shown to be discriminatory regarding other protected characteristics but the effect is similar. Such a complaint could, of course, be brought either under the Equality Act 2010 or under unfair dismissal law, or indeed under both. If discrimination is involved, compensation is potentially unlimited. If an employee is disabled and has been selected for dismissal as a result of assessment according to a matrix like that described at **14.4.5.2**, it is often possible to show that one or more of the marks obtained may adversely have been affected by the disability. There may also be a parallel discrimination claim, which has the advantage that compensation is not capped.

14.5.3.3 Unreasonableness

Unless the employee's case can be brought within the special rule we have just described, and if the stated reason of dismissal for redundancy seems genuine, we must return to the issue of reasonableness under s. 98(4) of ERA 1996. Each of the nine stages of the employer's checklist (except perhaps notification and redundancy payments) is worth examining for possible objections. The most likely stages for finding material failings may well be:

- selection (perhaps unit of selection);
- individual consultation;
- failure to look for alternative work.

The employment tribunal will examine those three key aspects of the employer's handling of the redundancy, whether or not they are expressly pleaded in the claim to the tribunal: see *Langston* v *Cranfield University* [1998] IRLR 172.

14.5.3.4 Remedies for unfair dismissal for redundancy

We noted in **Chapter 13** that the remedies for a successful claim of unfair dismissal were to be considered in sequence by the employment tribunal: reinstatement, re-engagement (if the employee so wished), and compensation. That rule applies in exactly the same way to a dismissal for redundancy as to any other reason.

In practice, except for cases like those at **14.5.3.2** above, orders for reinstatement are very uncommon where the reason for dismissal is redundancy. The employer would need to find someone else to dismiss if ordered to reinstate the employee, although occasionally re-engagement in a different job or at a different place of work may be feasible. The more common remedy where there has been a finding of unfair dismissal on grounds of redundancy is compensation.

14.5.3.5 Compensation in redundancy cases

In principle the rules applying to other unfair dismissals also apply to compensation where dismissal was for redundancy but has been found unfair. However, the following points occur:

(a) A statutory redundancy payment and a basic award of compensation for unfair dismissal are normally exactly the same figure. By s. 122(4) of ERA 1996 the redundancy payment is offset against the basic award. This will normally extinguish it entirely, except where the basic award has already been reduced for some other reason. The scope of this rule is unclear, since deduction by reason of the employee's contributory conduct is expressly excluded where the reason for dismissal is redundancy: s. 122(3).

(b) Any redundancy payment *in excess* of the basic award is to be offset against the compensatory award: ERA 1996, s. 123(7). This rule includes any contractual or *ex gratia* severance payment but not pay in lieu of notice: *Rushton* v *Harcros Timber* [1993] ICR 230. However, this offset, like other calculations affecting a compensatory award, is performed before application of the statutory maximum, so that the employer paying a substantial non-statutory severance payment may still have to pay the maximum compensatory award in addition if the employee's loss is considerable: *McCarthy* v *BICC* [1985] IRLR 94.

(c) There is provision in s. 123(3) of ERA 1996, apparently very little used, that in assessing the appropriate amount of a compensatory award the employment tribunal can include the excess of any redundancy payment (or, as we have been calling it, a severance payment) above the statutory payment if the employee had a potential entitlement to such a payment, or even an expectation of it. This last element of an expectation being sufficient makes the lack of use of the rule surprising. It appears to permit an employee whose dismissal for redundancy is found to be unfair to enforce against the employer a voluntary severance scheme even where that scheme has no contractual basis, provided the employee had some expectation, presumably reasonably founded, of being paid.

(d) The important decision of the House of Lords in *Polkey* v *A. E. Dayton Services* [1988] ICR 142, which we have already mentioned in connexion with individual consultation, also resolved a long-running argument about the effect of a finding that some procedural failing in fact made no difference to a final decision to dismiss. *Polkey* v *Dayton* determined that a procedural failing that truly made no difference to the result should be reflected in the amount of compensation awarded. Since then the tribunals have very often adopted an approach of trying to assess the chances, usually on the basis of a percentage probability (rather than the horse-racing equivalent of odds), that a correct approach might have led to a different result. This is particularly relevant to a dismissal for redundancy. If the dismissed employee was one of a unit of selection of three of whom one was to be dismissed for redundancy, and it is found that the method of selection was unfair, then it can be said that there was a 33 per cent chance the same result would have ensued if a correct method had been followed (unless of course there is evidence that the three were not in fact equally at risk). So, having assessed compensation on the basis of actual gross loss, the tribunal then reduces it by one-third to take account of that probability. Further guidance was given by the EAT in *Cox* v *London Borough of Camden* [1996] IRLR 389, and this case now sets out the correct sequence of calculations. In *Software 2000* v *Andrews* [2007] ICR 825 the employment tribunal had found that the method of selection was not unfair, but that it had been applied improperly. The EAT held that it was not enough to say simply that the claimant would or would not have been dismissed if the method had been applied properly; the tribunal should have assessed the possibility.

(e) Sometimes where the employer has failed properly to consult the individual it is found under the *Polkey* reasoning that consultation would have made no difference to the result. In such cases, compensation is normally limited to wages for a period that the tribunal estimates proper consultation might have lasted—usually about two weeks. Where it can be shown that the lack of consultation had a greater effect, compensation may be greater, as in *Elkouil* v *Coney Island Ltd* [2002] IRLR 174, where the employee was disadvantaged in looking for another job because the employer concealed the likelihood of redundancy for 10 weeks.

14.5.3.6 Civil action to recover a contractual severance payment

We have already noted when considering the matter from the employer's standpoint that there may be a contractual scheme of redundancy or severance payments higher than the statutory scheme. We also noted that employers (especially successor employers following a change of ownership) sometimes try to avoid meeting contractual duties, especially if the business is now less profitable than when the contractual scheme was first introduced.

Employees seeking to enforce a contractual entitlement to a superior severance payment can do so in the employment tribunals, but only up to the maximum amount of £25,000. Larger amounts will still have to be sought in the county court or High Court.

As we mentioned at item (c) in the list at **14.5.3.5**, it may be possible for an employee who can show unfair dismissal as well as redundancy to include the *expectation* of a superior severance payment as a head of compensation, even where the entitlement was not strictly contractual.

14.6 Summary

- Redundancy is a reason for dismissal and not an alternative to dismissal.
- There is a precise statutory definition of redundancy in terms of the requirement of a business for people to do certain work.
- The cases lay down a series of steps that employers are expected to take with some care in handling a redundancy. Experience suggests that employers most often fail on three of them.
- The first step is that it is essential to consult—to consult representatives if 20 or more people are being dismissed and to consult the individual in every case.

Consultation must be genuine or 'meaningful'—i.e., it must not be a sham and the outcome must not be predetermined.

- The second step is that the selection of those to be dismissed must be done carefully and in some organised way.
- Thirdly, the employer must seek alternatives to dismissal, including looking for alternative work.
- The redundant employee is entitled to a redundancy payment, irrespective of whether the dismissal is fair or unfair, calculated according to a statutory scheme that takes account of age, length of service, and weekly pay.
- The employee may be entitled to a company scheme redundancy payment (usually more generous than the statutory one but also usually off-set against the statutory payment).

14.7 Self-test questions

1. Which of the following examples involves a dismissal for redundancy and why?
    (a) The employer's business makes and packs foodstuffs for several supermarket and other outlets. One of the largest customers moves its contract elsewhere and the employer declares a redundancy of a quarter of the production workers.
    (b) The circumstances are the same as (a) except that there is no loss of a contract. The employer has decided to reduce costs in order to boost profits and because the factory is currently over-staffed. About a quarter of the workers will lose their jobs. The trade union objects strongly that there is no reduction in work and therefore no redundancy: such chasing of excessive profits is immoral.
    (c) The production supervisor has not been performing well. The managing director tells him that the post is being eliminated and he is redundant. The supervisor then learns that a production director is being appointed, with substantially the same duties but a bit more responsibility, including a seat on the local board of management.
    (d) The site in Bristol is being closed and the work is being transferred to another factory in Clevedon, about 13 miles away. The employer says there is no redundancy because work is available for everyone in Clevedon.
    (e) In the context of the reduction in numbers at (a) one of the quality control inspectors is to lose her job. She objects. She has never been involved in any of the work under the contract that is being cancelled; the work she does remains exactly as before and she cannot therefore be redundant.
2. Mr Vijay Patel comes to your office while you are out to talk about his recent dismissal for redundancy by St Werburgh's Electrical Apparatus Testing Shop Limited. Your secretary has arranged for him to come to see you tomorrow and meanwhile he has left for you to study beforehand a copy of his assessment form—**Figure 14.3**. You will note he scored 31 points; he was obviously close to retention as a colleague who scored 33 kept his job. Try to compile a list of all the possible grounds to argue unfair dismissal so that you can explore the evidence tomorrow.

ST WERBURGH'S ELECTRICAL APPARATUS TESTING SHOP LIMITED
ASSESSMENT FOR REDUNDANCY SELECTION – FEBRUARY 2011

Employee's Name V. PATEL Department Main Stores Clock No 789

Job Storekeeper Date of start 1.10.90 Date of birth 31.1.49

	Poor 1 point	**Satisfactory 2 points**	**Good 3 points**	**Excellent 4 points**	**Factor**	**Score**
1. Absenteeism	16 days plus X	6 – 15 days	2 – 5 days	0 – 1 days	X4	4
2. Output of work	Fails to meet targets X	Meets targets if constantly supervised (X, scribbled out)	Output above average	Always meets or exceeds targets; actively works to increase productivity	X3	6
3. Initiative and judgment	Judgment suspect; needs help in organising	Organises work fairly well and judgment usually sound X	Uses initiative when required. Uses common sense to advantage	A lot of initiative; a good organiser.	X4	8
4. Attitude	Unco-operative	Prefers the status quo but will change if forced to X	Keen to try new ideas and responds well to requests for change	Exceptionally co-operative with any request	X6	12
5. Potential	Will not progress further X	Limited promotability; more likely to remain in present job	Will be promotable with greater experience and/or training	Could undertake more senior job now	X5	5
					Total	31

Total 31

Assessed by Mike Street Stores foreman. Date 10.2.11

Figure 14.3 Redundancy selection matrix for self-test question 2.

THE INSOLVENCY SERVICE
www.insolvency.gov.uk

Restricted Commercial

HR1

Advance notification of redundancies

Trade Union and Labour Relations (Consolidation) Act 1992, Part IV, Chapter II

Note for employer

There is a statutory requirement for the Government to assist employees facing redundancy. In order to do this, advance notification of potential redundancies is required from you. Failure to comply with the statutory notification requirements below without good cause may result in prosecution and a fine, on summary conviction, of up to £5000, for the company and/or officer of the company.

The Redundancy Payments Service (RPS), acting on behalf of the Secretary of State for Business, Innovation and Skills, collects the information and distributes it to the appropriate Government Departments and Agencies who offer job brokering services and/or training services so that they can discharge their obligation to your employees. The information about your company is commercially confidential and may be used only for the purpose of assisting those facing redundancy. The other Government Departments and Agencies are bound by the same confidentiality terms as the RPS. You will be contacted directly by your local JobcentrePlus and other service providers in your local area with offers of assistance during this notification/consultation period.

Data Protection Act 1998 We will store the information you give us in a computer system, which will help us deal with it more efficiently. We may use the information for statistical purposes.

How to complete this form

1) Use a separate form for each establishment where 20 or more redundancies may occur within a 90-day period.

2) Use **black ink** and write your answers in CAPITALS, as this will make it easier for us to read.

3) Where tick boxes appear, please tick those that apply.

4) If there is not enough space for your answers, please use a separate sheet of paper and attach it to this form.

5) If the circumstances outlined in this form change, please notify us immediately.

6) Please return the completed form, by post to:
The Insolvency Service, Redundancy Payments Service, PO Box 15425, BIRMINGHAM, B16 6HP

or by fax on **0121 455 0531**

or by Email:**HR1@.insolvency.gsi.gov.uk** Please attach a read receipt to your e-mail if you require an acknowledgement.

NB. If you fax or email the form to us there is no need for you to send the original form by post.
Tel: 0121 456 4411 for assistance on completing the form.

Further Information on assistance for employers

For more copies of the form you can down load one from our website on http://www.insolvency.gov.uk/forms/forms.htm

Guidance on redundancy handling and assistance for employers can be found on the following websites:

- Business Link http://www.businesslink.gov.uk
- BIS http://www.bis.gov.uk/whatwedo/employment/employment-legislation/ice/index.html
- Local Development Agency http://www.englandsrdas.com
- Local Skills Agency http://inourhands.lsc.gov.uk
- Wales http://wales.gov.uk/topics/businessandeconomy/?lang=en
- Scotland http://www.scottish-enterprise.com/grow-your-business

Your legal obligations

1) You are required by law to notify the RPS of a proposal to dismiss 20 or more employees as redundant at one establishment within a period of 90 days or less.

2) If you operate from more than one site, each one is treated separately for notification and consultation purposes. An **establishment** is the site where an employee is assigned to work. You must complete a form for each site where 20 or more redundancies are proposed.

3) Your **Minimum period** for notification and consultation for:

- between **20 to 99** redundancies at one of your establishments, is **at least 30 days before** the first dismissal.
- **100 or more** redundancies at one of your establishments, is **at least 90 days before** the first dismissal.

4) You must notify us **at least 30/90 days before the first dismissal and before you issue any individual notices of dismissal**.

5) You must **send a copy of this notification to the representatives** of the employees being consulted.

6) If you have already notified us about one group of redundancies and you need to make further redundancies you should treat them as separate events. You do not need to add the numbers in the two groups together to calculate the minimum period for either group.

7) The **notification date** is the date on which we **receive your completed form**.

8) If it is not reasonably practicable for you to comply with the minimum notification periods you must make every effort do so as far as you are able. **You must give reasons why you could not provide the information on time**.

URN 09 / 1563-

A BIS SERVICE

1. Employer's details

Name:
Address:

Postcode:
Tel:
Email:

2. Employer's Contact details (MUST be completed)

Name:
Address (if different to 1):

Postcode:
Tel:
Email:

3. Establishment where redundancies are proposed
(Please tick relevant boxes)

a) Address at 1; ☐ b) Address at 2; ☐ c) Different to 1 or 2 ☐

Please write different address here:

Postcode:
Tel:
Email:

4. Timing of redundancies

a) Date of first proposed dismissal ☐

b) Date of last proposed dismissal ☐

c) If you have given less than the required 30/90 day notification period please give reason for late notification.

5. Method of Selection for redundancy

6. Staff numbers/redundancies at this establishment

Occupational group	Total Number of employees	Number of possible redundancies
Manual		
Clerical		
Professional		
Managerial		
Technical		
Apprentices/trainees		
Under 18		
Other		
Totals		

7. Nature of main Business

8. Closure of business

Do you propose to close this establishment?

Yes ☐ No ☐

9. Reason for redundancies

Please tick one or more boxes to show the main reason(s) for the proposed redundancies.

A	Lower demand for products or services	
B	Completion of all or part of contract	
C	Transfer of work to another site or employer	
D	Introduction of new technology/plant/machinery	
E	Changes in work methods or organisation	
F	Other (please give brief details below)	
G	Insolvency	

10. Consultation

a) Please provide the name(s) of

Recognised trade union	Name of Representative	Description of employee they represent

b) If you do not recognise trade unions for any groups of employees please give the name(s) of their elected representative below.

Name of elected Representative	Description of employee they represent

c) Have you given a copy of this form to all the appropriate representatives?

Yes ☐ No ☐

d) Have you started the consultation process with the appropriate representatives?

Yes ☐ No ☐

e) If yes, please give the date consultation started.

☐

f) Have you given individual notices of dismissal to the employees?
Yes ☐ No ☐

11. Declaration

I certify that the information given on this form is, so far as I know, correct and complete.

Signature: Date:

Position:

15

Takeovers and transfers of undertakings

15.1 Introduction

In this chapter we examine the consequences for employees and their contracts of employment when the ownership of a business changes. It is convenient to add the implications for employment of an employer's insolvency or death.

Why, it might be asked, is there a problem at all? If employer B buys employer A's business as a going concern, does the sale not include the employees as well as the premises, plant, equipment, and work-in-progress? One answer might be that slavery was abolished in this country rather a long time ago. A more technical response would be that if we apply the common law rule of privity of contract to the example above we find that, on ceasing the business that is being sold, A will no longer have anything for the employees previously involved in it to do. The new owner is not party to the original contract so the employees must all be dismissed, and the reason will be redundancy within the definition we considered in **Chapter 14**.

Without some form of regulation, if B wished to recruit some or all of A's former employees, it would be necessary to enter into new contracts with them. The employees would have no continuity of service with B prior to the date of their new employment and, given that A may have no funds to pay any redundancy payments or unfair dismissal awards, the employees' rights will have been affected adversely.

Such a result, in which any change in the ownership of a business results in the wholesale redundancy of all those employed by it is incompatible with modern legal principles of employment protection. So there are various statutory rules to give some continuity of employment and to reverse the common law rule in five broad categories of change of ownership—effectively to deem the new owner to have been the owner all along. Simple continuity is provided by ERA 1996, s. 218, but there are other matters we shall need to consider:

(a) What happens if the employer is a limited company and the ownership of shares in that company changes through some takeover or sale of shares? We shall look at this further in **15.2**.

(b) One legally-constituted employer must transfer a business activity to another such employer. This kind of change brings in a European Directive as well as the Transfer of Undertakings (Protection of Employment) Regulations 2006 (TUPE 2006). We shall look at these in **15.3–15.5**.

(c) What if there is a transfer between associated companies? (see **15.6**)

(d) What if the employer becomes insolvent and a business activity is available for acquisition from the receiver, liquidator, or administrator? The various possible kinds of insolvency will be examined briefly in **15.7**.

(e) What if the employer dies? (see **15.8**)

15.2 Share transfers

It is an axiom of company law that a limited company (both plc and Ltd) is regarded as a legal person. The company can sue and be sued in its own name, it can own property, and it can enter into contracts. All of those external activities are unaffected by changes in the shareholders' identities or ownership of shares.

Employees of a limited company look to the company as the legal employer and are not directly interested in who owns the shares of the company. It follows that a change in share ownership has no consequence for the position of the employees. Their rights and obligations relate to the legal person that employs them, and that has not changed. This principle applies equally to a small-scale sale of a few shares in a personal shareholding as to a change in the controlling interest, majority shareholding or even wholly-owned status of a limited company.

This principle is of great importance. In the UK (as contrasted with some of the rest of Europe) most changes in ownership of a business are in fact executed by a transfer of shares. The legal entity that employs employees therefore does not change, and neither do any of the conditions of employment. The courts have shown themselves unwilling to 'pierce the corporate veil' but they are quite prepared to examine critically something described as a share transfer—see for example *The Print Factory (London) 1991 Ltd* v *Millan* [2007] EWCA Civ 322, [2007] ICR 1331 (a share transfer by name but in reality a TUPE transfer).

This heading is always the starting point for analysis because clients often ask questions about TUPE 2006 which on closer examination prove to be about share sales where those regulations have no impact.

15.3 The Transfer of Undertakings (Protection of Employment) Regulations 2006

Before we proceed to look in more detail at the operation of TUPE 2006, it is useful to summarise their effect.

Where there is a *relevant transfer* (i.e., one covered by TUPE—which we shall define below):

(a) employment is *automatically transferred* (unless the employee objects) with full continuity of service;

(b) the transferred employment is on the *same conditions*—including trade union recognition but excluding pensions;

(c) any dismissal because of the transfer is *automatically unfair* (unless in narrowly defined circumstances);

(d) employee representatives of both transferor and transferee must be *consulted*.

It may help to give an example of how a TUPE problem may arise. Suppose an engineering company makes and sells both agricultural equipment, such as tractors, and garden machinery, such as lawnmowers. Its business is organised in two separate divisions for the two sets of products, with the agricultural division the more profitable of the two. It receives an offer for the garden machinery business from another garden machinery manufacturer. If the sale of the garden machinery division goes ahead this looks like a transfer which will be covered by TUPE 2006. That means that the employees in the garden machinery division who are transferred have their continuity of employment protected and their conditions of employment (pay, holidays etc.) remain the same as they were under their original employer. However, if the two activities were organised as subsidiary companies rather than as divisions of one company, then a sale of the **shares** involves no change in the legal identity of the employer so TUPE is irrelevant but continuity of employment is preserved in any event because the mere transfer of shares does not affect employment status.

Sometimes the transfer does not involve something as obvious as a division of a company but, rather, what is termed a *service provision change*. A good example might be a decision of the same engineering company to cease staffing its security gates with its own gatekeepers and to subcontract security to a specialist company. The difference between this and the first example is that the garden machinery business was an enterprise run (whether successfully or not) for profit; the security operation is an identifiable service to the factory but would never have viewed it as a business enterprise in its own right. Nevertheless, as we shall see, the effect of TUPE 2006 is to preserve the continuity of employment of the gatekeepers.

15.4 Relevant transfers

A 'relevant transfer' simply means one to which the Regulations apply. The various consequences we set out at **15.3** above follow if (but only if) the events that occurred fall within the definition of a 'relevant transfer' in reg. 3 of TUPE 2006.

There are two types of relevant transfer:

(a) a transfer of some business activity from *one legal person*, the transferor, to *another*, the transferee. This must be:
- an *economic entity*
- which *retains its identity*; and

(b) a *service provision change*.

We shall need to look at both possibilities.

15.4.1 Transfer from transferor to transferee

The first type of relevant transfer we need to examine is where there is a transfer of some business activity from *one legal person*, the transferor, to *another*, the transferee, and that which is transferred is an *economic entity* that *retains its identity*. The key questions and the analytical structure can be seen in **Figure 15.1**.

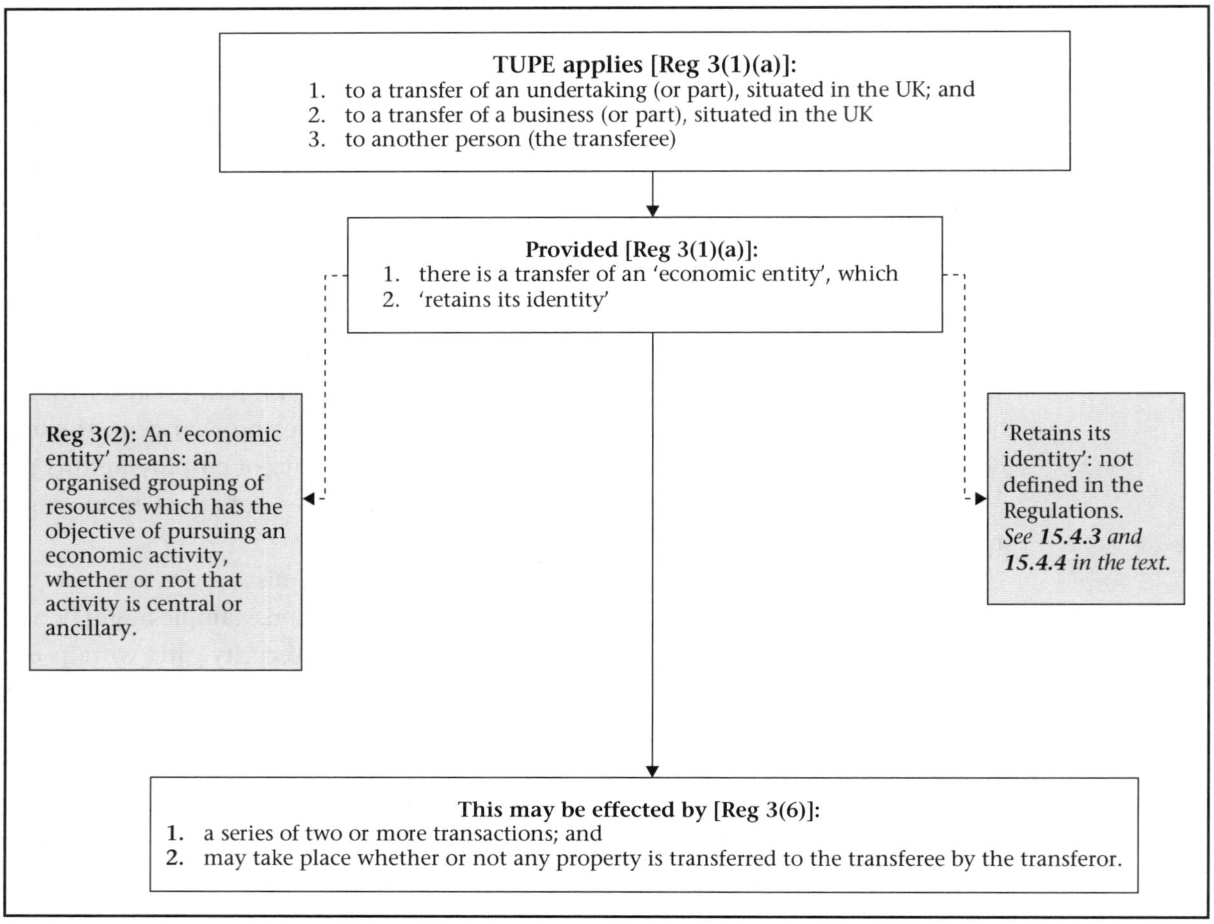

Figure 15.1 Relevant transfer.

15.4.2 An undertaking or business

The definition in reg. 3(1) of the scope of a relevant transfer provides that it applies to an undertaking or business (the whole engineering company in our example above) or to part of an undertaking or business (the garden machinery division). The undertaking must be situated immediately before the transfer in the UK, and there must be a transfer of an *economic entity* which retains its identity. This formula reflects Directive 2001/23/EC. It means that selling off one part of a business to another is likely to be a 'relevant transfer'; selling off one part of a business to *multiple* new owners probably would not be as there is no identity retained. So, there must be some 'before and after' element which looks substantially the same.

Regulation 3(2) states that an economic entity is 'an organised grouping of resources which has the objective of pursuing an economic activity, whether or not that activity is central or ancillary'. Note that the emphasis is on 'resources'. This grouping must have some form of autonomy and structure but the existence (or non-existence) of tangible property is irrelevant: reg. 3(6)(b). The identity of an entity emerges from factors such as its workforce, management style, the way in which its work is organised, its operating methods and any operational resources available to it. Even an organised group of workers (so, with no property involved at all) may constitute an economic entity e.g., a group of workers specifically and permanently assigned to a common task.

It is worth noting the EAT case of *Cheesman* v *R Brewer Contracts Ltd* [2001] IRLR 144 at this stage—a case that reviewed all the key ECJ decisions in this area and laid down very helpful guidelines on what was then the 1981 version of the TUPE Regulations on the meaning of 'economic entity':

(i) a stable economic entity whose activity is not limited to performing one specific works contract, an organised grouping of persons and of assets enabling (or facilitating) the exercise of an economic activity which pursues a specific objective ...;

(ii) . . . such an undertaking . . . must be sufficiently structured and autonomous but will not necessarily have significant assets, tangible or intangible;

(iii) in certain sectors, such as cleaning and surveillance, the assets are often reduced to their most basic and the activity is essentially based on manpower;

(iv) an organised grouping of wage-earners who are specifically and permanently assigned to a common task may, in the absence of other factors of production, amount to an economic entity;

(v) an activity of itself is not an entity; the identity of an entity emerges from other factors, such as its workforce, management style, the way in which its work is organised, its operating methods and, where appropriate, the operational resources available to it.

The Regulations apply to both public and private undertakings engaged in economic activity. However, an administrative reorganisation of public administrative authorities or the transfer of administrative functions between such bodies (such as with local government reorganisations) is not a relevant transfer: reg. 3(5).

15.4.3 Continuity of the economic entity

Once an economic entity has been identified the next question is whether it has retained its identity on the transfer. This issue requires consideration of the two key questions identified by the ECJ in the leading case of *Spijkers* v *Gebroeders Benedik Abattoir CV* [1986] 2 CMLR 296:

- can we identify a stable economic entity before and after the transfer; and
- has it retained its identity as a result of the transfer?

In *Spijkers* the transferor's business of running a slaughterhouse had ceased entirely. After a break in time the transferee took over all the employees except Mr Spijkers—but none of the customers. The Advocate General assigned to the case recommended 'a realistic and robust view' that involved considering all the facts and the ECJ held that there had indeed been a transfer within the Directive despite the break and the lack of transfer of goodwill. The new slaughterhouse business was sufficiently similar to the old one to say that there was a stable economic entity that had retained its identity. No one factor alone is decisive. It is necessary to look at everything—the function, assets, and employees before the possible transfer and the function, assets, and employees afterwards.

Although the *Spijkers* decision pre-dates both TUPE 2006 and the underlying Directive, we suggest that it remains good authority for interpretation of the statutory language in reg. 3, especially as that language can be traced back to the *Spijkers* decision. That is not to say that there have not been conflicting decisions since but the Court of Appeal usefully confirmed in *RCO Support Services Ltd* v *UNISON* [2002] EWCA Civ 464, [2002] ICR 751 that the key authority remains *Spijkers*.

It is confirmed in reg. 3(6)(a) that a transfer may be effected in two or more transactions, but we shall see from *North Wales Training and Enterprise Council Ltd* v *Astley* [2006]

UKHL 29, [2006] ICR 992 in **15.5.1.1** that this does not mean the transfer is gradual: it must always be possible to ascertain a time when it happens.

15.4.4 Some uncertainty

Prior to the replacement of TUPE 1981 by TUPE 2006, practitioners sometimes found it very difficult to say with any certainty whether a given set of circumstances fell within the definition of a relevant transfer or not. Things are now much better, but it would be wrong to imply that all the uncertainty had been removed.

Indeed, in the latest ECJ pronouncement (a German reference: *Klarenberg* v *Ferrotron Technologies GmbH* [2009] IRLR 301), the ECJ had to decide whether TUPE was engaged when the business transferred did not retain its autonomy in all respects. The ECJ held that TUPE could still apply, that there must be 'a functional link between the various elements of production transferred (e.g., labour and material) that enables the transferee to use those elements to pursue an identical or analogous economic activity' and it is for the national court to judge whether there is an identity that has been retained following the transfer. So, just because the entity is merged into the transferee's business does not mean *per se* that the identity has been lost—though it makes the task of proving factually that the 'functionality' continues much more difficult.

An older example of a case where the ECJ found there was no transfer within the meaning of the Directive is *Ledernes Hovedorganisation* v *Dansk Arbejdsgiverforening* [1996] ICR 333 (*Rygaard's* case). Here the supposed economic entity being transferred consisted of a part of the work under one specific building contract, transferred with a view to its completion. It was held that the item transferred, consisting of two apprentices and one employee together with some materials, lacked the stability to constitute an economic entity. The Directive did not apply. So, stability became a key factor.

The extent of uncertainty must not be exaggerated. In most cases in practice it is reasonably clear whether the circumstances constitute a relevant transfer or not. The problems occur inevitably at the margins. Occasionally large sums of money may hang on the question whether the transferor's employees have continuity of employment and you will find in practice that the application of TUPE 2006 has become a matter of great interest in large firms of solicitors, both to the employment department and to those concerned with mergers and acquisitions. Many commercial contracts for the sale of businesses now contain indemnity clauses in relation to the effect of TUPE 2006 and you will be concerned with trying to assess the risk to your client.

15.4.5 Service provision change

The second type of 'relevant transfer' is a 'service provision change'(SPC). This arises where, for example, the company decides not to continue with in-house operations such as cleaning or portering and instead to offer contracts to perform these activities to other outside companies on tender. Regulation 3(1)(b) states that every SPC is capable of qualifying as a relevant transfer if it consists of a transfer:

(i) of activities from the client to a contractor (what is termed 'outsourcing'—where the company gives up running its own security and gets in specialist firms); or

(ii) from one contractor to a subsequent contractor ('re-tendering'—where the contract with the security firm comes to an end and the company looks around for a better deal); or

(iii) transfer or transfer **back** of activities from a contractor to client ('in-sourcing'—where the company discovers problems with outsourcing and 'brings back' the service under its own control).

Thus, say company A decides it is cheaper to outsource its cleaning and asks for tenders on the cleaning contract. Another well-established cleaning company (B) gets the contract. What happens to the cleaners employed by company A? The answer is that, if the requirements of TUPE are met then the cleaners are transferred to company B. This has obvious implications for company B, as they now have both a new commercial contract and more staff.

There is no express definition of 'activities' or of 'service provision' but it seems that almost all provisions of services can be covered, including commonly sub-contracted activities like catering, cleaning, and security. The EAT case of *Metropolitan Resources Ltd* v *Churchill Dulwich Ltd* [2009] IRLR 700 held that the fact the new contractor performs some additional duties is unlikely to negate the application of reg. 3(1)(b) and that it is a matter of fact whether the service provided after the 'transfer' is fundamentally or essentially the same as before that event (which it needs to be to bring TUPE into play). In *OCS Group UK Ltd* v *Jones* EAT/0038/09, [2009] All ER (D) 138 (Sep), therefore, when a restaurant service in a company was replaced by a kiosk run by an outside enterprise and selling pre-prepared sandwiches the activities were held to be different so that TUPE did not apply.

15.4.5.1 What are the exceptions regarding SPC?

Exceptions are provided in the regulations:

- The first is that before every SPC there must exist **an organised grouping of employees** in Great Britain whose principal purpose is the work for the client. An example might be the following. Suppose that some aspect of the cleaning of an office is carried out by a cleaning company with a team of people that goes around a number of workplaces with specialist equipment. If the occupier of the office decides to change contractor (re-tender) there is no grouping of employees whose principal purpose is that work and therefore no SPC.
- It would be different if the contractor employed people to work exclusively at that office; then there would be an 'organised grouping of employees'. One might be forgiven for thinking that one person could not constitute an 'organised grouping', but the ECJ case of *Schmidt* v *Spar- und Leihkasse der Früheren Ämter Bordesholm, Kiel und Cronshagen* (Case C-392/92) [1995] ICR 237 established that the Directive did protect the job of a single office cleaner when a bank 'privatised' its cleaning operations.
- The second exception is to exclude activities concerned with a single specific event or task of short-term duration. It seems that the definition requires *both* something single *and* specific *and* for it to be of short-term duration. The BIS guidance suggests, for example, that where a client engages a contractor to organise an event or conference on its behalf then the engagement of a different contractor for a subsequent conference would not trigger TUPE. This works well where the event is of short-term duration but the obvious point is that the longer the arrangement lasts the less if fits this definition and the more likely TUPE will apply.
- The last exception excludes as a possible SPC the supply of goods. A Department for Business Innovation and Skills guidance note gives an example of a contractor engaged to supply sandwiches and drinks to a client's canteen for sale by the client's own staff. If that contract is terminated TUPE does not apply. However, where the contractor operates the client's staff canteen and the contract is given to another

company this would give rise to a service provision change and, therefore, would constitute a relevant transfer.

Note: it is the concept of 'activity' that is central to service provision changes. One does not also need to look for 'economic entity'. This can be seen in the wording of the regulations themselves, where an 'economic entity' requires an 'organised grouping of **resources**' and a SPC requires an 'organised grouping of **employees**'. Equally, the SPC rules provide supplementary protection so, even if a transfer does not fall within the heading of a SPC (because, say, of one-off event exemption) the 'transfer' still has to be considered under the ordinary head.

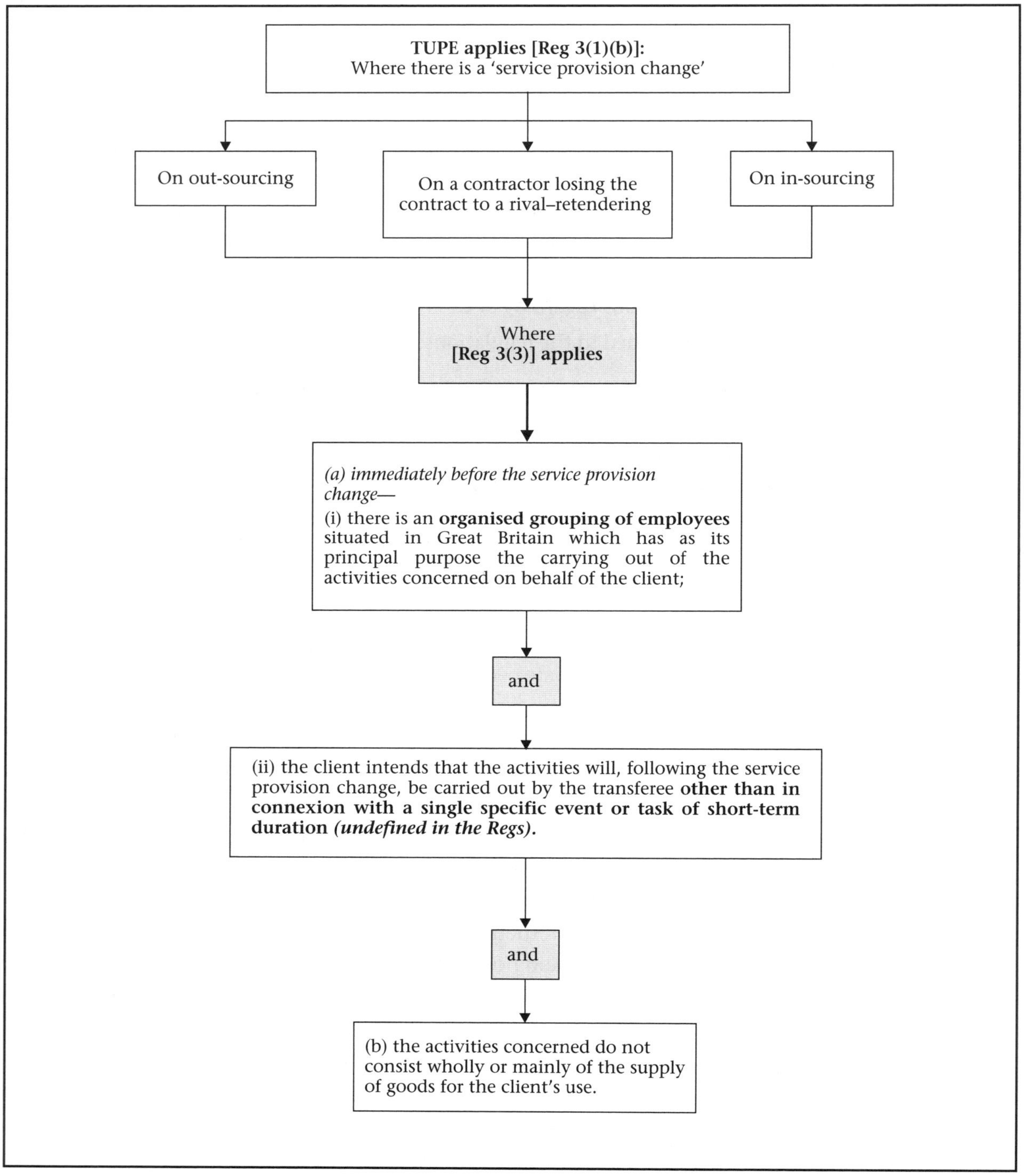

Figure 15.2 Service provision change.

15.5 The consequences

We have already noted that if a transfer of a business falls within the definition of a relevant transfer there are four consequences, which we now need to examine in detail.

15.5.1 Automatic continuity of employment

Wherever there is a relevant transfer, TUPE 2006, reg. 4 provides that the transferor's responsibilities under contracts of employment pass automatically to the transferee. The rule is expressed as applying to all those employed *immediately before* the transfer *assigned to* the organised grouping transferred and unless *the employee objects*. Each of those elements emphasised requires further examination.

15.5.1.1 'Immediately before'

Not surprisingly, the expression has been exposed to some scrutiny in the cases and an argument as to how short a time constituted employment immediately before a transfer was finally resolved in *Secretary of State for Employment* v *Spence* [1986] ICR 651. The Court of Appeal held in that case that it was to be taken quite literally. A gap of even an hour or two was sufficient to break continuity.

An important qualification of that rule was introduced by the House of Lords in *Litster* v *Forth Dry Dock* [1989] ICR 341, however. In that case, the use of a purposive interpretation led to the imaginary insertion of additional words into TUPE 1981. The words do now appear in TUPE 2006 in reg. 4(3) so as to include both those employed immediately before the relevant transfer and also those *who would have been so employed if they had not been unfairly dismissed in the circumstances described by reg. 7(1)*, which we shall consider at **15.5.3** below. So, if the transferor dismisses all the staff a short while before the transfer in the hope that those staff are therefore not covered by the regulations that employer will have misjudged the effect of TUPE. (See also **15.5.4.1** for an important question left unanswered by *Litster.)*

It was noted above that a relevant transfer did not have to occur in a single transaction but could result from a series of events. In *Celtec Ltd* v *Astley* (C-478/03) [2005] IRLR 647 the precise date of the transfer became important in relation to former employees of the Department of Employment seconded to privatised Training and Enterprise Councils in 1990. After some dispute whether a transfer could happen gradually or whether it must always be possible to ascertain a single date, the House of Lords referred the matter to the ECJ who decided that 'the date of transfer' in art. 3(1) of the Directive is always a particular point in time when responsibility as employer moves from the transferor to transferee. In the particular case, when it returned to the House of Lords as *North Wales Training and Enterprise Council Ltd* v *Astley* [2006] UKHL 29, [2006] ICR 992, the employees were allowed the full continuity of service they claimed.

15.5.1.2 Which employees are transferred?

In some cases it is obvious what it is that constitutes the economic entity transferred. In other cases it is not so clear, and there may be people who work both in the part of the transferor's business that is transferred to the transferee and in the part that the transferor retains. For example, in the two-division agricultural equipment and garden machinery company that we described earlier in the chapter, there may be departments such as buying or finance that support both divisions. It is important to know whether such employees are transferred or not.

The answer to this is found in reg. 4(1). The employees transferred are those *assigned to* the economic entity. The formula is that set by the ECJ in *Botzen* v *Rotterdamsche Droogdok Maatschappij* [1985] ECR 519. It is essentially a matter of the employee's function rather than of the terms of the contract. Thus a mobility clause in the contract that is not in fact operated is irrelevant: *Securicor Guarding Ltd* v *Fraser Security Services Ltd* [1996] IRLR 552.

The application of the test of assignment to the part of the undertaking transferred does not require the employee to work *exclusively* for that part: *Buchanan-Smith* v *Schleicher & Co. International Ltd* [1996] ICR 547. It is a matter of fact for the employment tribunal to decide. Similarly, where a transfer involves two or more transferees, it is for the employment tribunal to decide which employees go to which using the same test of *assignment*: *Kimberley Group Housing Ltd* v *Hambley* [2008] ICR 1030. It was not good enough in that case for the employment tribunal to have split liability between two transferees on a *pro rata* basis.

15.5.1.3 The employee's objection

At one time the transfer of employment of the employee from transferor to transferee was entirely *automatic*. In effect none of the three parties involved had any choice in the matter. Now the employee is given a statutory right to object, but in a strange form. Under reg. 4(7) it is provided that an objection to being transferred has the effect of ending the contract but that it is not for any purpose to be regarded as a dismissal. An objection must consist of an actual refusal to be transferred, and not merely an expression of concern or unwillingness: *Hay* v *George Hanson (Building Contractors) Ltd* [1996] ICR 427.

15.5.1.4 Objecting and resigning

In addition to the simple right of refusal, reg. 4(9) preserves the employee's right to resign and to claim constructive dismissal if some *substantial* change is made in working conditions which is to the employee's material detriment. Thus in *University of Oxford* v *(1) Humphreys and (2) Associated Examining Board* [2000] IRLR 183 the employee successfully claimed damages for wrongful/constructive dismissal against the transferor when his terms of employment were altered to his detriment. The same rules apply here as under domestic unfair dismissal law. In *Rossiter* v *Pendragon plc* [2002] EWCA Civ 745, [2002] ICR 1063, the Court of Appeal, for instance, held the transferee-employer's revision of a commission scheme was not a breach of a salesman's contract: he was not entitled to resign under the concept of constructive dismissal. In any event, said the Court, he had affirmed the contract by working under it for 16 months. It is provided in reg. 4(11) that all these rules are without prejudice to the right of an employee to resign and claim constructive dismissal in the event of a repudiatory breach by the employer apart from TUPE 2006.

15.5.2 Maintenance of terms and conditions of employment

All employees whose continuity of employment is preserved on a relevant transfer take with them their existing terms and conditions of employment, entirely unchanged except for one matter we shall consider at **15.5.2.3** below.

15.5.2.1 Individual and collective matters

In this country contractual relationships between employer and employee are considered to be individual, even where employees are treated as a group for some purposes. The European origin of TUPE 2006 means that this rule extends to some collective matters as well as individual terms. So all collective agreements are maintained (including trade union recognition) until the date that agreement was due to end or until a replacement is negotiated. Collective agreements are of course generally not legally binding in the UK, but some aspects of these may have been incorporated into individuals' contracts of employment. Care must also be taken with the wording of the collective agreement. In *Alemo-Herron* v *Parkwood Leisure Ltd* [2009] IRLR 322, for instance, a transferee company (in a chain of transfers) inherited employees whose contracts had originally been subject to a collective agreement negotiated by the original transferor and a national council. That expired and was renegotiated. The transferee company then found itself bound by that newly-negotiated collective agreement to which they were not even a party, partly because the employees' original terms referred to the relevant collective agreement as one being 'negotiated from time to time'. This last phrase meant that the expiry of one of the original collective agreements did not bring the transferee's responsibilities to an end.

15.5.2.2 New recruits

The continuity of terms and conditions applies to those transferred at the time of the transfer. Those subsequently recruited into employment cannot claim the same terms: *Landsorganisation i Danmark* v *Ny Mølle Kro* [1989] ICR 33.

15.5.2.3 Pensions as an exception

TUPE 2006, reg. 10 excludes from the automatic transfer of terms and conditions almost anything to do with occupational pension schemes. The exclusion is restricted to provisions concerned with old age, invalidity, or survivors' benefits, a clarification apparently designed to ensure that superior redundancy payment schemes linked to early retirement were not included and to bring British law into compliance with the decision of the ECJ in *Katsikas* v *Konstantinidis* [1993] IRLR 179. In *Beckmann* v *Dynamco Whicheloe Macfarlane Ltd* (Case C-164/00) [2002] IRLR 578, the ECJ held that even a pension paid early under an early retirement arrangement in a redundancy was not covered by the exception, as it was not an old-age benefit.

The Transfer of Employment (Pension Protection) Regulations 2005, implementing provisions under the Pensions Act 2004, cover the protection of pensions following a relevant transfer. Employees who were members of an occupational pension scheme before the transfer are entitled to have a scheme provided by the transferee, but there is no obligation on the transferee to match the transferor's scheme. The transferee is free to choose the type of pension scheme (defined benefit, money purchase, and so on), provided that it meets a statutory standard under the Pension Schemes Act 1993 (as amended by the Pensions Act 1995). An earlier suggestion that the transferee's scheme should provide benefits that are of overall equivalent value to those of the pre-transfer scheme was abandoned. (The detail of the statutory standard is outside our scope, but in many cases it will require the transferee to continue the transferor's 'relevant contributions' to a pension fund, up to a limit of 6 per cent of basic pay.) Many employees who enjoyed good defined benefit schemes prior to a transfer will find the new rules give little additional protection. Under TUPE 2006, reg. 10(4), employees transferred are not permitted to bring claims against the transferor for breach of contract or constructive unfair dismissal based on loss of pension rights.

15.5.2.4 Maintenance of terms and the possibility of variation

TUPE 2006, reg. 4(2) preserves the employee's contract of employment so that the terms of employment with the transferee after the transfer or for a reason connected with it are exactly the same (except for pensions) as those with the transferor beforehand.

Let us return to the earlier example we used earlier. The engineering company wanted to sell the garden machinery business because it was not sufficiently profitable. The transferee wanted to buy it because it saw a way to make it more profitable. The difference in profitability will not be achieved by magic. The new owner will need to cut costs by integrating the undertaking transferred into the existing garden machinery business. Employees will need to be interchangeable between old and new businesses, but this may well be unrealistic if conditions of employment are sufficiently different as to cause resentment between the two groups of employees. Very often one group will have a better condition under one head and a poorer condition under another. The employer may well be able to obtain the agreement of individuals or their trade union to some programme of harmonisation. TUPE prevents the new employer simply standardising the terms of the transferred employees to match those of the new business if this would mean the transferred employees suffered a detriment.

The transferee-employer will eventually have to find a way to harmonise the terms of both sets of employees. But even when the transferee-employer 'buys' new terms they may still not be enforceable: in *Crédit Suisse First Boston (Europe) Ltd* v *Lister* [1999] ICR 794, the Court of Appeal had to consider a case in which the transferee had given employees additional benefits in return for a post-termination restraint. The transferee now tried to enforce the latter. The Court held that the change in terms and conditions was by reason of the transfer, and therefore void. So, even when the overall package balances out the gains and losses (or even marginally benefits the affected employees) that does not mean it complies with TUPE as TUPE concentrates on individual terms and conditions.

There are, however, instances where an employer may be permitted to make changes (otherwise the business may grind to a halt). We shall look at which changes are permitted under TUPE 2006 at **15.5.4** below ('variation of contract'). We cannot do this yet because, first, we need to consider what are 'automatically unfair dismissals' in this context and what possible general defences are open to the employer.

15.5.3 Automatically unfair dismissal

By reg. 7 of TUPE 2006, any dismissal of an employee by transferor or transferee *because* of the transfer or for a reason connected with it is automatically unfair, **unless** it can be shown to be for an 'economic, technical or organisational reason entailing changes in the workforce'—the 'eto' defence. So, 'automatic' does not actually mean 'automatic' but the application is quite strict. If the 'eto' defence does not apply, dismissal is always *automatically unfair*. If the 'eto' exception does apply, this is deemed to be a fair reason under s. 98(2) of ERA 1996 (categorised as either redundancy or some other substantial reason) and the tribunal will proceed to consider whether the employer acted reasonably as per any other unfair dismissal action. The requirement for qualifying service of one year also applies as with other complaints of unfair dismissal.

In *Morris* v *John Grose Group Ltd* [1998] ICR 655 the EAT was required to consider a dismissal by receivers *before* any transfer had been arranged. They rejected the contention that the equivalent of reg. 7 presupposed the existence of a particular transfer and held that it still applied if dismissal was because of a transfer still to be arranged.

15.5.3.1 Economic, technical, and organisational reasons

The words 'economic, technical or organisational' are taken literally from the Directive and it is not immediately clear what they are intended to mean in the law of this country. **Each of them must also involve changes in the workforce, not just the**

individual's contract: *Berriman* v *Delabole Slate* [1985] ICR 546. Some Government guidance given earlier on the application of TUPE 1981 to privatisations in the public sector gave three examples:

(a) An *economic* reason might arise where demand for the employer's output has fallen to such an extent that profitability could not be sustained unless staff were dismissed.

(b) A *technical* reason might arise where the transferee wishes to use new technology and the transferor's employees do not have the necessary skills.

(c) An *organisational* reason might arise where the transferee operates at a different location from the transferor and it is not practical to relocate the staff.

So there are two analytical steps: (i) was there, say, an organisational reason; (ii) did this entail a change in the workforce? *Berriman* v *Delabole Slate* dealt with this second question. The transferee sought to standardise conditions of employment for newly transferred and existing employees and Berriman resigned, claiming constructive dismissal. The Court of Appeal held that the actual reason for dismissal was not one entailing changes in the workforce, just changes in the individual's contract ('workforce', it was said 'connotes the whole body of employees as an entity). In *Crawford* v *Swinton Insurance* [1990] ICR 85 the EAT expanded upon this in saying that there can be a 'change in a workforce' if the same people are kept on but they are given entirely different jobs to do. The workforce has to be looked at as an entity and it then has to be seen whether the reason in question is one that involves a change in that workforce. There may well be a change in a workforce if the same people are kept on but they are given entirely different jobs to do.

That has been the settled position (though awkward for transferee employers): it is the whole workforce (combining new and existing employees) that has to be considered. However, in *Nationwide BS* v *Benn* [2010] UKEAT/273/09 the EAT appears (very questionably) to have moved away from this. This case involved the transfer of staff from the Portman Building Society to Nationwide, with a change in the bonus scheme for the transferred employees being imposed (the employees of Nationwide prior to the transfer already being on that bonus scheme). The argument was that this entailed a change in the transferred workforce but not the workforce as a whole. The EAT (without much elaboration) held that 'Regulation 7(2) does not state that the organisational reason must entail changes in the entirety of the workforce' and held that the 'eto' defence applied.

In many actual examples there is a conflict between two very practical sets of considerations. The transferor wants to dispose of the undertaking because it is not sufficiently profitable. The transferee sees a prospect of making it profitable by combining it with an existing business and achieving some economies of scale, in other words by employing fewer people in the combined business.

To put too strict a test on the employer would discourage transfers and improved efficiency in business; to put too easy a test would undermine the whole purpose of TUPE 2006 and the Directive. The compromise the tribunals seem to have evolved puts a fairly broad interpretation on an 'eto' *reason* but then investigates quite thoroughly whether the employer behaved *reasonably*. This happened in *Meikle* v *McPhail* [1983] IRLR 351, where the business was a public house and its small size was held to be a relevant factor in determining reasonableness in dismissing a barmaid.

The Court of Appeal has examined the scope of economic reasons within the 'eto' exception. In *Warner* v *Adnet Ltd* [1998] ICR 1056 they confirmed that 'eto' cases form an exception to the general rule of automatic unfairness and that consequently reg. 7(1) and reg. 7(2) are not mutually exclusive. The dismissal of an accountant in that case was for redundancy, and was held to be fair (despite a lack of consultation) because of the urgency of the transferor's financial problems. In *Hynd* v *Armstrong* [2007] CSIH 16, [2007] IRLR 338 the claimant had been a solicitor in the transferor's firm who dismissed him before the transfer because he was surplus to the requirements of the transferee. It was held that it was not within the 'eto' exception for the transferor to anticipate the transferee's future business requirements in this way: transferor and transferee could each use it only in relation to their own future conduct of the business. The Court of Session contrasted the position in *Warner* where the transferor's dismissal of the claimant for redundancy was required in any event, quite apart from the transfer.

15.5.4 Variation of contractual terms

Now that we have seen the possible defences open to an employer regarding an unfair dismissal claim, we can return to try to answer the question we left hanging at **15.5.2.4**. When, following a relevant transfer, can the employer change terms of employment for transferred employees? There is express provision in TUPE 2006, reg. 4(4) and (5) that appears designed to try to provide an answer. A variation of the employee's contract is **void** in either of two circumstances;

(a) the reason is the transfer itself; or

(b) the reason is connected with the transfer and it is not an 'eto' reason entailing changes in the workforce.

However, the employer and employee are permitted to agree a variation if:

(a) the reason is connected with the transfer and it is an 'eto' reason entailing changes in the workforce; or

(b) the reason is unconnected with the transfer. A reason *unconnected* with a transfer could include the sudden loss of an expected order by a manufacturing company or a general upturn in demand for a particular service or a change in a key exchange rate.

This formula seems strange. One can see that the regulations are designed to confer protection on the terms and conditions of employment of the employees who are the subject of a relevant transfer and that the affected employees cannot generally agree diminutions to their contractual rights. However, it is not immediately clear why it is permitted to vary a contract for an 'eto' reason entailing changes in the workforce if the reason is merely connected with the transfer, but not if it *is the transfer itself*. There is no hiding the fact that this is still a fine distinction in some cases.

15.5.4.1 The unresolved question from *Litster*

The Court of Appeal decision in the joined cases of *British Fuels Ltd* v *Baxendale*; *Wilson* v *St Helens Borough Council* [1998] ICR 387 brought out into the open a difficult question that had remained unresolved since the decision in *Litster* v *Forth Dry Dock* [1989] ICR 341. It was this: where an employee is dismissed shortly before a transfer by the transferor, did (what is now reg. 7) operate to give the employee a remedy against the transferor for unfair dismissal, or did the rule in *Litster* make the dismissal a nullity, so that automatic transfer of employment occurs, and any remedy is then against the transferee? This may matter, depending on who has the money to pay any compensation.

The *British Fuels* cases involved dismissals for redundancy (Baxendale and another employee, Meade) by the transferor with 're-engagement' by the transferee on different, less attractive terms. The question in both cases was whether, having accepted the new terms with the transferee this had varied their entitlement to the terms they had enjoyed with the transferor. So, the first point that had to be considered was whether the dismissals for redundancies were a nullity.

The House of Lords gave a clear answer to this unresolved question at [1998] IRLR 706: a dismissal that offends reg. 7 is *unfair* but nevertheless *legally effective;* it is not a nullity. This means the transferee must meet all the transferor's contractual and statutory obligations unless either the employee objects to being employed by the transferee or there is an economic, technical or organisational reason for the dismissal entailing changes in the workforce. The contract of employment is kept alive but only for the purpose of enforcing rights for breach of it or enforcing statutory rights dependent on it. The liability that is transferred by virtue of TUPE to the transferee is to pay damages for wrongful dismissal or compensation for unfair dismissal.

15.5.4.2 When can a transferee change the terms?

Although the House of Lords very helpfully gave a clear answer to the question whether a pre-transfer dismissal is at risk of being nullified, they did not dispose so finally of the question we posed at **15.5.2.4**, viz, when can the employer safely change terms and conditions after a relevant transfer?

The question was of course raised by the cases of each of the three applicants in *British Fuels/Wilson* but it became irrelevant in relation to *Wilson* and *Meade* because of the decision on the first point that their dismissals were not a nullity and in relation to *Baxendale* because of a finding of fact by the employment tribunal that he had validly accepted a variation of conditions. Comments on the issue of when conditions can lawfully be varied were therefore *obiter*. Lord Slynn of Hadley (with whom the other Law Lords agreed) rejected the argument that the automatic preservation of rights and duties under (what is now) reg. 4 was restricted to the time of the transfer. A purported variation would still be invalid if *due to the transfer and for no other reason even if it came later*. He accepted that there must come a time when the link with the transfer could be said to be broken, but said that, if the appeal turned on that point, he would refer it to the ECJ under art. 234. He did not venture any further guidance on it.

In practice the question remains a very real one in circumstances such as we discussed earlier. In most examples, the transferor wants to dispose of some business undertaking because it is not sufficiently profitable. The transferee is prepared to take it over in order to put into effect some rationalisation plan that will improve efficiency. The rationalisation does not necessarily involve dismissing anyone. It sometimes will, but it may also involve harmonisation of conditions of employment, especially if the transferee wants to amalgamate the transferred undertaking with an existing enterprise.

The solicitor will be asked when it is safe to take such steps. After *British Fuels* it seems that the answer has to be a pragmatic one based on common sense. If the variation is *due to* the transfer and for *no other reason* it is invalid according to Lord Slynn's dictum. If it is for an 'eto' reason involving changes in the workforce, it is possible to read across the language of reg. 7 into reg. 4 and the variation will not be due solely to the transfer. We can now recognise Lord Slynn's dictum as lying behind the formula we encountered in reg. 4(4), (whose rationale was not immediately clear). There is no exception within that formula for harmonisation of the conditions of transferred employees with those of the transferee's existing workforce, despite the likely importance of that process to a transferee who wants to maintain good employee relations. However, the more time has passed since the transfer, the more difficult it will be for a claimant to show that the variation was due solely to the transfer. This, however, can raise another problem: the vexed question of equal pay in this context, e.g., the transferred employees find they are paid less than their equivalents when they 'join' the new company. Although TUPE can be used as a defence to an equal pay claim at the time of the transfer this will not last indefinitely and the transferee will be required to take action to remedy the pay gap reasonably quickly. This will usually mean bringing the transferred employees up to the pay level of the established ones.

It would be futile to pretend that the difficulty of providing clear advice in these cases has been removed. In *Boor* v *Ministre de la Fonction publique et de la Réforme administrative* (C-425/02), [2005] IRLR 61, for instance, the ECJ was asked whether the Acquired Rights Directive precluded the Luxembourg Ministry of National Education from reducing the pay of an employee transferred from a private not-for-profit organisation, because she was now placed on a public sector contract governed by national pay scales under national law. The ECJ held that Directive 77/187 did not preclude such a reduction, provided the competent authorities took account of the purpose of the Directive, and in particular the employee's length of service if pay depended on it. However, if there was a substantial reduction in the employee's remuneration, that fell within art. 4(2) of the Directive, entitling the employee to resign and claim constructive dismissal. No British solicitor specialising in mergers and acquisitions is likely to get much help in advising clients from this case but it demonstrates the practical difficulty of balancing the employees' rights and business needs.

15.5.5 Joint and several liability

It is possible under art. 3.1 of the 2001 Directive for member states to legislate that transferor and transferee share joint and several liability for obligations to employees. There is no such provision in TUPE 2006, where reg. 4(2) provides simply that all rights, powers, duties and liabilities pass from transferor to transferee on the transfer. Indeed in *Bernadone* v *Pall Mall Services Group* [2000] IRLR 487, the Court of Appeal held that the rule even extended to liability (and consequently an insurance indemnity) in respect of a personal injury, because it was 'in connexion with' the contract of employment.

In *Allan* v *Stirling District Council* [1995] ICR 1082 employees sought to enforce rights against the transferor on the basis of the Directive. The Scottish Court of Session overruled the EAT and held that the power given to member states by the Directive was permissive and not mandatory, and could not therefore contradict the clear provision of reg. 4(2). Once the transfer has taken place, the transferor no longer has any rights or duties under the employees' contracts of employment.

15.5.6 Consultation of employee representatives

The employers—both transferor and transferee—are required to consult their respective employee representatives about the forthcoming transfer. The duty ends once the transfer date has arrived (so there is no duty, for instance, on the transferee to consult those being transferred, either before or after the transfer). This duty is not unlike the requirement to consult representatives about proposed dismissals for redundancy but no minimum time periods are defined. The main practical problem is that commercial negotiations often need to remain confidential, and it is consequently almost impossible for either employer to inform anyone until the deal has reached a point at which consultation is unlikely to change the result. If no trade union is recognised, the employer must arrange for employee representatives to be elected and failure to do so can lead to an award of compensation to individuals: *Howard* v *Millrise Ltd* [2005] ICR 435.

15.5.7 Employee liability information

Regulation 11 TUPE 2006 requires the transferor to notify the transferee in writing or in some other readily accessible form of certain key information about each employee assigned to the economic entity transferred (and therefore covered by the transfer). That information consists of:

(a) the identity and age of each employee;

(b) particulars of employment as in the written statement issued to the employee;

(c) information about any disciplinary procedure or grievance procedure involving the employee during the previous two years;

(d) information about any court or tribunal claim brought by the employee during the previous two years or likely to be brought; and

(e) information about any relevant collective agreements.

15.6 Transfer between associated employers

Within large groups of companies, reorganisations of company structure are common, and in some cases frequent. There may be tax advantages or some administrative benefit in shifting responsibilities from a parent company to a subsidiary or vice versa, or between subsidiaries. Sometimes the company is organised into divisions or different establishments of the same limited company. There is no legal significance at all in a shift of administrative responsibility within one limited company; but technically any transfer of employees from one limited company to another is covered by TUPE 2006, even if the companies are associated.

Few employers properly comply in such circumstances with the TUPE 2006 requirements, although it is probably only the duty to consult recognised trade unions that has any practical significance. Most regard it as purely administrative. Even so, there is a duty on them to inform employees of any change in the identity of the employer within one month of its happening: ERA 1996, s. 4.

Whenever any employee's employment moves from one company to another associated company, continuity of employment is preserved: ERA 1996, s. 218(6). This rule applies irrespective of the circumstances. So an employee of one company in a group who happens to get a job in another group company will have continuity of employment preserved, even if the move resulted from an advertisement on the open market and was not in the usual sense a transfer initiated by the group.

15.7 Insolvency

One of the circumstances where the ownership of a business certainly undergoes some change is when the employer becomes insolvent. Insolvency is, of course, a very complex aspect of company law and we shall not attempt to deal with it in any detail here. We are concerned only with the position of the employees when an insolvency occurs, and there are two questions we shall want to answer:

(a) Does the employment of the employees come to an end on insolvency, or is it possible for them to continue to be employed—and, if so, by whom and on what conditions?

(b) What rights have the employees against the assets of an insolvent business for arrears of pay, outstanding holiday pay and other debts owing to them, especially in comparison with other creditors?

Before we proceed to address those questions it is convenient to put them in context by describing the various kinds of insolvency that now exist.

15.7.1 Kinds of insolvency

There are four main kinds of insolvency that we shall need to consider in outline:

15.7.1.1 Bankruptcy

This applies only to individual traders and to partnerships. It is less important for our purposes than the kinds of insolvency affecting companies.

15.7.1.2 Administration

This is the newest of the procedures, having been introduced in the Insolvency Act 1986. The intention is to provide a temporary means by which companies in difficulty but capable of being rescued can indeed be saved. The issue of an administration order requires a reference to the court leading to the appointment of an administrator, who has extensive powers to run the business and is deemed to act as an agent of the company.

15.7.1.3 Receivership

A receiver is appointed to receive the income of a company, to realise its assets and to meet its debts in a statutorily defined sequence of priorities. There are various ways that the receiver can be appointed, some leading to a receiver who is deemed to be an officer of the court and some as an agent of the company. In practice it is now very rare to find anyone other than an *administrative receiver*, a category introduced by the Insolvency Act 1986 and given the power to continue to run the business. An administrative receiver is not the same as an administrator, the first being an open-ended appointment and the second normally requiring a conclusion within three months.

15.7.1.4 Liquidation or winding up

This is the final ending of the existence of the company and may be set in train by court order (compulsory winding up) or through a voluntary winding up if the directors believe the company can pay its debts.

15.7.2 The effect on contracts of employment

If the employer is an individual or a partnership that becomes bankrupt, the employment comes to an end.

The reason why the basis of appointment of the administrator, receiver or liquidator (the 'specialist') is important is that appointment by the court leads, under a long-standing rule, to the automatic termination of employment of the employees: *Reid* v *Explosives Co. Ltd* (1887) 19 QBD 264 and *Golding and Howard* v *Fire Auto and Marine Insurance (in liquidation)* (1968) 4 ITR 372. The reason for dismissal is redundancy; but the employee's right to a redundancy payment will depend on having the necessary two years' service, and the ability to obtain it will depend on the matters we discuss in **15.7.3** below.

In all other cases the specialist's appointment as agent of the company has no effect on the employees' contracts of employment: *Re Foster Clark's Indenture Trusts* [1966] 2 All ER 403.

The Insolvency Act 1986 expressly provides that an administrative receiver is personally liable in relation to any contract of employment 'adopted' in connexion with performing his functions. Adoption cannot occur within 14 days of the administrative receiver's appointment but is otherwise not defined. Until recently it had been unclear whether some specific act of adoption was required or whether mere continuance beyond 14 days was sufficient. As there was some authority for the second possibility, administrative receivers usually issued a disclaimer to prevent adoption. However, in *Powdrill* v *Watson* [1995] ICR 1100, the House of Lords held that adoption is a matter of fact if employees are continued in employment for more than 14 days. A full or partial disclaimer was ineffective.

Very often the specialist dismisses at least some of the employees in an effort to reduce the outgoings of the business. This is normally a redundancy. Employees have the same rights to notice and to statutory redundancy payments that we discussed in earlier chapters. Although it is usually the rule that legal proceedings cannot be brought against an insolvent company without the leave of the court, it appears that this does not prevent a dismissed employee from complaining to the employment tribunal, except in connexion with a compulsory liquidation. For example, the employee may wish to complain of unfair selection for redundancy—see **Chapter 14**.

Although one of the specialist's main objectives is to get the insolvent company into such a state that it can be sold as a going concern it is dangerous to dismiss employees solely for this purpose because of the effect of TUPE 2006: *Litster* v *Forth Dry Dock* [1989] ICR 341.

15.7.3 Rights of employees to outstanding debts

When the employer becomes insolvent, various creditors may be competing for the assets. The rights of the employees can be considered in two parts:

(a) rights against the assets of the insolvent employer; and

(b) rights to claim from the National Insurance Fund.

15.7.3.1 Rights of employees against assets of the insolvent employer

In any insolvency there is a strict order of priority in which the specialist must seek to meet the claims of outstanding creditors. In outline the sequence is as follows:

(a) the costs of realising the assets;

(b) other costs and remuneration of the specialist;

(c) claims from holders of fixed charges;

(d) preferential claims;

(e) claims from holders of floating charges;

(f) unsecured claims.

Each item in that list must be met in full before the next item is considered at all. If there is insufficient in the assets to meet the whole of an item it must be met in proportion to the amount that is available. So, for example, if there is enough on liquidation to meet the first three items but then only half the amount required for preferential claims, they will be satisfied only as to half their full amount and holders of floating charges and unsecured creditors will receive nothing at all.

Under sch. 6 of the Insolvency Act 1986, certain debts due to employees count as preferential debts for the purposes of that sequence:

(a) remuneration (defined to include wages and salary and various other items) in respect of the period of up to four months prior to the appointment of the receiver or liquidator, subject to the statutory maximum of £800;

(b) accrued holiday pay.

Any claim from an employee in addition to those amounts can still be pursued, but will rank as an unsecured claim and will be amongst the lowest priorities.

15.7.3.2 Rights against the National Insurance Fund

Very often the assets of an insolvent employer are insufficient to meet the debts due to preferential creditors, including employees. Even where that is not the problem, the process of liquidation is often so slow as to leave some employees in financial difficulty because of the absence of immediate income.

Some help is provided by s. 182 of ERA 1996, which provides some limited immediate payment to the employee from the National Insurance Fund, which then stands in the employee's shoes in seeking redress from the insolvent employer. Insolvency is defined for this purpose as meaning bankruptcy or any of the corporate states of insolvency defined at **15.7.1** above, but not merely that the employer cannot meet debts. This provision meets the requirements of European Directive 80/987/EEC.

Payments available from the National Insurance Fund are in all cases limited to the statutory maximum week's pay of £380 which we have encountered elsewhere, and are as follows:

(a) arrears of pay for up to eight weeks;

(b) minimum statutory notice as in s. 86 of ERA 1996;

(c) holiday pay for up to six weeks;

(d) a basic award for unfair dismissal;

(e) statutory redundancy pay: ERA 1996, s. 166;

(f) certain unpaid pensions contributions—those due from the employer and those employee's contributions already deducted but not paid over by the employer;

(g) statutory maternity pay.

15.8 Death of the employer

The rights of the employee when the employer dies are set out in s. 206 of ERA 1996. The rights of personal representatives of a deceased employee are covered in s. 207.

The death of an employer obviously changes the status of the employee only if the employer was acting as a sole individual. If the employer was a partnership, the usual rule of survivorship provides that the remaining partners become the new employer; if the employer traded as a limited company, the death of a major shareholder does not affect the continuing existence of the company.

The essence of the statutory rules is that rights enjoyed by the employee against the employer can be maintained against the personal representatives. This includes employment tribunal proceedings, subject only to the rule that in a case of unfair dismissal, reinstatement or re-engagement cannot be ordered against personal representatives.

If the death of the employer results in the ending of the employment, that is to be treated as a dismissal for redundancy: ERA 1996, s. 136(5). This will usually apply to domestic servants and the like. However, if the employment is a business the personal representatives are more likely to want to keep it going to maximise its resale value, and there is continuity of employment in such cases. The liability of the personal representatives to make a redundancy payment can be avoided if the employee unreasonably refuses an offer of suitable continuing employment. However, the employment will not be continued by default: there needs to be some agreement between the employee and the personal representatives to continue: *Ranger* v *Brown* [1978] ICR 608.

15.9 Summary

Although this chapter deals with several kinds of change in the ownership of a business, the main topic is the Transfer of Undertakings (Protection of Employment) Regulations 2006 (TUPE 2006).

We noted that the effect of TUPE 2006 is:

- where there is a *relevant transfer*, i.e., the transfer of either (i) an *economic entity* that *maintains its identity*, or (ii) a *service provision change*;
- employment is *automatically transferred* (unless the employee objects) with full continuity of service;
- the transferred employment is on the *same conditions*, including trade union recognition, but excluding pensions;
- any dismissal because of the transfer is *automatically unfair* unless for an *economic, technical, or organisational reason entailing changes in the workforce*;
- there is limited scope for the transferee to alter the terms and conditions of any transferred employees; and
- employee representatives of both transferor and transferee must be *consulted*.

In diagrammatic form this becomes:

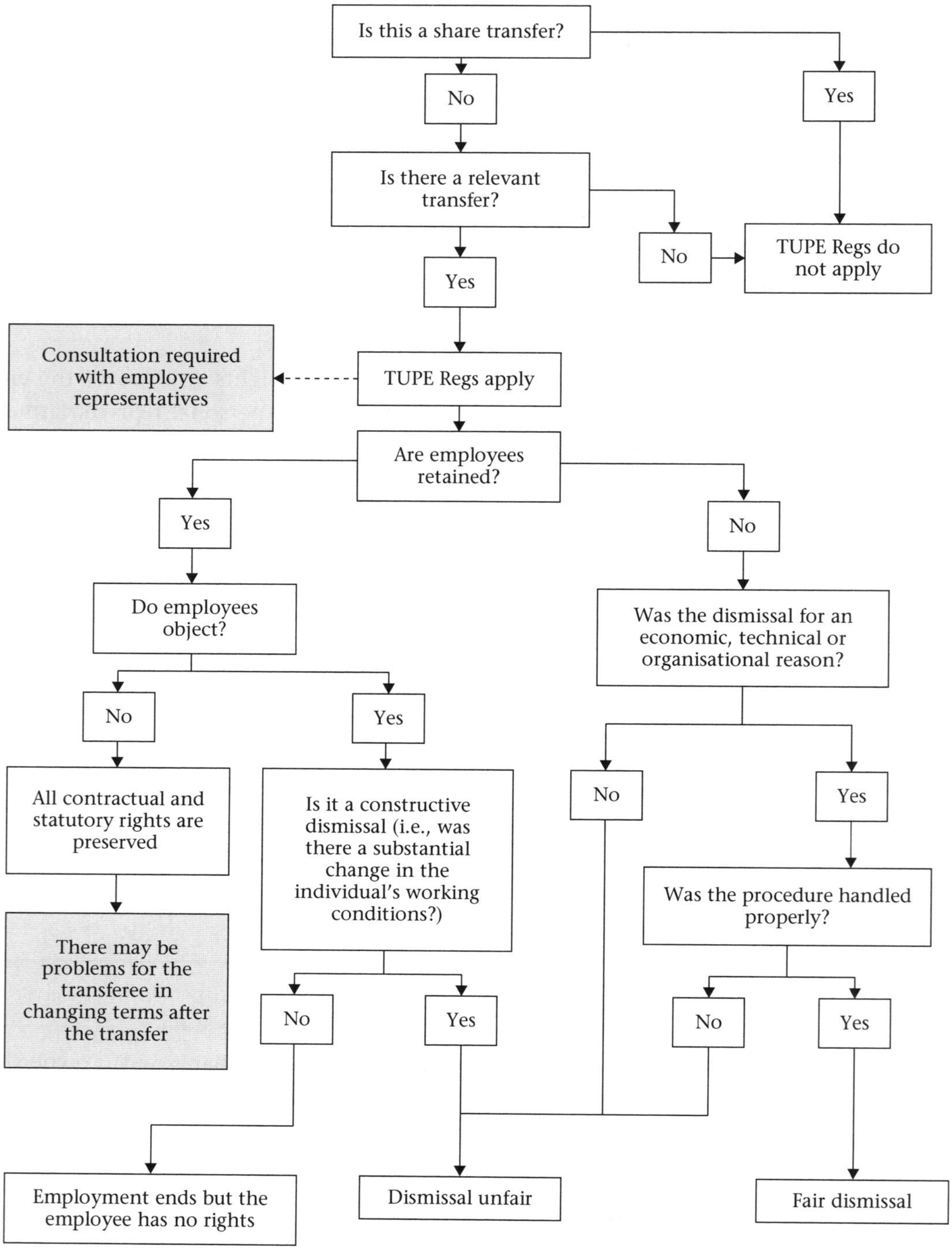

Figure 15.3 Diagrammatic summary.

15.10 Self-test questions

1. Is there any single test you can apply when a business (or part of one) changes hands to decide whether there has been a relevant transfer within the meaning of TUPE 2006?
2. A client comes to you wanting to discuss his proposed purchase for a very favourable price of an unprofitable part of an existing business, in the hope of amalgamating it with his current business and making it profitable through economies of scale. Your detailed enquiries indicate quite clearly that the purchase will be a relevant transfer within the meaning of TUPE 2006. What key employment law consequences would you bring to the client's notice as a result of that conclusion?

16

Employment tribunal procedure

16.1 Introduction

The feature that links most of the rights of employees set out in this book is that the remedy for infringement is a complaint to the employment tribunal. There are, of course, a few items where this is not the case—mostly matters involving alleged breach of contract. The procedure there is to be found in any standard work on civil procedure and the key points have been noted in **Chapters 5** and **10** (and **8** and **9** regarding confidentiality and restraint of trade), but the employment tribunals are unique to employment law and we need in this chapter to describe their operation and procedure.

New rules of procedure in the tribunals came into effect in October 2004. It would be comforting to report that the new arrangements have settled in nicely and that we now have a clear idea of how the 2004 rules operate. Comforting but still not true. The problem seems to be that in some respects the 2004 rules are very strict, and allow tribunals much less discretion than the previous 2001 version. There certainly seems to be some variation among different regions and different individual employment tribunal judges. This chapter therefore works on the basis that the new rules operate as written, noting the points where it seems that some variation may occur.

For our purposes the claimant presenting a claim to the tribunal is nearly always the employee (or, in appropriate cases, the applicant for a job, the 'worker', or the ex-employee) and the employer is the respondent. However, if the ex-employee brings a claim for breach of contract in a tribunal, the employer may counterclaim, but the employer cannot initiate proceedings.

There are a few jurisdictions in which an employee can bring proceedings in the employment tribunal against a trade union or a trade union against the employer, but the number of such cases in practice is so small that we shall ignore both possibilities.

The solicitor is most likely to become involved on behalf of either side once something has already gone wrong in the employment relationship. As in any other branch of the law, litigation is the last resort and clients should be advised not to ignore obvious and less formal solutions. We have always regarded it as good practice to suggest that the employee should complain personally to the boss or use the trade union to pursue a grievance. The ACAS code of practice about discipline and grievances suggests that voluntary procedures should be used before starting tribunal proceedings. So, as we saw in **Chapter 13**, a claimant who successfully complains of unfair dismissal will find compensation reduced if there is no good explanation for not having used the employer's appeal procedure. Both sides, though, will need to take care to ensure that discussions held 'without prejudice' do not adversely affect them if tribunal proceedings follow.

The 'without prejudice' rule only applies once a dispute can be said to exist and in any case does not protect from disclosure any remark that involves unlawful discrimination: *BNP Paribas* v *Mezzotero* [2004] IRLR 508.

If those informal steps fail, an application to the tribunal becomes inevitable and we shall set out the procedure to be followed in the remainder of the chapter, which takes the following form:

- the constitution and workload of the employment tribunals;
- bringing a claim;
- presentation of the claim on time;
- acceptance of the claim;
- the response;
- acceptance of the response and default hearings;
- case management;
- pre-hearing reviews;
- conciliation and the role of ACAS;
- the hearing;
- the tribunal decision;
- costs and preparation time orders;
- the remedies available to the tribunal;
- challenge of an employment tribunal decision;
- a summary of main jurisdictions, time limits, and awards.

In trying to understand how the procedures work it will be helpful to use four imaginary examples, three of them complaints of unfair dismissal:

- Amrita was dismissed for redundancy;
- Basil for alleged dishonesty;
- Catherine claims constructive unfair dismissal;
- Dmitri complains of disability discrimination.

The detailed facts will emerge as we introduce and develop the cases.

16.2 Constitution and workload of the employment tribunals

16.2.1 History

The current workload of the employment tribunals is broad. As we explained at the start of the book, the employment tribunals were known as industrial tribunals until 31 July 1998. They still use that name in Northern Ireland. Since 1 October 2004 the operation of the employment tribunals has been governed by the Employment Tribunals (Constitution and Rules of Procedure) Regulations 2004 (SI 2004/1861) (the ET Regs 2004), which contain in sch. 1 the Employment Tribunal Rules of Procedure (ET Rules 2004) and, as from April 2009, the Employment Tribunals (Constitution and Rules of Procedure) (Amendment) Regulations 2008 (SI 2008/3240) (the ET Rules (Amendments) 2008). We shall not concern ourselves with the special rules for certain specific jurisdictions that are contained in schs 2 to 6 of the ET Rules 2004. The provisions apply to the whole of Great Britain.

16.2.2 The composition of the tribunals

Under the Tribunals, Courts and Enforcement Act 2007 (TCE 2007), the employment tribunal system is a distinct part of the unified tribunal system administered by the Tribunals Service of the Ministry of Justice. Its judicial side is headed by the President.

The system in England and Wales is organised into 27 offices, some of which have the status of regions. Under TCE 2007 the former tribunal chairmen have been known since December 2007 as employment judges. Each region is headed by a regional employment judge, and there are also several full-time employment judges and a number of part-time employment judges. By reg. 8 of the ET Regs 2004 an employment judge must be a barrister or solicitor of seven years' standing. The part-time employment judges in fact consist of some practising lawyers and some retired, former full-time employment judges.

When the tribunal sits it must be chaired by the President or another employment judge, who normally is accompanied by one person from each of two lists (or 'panels') of people representative of employers' organisations and of employed people's organisations. In interim matters and uncontested cases the employment judge sits alone. There has been increasing use of the provision under ETA 1996, s. 4(2) as amended by the Employment Rights (Disputes Resolution) Act 1998 (ERDRA 1998), s. 3, whereby employment judges sit alone in other matters and that is now normal practice in relation to protection of wages and breach of contract questions. It is possible for employment judges to sit alone if parties consent in other matters including unfair dismissal. They sometimes sit with one other member, usually where the third member has become indisposed or is forced to withdraw for some reason.

16.2.3 Procedure at the tribunals

The employment tribunals were originally intended to provide a means of resolving employment disputes that was informal, speedy, and cheap. To an extent they still do, but the informality is more apparent to lawyers who compare them with the courts than to the general public who often find them daunting. Under ET Regs 2004, reg. 3, their overriding objective is to deal with cases justly.

The ET Regs 2004 increased the emphasis on case management by the tribunals. In many ways this mirrors the Woolf reforms in the courts. Although the pre-2004 old rules gave tribunals a wide power to determine their own procedure and many employment judges had already adopted 'Woolf-type practices', the problem for practitioners has been that individual employment judges have different preferences, and it is still sometimes difficult to know how cases will be handled in an unfamiliar region. Such tight procedural management is often very unpopular with clients (both claimants and employers) who prefer an informal style in which they feel they can have their say. Sometimes they feel that cases are won or lost on legal technicalities rather than the merits.

As in the courts, terminology is changed to make it less arcane; interlocutory proceedings, for example, have now become interim hearings. A claim (previously an originating application) is presented by the claimant, usually using form ET 1 and the respondent replies in a response, form ET 3.

Under reg. 13 of ET Regs 2004 the President has the power to make practice directions. We expected that the power would be used very soon after the new rules came into effect on 1 October 2004 so as to start to standardise practice across the country, especially in matters like the use of witness statements where practice has varied considerably—see **16.8.10** below. In fact nothing has been issued. We understand that the President prefers to write informally to regional employment judges commending examples of good practice rather than to be prescriptive by issuing practice directions. Thus far, this 'softly softly' approach has left in place many regional variations.

We shall note the most important aspects of the tribunals' procedure as we work through the progress of a case in the following sections.

16.2.4 Jurisdictions

Although, as we have noted, there is a wide range of jurisdictions for the employment tribunals, the largest part of their workload is concentrated on relatively few issues. As we go to press the statistics for employment tribunal applications during the year April 2008 to February 2009 have been published—see **Table 16.1**.

16.2.5 Appeals

An appeal from a decision of the employment tribunal lies on a point of law only to the EAT, and thereafter in the usual way to the Court of Appeal and the Supreme Court. We shall consider briefly the mechanism for appealing to the EAT in **16.15.2** below.

16.2.6 Scotland

The substantive statute law that we have been considering throughout this book applies equally to Scotland as to England and Wales. There are, of course, a few differences as to the common law.

Although, as we noted at **16.2.1** above, ET Regs 2004 apply equally to Scotland as to England and Wales, the Scottish structure of employment tribunals is separate, with its own Central Office in Glasgow and its own President. Appeals lie to a Scottish division of the EAT, then to the Court of Session and finally to the Supreme Court. In a statement arising out of *Davidson* v *City Electrical Factors Ltd* [1998] ICR 443, however, the President of the EAT has explained that there is one EAT and not two, so that a judgment of the EAT wherever it sits has an equal effect in law in Scotland and in England and Wales. We should refer to 'the EAT sitting in Scotland' and not to a 'Scottish EAT'.

Practitioners may occasionally find themselves called upon by clients in England and Wales to deal with cases in Scotland. For example, a company with its only premises in

Table 16.1 Workload of the employment tribunals in 2008–09 (claims accepted).

Unfair dismissal	52,711	20%
Redundancy pay	10,839	4%
Deductions from wages	33,839	13%
Discrimination: race, sex, disability, part-time etc.	36,095	14%
Equal Pay	45,748	17%
Breach of contract	32,829	12%
Working Time Regulations	23,976	9%
All other jurisdictions, i.e., miscellaneous employment rights, and trade union issues	30,505	11%
Total	266,542	100%

Source: The Tribunals Service.

the south of England that dismisses a service engineer who used his home in Edinburgh as a base for work in that area will find an employment tribunal claim sent to a Scottish tribunal (see **16.3** for the reasons why). We expect that the few remaining differences in practice in Scotland will become less significant under the common rules of procedure, but practitioners straying north of the border must expect any reference they make to documents, costs, or staying proceedings to be corrected to 'productions', 'expenses', and 'sisting' proceedings.

16.3 Bringing a claim

The means of bringing an action in the employment tribunal is to present a claim to the appropriate local office of the tribunals, determined by reference to the postcode of the place of work or former place of work. Very clear guidance for claimants can be found at the employment tribunal website (www.employmenttribunals.gov.uk), which is worth visiting. It includes the standard form ET 1, use of which is now mandatory under r. 1(3). The key pages of the current version (omitting three final blank pages for additional information to be supplied) are reproduced below by kind permission of the Employment Tribunal Service, who advise readers to check that it is still the latest version. Forms may be downloaded from the website, completed, saved for later return, and sent to the relevant parties.

The form contains sections specific to particular kinds of claim. It is designed to be user-friendly and straightforward. We provide a blank form below and most of the points require no discussion (e.g., details of the claimant). The more substantive boxes do need explanation and to show the variety of claims and how they operate we will demonstrate how the key boxes should be completed by using four different claimants.

16.3.1 How much information is required?

There is a list in r. 1(4) of ET Rules 2004 of the matters that have to be covered in a claim and provision is made for all of them in the mandatory form ET 1. Express provision is made for multiple claims by the claimant against the same employer and for multiple cases arising from the same or similar circumstances of which this is one. Names and addresses must be given for each claimant.

If you take a look at the version of the ET 1 in use as from April 2009 you will see that it is constructed in a way which seeks not to deter applications.

Items 1 (claimant's details), 2 (respondent's details), 3 (employment details), and 4 (earnings and benefits) are all straightforward—though sometimes employees have difficulty in: (a) establishing exactly what they were paid or when they started at that organisation and (b) what the significance of item 4.9 is (what the claimant wants if successful).

16.3.2 The claim (item 5)

Previously there were separate items to fill in according to whether the claim was for unfair dismissal, discrimination etc. Now, one is asked to tick one or more boxes in 5.1. Item 5.2 then allows for details of the complaint to be made and we shall return to how this can be filled in soon.

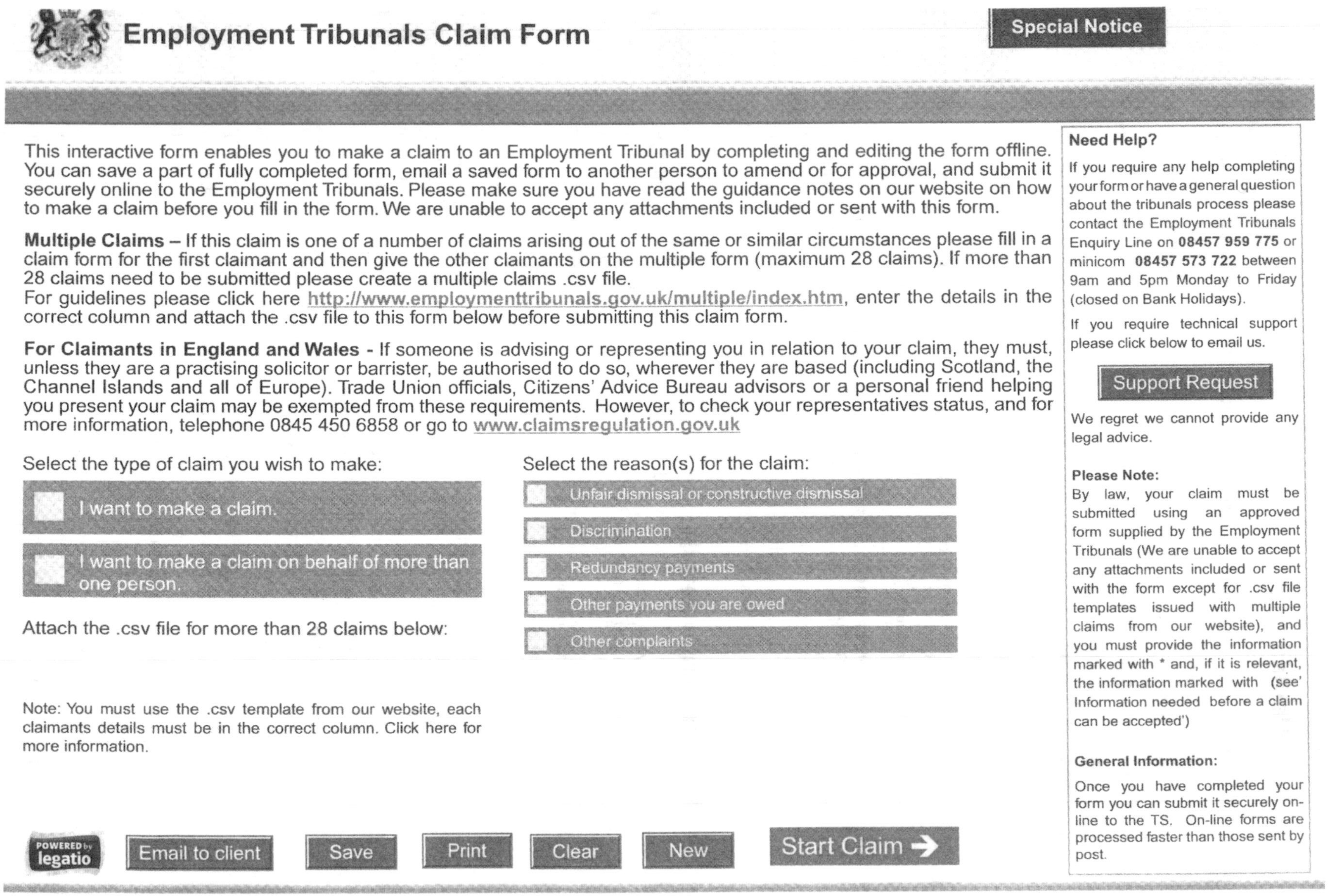

Employment Tribunals Claim Form

Special Notice

This interactive form enables you to make a claim to an Employment Tribunal by completing and editing the form offline. You can save a part of fully completed form, email a saved form to another person to amend or for approval, and submit it securely online to the Employment Tribunals. Please make sure you have read the guidance notes on our website on how to make a claim before you fill in the form. We are unable to accept any attachments included or sent with this form.

Multiple Claims – If this claim is one of a number of claims arising out of the same or similar circumstances please fill in a claim form for the first claimant and then give the other claimants on the multiple form (maximum 28 claims). If more than 28 claims need to be submitted please create a multiple claims .csv file.
For guidelines please click here http://www.employmenttribunals.gov.uk/multiple/index.htm, enter the details in the correct column and attach the .csv file to this form below before submitting this claim form.

For Claimants in England and Wales - If someone is advising or representing you in relation to your claim, they must, unless they are a practising solicitor or barrister, be authorised to do so, wherever they are based (including Scotland, the Channel Islands and all of Europe). Trade Union officials, Citizens' Advice Bureau advisors or a personal friend helping you present your claim may be exempted from these requirements. However, to check your representatives status, and for more information, telephone 0845 450 6858 or go to www.claimsregulation.gov.uk

Select the type of claim you wish to make:

- I want to make a claim.
- I want to make a claim on behalf of more than one person.

Attach the .csv file for more than 28 claims below:

Note: You must use the .csv template from our website, each claimants details must be in the correct column. Click here for more information.

Select the reason(s) for the claim:

- Unfair dismissal or constructive dismissal
- Discrimination
- Redundancy payments
- Other payments you are owed
- Other complaints

POWERED by legatio

Email to client | Save | Print | Clear | New | Start Claim →

Need Help?

If you require any help completing your form or have a general question about the tribunals process please contact the Employment Tribunals Enquiry Line on **08457 959 775** or minicom **08457 573 722** between 9am and 5pm Monday to Friday (closed on Bank Holidays).

If you require technical support please click below to email us.

Support Request

We regret we cannot provide any legal advice.

Please Note:
By law, your claim must be submitted using an approved form supplied by the Employment Tribunals (We are unable to accept any attachments included or sent with the form except for .csv file templates issued with multiple claims from our website), and you must provide the information marked with * and, if it is relevant, the information marked with (see' Information needed before a claim can be accepted')

General Information:
Once you have completed your form you can submit it securely on-line to the TS. On-line forms are processed faster than those sent by post.

1 Your details

1.1 Title: Mr ☐ Mrs ☐ Miss ☐ Ms ☐ Other ☐

1.2* First name (or names):

1.3* Surname or family name:

1.4 Date of birth (date/month/year): D D - M M - Y Y Y Y Are you: male? ☐ female? ☐

1.5* Address: Number or Name

Street

\+ Town/City

County

Postcode

1.6 Phone number including area code **(where we can contact you in the day time)**:

Mobile number **(if different)**:

1.7 How would you prefer us to communicate with you? (Please tick only one box) E-mail ☐ Post ☐

E-mail address:

@

2 Respondent's details

2.1* Give the name of your employer or the organisation you are claiming against.

2.2* Address: Number or Name

Street

\+ Town/City

County

Postcode

Phone number:

2.3● If you worked at a different address from the one you have given at 2.2, please give the full address and postcode.

Postcode

Phone number:

If there are other respondents please complete **Section 11.**

3 Employment details

3.1 Please give the following information if possible.

When did your employment start? D D - M M - Y Y Y Y

Is your employment continuing? Yes ☐ No ☐

If your employment has ceased, or you are in a period of notice, when did it, or will it, end? D D - M M - Y Y Y Y

3.2 Please say what job you do or did.

4 Earnings and benefits

4.1 How many hours on average do, or did, you work each week? ☐☐ hours each week

4.2 How much are, or were, you paid?

Pay before tax £ ☐☐☐ , ☐☐☐ .00

Normal take-home pay (including overtime, commission, bonuses and so on) £ ☐☐☐ , ☐☐☐ .00

Hourly ☐
Weekly ☐
Monthly ☐
Yearly ☐

4.3 If your employment has ended, did you work (or were you paid for) a period of notice? Yes ☐ No ☐

If 'Yes', how many weeks' or months' notice did you work, or were you paid for? ☐☐☐ weeks ☐☐ months

4.4 Were you in your employer's pension scheme? Yes ☐ No ☐

Please answer 4.5 to 4.9 if your claim, or part of it, is about unfair or constructive dismissal.

4.5 If you received any other benefits, e.g. company car, medical insurance, etc, from your employer, please give details.

4.6 Since leaving your employment have you got another job? Yes ☐ No ☐
If 'No', please now go straight to section 4.9.

4.7 Please say when you started (or will start) work.

4.8 Please say how much you are now earning (or will earn). £ , .00 each

4.9 Please tick the box to say what you want if your case is successful:

a To get your old job back and compensation (reinstatement)

b To get another job with the same employer and compensation (re-engagement)

c Compensation only

5 Your claim

5.1* Please tick one or more of the boxes below. In the space provided, describe the event, or series of events, that have caused you to make this claim:

a I was unfairly dismissed (including constructive dismissal)

b I was discriminated against on the grounds of

Sex (including equal pay)	Race
Disability	Religion or belief
Sexual orientation	Age

c I am claiming a redundancy payment

d I am owed

notice pay

holiday pay

arrears of pay

other payments

e Other complaints

5.2* Please set out the background and details of your claim in the space below.
The details of your claim should include **the date when the event(s) you are complaining about happened**; for example, if your claim relates to discrimination give the dates of all the incidents you are complaining about, or at least the date of the last incident. If your complaint is about payments you are owed please give the dates of the period covered. Please use the blank sheet at the end of the form if needed.

5.3 If your claim consists of, or includes, a claim that you are making a protected disclosure under the Employment Rights Act 1996 (otherwise known as a 'whistleblowing' claim), please tick the box below if you wish a copy of this form, or information from it, to be forwarded on your behalf to a relevant regulator (known as a 'prescribed person' under the relevant legislation) by the Tribunals Service.

☐

6 What compensation or remedy are you seeking?

6.1 Completion of this section is optional, but may help if you state what compensation or remedy you are seeking from your employer as a result of this complaint. If you specify an amount, please explain how you have calculated that figure.

7 Other information

7.1 Please do not send a covering letter with this form. You should add any extra information you want us to know here. Please use the blank sheet at the end of the form if needed.

8 Your representative

Please fill in this section only if you have appointed a representative. If you do fill in this section, we will in future only send correspondence to your representative and not to you.

8.1 Representative's name:

8.2 Name of the representative's organisation:

8.3 Address: Number or Name

Street

+ Town/City

County

Postcode

8.4 Phone number **(including area code):**

Mobile number **(if different)**:

8.5 Reference:

8.6 How would they prefer us to communicate with them? E-mail ☐ Post ☐
(Please tick only one box)

E-mail address:

@

9 Disability

9.1 Please tick this box if you consider you have a disability Yes ☐
Please say what this disability is and tell us what assistance, if any, you will need as your claim progresses through the system, including for any hearings that may need to be held at Tribunal Service premises.

10 Multiple cases

10.1 To your knowledge, is your claim one of a number of claims against the same employer arising from the same, or similar, circumstances? Yes ☐ No ☐

11 Details of Additional Respondents

- Name of your employer or the organisation you are claiming against.
- Address: Number or Name
  Street
  \+ Town/City
  County
  Postcode

  Phone number:

- Name of your employer or the organisation you are claiming against.
- Address: Number or Name
  Street
  \+ Town/City
  County
  Postcode

  Phone number:

- Name of your employer or the organisation you are claiming against.
- Address: Number or Name
  Street
  \+ Town/City
  County
  Postcode

  Phone number:

Please read the form and check you have entered all the relevant information.
Once you are satisfied, please tick this box.

Data Protection Act 1998. We will send a copy of this form to the respondent(s) and Acas. We will, if your claim consists of, or includes, a claim that you have made a protected disclosure under the Employment Rights Act 1996 (and you have given your consent that we should do so) send a copy of the form, or extracts from it, to the relevant regulator. We will put the information you give us on this form onto a computer. This helps us to monitor progress and produce statistics. Information provided on this form is passed to the Department for Business, Innovation and Skills to assist research into the use and effectiveness of employment tribunals.

Additional information for sections 5.2 and 7.

Additional information for sections 5.2 and 7.

Additional information for sections 5.2 and 7.

Equal Opportunities Monitoring Form

You are not obliged to fill in this section but, if you do so, it will enable us to monitor our processes and ensure that we provide equality of opportunity to all. The information you give here will be treated in strict confidence and this page will not form part of your case. It will be used only for monitoring and research purposes without identifying you.

1. What is your country of birth?

- England
- Wales
- Scotland
- Northern Ireland
- Republic of Ireland
- Elsewhere, *please write in the present name of the country*

2. What is your ethnic group? Choose ONE section from A to E, then ✓ the appropriate box to indicate your cultural background.

A White

- British
- Irish
- Any other White background *please write in*

B Mixed

- White and Black Caribbean
- White and Black African
- White and Asian
- Any other Mixed background *please write in*

C Asian or Asian British

- Indian
- Pakistani
- Bangladeshi
- Any other Asian background *please write in*

D: Black or Black British

- Caribbean
- African
- Any other Black background *please write in*

E Chinese or other ethnic group

- Chinese
- Any other, *please write in*

3. What is your religion?
✓ box only

- None
- Christian (including Church of England, Catholic, Protestant and all other Christian denominations)
- Buddhist
- Hindu
- Jewish
- Muslim
- Sikh
- Any other religion, *please write in*

4. Sexual orientation

Which of these best describes you?
✓ box only

- Heterosexual
- Gay or lesbian or homosexual
- Bisexual
- Other

5. Disability

Do you have any health problems or disabilities that you expect will last for more than a year?
✓ box only

- Yes
- No

Employment Tribunals - Multiple Claim Form

Please use this form if you wish to present two or more claims which arise from the same set of facts. Use additional sheets if necessary.

The following claimants are represented by (if applicable) and the relevant required information for all the additional claimants is the same as stated in the main claim of

V

Title
First name (or names)
Surname or family name
Date of birth D D - M M - Y Y Y Y
Number or Name
Street
Town/City
County
Postcode

Title
First name (or names)
Surname or family name
Date of birth D D - M M - Y Y Y Y
Number or Name
Street
Town/City
County
Postcode

Title
First name (or names)
Surname or family name
Date of birth D D - M M - Y Y Y Y
Number or Name
Street
Town/City
County
Postcode

ET1a v01

Title
First name (or names)
Surname or family name
Date of birth
Number or Name
Street
Town/City
County
Postcode

Title
First name (or names)
Surname or family name
Date of birth
Number or Name
Street
Town/City
County
Postcode

Title
First name (or names)
Surname or family name
Date of birth
Number or Name
Street
Town/City
County
Postcode

Title
First name (or names)
Surname or family name
Date of birth
Number or Name
Street
Town/City
County
Postcode

This represents a return to the more relaxed pre-2004 rules of identifying the category or categories of claim that the claimant was making so that the respondent could not complain of being taken by surprise. Whether this does really allow the respondent enough detail is debatable, though the respondent can always seek to obtain more information later. However, the balance between too much and too little detail is difficult to describe in the abstract and an example may help.

EXAMPLE

Consider the following draft prepared by Amrita herself for **items 5.1** and **5.2** on her ET 1 when her claim is solely of unfair dismissal. She ticks box **4.9.c** (to show she is seeking compensation only) and **5.1.a** (unfair dismissal claim). Under **5.2** she states:

I was called into my manager's office in the afternoon of 23 November and was told that I was being dismissed as redundant. I was told to collect my personal belongings at once and to leave the premises before the end of the afternoon. I do not accept that I was fairly selected. There was no individual consultation before notice was given to me. At the time of my dismissal there were sub-contractors working in the design office in jobs that I could easily have filled.

This is a good statement, brief and devoid of legal jargon. It succinctly sets out the essential facts of the case and clearly identifies the items that the claimant is putting in issue. By implication at least it therefore also identifies those that are not being challenged. The matters put in issue are three:

(a) unfair selection;

(b) lack of individual consultation;

(c) failure to look for alternative work.

The statement does not challenge matters such as the following:

(a) that the dismissal was not truly for redundancy (although, as we have noted, the burden of proof of a reason for dismissal always rests with the employer and the tribunal may always require the employer to prove it);

(b) that the claimant's selection was automatically unfair by being based on trade union activities;

(c) that Amrita's selection involved any discrimination on grounds of race, sex, or disability, all of these being arguments that if successful could lead to unlimited compensation.

A solicitor representing a claimant like Amrita will not normally be permitted to raise such arguments at the hearing without warning. The respondent will be unprepared to defend them and will object. If the arguments are allowed at all, the hearing may then be adjourned until another day. Whilst costs are not normally awarded in the employment tribunals, extra costs resulting from such an adjournment may well have to be borne by the party responsible for it.

Note that while the statement clearly defines the issues for an eventual tribunal hearing, it does not attempt to identify in advance all the arguments that may be used. One reason used to be that it was tactically advantageous to deny the respondent's witnesses the chance to prepare for cross-examination. Thus, for example, if Amrita's selection depended on use of the type of matrix we encountered in **Chapter 14**, her solicitor would wish to cross-examine the manager who completed it about some of the entries—whether records were properly researched, whether a reason for poor attendance was investigated and so on. The argument was that the respondent could not complain about lack of notice of such questions in the ET 1 or elsewhere without scoring an own-goal; the answers should have been in the manager's mind when making the selection.

Current practice in the tribunals, especially the exchange in advance of witness statements that we shall mention shortly, now makes it more difficult to surprise a witness with such questions; in any event the effect is lessened if Amrita never raised them during any appeal against dismissal. A more important reason nowadays for not setting out the arguments at this early stage is that it is difficult to produce an exhaustive list while preparation of the case is incomplete, and it is better not to be so precise now than to keep needing to add to a list as the case progresses. Nevertheless it is useful for a solicitor representing Amrita to start now giving some thought to when and how to identify specific points of which the respondent needs warning—such as an argument that another, named employee was treated differently a year or two ago.

It is usually a good idea to avoid statements that leave the reader unclear what exactly it is you are talking about. References to 'certain shortcomings', for example, merely invite the other side to apply for additional information (see **16.8.3** below) about precisely what shortcomings you mean. In the above example it is possible to argue that the reference to sub-contractors is unclear in this way, and that might be a criticism. In practice, though, the employer is probably well aware of exactly who is meant, as there are unlikely to be many people fitting the description.

Amrita's ET 1 was drafted by the claimant and written in the first person. Often solicitors will find that they are not consulted until the ET 1 has already been presented, and not every claimant is as precise as this, so that you may have to decide later whether to seek leave to amend an inadequate ET 1. In other cases you may be asked to draft the ET 1 yourself, in which case you will probably do it in the third person. As with most other forms of legal drafting, there is no single right or wrong way to complete employment tribunal documents and different practitioners have different preferences, especially in relation to how much detail to include at an early stage and how much to keep until the hearing. Nevertheless, we can summarise points that emerge from the example like this:

(a) Be as succinct as possible. As a rule of thumb, it should not usually be necessary to expand beyond the space provided at item 5.2 on the ET 1, although an increasing number of representatives now do so. (Beware that any expansion beyond the blank additional pages of the ET 1 may be regarded as not meeting the requirement to use only that form.)

(b) Ensure that nothing so important is omitted as to entitle the other side to complain of being taken by surprise.

(c) Do not disclose unnecessarily facts that would more effectively be used with some surprise value in cross-examination.

(d) Avoid loose ends which almost invite the other side to apply for additional information. For example, the passive voice 'The claimant was told' invites the question, 'Who told her?' Unless the answer is obvious or well known to the other side, it is better to use the active voice from the outset: 'The manager told the claimant.'

16.3.3 The remedy being sought (item 6)

At item 6 on the form ET 1 the claimant is asked to state what compensation or remedy is being sought. Completion of this part is optional, which is just as well as most claimants will not know the significance of it. The claimant should have identified the preferred remedy under item 4.9 but, as we noted above, claimants will hardly ever recognise the legal significance of the terms 're-instatement' and 're-engagement'. Item 6 allows for a more discursive approach which may aid the tribunal.

As we noted in **Chapter 14**, there is a tactical advantage to the claimant in asking for reinstatement or re-engagement, even if not having any real wish to go back to work for the same employer: the amounts of compensation awarded if the employer has failed to carry out an order for reinstatement or re-engagement are substantially increased. So such a request at this stage may assist in the negotiation of an out-of-tribunal settlement: see **16.10** below.

16.3.4 Representation (item 8)

At item 8 the claimant is asked to name a representative if one exists. The ET Rules 2004 do not specify who may appear in the employment tribunals, but in practice representatives include counsel and solicitors, representatives of trade unions, employers' associations, and Citizens' Advice Bureaux and various personnel consultancies. Contingency-based fees have been common; these are now regulated by the Damages-based agreement Regulations 2010 (SI 2010/1201) under the auspices of ss. 58AA(4) and 120(3) of the Courts and Legal Services Act 1990. The Regulations apply to those providing advocacy, litigation or claims management services in employment tribunals. They set out what information must be supplied to the client, the form the agreement must take, and rule that an agreement that does not comply with the Regulations will be unenforceable. However, although the Regulations place a cap of 35 per cent on the percentage of costs deductible from the amount the client receives (including in settlement), solicitors can adopt alternative funding arrangements. Thus a contingency fee based on 'no win no fee' falls outside the scope of these Regulations (provided the amount of costs or success fee is not determined by reference to the amount the client is awarded e.g., through a scaling mechanism).

As legal aid is not available in the tribunals and costs have rarely been awarded (see **16.13** below), many claimants choose to appear in person, being reluctant to incur the cost of instructing lawyers. Employers sometimes do so too. It will be found in practice that employment judges have always aimed to meet the objective of ET Regs 2004, reg. 3(2)(a) to ensure that the parties are on an equal footing and try to compensate for any disadvantage suffered by an unrepresented party, especially a claimant. The procedural rules are applied less strictly than to any professional representative but this does not mean the tribunal will do the work for the claimant. Thus in *Mensah* v *East Hertfordshire NHS Trust* [1998] IRLR 531, the Court of Appeal (unlike the EAT) refused to allow a claimant to reopen a ground of complaint merely because the employment tribunal had allegedly not been astute in ensuring that she covered during the hearing all matters contained in the claim form.

16.4 Presentation of the claim on time

It is important that the claim is presented on time. 'Presentation' consists of delivering the originating application to the tribunal office, by hand, through the post, by fax, or using the internet. In the case of the post it is the time of arrival and not the time of posting that counts. We shall return to issues concerning the internet at **16.4.2** below.

If we look at the first six groups of jurisdictions of the tribunals set out in **Table 16.1** above, which together account for more than 90 per cent of the workload, we find that each has its own rule and we need to look at them in turn.

16.4.1 The various time limits

16.4.1.1 Unfair dismissal

A claim can be presented on or after the date notice is given, even if that is before the employment terminates. It must be presented to the tribunal office within *three months* beginning with the effective date of termination, or such further period as the tribunal considers reasonable if presentation within three months was *not reasonably practicable*: ERA 1996, s. 111(2).

16.4.1.2 A claim for a redundancy payment

A claim must be made within *six months* beginning with the relevant date, or within a further six months if the tribunal considers it *just and equitable*. A 'claim' in this context is widely defined: it includes a demand directly of the employer, a claim in the tribunal for a redundancy payment, or a complaint to the tribunal of unfair dismissal: ERA 1996, s. 164.

16.4.1.3 Protection of wages

A claim about a deduction from wages must be presented within *three months* beginning with the most recent date of payment of wages from which the unlawful deduction was allegedly made, or such further period as the tribunal considers reasonable if satisfied that it was *not reasonably practicable* for the claim to be presented within the three months: ERA 1996, s. 23.

16.4.1.4 Discrimination claims

Discrimination claims based on the 'protected characteristics' contained in EqA 2010 (see **Chapter 6**) share a common time of three months running form the alleged discriminatory act. Extensions are possible if the tribunal considers it just and equitable to allow for this. If the discrimination was continuous over a period, time runs from the most recent occurrence: *Barclays Bank* v *Kapur* [1991] ICR 208. So, if discrimination occurs through the employer's refusal of a request by the employee, time starts to run again *every* time the employer reconsiders the request and refuses again: *Cast* v *Croydon College* [1998] ICR 500.

There is *no time limit* in relation to proceedings brought directly under the European Treaty or a European Directive, but the ECJ normally regards such procedural matters as appropriate for determination by the member states.

A particular problem has arisen in relation to the time limit within which claims must be brought when decisions of the ECJ or domestic courts in effect create new rights, e.g., the right to equality in pensions' schemes following *Barber* v *Guardian Royal Exchange Assurance Group* [1990] ICR 616. The approach seems to be one of regarding time as running from the point when the claimant ought to have been aware that a right existed.

16.4.1.5 Discrimination against part-time and fixed-term workers

The same rule of a claim within *three months* (or, in this case, *six months* if concerning a member of the armed forces) and extension if the tribunal considers it *just and equitable* exists under these regulations as for the other categories of discrimination.

16.4.1.6 Equal pay

A claim may be presented at any time during the continuation of employment. A claim must be presented within *six months* of the termination of the employment. There is *no extension* of this period: Equal Pay Act 1970, s. 2.

16.4.1.7 Breach of contract

The rule here is the same as for unfair dismissal. See **16.6.3** below for the time limit regarding any counterclaim by the employer.

16.4.1.8 Claims under the Working Time Regulations 1998

Under reg. 30(2) a claim must be presented within *three months* (or *six months* for the armed forces) of the alleged start of infringement, with a possibility of extension if it was *not reasonably practicable* to present before the end of that period.

16.4.2 Presentation within time and the possibility of extension

As we noted at the start of this section, the rule about presentation in time is important. The reason is that it has been held to be a rule about *jurisdiction* and not merely *procedure*. If it were procedural, the tribunal could refuse to let a respondent employer use the time limit as a defence if it felt that the lateness was wholly or partly the respondent's fault or that the respondent's conduct had ignored the time limit. As the rule is jurisdictional there is no such flexibility and it must be applied strictly. Nevertheless, the effective date of termination in an unfair dismissal application is a matter of fact, not law, and an agreement about that was binding on the parties in *Lambert* v *Croydon College* [1999] ICR 409.

There are two aspects to the operation of the time limit and we shall consider each in turn:

(a) whether the claim was presented in time; and, if not,

(b) whether time should be extended in the circumstances.

Where a time limit is expressed as beginning on a particular date, it has been held to mean precisely that. Thus, if the employee was dismissed on 3 April and wishes to complain of unfair dismissal, a claim must be presented at the tribunal on or before 2 July. Presentation on 3 July is one day after the end of the three-month period *beginning on* 3 April, and a claim received then would be out of time. It is calendar months that count, notwithstanding variations in their length. So, for example, periods of three months beginning with an effective date of termination between 29 November and 1 December will all end on 28 February (in a non-leap year). The rule about statutory periods of time starting *on* a date is different from that under ET Regs 2004, reg. 15, which provides that any period defined under ET Rules 2004 or in a tribunal decision *excludes* the start date.

The rules about the application of time limits when a claim is presented by post were reviewed in *Consignia plc* v *Sealy* [2002] EWCA Civ 878, [2002] ICR 1193. It is now to be assumed as in CPR, r. 6.7 that first-class post arrives on the second day after it is posted, excluding Sundays, bank holidays, Christmas Day, and Good Friday. So a claim due to be received on a Saturday or Sunday will be in time if it is posted first class no later than the previous Thursday, even if the tribunal office does not open it until the Monday or it is unexpectedly delayed even longer. For this reason the tribunals retain the envelopes in which claims arrive.

If you have visited the Employment Tribunal Service (ETS) website (www.employmenttribunals.gov.uk) you will have seen that claimants are encouraged to present claims by e-mail. Solicitors should be warned that electronic methods allow for very accurate fixing of the time of presentation. In *Beasley* v *National Grid Electricity Transmissions* [2007] All ER (D) 110 (Aug) the EAT approved an employment judge's rejection of a claim presented 88 seconds too late.

In *Tyne and Wear Autistic Society* v *Smith* [2005] ICR 663, the form ET 1 was completed online and was sent by e-mail to the 'host' used by ETS, but for some internal reason was not passed on to ETS itself. The EAT accepted that the claim could be presented electronically but it must reach the website and be accepted there; in *Smith's* case the claimant had done all that was required and the claim was in time. By contrast, in an unreported case, *Mossman* v *Bray Management Ltd* EAT/0477/04, the EAT held in December 2004 that a claim had not been presented in time when the claimant failed to notice that a claim had not been acknowledged as received. This seems a harsher decision than in *Initial Electronic Security Systems Ltd* v *Avdic* [2005] IRLR 671 where the EAT held that an e-mail claim could be expected to arrive within 30–60 minutes of transmission, and that the claimant was in time when she sent her ET 1 eight hours before the time-limit expired, albeit unsuccessfully.

The detailed time limits we considered at **16.4.1** contained two broad definitions of an exception:

(a) the 'just and equitable' rule in relation to redundancy payments and all the various heads of discrimination; and

(b) the 'not reasonably practicable' rule in relation to unfair dismissal, the protection of wages, breach of contract, and claims under WTRegs 1998.

Those two rules are of very different severity and we shall consider each in turn.

16.4.3 The 'just and equitable' rule

In relation to claims for redundancy payments and claims of discrimination, the relevant time limit can be extended if the tribunal considers it *just and equitable* to do so.

The discretion allowed to the tribunal by this formula is very broad: *Hutchinson* v *Westward Television* [1977] ICR 279. Furthermore, there can be circumstances in which the extension may be lengthy, so that cases considerably out of time can still be heard. In *Southwark London Borough Council* v *Afolabi* [2003] EWCA Civ 15, [2003] ICR 800, the claimant was allowed to present a claim of racial discrimination almost nine years late because the facts only came to light when he inspected his personal file. In *Chohan* v *Derby Law Centre* [2004] IRLR 685 the EAT accepted a late claim under this rule where delay was due to bad advice the claimant had received from her legal adviser. Respondents need to be warned that some flexibility may be allowed in claims of disability discrimination. In *Department of Constitutional Affairs* v *Jones* [2007] EWCA Civ 894, [2008] IRLR 128 the claimant's late presentation of a claim under DDA 1995 (related to a depressive illness) resulted in large part from his reluctance to admit to himself or anyone else that he was disabled, and the Court of Appeal approved the exercise of discretion to allow him to present a claim late, while indicating that discretion was not to be exercised without limit.

16.4.4 The 'not reasonably practicable' rule

By contrast with the rule in those three jurisdictions, the rule in relation to claims of unfair dismissal, of unlawful deductions from wages under ERA 1996, Part II, or of breach of contract or WTRegs 1998 is much stricter. An extension of time is permitted only if:

(a) it was not reasonably practicable to present in time; and

(b) the length of the extension is reasonable.

The meaning of 'not reasonably practicable' has been exposed to much scrutiny in the cases over a long period of time. An early example was *Dedman* v *British Building* [1974] ICR 53, in which Lord Denning MR held that when a claimant, through no fault of his own, was ignorant of the time limit for presentation, that was enough to make it not reasonably practicable for him to meet it. Fault therefore became an important criterion. If the claimant's lateness was not his fault he might well get through; if he or his advisers were in some way at fault that would usually be fatal. The discovery of new facts (e.g., that a redundancy was actually a sham) would also justify a tribunal awarding an extension of time. The EAT case of *Cambridge & Peterborough NHS Trust v Crouchman* [2009] UKEAT/108/09 lays down extensive and helpful guidelines on this.

For some time the EAT took the view that late submission owing to bad legal advice meant the claim would not be admitted—the claimant being left to pursue a claim against the solicitor for negligence. Recent authorities have regarded that as an unjustified windfall for the employer and take the opposite view.

The second half of the statutory discretion is also important. If it is established that presentation within the statutory period is not reasonably practicable, the period should be extended only by as much as is *reasonable*. The claimant must act without delay once presentation becomes reasonably practicable: *James W. Cook (Wivenhoe)* v *Tipper* [1990] IRLR 386. So, for example, a claimant who claims ignorance of the time limit must act as quickly as possible on learning of it.

A particularly difficult category of case for exercise of either statutory discretion occurs where a decision of the ECJ or one of the higher courts in this country effectively establishes a new jurisdiction. So, for example, until the decision of the House of Lords in *R* v *Secretary of State for Employment, ex parte Equal Opportunities Commission* [1994] ICR 317, it was generally believed that most part-time employees did not have the right to present a claim of unfair dismissal. In *Biggs* v *Somerset County Council* [1996] ICR 364 an employee who was dismissed in August 1976 argued that her complaint of unfair dismissal was in time because, as a part-time teacher working 14 hours per week, her right to claim only ran from the date of the House of Lords' decision on 1 June 1994 and her claim was presented within three months of that date. Her claim was brought under art. 141 of the EC Treaty, and therefore did not need to wait for UK legislation about part-time workers. The Court of Appeal held that time ran from her dismissal in 1976 and the 'not reasonably practicable' rule could not be stretched to the extent she suggested. A different result occurred with the 'just and equitable' rule: *Director of Public Prosecutions* v *Marshall* [1998] ICR 518.

16.5 Acceptance by the tribunal office of the claim

Under rr. 2 and 3 of ET Rules 2004 a new step was added to the tribunal procedure. Hitherto, receipt of the claim (then known as the originating application) involved the tribunal office merely in the administrative tasks of stamping it with the date, giving it a reference number and a code indicating the nature of the complaint, and notifying the employer accordingly. Now the office is given a duty to examine the content of the claim and to consider whether it can be accepted.

Any administrative decision within the tribunal office not to accept a claim must be referred to an employment judge who makes the final decision. The grounds for refusing to accept are set out in r. 3:

(a) the claim is not made on the prescribed form;

(b) it does not include the relevant information;

(c) the tribunal has no jurisdiction to consider it.

If rejection is on ground (a), the claimant is told the reason and sent a copy of the form. Although employers have sometimes complained that it is too easy for disgruntled employees to bring cases to the tribunal that stand no prospect of success, this provision allows tribunals to reject claims only because of formal failings and not because they lack merit. Some employment judges have been interpreting the requirements of r. 1(4) regarding (b) above with great strictness, and have refused to accept claims that do not contain the required information. However, the EAT has criticised excessive strictness and in *Richardson* v *U Mole Ltd* [2005] IRLR 668, for example, accepted a claim that did not expressly state that the claimant had been an employee of the respondent, although it was clear from the context. The tribunals do not seem to be given any discretion under ET Rules 2004, and the slightly strange EAT suggestion is that they should exercise the power to review decisions in the interests of justice. See also **16.15.1** on 'Application for review'.

16.6 The response

If the claim is accepted, the tribunal office stamps it with the date, gives it a reference number, and sends a copy with a covering letter (ET 2) to the employer named on the form together with a blank response form (ET 3) and an explanatory booklet. Use of the form ET 3, like that of ET 1 as discussed earlier, is now mandatory. With permission from the Employment Tribunal Service we have reproduced a copy of the form below.

The response must be presented to the tribunal office within 28 days of the date the copy of the claim was sent to the employer—r. 4(1). Failure to do so will lead to a default judgment being made (see **16.7.2** below). The employer may apply for an extension of time to present a response but must do so within the 28-day period and give an explanation—r. 4(4). Under the new r. 4A inserted by ET Rules (Amendments) 2008, where the respondent is legally represented they will have to notify all other parties of the application with the reasons why it is being made and the manner in which objections to the application may be lodged. They must inform the parties that any objections must be in writing and copied to all parties and they must confirm to the Employment Tribunal Office that this has been done. If the respondent is not legally represented the tribunal fulfils this role. Employers have sometimes failed to recognise the importance or urgency of tribunal communications and in some large companies internal post often seems to take a long time to get papers to the right individual. Papers sometimes sit waiting for the right person to return from holiday. Solicitors instructed to act for client employers when only a very short time is left to draft a response will wish to emphasise to the client the importance of acting more speedily next time.

16.6.1 The use of form ET 3

Completion of form ET 3 is as straightforward as that of ET 1. There are, however, a few points worthy of note:

At item 1.1 it is necessary to enter the claimant's name and then at 2.1 the employer's name and at 2.2 the address. The name and address to which the notices have been sent will be those the claimant has given on the ET 1 and may be incorrect. Claimants

Employment Tribunals Response Form

Special Notice

You can make a response to an Employment Tribunal by completing and editing the form offline. You can save a part or fully completed form, email a saved form to another person to amend or for approval, and submit it securely online to the Employment Tribunal Service.

Please make sure you have read the guidance notes on our website or in our booklet on how to make a response before you fill in the form.

In order to proceed you must enter the case number and names of the parties printed on the form and letter we sent you.

Case number

Names of parties V

Tribunal office dealing with claim --please select--

POWERED by legatio

Print New Continue →

Need Help?

If you require any help completing your form or have a general question about the tribunals process please contact the Employment Tribunals Enquiry Line on

0845 795 9775

minicom 08457 573 722

between 9 am and 5 pm Monday to Friday, our lines are closed on Bank Holidays.

If you require technical support please click below to email us.

Support Request

We regret we cannot provide any legal advice.

Please Note:

By law, your claim must be submitted using an approved form supplied by the Employment Tribunals Service, and you must provide the information marked with * and, if it is relevant, the information marked with ● (see 'Information needed before a claim can be accepted')

General Information:

Once you have completed your form you can submit it securely on-line to the ETS. On-line forms are processed faster than those sent by post.

Case number:

1 Claimant's name

1.1 Claimant's name:

2 Respondent's details

2.1* Name of Individual, Company or Organisation

Contact name:

2.2* Address: Number or Name

Street

+ Town/City

County

Postcode

2.3 Phone number including area code **(where we can contact you in the day time):**

Mobile number **(if different):**

2.4 How would you prefer us to communicate with you? (Please tick only one box) E-mail Post

E-mail address:

@

2.5 What does this organisation mainly make or do?

2.6 How many people does this organisation employ in Great Britain?

2.7 Does this organisation have more than one site in Great Britain? Yes No

2.8 If 'Yes', how many people are employed at the place where the claimant worked?

3 Employment details

3.1 Are the dates of employment given by the claimant correct? Yes No
If 'Yes', please now go straight to section 3.3.

3.2 If 'No', please give dates and say why you disagree with the dates given by the claimant.

When their employment started D D - M M - Y Y Y Y

When their employment ended or will end D D - M M - Y Y Y Y

3 Employment details (continued)

Is their employment continuing? Yes ☐ No ☐

I disagree with the dates for the following reasons.

3.3 Is the claimant's description of their job or job title correct? Yes ☐ No ☐
If 'Yes', please now go straight to section 4

3.4 If 'No', please give the details you believe to be correct below.

4 Earnings and benefits

4.1 Are the claimant's hours of work correct? Yes ☐ No ☐

If 'No', please enter the details you believe to be correct. ☐☐ hours each week

4.2 Are the earnings details given by the claimant correct? Yes ☐ No ☐
If 'Yes', please now go straight to section 4.3

If 'No', please give the details you believe to be correct below.

Pay before tax £ ☐☐☐,☐☐☐.00

Normal take-home pay (including overtime, commission, bonuses and so on) £ ☐☐☐,☐☐☐.00

Hourly ☐
Weekly ☐
Monthly ☐
Yearly ☐

4.3 Is the information given by the claimant correct about being paid for, or working, a period of notice? Yes ☐ No ☐
If 'Yes', please now go straight to section 4.4

If 'No', please give the details you believe to be correct below. If you gave them no notice or didn't pay them instead of letting them work their notice, please explain what happened and why.

4.4 Are the details about pension and other benefits, e.g. company car, medical insurance, etc, given by the claimant correct? Yes ☐ No ☐
If 'Yes', please now go straight to section 5.

If 'No', please give the details you believe to be correct below.

ET3 v03 002

5 Response

5.1* Do you resist the claim? Yes ☐ No ☐
If 'No', please now go straight to section 6.

5.2● If 'Yes', please set out in full the grounds on which you resist the claim.

ET3 v03 003

6 Other information

6.1 Please do not send a covering letter with this form. You should add any extra information you want us to know here.

7 Your representative

If you have a representative, please fill in the following.

7.1 Representative's name:

7.2 Name of the representative's organisation:

7.3 Address: Number or Name

Street

Town/City

County

Postcode

7.4 Phone number:

7.5 Reference:

7.6 How would you prefer us to communicate with them? (Please tick only one box)

E-mail Post

E-mail address:

@

Please read the form and check you have entered all the relevant information.
Once you are satisfied, please tick this box.

Data Protection Act 1998. We will send a copy of this form to the claimant and Acas. We will put the information you give us on this form onto a computer. This helps us to monitor progress and produce statistics. Information provided on this form is passed to the Department for Business, Enterprise and Regulatory Reform to assist research into the use and effectiveness of employment tribunals. (URN 05/874)

ET3 v03 004

Additional space for notes.

Additional space for notes.

Additional space for notes.

sometimes give a trading name for the company that has no standing to defend litigation. This is the opportunity to make any corrections. Solicitors will find that some large companies reorganise themselves remarkably often, and it may take some effort to get proper instructions about the identity of the employer, ending with 'Limited' or 'plc', but it is better to do the investigation now than to suffer the indignity at a tribunal hearing of being unable to identify your client properly. There are further details required about the nature of the organisation under items 2.5–2.8. These items may prove to be more important than they first appear. For instance, in many instances a tribunal is meant to decide on, say, fairness of procedure with an eye on the size and nature of the employer's organisation and, if the claim is for redundancy then the number of sites (and any requirements to work on different sites) may be critical.

Items 3 and 4 allows the employer to correct any misinterpretation of employment details supplied by the claimant (who may not have understood the payments system correctly).

Item 5 covers the employer's response, beginning with whether the claim is resisted or not and, if resisted, why. The employer may, for instance, argue that there was no dismissal—that the employee resigned. So the employer would tick the 'resist claim' box in 5.1 and then explain this in 5.2. The practical significance of this answer is that if the claimant claims to have been dismissed and the employer denies it, the claimant will have to prove dismissal and will have to open the case at the hearing. If the employer admits dismissal, the employer begins in order to prove the reason for dismissal. The employer will usually wish to deny dismissal if:

(a) challenging a claim of constructive dismissal;

(b) the employee resigned voluntarily or there was a termination by mutual consent;

(c) the contract ended through frustration;

(d) the claimant is regarded by the employer as still employed.

It is not just constructive dismissal claims that would follow this line, of course. The employer may be resisting an ordinary claim for unfair dismissal, or discrimination etc.; the key point to item 5.2 is that here the employer is required to set out the grounds of resistance and this requires some detailed consideration.

16.6.2 Grounds of resistance (response)—item 5.2

The general remarks above about completion of a claim apply equally to the response, and especially to the descriptive part. Parties are not expected to meet High Court standards, but, especially where lawyers are acting for the employer, tribunals will expect the points at issue to be identified clearly. This still leaves considerable scope for individual practitioners to follow their own preferences.

We shall discuss technique by reference to our first three examples: Amrita whose ET 1 we thought at **16.3.2** was well-drafted, and two others, Basil and Catherine, where the ET 1s are badly-drafted. Basil's is too long; Catherine's is too brief.

16.6.2.1 An ET 3 for Amrita

Item 5 of Amrita's ET 1 read:

> I was called into my manager's office in the afternoon of 23 November and was told that I was being dismissed as redundant. I was told to collect my personal belongings at once and to leave the premises before the end of the afternoon. I do not accept that I was fairly selected. There was no individual consultation before

> notice was given to me. At the time of my dismissal there were sub-contractors working in the design office in jobs that I could easily have filled.

Consider the following as a response to that ET 1:

> The Respondent company suffered a severe loss of business as a result of the cancellation of a large order by a major customer in September 2009 and was forced with much regret to reduce the size of its workforce by approximately 10 per cent.
>
> The Applicant's dismissal on 1st December was for redundancy. It was essential if the company was to remain in business and was not unfair.

This response is inadequate. While some practitioners prefer to leave as many of their options open as possible, brevity to this extreme is disliked by the tribunals. It deals with the *reason* for dismissal, perhaps in more detail than is necessary, but makes no attempt to show that the employer *acted reasonably* in dismissing for that reason. The tribunal would probably react by asking for additional information (see **16.8.3** below) of *how* it is alleged the employer acted reasonably. This may include questions that the employer might have preferred to leave to be answered at the hearing.

It is therefore better to prepare a fuller response which deals with those matters in the way the employer chooses. The ET 3 should show that the employer knew how to handle a redundancy reasonably and aimed to do so, especially in relation to the matters put in issue by the ET 1. Consider the following second attempt:

> On 16th November 2009 the Respondent company announced a redundancy of 20 people because of the cancellation of an important order and started consultation with the recognised trade unions. The unions declined to agree a method of selecting who was to be dismissed, but urged the Respondent to select speedily and to allow those selected to leave as soon as possible immediately after interview on 23rd November so as to maximise the value to them of severance payments by avoiding tax.
>
> The Claimant was employed as a design engineer and the Respondent decided to reduce the number so employed from eight to seven. All eight were marked for their length of service, attendance record, quality and quantity of work, and their versatility. The Claimant scored the lowest total mark and was therefore selected for dismissal.
>
> She was called to an interview on 23rd November. She declined the offer of being accompanied by another employee. The reason for the redundancy and the selection method were explained to her. She was told she was at risk of redundancy and did not need to attend at work during a consultation period. She had the right to appeal against selection, and to remain in employment while the appeal was heard. She did not appeal, or raise any other questions and, in the absence of any alternative, her dismissal was confirmed on 1st December.
>
> At the time of the claimant's dismissal, two sub-contract design engineers were working in the design office. They were engaged in the final stages of a specific project which was expected to last only two more weeks and which in fact ended at the Christmas holiday. The claimant would have required training to undertake that work and it could not have been completed in the available time.
>
> In all the circumstances the claimant's dismissal for redundancy was not unfair.

This is much better. Unlike a High Court defence it does not follow exactly the same sequence as the ET 1 it is answering and admit or deny each element one by one. Indeed, it appears to tell a remarkably different story. Yet it demonstrates that the employer was aware of some at least of the legal requirements of handling redundancy reasonably and attempted to satisfy them. It states clearly the employer's point of view about the key contentions we spotted in the ET 1 but does not waste time asserting things that are not in issue in any event. Nor does it gratuitously expose the weaknesses the solicitor has uncovered in the respondents' case. We shall see later that it will probably prompt Amrita's solicitor to ask for inspection of documents, but, apart from that, the case is now ready for hearing.

It is a good test of a well-drafted ET 1 and ET 3 that, taken together, they clearly establish the points at issue.

16.6.2.2 An ET 3 for Basil

Basil was dismissed for theft of company products. The employer understood the requirements of *British Home Stores* v *Burchell* [1980] ICR 303 and aimed to comply with them (see **12.6** for details—misconduct and fairness).

Basil, by contrast, has never heard of *BHS* v *Burchell* and is simply aggrieved that he has lost his livelihood in circumstances where the police say there is insufficient evidence to press criminal charges. He submits an ET 1 claiming unfair dismissal. His entry in item 5.2, completed in a spidery handwriting, runs on for two more sheets. The following is a considerable précis:

> He stresses his long and hitherto unblemished record of employment with this company and earlier employers going back thirty years. He was a willing and co-operative worker and the quality of his workmanship has never been questioned. The evidence against him is scanty. In any event, dismissal is an excessive penalty for petty pilfering. Minor theft and other corrupt practices are widespread in the workplace and he threatens to reveal misconduct by senior people. No disciplinary action has been taken against anyone else. Perhaps he was set up.

Dealing with long and rambling claims like this is often difficult. Basil's statement is so wide-ranging that it is impossible to discern his real complaint. He does not expressly deny theft, but it would be unfair to assume that such an omission by an unrepresented claimant was deliberate. One device is to ask for additional information, specifying precisely what are the grounds for complaining of unfair dismissal, perhaps even seeking leave to delay completion of the ET 3 until it is supplied. In other cases it is better tactically to ignore irrelevant grouses. The claimant may well have been upset by the dismissal and have included in the ET 1 various things written in the heat of the moment that will not in fact be pursued.

Basil's case is probably more of the second kind than the first. The employer will probably want to refute the allegations of widespread dishonesty, more for the record than for this case. (If Basil did not mention such allegations at disciplinary interviews or any appeal hearing, the usual rule that fairness is to be judged by reference to the employer's knowledge *at the time of dismissal* will mean that he gains little by raising them for the first time here.) If there is a serious prospect of accusations being made at the hearing that could take the employer by surprise, it may be necessary to ask later for information.

Applying the above reasoning, Basil's employer's solicitor may decide to produce an ET 3 which denies general dishonesty in the workplace but otherwise concentrates entirely on showing that the employer tried to comply with the *BHS* v *Burchell* tests and followed a correct procedure:

> The Respondent company manufactures small domestic electrical appliances. Because of its susceptibility to petty theft, random security checks are undertaken from time to time.

On 5 November such a random search found the Claimant leaving the works with a machine, in its sales carton, in his bag. He was suspended on full pay while his departmental manager obtained written statements from the security officer and others involved and checked computerised stock records. The statements were sent to the Claimant.

The Claimant was called to a disciplinary interview on 12 November which he attended with his shop steward. His manager invited his comments. He said he did not know the item was in his bag and could not explain how it got there.

During an adjournment the manager and a colleague considered the Claimant's explanation and decided they did not believe it. On resumption the manager told the Claimant they concluded he was trying to steal the machine and he was summarily dismissed.

The Claimant exercised his right of appeal but was unsuccessful.

It is not admitted that dishonesty is widespread or tolerated in the works as alleged or at all.

16.6.2.3 An ET 3 for Catherine

The third of our examples concerns an ET 1 which, by contrast with Basil's, is extremely brief and really gives the employer little indication of Catherine's complaint. Her ET 1 reads like this:

> ***Item* 5.1**
>
> *Catherine has ticked box 5.1.a: 'I was unfairly dismissed (including constructive dismissal)'*
>
> ***Item* 5.2**
>
> Since Mike Jones became my manager two years ago he keeps picking on me for all the unpleasant jobs that the other girls do not want to do. Obviously he does not like me and prefers the younger ones. I have complained about this treatment on several occasions but nothing is ever done. On 11 January he told me to change jobs. This was the last straw and I resigned. Because I have complained informally so many times without anything being done that I needed to react firmly at the time.

The employer cannot proceed to the tribunal hearing with a claim as vague as this. At some stage it will be necessary to establish answers to three questions:

(a) What exactly is Mike Jones supposed to have done?

(b) When, how, and to whom were the complaints made?

(c) Is the implied complaint of age discrimination going to be pursued? In theory Catherine should not be allowed to pursue such a claim if item 5.1.b of the ET 1 is left blank but tribunals have not always been so strict as regards previous versions of the ET 1.

The mechanism for dealing with such vagueness is through a request for additional information: see **16.8.3** below.

Meanwhile, it is a question of tactics whether or not the employer prefers to delay completion of the ET 3 until that information is supplied. It is of course the claimant's responsibility to show that she was dismissed, and not the employer's to show that she was not. In view of that burden, a blanket denial by the employer may seem to be enough:

> It is not admitted that any act or omission by the Respondent employer entitled the Claimant to resign without notice as alleged or at all.

Note the addition of 'as alleged or at all'. This is a standard device in any drafting, and avoids a trap called the *pregnant negative*. If the employee alleges in the ET 1 that something was done to her by a named person on a Friday afternoon in the office, and the ET 3 denies it in precisely the same terms, someone reading the statement may conclude that the event did indeed take place, but the claimant has made some minor error of detail, perhaps with the date, or time or place.

At one stage, when tribunal proceedings were much more informal and hearings more exploratory, such a brief response would probably have been accepted. Now, with the emphasis on case management and clarification of issues in advance of hearing, a tribunal office is unlikely to accept it (see **16.7** below) and will insist on more information. In any event an employer who knows the background to Catherine's complaint would probably wish to demonstrate a coherent and reasonable approach to her and think it tactically better to produce a fuller version of item 5 on the ET 3:

> The Claimant was employed as a machine operator and it was a term of her employment that she could be moved at any time from one machine to another and from one shift to another. Whilst the departmental manager usually tries to accommodate the personal preferences of the operators in terms of allocation to machines, this is not always possible and the terms of the contract sometimes have to be adhered to.
>
> During October the Claimant repeatedly declined requests to move to a particular stapling machine. The manager realised that this refusal was causing ill-feeling amongst other operators and told the Claimant she would have to move. He offered to try to resolve any particular difficulties the Claimant might have in complying with such a request but she raised none and persisted in her refusal. The Respondent has a well-used grievance procedure which requires any grievance to be sent in writing to the human resources department but the Claimant has never registered any complaint under it.
>
> On 11 January the manager therefore instructed the Claimant to move.
>
> The said instruction was within the terms of the Claimant's contract of employment. Neither that instruction nor any other act or omission by the Respondent entitled the Claimant to resign without notice.
>
> If, which is not admitted, the said instruction constituted a dismissal, it was for the substantial reason of needing to share out unpopular work and was not unfair.

The final paragraph of that revised version may be important. As we emphasised in **Chapter 11**, a constructive dismissal is not necessarily unfair. Sometimes, in cases of alleged constructive dismissal, it is therefore necessary to plead '*in the alternative*' so that the defence about fairness is in place lest the issue of whether there was a dismissal is lost. Occasionally, if the employer omits to do this, the tribunal office will write asking whether it is wished to do so.

16.6.3 Breach of contract counterclaim by the employer

As we noted in **Chapter 5**, employees can bring certain breach of contract claims *in the employment tribunal* as well as in the courts provided the claim '**arises or is outstanding on the termination of the employee's employment**'. Item 5.1.c of the ET 1 should be ticked as relevant (e.g., 'I am owed arrears of pay').

The novel feature of the breach of contract jurisdiction is that the employer is permitted to make a counterclaim against the employee, but only if the employee's claim alleges breach of contract, and not (for example) if the ET 1 is about unfair dismissal alone. Counterclaims are covered by ET Rules 2004 in r. 7, which requires very little except that the counterclaim should be in writing and permits the President to make a practice direction about counterclaims. The requirement as to timing seems not to have been changed from the 1994 Regulations, so that it must be presented by the employer to the tribunal office within six weeks of the date that the employer *received* the copy of the claim. The counterclaim cannot relate to the topics listed in **Chapter 5** at **5.8**, which remain actionable in the courts alone, especially:

(a) intellectual property;

(b) restrictive covenants.

16.7 Acceptance and non-acceptance of the response

We have already noted at **16.5** the provision under ET Rules 2004 for the tribunal to accept the claimant's claim. There is an equivalent provision in r. 5 for the tribunal to accept the respondent's response.

16.7.1 The acceptance procedure

The procedure for acceptance of the response is parallel to that for acceptance of the claim, and there are three grounds for the tribunal office to decline to accept:

(a) the response is not on the prescribed form;

(b) it does not include all the required information; or

(c) it was not presented within the time limit.

As with acceptance of the claim, acceptance of the response does not depend on the merits of the case. If it is rejected on ground (a) above, the employer is told the reason and sent a copy of the appropriate form. Note the point made at **16.6** above about acceptance of late responses.

16.7.2 Default judgments

Under ET Rules 2004, r. 8, where a response has not been presented within time, or where a response has not been accepted, or where the response is that the claim will not be defended then any claim must be referred to an employment judge for a default judgment (without a hearing). This may deal with liability alone or liability and remedy; it is at the employment judge's discretion. The employer (who technically has not even become a respondent) will not be heard. The judgment will be reached on the basis of information available to the tribunal, which presumably means the information contained in the ET 1, although it is also possible under r. 10 for the tribunal itself to ask the claimant for additional information. Default judgments can, however, be avoided: for instance, if the tribunal has no jurisdiction to hear the claim or there is sufficient evidence that the claim form was not received by the respondent (or, of course, that the parties have settled).

The only opportunity for the employer subject to a default judgment to be heard about the case is by applying for a review of the default judgment under r. 33. The application must be in writing and be presented within 14 days of the date the default judgment was sent to the parties. It must include a response to the claim, an application of an extension of time to present it and an explanation of why it was not presented within time.

The discretion allowed to the tribunals under ET Rules 2004 to review default judgments is limited and an application for review must include with it the respondent's proposed response to the claim. The employment judge may refuse, vary or revoke the default judgment. Rule 33(8) also allows an employment judge on his own initiative to review a default judgment on grounds laid out in r. 34 (e.g., the decision was wrongly made because of an administrative error or there is new evidence or the interests of justice so require this).

An aspect of the rule regarding default judgments that does not seem to be covered in ET Rules 2004 is the interrelationship with employers' counterclaims. As the time limit for an employer to present a counterclaim is just over two weeks longer than the time to present a response to the claim, it seems to be possible for a claim to have entered the default judgment procedure in the absence of a response, but for a valid counterclaim still to be raised. These circumstances do not yet seem to have arisen in any reported case.

16.8 Case management

We have already noted in the imaginary cases we have been considering that the ET 1 and the ET 3 do not always adequately define the issues that need to be explored at a hearing to decide a case. Often the parties need to communicate with one another, or in default of agreement the tribunal must ensure that a case is properly prepared. In rr. 10–13 of ET Rules 2004 under the title 'Case Management' we find grouped together a number of powers given to employment judges to make orders for the efficient handling of cases. A list of orders is set out in r. 10(2), but it expressly states that the items listed are examples and the full range envisaged by s. 10(1) could therefore be even more extensive. Orders can be made on consideration of the papers or at a case management discussion. Rule 11 sets out the manner in which the parties must respond. The list of possible orders is comprehensive and includes the manner in which proceedings are to be conducted including setting time limits, linking together of cases and separation of issues in a case. Particular matters that we need to consider further are these:

(a) case management discussions;

(b) provision of additional information;

(c) witness orders ('attendance of any person to give evidence');

(d) disclosure of documents;

(e) supply of written answers to questions;

(f) dealing with part of the proceedings separately;

(g) pre-hearing reviews;

(h) leave to amend claim or response;

(i) witness statements; and

(j) penalties for non-compliance.

In many regions some simpler categories of cases by-pass this procedure entirely. Straightforward claims of unlawful deduction from wages or breach of contract, for example, are put into a 'fast-track' system whereby they are simply listed for hearing and some regions set aside time on a fixed day each week to deal with a large number of such cases.

16.8.1 Cooperation between the parties

Before we start to look at the list from the standpoint of orders made by the tribunal it is worth repeating that in practice these steps often start, especially if the parties are legally represented, with an exchange between parties or representatives.

We have already observed, for example, that Catherine's ET 1 was so lacking in detail that the respondent employer was having difficulty in filling in the ET 3. The respondent requires more information, and we shall see shortly in **16.8.3** and **16.8.6** how the tribunal can be asked to order its disclosure. However, the employment judge will expect, especially if the parties are represented, that, before the respondent seeks an order, the claimant will have been asked to comply voluntarily. The employment judge will want to know what was in the request and in the reply to it, and any order may cross-refer to the request.

16.8.2 Case management discussions

A case management discussion (CMD) is a hearing to consider making any of the orders we have been discussing or any other orders about the handling of a case. Such hearings used to be known as hearings for directions, prior to the express provision for them in ET Rules 2004, r. 17(1). They may be instigated by the tribunal or they may be requested by the parties, provided the requirements of r. 11 concerning all applications for orders are satisfied.

(a) An application for any order must be made at least 10 days before the hearing at which it is to be considered.

(b) It must be in writing, be sent to the tribunal office and include the reference number and the reasons for the request.

(c) An application for a CMD must identify what orders will be sought at it.

(d) An application for an order must explain how it will assist the tribunal in dealing with proceedings efficiently and fairly.

(e) Legal representatives must notify other parties of any application for an order (except a witness order) with the reasons for it and notify them of their right to object within seven days.

A CMD is held by an employment judge alone; it may be in private and it cannot determine the rights of a case. That last rule has not prevented employment judges in some regions from expressing an opinion about the merits of a case with a view to encouraging settlement, not necessarily having regard to all the complexities of that matter described in **16.10.3**. There is provision in r. 15(1) for a CMD to be held using electronic communications and this rule permits continuation of the recent practice whereby they are usually in the form of conference telephone calls (indeed, following the 2008 amendments r. 15 now permits any kind of hearing to be conducted by the use of electronic communications).

At one stage CMDs were held only exceptionally, reflecting the cost to the parties of attending a hearing in person at the tribunal office and the time requirement for the employment judge. There was even a worry in some regions that the use of telephone conferences offended the requirement to hold hearings in public, but that was resolved and they are now used extensively in all cases of any complexity.

As an example of the usefulness of a CMD it is time to introduce our fourth claimant. Dmitri is a salesman in a furniture shop who has applied several times for promotion to supervisor but has been unsuccessful. He alleges in the ET 1 that his departmental manager told him that he was rejected because of his high level of sickness absence since he developed a serious intestinal disorder, and he claims discrimination on grounds of disability contrary to DDA 1995. The ET 3 says that Dmitri was turned down on his merits and denies that the manager ever made such a statement; it also denies that Dmitri is a disabled person within the meaning of DDA 1995. In cases like this it is very common for the tribunal to take the initiative in calling a CMD at which the employment judge will check that the employer continues to deny that Dmitri is disabled and a timetable will then be set to deal with that issue. Dmitri's solicitor will be instructed to serve the necessary medical evidence on the employer by a defined date and the employer will be given a deadline to respond, conceding disability or not. The employer may be warned about an order for costs if a challenge to Dmitri's status is regarded as unreasonable. The tribunal may then decide to hear the question of Dmitri's disabled status and the merits of the discrimination case as separate issues and will require the parties to estimate the time needed for both hearings in the case. Dates will be set for hearings, for agreeing documents and for exchange of witness statements (see later) and the employment judge will ask whether there are any other orders required by the parties. The tribunal will then be very reluctant to change any of these agreed arrangements unless one party can show an extremely good reason for doing so.

It will be seen from the example that solicitors taking part in a CMD need to be well-prepared. Employment judges usually expect to end a CMD by fixing a date for a hearing, which requires the solicitor to have established the availability of witnesses, and that in turn requires the solicitor to know enough about the case to have decided which witnesses need to give evidence. Sometimes such case management seems to add to the costs of cases that may well not in the end proceed to a hearing.

16.8.3 The provision of additional information

The tribunal will order a party to provide further information if the ET 1 or ET 3 does not give the other side sufficient to prepare for the hearing. Hitherto 'further and better particulars' (as the information used to be known) necessarily involved some kind of development of something already contained in either ET 1 or ET 3; the new name seems likely to allow much broader requests to be made, and the older fine distinctions no longer matter.

In our examples there is plainly a need for the employer to request additional information in Catherine's case. This is done either in the body of a letter or more formally. In either case the request itself will look something like the request below. You will remember that Catherine's entry in item 5.2 of her ET 1 was:

> Since Mike Jones became my manager two years ago he keeps picking on me for all the unpleasant jobs that the other girls do not want to do. Obviously he does not like me and prefers the younger ones. I have complained about this treatment on several occasions but nothing is ever done. On 11 January he told me to change jobs. This was the last straw and I resigned. Because I have complained informally so many times without anything being done that I needed to react firmly at the time.

REQUEST FOR ADDITIONAL INFORMATION

ABOUT THE CLAIM

Under Item 5.2

> Of 'I resigned': describing precisely with dates and the names of persons involved each and every act or omission by the Respondent employer which allegedly entitled the Claimant to resign her employment without notice.

> Of 'I have complained about this treatment on several occasions': specifying the subject matter of the complaints, when and to whom they were made, whether orally or in writing, and what was the result in each case.

We have deliberately not requested any additional information to establish whether Catherine is in fact pursuing the implied claim of age discrimination. The likelihood is that the discrepancy between the implication at item 5.2 on the ET 1 and the blank in item 5.1.b may be sufficient to prompt an employment judge to call a CMD at which it will be explored. If she says she wishes to pursue the point her representative may in effect be invited to apply to amend the ET 1 accordingly—see **16.8.9** below. If she does not do so, she will not be permitted to raise it without warning at a hearing. So there is no benefit to the respondent in seeking information about it.

We noted above that one of the objectives of making such a request direct of the other party is to prepare the ground to ask for an order if the other party does not comply voluntarily. Such a request can be made during any CMD or as a written application to the tribunal office that complies with the requirements of r. 11 set out at **16.8.2.**

16.8.4 Witness orders

The employment tribunal can issue witness orders against witnesses, usually those who are not willing to attend a hearing voluntarily. The difference between this order and the other orders we are considering is that this is not issued against the other party but directly to the witness. The party applying for the order is not required by r. 11 to notify the other party. Thus the employer may find that witness orders have been issued to several members of staff on the claimant's application and without the employer having any opportunity to express a view.

Basil's case provides two examples of the kind of instance where this rule may be used.

Basil has alleged that dishonesty is widespread in the workplace. If he wishes to proceed with this contention, he may well want to call as witnesses other employees who would not wish to attend voluntarily. A witness order forces them to attend, to give evidence, and (if the order so provides) to bring documents with them.

The employer may also find it necessary to apply for a witness order. Perhaps a shop steward of the trade union would admit that dishonesty is not widespread or would give evidence against Basil's conduct during the disciplinary procedure. The shop steward might well feel it was wrong to give evidence voluntarily against a union member, but would respond favourably if a witness order was issued.

An application to set aside a witness order must be made by the individual to whom it is issued. In practice, however, there is no problem if an employer coordinates applications from an excessive number of staff called to give evidence.

16.8.5 Disclosure of documents

As in the county court, each party in the employment tribunal is entitled to know what documents the other party has in its possession that are relevant to the case and, subject to very limited safeguards, to inspect them. In practice parties almost always comply by supplying the other with photocopies. If disclosure is not given voluntarily, it can be ordered by the tribunal. This rule often causes practical problems: employers frequently regard documents as confidential and resist disclosure, while the tribunals take a different view.

For example, Amrita was selected for dismissal for redundancy because her score on an assessment was less than that of seven colleagues. She will naturally want to see how the other seven were marked. The employer, on the other hand, will regard the other forms as confidential to the seven individuals and will resist disclosure. This disagreement has been explored in the cases.

The tribunal can order disclosure of documents *or information*, and we shall see at **16.8.6** that they can also order a party to answer questions. The rule is to be used for documents that can be identified and not for 'fishing'. Thus it is for the parties to make specific requests and usually disclosure depends on the initiative of the party wanting to see a document. There is an increasing tendency, however, especially in some regions, towards the practice in the courts of requiring parties to disclose to each other all relevant documents in their power, possession or control. In *Scott* v *Commissioners of Inland Revenue* [2004] EWCA Civ 400, [2004] IRLR 713 the employer was criticised for not disclosing a revised retirement policy that had an effect on the claimant's expected future working life before retirement and therefore on compensation.

There is no immunity for confidential documents, although sometimes the tribunal will inspect them before ordering disclosure: *Science Research Council* v *Nassé* [1979] ICR 921. If the names of other people in documents are not necessary, they can be obliterated: *Oxford* v *DHSS* [1977] ICR 884. Documents may be anonymised or redacted to protect the confidence of informants. The employer was not required to disclose the identity of witnesses in *Asda Stores Ltd* v *Thompson* [2002] IRLR 245, where dismissals resulted from the alleged use of hard drugs. Whilst documents passing between a client and the lawyer in connexion with litigation are *privileged* and cannot be included in an order for inspection, this rule is restricted in the tribunals to lawyers and does not apply to other representatives: *New Victoria Hospital* v *Ryan* [1993] ICR 201.

Amrita's case raises an issue about disclosure of documents that is common in cases of dismissal for redundancy: can she insist on seeing the assessment forms for the others in her unit of selection? She will argue that such information is essential to the preparation of her case, while the employer may feel that disclosure breaks the confidence owed to the other employees. In *British Aerospace plc* v *Green* [1995] ICR 1006 the employer sought to avoid disclosure of other forms. The Court of Appeal declined to support the tribunal's order for disclosure of the forms. The tribunal was concerned only with the question of whether an assessment system was properly applied, and should not scrutinise its workings officiously; disclosure of the forms of those retained in employment was unnecessary for this purpose. Despite that authority, many tribunals seem in practice to have found reasons to distinguish *Green* and have continued to order disclosure. Thus, for example, in *John Brown Engineering Ltd* v *Brown* [1997] IRLR 90, the EAT in Scotland supported an employment tribunal finding that withholding other employees' marks rendered the appeal procedure 'a sham'. If disclosure is required for an internal appeal, it is difficult to see how it could be refused for tribunal proceedings. A middle course that the tribunals sometimes adopt is to order disclosure of forms with names and other personal details obliterated. Obviously Amrita is bound to respect the confidentiality of any documents she receives and will expose herself to action if she discloses them outside the tribunal case.

16.8.6 Supply of written answers to questions

The tribunal may order either party to answer questions posed by the tribunal. In practice, the tribunal may require the applicant to produce a schedule of losses (which quantifies the claim) but most other questions are prepared and posed by the other party. Quite often the dividing line between questions and additional information becomes blurred, and requests are made that fall somewhere between the two.

In some kinds of case it is useful to be able to serve questions that could not possibly be described as additional to ET 1 or ET 3. A solicitor acting for Dmitri may well want to exploit this provision, perhaps asking for statistical information about numbers of disabled and non-disabled people who have been promoted. As we noted in **Chapter 6**, the employer cannot be forced to reply to the statutory questionnaire in a discrimination case. However, if Dmitri asks some of the same questions under this provision, the tribunal can require the employer to answer. There are also occasions when the rule can be used to agree non-contentious matters of fact between the parties, thus reducing the evidence that needs to be given at the eventual tribunal hearing and possibly saving a lot of time. Solicitors will generally resist answering questions that really amount to cross-examination in advance.

16.8.7 Dealing with part of the proceedings separately

We have already encountered this possibility in the context of the CMD we discussed for our fourth imaginary example at **16.8.2** above. Dmitri claims to be a disabled person within the meaning of DDA 1995, and the employer challenges that claim. The issue whether he falls within the statutory definition is clearly a matter of some importance; if he does not, the whole of the remainder of his claim fails and there is no point in the parties' wasting time preparing for a hearing about the merits or of course in the tribunal's holding such a hearing. So that point is decided first as a separate matter, and (although the term does not appear in ET Rules 2004) this is usually called a preliminary hearing.

Preliminary hearings have often taken place about issues of jurisdiction, such as whether a claim was presented in time or whether a claimant has sufficient service to make a particular claim. Under ET Rules 2004 we may find that some of those issues are considered by the tribunal when deciding whether to accept a claim, and the only hearing would then be on an application to review a decision not to accept.

A preliminary hearing is a full hearing of the tribunal, but it can often be heard by an employment judge sitting alone, especially since the widening of that power by ERDRA 1998, s. 3. The EAT held in *Sutcliffe* v *Big C's Marine* [1998] ICR 913 that employment judges should not sit alone if contentious issues of fact are involved.

16.8.8 Pre-hearing reviews

One of the case management orders available to a tribunal is an order to hold a pre-hearing review (PHR). There are special provisions about PHRs in ET Rules 2004, rr. 18–19 and we shall consider them separately at **16.9** below.

16.8.9 Leave to amend a claim or response

Among the case management orders listed at ET Rules 2004, r. 10(2) is (q) the giving of leave to amend a claim or response. At a time when tribunals were more informal, such amendments were unimportant; new arguments were often raised at a hearing. Now, it would be inconsistent with the modern style of case management for parties to be taken by surprise, and it is necessary to apply to amend a claim or response if in the course of preparation for a hearing you find that the original version inadequately covers the case you wish to make. This often happens if the client drafted a claim or response and sent it in to the tribunal before you were instructed.

Sometimes it can be difficult to know whether the omission is important enough to matter, or whether it puts you at a tactical disadvantage to seek leave, or even looks incompetent to your client unless done carefully. Catherine's case is a good example where amendment is undoubtedly necessary, as we noted at **16.8.3**. If she is serious about her allegation of discrimination items 5.1 and 5.2 need completion and expansion. The employer will want if possible to resist the broadening of her claim in this way. So we must ask what grounds there are to object, and how the tribunal decides the matter.

The authority on this matter is *Selkent Bus Co. Ltd* v *Moore* [1996] ICR 836 and the tribunal will not allow an amendment that has the effect of circumventing the usual rules about time limits. So, if a claimant completes an ET 1 about one jurisdiction and is then out of time to present a claim about something different, the tribunal will not allow an amendment to the first so as to bring in the second by the back door. It is different if the first is so expressed as to include the second, so that the second claim is in fact merely a tidying-up of the legal process. Catherine's case is debatably of this latter kind: even though 'discrimination' is not identified as a claim in item 5.1 of the ET 1 the references in item 5.2 such as, 'Obviously he does not like me and prefers the younger ones' arguably contain sufficient to put the respondent on notice that there is an element of discrimination in her allegation and leave to amend the ET 1 will not be refused. In *Ali* v *Office of National Statistics* [2004] EWCA Civ 1363, [2005] IRLR 201, the Court of Appeal reviewed all the relevant authorities and held there was no material difference between the test of whether allowing an amendment was *just and equitable* and the test of a *balance of injustice and hardship* suggested in *Selkent*. In *Lehman Brothers Ltd* v *Smith* EAT/0486/05 it was held that the tribunal must always look at the balance of prejudice and hardship, so that the question whether a new claim is out of time is not determinative; an amendment was allowed in that case.

16.8.10 Written witness statements

There is an express reference in the list at r. 10(2)(s) to an order for the preparation or exchange of a witness statement. In some tribunal regions it is now almost invariable practice with all cases except those put into the 'fast-track' (see **16.8** above) to issue an order requiring agreement between the parties about a bundle of documents for the hearing and the exchange of witness statements. Occasionally the parties are ordered to prepare a schedule of agreed facts or events in the case. Dates are set for all these steps to be completed.

Recent practice has varied considerably among regions and we had expected that a practice direction issued by the President under ET Regs 2004, reg. 13 might introduce some standardisation. No practice direction has been issued and we do not expect that the letter to regional employment judges commending good practice will remove the differences. So solicitors must for the time being read such orders carefully. In the Leeds and Bedford regions, for example, the order has often required a bundle to be agreed four weeks after presentation of the ET 3 and witness statements to be exchanged two weeks later. In Bristol and Birmingham the bundle must be agreed 14 days before the hearing and witness statements must be exchanged seven days before hearing. In Cardiff no such orders are usually made at all.

We shall return to both bundles of documents and written witness statements when we discuss preparation for the hearing in **16.11** below.

16.8.11 Penalties for non-compliance with an order

The penalties for failing to comply with any of these orders are laid down in ET Rules 2004, r. 13 and there are three possibilities open to a tribunal.

(a) Costs may be awarded.

(b) After notice is given to the defaulting party, the whole or part of the claim or response may be struck out, but this can only be done at a hearing or PHR.

(c) If the order itself provides that failure to comply will lead to striking out, then the claim or response can be struck out on the date of non-compliance without further ado.

In practice striking out for failure to comply with an order has been very rare indeed and costs have usually been considered the appropriate penalty. Unusually, in *Blockbuster Entertainment Ltd* v *James* [2006] EWCA Civ 684, [2006] IRLR 630, the employment tribunal struck out a claim where it found that the claimant showed 'wilful and deliberate disobedience' of an order for disclosure for documents and failed also to comply with other orders. The Court of Appeal regarded the power to strike out as a draconic power, not to be readily exercised, and only to be used when it was a proportionate response—which it was not in this case. On the other hand, threatening to hit one's ex-manager outside the tribunal has proved a good ground for strike out.

The Court of Appeal has also confirmed that the CPR rule on striking out—r. 3.9(1)—does not apply to tribunal procedure: *Governing Body of St Albans Girls' School* v *Neary* [2009] EWCA Civ 1190, [2010] IRLR 124.

16.9 Pre-hearing reviews

Pre-hearing reviews (PHRs) are interim hearings and the provisions regarding the holding of a PHR are to be found in ET Rules 2004, r. 18. The idea is to discourage parties from pursuing hopeless cases.

Either party can apply for a PHR, or the tribunal can take the initiative itself. In practice very few claimants apply. The tribunals have in the past seldom instigated PHRs themselves and in many regions have been reluctant to grant respondents' applications. Recently they have been used more extensively. In Bristol, for example, where PHRs are often held as telephone conferences, the tribunal has indicated it will hold them as a normal course in claims of unfair dismissal involving the rule in *British Home Stores* v *Burchell* [1980] ICR 303, where the facts seem largely agreed. So Basil's case would probably proceed to a PHR if his employment was in that region.

Under r. 18, a PHR is to be conducted by an employment judge alone, unless one party makes a written request ten days beforehand for a hearing by a full tribunal or the employment judge decides that substantive issues of fact have to be decided and that a full tribunal is desirable. A PHR is to be held in public but it can use electronic communications. So the employment judge must conduct any telephone conference from a room to which the public has access using equipment which allows the public to hear all parties.

The purpose of a PHR is to carry out a preliminary consideration of the case. Under the old rules of procedure this was confined to the ET 1, the ET 3 and written representations and/or oral argument, with a view to identifying contentions that stood no reasonable prospect of success and warning the appropriate party accordingly. The provision under ET Rules 2004 is less narrow and allows the employment judge or tribunal to look at evidence and to reach a broader set of conclusions:

(a) to determine interim or preliminary matters;

(b) to perform any of the functions of a CMD;

(c) to require a party to pay a deposit as a condition of proceeding with a contention that has little reasonable prospect of success; and/or

(d) after giving due notice, to strike out all or part of a claim or response which is scandalous, vexatious or has no reasonable prospect of success, or has been conducted scandalously, unreasonably or vexatiously, or which has not been actively pursued (see r. 18(7)(b)).

The deposit that the employment judge or tribunal can order is up to £500, subject to enquiry about the party's ability to pay, and it has to be paid within 21 days of the date the decision is sent to the parties in writing. If the deposit is not paid, the claim, response or part concerned is struck out. Most such orders are made against the claimant and it is unusual for the deposit to be paid, so that the claim is struck out, but if the deposit is paid and the case proceeds to a hearing where that contention fails, the party concerned may lose the deposit as a contribution to costs.

If a PHR considers the possibility of requiring a deposit, whether or not such an order is made, no employment judge or member of the tribunal who heard the PHR may then sit at the full hearing of the case.

The most radical of the above provisions is (d): the right to strike out various categories of case, including those with no reasonable prospect of success. We see no evidence that employment judges are now any less reluctant than before to strike out any but the very obviously hopeless cases.

16.10 Conciliation and the role of ACAS

16.10.1 How ACAS becomes involved

Under all the jurisdictions of the employment tribunals we have been considering in this chapter there is a standard procedure under ETA 1996, s. 18 that a copy of every claim to the tribunal is sent by the tribunal office to ACAS. It is the job of the ACAS conciliation officer to seek to reach an agreement between the parties to settle the complaint without its being determined by the employment tribunal. Conciliation was extended to cover claims to redundancy payments as well as all the other jurisdictions by ERDRA 1998, s. 11.

The conciliation officer makes contact as a matter of course with both parties, usually telephoning professional representatives and arranging to meet unrepresented parties. This initiative avoids either party creating the appearance of lack of confidence in their case. The role of the conciliation officer is to try to promote a settlement and not to adjudicate on the merits of the case. In practice this is often too fine a distinction to draw and some debate on the merits takes place.

The ACAS officers use a number of standard forms, often referred to by their initials. Form COT 1 is the office record for ACAS, but the others may be seen by the parties.

COT 2 is the form used to record reinstatement or re-engagement of the claimant.

COT 3 is used to record terms of a settlement, usually involving some payment of money, but sometimes other matters like the provision of a reference (either in addition to money or instead of it) or confidentiality as to the terms.

COT 4 is used to record a withdrawal by the claimant.

As soon as the conciliation officer reaches some settlement of the claim, the tribunal office is notified and the case is held in abeyance pending receipt of the appropriate form, signed as necessary by one or both of the parties.

16.10.2 Binding settlements

Most of the statutory rights we have been considering in this book are subject to the rule that the parties cannot contract out of them. For example, the right to complain of unfair dismissal is protected by s. 203 of ERA 1996. Exceptions, where they exist at all, are closely defined.

Because of the breadth of that rule, even an agreement between the parties to settle terms of dismissal will not preclude a later change of mind by the ex-employee who can then start tribunal proceedings. There are two exceptions, where settlements are binding. The first is in relation to agreements reached with the involvement of ACAS. However, ACAS has become unwilling to act merely as a 'rubber stamp' in giving its formal blessing to agreements already concluded between the parties and declines to prepare a COT 3 settlement in relation to negotiations it has not led, partly because of worries about the resulting workload and partly because to do so might exceed its statutory powers. This has caused practical problems where both sides have wanted a COT 3 settlement and ACAS has felt unable to help.

The second exception is contained in ERA 1996, s. 203(2)(f), which provides that a 'compromise agreement' is binding if reached with the advice of the applicant's *relevant independent adviser*. The adviser concerned must be covered by insurance, and the agreement itself must be in a form that complies with each of the requirements of s. 203(3). Under amendments introduced by ERDRA 1998 into s. 203(3A) and (3B), advisers covered by this rule include not only lawyers (as hitherto) but also trade union officials and workers in advice centres, except in relation to their own employees. There is sometimes a problem under either method when such representatives purport to have the authority to settle on their members' behalf, but have not properly obtained it—see *Gloystarne & Co. Ltd* v *Martin* [2001] IRLR 15.

16.10.3 Considerations for the parties about whether to settle

The decision whether to fight a case in the employment tribunal or to seek to settle before the hearing may be a complex one for both parties.

In the simplest cases the matter is merely one of the amount of money involved. Suppose, for example, that the claim is of unfair dismissal, and both sides are considering the possibility of settlement through the involvement of ACAS.

The claimant may consider that the likely award of compensation from the tribunal if the claim is successful may be £5,000, but that the chances of success are only 50:50. Maybe, therefore, a definite promise of £2,500 is as good as taking a chance on £5,000. However, the costs of contesting the case in the tribunal may be £1,000 more than has already been incurred. This suggests that settlement at anything in excess of £1,500 may be worthwhile.

The employer's estimate of the likely award may be lower (perhaps £4,000) and the estimate of the chances of losing rather higher (say three to one). So applying the odds of one-in-four to the likely award suggests a settlement of £1,000. The employer may also be likely to incur additional costs by contesting the case, perhaps £1,000. So the employer will be attracted by the prospect of settling at anything below £2,000.

The conciliation officer has a relatively easy task in such a case. Where the parties eventually come together in the range between £1,500 and £2,000 will obviously reflect their respective skills as negotiators.

Cases in real life are rarely quite so simple. Both parties have a much more complicated agenda and will look to their solicitors for advice. The issues involved in such a decision may be significantly different from those in most civil litigation, and the solicitor may wish to encourage the client to try to analyse some of the factors involved. **Table 16.2** below provides a model for use in complaints of unfair dismissal; cases like Dmitri's where it is necessary to preserve a continuing relationship between the parties raise even more complex issues.

16.10.3.1 Other issues

In assisting clients to analyse issues like those listed above, solicitors will wish to discourage reliance on irrelevant reasoning:

(a) Claimants such as Basil (**16.6.2.2**) sometimes want to go ahead to clear their names, especially against implications of dishonesty. Such logic displays a widespread but erroneous view of the role of the tribunals. The solicitor will have to try to explain the principles of *British Home Stores* v *Burchell* [1980] ICR 303. However, it is difficult for claimants to understand that tribunals are concerned only

Table 16.2 Issues for both sides in deciding whether to settle a tribunal claim.

Issues for the claimant	*Issues for the employer*
How much will be awarded if I win?	How much is at stake if we lose, including any special or additional awards or orders for reinstatement or re-engagement?
What are my chances of winning?	What are the chances of losing?
What are the legal costs of continuing the fight?	What are the legal costs of fighting?
What are the costs or disadvantages of losing a day or more in the hearing, especially in a new job?	What is the cost in management time?
What is the effect of the Recoupment Regulations (see **16.14.1**)?	
How much might the other side offer?	How much will the claimant accept?
Will the publicity of a tribunal hearing, probably reported in the local press, adversely affect my chances of future employment or my security in my present job?	Will publicity be damaging in the local labour market, with customers or with the boss at group headquarters?
Can I and any witnesses face the personal strain of a tribunal hearing?	Might fighting the case require us to call witnesses we would rather not use, e.g., the fellow employee who originally brought dishonesty to our notice or to disclose confidential documents?
Has the employer more to lose than I have by going to the tribunal?	What precedents are set by being seen to have settled out of court for any future cases where employees will expect like treatment? Will the manager who originally made the decision to dismiss feel that his or her authority has been compromised?
	Shall we lose the opportunity of training supervisors in the importance of following procedures by avoiding a tribunal hearing? Does settlement compromise the integrity of our disciplinary procedure or damage the motivation of other employees?
Is my former employer likely to be offended by my refusal to settle in a way that may prejudice any future reference? (Victimisation is in theory forbidden but is difficult to prove.)	

to assess the *reasonableness* of the employer's belief and not its objective proof to a criminal standard.

(b) Both parties often see the issue for the tribunal as one of principle and are keen to get their own back on the other side. It needs to be explained that this too is not the role of the tribunals. As time passes, however, both sides probably become more pragmatic and less concerned about the supposed principles.

16.10.4 Drafting a settlement

A compromise agreement must meet the requirements of ERA 1996, s. 203(3) as to its format. This requires that:

(a) the agreement must be in writing,

(b) the agreement must relate to the particular proceedings,

(c) the employee or worker must have received advice from a relevant independent adviser as to the terms and effect of the proposed agreement and, in particular, its effect on his ability to pursue his rights before an employment tribunal,

(d) there must be in force, when the adviser gives the advice, a contract of insurance, or an indemnity provided for members of a profession or professional body, covering the risk of a claim by the employee or worker in respect of loss arising in consequence of the advice,

(e) the agreement must identify the adviser, and

(f) the agreement must state that the conditions regulating compromise agreements under this Act are satisfied.

A solicitor preparing such an agreement or the wording for a COT 3 must give some thought to the question of what it should cover. In relation to a dismissal, for example, an employer will want any payment to settle all claims (whether or not yet made) for unfair dismissal, wrongful dismissal, discrimination of any kind, and any contractual or similar claim that may be outstanding on the termination of employment. Employees, on the other hand, will wish to ensure that any such broad definition does not preclude them from enforcing their future pension rights or from litigation about some future industrial disease or personal injury. Many solicitors acting for employees and also ACAS conciliation officers ask for these matters to be excluded expressly. The courts have tended to construe compromise agreements strictly against the party (usually the employer) seeking to rely on them, and the express exclusion of claims of a different nature or which have not yet arisen is probably unnecessary. In *University of East London* v *Hinton* [2005] EWCA Civ 532, [2005] ICR 1260 the Court of Appeal held that a specific type of claim (in that case one of public interest disclosure under ERA 1996, s. 47B) was only compromised if particularly specified.

It is unlikely, whatever words are used, that a settlement will preclude a party from pursuing an action which was not known about and could not be known about at the date of the agreement. See, for example, the House of Lords decision in *Bank of Credit and Commerce International* v *Ali* [2001] ICR 337. Former employees were permitted to pursue a claim for damages for disadvantage on the labour market caused by widespread publicity about corruption and dishonesty at the bank, despite accepting terms 'in full and final settlement'. When signing the agreement neither party could realistically have supposed that such a claim was a possibility. Claims unknown to the claimant at the time of signing a compromise agreement can only be compromised by 'extremely clear words'. In practice the wording used in compromise agreements has been given more searching scrutiny than that on forms COT 3.

16.10.5 The arbitration alternative

In May 2001, there was brought into force a scheme of arbitration in unfair dismissal applications provided for under s. 7 of ERDRA 1998 as an alternative to tribunal proceedings: see ACAS Arbitration Scheme (England and Wales) Order 2001 (SI 2001/1185). The parties may agree, through the ACAS conciliation officer, to submit a dispute about unfair dismissal to binding arbitration, which ACAS will then arrange but not itself conduct. The scheme took a long while to develop because of worries that the denial of a fair trial, albeit by agreement, might breach the HRA 1998, and the result is consequently somewhat cumbersome. It has been very little used.

16.10.6 Withdrawal

Claimants can withdraw their claims at any time, and frequently do so, whether on their own initiative or as a result of the involvement of ACAS. It is in theory possible for the respondent to claim costs, but this almost never happens, and costs have rarely been awarded: see **16.13** below. In *Ako* v *Rothschild Asset Management Ltd* [2002] EWCA Civ 236, [2002] ICR 899, the Court of Appeal advises a tribunal to ask an applicant about the circumstances of withdrawal, as a cause of action estoppel will arise if the application was dismissed judicially on the applicant's withdrawal, but not if it was merely discontinued. Now, under ET Rules 2004, r. 25 dismissal of the claim no longer follows automatically on the claimant's withdrawal, but requires an application from the respondent under r. 25(4). However, the tribunal has no discretion to set aside a withdrawal if the claimant has a subsequent change of mind—*Khan* v *Heywood & Middleton Primary Care Trust* [2006] EWCA Civ 1087, [2006] IRLR 793.

Where the case has been settled through ACAS r. 25A operates so that automatic dismissal of the claim still occurs subject to proper notification being given to the tribunal.

Care should be taken in relation to complaints of breach of contract. In *Patel* v *RCMS Ltd* [1999] IRLR 161, the EAT held that the employer's counterclaim survived the employee's withdrawal. Obviously a settlement providing for mutual withdrawal would have been a safer option for the applicant than unilateral action.

16.11 The hearing

If the efforts of ACAS prove unsuccessful the claim now proceeds to a hearing in the employment tribunal. If the ET 1 and ET 3 are reasonably well drafted and the case management procedures have been used properly, it should by this stage be fairly clear what the issues for the tribunal are going to be.

For example, in Amrita's case a key issue is whether the assessment that led to her selection for redundancy was fairly and properly carried out. The employer will presumably call as a witness the person or people who performed it; Amrita herself, and possibly other witnesses, will want to challenge its fairness, partly by their own evidence and partly by challenging the employer's evidence. Both sides may wish to produce documents to support their contentions.

We now need to examine how that all happens in practice. We shall do so by reference to the main hearing (denoted hearing by ET Rules 2004, r. 26) of the merits of a claim, but we have already noted at **16.8.7** that the tribunal can order under r. 10(2) that part of the proceedings should be dealt with separately. Each part, like any CMD or PHR, then qualities as a hearing under r. 14(1) and the following remarks apply to each part.

16.11.1 Preparations

By the ET Rules 2004, r. 14(4), the tribunal office is required to give the parties 14 days' notice of a hearing except a CMD, unless the parties agree to shorter notice. Many dates of hearing are fixed in the course of a CMD, so that the parties have already agreed their availability, but some are notified by post or e-mail. If the parties have not been consulted about a date, the tribunal office is normally very amenable to granting one postponement, although some regions have been known to require detailed justification for such a request. The request is more likely to be granted if the party making it has consulted the other parties and is able to write as soon as possible after the notification, proposing an alternative date or dates. The tribunal offices are much less willing to grant late requests, and will require detailed justification for any request to postpone an agreed date, including evidence of the illness or other non-availability of a witness. No postponement will usually be granted, for example, if a witness has booked a holiday *after* the tribunal date was fixed.

Increasingly notices of hearing include the employment judge's estimate of the likely length of hearing and it is for the parties to say so if they disagree for any reason. Many employment judges are already limiting cross-examination and speeches to ensure that cases are completed in the time allocated.

Hearings are normally public and the press is admitted. Under r. 16(1) of ET Rules 2004 hearings may be in private in tightly defined and exceptional circumstances. Under r. 50 hearings may be subject to restricted reporting orders where allegations of sexual misconduct are involved. In *X* v *Commissioner of Police of the Metropolis* [2003] ICR 1031 the EAT held that this provision should be used to ensure applicants were not deterred from bringing such cases, a protection required by art. 6 of the European Equal Treatment Directive 76/207/EEC.

We noted when discussing the operation of a CMD above that it was important for a solicitor acting for either party to have given careful thought at a very early stage to the presentation of the client's case at an eventual tribunal hearing.

Appearing for a client at a tribunal hearing is all about *persuasion*. You have to persuade the employment judge or a tribunal of three, none of whom has any personal interest in the outcome, to adopt your client's version of the facts and your interpretation of the law rather than your opponent's. You have three tools available to you: the documents, the evidence of witnesses, and the authorities. Without compromising your personal integrity you have to decide how to use each of them most effectively in support of your case.

16.11.2 Documents

We have already discussed at **16.8.10** the orders that tribunals often issue for parties to agree a joint bundle of documents. There is an increasing tendency for the order to limit the permitted size of the bundle, perhaps to a total of 40 pages in a tribunal scheduled for hearing in a single day, and 90 pages for a two-day hearing, with any extra pages requiring express permission from the tribunal. Where requested, with reasons, such permission is not usually refused, but of course good reasons must be supplied. This does not usually cause a problem where both parties are represented, as representatives are willing to compromise, but sometimes it happens that unrepresented claimants make unreasonable demands. In such a case you will wish to write formally proposing fewer documents so that it is clear to the tribunal where the fault lies in failing to comply with their order. The tribunals are less strict than the courts in operating the 'best evidence' rule, and photocopies of documents are usually sufficient, but it is a wise precaution to take originals to the hearing in case any issue of authenticity arises.

Sometimes certain documents are obviously required. Thus in Basil's case the employer's disciplinary procedure, any rules stipulating what conduct may lead to summary dismissal and the notes of disciplinary meetings will probably be required by both parties. Irrelevant material should be left out—both because the tribunals dislike needlessly large bundles and because the persuasive power of anything good is reduced if it is buried in a lot of paper. So if, for example, the procedure and rules are contained in an employee handbook, it is a good idea to take a copy of the handbook to the hearing in case anyone wants to see the whole, but only the relevant parts should go into the bundle.

Contemporaneous documents have much greater persuasive power than anything written up after the event. So working documents concerned with Amrita's selection may be very helpful in showing how carefully the employer approached the task. Any manuscript notes taken by either side during the crucial meeting with the departmental manager in Dmitri's case will far outweigh typed notes prepared subsequently.

Documents should be assembled in a folder, in chronological order, with an index at the front and with the pages (rather than the documents) numbered in sequence. It will be found that this makes reference during the hearing as simple as possible.

16.11.3 The order of proceeding and burden of proof

Under ET Rules 2004, r. 14(4) it is provided that either party may send in to the tribunal written representations as an alternative to attending in person. They must be lodged at the tribunal office at least seven days before the hearing. In practice this is a very unsatisfactory alternative and should be used with great reluctance.

Apart from that possibility, the parties turn up on the day appointed to give their own evidence, to cross-examine witnesses for the other side, and to address the tribunal. Although the tribunal is given wide powers under the rules to determine its own procedure, that power is in practice much circumscribed by custom and some case law (e.g., that a party stating that he will not be calling evidence will usually be bound by that statement).

In practice the order of proceeding is standardised. Generally speaking it is for the party on whom the burden of proof rests to start the proceedings. Thus, in relation to deductions from wages, discrimination, and equal pay it is for the *claimant* to start by making out a case. In dismissal cases (unfair dismissal and claims for redundancy payments), it is for the *claimant* to go first if it is necessary to prove dismissal, i.e. if the employer denies dismissal. If the employer admits dismissal, the *employer* goes first to prove the reason for dismissal. This rule is of long standing and pre-dates the present statutory provision about burden of proof.

16.11.4 Opening statement

In the past the party opening proceedings often made an opening statement, as in the county court. Occasionally employment judges still permit that to happen and it can be helpful in identifying the real issues in a case. Increasingly, though, and especially where witness statements and the bundle are handed in to the tribunal in advance, employment judges regard opening statements as superfluous and prefer to get on with the evidence. Solicitors may sometimes be permitted to draw the attention of the tribunal to key parts of the bundle before the evidence starts.

16.11.5 Evidence-in-chief

The two sides will need to decide what facts they need to prove in order to establish their cases and to decide what witnesses need to be called. As in the courts, this evidence given on behalf of the party calling the witness is called evidence-in-chief.

16.11.5.1 The rules of evidence

The rules of evidence followed in the employment tribunals are based on those in the county courts, but are less rigid. Rule 14(2) states that the tribunal 'shall not be bound by any enactment or rule of law relating to the admissibility of evidence in proceedings before the courts'. Thus the rule against hearsay is not strictly followed, and evidence is often permitted that would be forbidden in the courts. Indeed, the definition of hearsay is complicated by the slightly special nature of the issues the tribunals often need to investigate. If a manager decided to dismiss a claimant because of a report made to him by a subordinate about the claimant's behaviour, the content of the report may sometimes be direct evidence of the manager's reasoning in deciding to dismiss, rather than hearsay evidence of the claimant's behaviour.

During evidence-in-chief, the solicitor should follow the normal rule of not asking leading questions, except when presenting background evidence about non-contentious aspects of the case. Even then it is courteous to ask the tribunal's permission before leading a witness.

16.11.5.2 Written witness statements

At one stage the tribunals required all evidence to be given through oral examination. Most regions now order witness statements to be exchanged between the parties who may be required to arrive early and to hand in copies of the bundle and of the witness statements so that members of the tribunal can read them before the start of the hearing. The tribunal may then require witnesses to read the statements aloud under oath or, increasingly, they take the statements as read and move straight on to cross-examination. Representatives are sometimes not permitted to ask additional questions by way of examination-in-chief without leave of the tribunal, although such leave is usually given in relation to points raised by the other side's statements. Such procedures do not add much to informality in the tribunals.

The variation in procedure causes problems for solicitors and other representatives. The style of a witness statement prepared for reading aloud may be rather different from one prepared for the tribunal to read for itself. It is always a good idea to try to find out local practice before appearing before any tribunal for the first time.

16.11.6 Cross-examination

The rules of cross-examination are the same as in the courts and it is important that key elements in your case are 'put to' the witnesses of the other side so that they have a chance to refute them. With an unrepresented claimant the tribunal will sometimes permit recall of the witness for the purpose, as the claimant may not have understood the requirement, but solicitors may not be given that flexibility.

16.11.7 Questions from the tribunal and re-examination

The final stage of evidence from each witness is for the party calling that witness to tidy up loose ends resulting from cross-examination. This gives the representative the chance to give the full story of any matter raised during cross-examination in a way that tells only half a story. For example, if Basil's solicitor puts to one of the respondent's witnesses during cross-examination some unexpected version of the facts which appears to clear Basil of blame, the respondent's solicitor may try to draw the sting from the new argument by obtaining in re-examination (without asking a leading question) confirmation that the argument was never made by Basil in his disciplinary or appeal hearings. It is not permitted to raise completely new material at this late stage. While the tribunal may permit an unrepresented claimant to do so, and then give the other side a chance of further cross-examination, a solicitor will not normally be allowed to make this mistake.

At some stage the employment judge and members of the tribunal will wish to ask questions of the witness. Practice varies considerably. Some employment judges interrupt continuously during evidence-in-chief; others wait until the end. The lay members are not usually given their chance until the end. There is no uniform practice as to whether re-examination or questions from the tribunal come first.

16.11.8 Closing addresses

When all the evidence has been presented, the two parties or their representatives each have the chance to address the tribunal. This gives them the opportunity both to review the evidence and to refer to any statute and to relevant authorities. Recent practice in the tribunals has been to discourage excessive dependence on the authorities and to concentrate on the statutory provisions. It is therefore unwise to encumber a closing address with references to the very well-known cases like *British Home Stores* v *Burchell* or *Williams* v *Compair Maxam*. It is also unnecessary to waste time on authorities where a decision really rests entirely on the facts. Some employment judges limit the time allowed. Skeleton arguments are still not the norm, but their use has become more common.

It is usual for the party that went first at the beginning of the hearing also to have the last word by giving the second closing address. This practice is not invariable, however, and some employment judges, especially in Scotland, prefer to reverse it.

16.12 The tribunal decision

We have been used to calling the final result of a tribunal hearing the decision, but that term is not used in ET Rules 2004. Instead in r. 28(1) we find definitions of 'judgments' and 'orders'. The first represents a final determination of the whole or part of a claim and may include an award of compensation, a declaration or a recommendation, while the second is an interim decision, most often resulting from a CMD or PHR.

Under r. 28, the tribunal may issue its judgment or order orally at the end of the hearing (almost always after an adjournment to consider it), or it may reserve its decision and issue the judgment or order in writing later. Judgments must always be recorded in writing, and reasons must be given, but there is no longer any requirement for the reasons for an oral judgment to be recorded in writing unless one party so requests either at the hearing or within 14 days, or the EAT so orders. There is no obligation on the tribunal to give reasons for an order unless a request for reasons is made at the hearing.

A judgment may simply be on the merits of the case, so that the tribunal announces whether it finds for the claimant or dismisses the case, or (if it finds for the claimant) it may go on to announce a remedy. A subsequent hearing is sometimes arranged as to remedy, leaving the parties time meanwhile to try to negotiate a settlement.

The tribunal may reach a unanimous decision, or it can decide by a majority. Employment judges usually work hard to try to achieve unanimity. Where a tribunal is reduced to an employment judge and one other, the judge has a second, casting vote. Despite a growing tendency for decisions to be announced at the end of a hearing, the Court of Appeal has suggested that a reserved decision is to be preferred if the lay members form a majority and the employment judge preparing the decision is in the minority—*Anglian Home Improvements Ltd* v *Kelly* [2004] EWCA Civ 901, [2005] ICR 242.

Where reasons are given, the rule until now has been that they must contain enough detail to allow the parties to see how the decision was reached, but need not necessarily address each and every contention advanced at a hearing: *Meek* v *City of Birmingham District Council* [1987] IRLR 250. The tribunal may correct clerical errors in a decision but is otherwise *functus officio* having given its decision and may not change it.

16.13 Costs and preparation time orders

16.13.1 The 2004 rules

Costs have always been a tricky issue in employment tribunals. Recent experience suggests a long-running battle between the legislators (who see costs as a good way of discouraging hopeless cases and thereby reducing the massively increased public expenditure on the employment tribunal service) and most employment judges, especially those who support widespread access to justice, who have been reluctant in practice to award costs unless parties behave outrageously. So everything hinges on the question whether the new rules are applied more often in practice than their predecessors. We therefore propose to restrict ourselves to a fairly brief section on this topic.

16.13.2 The meaning of costs and preparation time

Costs are defined in r. 38(3) to mean fees, charges, disbursements, or expenses incurred in relation to tribunal proceedings and a tribunal may make a costs order only in favour of a party which is legally represented. A costs order can be made up to £10,000 without detailed assessment under the Civil Procedure Rules—more with such assessment (r. 41).

A preparation time order can be made in favour of a party which is not legally represented, but not in addition to a costs order in favour of the same party in the same case. Preparation time is time spent by the party or its employees or advisers in preparation for a hearing but not at the hearing itself—r. 42(3). A preparation time order has to be calculated by multiplying the number of hours actually spent by £29 (increased by £1 every April), subject to a maximum of £10,000.

16.13.3 When costs are awarded

Despite other changes to the rules, there has been no major change in the general provision as to when costs (or equally, a preparation time order) may be awarded. Costs *must* now be awarded against an employer if postponement or adjournment of a hearing was because the employer failed without a special reason to provide evidence about availability of the job in a case of unfair dismissal where the claimant sought reinstatement or re-engagement. Costs *may* (much as before) be awarded against a party or representative who has acted vexatiously, abusively, disruptively, or otherwise unreasonably or if the bringing or conducting of proceedings has been misconceived—r. 40(3) for costs and r. 44(3) for preparation time.

In *Nicolson Highlandwear Ltd* v *Nicolson* [2010] IRLR 859 Lady Smith put an interesting gloss on this. The case concerned an employee who was found to have been unfairly dismissed but to have contributed 100 per cent to his dismissal (odd though that sounds). Costs to the employer were refused but Lady Smith pointed out that there are three remedies only available to an employee claiming unfair dismissal and 'seeking a declaration as to unfairness' is not one of them, so pursuing a case to 'clear one's name' may lead to an award of costs where the action is unsuccessful in real terms. As the editors of the IRLR comment, this ignores the industrial reality that it may be important for future employment to try to rid oneself of a 'dismissal' tag and also ignores earlier authority that even where an offer of the maximum compensation was made to an employee that did not make pursuing a claim frivolous in itself.

A new provision allows for the award of wasted costs *against a representative* and not the party in the event of any improper, unreasonable, or negligent act or omission by the representative. In 2008–09 costs were awarded to claimants on 102 occasions and to respondents 265 times—with most awards to either party being below £2,000.

16.13.4 Applying for costs

Under ET Rules 2004, r. 38(7) or r. 42(5) respectively, an application for costs or a preparation time order can be made during proceedings, at the end of a hearing or in writing to the tribunal office within 28 days from the issue of the judgment.

Past experience suggests that the highest chance of success in an application arises when the tribunal has held a PHR and the other side has been ordered to pay a deposit, has paid it and has then lost the case on the grounds predicted. It doesn't happen often but it is a pleasant dream.

More often the threat of an application for costs on the ground that the other side has been pursuing the case unreasonably has been much more significant in practice, especially where you are having difficulty in getting the other side to negotiate seriously about a settlement.

In the courts, where the possibility exists of paying money into court, this procedure involves the writing of a formal letter threatening an application for costs if the offer is rejected, as in *Calderbank* v *Calderbank* [1976] Fam 93. In *Kopel* v *Safeway Stores plc* [2003] IRLR 753, the EAT suggested that this procedure cannot be copied in the tribunals where there is no system of paying money into the tribunal, but in fact a similar procedure to the *Calderbank* letter is sometimes operated.

In *Beynon* v *Scadden* [1999] IRLR 700, the claimants' trade union, Unison, supported them in a complaint of a breach of the consultation requirements under TUPE. The case was in fact hopeless because the transfer of the business was achieved by a share transfer and so was not covered by TUPE. The employment tribunal had found as a fact that the reason Unison pursued the case was the collateral purpose of achieving union recognition. That finding was enough for the EAT to support an award of costs, based on vexatious conduct by the claimants or their representatives. In *Kovacs* v *Queen Mary & Westfield College* [2002] EWCA 352, [2002] ICR 919, the Court of Appeal approved the reasoning in *Beynon* and held that an award of costs did not require the tribunal to assess a party's ability to pay, something that is now permitted by r. 41(2) and r. 45(3) but is not mandatory.

16.14 The remedies for the tribunal

We have already considered the appropriate remedies relevant to the various jurisdictions in earlier chapters, but several points remain to be made here.

16.14.1 Recoupment of benefits

Under the Employment Protection (Recoupment of Jobseeker's Allowance and Income Support) Regulations 1996, the full amount of a monetary award of compensation may not be payable to a claimant who succeeds in a claim of unfair dismissal. The tribunal is required to assess the approximate amount of jobseeker's allowance and income support benefit the claimant has received between the date of dismissal and the date of hearing. This figure is called the 'prescribed element'.

The compensatory award is assessed without regard to any benefits the claimant may have received during that period. Only the excess of the compensatory award over the prescribed element is payable immediately to the claimant at the end of the hearing. The Department of Social Security then sends the employer a demand in respect of benefits actually paid to the claimant, an amount that may not exceed the prescribed element. The employer pays that amount to the DSS, and any surplus remaining to the claimant.

Since the Recoupment Regulations apply to tribunal awards and not to conciliated settlements, it is an inducement to both sides to settle and to avoid their effect.

16.14.2 Payment of interest

Under the Employment Tribunals (Interest) Order 1990, interest is payable on tribunal awards still outstanding on a date 42 days after a decision is issued to the parties. The rate of interest is as laid down for other similar purposes in relation to court awards and varies from time to time.

16.14.3 Remedy hearings

The maximum amount of the compensatory award that can be made in cases of unfair dismissal is £65,300. However, although a few cases result in very large awards, the average amount actually awarded in 2008–09 for unfair dismissal cases was £7,959, and the median was £4,269. The tribunals often require a claimant to prepare at an early stage of preparation a schedule of loss. Calculation at the hearing is speeded up because the relevant facts have already been ascertained.

In discrimination cases unlimited compensation has been available since 1993. In *Buxton* v *Equinox Design Ltd* [1999] ICR 269 the EAT stressed the need for proper management by the tribunal of the assessment of compensation in a disability discrimination case. It was not good enough to assess future unemployment on the basis of 'guestimate'; some medical evidence was required about the claimant's employability, given his multiple sclerosis.

A tribunal decision about remedy has usually required additional evidence beyond that used at the hearing on the merits of the case. Is reinstatement or re-engagement feasible? If not, and the tribunal moves on to the assessment of compensation, what was the state of the employment market locally and how much did the claimant do to mitigate loss? Now, as a stricter approach starts to be taken, even more evidence may be required in some cases. For example, if the employer loses in Basil's case, the evidence called about the alleged theft at the hearing on the merits will have concentrated on the reasonableness of the employer's belief. In assessing contributory fault, the issue is one of fact: did Basil steal or not? That may require different witnesses whom neither side needed to call at the first hearing.

The availability of a much higher limit may also give rise to some new heads of compensation. In *Sheriff* v *Klyne Tugs (Lowestoft) Ltd* [1999] IRLR 481, the Court of Appeal held that compensation for psychiatric damage as well as injury to feelings fell within the jurisdiction of an employment tribunal in a case concerning racial discrimination.

16.14.4 The effect of tax

At **13.6.1** above we dealt with the general principles of taxation of compensation awarded by the tribunals in cases of unfair dismissal. It is still relatively unusual for these rules to apply in practice: most awards are well below £30,000 and therefore are not taxable in the applicant's hands. Reference should be made to the earlier chapter if there is a need to consider 'grossing up' to compensate for the effect of tax.

16.15 Challenge of a tribunal decision

There are two ways a tribunal judgment or decision can be challenged after it is given: it can be reviewed by the tribunal, or an appeal can be taken to the EAT.

16.15.1 Application for review

The power for a tribunal to review a decision is contained in r. 34 of the ET Rules 2004. The application must be made in writing within 14 days of the issue of a decision. The application must be on one or more of the following grounds:

(a) an administrative error has occurred;

(b) a party did not receive notice of proceedings;

(c) the decision was made in the absence of a party;

(d) new evidence, not reasonably foreseeable, has come to light;

(e) the interests of justice require a review.

Until the ET Rules 2004 came into force this power was very restricted and some employment tribunals have operated under the ET Rules 2004 as if the same restricted power to review still operated. However, a broader approach is now being adopted by the EAT. In *Sodexho Ltd* v *Gibbons* [2005] ICR 1647 the EAT interpreted the power to review in the *interests of justice* in the light of the overriding objective. This has the effect of mitigating some of the strict requirements of the ET Rules 2004, including those about ET 1 and ET 3. In that case the tribunal had rightly reviewed a strike-out judgment after it emerged that the claimant's solicitors had not received the notice requiring him to pay a deposit, because he had given the wrong postcode for their office in his claim. In *Onwuka* v *Spherion Technology UK Ltd* [2005] ICR 567 the EAT allowed a review to amend a claim to add an additional respondent.

Whilst other applications for review can be considered and refused without a hearing, an application for review of a default judgment must always be considered at a public hearing—r. 33.

16.15.2 Appeal to EAT

If the decision of an employment tribunal contains an error of law, an appeal lies to the EAT. Under a Practice Direction issued by the EAT in May 2008, all notices of appeal in the appropriate form must be accompanied by the claim form ET 1, the response ET 3, and the employment tribunal judgment, decision, or order appealed against, with written reasons or an explanation of why any of that list is not included. Appeals have to be entered within 42 days of the date the employment tribunal sent an order or decision to the parties, or within 42 days of the date written reasons for a judgment were sent to the parties. Employment tribunal judgments are usually sent to the parties with an accompanying leaflet explaining how standard forms can be obtained from the EAT at Victoria Embankment in London.

The full rules about appeals to the EAT are outside the scope of this book. Suffice it to say that full compliance is essential. The President has recently stated that many appellants are not complying with the Practice Direction concerning inclusion of the claim and response and that the EAT intends to operate the rule from *Kanapathiar* v *London Borough of Harrow* [2003] IRLR 571, under which an appeal lodged without the correct papers is not considered to be lodged at all. A further appeal which complies may then be out of time.

Parties often express a wish to appeal on the basis that they do not like the judgment of the employment tribunal and wish for a second opinion. It has to be explained to them that this is not the function of the EAT, which will not interfere with a properly reached judgment of the employment tribunal on the facts of the case. It is also almost always impossible to raise at the EAT new points of law that were not raised at the employment tribunal: *Jones* v *Governing Body of Burdett Coutts School* [1998] IRLR 521.

16.16 A summary chart of the main jurisdictions

Jurisdiction	*Source*	*Service condition*	*Time limit for IT application*	*Extension of time*	*Maximum award**
Unfair dismissal	ERA 1996, s. 94	1 year	3 months from EDT	'not reasonably practicable'	£76,700** unless re-employment ordered
Redundancy payment	ERA 1996, s. 135	2 years	6 months from RD	'just and equitable'	£11,400

Deductions from wages	ERA 1996, Part II	Nil	3 months from payday	'not reasonably practicable'	Unlimited
Racial discrimination	RRA 1976	Nil	3 months from act complained of	'just and equitable'	Unlimited
Sex discrimination	SDA 1975	Nil	3 months from act complained of	'just and equitable'	Unlimited
Equal pay	Equal Pay Act 1970	Nil	6 months after termination	None	Unlimited
Disability discrimination	DDA 1995	Nil	3 months from act complained of	'just and equitable'	Unlimited
Breach of contract	ITA 1996, s. 3 and 1994 Order	Nil	3 months from EDT	'not reasonably practicable'	£25,000
Working time	WTRegs 1998	Nil	3 months from infringement	'not reasonably practicable'	No general limit

* These are the figures from 1 February 2010.

** The 'unfair dismissal' figure is made up of a maximum basic award of £11,400 and a maximum compensatory award of £65,300. Both figures are subject to annual change.

Index

A

B

C

D

T